Active Index Investing

Maximizing Portfolio Performance and Minimizing Risk through Global Index Strategies

STEVEN A. SCHOENFELD

WILEY

John Wiley & Sons, Inc.

Published by John Wiley & Sons, Inc., Hoboken, New Jersey.
Published simultaneously in Canada.

For general information on our other products and services, or technical support, please contact our Customer Care Department within the United States at 800-762-2974, outside the United States at 317-572-3993 or fax 317-572-4002.

Wiley also publishes its books in a variety of electronic formats. Some content that appears in print may not be available in electronic books. For more information about Wiley products, visit our web site at www.wiley.com.

Library of Congress Cataloging-in-Publication Data:

Active index investing : maximizing portfolio performance and minimizing risk through global index strategies / edited by Steven A. Schoenfeld.
   p.   cm.
Published simultaneously in Canada.
Includes index.
ISBN 0-471-25707-9 (cloth : alk. paper)
1. Investments. 2. Portfolio management. 3. Risk management. I. Schoenfeld, Steven A.
HG4521.A22   2004
332.63'27—dc22

                                  2003026645

Printed in the United States of America.

10 9 8 7 6 5 4 3 2 1

To the memory of the thousands of innocent victims of terrorism who have fallen during this decade. I hope that despite their personal tragedy, the call to moral clarity of this despicable violence will mean that their deaths were not in vain.

All of the Editor's net proceeds from this book will be donated to several charities established for direct relief of terror victims in the United States, the Middle East, Europe, and Southeast Asia.

Contents

Foreword

The Role of Indexing and Benchmarks in Developing Sound Investment Approaches

Don Phillips
Morningstar

Simple ideas can have profound consequences. Just consider the revolutionary effect that indexing has had on the investment markets. From the simple notion of creating a benchmark of the market, a host of radical changes have emerged to give investors greater control in managing risk, return, and cost in their portfolios. Indexing also has raised the bar for active managers. The changes have been profound, positive, and permanent. From almost any angle, the power of indexing and its impact on investors, financial markets, and investment products are difficult to overstate.

Indexes serve as a gauge of the market, but they also do much more. They are the basis for asset allocation research. Much of what we now know about the relative impact of asset, sector, and security selection on portfolio performance is the result of analytical work derived from indexes. They are also tools for performance measurement, creating increasingly better standards by which to evaluate managers. But, perhaps most significantly, indexes are now often the basis for investment vehicles. No longer can a fund manager take credit simply for offering the investor broad-based exposure to the market. Today, that service can be had for pennies on the dollar through index funds. Money managers who want to charge higher fees must demonstrate that their services provide added performance benefits. In a very real sense, the growing popularity of indexes and index investing has forced all money managers to raise the level of their game.

Indexing has been at the heart of a process that is moving the investment profession from art to science, which in turn brings significant value to all investors. Beyond the considerable cost savings of index-based products versus conventionally managed ones, indexes yield many other significant benefits. By establishing clear benchmarks, indexes serve as performance measurement tools that bring a needed precision to manager evaluation, increasing the likelihood that an investor will identify and retain high-quality managers. In addition, managing to a stated benchmark helps ensure that the manager's and the client's understanding of a fund's objectives are in sync, thereby making it easier to understand what role the fund will play in a portfolio. Proper and appropriate benchmarking is a powerful tool for increasing an investor's chances of investment success.

But where indexes get really interesting is when theory turns to practice. The wave of investment products based on indexes has been remarkable, both for its variety and popularity. With index funds, exchange-traded funds (ETFs), and a host of index-based derivative instruments, the tool kit at an investor's disposal has never been broader or deeper. While some money managers may perceive index-based alternatives as a threat, investors should cheer their arrival. Even if an investor continues to favor active managers, the availability of lower-cost index strategies only improves the investor's chance of success.

The benefits of index strategies are perhaps greatest if investors think of index-based products not as being on a straight-line spectrum that runs from actively managed funds to passive indexes, but instead as being on a horseshoe-shaped spectrum. One prong offers low-cost index strategies and the other prong offers exceptional managers at reasonable costs. Either approach is attractive and the two can easily be combined. Think of Jack Bogle representing one approach and Warren Buffett the other. What smart investors will do is purge their portfolio of the bottom part of the horseshoe, which delivers not particularly creative or effective management at high fees. Sadly, that's the vast majority of funds out there. Still, with the advent of index funds, and the added pressure on good managers to deliver strong returns with reasonable risk, the number of suitable choices facing an investor has never been greater.

Indeed, index-based investment products are powerful tools that can offer greater precision at lower cost than actively managed portfolios, and as several chapters in the book indicate, one can build "active index" portfolios that are more efficient investment strategies. To exclude index vehicles from your arsenal without proper consideration of their merit would be foolhardy. For one, index products offer purity of style or asset-class exposure. With an index fund, what you see is what you get—it is the ultimate in truth in labeling. Index-based products also remove the ambiguity over who is making the asset allocation decision. There is no need to worry about a manager going to cash when your intent is to be fully invested. Indexes also can remove security selection risk for all or any part of the portfolio. If you think biotech will rally but are unsure which stocks will do the best and want to avoid the risk of selecting a manager who picks wrong, an index-based solution is at your disposal. Whether you use index funds/ETFs as your entire portfolio, as building blocks of a portfolio, or as a way to fine-tune an already established portfolio, indexes and the products built from them are invaluable tools in your investment tool kit.

A significant reason to include indexes among your choices is the transparent availability and legitimacy of their performance record. Indexes offer long histories of how a certain approach to the market works in all sorts of environments. Whereas the returns of actively managed funds lose legitimacy as managers come and go or styles change, the consistency of an index strategy makes the entire record of the index germane to the investment decision. If you want to get a sense of the stock market's long-term potential, you should turn to a series of broad market indexes. If you want to get a sense of the Fidelity Magellan Fund's long-term potential, you must first disentangle the Peter Lynch years from the Morris Smith years from the Jeff Vinik years and the Bob Stansky years. One is left with a lot less fully applicable data than may at first appear. This facet of indexes is a boon to investors who want to understand the long-term implications and potential of their choices.

A final reason, which I have already touched on but which bears repeating, is the significant cost savings of index strategies. At a time when mutual fund expenses continue to creep inexorably upward, the low-cost alternative of index investing appears increasingly attractive. Within the world of indexing, there is true cost competition. Who would pay 120 basis points for exposure to the same index that another firm offers for 20? In an era of lower expected absolute returns for both stocks and bonds, the cost savings of index strategies makes tremendous sense. There's also the issue of tax efficiency, another score on which indexes have saved investors huge sums of money while putting more pressure on active managers to focus on the tax costs of their own trades. Lowering costs and tax burden are two sure things investors can do to enhance return without incurring added risk—which is essentially a "free lunch." Index-based investment products are a great tool for capturing these two free lunches.

With all the positive changes that the index revolution has brought to investing, you might expect the field to be crowded with books documenting the origins and subsequent ascent of indexing in the marketplace, but that is hardly the case. While the field may still not be crowded, it can certainly no longer be claimed to be underserved. Steven Schoenfeld has produced a remarkable book that features not only his own considerable insights, but also the perspectives of numerous leading practitioners from all spheres of the indexing and investing world. The book's scope is immense, covering the genesis of indexing, the use of indexes as benchmarks, the development of an ever-expanding range of index products, and the details of index-based portfolio management. Finally, examples and case studies illustrate how the world's most sophisticated investors use indexing to minimize costs and risks and maximize returns.

Fittingly for a project so broad, the book's scope doesn't end with these pages, but is continued in the book's E-ppendix—www.ActiveIndexInvesting .com—supported by IndexUniverse.com. This Electronic Appendix expands and updates the book's topics, allowing even more voices to help chronicle the ongoing development of this fascinating and dynamic field. In fact, the concept of a web-based supplement to the book was so compelling that Steven chose to partner IndexUniverse.com with the *Journal of Indexes* to develop a unique online resource where the financial industry and investors can gain and exchange knowledge about indexing.

The book itself is encyclopedic. *Active Index Investing* not only covers the history of indexing to date, but also marks out the terrain the industry is likely to cover in its continuing evolution. If you follow the investment markets and want to see how indexes and index-based tools and strategies will continue to shape the markets, you have found what will surely become one of the definitive books on the topic. I am sure that you will gain from the journey.

Preface

How does someone end up editing a 31-chapter investment book that encompasses a comprehensive array of theories, products, and practices spanning all of the world's major asset classes? Well, to some extent, unintentionally. The project started a bit more modestly with "only" 24 chapters and was originally focused on global equity indexing. But as I developed numerous outlines and discussed the project with industry peers, the importance of producing a comprehensive survey of index-based investment became evident—and the project expanded accordingly.

The initial motivation to embark on this project developed during my six years as an investment strategist and manager of institutional equity index funds. At the same time that my colleagues and I were diligently capturing every basis point for our clients' portfolios, I was meeting with consultants, clients, and other investment professionals who frequently considered index funds essentially a commodity. They often differentiated these funds only by price—the management fees, which were often measured in fractions of a basis point.

My former colleagues and I at Barclays Global Investors (BGI) would provide detailed advice on benchmark selection and overall investment policy, and assist clients with complete investment solutions. These included standard or customized index funds, benchmark evolution, and portfolio transition services. My team of investment strategists and portfolio managers also interfaced with all of the major index providers, sharing information on corporate actions, advising them on methodology, evaluating the prospects for new benchmarks, and sometimes complaining loudly when their index changes were not well aligned with market realities. During the late 1990s and early 2000s, we spent a lot of time explaining to clients how we delivered significant value—consistent performance, low fees, cost-effective investment/redemption through crossing, efficient shifts between benchmark indexes, and enhanced returns through securities lending and efficient trading. We also launched some of the most efficiently managed exchange-traded funds (ETFs) that were used by both institutional and retail clients.

We knew that through our hard work, we were saving our clients millions of dollars each year. Yet indexing—whether U.S. large-cap, European developed markets, long-term Canadian bonds, or Asian emerging markets—continues to be viewed as a passive investment process. In reality, whether one looks at the benchmark decisions, portfolio management, or asset allocation strategies that we were involved with, our approach to indexing was "anything but passive," and this became our group's slogan at the time.[1]

I was therefore constantly looking for ways to demonstrate the value that index-based strategies delivered for investors and gave many presentations with this message. My colleagues and I also wrote numerous articles and research papers that highlighted the sophistication of indexing, and how the "active versus index" debate was obsolete. In some ways, these presentations and articles were the genesis of the book project, and the "nonpassive" nature of index management and applications became the inspiration for the book's title.

But the specific catalyst came in early 2001 when Bill Falloon at John Wiley & Sons approached me with a proposal for a book on indexing. I was favorably disposed to both the idea and the messenger, as I had worked closely with Bill when I was a trader and writer in Singapore in the late 1980s, and he was a writer and editor at *Intermarket Magazine* in Chicago. Yet I initially refused, remembering how much work my first book had been. But the idea stayed with me, and the continuing challenges in conveying the value of index-based strategies to some of the most sophisticated financial institutions reminded me that a book that "explained it all" might be a useful contribution to the financial community. I also talked to colleagues throughout the industry—friends at asset managers, pension plan sponsors, institutional brokers, index providers, exchanges—and they almost universally agreed that there was a need for such a book. As one colleague reminded me, although indexing accounted for about 25 percent of institutional equity assets and over 12 percent of mutual fund assets, there was no comprehensive, professional-level book on index-based investments.

I made the final decision in late spring 2001, during a trip to Southeast Asia. Sitting at the Foreign Correspondents Club in Phnom Penh, Cambodia, I realized that if I did not embark on the project, I would regret it in the long term. I then asked the people in the industry who were most supportive of the project to contribute to the book—and many accepted. As mentioned, the project initially focused on equity indexing—benchmarks and portfolio management. But as I got deeper into developing the framework for the book, I realized that ignoring other asset classes would be suboptimal. So at first I added chapters on fixed-income benchmarks and index portfolio management. And sure enough, once this expansion started, I added chapters or sidebars on commodity indexes, real estate indexes, and hedge fund benchmarks.

In early 2003, I left BGI and joined an innovative venture focused on index-based separate accounts which were actively managed for tax efficiency. The idea was to bring the power and efficiency of customized indexing (which I had implemented in a variety of ways for institutional clients) to the advisor marketplace and the "wrap account" programs at major retail brokerage firms. During this time I learned a lot more about the financial products that are sold to individual investors, and the generally high costs and subpar performance that these services generate. I became even more convinced that index-based products—whether separate accounts, index funds, or ETFs—should play a much larger role in the portfolios of most individual investors. This experience shifted some of the book's emphasis toward the plight of these investors and led to the inclusion of ideas on "best practices" for financial advisors and individuals, based heavily on the lessons learned by large sophisticated institutional investors.

This book encompasses views from most of the major index fund managers, including my former colleagues at BGI and my former competitors at State Street Global Advisors, The Vanguard Group, and Northern Trust Global Investments. The major global index providers such as Dow Jones, Standard & Poor's, FTSE, Russell, and MSCI are all represented, either in chapters and sidebars, or in the "web-only" sidebars found in the book's "E-ppendix" (Electronic Appendix). A diverse group of plan sponsors, broker-dealers, academics, and financial advisors round out this great group of contributors. All in all, over 50 contributors from more than 20 organizations are involved in the book and its supporting web site: www.ActiveIndexInvesting .com, powered by IndexUniverse.com. The views of all the different players in the large world of indexes and index-based investing are represented. This broad and deep perspective provides comprehensive insight into the unique art and science of index-based investments.

When I embarked on this project in 2001, I certainly could not anticipate that scandals and allegations concerning the mutual fund industry in late 2003 would also make the book's recommendations for individual investors so timely and relevant. But now, in 2004, sophisticated financial advisors and individual investors view index funds and ETFs as key elements in their search for a better way of investing. Because of their transparency, precise performance objectives, and low costs, index funds have always had to discourage market timers and develop fair and effective solutions to stale pricing and the late trading practices that could engender.

Traditional index funds have long had safeguards in place to prevent the abuses of shareholders that have caused the outcry. These include investment/redemption fees and minimum holding periods. In addition, a certain type of index fund—which I categorize as *focused* funds (e.g., the inverse and leveraged funds offered by Rydex, ProFunds, and Potomac)—already accommodated active traders, and their fund structures are designed for frequent investor activity. Similarly, index-based exchange-traded funds (ETFs) have a totally transparent price and trading structure, and can be traded all day without harming long-term investors in the funds. Furthermore, index funds and ETFs have always been "no-load," and their low fee structure could never be a part of the "pay to play" practices (and mentality) that dominated mutual fund sales and marketing approaches.

Finally, regardless of the efficiency and fairness advantages of index fund structures, after the brutal bear market of 2000–2003, investors have been looking for a better way to achieve their long-term investing objectives. Thus, a key message of this book is that through indexing and index-based vehicles, there *is* a better way for individual investors to achieve some of the same efficiencies enjoyed by large investors. They do not have to suffer with high fees and low risk-adjusted returns, let alone the hidden costs of high loads and payments by mutual funds for "shelf space" at broker-dealers.

Two of the closing chapters of the book propose this "better way" and stress an overall investment approach based on index funds. Chapter 29 is an "investment recovery plan" geared to individuals who are tired of the mutual fund trap. It is excerpted from an important book written by two former U.S. Treasury Department officials. Chapter 30 proposes four axioms for long-term investment success—a holistic approach that I call "indexing at the core." It is suitable for both individual investors and their advisors.

Another somewhat unintended outgrowth of the book project was my involvement in a media enterprise focusing on the world of index products, anchored by the web site that I originally developed to support the book—IndexUniverse.com. The idea for this site stemmed from my experience in coauthoring a book on Asian-Pacific derivatives markets in the early 1990s.[2] The book had a huge 180-page appendix, providing detailed information on exchanges, futures contracts, underlying indexes, and regulatory structures. Much of the data was obsolete by the time the book was in readers' hands, but in that pre-Internet age, there was no way to update the material. As I embarked on this book, knowing that the world of index products is constantly changing, I wanted to avoid this problem—and save some trees as well. So the idea of an "E-ppendix" was born. The book therefore has a relatively short appendix, featuring abridged glossaries and bibliographies, with the bulk of supplemental materials on the web, at www.ActiveIndexInvesting.com, supported by the IndexUniverse.com platform (see "How to Use This Book"). This concept has proven itself many times over in producing the manuscript, especially as its scope expanded dramatically. Through this site I was able to expand content beyond the confines of the pages before you and even update material between manuscript submission and final publication.

As part of the E-ppendix concept, I began to develop IndexUniverse.com during 2002 and 2003. Initially focused on supporting the book, conversations with industry peers convinced me that the world of indexing had a strong and genuine need for an online community that could bring together investors, exchanges, index providers, and fund managers. Somewhat like the unintended expansion of the book itself, the web site has developed steadily in scope and scale. Initially, IndexUniverse.com was going to be the E-ppendix, but as the world of finance and indexing moves so fast, I saw the need for more editorial and technological infrastructure to maximize the usefulness of the site to the industry. As I recognized the potential, I also realized that I could not subsidize IndexUniverse.com in perpetuity, and looked to make it a commercial venture.

In August 2003, I partnered the site with Index Publications LLC, the publisher of the *Journal of Indexes* and the *Exchange Traded Funds Report (ETFR)*. IndexUniverse.com now includes extensive content from these two key industry publications, as well as its own unique editorial content, industry research, data resources, and investor tools. IndexUniverse.com is linked to subsites for the print publications (www.journalofindexes.com) as well as the book's E-ppendix site at www.ActiveIndexInvesting.com. I am hopeful that this blend of hard-copy book and web-based supplement will provide continuing value to readers, and perhaps serve as a new model for professionally oriented financial books.

Although indexing is global in nature, this book is written primarily from a North American investor's perspective. However, many global examples are provided, especially in some of the sidebars. Furthermore, another benefit of having the book supplemented by the web sites is that IndexUniverse.com—which has operations in the United States, Europe, and Latin America—has substantial international coverage and perspective.

I hope that you find this book useful as a source of background on the development of indexing as well as the wide array of index products and their uses. Readers will learn that indexing is a sophisticated and active investment process, whether it involves the discipline of managing index portfolios or the art and science of assembling "portfolios of indexes." At minimum, it should provide a sense of the enormous breadth, depth, and dynamism of the indexing field. I also hope that *Active Index Investing* will stimulate your ideas on how best to use index-based products and therefore minimize risks and costs and maximize your portfolio's performance.

HOW TO USE THIS BOOK

As you might be able to discern from its heft, this book covers a lot of material. Benchmarks and index products for all major asset classes are discussed, as well as the ways that sophisticated investors use these products. The book has five parts that cover distinct areas of knowledge. While the parts build on each other, and ideally one would read the book in sequence,

I think of this book as "Five Books in One." The parts essentially stand alone (and in a way, could have each been stand-alone books) but also have lots of cross-references that direct the reader to other relevant information throughout the book.

Each discrete part has an Introduction that sets the stage for the broad topics and ties the chapters and accompanying sidebars together. In addition, Chapters 1 and 31 fall outside the five parts and serve as a thematic introduction and conclusion for the entire work. Chapter 1 outlines the themes of the book, the different meanings and interpretations of *active indexing,* and the different strands of Parts One through Five. Chapter 31 briefly reviews how far the indexing revolution has advanced and provides an extensive—and opinionated—vision for the future of indexing.

But the book does not end with Chapter 31. The Glossary and Bibliography provide a resource for terms and references in the book, supplemented by the expanded Glossary and Unabridged Bibliography and Research Resources in the E-ppendix. Each chapter has its own area on the E-ppendix, which includes relevant web-only sidebars. The E-ppendix is available on the book's dedicated web site—www.ActiveIndexInvesting.com—which is heavily integrated with further resources from IndexUniverse.com. As noted previously, I initially developed the latter site simply to support the book, but the site is now partnered with the *Journal of Indexes* and *Exchange Traded Funds Report,* to become the ultimate portal to the world of indexing . . . and beyond.

The content and structure of the E-ppendix are outlined in detail in the "Guide to the E-ppendix" at the back of this book. It has numerous features that will help the book maintain its relevance longer than most books of this type. Each chapter has a section in the E-ppendix that includes supplemental data, additional research by authors or their institutions, and "uncut" or expanded versions for some chapters. Where needed, updates and errata are provided. Some chapters also include web-only sidebars that enhance material in the book, as well as related Internet links for further information. The E-ppendix also includes several special sections for particular categories of readers, including one for indexing novices, one for industry professionals, and another for academia. These resources can be enhanced by you—the reader—through submission questions and opinions for the book's Discussion Boards. Finally, the E-ppendix has a "Feedback" feature that allows readers to provide their opinions, additional information, and suggestions, as well additional references and definitions for the Bibliography and Glossary. I also anticipate that some of the material in the errata entries for the book will be provided through this feedback mechanism—and I thus invite readers to help me continually improve the book through the E-ppendix.

Acknowledgments

A book project that spans more than three years from conception to publication invariably involves the effort of many people—colleagues, friends, industry counterparts, and publishers. And when the editor is trying to coordinate these efforts across time zones and oceans, the communications challenges and burden on those who have assisted tends to be that much greater.

Although I have tried to acknowledge all those who have helped make this dream a reality, I am aware that I may have forgotten some people. At the outset of these acknowledgements I therefore both thank them for their assistance and apologize for my oversight. A few other key supporters of the project preferred to remain anonymous, but I will make my thanks to them public—Thanks!

I must start with my family and friends not only for their support and encouragement, but also for their forbearance. The workload and challenges of this project meant numerous instances of canceled plans, unreturned phone calls, and missed e-mails. My parents, my brother, and four sisters provided a big dose of emotional support and cheerleading when needed.

Everyone I acknowledge in this section helped me achieve this goal, but a handful of people were essential in making this book and web site a reality, and therefore deserve special recognition.

Since early 2003, John Spence has been a superb editorial assistant, project manager, and coordinator of many book-related tasks, large and small. He also kept my spirits up during times when the scale of the project seemed overwhelming. John was also my partner in developing many of the elements of IndexUniverse.com, and in writing most of the initial news articles on the site.

Yasue Pai was first editorial assistant for the book, and project manager for the IndexUniverse.com site. In 2002, she helped me design the first version of IndexUniverse.com and wrote some of the first copy for the site. Yasue also applied her global outlook and skills in working with contributors around the world. I've now worked with Yasue on and off for over a decade, and like everyone else named here, I consider her a friend as much as a collaborator in work projects.

Jim Wiandt, publisher and editor of the *Journal of Indexes,* was an early and enthusiastic supporter of the project. He published some earlier versions of several book chapters and was a steady voice throughout the process, reminding me of the strong need for such a book. He also took on a selfless coordinating role for the project during a particularly challenging period in mid-2003. In addition, Jim provided a substantial amount of last-minute comments on draft chapters in the homestretch of the project. Little did we know at the outset that his involvement in the book project would also result in a business relationship. As noted in the Preface, we saw the potential and need for an independent indexing web site, and we decided to increase our collaboration and partnership to develop IndexUniverse.com into a valuable resource for the financial industry.

Christina Polischuk is a former colleague in two previous firms who also worked closely with me on the book project. Through it all, she has been a very good friend. Christina is an amazing reviewer, providing tough but helpful comments and edits, while showing deep respect for the reader's point of view. She also knows indexing from the perspective of both an asset manager and the client's point of view and improved the message of many parts of the book. For this, the authors of the chapters she helped with and I are very grateful.

Robert Ginis has been a friend and colleague for a dozen years and shares my passion for indexing and global investing. Aside from the chapters and sidebar that we coauthored, Rob generously agreed to review several other chapters. He also was a constant source of encouragement for my efforts on both the book and web site projects. I greatly appreciate his support, his friendship, and our partnership in building a shared vision for Global Index Strategies.

Paul Danziger Weil helped develop much of the programming backbone of IndexUniverse.com and the book's E-ppendix. He also was always available for emergency computer repair, most notably the salvaging of files on a hard drive after a particularly bad computer virus and crash during the manuscript's compilation.

Supplementing Paul's work was Fernando Rivera, Carolina Guerrero, and the entire team at StarNetSys who designed the "look and feel" and the technological infrastructure of both IndexUniverse.com and ActiveIndexInvesting.com.

David Kurapka—a great finance/economics writer—provided invaluable editorial help with a few key chapters. During the project, he also responded positively to my occasional requests for "power editing." On short notice, he came through with major improvements, as befits a former speechwriter for two Secretaries of the Treasury.

I must also thank all of the executives and staff at my publisher, John Wiley & Sons, for their multifaceted efforts on behalf of this project. My editor, Bill Falloon pursued the book aggressively and helped me see the opportunity to bring index fluency to a broader audience. Melissa Scuereb was a superb editorial assistant, working closely with John Spence and me to process the huge manuscript into production and working diligently to support many other elements of the book's transformation into the final text. Senior Editor Pamela van Geissen (who has now had to deal with me on two book projects in two decades) provided impetus and guidance when the effort hit the inevitable rough spots. Peggy Garry provided first-rate advice on numerous complex copyright issues that were inevitable with a book of this length. And the copyediting and production staff, particularly Mary Daniello of Wiley and Pam Blackmon and Nancy Land and their colleagues at Publications Development Company of Texas, made the endgame of this project as smooth and as painless as possible.

All the contributors to this book took time out of their busy schedules to share their views and experience with index-based investing. A few contributors helped in ways beyond just their writing and went "above and beyond the call of duty" to assist with chapter ideas, turn around drafts in hyperspeed, arrange republication rights, secure and/or assist other book contributors, and generally support this endeavor. Their encouragement was a source of additional energy to propel me forward. And, of course, they share my interest and passion for the world of indexing. They are, in alphabetical order:

Mark Anson	Adele Kohler
Sanjay Arya	Kevin Maeda
Greg Baer	John Prestbo
Nancy Calkins	Lori Richards
Pam Cloyd	Matt Scanlan
Mark Friebel	Larry Siegal
Gary Gensler	Mark Sladkus
Simon Hookway	Stephen Wallenstein
Jim Keagy	Joy Yang

Scores of other friends and colleagues assisted by reviewing chapters and providing theoretical or practical input, comments, graphics, and data. This list also includes supporters of the book's related web sites—www.ActveIndexInvesting.com, www.IndexUniverse.com and affiliated sites, in their past and current incarnations, as well as business colleagues and counterparts who have helped make my involvement in this dynamic industry more meaningful. Finally, I've included some dear friends who have tolerated having an author and editor in their life for the past three years—and perhaps a few more years going forward.

Thanks to everyone listed here:

Paul Aaronson, Standard & Poor's

Allison Adams, Institutional Investor

Scott Balentine, Barclays Global Investors

Jeremy Baskin, Northern Trust Global Investments

Michael Belkin, The Belkin Report

Steve Berkley, Lehman Brothers

Herb Blank, QED International

Jim Bogin, Legend Capital

Bruce Calkins, Moller International

Kevin Carter, Active Index Advisors

Tom Christofferson, JP Morgan

Dennis Clark, Advisor Partners

Jonathan Cohen, Barclays Global Investors

Lynn Cohn, Standard & Poor's

Bo Chung, Standard & Poor's

Renee DeBruin

Oscar Ehrenberg

Todd Ewing, San Francisco Chamber of Commerce

David Feltman, Barclays Global Investors

Henry Fernandez, MSCI

Ambassador Richard Fisher, Kissinger McLarty Associates

Don Friedman, Strategic Research Institute

Jennice Fuentes

Debbie Fuhr, Morgan Stanley

Sharon Gibson

Kristen Gilbertson, Stanford University Endowment

Michele Glicken

Leonard Gold

Mark Goldhaber, GE Capital

Jonathan Gosberg

Andrew Greenberg, Greenberg Brand Strategy

David Greenspan

Ellie Halevy

Kris Heck, Barclays Global Investors

Rep. Baron Hill, U.S. House of Representatives

Christine Hudacko, Barclays Global Investors

Mas Iwata

Jeff Jacobs, Merrill Lynch

Craig Jacobson

Bruce Johnson, Albourne Partners

Allison Jones Maitlandt, Information Management Network

David Karl, Pacific Council on International Policy

Jay Katz, Jacobs, Persinger and Parker

Farida Khambata, International Finance Corporation

Cary Klafter, Intel

Charles Kleinhaus

Zev Kleinhaus

Lee Kranefuss, Barclays Global Investors

Shannon Laughlin, Standard & Poor's

Bruce Lavine, Barclays Global Investors

Peter Leahy, State Street Global Advisors

Patricia Lee, International Finance Corporation

Lee Yuit Chieng, Barclays Global Investors

Hayne Leland, UC Berkeley/Haas School of Business

Steve Leonard

Claire Leow, Bloomberg News

Patrick Lighaam, Barclays Global Investors

Lisa Peller London, Finnegan-Henderson

Abraham Lowenthal, Pacific Council on International Policy

Miriam Lev, Bank Hapoalim

Terry Marsh, Quantal International/UC Berkeley

Lisa Mazzocco, Los Angeles County Employees Retirement Association

Tim McCarthy

Bill Miller, Morgan Stanley

John O'Brien, UC Berkeley/Haas School of Business

Kaz Okamoto, Barclays Global Investors

Yair Orgler, Tel Aviv Stock Exchange

Steve Paradis, JPMorganChase

Florence Pan, U.S. Department of Justice

Gwenn Paness, Institutional Investor

J. Parsons, Barclays Global Investors

Michael Petronella, Dow Jones Indexes

Mark Peller

Linh Pham, Barclays Global Investors

Michelle Phillips

Jim Pollison, Barclays Global Investors

Stephane Prunet, AXA Rosenberg

Roy Regev, KSM Financial/Excellence Nessuah

Robert Saffer, Lehman Brothers

Bruce Schoenfeld, CDP Capital

Brian Schreiber, AIG

Andrew Schulman, ThinkBank

Bob Shakotko, Standard & Poor's

Ofer Simchony, Tel Aviv Stock Exchange

Maya Skubatch, Wilson Sonsini Goodrich & Rosati

Stephen Smith

Sara Soibelmann

Andrew Sollinger, Thomson Media

John Sulski

Ruenvadee Suwanmongkol, Thai Securities and Exchange Commission

Tom Taggart, Barclays Global Investors

Larry Tint, Quantal International

Alan Tonelson, U.S. Business and Industrial Council

Jeff Torchon, Barclays Global Investors

Lois Towers, Barclays Global
Investors
Robert Tull, American Stock
Exchange
Cliff Weber, American Stock
Exchange

Lisa Weitzman
Al Wheeler, Jacobs, Persinger and
Parker
Deborah Yang, MSCI
Janice Yecco, Florida State Board of
Adminstration

Despite the myriad contributions of those named in the preceding list—and the book's contributors in the next section—I am solely responsible for any errors or omissions in the text. I apologize in advance for the inevitable mistakes that emerge in a work of this nature and scope.

Luckily, as noted previously, the book has a linked web site, and you are encouraged to provide feedback on any factual errors, or even points of disagreement. As discussed previously, on the book's E-ppendix, each chapter has an update and errata section, where authors can update material in the chapter, and I will post relevant reader feedback. The world of indexing has benefited greatly from debate and exchange of ideas, and I will be honored if my mistakes can stimulate dialogue and positive change.

Finally, I want to reiterate my thanks to all the contributors to the book—both chapter contributors and sidebar contributors—for their effort and commitment on behalf of this project. Their names and affiliations follow, and their detailed biographies (with photographs and updated titles/affiliations) are provided on the book's E-ppendix, at www.ActiveIndexInvesting.com (also accessible via www.IndexUniverse.com).

NOTES

1. The ultimate expression of this activeness was our transition of tens of billions of dollars of client assets in 2001 and 2002 from MSCI and FTSE global indexes to their new float-adjusted successor benchmarks. While doing this, we minimized transaction costs and avoided wealth erosion from potential index change front-runners lurking in the marketplace. This major index event is discussed in Chapters 5, 9, 12, and 21.
2. Keith K. H. Park and Steven A. Schoenfeld, *The Pacific Rim Futures and Options Markets* (Chicago/Cambridge, UK: Probus Publishing/McGraw-Hill, 1992, and Singapore: Heinemann Asia/Reed International, 1994).

Contributors

The following is a list of the contributors to this book. Whether they are authors or co-authors of a chapter, or a contributor of a sidebar, I am grateful to each and every one of them for joining me in this project and sharing their insight and knowledge with the book's readers.

These professionals represent a wide range of functions and backgrounds from across the indexing industry—including portfolio managers, analysts, index calculators, university professors, financial advisors, editors, and other industry practitioners to name but a few. As readers will know, the financial industry is dynamic, and successful professionals are anything but static in their roles. As the book was in the final editing stage, it was not possible to assemble comprehensive, updated biographical information for this group of more than 60 talented investment experts. Therefore, a simple list of the contributors and their institutional affiliation (where appropriate) is provided below. This list is supplemented by the CONTRIBUTORS section of the book's E-ppendix at www.ActiveIndexInvesting.com, where complete biographical information is provided. This biographic information is also accessible via the IndexUniverse.com web site. For some contributors, photographs and additional research papers are available. The E-ppendix will also facilitate continuing updates from contributors on their specific topic areas. More information on the book's "web-only" sidebar contributors will also be updated and enhanced as this aforementioned section grows.

Mark Adams
Active Index Advisors

Mark Anson
California Public Employees'
  Retirement System (CalPERS)

Sanjay Arya
Morningstar Indexes

Yasushika Asaoka
Pension Fund Association of Japan

Gregory Baer
Co-author of *The Great Mutual
  Fund Trap*

David Blitzer
Standard & Poor's

Eric Brandhorst
State Street Global Advisors

David Burkart
Barclays Global Investors

Nancy Calkins
Washington State Investment
Board (WSIB)

Michael J. Chasnoff
Truepoint Capital

Lisa Chen
Barclays Global Investors

Melinda Chu
Standard & Poor's

Pamela Cloyd

James Creighton
Northern Trust Global Investments

Partha Dasgupta
Barclays Global Investors

Eleanor de Freitas
Barclays Global Investors

Francis Enderle
Barclays Global Investors

Joyce Franklin
JLFranklin Wealth Planning

Mark Friebel
Barclays Global Investors

Gary Gensler
Co-author of *The Great Mutual
Fund Trap*

Binu George
AXA Rosenberg Investment
Management

Khalid Ghayur
MSCI

Robert Ginis
Global Index Strategies

William Hahn

Joanne M. Hill
Goldman Sachs

Simon Hookway
MSS Capital Management

Edward Hoyt
California State Teacher's
Retirement System (CalSTRS)

John Jacobs
Nasdaq Financial Products

Yigal Jhirad
Morgan Stanley

Creighton Jue
Barclays Global Investors

James S. Keagy
Barclays Global Investors

Adele Kohler
State Street Global Advisors

John Krimmel
Illinois State University Retirement
System

S. Jane Leung
Barclays Global Investors

Kevin Maeda
Active Index Advisors

Vache Mahseredjian

Mark Makepeace
FTSE International

Tom McCutchen
Barclays Global Investors

Barbara Mueller
Goldman Sachs

Michael Mueller
Oregon State Treasury

Niklas Nordenfelt
Wells Fargo

Patrick O'Connor
Barclays Global Investors

Omer Ozkul
Morgan Stanley

Elizabeth Para
Barclays Global Investors

Don Phillips
Morningstar

Gardner Platt

Brad Pope
Barclays Global Investors

John Prestbo
Dow Jones Indexes

David Qian
Morgan Stanley

Chad Rakvin

Lori Richards
Russell Indexes

Aje K. Saigal
Government of Singapore
Investment Corporation

Gus Sauter
The Vanguard Group

Matthew Scanlan
Barclays Global Investors

Amy Schioldager
Barclays Global Investors

Larry Siegel
The Ford Foundation

Mark Sladkus

John Spence
IndexUniverse.com

Peter Wall

Stephen Wallenstein
Duke University Global Capital
Markets Center

Amy Whitelaw
Barclays Global Investors

Jim Wiandt
The Journal of Indexes/
IndexUniverse.com

Hugh Wilson
State Street Global Advisors

Joy Yang
AXA Rosenberg Investment
Management

Yi Zheng

Mark A. Zurack
Columbia University School
of Business

About the Editor

Steven A. Schoenfeld is a Managing Partner of Global Index Strategies, which provides consulting services to asset managers, brokerages, institutional investors and exchanges on benchmark design and selection, asset allocation, product development, and marketing strategies. He is also a Senior Research Fellow of Duke University's Global Capital Markets Center, and the Founder and Editor-in-Chief of IndexUniverse.com, the definitive online resource on indexes, index products, and index-based investment strategies.

In 2003, Steven served as Chief Investment Officer of Active Index Advisors (AIA), focusing on customized, tax-optimized enhanced index portfolios. He was responsible for AIA's investment and product development activities and supervised the portfolio management process. Through January 2003, Steven was a Managing Director of Barclays Global Investors (BGI). He served in a variety of portfolio management and investment strategy roles at BGI, with a focus on global equity indexing. This included several years of responsibility for BGI's international equity index products, encompassing $65 billion in developed international and emerging markets portfolios and *iShares* exchange-traded funds. Steven also served for three years as BGI's Global Coordinator for Index Methodology and Vendor Relationships.

Prior to joining BGI in 1996, Steven worked for five years at the International Finance Corporation (IFC)—the private sector affiliate of the World Bank. While there, he helped develop the IFC Investable Emerging Market Indexes (now the S&P/IFC Emerging Market Indexes) and structured the first index funds and derivatives based on the IFC Indexes. Before joining IFC, he worked for seven years in the derivatives industry, including three years as an independent floor trader in Japanese stock index futures at SIMEX (now the Singapore Exchange).

Steven holds a BA in History and Government from Clark University, and studied at the London School of Economics. In 1985 and 1986, he was a Fulbright Scholar in Economics at the National University of Singapore, and in 1992, he received an MA in International Relations from the Johns

Hopkins University School of Advanced International Studies (SAIS). He is coauthor of *The Pacific Rim Futures and Options Markets* (Probus Publishing/McGraw-Hill, 1992) and has contributed chapters and articles for numerous books and financial publications. Steven is a member of the Duke University Global Capital Market Center's Advisory Board, the American Stock Exchange's New Product Development Committee, and the FTSE Global Equity Indices Committee.

More background information about the editor is available in the EDITOR section of the book's E-ppendix at www.ActiveIndexInvesting.com. This section includes a number of Steven's previous writings and presentations, links to his organizational affiliations, and some colorful highlights from his global trading, traveling, and investing experiences.

CHAPTER 1

Indexing *Is* Active

The Meaning of *Active Indexing* and the Interconnected Themes of the Book

Steven A. Schoenfeld

THE IMPACT OF INDEXING

This chapter provides an overview of the key themes and topics of *Active Index Investing*. Its purpose is to help the reader gain a better understanding of the multiple dimensions of indexing, which are then explored comprehensively in the rest of the book.

The impact of index investing has gone well beyond index-based portfolios; its transparency and efficiency have dramatically changed the investment landscape. Benchmarks have moved from being theoretical constructs to become truly transparent and efficient investment alternatives. What better method of measuring active manager performance could be devised than a yardstick for asset class exposure? Index-based portfolios have shone a bright light on the value added (or lack of value added) by managers who were charging active fees yet hugging their benchmarks—a practice known as "closet indexing."

The lower costs of index funds brought new transparency and focus on trading costs for all institutional investment vehicles. Institutional investors have saved enormous sums in the first quarter century of indexing.[1] This also led to the growth of new products and new techniques for adding value to the investment process. Among the most notable are portfolio trading, securities lending, and structured transition trades.

The same focus on efficiency of exposure and risk management led to the development of stock index futures and options. And the development

1

of exchange-traded funds (ETFs), which started as an evolved blend of the techniques of both portfolio trading and index derivatives, has extended the benefits of indexing to a huge new group of potential users. Furthermore, ETFs, unlike previous index vehicles such as index mutual funds, are appropriate and efficient for both institutions and individual investors: The participation of one type of user does not disadvantage the other. Finally, although indexing started with equities, it has expanded into most other asset classes and virtually every equity market in the world.

The growth and development of indexing has been both a theoretical and practical financial revolution, and it is steadily advancing. Thus, it is important to understand the fundamentals of indexing, as well as the products and their varied uses. This knowledge will help the reader recognize just how dynamic the field is and why indexing truly is active.

This chapter starts the journey by first explaining the book's title—*Active Index Investing*—with a description of the three ways in which indexing is anything but passive. The second part of the chapter provides a broad overview of the core themes and information in Parts One through Five of the book.

WHAT DOES ACTIVE INDEXING MEAN?

Index-based products are commonly referred to as passive, which implies a static, even boring, approach to the market. Although Chapters 2 through 4 demonstrate how this "passivity" can actually deliver better long-term investment performance, many investment professionals secretly suspect that indexing is a lazy man's game. They perceive it as a cop-out that somehow means "leaving something on the table"—in this case, the potential for outperformance. This has led to decades of debate between proponents of active management versus believers in indexed approaches. In fact, some of the early opponents of indexing called it "un-American" and "guaranteed mediocrity." To which Nobel Laureate Paul Samuelson replied, "People say that you're settling for mediocrity [with indexing]. Isn't it interesting that the best brains on Wall Street can't achieve mediocrity?"

This book *will not* engage in that debate. As Chapter 3 indicates, for sophisticated investors, this debate is over, and the conclusion is both simple and elegant. What maximizes the efficiency of an overall portfolio is not "index versus active," but instead, a combination of both approaches. This book shows the reader how smart cost- and risk-sensitive investors use the power of indexing to maximize portfolio performance and minimize risk.

As noted in the Preface, the term *active indexing* is most decidedly *not* an oxymoron. It can describe the active nature of managing index-based portfolios, and it also can describe a philosophy or approach that uses index-based tools in creative (decidedly nonpassive) ways to change the risk/return profile of an investment. It can mean many different things to different market participants, but I define it in three basic ways that reflect a high degree of activeness (the key phrases are in italics):

1. *Benchmark construction and selection is active.* The choice of benchmarks (for indexing and for asset allocation and performance measurement) involves substantial active decision making. In using index strategies, investors make important, active decisions about strategic benchmarks, weightings, and rebalancing of asset allocations. Even when using exclusively active managers, the choice of benchmark for the manager—and for the asset class within the overall portfolio—greatly influences the investment outcome. The index industry is dynamic, with continual development and refinement of both benchmarks and the index products linked to them. As more products are launched, and as indexing expands to virtually every asset class, the need for investors to make informed decisions on benchmarks will only grow. Asset owners cannot be passive about the benchmark decision.

   Part Two of the book provides background on benchmarks. It includes the discussion and analysis of the benchmarks that are available to investors, the different metrics for assessing indexes that demonstrate the activeness of this decision process, and the need for independent analysis.

   Part Three of the book provides an overview of the huge variety of index-based products and strategies and how they are developed and used. Readers will see how active the innovation and creativity of the financial community can be when applied to indexing.

2. *Managing index funds is active.* Managing index-based portfolios is an extremely active process. Because tracking benchmark indexes requires a high investment quotient (IQ), index portfolio managers often have more insight into market microstructure—trading, operational constraints, liquidity, corporate actions—than most traditional active investors.

   Part Four of the book focuses on this little-understood dimension of index-based investment. Readers will likely be amazed at the degree of effort and skill needed to manage portfolios that accurately track equity and fixed-income indexes.

3. *The use of index products can be as active as the investor wants it to be.* Active and sophisticated decision making by investors undergirds their use of index-based products and strategies. Investors who choose an index-based approach in no way abdicate the quest for outperformance. In fact, integrating indexing and enhanced indexing within a total portfolio approach to risk budgeting allows them to better segment the beta or market

exposure from their sources of alpha or excess return.[2] Determining the right index products and optimal proportion of allocation to index-based strategies is a vital decision. Using appropriate indexing approaches can be one of the most important ways to achieve outperformance.

In Part Five, sophisticated investors illustrate how index products and strategies can help manage risk, minimize costs, and maximize performance in the only way that matters—relative to the risk taken.[3]

By the end of the book, the reader will understand all these definitions of active indexing and will have one or more favorite examples for each of the preceding meanings.

Although the issues of index-based portfolio construction differ greatly from the decisions and products of traditional active management, its dimensions are all active—there is nothing passive about them.

ACTIVE DECISIONS IN INDEXING—TOUGH CHOICES, LIMITLESS CREATIVITY

The myriad choices of benchmarks, allocation schemes, and methods of rebalancing can seem overwhelming. These diverse and multiple options reflect the continual evolution of both index products and the theories behind them.

This complexity and the many nuances highlight the activeness of every indexing decision. The use of index products and strategies almost always has an active element, and often, index-based products are the most efficient way to maximize return and minimize risk.

As active benchmark decisions are not explicitly discussed in subsequent chapters, a short description follows here. Further explanation of the actual implementation of alternative benchmark structures can be found in Chapters 14 and 18.

Indexing started as a way to achieve diversified, transparent, efficient core exposure to asset classes—initially domestic equity, and then international and global equity and fixed income. But indexing has evolved in many active ways; among the most interesting is the blending of index benchmarks and tools with various levels of active decisions. This phenomenon developed through the interaction and debate of many players: academics (discussed in Part One), index providers, consultants, fund managers, and asset owners.

Index benchmarks have numerous differences—investors need to understand the methodologies before making decisions. And as ETFs penetrate further into the retail marketplace, this need will become more pressing.

Choosing benchmarks and investment strategies will become increasingly complex. Parts Two and Three of the book describe many nuances involved with these choices and explore ways to build portfolios on them. The following short list shows some of the choices that investors face in determining appropriate benchmarks (standard or custom) and the investment strategies linked to them:

■ Reliance on known quantities—use of name brand indexes.
■ Alternative weights, both within markets and across markets.
■ Country inclusions/exclusions for investment or policy reasons.
■ Sectors/industries (subsectors).
■ Size/capitalization range.
■ Style and style rotation.
■ Screened portfolios, whether for social policy or investment prudence (e.g., bankruptcy/value, corporate governance).

To visually portray the array of choices, Table 1.1 summarizes the range of size, style, sector, and country coverage of the major global index families. And each of these factors can be custom implemented—using alternative weights or excluding certain characteristics—either as a benchmark or within an index strategy. Each subindex can also be used to complete an investor's existing allocations, a strategy that is discussed in Chapter 18. Index providers and index fund/ETF managers will continue to innovate, and thus, this list might be obsolete relatively soon. IndexUniverse.com provides news and updates on benchmarks and index products.

Table 1.1 excludes highly popular domestic U.S. benchmarks such as Russell or Wilshire Indexes (all of which are discussed in Part Two, and are thoroughly covered in the Index Research section of www.IndexUniverse.com.

TABLE 1.1   Array of Choices in Standard and Custom Indexes

	Cap Range (Size)	Style (Value/Growth)	Sectors	Market Coverage	Specialized/ Screened
Dow Jones	L/M/S/total	V/"Neutral"/G	10	>30	Sustainability, Islamic, custom
FTSE	L/M/S/total	V/G	10	>45	Socially responsible, custom
MSCI	L/M/S/total	V/G	10	>45	Custom
S&P	L/M/S/total	V/G	10	>45	Custom

Note: L = Large cap; M = Mid cap; S = Small cap; V = Value; G = Growth. "Neutral" is also commonly referred to as "core." Market Coverage is the number of stock markets that the index series includes in both data and broadest "multi-market" index.

Once investors have chosen an alternative or customized benchmark, they face major rebalancing choices:

(handwritten margin note: rebalancing choice)

- ■ *Rebalancing approaches within strategy.* For example, there are different types and frequencies of calendar-based approaches (trigger bands) that seek to capture mean reversion between sectors and/or countries.
- ■ *Rebalancing/funding approaches between asset classes strategies.* This total portfolio perspective can use investor cash flows to rebalance between and among asset classes—domestic and international equities, fixed income, real estate securities, and others. Using new funding to rebalance with index products can be a highly efficient way to achieve the long-term benefits of multi-asset class index or index and active strategies. This approach is discussed in Chapter 28 and in more detail in Chapter 30.

Working alone, or with their asset managers or financial advisor, investors have virtually limitless opportunities for creative solutions, with transparent, cost-effective, and efficient investment vehicles. Furthermore, even the most heavily customized indexing strategy can share in the liquidity pool of other index portfolios. Whether trading a publicly listed vehicle that benefits from institutional participation or working within an institutional product structure, index-based approaches benefit from the two-way activity flow of various users. Many times, this activity can facilitate cross-trading between large index investors trading in the opposite directions.[4]

This short discussion illustrates the limitless variations around an indexing approach. Whether a portfolio is 100 percent index-based, or a blend of index or active, there are many important choices in benchmark selection and implementation—some of them highly complex. This is a key element in the definition of the term *active index investing.*

THE INTERCONNECTED THEMES OF PARTS ONE THROUGH FIVE

The book is divided into five parts—which as mentioned in the Preface could have each been a stand-alone book. Clearly, purchasers of the book have "made a good trade." The five parts are as follows:

Part One: The Indexing Revolution: Theory and Practice.
Part Two: Benchmarks: The Foundation for Indexing.
Part Three: The Ever-Expanding Variety and Flexibility of Index Products.

Part Four: Managing Index Funds: It's Anything but Passive!
Part Five: Pulling It All Together: How to Use Index Products to Build
 an Efficient, Risk-Controlled Investment Strategy.

Throughout, the book highlights the myths and misperceptions about indexing and provides insight into the core benefits of index-based strategies.

The theory behind indexing evolved largely from the study of equity markets, which tends to give this book an "equity-centric" focus. It does, however, cover most other major asset classes; more important, the core theories that underlie equity indexing are equally relevant for other asset classes, including fixed income, real estate, and commodities. Part One provides a comprehensive overview of the foundations and principles of indexing, including a consolidation of the theoretical and business history of indexing. Contributors explore the enduring logic and accelerating sophistication of indexing and tackle the critics of indexing with solid empirical data and numerous real-world examples.

The detailed presentation of benchmarks in Part Two shows how indexes are the foundation for almost all investment activity. The nuances of index construction and maintenance methodology are described as well as the seven key criteria for choosing the right benchmark index for specific investing needs. This decision is an *active* choice that has significance, regardless of whether the investments are in index funds or in active funds benchmarked to an index.

Part Two starts with a focus on equity indexes, but its scope broadens to include most major asset classes and areas of investment. Investors building multiple asset class portfolios rely on benchmarks when performing asset allocation studies that determine their commitment to various categories of assets. Again the reader will see how and why the benchmark decision is an active one, and why it matters so much.

In Part Three, the focus shifts to an overview of the ever-growing range of index-based investment products. Indexing has shaken up sleepy corners of the investment industry by bringing transparency and accountability to investment managers. Through three decades, innovative index product development has been a source of disruptive technology that serves the greater good of asset owners. And while the process started with equity markets, it is rapidly spreading to all major investable asset classes, including alternative investments such as real estate and hedge funds.

The purpose of Part Three is to define and highlight the broad categories of index products—funds, derivatives, ETFs, and so on—and the asset classes that they track. An effort is made to cover global trends and developments, even though this book retains a North American investor's perspective.

From the outset, the book makes no effort to be all-inclusive. This would have been virtually impossible. The largest institutional index fund management firms track hundreds of benchmarks for more than a thousand clients, and although retail index mutual funds may have fewer variants, they still have large fund families. ETFs are somewhere in between. But more critically, the product sets are always evolving, and thus this part of the book depicts the scope and scale of index-based products. It highlights some particularly interesting product and strategy types, such as ETFs, enhanced indexing, and the indexing of alternative asset classes. Chapter 18 delves deep into the ways that index products can be used to facilitate sophisticated strategies—what I call *active indexing*.

Part Four focuses on the art and science of managing index-based portfolios. It provides an insider's perspective of the techniques and challenges in building and maintaining index funds, ETFs, and custom index-based portfolios. It also demonstrates that this craft is certainly "anything but passive." The six chapters in Part Four all were written by current or former index portfolio managers. The subject matter covers the major asset classes and product types including U.S. and international equities, fixed-income, ETFs, and index-based separate accounts.

As far as I know—and I asked a lot of people before embarking on this project—there has never before been such a detailed and comprehensive exploration of the index portfolio management investment process. The contributors have provided robust examples and even some entertaining war stories from the front lines of the battle to minimize costs and maximize tracking. Topics include index construction methodology, client needs and motivations, the underlying market microstructure, trading and transaction costs, and macroeconomic and other market-moving forces.

Part Five, the final section, is an exploration of why and how sophisticated investors use index-based products to minimize costs and risks, and maximize portfolio performance. In these seven chapters and six sidebars, readers see the perspective of large public institutional investors, financial advisors, and authors writing from the individual investor's viewpoint. In what may prove to be the most valuable part of the book for some readers, the contributors provide numerous real-world examples of indexing for asset allocation, risk budgeting, and tax minimization. They also describe the key factors that plan sponsors and their consultants should use when choosing index-based instruments.

Speaking for the needs of individual investors, two former U.S. Treasury Department officials who have fully explored the traps that most mutual fund investors fall into propose a better—indexed—way to achieve better long-term results for savings and/or retirement.

Part Five also proposes a universal investment philosophy that is relevant for institutions, financial advisors, and individual investors—what I call *indexing at the core*; and this section and the book conclude with an opinionated projection of the future of indexing. Not surprisingly, the chapter envisages the probability of continued expansion and democratization of index-based products and strategies.

ON TO THE REVOLUTION

After reading this overview, you should have a better sense of the three definitions of active indexing; active benchmark choice, the active process of managing index portfolios, and the active use of index products for everything from broad-based asset allocation to short-term tactical trading.

Investors should keep this multifaceted concept in mind when consulting the five parts of the book—in whatever order makes the most sense to them. Each one covers material that could have been a book in itself, and there are numerous cross-references to related chapters throughout. As befits a dynamic, rapidly growing industry, the editor and contributors will endeavor to update chapters of the book in the "E-ppendix," which is hosted on and supplemented by other features and data on www.IndexUniverse.com.

We now move into Part One of the book, which documents the efforts of then-radical academics and investment professionals who began this revolution. Their theories and innovations continue to drive the inexorable advance of index investing even today. Chapter 2 provides insight into the "profound, positive, and permanent" revolutionary effect of indexing introduced by Don Phillips in the Foreword. The subsequent chapters show how the industry has built on those foundations to continually develop products and strategies "that have given investors greater control in managing risk, return, and cost in their portfolios."

NOTES

1. In a study conducted in 1998, "25 Years of Indexing: An Analysis of the Costs and Benefits" by PricewaterhouseCoopers, and commissioned by Barclays Global Investors, the authors estimated that the total savings for U.S. institutional tax-exempt investors ranged between $81 billion and $105 billion since the launch of the first cap-weighted index fund in 1973. These savings include transaction costs, management fees, and the performance difference between index and active strategies. They similarly estimated that the then "current" annual savings are between $14 billion and $18 billion (p. 27).

2. These terms are fully explained in subsequent chapters, particularly in Chapters 2 and 14.
3. Return relative to risk incurred is generally measured as an information ratio. This measure is defined and discussed in Chapters 14 and 15.
4. Crossing—which saves enormous amounts of money for institutional index fund clients—is discussed in Parts Four and Five of the book.

PART

One

The Indexing Revolution
Theory and Practice

Steven A. Schoenfeld

After over a third of a century of indexing, we are seeing the start of a revolution. The first index fund was launched in 1971, and perhaps the concept was revolutionary, but how then can the revolution just be starting? Part One focuses on the finance theory that is the foundation for index-based investment and explores the enduring logic and accelerating sophistication of indexing. One of the most interesting elements in the growth of indexing has been the constant interplay between academia and practitioners. In fact, many indexing pioneers—past, present, and, likely, future—have blended careers in the ivory tower and the trenches of Wall Street.

As background and perspective on some of the major milestones in the history of indexing, I have provided a time line of key developments in products and investment practice (see the table on page 12).

Chapter 31 includes a more detailed version of this time line, extended further into the future. That chapter looks deeply into future trends in the industry and bravely (naively?) makes predictions about product innovation and asset growth.

Chapter 2 provides a comprehensive overview of the theoretical and practical foundations that started the indexing revolution. This history is both interesting and entertaining. Chapter 3 picks up the story by showing the ever-evolving uses of indexing and begins to unwind the twentieth-century "index versus active" debate that, frankly, is obsolete.

Time Line of Index-Based Vehicles and Strategies

Time Period	Major Developments
1970s	The first institutional (1971/1973) and retail index fund (1976)
	First international equity index fund (1979) and "tilted" index fund (enhanced indexing)
1980s	Stock Index futures and options (U.S.–1982, U.K.–1984, Japan–1986)
	Expansion of index funds
	First fixed-income index funds
	First socially screened portfolios (South Africa-free)
1990s	Bull market spurs massive growth of index fund assets and deeper penetration of indexing in Japan and Europe
	Launch of ETFs in Canada and United States (TIPS, SuperShares, SPDR) (1991–1993)
	Investable emerging market indexes and first EM index funds (1991–1994)
2000–2004	Global ETF explosion (equity and fixed income)
	Major global and local benchmark indexes move to float-adjustment (the biggest index change[s] ever)
	Options and SSFs on ETFs brings liquid derivatives to more specialized/focused indexes
	Universal accounts (combining separate accounts, ETFs, and mutual funds)
	Launch of commodity and currency ETFs

Chapter 4 addresses some of the last remaining myths about indexing by demonstrating with empirically and anecdotal evidence how index-based strategies work in all market environments.

Part One provides a solid foundation in the history, rationale, and dynamism of indexing. It will hopefully propel the reader—with enthusiasm—into the more technical parts of the book. By the time you reach the final chapter, you are likely to be as excited as I am about the next stage of the indexing revolution.

CHAPTER 2

The Foundations of Indexing

Theoretical and Practical
Underpinnings of a Heretical Concept

Binu George, Steven A. Schoenfeld, and Jim Wiandt

_____ Editor's Note _____

This chapter chronicles the evolution of the investment theories that explain why index investing is the most rational method of fund management. Harry Markowitz's theory of efficient portfolios and subsequent research by William Sharpe, Paul Samuelson, and others laid the philosophical foundations of index investing. Wells Fargo Bank's launch of the first index fund in 1971 was followed almost immediately by funds at Batterymarch and American National Bank. Vanguard established its first retail index fund in 1976, while international and fixed-income indexing started in the early 1980s. Since then, hundreds of index futures, options, swaps, exchange-traded funds (ETFs), and other index products have put theory into practice. The essential principle underlying indexing—a focus on minimizing costs and controlling risks—remains unchanged and is now shared by index and active managers alike. The industry's future is no longer a simple debate between index and active investing. It is about ensuring that the investor chooses the appropriate mix of the two approaches. This theme concludes the chapter and is developed throughout the book.

_____

The authors would like to acknowledge John Spence and Yi Zheng for their research assistance in developing this chapter.

Although the origins of index investing go back to the early 1950s, stock indexes have been around since the late nineteenth century. In 1884, Charles Dow, founder of the *Wall Street Journal,* and Edward Davis Jones first began listing the Dow Jones Average, a price-weighted index of 11 large railroad companies. With his new benchmark, Dow hoped to give investors an overall view of what the market was doing on any given day. In 1896, Dow Jones created the industrial average (with 12 stocks) and separated the railroad stocks into a separate average, which was renamed the Transportation Index. Daily publication of the Dow Jones Industrial Average (DJIA) began in the *Wall Street Journal* on May 26, 1896. The DJIA expanded to 20 stocks in 1916, and to 30 in 1928. The index still lists 30 stocks on a price-weighted basis, although the only company remaining from the original 12 is General Electric (see Table 2.1).

Although investors still use the Dow as a point of reference to take the market's pulse, many now view the S&P 500 as the best yardstick for U.S. equities. In 1913, Alfred Cowles conducted the meticulous research that would later form the basis of Standard & Poor's stock indexes. Not until the 1960s, however, would the technology be available to compute market capitalization-weighted indexes like the S&P 500 in real time.

Since those early days, a mind-numbing array of index-based products—from index funds and ETFs to options, futures, and options on index ETFs—have been launched around the world. At the same time, numerous providers

TABLE 2.1   What Happened to the Original 12 Companies in the Dow Jones Industrial Average?

Company	What Became of It?
American Cotton Oil	Distant ancestor of Bestfoods
American Sugar	Evolved into Amstar Holdings
American Tobacco	Broken up in 1911 antitrust action
Chicago Gas	Absorbed by Peoples Gas, 1897
Distilling and Cattle Feeding	Whiskey trust evolved into Millennium Chemical
General Electric	Going strong and still in the DJIA
Laclede Gas	Active, removed from DJIA in 1899
National Lead	Today's NL Industries removed from DJIA in 1916
North American	Utility combine broken up in 1940s
Tennessee Coal & Iron	Absorbed by U.S. Steel in 1907
U.S. Leather (preferred)	Dissolved in 1952
U.S. Rubber	Became Uniroyal, now part of Michelin

Source: Dow Jones Indexes.

have constructed thousands of indexes to meet these burgeoning product and benchmarking needs. Most important, an entirely new investing philosophy has grown around indexing, and has fundamentally changed how sophisticated investors look at the market. This philosophy, which has gained ground in both institutional and retail investing circles, is an interesting mix of faith in efficient markets, sober examination of the facts of performance attribution, and a good dose of common sense.

The tidal movement toward index investing owes its start to a serendipitous meeting between a graduate student in search of a thesis and his advisor's stockbroker. A casual conversation, struck up while they were both waiting to see the advisor, ultimately led to a radical transformation of the investment management industry.

Harry Markowitz was the graduate student at the University of Chicago, and he started his project by perusing the standard research reports published in the industry. He was struck by the focus on return as the primary consideration in choosing assets. When the portfolio managers of the day looked at risk, they did so subjectively without fully understanding the interrelationships between securities. Markowitz's contribution was to describe how a well-diversified portfolio reduced the risk of equity investment. He wrote his seminal paper, "Portfolio Selection," in 1952 while still a student. The name suggested that investors should search for the best *portfolio,* and not just the best *stocks.*[1]

The best portfolio would provide investors with the optimal trade-off between return and risk. Investors choose different portfolios because everyone has different goals and varying tolerances for risk. A young investor with a long horizon and a bright future would presumably invest in a portfolio that would offer high returns, but at the cost of steep risk (measured by the portfolio's standard deviation). On the other hand, a retired investor might not be willing to stomach the ups and downs of a high-risk portfolio and would settle for a low-risk, low-return basket of securities. The set of possible choices is depicted in Figure 2.1 as the curve AZ. This diagram is commonly known as the Efficient Frontier Curve, with the point on the curve which touches the preference line (point U) being the point of maximum utility for the particular investor.

This new theory ran counter to the then-prevailing wisdom that an investor should only buy a few firms that could be researched and examined in depth. Investors typically bought only companies that they understood, without considering how each addition affected the overall risk of the portfolio. In addition to the prevailing logic-based dissonance, other reasons prevented Markowitz's ideas from gaining a firm footing for several years. Most importantly, the technology prevalent at that time was inadequate to cope with the needs of Markowitz's theory. Analyzing a 100-security portfolio would

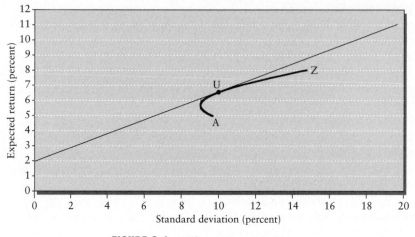

FIGURE 2.1   Efficient Frontier Curve

require the calculation of 100 expected returns, 100 standard deviations, and 4,950 correlations. Number crunching of this magnitude simply could not be done within a reasonable time frame on the technological platforms of those years. In addition, transaction costs were prohibitively high. Commissions averaged 2 percent per transaction. By definition, a well-diversified portfolio would require more transactions than a concentrated portfolio. The additional costs would negatively impact the benefits of diversification.

James Tobin, an economist at Yale, agreed with Markowitz on the benefits of portfolio diversification and about not keeping all of one's eggs in the same basket. However, he wanted to explore ways to adjust a portfolio's risk level aside from simply altering the mix of risky securities. He proved that an investor could attain any desired point of risk by simply altering the proportion of cash and stock in a portfolio. Furthermore, the investor would be better off lowering the risk level with cash, instead of shifting the mix of securities.[2]

William Sharpe, a student of Markowitz, made the next major contribution to quantifying portfolio risk. He was awarded the Nobel Prize in 1990 for developing the theory that came to be known as the Capital Asset Pricing Model (CAPM). It stated that the uncertainty of stock returns is caused by two types of risk factors—systematic and unsystematic.[3] Systematic risk is the risk that an investor takes on from simply being a part of the stock market. This includes general shocks such as an unexpected rise in inflation or threat of war. Unsystematic risk, on the other hand, is specific to a particular stock. Examples of this risk are rumors of management changes and product failures. Systematic risk should be rewarded, as that is the compensation for being exposed to the vagaries of the general economy. Because unsystematic risk could be reduced to zero in a portfolio simply by holding securities that encompass all aspects of the market, it should not be rewarded.

In 1965, Paul Samuelson published his paper on the information inherent in stock prices. He said that the intrinsic value of stocks is nothing but their market price at any moment.[4] The near constant fluctuations occur because there is continuing disagreement on the intrinsic value between buyers and sellers. The only price at which equilibrium is reached is the market price.

Eugene Fama expanded this argument. He coined a phrase with his new theory: the *Efficient Market Hypothesis* (EMH), which has three levels—weak, semistrong, and strong.[5] The weak form suggests that past price behavior is already incorporated into stock prices. The semistrong version says that the market also reflects all current information, such as earnings reports and new product releases. The strong version holds that it is not possible to benefit from "monopolistic information" either. Monopolistic information here is defined not just as information from all sources, but also as the ability to translate that information into valuable asset selections. The academic community debated which level of efficiency applied to stock prices, while the investment community, for its part, continued to blithely ignore the entire topic. The extended bull market that continued into the mid-1960s had contributed to a conviction in many quarters that professionals who were willing and able to identify outperforming stocks could easily beat the market. Only after a painful bear market did professionals start to differentiate between luck and skill.

Alas, when the theoretical dust finally settled, it became all too clear that because, by and large, the market *is* efficient, it is difficult to systematically exploit inefficiencies. They are quickly priced out of the market and are fleeting at best. The overriding basic theory that ties index investing to EMH is that the market simply can't outperform or outguess itself. On average, investors are going to earn market returns minus whatever their costs may be. And the more active the investors are, the more transaction, market impact, and tax costs they will have to deal with. This factor must be combined with EMH's basic precept that all information for any equity's present and future earnings potential in the macroeconomic picture has been priced into the stock's current value. Thus, in principle, a stock's price is balanced like a seesaw, with equal probability of going in either direction, depending on any new information that comes in. Thus, not only must active investors overcome higher costs, basic EMH theory holds that it is nigh impossible to guess correctly over any long-term period about market or specific equity movement.

This idea gives rise to the basic philosophy that is fundamental to index-based investing, and it is as simple as it is revolutionary. Whether or not an investor believes in an efficient market, the logical course in investing is to first manage the controllable variables by dampening risk through diversification, while minimizing turnover, transaction costs, and tax implications. Achieving these goals is the core logic supporting index investing and index-based products. Many not-so-passive investors are using the increasingly diverse array of index products because of their diversification across a relevant asset class, their low turnover, and low-cost tax efficiency. As this book describes in detail, in addition to being the basis of a portfolio, these index products can be used to customize a portfolio to a specific investor's asset allocation needs, to form the core of a portfolio that otherwise invests actively, or to form components of a highly active strategy for making style, sector, or country bets.

All these subsequent developments were beyond the wildest imagination of the first proponents of both modern portfolio theory and EMH. In the earliest days of index investing, unfamiliarity with these intellectual concepts in actual investing circles and a correspondent distrust of the unfamiliar delayed the launch of index products. Then once they were launched, gaining sufficient assets took many years. However, indexing had to start from somewhere, and it all really began with the theoretical underpinnings of portfolio theory and EMH articulated by Markowitz, Samuelson, Sharpe, and Fama.

The financial analysis department of Wells Fargo Bank performed trailblazing work on fund management through a confluence of the right people and circumstances. John McQuown, William Fouse, and James Vertin were the principals behind this effort. Wells Fargo launched the first index fund on July 1, 1971, with a $6 million contribution from Samsonite Corporation. The fund was based on an equal-weighted NYSE (New York Stock Exchange) Index.[6]

Young Charles Schwayder, son of the head of the Samsonite Corporation, attended the University of Chicago's business school, which was a hothouse for much of the theory underlying index investing. He was convinced by the basic theory and was anxious to work with McQuown and Bill Fouse to launch the world's first index fund (see Sidebar "The Inside Scoop on the First Index Fund").

The fund held an equal proportion of its assets in each of the approximately 1,500 names listed on the New York Stock Exchange, as that seemed to be the most appropriate representation of the overall market. The maintenance of the fund quickly proved to be a "nightmare." Typically, the return of each stock was unique and divergent from that of the other stocks. This meant that the portfolio had to be constantly rebalanced—winners sold and losers purchased to maintain equal weights. Excessive transaction costs caused the equal-weighted strategy to be abandoned in favor of a market capitalization-weighted fund. As long as dividends are reinvested, such a fund automatically

THE INSIDE SCOOP ON THE FIRST INDEX FUND: WILLIAM FOUSE TELLS THE STORY

Jim Wiandt

This is how Bill Fouse described the situation: "John McQuown, who was working with the Management Sciences Department, had been hiring financial consultants to help advise him on what type of investment management Wells Fargo ought to be doing. Meanwhile, Mr. Vertin was not sympathetic to this at all. But McQuown had the ear of Ernie Arbuckle, the chairman of Wells Fargo at the time, and Dick Cooley, who was president, and was telling them that they had to get their investment operation up to snuff. At that time, I [Fouse] was at Mellon in Pittsburgh, and I was interested in going in the direction of Modern Portfolio Theory application. The people in charge of the trust division at Mellon were decidedly against that. So I really wanted to do something with my career at Mellon and was lucky enough to meet McQuown. I knew that Wells Fargo's Management Sciences Department was doing investigative work in the area. McQuown wanted to place me right in the Financial Analysis department under Vertin. At the time, I didn't realize what sort of battle royal I was getting into. He got me into the department because he had the ear of the president and chairman of the board of the company. I arrived in December 1970, and by that time McQuown and the Management Sciences Department had been working primarily with Myron Scholes and Fisher Black."

So with a disciple firmly planted on the investment side at Wells Fargo, the groundwork had been laid for the world's first index fund— a cumbersome, equal-weighted affair that was launched the next year.*

---

* Bill Fouse went on to help found Mellon Capital Management, and Wells Fargo evolved to become today's Barclays Global Investors.

grows in line with market performance and needs no rebalancing, hence the term *self-rebalancing*. In 1973, Wells Fargo established the Stagecoach Fund, a market cap-weighted closed-end mutual fund tracking the S&P 500, and it remains a model for almost all the index funds that have followed. Subsequent chapters in both Part Two and Part Four discuss the inherent advantages of cap-weighted benchmarks and index funds.

American National Bank of Chicago (which was ultimately absorbed by Northern Trust) launched the first publicly marketed index fund. It, too, was based on the S&P 500 index, in a fully replicating strategy.[7] It used a converted commingled trust fund structure and thus could be broadly marketed.

David Booth and Rex Sinquefield, two other University of Chicago Graduate School of Business alumni (1971 and 1972 respectively), were also dedicated proponents of EMH. Booth left graduate school and went to work for Wells Fargo on the first index funds. Sinquefield similarly went right into the index business, creating an S&P index fund with American National in 1973 that came out about the same time as the first S&P fund at Wells Fargo. Less than 10 years after graduation, they teamed up to take indexing in a different direction and build their own company.

Booth and Sinquefield founded Dimensional Fund Advisors (DFA), which had its theoretical underpinnings in research by Rolf Banz and Mark Reinganum. They documented that the return of small-cap stocks was superior to that of large-cap stocks by approximately 3 percent annually. Finally, Professors Eugene Fama, Ken French, and Robert McCormick of (once again) the University of Chicago wrote a seminal paper that formed the basis of DFA's new investment philosophy and put academic theory into practice. The paper outlined a three-factor model based on risk, size, and financial health that largely determined the returns of stocks.

By the mid-1970s, disillusionment with active management was beginning to set in. After adjusting for inflation, stock prices in 1974 were at the same level as 1954. It was a very different environment from the heady 1960s, and active funds were not holding up well under the brutal pressure of a prolonged bear market. The indexing business was the beneficiary of this underperformance, growing steadily from a humble $6 million in 1971 to reach $10 billion by 1980. Other changes in the investing environment (e.g., deregulation of commissions and regulators' acceptance of indexing as a prudent investment approach) aided this phenomenal growth.

Stock commissions were deregulated on May 1, 1975. The typical commission before then—about 2 percent of the trade—strongly affected the indexing business because indexed portfolios held such a large number of stocks.[8] The regulatory change that cleared the way for indexing was a statement that "prudence" in mutual funds would be determined on the basis of diversification, as opposed to an examination of the merits of individual stocks.

The indexing wave did not leave individual investors behind for very long, thanks in part to two Princeton alumni who brought index theory and index funds to retail investors. Economist Burton Malkiel's landmark 1973 book, *A Random Walk down Wall Street,* summarized the growing wealth of academic research in language that investors could digest.[9] Malkiel is credited with introducing the investing public to market efficiency and the new empirical concepts of stock market risk and return. Malkiel's main point was a jolt for many investors: The stock market, although generally trending upward, is random and unpredictable in the short term, much like the path of a drunk attempting to find his way home. The release of new information, which is itself unpredictable, determines stock prices. Malkiel's inevitable conclusion was that actively managed mutual funds and stock picking are a waste of time; cheap and diversified index funds are the superior choice for long-term investors.

As Burton Malkiel brought the concept of indexing to the general public, academia continued to turn out a steady stream of research and mainstream articles that questioned the benefits of stock picking and active management. In 1974, Paul Samuelson, Nobel Laureate in economics, published his landmark article "Challenge to Judgment," which urged the financial community to introduce a mutual fund tied to the broad S&P 500 index, thus planting the seed for the first index fund.[10]

Indexing achieved further credence when studies showed that asset allocation is the primary determinant of the variation of portfolio returns. A widely quoted (and often misunderstood) study by Brinson, Hood, and Beebower published in the *Financial Analysts Journal* found that investment *policy,* or asset allocation, dwarfs the effect of investment *strategies,* such as individual stock selection or market timing. The authors found that asset allocation policies—the major asset classes include stocks, bonds, cash, and real estate—account for 93.6 percent of the *variation* in portfolio returns over time.[11] In other words, investors should spend more time thinking about asset allocation and less time guessing the market's direction or fretting over individual stock picking. Chapter 30 addresses some of the misunderstandings and misinterpretations of this landmark study.

In a comprehensive study of mutual fund performance, Mark Carhart found no evidence of persistence of fund outperformance after adjusting for the common Fama-French risk factors as well as for momentum. The study demonstrated the importance of fund costs and also showed that "survivorship bias," or not accounting for underperforming funds that were liquidated or merged out of existence, can skew the results of active/passive studies in favor of active managers.[12]

In 1975, Charles Ellis wrote an important article about active management, called "The Loser's Game," for the *Financial Analysts Journal.* He showed that 85 percent of active managers had failed to beat the S&P 500 index over the previous 10 years. Ellis argued that investing in the stock market is a zero-sum game because, in aggregate, all investors earn the market's return. For every loser, there must be a winner—not all investors can outperform because they are the market.[13] Investors should not try to outguess the market; instead they should reflect the market at the lowest cost through passive index funds.

In 1976, John Bogle at the Vanguard Group, disillusioned with active fund underperformance, introduced the first index fund for individual investors. He was influenced by Malkiel's seminal book and eventually teamed up in a close association with him.[14] Its mandate was to track the S&P 500 without making any claims of expected outperformance. Although the Vanguard S&P 500 was the largest mutual fund in the United States at the beginning of 2003, with nearly $82 billion in assets according to Morningstar, the fund came from humble beginnings. It managed to scrape together just $11 million at the initial offering in 1976, much less than Bogle had hoped for.

Like the index fund he created, however, Bogle's story is that of the underdog who eventually came out on top. After reading a *Fortune* magazine article on the mutual fund industry in 1949, Bogle decided to devote his Princeton senior thesis to the topic, and he took a job within the industry soon after graduation. However, after following with interest the EMH academic research and experiencing firsthand the failure of active management while at Wellington Management, he left to form the Vanguard Group in 1974. In many ways, the firm was modeled on concepts from Bogle's Princeton thesis—with index funds providing the ideal vehicle to obtain market returns at the lowest cost (the firm also offers relatively low turnover and cheap active funds). Vanguard is currently second in retail mutual fund assets behind Fidelity, and its index funds include the top performers among their peer groups over long periods, just as Bogle envisioned.

Bogle became the primary spokesperson for the index philosophy; and even after retiring as CEO of the Vanguard Group, he continued to make speeches around the country to get the message out. Bogle always kept things simple and clear for retail investors. He pointed out that nearly all of them would be better off to just put their money into a broadly diversified, low-cost portfolio and leave it there. Even today, the Vanguard group continues its effort to educate retail investors who are paying too much and making too little from their investments. The message has penetrated institutional circles, where by some measures, indexed assets are now approaching 30 percent of the total assets in the United States (as opposed to still less than 10 percent for U.S. retail mutual fund investors, and just 4 percent of the overall invested stock market assets).[15]

Indexing had been built on a solid theoretical foundation and reinforced by substantial empirical evidence from active managers' returns. In 1991, a paper by William Sharpe made another case for indexing.[16] Brilliant in its clarity and simplicity, it was based on plain logic with no reliance on financial concepts or fancy equations full of Greek symbols. It proved that the average active dollar has to produce a performance identical to the average indexed dollar before costs and fees.

As an example, Sharpe and others ask investors to consider all managers whose mandate requires them to be measured against the benchmark of country X. Let's assume that we use an "advanced emerging market" such as Brazil or Israel. (We use a supposedly inefficient emerging market to demonstrate how this theory works in all markets.)[17] The demonstration runs like this: One

AN INTERVIEW WITH JOHN BOGLE
Jim Wiandt

Wiandt: What was the most significant obstacle you had to overcome to be successful with the Vanguard index funds?

Bogle: We had to overcome public opinion and industry horror about the idea, called "Bogle's Folly" in the beginning. When our Index 500 Fund began, it was criticized by virtually everyone. Inertia was the biggest problem—we had to get across the idea of indexing as a *way of investing,* not merely a *product.* It has increasingly *become* a product, and I don't really like that. But such a large change in the way people think always takes some getting used to.

Wiandt: When it first came out, people were talking about it being like communism, that it didn't represent the free market.

Bogle: Yes, communism. The rewards go to the owners, not the managers. "Stamp Out Index Funds," as the vintage poster outside my office says. The other thing is that many investors didn't understand investing well enough to know that as a group they cannot win. Indexing is based on a very simple formula, namely, "gross return minus cost equals net return."[a] And you know what? Investors as a group lose by the exact amount of their costs . . . which are about a billion dollars a day. So did indexing win today? Yes, it won today, and by another $1 billion. It's pretty easy. The data says that indexing wins . . . but it wins by much more than the data shows. Because the data has survivor bias, incubation bias, and cash flow bias (many investors buy high and sell low). Investors' dollar-weighted returns are a fraction of the funds' advertised time-weighted return. Indexing wins by so much that it's staggering.

Wiandt: To you, what is the definition of good index fund management?

Bogle: No index fund management. Don't do something. Just stand there. That's essentially what you can do in a total stock market index. You can buy the stocks in the appropriate weight, and if there's a merger, that doesn't do anything at all to the index, you don't have to change anything in the fund. There are no changes. It just takes care of itself. A bit of rebalancing might have to be done

---

[a] This is the same concept of "The Arithmetic of Active Management" as described within the chapter and cited in Note 16.

(Continued)

if a company gets bought out for cash, for example, but that rarely happens to any of the larger companies. An S&P index fund, on the other hand, requires a small amount of management. When a new company is added, a small company usually goes out, and requires only a very small reduction in all of the other 499 holdings. So I don't believe in managing indexes. I believe the idea of indexing in its purest form is to keep your hands *off* the portfolio. Now in bond index funds, you *can't* buy the whole bond universe. There are just too many bonds to do so efficiently. So you match it as well as you can. But do it to match the characteristics of the index. And never put a bond in there that yields a little bit more. If you do that, surprise! It has more risk. *(Editor's note: See more about fixed-income indexing in Chapters 10 and 22.)*

Wiandt: What further innovations do you see coming to the industry? Do you think innovation is a good thing?

Bogle: The total market index is by definition the perfect investment, and the S&P 500 is virtually as good. They cannot be improved on. They will give you virtually all of the market's return, provided that the costs are minimal. No other form of indexing will give you that. Shifting back and forth between styles makes no sense. If you try to go back and forth, get into growth, or get into value at the right time—I'm persuaded that that can't be done. Yes, you may be lucky and buy a growth index, and have growth outperform for a while, or you may be lucky and buy a value index, and have value do better for a while. But in the long run, they're all likely to provide the same returns. You also take a big risk in overweighting styles or market caps. You're essentially betting that the market weight is wrong, and I don't know anyone who's been successful betting against the market over the long term. And trading them is not going to work.

The job of the investor is to get the market return, and we have it in indexing . . . a virtual guarantee (unless the index management is messed up) of giving you the market return. And there's no excuse for messing up the index management. So if that's all you can aspire to, and because of high costs that's by definition much more than investors as a group can aspire to . . . accept it! Because of costs, you probably have, the statistics suggest, about a 4 percent chance of beating the market over 50 years. Is there any point in not just garnering the market return, when you have one chance in 25 of beating the market, when the other 24 chances have you losing? I can't imagine making that kind of bet. If you have the perfect investment, and I think the total market index fund is the perfect investment, why innovate? It's an interesting idea, and we seem blind to that fact in this industry. We're constantly creating new funds that seem to say, "Here's a better way to do it." There's not a better way to do it.

Wiandt: Why have 21 index funds at Vanguard then, for example?

Bogle: Well, I have to take the responsibility for that. They were formed on what seemed to me at the time to be very sound reasoning. Take the small-cap fund, for example. If an investor had a well-diversified portfolio, let's say he had a high-cost fund and was going to sell, and he decided he wanted small-cap exposure, the best way to get that exposure for that narrow part of his portfolio was through small-cap indexing. Or perhaps an investor who is young might want a growth index fund for a taxable account, which is a little more volatile, minimizes taxable income, and *should* be very tax efficient. An older investor might want a value fund, which brings higher income, a little less volatility, and a bit more protection. So you could put your money into a growth index fund, when you're young, at least in your taxable account, and gradually shift over to a value index fund when you retire.

Unfortunately, what got in the way of that seemingly sound idea is that first, the indexes were flawed by their construction—arbitrarily saying that 50 percent of the S&P 500 must be value, and the other 50 percent must be growth. Second, people were not using them for that purpose . . . *clearly.* They were instead chasing whichever style had performed the best in the past. If growth was doing well, they were investing their money in growth; if value was doing well, they were putting their money in value. With the new growth and value indexes and the small-cap indexes that Vanguard is moving to, the basic investment principle should be okay. But many investors, I'm afraid, are still going to be playing the market. Should we have those funds? Good question. Maybe, maybe not. But I'll take the responsibility for starting them.

Wiandt: What do you see as the biggest success of the index industry?

Bogle: Well, the biggest success so far is that little index fund we started on the next to the last business day of 1975—now the biggest fund in the world. That's not a bad accomplishment. However, over time, the biggest success will clearly be the total stock market index fund. People will gradually put more and more

(Continued)

money into the total stock market index fund. It doesn't have a large-cap bias over the market, which in the long run doesn't matter, but in the short run probably matters. It should have less turnover than our 500 Index Fund, and it does—around 3 percent versus perhaps 6 percent or 7 percent.

Wiandt: And what do you believe is the largest shortcoming of the index industry?

Bogle: The largest shortcoming of the index industry is playing so many games. Targeting microscopic segments of the market, from South Korea to the Nasdaq index, completely defeats the purpose of indexing. Of all the probably 100 different kinds of stock index funds out there, only two meet my definition of the right index funds. The other 98 index products are going to lead most people astray. Hope may spring eternal, but it is not something a successful investor will want to rely on.

Wiandt: Where do you see the index industry going in the next 5, 10, 30 years?

Bogle: Broad market indexing is going to grow every year. I just can't see how it can fail to grow. As I said in a recent *Fortune* article, "investors won't act contrary to their own best interests forever." They will live and they will learn. So it's important for us to go out and educate them. It takes a lot longer and is a lot more expensive for investors to learn from their own hard experience! Learning on your own is very expensive. It's far better to learn from the experience of others, the Nobel Laureates and Warren Buffett, they're all in the same camp here. Benjamin Graham said about indexing— right after our index fund started—that logically, having the market outperform itself doesn't make any sense. It simply can't happen, for it would be a logical contradiction to expect the average investor to outperform the index. Investors as a group must lose, and will continue to lose to the market's return by the amount of the high costs of financial intermediation. The case is ironclad. There's no way around it![b]

---

[b] John C. Bogle, founder of the Vanguard Group, spoke with Jim Wiandt in an interview that originally appeared in the second quarter, 2003 issue of the *Journal of Indexes*. The full interview is available from www.IndexUniverse.com and www.journalofindexes.com.

divides all investors in Brazil into two categories, active and index managers (some might be local and some might be foreign), and either they hold the benchmark (index) or they deviate from the benchmark (active). This assumes that the benchmark index is an accurate representation of the market.

We know that all the active managers (again, some local and some foreign) combined into one notional portfolio will achieve the market returns. The indexers' holdings are identical to that of the benchmark because they hold the same stocks in the same proportions. That leaves the active management piece, which also, as a whole, has to be the same as the benchmark. This is because the two pieces together make the benchmark, and because the index piece mirrors the benchmark, the active piece has to do as well. And, of course, if index and active have the same holdings, they will generate the same performance.

The picture for active managers actually gets worse when costs and fees are considered less, which we know to be higher, as they will be actively trading among themselves, and their management fees will be higher. In developed markets, active fees are typically 0.25 percent to 1 percent higher than index fees. Furthermore, active turnover is usually 2 to 4 times higher than index turnover, increasing costs and lessening tax efficiency. These significantly higher fees and costs translate into a greater hurdle for active managers. Thus, mathematically the aggregate of all index managers will outperform the aggregate of all active managers.

Realization of the corrosive impact of greater costs and fees (especially over longer time periods) combined with an awareness of the lack of compensation for unsystematic risk has led to a new breed of active management. The goal here is to aim for outperformance, but with a strict control over the risk taken and a dedication to minimizing the transaction costs incurred. This structured approach to portfolio management, with its focus on risk and costs, is an outgrowth of the principles underlying indexing.

The industry's future is no longer a simple debate between indexing and active. It is about ensuring that the investor chooses the appropriate mix of the two approaches. This theme is discussed in the following chapter and developed throughout the book. Although efficiency of markets is a good initial assumption, there are temporary misevaluations and pockets of inefficiency. This does not mean that these areas are easily identified or that, once identified, they can be invested in at a price that is low enough to be profitable. For managers to add value even after all costs and fees are taken into consideration, it is imperative that rigorous risk control and minimization of transaction costs accompany identification of the return potential.

Whereas the universe of managers can be winnowed down by selecting the ones with a focus on the three pillars of performance, identifying managers obviously still involves risk. This is because managers' past records are not necessarily good guides to their future performance. The concept of risk budgeting comes to the investors' rescue here. Risk budgeting states that investors want to undertake a certain level of risk based on their investment horizon, risk tolerance, tax status, current wealth/funded status, and so on. In addition, investors need to consider choices that run the gamut from pure broad-based indexing to the use of supercharged active tools. Each of these choices has a certain risk and expected return associated with it. An optimal portfolio will incorporate all these forecasts and find the solution that most satisfies the objectives given the constraints that are faced. This approach can be applied at the total portfolio level, and/or within specific asset classes. It is discussed in more detail in Chapters 3, 30, and 31, and in a variety of sections on www.IndexUniverse.com.[18]

So, half a century after Markowitz's opening salvo against the traditional active style of investing, there still is a place for actively managed investments to fit within a portfolio that carefully balances risk and return as efficiently as possible. But, this is no longer your grandfather's investment portfolio that consisted of a few funds, each of which held a few stocks and ignored any clear measure of risk or costs. It is now an investment portfolio that focuses above all on sensible asset allocation and employs an optimal mix of index and structured active funds so as to be a precise fit with your risk budget.

NOTES

1. Harry M. Markowitz, "Portfolio Selection," *Journal of Finance* (March 1952).
2. James Tobin, "Liquidity Preferences as Behavior Toward Risk," *Review of Economic Studies* (February 1958).
3. William F. Sharpe, "Capital Asset Prices: A Theory of Market Equilibrium under Conditions of Risk," *Journal of Finance,* vol. 19 (September 1964).
4. Paul Samuelson, "Proof That Properly Anticipated Prices Fluctuate Randomly," *Industrial Management Review* (1965).
5. Eugene Fama, "Efficient Capital Markets: A Review of the Theory and Empirical Work," *Journal of Finance* (May 1970).
6. The division was within the Trust Division at Wells Fargo, which was to go through different ownership structures before evolving to become today's Barclays Global Investors, although the pioneering staff went on to build a diverse group of financial firms.
7. "Passive Far from Passe," *Pensions & Investments* (October 19, 1998): 112–113.
8. A mitigating effect was that the ongoing turnover was quite low.
9. Burton G. Malkiel, *A Random Walk down Wall Street* (New York: W.W. Norton & Company; 1st–8th editions, 1973–2003).
10. Paul A. Samuelson, "Challenge to Judgment," *Journal of Portfolio Management* (Fall 1974).

11. Gary Brinson, L. Randolph Hood, and Gilbert L. Beebower, "Determinants of Portfolio Performance," *Financial Analysts Journal* (July/August 1986).

12. Mark M. Carhart, "On Persistence in Mutual Fund Performance," *Journal of Finance* (March 1997).

13. Charles D. Ellis, "The Loser's Game," *Financial Analysts Journal* (July/August 1975).

14. John C. Bogle, *Common Sense on Mutual Funds* (New York: John Wiley & Sons, 1999).

15. John C. Bogle, "An Index Fundamentalist Goes Back to the Drawing Board," *Journal of Portfolio Management,* vol. 28, no. 3 (Spring 2002).

16. William F. Sharpe, "The Arithmetic of Active Management," *Financial Analysts Journal* (January/February 1991).

17. Larry Tint, previously of Sharpe-Tint and BGI, now with Quantal, has used this example with even less efficient emerging markets, such as Zimbabwe.

18. In the book's E-ppendix, www.ActiveIndexInvesting.com, see, in particular, the features and commentaries in the "For Professionals" and "For Academia" areas.

CHAPTER **3**

The Ever-Evolving Uses of Indexing

Why the Active versus Index Debate Is Over

Matthew Scanlan, Binu George, Francis Enderle, and Steven A. Schoenfeld

_____ **Editor's Note** _____

This chapter covers the growth of indexing from its humble beginnings, which were described in Chapter 2. We highlight the debate over indexing's appropriateness for different market environments and various asset classes, discuss the advantages of index products, and describe the factors that have contributed to their meteoric growth. We examine indexing's performance in both rising and falling markets and explore the claims that while indexing may be appropriate for U.S. large-cap equity investing, it somehow isn't appropriate for U.S. small-cap or international equities. The myths and conventional wisdom about the latter are discussed in detail. While there is a brief discussion of index derivatives and ETFs, these subjects receive more thorough analysis in Parts Three, Four, and Five. The focus in this chapter is on how investors use indexing in increasingly sophisticated and creative ways, and how indexing should be a key part of an overall investment strategy. We stress that the active versus index debate is (or certainly should be) over. Instead, indexing needs to be part of a mosaic in a holistic investment strategy

_____

This chapter is a modified and updated version of an article published by Barclays Global Investors entitled "Indexing in the Twenty-First Century" in March 2002. The authors gratefully acknowledge the assistance of David Kurapka, Linh Pham, and John Spence in the production of this chapter and its accompanying data and tables.

that encompasses broad universes of assets and asset classes (see also Chapters 26 and 30 on how indexing can be the "core" of one's portfolio). Other contributors to the book also draw on these concepts and themes.

The long global equity bull market, inconsistent performance by active managers, and the ever-compelling cost benefits helped index-based investing grow meteorically through the 1990s. The bearish and volatile market environment in the early 2000s, however, raised new questions and critiques about the future of indexing: Was its rise a short-term, cyclical dalliance or a signal of long-term structural change in the management of investments? And could it be possible that indexing actually had a role in some of the stock market overshooting of the late 1990s?

This chapter provides a broad outlook on the future of indexing. It begins by examining the advantages of indexing and some of the market factors that have contributed to indexing's explosive growth during the past decade. It discusses why indexing has not been used nearly as much outside the United States and why that is likely to change. We describe some of the basic types of index products, foreshadowing the more detailed coverage in Part Three. We then look at how investors are using indexing in increasingly sophisticated and creative ways (setting the stage for Part Five), and outline how index-based investment can be a key part of an overall investment strategy, which is also expanded on in Part Five.

THE GROWTH OF INDEXING

As described in the previous chapter, in the 1970s, indexing was mainly the provenance and obsession of academics. By the late 1980s, however, both mainstream retail and institutional investors were increasingly embracing it. Figure 3.1 demonstrates that, even after factoring in market returns, indexing has had a growth rate of 20 percent in the tax-exempt marketplace from 1988 to 1999, with market-related contraction in the subsequent three years.

Institutional managers have traditionally led retail participants in investing trends, and indexing is no exception. Four main factors have contributed to the growth of indexing: ease in risk budgeting, lower management fees and expenses, ease in manager evaluation, and competitive performance against active managers.

Ease in Risk Budgeting

Institutional investors are concerned about both the total risk of their investment portfolio (which may hold several different asset classes and many

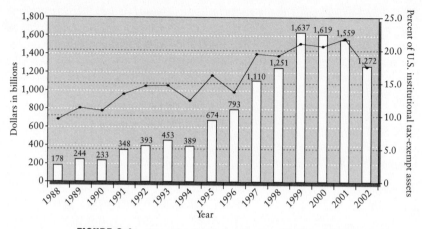

FIGURE 3.1   Growth of U.S. Institutional Indexed Assets
Source: Pensions & Investments, annual May Surveys.

managers within those asset classes) and relative or active risk, which relates to the variation between the returns of the benchmark to which a manager is held accountable and the actual returns.

The magnitude of the deviation from the benchmark is directly related to the number and size of the bets the manager makes instead of merely replicating the benchmark. The bets may be related to several different conditions or factors and may be made intentionally or unintentionally. The factors on which the managers make bets may be explicit, such as holding a concentrated portfolio of large-capitalization securities or buying securities outside the underlying asset class (holding cash or fixed-income securities within an equity benchmark). Bets may also be implicit, such as by holding a diversified portfolio of stocks over several sectors that all contain significant exposure to a change in interest rates (e.g., finance or automotive). The only way a manager can eliminate active risk is to fully replicate the underlying benchmark, which is precisely what an index manager does.

Nevertheless, it is important to emphasize that this discussion of portfolio risk is *not* attempting to pit active forms of investment management against indexing. In fact, the two can—and should—work in tandem.

Indexing has provided many institutional pension plan sponsors with new techniques for plugging risk holes in active portfolio groupings through specialized index accounts. An overall investment plan may have a broad-based equity benchmark like the Russell 3000 or the Wilshire 5000, yet also have a collection of active managers who hold a disproportionate concentration of large-capitalization stocks. Small- and large-capitalization index funds can be used to diversify these holdings and attain broader exposure in line with the stated broad-capitalization benchmark. With the advent of specialized benchmarks that denote style and capitalization groupings within the domestic and international capital markets spectrum, indexing can actually be employed to create a more comprehensive active approach to fund management. Chapter 18 develops this concept and provides a robust example of how a plan sponsor took such an approach to address an undesired growth tilt in its international equity allocation.

Lower Fees and Costs

The manager's fees, whether active or index, can be highly variable and are based on a combination of elements including the manager's performance track record, reputation, capacity for new investment relationships, personnel and overhead costs, service requirements, and the degree and sophistication of a manager's investment process and research. Typically, the fees of an active manager are substantially higher than the fees of an index manager because indexing involves fewer underlying costs.

Nevertheless, indexing requires significant resources to produce benchmark performance efficiently and consistently. Indexes are not static but rather involve many constituent security changes over the course of a year. Managing these changes without adversely impacting portfolio performance requires considerable skill. Index managers must also account for cash flows into and out of a portfolio and thus need to retain a degree of liquidity. Index benchmarks do not take this factor into account and performance statistics generally require full investment in constituents at all times. Finally, most securities produce some proportion of their return as income from dividends or interest payments, and these must be effectively reinvested in index constituents to avoid a cash buildup within the portfolio.

Although meeting these challenges requires a skilled and experienced investment staff (as all six chapters in Part Four emphatically demonstrate), generally index management still involves much lower research costs than active management, particularly as index managers reach a certain level of economies of scale. Active managers must continually develop new techniques to produce excess returns. Since several active managers are always simultaneously pursuing these returns, any advantage may quickly dissipate when it becomes apparent to other active managers.

In addition, active managers typically have substantially more portfolio turnover as they constantly act on their investment opinions, and thus they incur higher turnover-related costs. Index managers generally realign portfolio composition only to reflect index changes. For tax-sensitive portfolios, this benefit also helps avoid the constant recognition of investment gains, and in the case of taxable separate accounts, tax-loss harvesting can even produce after-tax "index alpha" (see Chapters 24 and 27).

Efficient management of portfolio turnover is a critical component in the ultimate success of any investment manager. Index and quantitative active managers pursuing disciplined, consistent, and risk-controlled outperformance of a benchmark have generally approached the trading as a science. They focus on minimizing explicit costs (commissions and execution spreads) as well as implicit costs like market impact (the extent to which the volume of a trade pushes the bid or ask price against the trader).

Crossing Opportunities   Crossing opportunities provide additional savings for a plan sponsor. Crossing involves matching buyers and sellers—either within one investment management firm or through industry-developed "crossing networks"—saving both the buyer and seller any bid/offer spread, commission costs, and market impact associated with these trades. Through special agreements granted by government regulatory agencies, some quantitative investment managers who rely solely on formula-driven portfolio construction techniques can conduct cross-trading internally and also realize such savings.

Securities crossing has become a powerful tool in the management of large index and quantitative (or risk-controlled active) portfolios. Index-based managers have a tremendous advantage relative to traditional active managers who do not have access to crossing. The savings associated with securities transactions by such managers can often be substantially greater than their management fees. The benefits of crossing are discussed in Part Four, and in Chapter 26.

Relative Ease in Choosing Managers

Indexing also eliminates several criteria that enter into searches for managers of investment mandates. Compared with active managers, who pursue wide-ranging asset selection or allocation strategies, index managers are fairly transparent and do not require the same degree of scrutiny of the investment process:

- *Comparative risk characteristics.* Index managers who fully replicate benchmarks will have an essentially identical risk profile to the benchmark, thus eliminating the need for risk-factor analysis.
- *Sources of performance.* It is also easy to evaluate an index manager's performance because there should be little deviation from the benchmark's overall return. Most tracking errors result from three sources:

1. Excess cash in the portfolio.
2. Transaction costs.
3. Small portfolio misweightings.

This contrasts with the onerous process of judging active managers, which involves studying a combination of stock selection, sector rotation, market timing, and asset allocation. Moreover, each category has myriad shades, and a manager's style may change over time as personnel depart or in response to market conditions. Chapter 26 highlights this substantial benefit of indexing.

Superior Performance

Finally, as discussed, one of the key drivers in the growth of indexing has been investors' frustration with traditional active manager performance. The strong bull market in stocks in the United States during the 1980s and 1990s challenged managers who rely on fundamental approaches to out-perform domestic indexes. As shown in Table 3.1, when examining a uni-verse of active equity managers against a popular index (in this case, the S&P 500 index), the benchmark ranks close to—but almost always above—the median active equity manager, whether the comparative period is short term or longer term.

Furthermore, the myth that active managers do outperform in bear markets is just that—a myth. The following section as well as Chapter 4 provides compelling evidence that active managers did not fare much better in the brutal bear market of the early 2000s.

Some talented managers have delivered on their promise of consistent outperformance of their stated benchmark. Nevertheless, the performance

TABLE 3.1   Active Large Cap Funds versus S&P 500 Index

Funds versus the S&P 500							
	Period						
	One Quarter	Year to Date	One Year	Three Years	Five Years	Seven Years	Ten Years
S&P 500 index (official) return	−3.15	−3.15	−24.77	−16.09	−3.77	5.60	8.53
Percentile ranking	58	58	63	68	74	66	66
Number of funds in universe	406	406	405	377	334	283	217

Source: BGI, Wilshire data as of 3/31/03.

gulf between the index and the universe of active equity managers is even worse when taking into account survivorship bias. By considering only managers who are still in business, managers who consistently underperform and must cease operations fall out of the universe and new managers replace them.

MYTHS AND MISPERCEPTIONS ABOUT INDEXING

Although the reasons for indexing growth seem persuasive, these have not convinced all the gainsayers. In the following subsections, we critique the most common objections.

Indexing Only Works during Bull Markets

Many critics of indexing argue that in strong bull markets active managers typically have trouble posting favorable returns relative to a benchmark. This common myth is based on the perception that active managers tend to be more defensive during periods of market underperformance, extreme volatility, or general nontrending market performance and thus post better results than "blind" indexing strategies.

However, as Figure 3.2 shows, active manager equity performance is historically not dependent on market direction.

One can thus assume that indexing's performance relative to active managers is not dictated by market direction. Figure 3.2 seems to indicate that indexing performs strongly relative to active management in advancing markets, yet not as strongly in declining environments. Several theories have been advanced for this phenomenon, but a widely accepted reason has been the relative cash holdings of active managers versus indexers. Theoretically, index managers should hold no cash reserves, although in practice, a small cash reserve is necessary to accommodate clients' participation and withdrawal activity as well as dividend or interest accruals. In contrast, active managers often hold a significant level of cash, and many incorporate a tactical cash strategy as part of their investment program. When active managers find that securities' valuations are not compelling for investment, many of them will convert a large piece of their portfolio to cash. These material cash holdings create a cushion in declining markets and a performance drag in rising markets. According to data from mutual fund trackers (most notably Morningstar), many active stock funds hold cash positions in excess of 20 percent, with a few over 50 percent. This market environment issue is developed in greater depth in Chapter 4.

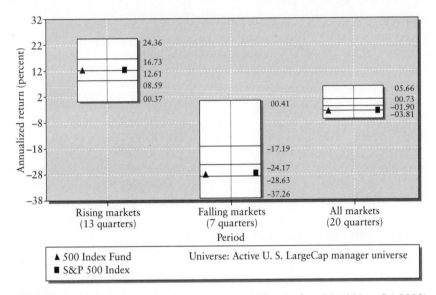

FIGURE 3.2   S&P 500 Index Performance over Market Cycles (Q2 1998 to Q1 2003) *Source:* BGI, Wilshire data.

Indexing's Success Will Drive out Successful Active Managers

In fact, most investment money is still actively managed, and professional security analysts and money managers are not even close to being driven out of their industry. As mentioned previously, less than 10 percent of equity assets in the United States are indexed.

Indexing Only Works in Efficient Markets

The international adoption of indexing has been significantly slower than in the United States although indexed investing makes a great deal of sense in non-U.S. markets. Just as in the United States, investing abroad is subject to Sharpe's "Arithmetic of Active Management" (described in the previous chapter); the average active manager will match the return of the index before fees and costs. Furthermore, the cost differentials between active and index portfolios are even more pronounced in non-U.S. markets. Why, then, are pension plan sponsors less willing to adopt indexing in foreign portfolios?

The answer lies in performance, especially that of traditional active managers in the 1990s. On average, they outdistanced international benchmarks such as MSCI's (Morgan Stanley Capital International's)

EAFE (Europe Australasia Far East) Index quite handily. This has led to the belief that indexing does not merit a role in international investing because stock markets abroad are less efficient.

Whereas over the five years ending September 30, 2001, EAFE's performance was near the bottom of all managers,[1] in the three years, at the end of that period, EAFE improved to become a third-quartile performer. And for the subsequent quarter of 2001, and all of 2002 EAFE performed above the median.[2] The pattern has continued to shift toward "normal" (i.e., with a bell-shaped distribution curve of underperforming and outperforming managers) during 2003.

Three factors have helped EAFE push its way into the higher ranks of performance and are transforming investments in international equity markets: weighting of Japan, diminishing stock opportunity set, and increased efficiency. As a result, it is becoming much harder for traditional active managers to beat EAFE and other international benchmarks.[3]

Weighting of Japan   The major reason EAFE has been relatively easy to beat in the past decade—but is unlikely to be so moving forward—has been the underweighting of Japan by traditional active managers.

Since the early 1980s, median active managers (in fact, nearly all active international managers) have consistently underweighted Japan in their portfolios. During the 1980s—the decade of the "rising sun"—and a period of bull markets in Japan, that underweight brought about severe underperformance for the average manager.

During the 1990s, Japan experienced a reversal, a decade of bear markets. The active manager community had maintained the underweighting, though, and discovered the "wrong" (or unlucky) bet made in the 1980s had now turned into the "right" (or lucky) bet in the 1990s.

That degree of recent outperformance is unlikely to continue going forward. Japan's weight in EAFE is now down to about 22 percent from a high of 65 percent. (Chapter 12 provides an excellent analysis of the "Japan in EAFE" phenomenon, and the "solutions" that the index investment community developed for the issue.) Traditional active managers who, according to InterSec data, previously were underweighting Japan by 10 to15 percent in their portfolios are now—given Japan's dramatically reduced weight in the index—more comfortable with a 3 to 4 percent underweight. Even supposing these managers were to increase their underweight, it is unlikely that they could repeat the success of the 1990s because if Japan were to fall at the same rate in the 2000s, it would end up with a weight in EAFE of only about 7 percent. Japan is still the world's second largest economy and forms 30 percent of EAFE when weighted by GDP, suggesting that this is a highly improbable scenario. As of this chapter's writing, in fact, the opposite has happened. After a sharp rebound in Japanese equities in 2003, active managers remained underweight Japan and were forced into chasing the market up to build their allocation closer to benchmark weight. Although the statistics are not in yet (but will be documented on www.IndexUniverse.com), it would appear that traditional active international managers are having as much difficulty beating their benchmarks as their domestically focused peers. To us, this simply means that the immutable laws of "the arithmetic of active management," which was discussed in the previous chapter, are working in this asset class, too.

Diminishing Stock Opportunity Set outside the Benchmark A second reason EAFE has been relatively easy to beat in the past decade has been the presence of numerous large, liquid stocks outside the benchmark. Consider 1999—a great year for traditional managers. The key driver worldwide that year was the technology, media, and telecommunications sector. For an international manager, the largest country in their portfolio was Japan and the largest wireless stock in Japan was NTT DoCoMo. Amazingly, this stock was excluded from EAFE. An investment in this stock yielded an astonishing 365 percent return in 1999 versus a return of 25 percent on EAFE. A mere 1 percent exposure to this stock would have helped a manager outperform the benchmark by 3.4 percent.

The reason NTT DoCoMo was omitted from the index is that MSCI targeted 60 percent coverage of each underlying industry. In Japanese telecommunications, NTT (NTT DoCoMo's parent) used up most of the room. With new indexing methodology, the room gets expanded to 85 percent and the existing stocks typically shrink in weight as they get adjusted for free float. Both changes mean that there is now more room for many large liquid stocks such as NTT DoCoMo, Cable & Wireless, and Shell to enter the benchmark universe. In fact, research indicates that the available opportunity set outside the benchmark for traditional managers—the pool of large, liquid stocks—has shrunk by 60 percent.[4]

Improving Efficiency of International Markets The final factor is the rise of globalization and competition, which has narrowed the efficiency gap between U.S. and developed international equity markets. National borders have become more porous, and plan sponsors around the world are increasing their international allocation. While true for the United States and the United Kingdom, it is especially evident in the EMU (European Monetary Union). In the Netherlands, the international equity allocation has increased in the past five years from 50 percent to 80 percent. Signs of this shift are visible in transaction costs, which have fallen by 21 percent in the EAFE markets since 1998, and in the more rapid absorption of earnings and economic information into stock prices. The big holes of inefficiency are getting smaller and closing more rapidly, thereby raising the pressure on traditional managers accustomed to large, simple bets.

Based on these three factors, the average international active manager, going forward, should have a record relative to the benchmark that more resembles any other asset class. Whereas these factors are affecting traditional active managers, they do not affect the prospects of risk-controlled, structured strategies because they tend to hold well-diversified positions consisting of multiple small bets, as opposed to a few large bets. Thus, the structured approach does not suffer losses from the inability to make big bets on certain stocks now entering the EAFE, or on Japan because it has fallen in weight, or on nonbenchmark countries that will be included in a more precise benchmark. Nor is there any need to absorb the disappearance of big holes of inefficiency.

In short, the case for indexing and other risk-controlled strategies is as strong for international stocks as it is for U.S. equities. And even in areas that the industry generally considers to be the least efficient markets, such as U.S. small cap and emerging markets, index-based strategies can provide the same low-cost, efficient core exposure to these subasset classes.[5]

INDEX-BASED INVESTMENT VEHICLES

As indexing has grown, investors have begun using index-based products beyond index funds in increasingly sophisticated methods to enhance performance, control risk, and lower costs. Two of the most common methods are exchange-traded funds (ETFs) and index derivatives. ETFs are thoroughly covered in Chapters 16, 23, and 25; derivatives and other index vehicles and their uses are discussed extensively in Chapters 14 and 25.

Exchange-Traded Funds

As shown in Figure 3.3, ETFs are one of the fastest growing index investment vehicles used by institutional and individual investors. In fact, during the bearish market environment of the early 2000s, ETFs were one of the few consistently growing financial products, as is visible in Figure 3.3. Updated data on ETF assets can be accessed via IndexUniverse.com and its affiliated sites.

As will be discussed in great detail in Part Three of the book, ETFs offer numerous advantages for institutional or other sophisticated investors. Unlike traditional mutual funds that allow investors to purchase or redeem their units only at the close of the trading day, ETFs can be bought or sold throughout the day, thus providing investors with intraday liquidity. ETFs

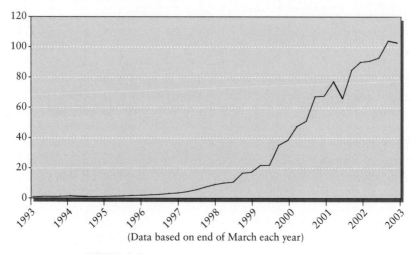

(Data based on end of March each year)

FIGURE 3.3   U.S. Listed ETF Assets (in Billions)

also have a lower expense ratio than most mutual funds. By virtue of the redemption process for ETFs, which transfers the securities with the lowest cost basis out of the portfolio, ETFs are more tax efficient than mutual funds and often pay out little or no capital gains. Last, because all ETFs are listed on an exchange, investors can transact these funds from their existing brokerage accounts without having to establish any new arrangements.

Index-Based Derivatives

In addition to considerations surrounding market impact, index futures have also contributed to keeping index management costs low. Instead of requiring investors interested in index replication to hold all constituent securities in an underlying benchmark, index futures trade as a package instrument representing the total return of an index or security basket and can greatly reduce trading costs. The futures holder is responsible for maintaining a margin deposit on a fraction of the underlying notional value of the investment as well as for covering changes in its value.

Trading volumes in futures markets have exploded over the past 15 years and generally provide the marketplace with an additional dimension of liquidity in portfolio management. Figure 3.4 demonstrates this growth in U.S.-listed stock index futures.

Chapters 14, 18, and 25 provide substantial background information on index-based equity derivatives, as do several exchange and index vendor

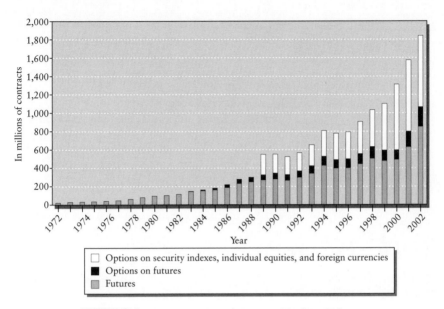

FIGURE 3.4 U.S. Futures and Options Trading Volume

web sites, links to which are provided on www.ActiveIndexInvesting.com and www.IndexUniverse.com.

THE MARRIAGE OF INDEX AND ACTIVE INVESTING

Traditionally, indexing has often been viewed as a rejection of the concept of active investing, thus setting up the continuing "index versus active" debate. On the indexing side are those who note that the average participant in the markets will achieve only the performance of the market average itself because investing is a zero sum game. Further, after accounting for the drag of management fees and trading costs, traditional active management, on average, is bound to underperform the benchmark. On the other side of the debate are the traditionalists, who disdain the indexer's effort to be "just average" and see active management as valuable wherever there might be inefficiency.

These views are thoroughly reconcilable. There is room among the managers who comprise the average for a few to be exceptionally skillful, able to consistently outperform their benchmarks over time. To maintain the macroconsistency of the average, such exceptional performance has to be earned at the expense of equally unskillful counterparts. This insight—that there can be predictable manager outperformance, but that it is conditional on exceptional skill—sets the stage for a dramatic reconciliation in the previously polarized roles of both index and active management in the portfolio. In the past five years or so, this new view has come to dominate the manager structure thinking of many of the largest and most sophisticated investors. Most of them believe that they have the ability to choose active managers who have the greatest skill at picking securities.

Thus, investors are increasingly using indexing as part of an overall investment strategy in complete harmony with active investing. This is one of the reasons for the book's title, and for the Ying-Yang symbol's use on the book jacket. The precise roles of indexed and active products depend on the asset owner's investment objectives, which are generally determined by funding level, size, and maturity. Here are three major uses of indexing and index funds that demonstrate how they can work in tandem with active investing.

Single or Multiple Asset Class Core Holding

Many investors use index funds to provide a core position in one or more asset classes around which they can add satellite active managers. In this structure, the index fund delivers benchmark returns while the active managers are expected to add value above their relevant benchmark. Frequently the index fund, with its market-level risk, prompts the investor to give the active manager(s) a higher risk mandate than would be the case without the index fund.

Core-Satellite investing has become standard practice among a broad set of investment professionals; in fact, the term has become so popular that it is already being misused.

Chapters 28, 29, and 30 highlight how "indexing at the core" can ensure healthy and stable portfolios for almost all types of investors—institutional and individual—and the latter chapter even provides some sample portfolio weights for different types of investors.

Asset Allocation Overlay

Strategic asset allocation plays a central role in determining long-term portfolio performance. However, with disparate returns across different asset classes, the portfolio mix soon starts to deviate from the target allocations. Plan sponsors who want to adhere to their allocations often find that the costs of reassigning mandates among various managers can be prohibitive. Thus, many institutions have let their actual asset allocation drift significantly from stated policy benchmarks.

The relatively low costs attached to index management have led it to become a useful solution to this challenge. Institutions that maintain core index positions in broad asset classes can rebalance to their stated benchmarks by simply reassigning asset surpluses into temporary index accounts that adjust asset exposure while awaiting assignment to managers. They can accomplish this through index funds or by using index derivatives as an overlay to the existing account balances. These approaches enable institutional investors to maintain a tighter profile to their stated asset allocation policy, without the costs of firing existing asset managers, having active managers reduce their mandates (placing downward price pressure on their own portfolio holdings) or conduct new manager searches for different allocations.

Another feature of index funds in the management of asset allocation involves their tactical use for enhancing total performance while reducing plan risk. An institutional investor may have a 60 percent policy allocation to equities and a 40 percent policy commitment to a fixed-income benchmark, but might desire having the latitude to change that allocation tactically should the projected return and risk characteristics of the capital markets change significantly. Once again, low-cost index funds or index derivatives can be employed to temporarily alter the overall plan asset allocation if the relative risk-adjusted expected return of one asset class outweighs another. This tactical adjustment can capture these modified outcomes without disrupting the performance characteristics of the existing manager mix. Part Three provides details and robust examples of this use of indexing in Chapter 18, particularly that chapter's sidebar interview with Aje Saigal of the Government of Singapore Investment Corporation.

The Optimization Approach

Perhaps the favored approach involves estimating the "optimal" combination of managers, where optimality is viewed in the dimensions of expected alpha versus active risk. Instead of looking at one manager at a time, this optimization approach looks at the combination of managers as a portfolio that should have desirable risk and return characteristics in sum. The objective function of this optimization is to maximize the portfolio's expected alpha while controlling its active risk (see Figure 3.5).

Figure 3.5 demonstrates this process by portraying an institutional sponsor's optimal allocation across candidate investment managers. The efficient frontier combines five managers in different proportions to build alpha-maximizing portfolios at many different levels of active risk. Manager 1 is an index provider, Manager 2 is a highly risk-controlled (enhanced index) manager, whereas Managers 3 through 5 maintain traditional active investment styles. As this figure illustrates, levels of active risk can be budgeted as low as zero (the risk involved in the index fund, the risk-free asset in active risk

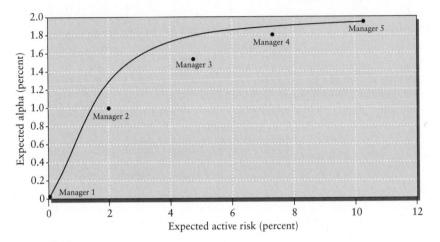

FIGURE 3.5 Optimal Allocation across Candidate Investment Managers

space). Or they can be as high as that represented by the investment manager candidate who has the highest level of active risk among those in the pool.

In between, where most sensible investors are going to choose to be, there will be a balance of both active and index managers, with the relative balance weighted to accomplish the best possible trade-off of expected alpha for active risk. Just how much additional active risk are we willing to take, in striving to add to our portfolio's expected alpha? Where on the frontier is the best trade-off? Usually the efficient frontier will level off well before it prescribes a portfolio that is 100 percent active, such a portfolio being seen then as too risky to justify its low incremental alpha.

Studying the mathematics of this optimization reveals that the favored managers will combine high expected information ratios and low levels of active risk. Thus, risk-controlled active managers (sometimes called *enhanced indexing*) and market-neutral long-short managers (usually equitized) have earned their growing roles in investor portfolios.[6] Yet the role of traditional active managers, while being less prominent, is supported wherever their skill is identifiable and repeatable.

The estimation and other issues that are required for this approach are reasonably well understood and entirely implementable. The discipline involved will deliver value to investors with better-behaved portfolios that capture more of the investor's insights into the sources of quality manager alpha. The best of these approaches also solve the practical problems of accommodating managers whose individual benchmarks are different from the sponsor's overall benchmark. Consider the case of a large-cap growth manager being considered for a portfolio benchmarked to the Russell 3000. Flexible methods of manager structure optimization handle this situation readily, assuring that a growth manager is balanced by a value manager and so forth.

This *manager structure optimization* or risk-budgeting approach is focused on the investor's needs to control risk and return, and it rejects the "indexed versus active" perspective as an irrelevant manager-centric argument between competing providers. It is more useful to the investor to seek the marriage of index and active investing, where both work together to serve the fund's objectives.

This marriage is valuable whenever investors believe that picking skillful active managers is possible (which includes most investors). Any manager who doesn't have such a belief should simply hold the lowest-risk portfolio, an index fund matched to the asset class benchmark. The theoretical and empirical evidence for this latter approach was well documented in the previous chapter.

CONCLUSION: CALLING A TRUCE TO THE DEBATE

Indexing will likely be the foundation for the investment strategies of the future, and the level of sophistication in combining global indexing with active management will undoubtedly increase going forward. Although there are critics of indexing, no one will deny the impact that its growth has had on the investment industry. The key benefits of indexing—in performance measurement, cost control, reduced portfolio turnover, and flexibility—will continue into the future. Indexing is the most efficient way to capture market returns—often referred to as beta.

A cardinal rule of investing is that investors should hire managers whose information or research enables them to produce a return in excess of a benchmark by over- or underweighting particular securities, sectors, growth and value styles. Asset owners who are not highly confident of their ability to chose such outperforming managers, however, should hold an index position. These "default" index exposures are relatively easy to achieve through a variety of index products discussed in Parts Three and Five of the book. Chapter 30 further develops this concept, which the author calls "Indexing at the Core."

Whereas viewing the markets as being at least somewhat inefficient is a necessary condition for employing active managers, it is not a sufficient condition. It is also necessary to select managers with skill in exploiting these inefficiencies. Without skill, inefficient markets still present a zero sum game (a negative sum game after fees and costs).

There has been a tremendous evolution in indexing over the past 30 years, and no doubt there will be further refinement and utility in this form of investing over the next 30 years. One concept seems timeless, however: Investors should view indexation not strictly as a substitute for active management, but as an effective tool in a holistic investment strategy that invests in broad universes of assets and asset classes. Or, as Chapter 1 states: It's not "index versus active" but how one combines the two to maximize the efficiency of an overall portfolio.

NOTES

1. InterSec Data (Third Quarter, 2001).
2. InterSec Data (Fourth Quarter, 2002).
3. See Steven A. Schoenfeld, "Watch Out, Active Managers, for the New EAFE," *Pensions & Investments* (November 12, 2001).
4. BGI *International Equity Strategy Group* research, presented as "Globalization and the Changing Framework for International Equities" (Steven A. Schoenfeld, BGI Chicago Client Conference, November 2, 2000).
5. See, for example, on U.S. small caps Richard Ennis and Michael Sebastian, "The Small-Cap-Alpha Myth," White Paper (Chicago: Ennis Knupp & Associates, September 2001); on emerging markets, see Steven A. Schoenfeld, "Index-Based Investment in Emerging Stock Markets," *Emerging Markets Quarterly*, vol. 2, no. 1 (Spring 1998).
6. See Chapter 15 for a full discussion on the appropriate definition of enhanced indexing and how it differs from "risk-controlled active" and traditional active management.

CHAPTER 4

Market Uncertainty and the Role of Indexing

Adele Kohler

_____ Editor's Note _____

Like clockwork, each bearish market environment brings with it the claims that "this is when active managers will prove their worth" or that "indexing only works in rising markets." Chapter 3 went to some lengths to dispel those myths. In this chapter, Adele Kohler attacks them head on, writing from the perspective of 2003's respite from a brutal three-year U.S. equity bear market. She draws heavily on publicly available empirical evidence, as well as some unique data points regarding active manager cash levels during market turns. Her conclusion is consistent with that of Chapters 3, 25, 29, and 30—namely, that a core allocation to index-based strategies is the ideal way to maintain the integrity of a well-designed strategic asset allocation in any market environment.

This is a modified version of an article published by State Street Global Advisors (SSgA) as "Market Uncertainty and Indexing—A Light at the End of the Tunnel?" (July 2003), distributed to clients and available on www.ssga.com. The views expressed are the views of Adele Kohler only through the period ended July 2003, and are subject to change based on market and other conditions. The opinions expressed may differ from those with other investment philosophies. The information provided does not constitute investment advice, and it should not be relied on as such. It should not be considered a solicitation to buy or an offer to sell a security. It does not take into account any investor's particular investment objectives, strategies, tax status, or investment horizon. We encourage you to consult your tax or financial advisor. All material has been obtained from sources believed to be reliable, but its accuracy is not guaranteed. There is no representation or warranty as to the current accuracy of, or liability for, decisions based on such information. Past performance is no guarantee of future results.

The second quarter of 2003 seems to have marked the beginning of the end of the worst down market since the 1930s. The stock market decline that began in the aftermath of the technology bubble of the late 1990s appeared to have bottomed out and some optimism had resurfaced. But the uncertainty that characterized the 3-year bear market remained. The unique global socioeconomic and political conditions of this era contribute to feelings of increased risk among investors despite a market turnaround.

Times like these often lead to doubt and reevaluation. Investors review the course they are on to determine whether policy changes will better enable them to meet their goals. The recent down market and associated volatility fueled the continuing debate over whether index investing is an appropriate method for gaining equity exposure. The subsequent market turnaround of 2003 provides an opportunity to revisit this question and draw on performance results during a particularly unpleasant period in the history of equity investing.

THE DOWN MARKET ARGUMENT

Whenever the market suffers a period of substantial or sustained loss, the notion of a "stock picker's market" resurfaces. The down market is typically associated with a time of opportunity for active managers. And the appeal of downside protection can tempt investors into questioning their commitment to passive investing. The urge to seek out protection in a down market is a rational response. It is always easier to deal with a rising market than to suffer through an unusually stubborn down market. Nevertheless, the argument that active managers can consistently provide protection in bear markets remains unsubstantiated. Numerous studies show that, since the down market of 1973/1974, the average active manager return exceeded the market return in about half of the down markets to date. In addition, not only was the outperformance not statistically significant, but the results were based on data beset with calculation biases favoring active managers (survivorship bias).[1]

In the most recent down market, active managers fared no better this time around than they have in past down markets. Data adjusted for survivorship bias and published by Standard & Poor's help illustrate the consistency with which index returns exceed active fund returns net of fees. Over the past 1 and 3 years ending March 31, 2003, the indexes beat the majority of active managers. Also, the average return of active managers was lower in 18 out of 26 categories (the 26 categories being S&P's 13 categories, in both their 3-year and 5-year measurement periods; see Tables 4.1 and 4.2).

TABLE 4.1 Percentage of Active Managers Outperformed by Their
Respective Indexes

Fund Category	Comparison Index	One Year	Three Years
All domestic	S&P SuperComposite 1500	63.19	55.46
All large cap	S&P 500	60.19	55.02
All mid cap	S&P MidCap 400	63.03	67.95
All small cap	S&P SmallCap 600	61.40	72.95
Large cap growth	S&P/BARRA 500 Growth	79.66	59.80
Large cap blend	S&P 500	58.80	57.58
Large cap value	S&P/BARRA 500 Value	36.67	33.45
Mid cap growth	S&P/BARRA MidCap 400 Growth	68.35	82.95
Mid cap blend	S&P MidCap 400	62.35	66.28
Mid cap value	S&P/BARRA MidCap 400 Value	49.06	71.76
Small cap growth	S&P/BARRA 600 SmallCap Growth	90.27	90.73
Small cap blend	S&P SmallCap 600	56.12	72.88
Small cap value	S&P/BARRA 600 SmallCap Value	18.63	55.47

Source: Standard & Poor's. For period ending March 31, 2003. Outperformance is
based upon equal-weighted fund counts. Universe is comprised of mutual funds.

These results are consistent with the notion discussed in Chapter 2, that
the average return of all investors is the market (index) return, net of fees and
transaction costs. Therefore, we would expect the indexes to outperform the
average active fund, in any market environment—up or down. However, a
few myths still persist about the presumed edge of active managers in a
down market. The first is that active managers have more discretion to hold
cash in their portfolios and, therefore, can increase their cash holdings at the
start of a bear market. This assumes that: (1) active managers can successfully predict bear markets and (2) that they really have the discretion and the
inclination to move in and out of cash in response to those predictions. Neither assumption holds water. For the most part, institutional investors prefer
to remain fully invested at all times. Unless tactical asset allocation is specifically mandated, most money managers are restricted from allowing cash to
build, unequitized, in a portfolio.

A look at institutional managers' allocation to cash in the past
10 years illustrates the overall trend toward a reduction in cash positions
(see Figure 4.1). The data also show that if active managers were, in fact,
attempting to time their changes in cash held over the past decade, they

TABLE 4.2   One- and Three-Year Annualized Returns Ending March 31, 2003

Fund Category	One Year (%)	Index Return	Index Outperformance	Three Years (Annualized %)	Index Return	Index Outperformance
All domestic	−24.77	−24.39	0.38	−17.21	−15.04	2.17
All large cap	−24.67	−24.76	−0.09	−17.20	−16.09	1.11
All mid cap funds	−24.79	−23.45	1.34	−17.30	−5.40	11.90
All small cap	−25.52	−24.81	0.71	−16.61	−3.26	13.35
Large cap growth	−25.55	−23.61	1.94	−22.90	−20.90	2.00
Large cap blend	−24.08	−24.76	−0.68	−15.54	−16.09	−0.55
Large cap value	−23.72	−26.19	−2.47	−7.41	−11.26	−3.85
Mid cap growth	−26.56	−24.22	2.34	−22.89	−12.85	10.04
Mid cap blend	−24.99	−23.45	1.54	−14.44	−5.40	9.04
Mid cap value	−21.75	−22.97	−1.22	−0.61	2.96	3.57
Small cap growth	−29.10	−21.21	7.89	−24.17	−9.19	14.98
Small cap blend	−24.46	−24.81	−0.35	−11.82	−3.26	8.56
Small cap value	−21.97	−28.60	−6.63	0.84	1.52	0.68

Source: Standard & Poor's. For period ending March 31, 2003. Outperformance is based upon asset-weighted returns. Universe is made up of mutual funds. Updates to this data are available on www.IndexUniverse.com and www.spglobal.com.

clearly miscalculated. Money managers held more cash at the start of the bull market of the 1990s than at any other point since then. Cash positions steadily declined as the bull market raged on and were at their lowest levels at the start of the bear market in 2000.

BEING THERE WHEN THE MARKET TURNS

These results confirm what most investors already know. Predicting the peaks and valleys of market cycles is extremely difficult for even the most skilled money managers. Therefore, relying on active managers to position their portfolios in anticipation of market turning points may be unrealistic. In doing so, investors risk missing out on potentially rapid and often significant market upswings. To take a recent example, while many hoped that the end of the war in Iraq would give a much-needed boost to equities, few anticipated the swiftness and extent to which the "war dividend" would have an impact. Therefore, investors who weren't fully exposed to U.S. equities in anticipation of the pop in April 2003 may not have enjoyed the 8.2

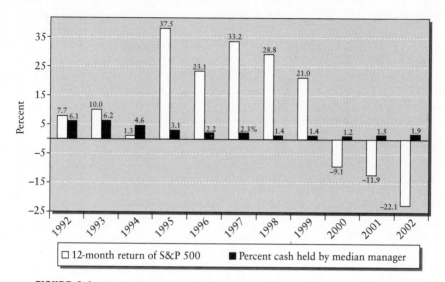

FIGURE 4.1 Active Manager Cash Reserves versus S&P 500 Performance
Source: New England Pension Consultants, SSGA.

percent return generated during that month. The difficulty of timing the market is brought into focus when we observe that three days in April were responsible for 84 percent of the return generated during that month.

Therefore, even if managers began to unwind defensive cash positions during April, they likely experienced some drag as they played catch-up with the market. Figure 4.2 shows what the return would be to an investor who missed the best performing days during the month. Investors can't predict when the critical up-days will occur. Therefore, just being there—having market exposure—is the best way to guarantee participation in a market turnaround. Figure 4.3 illustrates the impact of missing the early days of a market turnaround. The chart shows the cumulative effect of being unexposed at the start of the month and each consecutive day thereafter. Missing even the first day in April 2003 resulted in a 1.3 percent shortfall compared with the return for an investor who was fully exposed on April 1. Investors who are not invested in the first 2 days of the month fall short of the market return for that month by over 4 percent.

This is only one example, but it demonstrates how quickly active managers who hold cash balances can potentially find themselves trailing market returns. Unsuccessful timing decisions can cause active managers to fall short of the market over the long term. Additionally, some active managers cannot keep up during rising markets because they lack the necessary

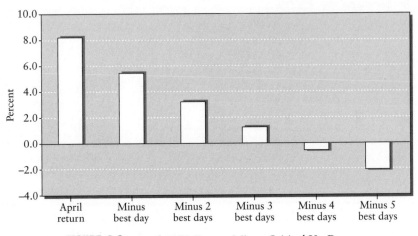

FIGURE 4.2   April 2003 Return Minus Critical Up-Days
Source: Factset, SSGA.

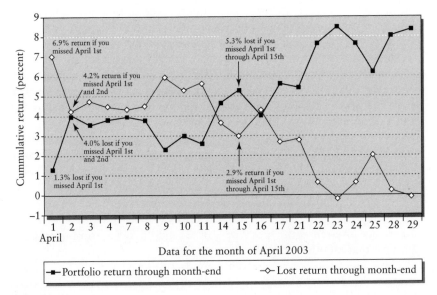

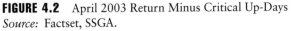

FIGURE 4.3   The Impact of Missing the Early Days of a Market Turnaround—
2003's Example
Source: Factset, SSGA.

stock-picking skills. The two problems combined can lead to significant shortfall over time. Since rising markets have been longer in duration and greater in magnitude than falling markets, downside protection is less relevant in the long term than simply keeping pace with the market over time. Most managers cannot produce enough alpha during market declines to make up for their performance shortfalls during rising markets. Since 1974, managers would have had to outperform in down markets by an average annualized return of 3.2 percent to compensate for underperformance during market expansions—a difficult hurdle to overcome.

INDEXING OVER THE FULL MARKET CYCLE

Having discussed the importance of keeping pace with the market, it is interesting to note the results of active managers throughout the duration of the last full market cycle. Standard & Poor's published results that were based on the returns of mutual funds in a variety of categories from March 1998 to March 2003. As visible on Figure 4.4, it was a bumpy ride for the overall market, as shown by the return of the S&P 1500 SuperComposite Index during the period (see Figure 4.4), but the indexes came out on top.

During the past 5 years of highs and lows, the indexes have beaten a majority of active funds in 8 out of 9 style categories (see Table 4.3).

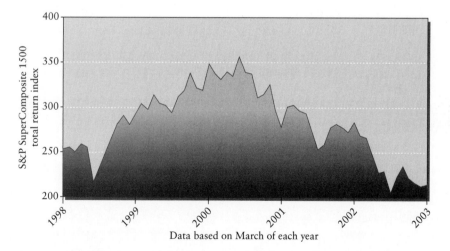

Data based on March of each year

FIGURE 4.4 The Volatile 1998 to 2003 Market Environment
Source: Standard & Poor's (S&P 1500 returns).

TABLE 4.3   Outperformance of Indexes Compared
with Active Funds

Fund Category	% of Funds Beaten by Index (March 1998 to March 2003)
Large cap growth	64.39
Large cap blend	58.40
Large cap value	52.07
Mid cap growth	97.16
Mid cap blend	86.11
Mid cap value	83.33
Small cap growth	72.20
Small cap blend	60.11
Small cap value	41.58

Source: Standard & Poor's.

Not only did the indexes outperform the majority of active funds, but the average return of active funds was lower than the index return over the 5-year period in all but two categories (see Table 4.4). Standard & Poor's now publishes this analysis each quarter as the "S&P Index versus Active" ("SPIVA") research papers, which are available through www.IndexUniverse.com.

TABLE 4.4   Lower Average Returns of Active Funds Compared
with Index Funds

Fund Category	Annualized Average Fund Returns		Annualized Index Returns
	Equal Weighted	Asset Weighted	
Large cap growth	−6.01	−5.23	−4.17
Large cap blend	−4.04	−3.88	−3.76
Large cap value	−3.19	−2.83	−4.09
Mid cap growth	−2.53	−3.09	4.03
Mid cap blend	0.13	−2.40	3.27
Mid cap value	−0.33	0.13	2.49
Small cap growth	−4.98	−5.00	−2.17
Small cap blend	0.75	−1.78	−0.88
Small cap value	0.51	1.12	−1.13

Source: Standard & Poor's.

BACK TO UNCERTAINTY

No one knows for sure whether the bear market of the early 2000s has finally given way to a sustained recovery. If it has, the issue of down market protection is mute—for the time being anyway. Although 2003 was a strong recovery year for markets, questions remain regarding the reach and durability of the current recovery across the world's major economies. Investors still fear the unknown and question whether indexing is an appropriate approach during a period when the possibility of market shocks seems greater.

The inherent uncertainty of financial markets, while at times unsettling, is the perfect backdrop for index investing. The reality is that no investment approach can guard against unanticipated events that cause large market shocks because, by definition, these events are unexpected. So, it is best to focus on long-term objectives in a way that continually reflects all known information. Indexing does this. Indexing is an investment solution that takes advantage of the market's ability to factor in all that is known and expected about price levels, interest rates, and all other factors "in the ever-changing basket of uncertainty at any given point in time."[2] It reflects the market's cumulative expectations for the future, given all the uncertainties.

Recall from Chapter 2 that the original motivation for passive investing was to achieve maximum diversification—a benefit inherent in the market portfolio. The only real and productive way to respond to true uncertainty is to diversify all the risks that are diversifiable. That is exactly what index-based investing does.

KEEPING A STRATEGIC FOCUS

All investors need to evaluate their portfolios regularly and make adjustments. However, any modifications should be based on changes in long-term expectations—not short-term uncertainties. While regular reviews may result in updated assumptions and ultimately adjustments to the portfolio, the first priority should be to ensure that strategic asset allocation reflects long-term expectations. This decision will have the greatest impact on long-term results.

Once determined, a core allocation to index funds is the ideal way to maintain the integrity of a well-thought-out strategic asset allocation. Indexing ensures that the portfolio is fully invested and fully diversified at low cost and with little monitoring. Active portfolios can also implement a plan's strategic asset allocation. However, it can be difficult to find managers who can (1) consistently outperform (or at least earn back their management fees) and (2) remain true to their style category. The uncertainty around whether a chosen manager will meet expectations only increases the chances of performance shortfall. In volatile times, plan sponsors and individual investors alike might prefer the low-maintenance, no-surprise approach that indexing provides.

NOTES

1. Eric Brandhorst, "Problems with Manager Universe Data," CFA, State Street Global Advisors (November 22, 2002). Available from www.ssga.com and the book's E-ppendix at www.ActiveIndexInvesting.com.
2. Catherine Gordon, "During Periods of Short-Term Uncertainty, Keep a Long-Term Focus," *Vanguard Investment Counseling & Research,* 2002.

Benchmarks
The Foundation for Indexing

Steven A. Schoenfeld

Part Two focuses on the relevance of benchmarks to the investment process and the legitimization of benchmarks through their application as
investment products. Even investors who have never used an index-based
product need to understand the important uses of benchmark indexes. As a
leading financial market researcher stated, "Benchmarks determine the performance of investment managers perhaps more than any other influence,
including managers' determination to succeed and the resources and skills
they bring to this task. We in the industry have largely overlooked this fact,
perhaps at our peril."[1]

Despite a primary focus on equity indexes, Part Two covers most other
asset classes in considerable detail.[2] More important, the overarching framework these nine chapters establish for understanding benchmarks—their uses
and their attributes—is universal and applicable to virtually any index and
asset class.

The first components of the universal framework are the *four uses of
benchmark indexes,* discussed in detail in Chapter 5:

1. Gauge of the market and investor sentiment.
2. Asset allocation and research.
3. Performance measurement.
4. Basis for investment vehicles.

As Chapters 5 and 6 make clear, choosing your benchmark—for any asset class—has huge implications for your overall portfolio because it provides "guardrails" for active managers and the underlying basis for index-based products. Thus, any investor requires appropriate parameters for assessing benchmark options. Part Two identifies *seven key criteria* of a satisfactory index:

1. Completeness.
2. Investability.
3. Clear rules and governance.
4. Accurate data.
5. Acceptance by investors.
6. Available liquidity and tradable products.
7. Low turnover and transaction costs.

Like the *four uses,* they were developed to be universal in scope—applicable on virtually any type of benchmark. Chapter 6 explores these seven criteria in detail including the inherent trade-offs between different criteria. Chapter 7 provides an alternative perspective for identifying an ideal benchmark. Within Part Two, these seven criteria are the basis for analyzing three key asset class benchmarks: U.S. equities (Chapter 8), international equities (Chapter 9), and fixed income (Chapter 10).

The sidebar in Chapter 7 identifies the major flagship index families (with additional contributions from key executives of the index providers themselves in the E-ppendix). The index calculation business is dynamic and competitive (and often highly profitable), and a key by-product of this competition is the continuous evolution of index methodology. Updates on the competition within the index business are available on IndexUniverse.com.

In addition to assessing the criteria for acceptable fixed-income benchmarks, Chapter 10 highlights the major differences between them and equity indexes, and a sidebar delves into an alternative asset class benchmark—commodity indexes. These latter indexes have become the basis for a variety of index funds and derivatives to gain efficient exposure to commodity returns.

The exploration of alternative assets in Chapter 11 provides a comprehensive assessment of hedge fund indexes; its sidebar discusses the new generation of investable hedge fund indexes, which are designed specifically to be the basis for index products.

Chapters 6 through 11 focus mainly on the second, third, and fourth uses of indexes. Chapter 12 focuses primarily on the first of the *four uses*—how indexes gauge the markets and investor sentiment, but in the process, exposes additional instances of the second and fourth use. Using over 30 years of history of global equity indexes as an example, this entertaining chapter demonstrates the application of benchmarks as research tools for assessing the underlying markets, sectors, and economic trends.

Chapter 13 breaks new ground in discussing the global phenomenon of Socially Responsible Investing (SRI) and how it has been applied in benchmarks and index investment products. Besides focusing on trends in the United States and Europe, the chapter includes some comments on SRI funds and benchmarks in Canada and Japan. A sidebar on Corporate Governance and its impact and implications for Indexation is also included within this chapter. The discussion of SRI indexes also foreshadows some of the key elements and trade-offs inherent in custom indexes discussed in Parts Three and Four.

By the end of Part Two, readers should understand the complexity and nuances of benchmark construction, recognize the relevance of benchmarks, and appreciate the vital importance of making the appropriate benchmark decision to suit an investor's objectives. After asset allocation, the benchmark decision is the most important decision for index-based products. The underlying benchmark essentially defines these products, and thus to make the best decision, investors should arm themselves with independently developed insight or research unaffiliated with the index provider or product sponsor.

NOTES

1. Mark Kritzman, Research Director for the Association for Investment Management and Research (AIMR), in Foreword to Laurence B. Siegel, *Benchmarks and Investment Management* (Research Foundation of AIMR, Charlottesville, VA, 2003).
2. One major asset class—currencies—is not covered in the book, although IndexUniverse.com has information on currency indexes, particularly the USDX (U.S. Dollar Index), which has futures trading based on the index at the New York Board of Trade.

The Vital Importance and Fundamental Uses of Benchmarks

Pamela Cloyd, Larry Siegel, and Steven A. Schoenfeld

_____ Editor's Note _____

By providing the essential foundation for understanding the crucial role of benchmarks in all types of investing, Chapter 5 sets the stage for all of Part Two. It starts by describing the four key uses of benchmarks: as a gauge of the market, as a performance benchmark, as an asset allocation research and implementation tool, and as the basis for investment vehicles. The chapter also reviews some of the recurring criticisms of benchmark usage, which often contain implicit or explicit criticisms of indexing itself and concludes with some guiding principles for the application of benchmarks. Two sidebars are included: The first explains why market capitalization weighting,

Substantial portions of this text are adapted from two key articles on benchmarks—a BGI *Global Solutions* article written by Pam Cloyd and Gerry Rocchi of BGI Canada in 2001 and an AIMR Research Foundation monograph by Larry Siegel. We attribute certain key points directly to them, but we also want to acknowledge their overall influence on the themes within this chapter. In addition, certain parts of this chapter (and the aforementioned AIMR monograph) are adapted from previously published BGI *Investment Insights,* including "Broad Capitalization Indices of the U.S. Equity Market," by Francis Enderle, Brad Pope, and Laurence Siegel (July 2002) and "International Equity Benchmarks for U.S. Investors" by Steven A. Schoenfeld and Rob Ginis (November 2002). Finally, the section on four key uses of benchmarks and indexes is adapted from the article "Perfection Impossible" by Steven A. Schoenfeld published in the second quarter, 2002, issue of the *Journal of Indexes.*

like democracy or capitalism, is not perfect, but still is better than any of the proposed alternatives; and the second focuses on the importance of float adjustment for benchmarks, using a robust example from the late 1990s.

WHERE YOU SIT DEPENDS ON WHERE YOU STAND

Indexation, both as an art and a science, has advanced substantially since the launch of the first index fund in 1971 (see Chapter 2). Because index funds are now so common, it must be hard for younger practitioners to imagine how radical an idea it once seemed even to measure performance against a benchmark, much less manage money against one. Jason Zweig, the financial historian and columnist for *Time* and *Money* magazines, recalls: "I believe it was not until [as recently as] the 1980s that mutual funds were required by the SEC [Securities and Exchange Commission] to calculate and report a number called 'total return.' When the SEC proposed that new rule, the fund industry met it with howls of execration. The most common refrain was that the investing public would not understand or would misinterpret a single total return figure. Previously, investors had either to calculate the number themselves or rely on services like Wiesenberger, Lipper, or the financial press."[1]

As indexed assets grew dramatically over the subsequent four decades, the critical importance of index construction methodology, along with the impact of index changes on index fund performance and markets, has also become better understood. Continual improvement in methodology benefits investment managers and their clients alike, and will undoubtedly continue in the years ahead. One should recognize, however, that while there can be indexes that are perfect for a specific investor application, there cannot and arguably *should not* be one perfect index—the diversity of investors' needs is too great.[2]

Index benchmarks are appropriate for a wide range of investment applications: monitoring market sentiment, evaluating performance, determining asset allocation policy, and implementing portfolio decisions. Thus, indexes with different approaches toward achieving "perfection" should be considered a good thing. Chapter 6 provides substantial detail on what we believe are best practices for index construction; Chapter 7 provides an alternative viewpoint. The subsequent chapters in Part Two use these key criteria to describe and assess major equity and fixed-income benchmarks.

This chapter explores the four benchmark applications along with the concepts and debates that surround their use. We focus primarily on broad stock market benchmarks that attempt to strike the balance between adequately representing a national equity market while remaining sufficiently investable to be the basis for index funds. An index that can effectively perform this dual role should be able to serve the multiple needs that investors have for their benchmarks, and thus should also be a successful index.

THE FOUR KEY USES OF INDEXES

The effort to measure the performance of stock markets, as opposed to individual securities, is at least as old as Charles Henry Dow's pioneering average, launched in 1884. The first Dow average was simply the average of the prices of 11 railroad stocks. This number provided investors with an updated barometer of the market every day. The calculation and popularity of this early market index seemingly reflected a general awareness that trends in the market had a bearing on the prices of individual issues, and not just the other way around.[3] Thus, from the beginning, indexes served multiple, interconnected purposes.

Today, dozens of index providers calculate thousands of market indexes representing every conceivable slice of individual markets, countries, regions, asset classes, and investment styles. In addition, a plethora of stock and bond indexes are calculated by local exchanges and financial firms in over fifty developed and emerging markets. Although this abundance reflects the explosive growth of the investment industry and suggests a healthy emphasis on quantifying investment results and processes, it also makes differentiation among the many indexes more challenging. Focusing on the following four major applications of indexes helps clarify the differences and reveals which indexes are appropriate in various circumstances.

Gauge of Public or Market Sentiment

From the beginning, market indexes have been widely used to answer the question, "What is happening in the world at this moment?" As early users of the Dow Jones could appreciate, reducing the prices of diverse securities in a market to a single statistic reveals the net effect of all factors at work in a market. These include not only hopes and fears specific to companies in the index, but also broader factors—war, peace, economic expansion and recession, and so forth—that potentially can affect stock and bond prices. Thus, a frequently updated stock market index indicates how people are reacting to current events—updated minute-by-minute on your mobile phone, wireless handheld organizer, customized computer homepage, or the evening TV news.

This use is particularly notable in times of stress. In early 2003, virtually every market movement around the world was attributed to investors' feelings about the second Gulf War in Iraq. Before the war, when the markets went down, media pundits said investors were pessimistic because of the upcoming war. Similarly, when the markets went up, it was said that investors were expecting a quick and positive outcome. The relatively short duration of the market drop in the days and weeks following the terrorist attacks of September 11, 2001, was seen as a signal that the nation's confidence had returned. But this use of indexes is not new. Depressed stock prices were also attributed to Allied setbacks in World War II and to the assassination of John F. Kennedy (and the strong rebound after the large one-day decline was taken as a sign that national confidence had not been destroyed). In all these cases, investors looked to stock indexes as an indicator of price levels and market sentiment.

There are also choices for investors who wish to predict—as opposed to observe after the fact—investor sentiment in the market. The Chicago Board Options Exchange (CBOE) Market Volatility Index (VIX) is seen as a barometer of anxiety or complacency in the market. It is derived by computing the implied volatility of eight call/put options on the S&P 100 with a mean expiration of 30 days. Since the value of an option increases with its volatility, the VIX tells us how much people value a basket of S&P 100 futures. The VIX is often used as a contrarian indicator: Higher values (when the market is sharply lower), such as figures of 40 and above, can represent *irrational fear* and can indicate that the market may be getting ready to turn back up. Lower values (when the market is on a steady uptrend), such as 15 or below, can represent complacency or *irrational exuberance* and may indicate the market is at risk of topping out and due for a fair amount of profit taking.[4]

Performance Measurement

One of the satisfying, and possibly unintended, consequences of having a market index available is that it answers the question, "Did I beat the market?" Although such comparisons have been possible since the earliest days of the money management industry, the modern science of performance measurement, evaluation, and attribution did not take shape until after the academic achievements of the 1960s—the Capital-Asset Pricing Model or CAPM (see Chapter 2) and related work—in determining to what extent, and why, a particular portfolio beat or was beaten by a market index. In the late 1970s and in the 1980s, as the technology for estimating active risk became accessible, and as the importance of the new academic theories (CAPM, efficient markets, and so forth) became widely appreciated, traditional active managers as well as "quants" and indexers began to use the technology. The consultant community led this expansion of quantitative investment analysis, which resulted in the near-universality of benchmarking that we see today in developed financial centers.

Nowadays, most professionals (but not all) consider measuring performance against an appropriate benchmark to be a crucial step in the investment process. Despite the evidence, however, some investors—perhaps unconsciously—still cling to the myth that wealth in the securities markets is *created,* as opposed to *traded.* They find it difficult to truly accept that one investor's gain can only be produced by someone else's loss. Yet, according to Sharpe's "The Arithmetic of Active Management," described in Chapter 2, it is arithmetically impossible for the average invested dollar to consistently beat benchmarks that include the entire set of securities from which investors select their portfolios (i.e., an appropriate benchmark). It is possible that the over 50 percent of investors who experience underbenchmark performance are convinced that it was just bad luck; they essentially believe, in the words of global investing pioneer John Templeton, *Next time things will be different.*

Benchmarking actively managed equity and fixed-income funds attacks these myths and has led to the exposure of poorly performing funds. It can reveal that what might have been called outperformance is often merely a by-product of "spicing up" returns by adding other asset classes—which cannot be done without adding risk.

In one example, many fixed-income managers in the United States consistently outperformed the Lehman Brothers Aggregate Bond Index between 1990 and 1998.[5] Much of that outperformance could be attributed to managers investing in securities not included in the index, such as high-yield bonds. An investment consultant said, "As a manager, if I'm reasonably insightful, I can take some credit risk and a little convexity, stir in a little duration, and lo and behold, I can beat the benchmark in my sleep before I actually have to think about making hard decisions."[6] As an important postscript, since 1998 many of the same managers have underperformed the Lehman Aggregate. The solution to this problem, as with other performance measurement exercises, is defining the benchmark to reflect the actual investable universe to some reasonable degree, which Lehman Brothers has attempted to do with the introduction of their Lehman Universal Index in 2000. During the early/mid 2000s, the refinement and sophistication of fixed-income benchmarks and index products has grown substantially, and this is discussed in Chapter 10.

Like Toto pulling aside the Wizard of Oz's curtain, unveiling the source of returns as well as the attendant risks tends to remove the cherished mystique that the investment industry has an enormous vested interest in maintaining. It is not surprising that some—though admittedly not all—of the most fervent advocates of the abandonment of benchmarks also stand to benefit the most from looser scrutiny. Perhaps the timing of the anti-index backlash is related to the exceptionally frustrating business environment faced by active managers during the market run-up of the late 1990s. During that period, the S&P 500 pulverized any value-oriented investment approach; for that matter, just about any bet away from the index was severely penalized.

Indexes actually drive the behavior of market participants in various ways, instead of just recording it. The sidebar by Larry Siegel accompanying the next chapter highlights the ways in which benchmarking and indexing can affect the capital markets, and this "index effect" is explored further in Chapters 8, 9, and in Part Four of the book.

Despite reasonable concerns about the S&P 500 as a benchmark and an investment vehicle, as well as its possible effect on investors, there is no adequate substitute for indexes, including the S&P 500, to compare performance. Such benchmarking allows for informed monitoring of manager performance and assists decision making in hiring, retaining, and firing managers. It also allows for tighter risk control relative to objectives, and for more precise allocation of investments. The ability to make better decisions, however, is underappreciated. Benchmarking helps investors identify managers with sustainable skill in generating superior results. This leads to greater confidence in decision making about manager performance, and potentially to greater skill in manager selection. As an example of how greater skill in manager selection can influence results, assume that an investor selects among managers generating returns that deviate from a benchmark with an 8 percent annualized standard deviation. Eliminating the bottom 10 percent of managers in that distribution would boost average returns by over 1.5 percent annually, a very significant difference in the long run.[7]

Performance monitoring should be done in a thoughtful context with adequate passage of time to evaluate decisions properly. Although institutional investors should evaluate investment decisions on a long-term basis and should sometimes encourage bold decision making, not squelch it, they still must monitor soundness of process and adherence to philosophy closely and continually. This is a process that absolutely requires benchmarks.

Measuring Asset Class Performance and Setting Asset Allocation Policy

A consistently well-constructed index allows the calculation of long-run rates of return and the comparison of market levels at various points in time—crucial information for analysts seeking insights into the behavior of securities and asset classes. In addition, investors use indexes to compare the risks of different asset classes and to measure the changes in risk of a given asset class over time; to calculate correlations and gains from diversification among asset classes; and to perform other analyses relevant to determining investment policy.

By reflecting the key drivers of investment return—style, size, sector, and country—narrower style or sector indexes help investors make meaningful and targeted decisions about the markets most relevant to them, particularly when evaluating specialty managers. Broad benchmarks, however, are generally more appropriate for setting asset allocation policy; complex benchmarks should be used at the policy level only for specific purposes or assumed added value. Specialty benchmarks, because of their sheer number and variety, are harder to implement suitably, but it would be foolish to discard such a valuable tool simply because it could be used improperly. As Einstein put it, "Everything should be made as simple as possible, but not simpler."

As discussed in Chapter 3, risk budgeting to create more efficient portfolios of managers focuses on the level of decision making most relevant to plan sponsors and consultants. Using portfolio optimization techniques to construct more efficient portfolios builds on a technology for quantitatively managing active risk or tracking error to the benchmark that was initially developed by Barr Rosenberg. A professor at the University of California, Berkeley, and founder of BARRA, Inc.—Rosenberg promulgated two key insights:

1. One should optimize active return against active risk, just as one optimizes policy, that is, market return, against policy risk.
2. Returns on securities are characterized by *extra-market covariance*: Security returns are correlated to factors *other* than the market factor. The market model says that security returns are correlated only to the market factor and are otherwise independent of one another. As a result, one can model any security as a bundle of factor exposures, plus an unexplained risk term. Such a model provides a better estimate of beta, for use in the CAPM to determine expected security returns, than can be obtained by calculating an ordinary historical regression beta for the security.[8]

There is a vital link between the two concepts: To solve the active return/active risk optimization problem, you need forecasts of return and risk for every security in your opportunity set, and you need forecasts of the correlation of every security with every other. For example, if the opportunity set is the 3,000 stocks in the Russell 3000, there are $[(3000 \times 2999)/2]$ or 4,498,500 correlations to forecast (setting aside, for the moment, the risk and return forecasts). This staggering number is too daunting to calculate. However, if you have a model that characterizes each security as a bundle, or vector, of 13 factors—the number of factors in BARRA's best-known U.S. equity model—then you have to forecast only the *correlations of the factors,* of which there are $[(13 \times 12)/2]$ or 78, plus the $[3000 \times 13]$ or 39,000 loadings, or degree of exposure of each security to each of the factors. This number is still formidable, but it is manageable with the requisite software (which, helpfully, is sold by BARRA, the company that Rosenberg founded, as well as

THE VITAL IMPORTANCE OF MARKET CAPITALIZATION-WEIGHTING
Larry Siegel

Between 1885 and today, by far the most important innovation in equity index construction has been that of the Standard Securities Corporation (later Standard & Poor's), which, in 1923, constructed the first market capitalization-weighted (cap-weighted) index. This index, a composite of 223 securities, evolved into today's S&P 500, which remains the flagship index with the most assets linked to it through index funds, ETFs, and listed and OTC index derivatives.[a] A cap-weighted index gives each company a weight in proportion to the total market value of that company's outstanding shares. Most of the broad market indexes in use today are market cap weighted. This is in contrast to the Dow Jones Industrial Average and Nikkei Stock Average, both of which implicitly weight each company by its stock price per share and are best viewed as indicators, not as benchmarks.

For several crucial reasons, market cap-weighting is the central organizing principle of good equity index construction. The first and simplest reason is macroconsistency: if everyone held a cap-weighted index fund and there were no active investors, all stocks would be held with none left over. With other weighting schemes, it is mathematically impossible for all investors to hold the index. It makes a certain amount of intuitive sense that cap-weighting reflects better the available opportunity set for investors.

Second—and far more important from a practical standpoint— cap-weighting is the only weighting scheme consistent with a buy-and-hold strategy. The manager of a full-replication fund needs to trade only to reinvest dividends, to keep pace with changes in the index constituents, and to reflect modifications in index weights caused by changes in the constituent companies' number of shares outstanding.

---

[a] The original index contained 233 stocks in 26 industry groups, but a narrower index, the S&P 90-Stock Composite Index (consisting of 50 industrial, 20 railroad, and 20 utilities), was the direct predecessor of the S&P 500, which started on March 1, 1957. The Ibbotson and Sinquefield and Ibbotson Associates studies link the S&P 90, from January 1, 1926, through February 28, 1957, with the S&P 500, from March 1, 1957, through the present, to form one continuous series representing large-capitalization stocks. All three indexes—the original S&P with 233 stocks, the S&P 90, and the S&P 500—are market capitalization-weighted. See Roger G. Ibbotson and Rex A. Sinquefield, "Stocks, Bonds, Bills and Inflation: Year-by-Year Historical Returns (1926–74)," *Journal of Business* (1976); and Ibbotson Associates, *Stocks, Bonds, Bills and Inflation: 2002 Yearbook* (Chicago, 2002).

As described in Part Four, a fully replicating fund holds every security in the index in proportion to its index weight. An optimized or sampled fund, which attempts to track an index using a subset of the securities in the index, may require more frequent rebalancing even if the fund is based on a cap-weighted index. In contrast, indexes that are not cap-weighted (such as equal-weighted indexes) require constant rebalancing because of ordinary changes in the prices of stocks. The cost of this frequent rebalancing can potentially destroy the value of using an index fund in the first place.

Finally, there is the theoretical basis. Despite the challenges to benchmarking, and to cap-weighted benchmarks in particular, that have arisen in the past decade, cap-weighted benchmarks will continue to have a preeminant place in investment management and analysis for a simple reason: *You cannot design a simple, rule-based, judgment-free portfolio that is demonstrably more efficient than the cap-weighted benchmark.* Some people have suggested equal-weighted benchmarks, book-value or earnings-weighted, or other types of benchmark such as international equity benchmarks that are GDP-weighted by country.[b] Equally weighted portfolios aside, proponents of such benchmarks cannot even agree on sensible rules for constructing them, much less prove that these portfolios are more efficient than a cap-weighted one.[c] Finally, the Capital Asset Pricing Model—despite its flaws—demonstrates that cap-weighted benchmarks are efficient. There is no theory (not even one proposed and untested) that claims some other simple, rule-based portfolio is efficient. For these reasons, benchmarking relative to cap-weighted indexes—as an important component of a broader performance-measurement discipline that also includes comparison to absolute-return and liability benchmarks—is very much here to stay.

---

[b] The definitive examination of the portfolio efficiency of equally weighted portfolios is that of J. D. Jobson and Bob Korkie, "Putting Markowitz Theory to Work," *Journal of Portfolio Management*, 7 (1981): 70–74. They find that under some conditions an equally weighted portfolio is as efficient as a cap-weighted one, or more so. The small-cap effect, which was very powerful in the time period leading up to Jobson and Korkie's work, may at least partly explain this result, which (if that is the correct explanation) would not be repeatable.

[c] There is another thread of thinking about benchmarks represented by Haugen (1999), who constructs an "efficient index" based on optimization, using estimates of security returns, risks, and correlations derived from fundamental factors. We would argue that this is just active management, since an investor who does not have access to Haugen's specific forecasts cannot determine what the benchmark contents will be. See Robert A. Haugen, *The New Finance: A Case against Efficient Markets* (Upper Saddle River, NJ: Prentice-Hall, 1999).

by competitive developers of several excellent variants).[9] Most investment managers shortcut the problem further by drastically reducing the number of stocks under consideration.

It is necessary to build factor models of securities to reduce the number of estimates needed to solve the active-risk optimization problem. Establishing this link and providing the technology to make the forecasts required by the factor model is Rosenberg's unique contribution to modern portfolio management practices. It is this technology that led to benchmarking—in the sense of managing active portfolios according to their degree of departure from cap-weighted benchmarks—as a widespread practice (see sidebar titled "The Vital Importance of Market Capitalization-Weighting").

Indexes as the Basis for Investment Vehicles

With the advent of CAPM and other theories suggesting it is difficult to beat the market on a risk-adjusted basis, market capitalization-weighted indexes turned out to be well suited for an important and revolutionary new use: index funds.[10] By matching the holdings of a well-constructed index, a portfolio manager can produce the return on the index, net of expenses. In the long run, this asset-class return, instead of the potential value added through stock-selection skill, forms the large majority of the gain from investing. Index-based funds deliver this benefit at extremely low cost, thus making it all the more difficult for active managers to earn their fee. Index funds as an easy alternative loom large over the shoulders of high-cost funds and/or underperforming managers. Furthermore, the introduction of index-based products to new asset classes such as emerging equity markets in the early 1990s creates more transparency for investors and puts active managers under more scrutiny.

Institutional investors disappointed in their active managers and vibrantly competitive index providers have helped drive the creation of index funds tracking every imaginable market segment, as described extensively in Part Three. Index fund managers and index providers are now the Baskin-Robbins of the investment management industry, but with many more flavors. Real estate investment trusts (REITs), small-cap stocks, any or all of the Lehman bond indexes, Japanese high-yield bonds, emerging market equities, the myriad equity sectors—all these (and more) are now available as index-based strategies. Moreover, many active funds—particularly the new breed of quantitative active, risk-controlled, and enhanced-index strategies—use an index as their starting point, deviating from index weights according to the degree of the manager's conviction that a particular stock is more or less attractive than the market as a whole. Chapter 15 discusses enhanced-index strategies.

What has changed most rapidly in the new century is the availability of a variety of low-cost index funds to individual investors through ETFs, a financial product category that swelled to over 280 different funds worth over $250 billion by the end of 2003.[11] The growth of index-based products—not just index and enhanced-index funds, but ETFs and index derivatives, is discussed in depth in Parts Three and Four. There are many uses for such products. Investors buy stock index futures or ETFs to gain market exposure far more cheaply than through traditional actively managed sector funds. ETFs are a convenient and cost-effective way for institutions to equitize cash and control risk, particularly during large portfolio restructurings, because unlike most funds, they trade like securities throughout the day. For the same reasons, active managers of all risk preferences also use them.

The newest ETFs are linked to fixed-income indexes, providing a hedging alternative that can be cheaper than futures and simpler than swaps. Even though fixed-income ETFs are legally equities, they are generally viewed as an appropriate part of a fixed-income portfolio because of their return stream. They are attractive for use in strategies for individual investors that encompass multiple asset classes, such as multistrategy accounts offered by investment advisors (for more information, see Chapter 24).

These *four key uses* of indexes provide a framework for rational assessment of the criticisms about the impact of benchmarks on both investor behavior and on the markets.

THE BENCHMARK BACKLASH

Despite their proven usefulness and popularity, benchmarks have come under increasing fire. Commentators, money managers, and other investment professionals have criticized an excessive attention to benchmarks and have blamed it for encouraging a disproportionate focus on short-term performance and overconcentration in portfolios while discouraging unconventional investment ideas. Benchmarks have even been blamed for inciting manias and lemminglike behavior, although the fact that there was no South Sea Island Index or Tulip 500 proves that manias do not need benchmarks to thrive. Indexes did not create that activity, nor do they support it. They reveal it.[12]

Overshooting is typically a case of widespread overconfidence on the part of nonindexers and others who pay almost no attention to benchmarks; the U.S. and global tech stock overshoot of 1999/2000 is a good example. After such a disaster, benchmarks, index funds, and benchmarked active portfolios became an easy target for critics. Who in their right mind would invest in such overpriced companies, even if avoiding them meant investors had to take the risk of having a large tracking error to a cap-weighted benchmark?

One (possibly too academic) answer is that many people had thought carefully about what the fair prices for technology and other popular growth companies should be and the prices at the time were the results of their analysis, as expressed through the supply of and demand for securities. Not that many investors were absolutely sure that the market was overpriced or that the cap-weighted benchmark was an ex-ante inefficient portfolio. Many value managers and tactical asset allocators, to their credit, were sure, but they appear to have been a minority.[13]

Let's concede that from March 2000, and for a period of time before and after, the cap-weighted benchmark was not a very good portfolio to hold, ex-ante, and that one would have arrived at that conclusion through conventional analysis (cash flow or dividend discount models, relative value or P/E analysis, etc.). Many—even most—investment professionals could have added alpha just by betting against the most obviously overvalued companies. Nonetheless, this was a once-in-a-generation anomaly. It is not a general indictment of Modern Portfolio Theory (MPT) or of benchmarks. No sensible person ever said benchmarks were always and everywhere the best portfolios. Following a benchmark exposes one to potential for overshooting in that market, but this is most true for narrow benchmarks. When overshooting occurs across a broad market, it indicates that overpricing is affecting the entire market, no matter whether index funds are used.

As a case in point, index funds do not inherently overweight large-cap growth stocks. Capitalization-weighting schemes always weight stocks in proportion to the market value. If some investors allocate more of their portfolios to large-cap growth stocks (or to a narrow index of these stocks) at the expense of allocations to other areas, demand could increase. However, this allocation issue exists whether index funds are used or not, and does not necessarily change the price of such stocks.

Another argument increasingly heard is that expected future market returns are low, so investors should concentrate on absolute returns, with cash as the benchmark. In the 1990s—and in fact throughout the historic 1982 to 2000 U.S. bull market—many traditional long-only equity managers delivered strong double-digit returns. Focusing exclusively on absolute returns would have made nearly every equity investor happy. But as the market dramatically lost trillions in market value from its peak in March 2000, the quest for another approach quickened.

Peter Bernstein, the highly respected market commentator and author of numerous books on investing, feels that the standard approach of selecting and evaluating managers largely on the basis of their performance against a benchmark is far too constraining and limits potential returns. Indeed, the Fundamental Law of Asset Management, as postulated by Richard Grinold and Ronald Kahn, states that a manager's alpha generation depends not just on investment insight, but on the breadth of investment decisions to which the insight can be applied.[14]

But breadth for the sake of breadth does not add value. Furthermore, indexes themselves do not discourage unconventional thinking. If superior results require contrarian ideas and wide deviations from benchmarks—for example, buying value stocks when the market is bidding up growth stocks—then index benchmarks merely highlight potential sources of added value.

Bernstein's proposal to allow managers to seek alpha across asset classes without regard to benchmark constraints presupposes that one can identify such considerable talent in advance. This can be tricky without a track record that can be readily evaluated against a benchmark. You don't have to be an efficient market believer to wonder, "If such managers exist, and they can be identified, would they not already be flooded with capital to invest, to the point that they either closed their doors to new investment, or totally diluted the value of their information?" Anyone shopping for good hedge fund managers has encountered this problem. Also, could institutional investors tolerate the risk level of such a mandate, which would include not just volatility of returns, but the risk of significant deviations from investment policy, and the career risk of being "alone and wrong," all of which can present major difficulties for real-world institutional investors?

We propose a compromise solution that includes nonstandard, possibly more aggressive investment approaches in the portfolio, but nevertheless measures their risk and return performances against a benchmark in the form of the information ratio.[15] Institutional pension plan sponsors and individual investors alike should tolerate significant deviations in performance by the managers whose ability they trust. Nevertheless, to reduce risk and costs—the elements of investing that can be directly controlled—larger-than-usual chunks of the portfolio should be placed in index funds and a combination of enhanced-index and risk-controlled active funds.[16] Richard Ennis has also been a strong advocate of this sensible-sounding approach, but it has not caught on to any overwhelming degree with institutional investors or their consultants. For affluent individual investors, index-based separately managed accounts can bring even more efficiency to this core portfolio, but as in the institutional world, the recognition of this benefit is just beginning to be accepted (see also Chapter 24).

There is certainly a place for absolute-return strategies in many portfolios, and low expected market returns can make these strategies more appealing. As a rebound strategy after a market drop, such strategies must be evaluated against a conscientious assessment of future risk premiums. If investors expect market returns to be low, the proportion of their portfolios dedicated to successful absolute-return strategies should increase, but that doesn't mean that they should be used in a vacuum. Even hedge fund investors will be assessing absolute-return strategies using past performance as a guide, and increasingly, peer-group universes and indexes as benchmarks.

Perhaps the antibenchmark attitude may also be a function of complacency from pension plan solvency of the late 1990s. In overfunded plans, there is the potential to lose focus on the purpose of investing, which is to meet future liabilities. The logical process of estimating liabilities, tracking changes, and determining the best-matching asset classes and their respective benchmarks begins to fade against the backdrop of double-digit market returns that routinely and significantly outpace liabilities.

If the roaring stock market is to blame for this attitude, a turnaround should be occurring, now that complacency has begun to give way to concern as plan sponsors have watched their paper profits evaporate in the early 2000s. Perhaps reminding investors that there are risks as well as rewards in the investing game will signal the beginning of a new era of disciplined investing. Investors of all types need to design a strategy that is appropriate to their funding objectives. They need to measure their performance continuously against their goals, measure the risks they have taken in pursuit of that performance, and perhaps most importantly, decide whether skill or luck was involved. Without benchmarks, it is virtually impossible to accomplish these tasks. There can be no information ratio to calculate, or even an alpha. Only with benchmarks can investors evaluate objectively how well their manager has performed.

GUIDING PRINCIPLES FOR THE APPLICATION OF BENCHMARKS

The investment decisions of other investors affect the market prices of assets for the rest of us, affecting the absolute level of achievable investment returns. So if investors tend to stick closely to their benchmarks, we all care which benchmarks they use, not just for relative performance, but for absolute performance as well. This is not a bad thing. Indexes encourage the most comprehensive and least artificial forms and methods of price discovery, which can benefit all investors.

The following five principles can guide investors in maximizing the benefits of benchmarks and modern portfolio theory:

1. Design an investment strategy most appropriate for the specific goals and requirements of the asset pool, taking into account all relevant factors.

THE IMPORTANCE OF FLOAT ADJUSTMENT:
THE YAHOO! EXAMPLE

To represent a truer and clearer picture of the shares available for purchase by the public, some index constructors remove closely held and illiquid shares when calculating a company's number of shares outstanding. In general, such a float adjustment makes an index more useful as a benchmark and as the basis for an index fund, since portfolio managers cannot typically buy shares held by founders, directors, employees, other corporations, and governmental bodies. Government and quasi-state holdings of corporate equities are a major consideration in many non-U.S. markets.

The importance of float adjustment, which many previously thought to be an unnecessary or even evasive complication in index construction, was noted (and was discussed in Chapter 3) in foreign markets.[a] Two examples are Japan in the late 1980s–early 1990s and Europe during the telecom privatization boom in the late 1990s. But few examples of the impact of not float-adjusting benchmarks are as powerful as that of the addition of Yahoo! Inc. to the S&P 500 index. On December 7, 1999—ironically, 58 years after another day of infamy—the most dramatic S&P 500 inclusion effect in history occurred. This was the day before Yahoo! was added to that index, replacing Laidlaw, the largest school-bus company. The price of Yahoo! rose by $67.25 per share, or 24 percent, to close at $348, as 66 million shares changed hands. Investors had previously run up the stock by 32 percent since S&P announced that it was including Yahoo! on November 30, 1999.

This mysterious price levitation was not caused by any special enthusiasm for the stock; it was just another constituent of the S&P index, and its special merits, whatever they were, were not under consideration that day. The inducement was that Yahoo! had been added to the S&P 500 at its full market-cap weight, without any adjustment for the *free float*, or number of shares held by stockholders who were at liberty to sell. The supply of shares, however, was only about 10 percent of the full market cap, since most shares were held by employees, venture capital firms, and other investors who were restricted from selling.

The result was a radical supply-demand imbalance, which manifested itself in the price spike just described. Float-adjusted indexes

[a] See discussion of Japan's weight in EAFE in Chapters 3, 9, and 12.

(Continued)

increased in popularity, and MSCI converted to a float-adjusted format not long afterward, although MSCI's action was primarily for other reasons. All the major international/global index families (MSCI, FTSE, Dow Jones Global, S&P/Citigroup) are float-adjusted. While float adjustment conveys substantial advantages to an index, some do not consider it a prerequisite of a well-constructed index for domestic investors in their home market. We believe differently, and certainly the "Yahoo! effect" demonstrates this need. Best practices in index construction methodology do—in fact *must*—include float adjustment. Standard & Poor's decision in early 2004 to float-adjust its "flagship" S&P 500 Index (as well as the S&P 400 and S&P 600) is a fitting testimony to the acceptance of this concept.[b]

[b] For information on the move to float-adjustment for the S&P 500, see articles and research on IndexUniverse.com.

2. Express this investment strategy in terms of broad investment benchmarks. The implementation benefits of using benchmarks are meaningful and can usually be captured with modest (if any) amendments to the investment strategy. For example, one of the broad market benchmarks discussed in Chapter 8 should be used for an all-market allocation to U.S. equities.
3. Where possible select active managers with demonstrated risk-adjusted skill (in excess of cost) who can deploy that skill over the broadest possible array of investments. Use subsidiary benchmarks to parcel out manager mandates and for completion strategies. Be aware of the indirect costs of adding complexity by adding benchmarks.
4. As discussed in Chapter 3, use a portfolio-based risk budgeting approach to balancing the use of active managers, index managers, absolute-return strategies, and benchmark-driven strategies.
5. As discussed in Chapters 3, 26, and 30, conserve costs and risk with indexing when uncertain about your ability to identify superior active managers.

After several decades of steady progress, benchmarking continues to add significant value for investors, and indexing continues to conserve costs, minimize uncompensated risk, and deliver on its promise of market exposure. The revolutions that these twin concepts introduced are alive and well, and their prescriptions for action are still powerful. Moreover, the application of benchmarking has now spread to alternative asset classes such as commodities and hedge funds, and the benefits of this will accrue to investors in these asset classes.

The four principal uses of indexes that should motivate us to distinguish one index from another are:

1. As a gauge of market sentiment.
2. To evaluate manager performance.
3. To set and monitor asset allocation policy.
4. As a basis for investment vehicles.

Selecting benchmarks to help achieve investment objectives requires time and attention. Whether an investor is trying to meet a liability or funding requirement or is targeting a wealth objective, selecting and designing benchmarks that are broad, investable, and appropriate is crucial to investment success. Chapter 6 dives deep into identifying the key criteria and inevitable trade-offs in modern index construction methodology and benchmark selection. Different indexes have different purposes; evolution in the marketplace and competition among index providers continue to drive ongoing improvement in methodology while providing optimal choice for users. As this chapter has emphasized, having appropriate benchmarks is vital for constructing efficient investment portfolios.

NOTES

1. Laurence B. Siegel, *Benchmarks and Investment Management* (Research Foundation of AIMR, Charlottesville, VA, 2003).
2. Steven A. Schoenfeld, "Perfection Impossible" *Journal of Indexes* (second quarter, 2002), pp. 14–22.
3. By "the market," we mean, technically speaking, the expected cash flows from the corporate sector, and the discount rate at which those cash flows are reduced to a present value by investors (reflecting the systematic risk to which those cash flows are subject).
4. More information on the VIX indicator and products to trade the VIX index is available at www.IndexUniverse.com and on www.cboe.com.
5. Callan, PSN, and Wilshire databases.
6. Howard Crane of Watson Wyatt Investment Consulting, "The Role of Benchmarks in the Twenty-First Century." For more information, see http://www.aimrpubs.org/cp/issues/v2002n5/abs/p0020066a.html#authors.
7. Gerry Rocchi, *BGI Global Solutions* (2001).
8. Barr Rosenberg, "Extra-Market Components of Covariance in Security Markets," *Journal of Financial and Quantitative Analysis* (March 1974); and Barr Rosenberg and Vinay Marathe, "The Prediction of Investment Risk: Systematic

and Residual Risk," *Proceedings of the Seminar on the Analysis of Security Prices* (University of Chicago, November 1975), pp. 85–226.

9. A good overview of the BARRA model is from www.barra.com/research /barrapub/risk_models.asp. Barr Rosenberg is no longer personally associated with BARRA. Other powerful optimizers which are commonly used in the financial industry are available from Wilshire Associates, Northfield, and Quantal International. In April 2004, BARRA was purchased by MSCI, a major provider of global indexes. See story on IndexUniverse.com.

10. Which the trust department of Wells Fargo Bank (which eventually evolved to become BGI), invented between 1970 and 1973. See William W. Jahnke, "The Development of Structured Portfolio Management: A Contextual View," *Quantitative International Investing* (Chicago: Probus, 1990), pp. 153–182 (see especially pp. 158–161). Background also provided in Chapter 2.

11. Morgan Stanley Equity Research, "Exchange Traded Funds," London (January 2004). See also Chapters 14, 16, 25, and 31.

12. Gerry Rocchi, BGI *Global Solutions* (Tulip 500 was actually Pamela Cloyd's notion, all the more appropriate given her residence and family relationships in the Netherlands). For those who are unacquainted with these manias in seventeenth-century England and eighteenth-century Holland, the same case can be made for the Japanese bubble of 1988/1989, and the Taiwanese bubble of 1990/1991. In those markets, at that time, indexation, benchmarking, and derivatives use was relatively minimal (and almost nonexistent in the Taiwanese case).

13. Among the investment managers who publicly took this position were Robert Arnott of First Quadrant, Pasadena, California; Clifford Asness of AQR Capital Management, New York; and Jeremy Grantham, of Grantham, Mayo, Van Otterloo, Boston.

14. Richard C. Grinold and Ronald N. Kahn, *Active Portfolio Management,* 2nd ed. (New York: McGraw-Hill, 2000).

15. Which we credit Larry Siegel with formulating, based on some of the same risk budgeting work described earlier in this chapter, and in Chapter 3.

16. For more on the distinction between index, enhanced index, and risk-controlled active, see Chapter 15 by Schoenfeld and Yang.

CHAPTER 6

Perfection Impossible

Best Practices for Index Construction

Steven A. Schoenfeld

None of us is as smart as all of us.

—Anonymous quote hanging in the office of James Vertin,
Head of Wells Fargo Management Sciences Department
and backer of the first index fund—circa 1971

_____ **Editor's Note** _____

Picking up where the last one left off, this chapter focuses on the key attributes that make up a "good index." There really is no such thing as a "perfect" index, since as we learned in the previous chapter, indexes have a variety of uses (the four key uses) and play a variety of roles for investors. Thus, a narrow, highly liquid large-cap equity index would be an appropriate benchmark for a tradable index derivative or ETF, but would be inappropriate for use in asset allocation studies aiming to measure the risk/ return of an entire stock market. However, there are fundamental characteristics of a good index—detailed in this chapter as the "Seven Key Criteria" for benchmark construction. Most of these key criteria are increasingly recognized as "best practices" within the investment industry. Furthermore, as

Substantial portions of this chapter originally appeared in the *Journal of Indexes*, Second Quarter 2002, as "Perfection Impossible—Why Simply 'Good' Indexes Can Result in a More Perfect Solution," as well as in BGI's "International Equity Benchmarks for U.S. Investors," *Investment Insights* (November 2002), by Steven A. Schoenfeld and Robert Ginis.

this chapter describes, there are natural, inherent trade-offs in choosing the "ideal index"—and in the end, the "perfect" index is one that resolves those trade-offs in an optimal way for an investor's specific needs. This chapter also includes two sidebars: The first, "Don't Stop at Seven: Other Factors to Consider," addresses the numerous additional criteria that can be used to assess benchmarks; the second, "The Impact of Index Reconstitution on Market Prices" by Larry Siegel, elaborates on the "index effect" and how benchmark reconstitution procedures can move markets. Several chapters in Part Four show how index portfolio managers work to minimize this impact on the performance of their funds.

Indexes have advanced tremendously since the launch of Charles Henry Dow's pioneering average in 1894. Particularly in the years since the launch of the first index fund in 1971, indexes and the art and science of indexation have risen to meet an ever-growing demand of uses, products, and indexed assets. As the financial industry is often in pursuit of the perfect index, improvements in index methodology benefit investment managers and their clients alike and undoubtedly will continue to do so in the years ahead.

The financial industry should, of course, pursue better index methodology, but we should not obsess over what inevitably would be a quixotic quest for a perfect index or index methodology. Investors use indexes for diverse purposes, and the needs of investors and the market evolve dynamically over time. Indexes must reflect this evolution and diversity. Competition among index providers and index managers will take care of the rest, ensuring that investors will have an optimal choice of indexes and index-based products.

The perfect index is in many ways "the impossible dream," but like Don Quixote, our pursuit of the ideal can make the world of indexes a much better place. This chapter discusses the uses of indexes, defines the characteristics of a good index, and covers the critical trade-offs in benchmark design. Finally, I discuss how to go about choosing an index that suits an investor's specific purposes. An index that is perfect for one investor might be completely inappropriate for another investor. Thus, when striving for perfection, we must continuously ask the question, "Perfect for what use?"

THE SEVEN KEY CRITERIA OF A GOOD INDEX

As discussed in the previous chapter, indexes can function as a gauge of market sentiment, as benchmarks for active management, as the basis for index funds, and as proxies for asset classes in asset allocation. Ideally, an index should be able to serve all four purposes simultaneously, as added fungibility makes the utility of the benchmark that much greater. When selecting indexes to use for one or more of these purposes, one must consider all their characteristics and determine which indexes best fit the investor's needs. Still, no equity index is perfect, as they all involve trade-offs.

How should one choose from among the competing alternatives? In addition to market capitalization-weighting, which was discussed in the previous chapter, is a prerequisite of a good index and is common to all indexes covered here, seven key criteria can help identify a good broad-capitalization equity benchmark. Although there are many minor criteria—described in the sidebar, "Don't Stop at Seven,"—it is useful to categorize the major criteria in the seven broad groupings that are described in the following subsections. Furthermore, Chapter 8 on U.S. Equity Benchmarks, Chapter 9 on International Equity Indexes, and to some extent, Chapter 10 on Fixed-Income Benchmarks, use these Seven Key Criteria as their framework for the assessment of key indexes.[1]

1. Completeness

Does the index accurately reflect the overall investment opportunity set, both in terms of market cap-range/country coverage and company inclusion? The more complete an index—the broader and deeper its coverage—the more effectively it represents the investable universe for both active and index managers. By spreading its allocation among most of the available securities and markets, a comprehensive index maximizes diversification. Completeness is probably the most important of the seven key criteria, as complete coverage of the targeted asset class is the foundation for the utility of indexes in all their potential applications.

2. Investability

Does the index include only those securities that investors can effectively purchase? For non-U.S. benchmarks, does the index screen out shares and market segments that are restricted for foreign investors? The goals of investability and completeness stand in juxtaposition, and the trade-off between the two often requires a user to make an explicit preference decision (and this inherent trade-off is discussed later in this chapter).

3. Clear, Published Rules and Open Governance Structure

How transparent are the rules that govern the benchmark? Are these rules well established and publicly available? Such rules provide predictability to both portfolio managers and asset owners and make it easier to anticipate how the benchmark will reflect changing market conditions. For an index to be truly useful to the various users of benchmarks, index construction rules should be fully transparent, especially during index reconstitution periods and during major corporate actions.

4. Accurate and Complete Data

For an index to be useful, return and constituent data must be accurate, complete, and readily available. Investors should have access to at least the following information: price/total/net dividend returns, consistent subindexes, high quality and efficient release of data, timely and transparent release of index changes, and historical returns. Although some believe that the ready availability of index data somehow hurts investors in index-based products, the opposite is true. The more investors understand the methodology and constituents of an index, the more comfort they have in products based on the index.

5. Acceptance by Investors

In general, investors prefer an index that is well-known and widely used. This gives investors faith in the index's ongoing integrity, since many market participants will scrutinize it. Furthermore, wide use enables effective peer group comparison. The performance of nonstandard indexes and index products is invariably compared with the standard benchmark. Academic and proprietary research, the basis for asset allocation studies, tends to focus on established benchmarks to provide relevant insights for investors. Finally, without broad acceptance of an index, there might be inadequate availability of supporting investment products based on the benchmarks (including active funds and derivative products).

6. Availability of Crossing Opportunities, Derivatives, and Other Tradable Products

Widely used indexes, especially within pooled investment vehicles, offer potential cost savings because they provide crossing opportunities within the fund complexes of large institutional investment managers. Crossing allows an institutional investment manager to equitably match buy and sell orders without the typical costs that would be incurred in the open market. Such indexes also generally create a more liquid, cheaper-to-trade OTC (over the counter) derivatives market, particularly in total-return swaps. The availability of listed index futures/options on some major benchmarks, and the proliferation of ETFs (exchange-traded funds) on virtually all major benchmarks/asset classes, further benefits asset owners and portfolio managers who use these accepted benchmarks. Ideally, a widely used benchmark fosters a virtuous circle of activity by a critical mass of investors, in turn creating the potential for crossing trades/activity. Broad acceptance of a benchmark creates a network effect between fund managers, sell-side brokers, and the cash and derivative markets that reduces transaction costs for movement into and out of index portfolios.

7. Relatively Low Turnover and Related Transaction Costs

All indexes incur a certain amount of turnover as they maintain index constituents in line with their stated methodology. In general, the lower the turnover, the lower the rebalancing costs, and the easier the index is to track. By design, a broader benchmark favors lower turnover, while an index that works within a narrowly defined market segment has greater turnover and transaction-related costs. Furthermore, an index with a predefined number of stocks (e.g., the S&P 500, the Russell 2000, the S&P Latin American 40) will, by definition, have some degree of additional turnover to maintain the fixed number of constituents.[2]

Index fund managers regularly provide detailed analysis of the major U.S. and international/global indexes for institutional clients along the lines of these and other criteria. Assessments of the major U.S. and international indexes is provided in subsequent chapters in Part Two. When investors pose the "What benchmark should I use?" question, it is inevitable to answer it with another question: "What is the intended purpose for the benchmark?" The discussion will then turn to the trade-offs inherent in any benchmark decision—does the client want a highly liquid tradable product for tactical allocation purposes or the maximum coverage of an asset class for strategic asset and liability modeling? On the other hand, perhaps a compromise can somehow accommodate both needs. Finally, some investors have such unique requirements (social screens, tax consequences, completion portfolios, etc.) that a custom index is required; obviously, a one-size-fits-all index would not be appropriate in these cases. Trade-offs and compromises permeate the decision process. It is critical to understand not only what you gain, but also what you give up in choosing a particular index.

As mentioned earlier, depending on a user's particular needs and preferences, he or she would "weight" the different elements of the Seven Key Criteria in a different way, especially given the inherent trade-offs between some of these *good* characteristics (which are discussed in the next section). However, beyond these seven major criteria, there are a myriad of specific

DON'T STOP AT SEVEN: OTHER FACTORS TO CONSIDER

The seven key areas of assessment may well be the most important factors in determining which benchmark is best in addressing the investment universe. However, these certainly are not the only factors that should be considered. In fact, the list of factors is almost endless. To give you an idea, in the following list are some of the other possible considerations along with the key criteria discussed in this chapter. While this list includes a score of criteria, many users will have others, and readers are invited to submit other factors to www.ActiveIndexInvesting.com for inclusion in this chapter's E-ppendix entry.

- Closing price convention.
- Real-time calculation/availability.
- Corporate action treatment.
- Timing of corporate action announcements.
- Brand recognition.
- Peer group usage.
- Foreign exchange treatment.
- Quality of client service.
- Structure and responsiveness of index committee.
- Data delivery method:
  –Cost of historical data series.
  –Cost of ongoing data support (*index alerts*, fundamental data, etc.).
- Regulatory status of derivative/tradable products.
- Style indexes/subindex availability.
- Compatibility with other asset-class benchmarks.
- Index maintenance transparency.
- Reconstitution frequency and timing.
- Concentration of large index constituents.
- Cost of investment/divestment.
- Custom index capability.
- Availability of *standard* socially screened index variants.
- Industry classification system and compatibility with other benchmarks.

(and not always *minor*) criteria that come into play, again, depending on the user's preferences. The sidebar, "Don't Stop at Seven," lists some—but not all—of these other criteria.

THE FIVE INHERENT TRADE-OFFS IN INDEX CONSTRUCTION AND SELECTION

In constructing a good index, there are always trade-offs in both methodology and implementation. These trade-offs, which are described in the following subsections, are critical in understanding why there cannot be a one-size-fits-all (or "perfect") index.

1. Completeness versus Investability

From a purely theoretical standpoint, the ideal index includes every security in its defined asset class. Few investors know exactly how many stocks are listed in the United States, but the Wilshire 5000, so named because it was originally composed of 5,000 stocks, contains over 6,000 stocks and thus includes more issues than any other widely distributed U.S. equity index.[3] However, many of the smaller stocks in the Wilshire 5000 are illiquid, and investors have a difficult time trading them. For these reasons, a somewhat less broad index is more investable and accessible. No full-replication index fund has ever been constructed for the Wilshire 5000 (nor should it be!). Similarly, there are well over 12,000 listed stocks in the total non-U.S. equity universe, and over 5,000 in the developed international universe.

2. Reconstitution and Rebalancing Frequency versus Turnover

Reconstitution, which is the process of periodically deciding which stocks meet the criteria for inclusion in an index, is a source of turnover (which is costly to investors) because the manager must trade to keep pace with changes in the index. However, timely reconstitution and rebalancing (the process of adjusting the weights of stocks in the index for changes in the number of shares outstanding) enables an index to track accurately the asset class it represents. There is a trade-off between such accuracy and trading costs. Reconstitution-related transaction costs are primarily a burden for small- and mid-cap indexes, for many emerging market indexes, and for style-specific indexes, all of which fall outside the scope of this chapter. In those indexes, companies with large weights in the index frequently cross the boundary that qualifies them for inclusion. Broad-cap indexes, in contrast, mostly experience turnover in their smallest-cap stocks, making turnover less of a problem when measured by the weight in the index of the stocks being traded. Nonetheless, turnover is costly whatever its source or frequency, and a cost advantage accrues to indexes that have less of it.

In terms of reconstitution-related turnover and trading costs, indexes that have no fixed limit on the number of stocks and that are all-inclusive in terms of their capitalization range have a small but notable advantage over indexes with a fixed number of stocks. This is because an all-inclusive index generally gains or loses stocks only as a result of new listings, delistings, and other changes in the identity of the stocks in the market or the market's industry composition.[4] The sidebar in this chapter "The Impact of Index Reconstitution on Market Prices" by Larry Siegel reviews some of the *unintended* consequences of index reconstitutions.

3. Precise Float Adjustment versus Transaction Costs

As float adjustment gains momentum and acceptance, *how* to apply free-float to benchmarks has become a prominent question. While this may seem relatively arcane, there is a significant potential cost impact of index providers going too far toward incorporating precise float adjustment (which is difficult to measure precisely anyhow). This, in fact, could be a case where *perfect* float adjustment is actually worse for users than simply *adequate* or representative adjustment.

4. Potential Index Effect versus Liquidity/Crossing Opportunities

The general tendency for a rise in the price of a stock bound for inclusion in an index and the fall of one that is to be dropped has been well documented. When an index is widely used, the price impact tends to be greater, but so are the crossing opportunities and the liquidity of index constituents, which can mitigate the market impact cost of rebalancing and reconstitution. Furthermore, the long-term price premium accorded to index membership may also compensate for the occasional—but unpredictable—deadweight cost of the index effect.

5. Objective and Transparent Rules versus Flexible Judgment-Based Methodology

Some broad-cap equity indexes are constructed using rules that are either rigidly or generally objective, whereas others are constructed using the judgment of their calculators. The advantage of objective rules is that any investor with access to the relevant data can predict, more or less accurately, what stocks will be added to and deleted from the index. This enables investors to trade in anticipation of (rather than in reaction to) additions and deletions, and in general to manage the index replication process in an orderly and efficient manner. Active managers also find it useful to be able to predict what will be in the index to which they are benchmarked.

Using judgment in selecting stocks for an index, however, enables constructors of judgment-based indexes to achieve certain traits that they claim are desirable but are not attainable with objective rules. Standard & Poor's, which uses judgment in selecting stocks for its flagship S&P 500, MidCap 400, and SmallCap 600 Indexes (and therefore also the S&P 1500 Composite, which incorporates all three), asserts that its indexes are superior in terms of stability, low turnover, and accurate representation of the real economy. The S&P indexes can achieve these traits specifically because the index construction staff does not act mechanically in selecting and removing stocks, and can take conscious steps to construct an index with the desired characteristics. Similarly, MSCI (Morgan Stanley Capital International) tends to use more judgment in the implementation of its major index changes, often in an effort to minimize turnover, and they increasingly consult the industry for feedback. More information on this philosophy of index construction is available in the book's E-ppendix at www.ActiveIndexInvesting.com.

As noted earlier, as well as in Chapters 3 and 5, the growth of indexing has led to market anomalies around major *flagship* index changes. By *flagship* indexes, I mean dominant local market benchmarks such as the S&P 500 and Russell 2000 in the United States, as well as the FTSE 100 in the United Kingdom, the DAX in Germany, and the Nikkei and TOPIX in Japan. When there are major changes to these indexes (such as calendar-based reconstitutions) or the addition/deletion of a major index constituent, the need for index-fund managers and derivative-trading desks to adjust their positions can lead to major price swings, as well as aggressive capital market cat and mouse games that rival children's cartoons. The sidebar, "The Impact of Index Reconstitution on Market Prices" by Larry Siegel describes some of these games and the implications for both index investors and other market participants.

WOULD PROPOSED INDEXATION SOLUTIONS DISTORT THE CORE ROLE OF BENCHMARK INDEXES?

As would befit a dynamic and innovative industry, a variety of proposed solutions to the shortcomings of indexes have been introduced in the past year or so. The problems they attempt to address generally focus on the transaction

THE IMPACT OF INDEX RECONSTITUTION ON MARKET PRICES[a]
Larry Siegel

As discussed in this chapter and in Chapter 5, individual stocks added to an index can rise in price dramatically on the announcement of their addition to the index, since index-fund managers are all trying to add the stock to their portfolios at the lowest possible cost. Stocks deleted from the index suffer a corresponding price decline. However, index funds that track rule-based indexes with predictable constituent changes should have a much less pronounced cost disadvantage from the inclusion effect because investors can act in advance of the changes. Furthermore, as more financial institutions focus time and capital on index changes, we have witnessed many unexpected results from index reconstitutions.

The reason for the inclusion and deletion effects (classified together as a reconstitution effect) is relatively obvious. An increase in the demand for a stock, caused by the need for index funds to hold that stock, is not met by any change in supply. Thus, the price rises. The market clears when active managers and arbitrageurs (hedge funds and proprietary trading desks), motivated by the desire to sell stocks that have gone up, provide indexers with enough of the stock to enable them to hold it in exactly the index weight.[b] The deletion effect is just the mirror image of the inclusion effect. The inflexibility of index-fund design (a virtue from some points of view) often makes a reconstitution effects inevitable.

One can interpret reconstitution-related price movements in either of two ways. The price-pressure hypothesis holds that "transitory order imbalances associated with index additions and deletions are the primary source of price movements."[c] The index-membership hypothesis holds that index membership itself is a source of value (due

---

[a] A substantial portion of this sidebar was adapted from the chapter, "The Impact of Benchmarking on Markets and Institutions," in Laurence Siegel, *Benchmarks and Investment Management* (Charlottesville, VA: AIMR Research Foundation, 2003).

[b] The major categories of arbitrageurs are (1) hedge funds and (2) the proprietary trading desks of brokerage firms.

[c] Anath Madhavan, "Index Reconstitution and Equity Returns" (2002), unpublished manuscript (available online at www.itginc.com/research/whitepapers/madhavan/RussellStudy.pdf), p. 3.

to greater liquidity or better information flow), so that an inclusion effect is permanent rather than transitory. The two hypotheses are not mutually exclusive; one might observe both.

The implication is that, relative to an idealized situation where there are no reconstitution effects, the investor overpays for index funds and receives too little. One researcher's estimate of S&P 500 underperformance due to the inclusion and deletion effects in recent years, expressed as an annual rate, was 0.32 percent over 1992–2002.[d] The amount of underperformance has been increasing, in some cases, as indexed assets have grown, but in other ways has been decreasing, as investors allocate their assets toward a variety of different benchmarks.

After paying the transaction cost caused by the inclusion/deletion effect, of course, an investor in an index fund gets the asset-class or style almost for free, since index funds have very low management fees. It is up to the investor to decide if this is a worthwhile trade-off.

Some index managers put a great deal of effort into trading disciplines that avoid these costs. Such *smart trading* tends to reduce the costs of all transacting, not just that associated with index reconstitution. Moreover, because large index fund management firms are *providers* (not just consumers) of liquidity, they may even be able to turn the tables on the arbitrageurs and capture, on behalf of their investors, some of the liquidity premium traditionally received by the *arbs*. Managers who are successful at this latter endeavor can beat the index (by a modest amount) without making any active bets.[e] In addition, while some of the overall observed reconstitution effect probably comes from active managers' demand as well, it is muted and there are active managers who profit from the effect as well as those who are hurt by it.

---

[d] Sandy Rattray, "Is Standard and Poor's Adding Return by Managing the S&P 500 Index?" *Goldman Sachs Derivatives and Trading Research* (January 27, 2003; originally presented at "The Superbowl of Indexing" Conference, December 2002).

[e] Since the index is calculated on a basis that assumes reconstitution-related costs have been paid, strategies that reduce these costs are seen as adding alpha. Some index-fund managers offer *index plus* products that explicitly aim to take more risk during index changes. These products are discussed in Chapter 15.

(Continued)

The sidebar within Chapter 5 describes the *single stock addition* phenomenon with the Yahoo! example. Next, I describe an example of a broader index reconstitution—the annual Russell Index changes— and its major impact on the underlying markets. The sidebar within Chapter 23 provides a more colorful example of this same annual event, from the perspective of an index-based ETF portfolio manager, during a particularly volatile year.

Russell Mania

Different in character, from the impact of adding/deleting a few names continuously into the S&P 500, is the annual reconstitution effect as one brokerage firm has called *Russell Mania*. It might seem that the Russell reconstitution would be relatively free of price distortions and other technical effects since it is based purely on market capitalization, which is observable by all interested parties in real time. However, Madhavan (2001) finds that:

> Equity returns [due to the Russell reconstitution] are concentrated in time, and are much larger in magnitude and in the number of stocks affected than the corresponding effects for S&P 500 index revisions. Specifically, a portfolio long additions and short deletions to the Russell 3000 index (constructed after the determination of new index weights at the end of May) had a mean return over the period 1996–2001 of 15 percent in the month of June. From March–June, the cumulative mean return exceeds 35 percent.[f]

These are *huge* numbers. One reason for the large effect is that stocks being added to the Russell 3000 are tiny so that they are disproportionately affected by either transitory or permanent changes in demand. However, an odd institutional artifact makes the Russell effect more complicated and more fun for arbitrageurs. Most large-cap portfolios are indexed or benchmarked to the S&P 500, not the Russell 1000; but a very sizable chunk of small-cap portfolios are indexed or benchmarked to the Russell 2000. Thus, when a stock moves from the Russell 1000 to the Russell 2000 because its relative market capitalization has declined, the demand for the stock *increases*.

It's understandable that index fund firms, active managers, hedge funds, brokers, and others would find themselves in an annual *mania* (every spring, culminating on June 30) to capture such returns, if they

---

[f] Madhavan, "Index Reconstitution and Equity Returns" (2002), p. 1.

> are the liquidity providers, or to avoid paying them as a cost if they are the liquidity consumers. Provision of liquidity for index fund reconstitution trades and related active-management trades has become a mini-industry in itself.
>
> As noted in the chapter, there are a variety of *solutions* to the index rebalancing impact, much of it involving switching to broader benchmarks or involving the evolution of index construction methodology. What is certain is that the markets and the industry will continue to pursue the efficient pricing of index changes, and when there are supply-demand imbalances, the impact can be significant.

costs and market impact of index changes, and thus the solutions are rooted in the belief that a change in approach would reduce that impact and cost as well as provide other benefits. The proposed solutions can be grouped in three broad categories:

1. Introduction of funds based on "silent" or proprietary indexes.
2. A switch to peer-based or average manager holdings-based benchmarks.
3. Adaptation of a pure passive approach to index portfolio management.

Response to the Concept of the Silent Index

Gary Gastineau, a respected author of many investment books and articles, has proposed limiting index transparency to minimize the index effect.[5] The basic tenet of efficient markets is transparent information flow and equal access to information source. Confidentiality of trading plans and opaqueness in index methodology creates inequity in information flows and increases uncertainty. Uncertainty raises risk and volatility, and higher risk and volatility increase trading costs and market impact, bringing us back around to the issue we wanted to eliminate. Recent research by Simon Hookway has demonstrated that pre-announced constituent changes have a substantially lower index effect.[6] For exchange-traded funds, which Gastineau is specifically addressing, transparency is not only an important feature of the ETF product, but also an integral part of the ETF mechanism. It lowers the cost to the investor because it enables precise hedging by market makers, who are willing to take on market risk with a known, hedgeable portfolio of stocks.

I am fundamentally opposed to the *self-indexing fund* idea because it becomes all too convenient to hide active risk behind the mask of a silent index. Gastineau alludes to the outperformance a silent index can offer, yet recent research by both Merrill Lynch and Goldman Sachs concludes that the S&P 500 index effects are diminishing, even as (or perhaps because) speculative capital targeting of major index changes has surged.[7] Any divergent return is the result of active risk, and the alpha could be either positive or negative. This ex-ante outperformance promise rings similar to the vibrant claims in late 2000 and early 2001 from the sell-side and competing index providers then claimed that Provisional EAFE (Europe, Australasia, Far East) would definitely outperform EAFE by at least 100 to 200 bp, when in fact it underperformed in the first phase (May 31, 2001, through November 30, 2001) by 6 basis points. In fact, during this dynamic time in the early 2000s, my colleagues and I at Barclays Global Investors calculated that when incidental country and sector bets (which provided a 35 basis point gain) were stripped out, the net stock add/delete impact (i.e., the pure index effect) was a negative 41 bps.[8]

Finally, the problem this solution attempts to address has not only diminished significantly, as mentioned, but is generally confined to the most popular indexes such as the S&P 500 and the Russell 2000. In response, many investors are moving to broader index strategies. These indexes are not affected by the turnover that prompts the buying and selling responsible for the index effect.

Peer-Based or Average Manager Indexes

The peer-based index proposes to use the determination of active mutual fund managers to efficiently determine what asset classes are, and what benchmark and investable indexes should contain. Gus Sauter describes this philosophy in Chapter 7. This logic would deem that the appropriate benchmark should simply measure what active managers are holding in their portfolios, that is, a variant of peer universes. While appealing in a Zen-like way (i.e. "it is what it is"), this approach would risk mimicking active managers' tendency toward herd mentality and would insufficiently capture the true universe of the asset class.

The main problem with this strategy is that ostensibly, the objective of both the theory and practice of index investing is to accurately reflect the investable opportunity set. Active managers tend to drift toward the latest fashion and do not stay put in their predefined asset classes. Another practical problem is related to predefining a size or style benchmark based on what managers actually hold, when the disclosure of these holdings at best has a significant time delay, and at worst, is opaque. As noted in both Chapter 5 and in the "Seven Key Criteria" elucidated in this chapter, transparency is vital for an efficient benchmark, yet peer-based benchmarks are by definition, ex-post. The alternative to this approach is the true meritocracy of manager competition against an accurate investable-universe index.

Allocation with Total Market Benchmarks and Pure Passive Portfolio Management Approaches

As an overall investment strategy, bypassing combinations of subasset class benchmarks (e.g., S&P 500 and Russell 2000) and replacing them with broad market indexes is sound, and this trend is strongly underway for both U.S. equity and international equity investment. The Russell 3000, Wilshire 5000, S&P 1500, Dow Jones Total Market Index, and MSCI All-Country World Index (ACWI) ex-United States and FTSE All-World have all made significant strides in attracting attention and assets recently. The low turnover, low costs, and high tax efficiency associated with these indexes, together with their broad diversification, make them appealing for many investors.

In an extension of broad market theory to index portfolio management, certain index fund managers are promoting a *pure passive* style of indexation. Essentially, it offers a relaxed approach to index changes, with the goal of lowering turnover, which would potentially minimize the index effect and ideally maximize portfolio wealth. This concept makes good sense in theory, but it is still far from clear that investors will accept significantly higher tracking error (especially negative tracking) when they retain brand-name indexes as their policy benchmarks. This potential outcome is similar to one of my concerns about silent indexes and the funds that may be based on them. Namely, in addition to potential cost/performance benefit from trading away from major index changes, higher tracking error will inevitably result from unintended (and therefore uncompensated) size/sector/style bets. This could result in underperformance well beyond the potential savings gained from avoiding specific index change events. Ultimately, as stated at the beginning of this chapter, competition between both benchmark methodologies and approaches to indexation is healthy, and the marketplace undoubtedly will decide the merits of the various products.

CHOOSING THE PERFECT INDEX FOR SPECIFIC NEEDS

When considering the broad array of uses, attributes, and inevitable trade-offs of indexes (while avoiding the silver-bullet claims of a single perfect index approach), how do you choose a perfect index to meet your specific needs?

The criteria generally accepted for choosing a broad-capitalization index depend on whether it is to be used as a benchmark for active management, as a portfolio (index fund), or as a proxy for an asset class in asset allocation. The best index, however, is one that can be used for all three purposes simultaneously, so that investors do not have to keep switching between indexes depending on the intended purpose at a particular time. This involves compromises, and thus it would be hard to expect such a multipurpose index to be the perfect index for each of the individual objectives. A good metaphor would be a Swiss Army knife: It has excellent utility for an array of tasks, but few of its tools are the absolute best for each specific use. Thus, most households will have a top-notch screwdriver, scissors, corkscrew, and so on, in addition to the all-purpose knife. The broad-market index contains many of the tools that can serve various investment needs, but the investor may also need a specialized—or even custom—index to provide the efficacy of a real screwdriver for certain tasks.

The alignment of strategic investment policy with major benchmarks (strategic–tactical–implementation) provides enormous utility to investors and asset owners. Ensuring that indexes are properly aligned provides significant value and is in many ways the second most important decision after asset allocation. Few people in the financial industry care more about benchmark methodology than I do. However, in my opinion obsession with the perfect benchmark is a misplaced use of industry resources, which could better be applied to continuous improvement of existing benchmarks. The industry could also focus on the development of custom solutions for specific client needs, and on refining the art and science of managing assets efficiently and consistently against the thousands of benchmark indexes available to investors.

Selecting an Asset Class Proxy

Some investors want the broadest possible index such as the Wilshire 5000 or the S&P/Citigroup (formerly Salomon Smith Barney) Broad Market Index (BMI) because they want the theoretically ideal market portfolio or because measures of aggregate wealth figure into their decision making. Breadth, however, should not be the sole deciding factor. All the genuine broad-cap indexes the industry offers to investors have essentially the same long-term historical and expected returns, as well as similar risk and correlation characteristics. Given this, other criteria are more important. Investors should favor the index that has the longest and most accurate history and other features (e.g., style and size subindexes, fundamental data, and industry and individual-company returns) that are important in their approach to studying asset classes.

It is important that the selected index be representative of the asset class it is intended to represent. The S&P 500, for example, is not a broad-cap index and should not be used as a proxy for the full spectrum of U.S. stocks. For international equities, some of the same principles apply. Whereas the S&P/Citigroup Broad Market Index (BMI) overs 95 percent of the investable universe, the 80 to 90 percent coverage of FTSE, MSCI, Dow

Jones Global, S&P Global, and S&P/Citigroup Primary Market Index (PMI) are generally sufficient for an asset class proxy, and the bulk of market participants have voted with their assets by using these only slightly narrower benchmarks (Chapters 8 and 9 assess the specific coverage range of these and other indexes for U.S. and international benchmarks).

Selecting an Active Benchmark or Index Fund and Exchange-Traded Fund

When investors are actually investing money, operational issues come to the forefront in selecting an index. The criteria for selecting an active benchmark and for selecting an index fund are closely related, because if an investor had no views on any stock, the active portfolio would presumably be identical to the index fund. The only difference is that active managers need more detail (including fundamental, industry, and company data) so they can evaluate bets made against the index and conduct performance attribution studies. For ETF products, the benchmark can be narrower, in both overall cap coverage and country/sector/style segments.

Other Operational Issues

Investors should choose an index that is easy to use. Some indexes are better supported by the index provider than others; for example, some of the index vendor's public web sites providing return and constituent data are more complete, accurate, timely, and convenient than others.[9] As noted, clear, objective, and widely disseminated rules for stock addition and deletion (and for other index-maintenance actions) make it more practical to manage the fund to the index, or to use the index as a benchmark. Flexibility and responsiveness of the index provider are also essential for creating and maintaining custom benchmarks to meet specific investor needs.

Finally, as previously mentioned, all other factors being equal, a high degree of acceptance by the broad investment community makes an index significantly more useful and valuable.

NEAR PERFECT CHOICES IN AN IMPERFECT WORLD

An open marketplace of index products (benchmarks and funds) with transparency of methodology and constituents, coupled with competition between index calculators/vendors and index fund managers, will continually improve benchmarks and the products based on them. It also will ensure that benchmarks respond to the constant changes in the underlying markets, such as cross-border mergers, country graduations, and the growth of new industries and sectors.

Diverse index choices are essential because each investor has unique needs that are best served by careful consultation with colleagues, managers, and consultants. Furthermore, fund managers and asset owners should continuously make their views known to index vendors; and the index providers should be open to this crucial input because it enables steady index improvement. Finally, the continual development of alternative approaches to index portfolio management—enhanced indexing, pure passive strategies, alternative weighting approaches, and even silent indexes or funds—will ensure that the marketplace will continue to assess the attributes and trade-offs of the varied approaches. In this robust environment of innovation and responsiveness, investors will be able to achieve their individually perfect benchmark and portfolio solution. Thus, as implied in the quote hanging on an office wall in 1971, through the efforts of all of us, the seemingly impossible dream could be achievable.

NOTES

1. These criteria formed the basis assessing indexes in "Benchmarks 101," published in the *Journal of Indexes* in the second quarter of 2001, in Steven Schoenfeld's "Perfection Impossible—Why Simply 'Good' Indexes Can Result in a More Perfect Solution" in the *Journal of Indexes* (second quarter, 2002), as well as earlier essays published by the Editor and his former colleagues at Barclays Global Investors.

2. When a merger, bankruptcy, or other corporate action removes a stock from a *numbered* index such as the S&P 500, it must be replaced with another constituent, usually from a *watch list* of eligible candidates. This incurs a slight additional turnover that an *unnumbered index* (such as the S&P/Citigroup PMI U.S. Index) would not incur. It should also be noted that some numbered indexes (like the Wilshire 5000) are only notional numbers, and in fact have more stocks than the number implies. In the case of the Wilshire 5000, it is quite a substantial difference.

3. The constituents of the Wilshire 5000 are *not* the totality of U.S. publicly traded securities as is widely assumed. Standard & Poor's maintains an internal equity database, but not an index, that contains approximately 9,000 U.S. common issues (including NYSE, AMEX, NASDAQ National Market, and NASDAQ Small Cap issues), plus over 1,500 American Depository Receipts (ADRs) and foreign stocks traded in the United States, for a total of over 10,500 common stocks. The Dow Jones internal database, of which its U.S. Total Market Index represents 95 percent by capitalization, contained over 6,000 stocks.

4. Including changes due to mergers, acquisitions, spin-offs, and so on, which have become increasingly complex in general, and for international/global indexes,

even more complex for cross-border corporate actions—some of which are discussed in Chapters 9 and 21.

5. Gary Gastineau, "Silence is Golden—The Importance of Stealth in Pursuit of the Perfect Fund Index," *Journal of Indexes* (second quarter, 2002) available on Journal of Indexes archive at www.IndexUniverse.com.

6. Simon Hookway, "Indexes, Targets, Benchmarks and Long-Term Investment Performance," London, 2002 (MSS Capital Ltd. [UK]—White Paper). Available at www.ActiveIndexInvesting.com (or via www.IndexUniverse.com) in this chapter's E-ppendix section.

7. Goldman Sachs Derivative and Trading Research, "S&P 500 Index Changes: Predicting and Capturing the Impact," *Annual Review and Outlook* (January/February 2001); and "Recap of the S&P Addition Effect in 2001: Is It History?" Merrill Lynch Portfolio Trading Strategy Comment (September 7, 2001). See also "Rules of the Race Have Changed for Index Fund 'Front Running,'" *Financial Times* (February 4, 2002).

8. Steven A. Schoenfeld, Robert Gimis, Niklas Nordenfelt, and Binu George "The World's Biggest Index Change Ever—BGI's Perspective on the MSCI Index Evolution" Barclays Global Investors International Equity Strategy Group White Paper (December 14, 2001). This paper fully documents the "doom and gloom" predictions of sell-side broker research on the anticipated "massive index effect," and tracks the actual performance of the index evolution, which greatly disappointed all those who attempted to front-run the changes. This paper is available from www.barclaysglobal.com and www.ishares.com, or from the author of this chapter.

9. Links to all of the world's major index provider web sites—as well as basic data and statistics—are available in the Index Research section on IndexUniverse.com.

CHAPTER 7

The Ideal Index Construction

Gus Sauter

_____ **Editor's Note** _____

As a contrast to the views expressed in Chapter 6, this chapter is a slightly condensed version of an article written by Gus Sauter in spring 2002 and published as "Index Rex" in the Journal of Indexes. *This article sparked considerable debate within the indexing community, much of which continues (and is covered in detail on IndexUniverse.com). Furthermore, certain index providers adapted several of Gus's proposals, and others are carefully observing the results. I hope that these contrasting views, and other index methodology issues raised throughout Part Two, help readers appreciate the key factors and nuances of benchmark design and construction. Certainly it will be apparent that index design, construction, and maintenance is a highly sophisticated endeavor—another element of indexing that is "anything but passive."*

The lengthy sidebar in this chapter describes the major index families and their flagship benchmarks. It gives readers who may be unfamiliar with the range of players in this dynamic field sufficient background to understand the nuances described in this part of the book. Further information on index providers is available through links in the book's E-ppendix at www.ActiveIndexInvesting.com and on IndexUniverse.com. This chapter's E-ppendix entry also includes "Web-Only Sidebars" by top executives from the various index providers, where they describe their benchmark families in more detail.

The bulk of the main text of this chapter was originally published in the *Journal of Indexes*, as "Index Rex" (second quarter, 2002) and is used with permission from the author and the publisher.

Over the century since the creation of the first U.S. stock index, new technologies made it possible to create indexes that more accurately captured the performance of the U.S. stock market such as the Standard & Poor's 500 Index, the Russell 3000 Index, and the Wilshire 5000 Total Market Index (in ascending order of comprehensiveness). Unlike the original Dow Jones average discussed in previous chapters, these indexes are weighted not by prices but by the market value of their constituents, and thus better represent the universe of securities available to U.S. investors.

In the mid- to late-1970s, however, a burgeoning industry of investment consultants recognized that these broad market indexes were inappropriate benchmarks for professional money managers. Most managers oversee portfolios that track not the broad market, but discrete sectors of it—perhaps stocks of a particular size, or stocks with pronounced growth or value characteristics.

The consultants addressed the mismatch between managers and benchmarks by creating indexes of stocks in various capitalization ranges and of different investment styles. Since then, the industry has created multiple indexes to track every sector, industry, and subindustry. The same has happened with bonds. There are few sectors of the financial markets that are not being sliced, diced, and tortured by an ever-growing list of index creators.

Despite the proliferation of indexes, these benchmarks have generally failed to reflect the way managers actually invest. On balance, they measure the wrong set of securities or, if not that, then the wrong way of managing those securities. As evidence, our research shows that the correlation between the performance of growth and value *managers* is much higher than the correlation between growth and value *indexes*. In other words, the growth and value indexes reflect a degree of difference in investment styles that doesn't exist in the real world. The same problems exist with indexes that represent other subsectors of the broad market.

It is indeed puzzling that two different indexes designed to provide insight into the same sector of the market (e.g., large-cap value stocks) can provide very different results. These discrepancies arise because of differences in the methodologies used to create the indexes. Over long periods, different value and growth indexes generally, though not always, provide similar results. In the short run, however, their differences cause confusion and limit their usefulness as benchmarks.

A PROPOSED NEW APPROACH

It is possible to create indexes that are meaningful benchmarks for managers who follow growth or value investment styles, focus on large- or small-cap stocks, or look for some combination of those characteristics. The starting point is this cardinal rule: *An index must reflect the way that money managers actually invest.*

This may sound like circular reasoning—defining value as what people call value. The reality, however, is that *growth* and *value,* and *small-cap* and *large-cap,* are what investment managers deem them to be. Modern portfolio theory doesn't define any of those terms. Managers do. The indexes that track these sectors should incorporate the thought processes of these managers. The best index is not necessarily the one that provides the highest return; it is the one that most accurately measures the performance of the style it is designed to track.

This chapter proposes guidelines for the construction of ideal indexes. With better tools, investors will be able to make better decisions about how their money is managed. Some indexes already incorporate some of these proposals, but no index incorporates all the guidelines.

These guidelines are not intended to make the lives of index fund managers easier. An index fund is a rational investment only if it provides an alternative to active management in a low-cost, relatively tax-efficient way, or if it offers exposure to a segment of the market in which active management is difficult, if not impossible. For example, microcap stocks are too illiquid to be managed actively in a portfolio with high turnover. Indexes designed only to simplify the lives of indexers probably would not meet these criteria. However, if the rules for creating indexes based on the behavior of active managers *also* simplify the indexers' job, then so much the better.

Rely on Objective, Not Subjective, Rules

An index can be rules-based and objectively maintained, with no ambiguity about when a stock should be included or excluded. Alternatively, an individual or committee can more subjectively reconstitute an index according to broad guidelines. Each approach has pros and cons.

A purely objective approach ensures absolute style integrity and total transparency, precluding debate about the merits of including one stock or another. However, it also can, but does not have to, result in short bursts of high turnover, raising costs, and tax inefficiency. Active managers, even those with high portfolio turnover, don't implement six months' or a year's volume of portfolio adjustments on a single day.

On the other hand, a subjective approach to index maintenance may allow for more orderly management of changes. This approach, however, is subject to committee decisions that do not represent the decision process of active management.

The most important characteristic of indexes tracking the market's subsectors—in essence, sectors created and defined by managers—should be that they accurately reflect the thought processes of active management. For that reason, style integrity is extremely important, and an objective set of rules for creating an index is preferable to the vagaries of a subjective process.

Adjust Weightings for Cross-Holdings/Float

In determining a company's size and capitalization category, it is necessary to take into account all of a company's outstanding shares because its economic size influences the stock's performance. However, a different standard should be used to determine the stock's weight in an index.

The investment universe available to active investors should be the starting point for all indexes. Many companies have shares that are closely held by individual investors, or cross-held by other corporations or governments. To the extent that these positions represent strategic long-term holdings that do not float on the market, they should not be used to calculate the stock's weight in the index, and thus its contribution to the index's return. They are not a part of active investors' opportunity set. Including these shares in a benchmark distorts its return relative to the universe of active investors because, in aggregate, the managers cannot own all the shares outstanding.

In truth, probably no index-related issue is less debatable than this. In fact, two major global indexes, the MSCI and FTSE indexes, have recently been reconstituted to adjust for shares that don't float. Although these changes resulted in hundreds of billions of dollars' worth of transactions for index and active funds, causing large transaction costs, those short-term costs will improve the long-term integrity of the indexes.

Define Market Capitalization as a Band, Not a Line in the Sand

Indexes based on market capitalization must be periodically reconstituted to ensure that they reflect the performance of the market segment they purport to measure. Both objectively and subjectively determined indexes currently capture this concept to varying degrees. In each case, the rebalancing usually results in significant market impact on the stocks affected as well as unnecessary turnover and transaction costs. This marketplace turmoil is not prima facie evidence of poor index construction, but rebalancing as it is now practiced does not reflect how active managers adjust their portfolios. Therefore, it leads to the creation of an inappropriate benchmark.

Active managers do not unanimously agree on the boundaries between two capitalization ranges. One manager might classify a $4 billion company as large cap, while another might consider it mid cap. To capture this ambiguity, an index's demarcation between capitalization ranges should be a band, not a line in the sand. If a stock's relative market capitalization changes so that it enters the band, the stock remains a constituent in the index to which it was previously assigned. It migrates to the other index only if it exits the opposite side of the band. A small-capitalization stock will remain in the small-cap index even if its market cap grows into the range that may have demarcated large cap when the index was first established. It will become a large-cap stock only if its market capitalization moves past the upper edge of the band.

The advantages of these bands would be twofold: First, they would reduce turnover during periodic index rebalancings, as stocks would not vacillate between one index and another based on minor changes in their market capitalizations. Second, and more important, these bands would more accurately reflect the way active managers think of their investment universe. Managers do not summarily throw a stock overboard because it crosses an imaginary line. They frequently continue to hold it even though a manager with a different investment style might consider it to be in a different index classification.

Building the Bands and Defining Capitalization Ranges

The capitalization bands should be based on the *relative sizes* of stocks, instead of on static dollar figures that may or may not be appropriate as the market rises and falls. The initial cutoff for a large-cap index could be the 700th-largest stock, as measured by total, as opposed to float-adjusted, market capitalization. Or it might be the stock representing the 85th percentile of the stock market's capitalization. (These boundaries are just suggestions, but they are roughly appropriate.)

The band around the large-capitalization cutoff could be plus or minus 150 stocks, or plus or minus five percentage points of market capitalization. A stock previously classified as small or mid cap would be added to the large-cap index once it became the 549th-largest stock, or the stock representing the 79th percentile of market capitalization. Similarly, a stock would be removed from the large-cap index when it became the market's 851st largest stock, or the stock representing the 91st percentile of market capitalization.

The small-cap index should be a complement of the large-cap index, with an initial cutoff of perhaps 700 for the largest stock and, as suggested earlier, 2,500 for the smallest stock. (The absence of a mid-cap index separating large- and small-caps may seem odd, but this construction better reflects active managers' capitalization exposure.) The cutoffs should be bounded by the 300-stock bands used in the large-cap index. While the top cutoff may seem high, it reflects the holdings of small-cap managers. In fact, the performances of the Russell 2500 and Wilshire 4500 Indexes—both of which include mid caps and small caps—more closely correlate to the performance of small-cap managers than does that of the strictly small-cap Russell 2000 Index. Stocks smaller than the 2500th stock could comprise a microcap index (a segment for which no index yet exists), as shown in Figure 7.1.

The mid-cap index would overlap the large-cap and small-cap indexes, with initial break points at perhaps the 400th-largest stock at the top and the 1200th-largest stock at the bottom, with both cutoffs surrounded by 300-stock bands. Figure 7.1 illustrates this concept. The first column shows the total stock market. The second column shows the universe of large-cap stocks; the third, that of small-cap stocks; and the fourth, that of mid-cap stocks. The dot-dash-dot lines show the initial cutoffs for each capitalization range. The dash-dash-dash lines show the bands or hurdles that a stock must cross to move from one capitalization range to another.

Some investors may be concerned that, because the mid-cap index overlaps the large- and small-cap indexes, the three together would not replicate the total stock market. But overlap is a problem that investors already face when combining two or more actively managed funds, or even when complementing an active fund with an index fund. Active managers follow no hard-coded rules about market capitalization. Two managers with different

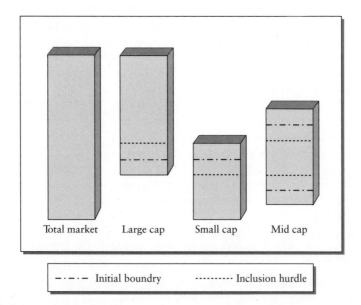

FIGURE 7.1   Range of Stocks Included in Capitalization Indexes Sorted by Size
Source: Journal of Indexes.

mandates will frequently consider the same stock to be in their target ranges. An investor who wants a total-market index is better off investing in one directly than trying to build one with subindexes. [*Editor's Note:* It should be noted that the use of subindex products could provide flexibility for tax loss swap transactions, which are discussed in Chapters 18, 24, and 28.]

DETERMINE STYLE IN TWO DIMENSIONS

Most widely accepted indexes consider value and growth stocks to be complements of each other. By this definition, a growth stock is anything that is not a value stock, and a value stock is anything that is not a growth stock. The delineation typically depends on a single factor, such as price/book ratio, or perhaps a combination of several factors blended into a single style rank for every stock, as depicted in Figure 7.2.

Active managers do not believe their world is flat. A value manager may hold a stock owned by a growth manager. The stock may fully satisfy the requirements of both. A value manager might require that a stock have a low price/earnings ratio, but would certainly not be dismayed to see that it also enjoyed strong growth prospects. Nor would a growth manager exclude a stock that met requirements for growth just because it sported a low valuation.

Using their independent criteria, value and growth managers occasionally fish from the same pond. Conversely, some stocks are attractive to neither. For active managers, stocks don't fall into rank on a simple line like that shown in Figure 7.2; instead, there is a two-dimensional delineation between value and growth.

Value managers emphasize a company's fundamentals relative to its current price, including price/earnings, price/book, price/sales, and dividend/ price (yield) ratios. They analyze companies based on these criteria and subject those that pass a certain hurdle to further analysis. Growth managers, by contrast, place the primary emphasis on characteristics such as earnings growth, sales growth, and margin growth. Working independently, value and

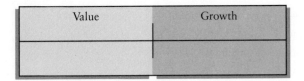

FIGURE 7.2 A Single Style Rank

growth managers analyze companies along their own growth or value spectra. Figure 7.3 shows a combined view.

In two dimensions, some stocks are pure value or growth, others are both value and growth, while still others appeal to neither growth nor value managers. Based on a stock's price ratios, a value manager might conclude that it is a value stock. Evaluating its sales and earnings growth, a growth manager might conclude that the same security is a growth stock. Using two distinct methodologies, both managers determine that the stock is a component of their universe. Style-based indexes should reflect this reality, instead of forcing a stock into one category or the other. Consequently, growth and value indexes, as subsets of broader indexes, should not be perfect complements.

Given this design, a combination of value and growth index funds will result in some overlap in holdings. It will also exclude some stocks. But that is true of actively managed portfolios as well. As in the case of market-cap-oriented funds, the combination of actively managed growth and value funds does not yield a complete nonoverlapping portfolio. Style indexes that are to be good benchmarks won't necessarily be perfect complements of each other. Index investors who want to combine value and growth should simply invest in a blended index.

This methodology would also allow us to create deep-value and aggressive-growth indexes by setting higher hurdles for those extreme styles. And as with the capitalization indexes, there should be bands around the growth and value demarcations.

Manage Stock Migration

Although market-cap and style-oriented bands would reduce turnover and better reflect the way active managers respond to changes in stock characteristics, there would still be those hard lines in the sand at the edges of a band. When a company crossed this edge, the stock would exit the index, and in the case of size indexes, migrate entirely from one classification to

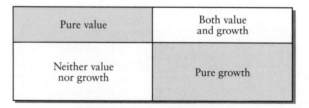

FIGURE 7.3 Combined View

another. Once again, this is not an accurate representation of how active managers respond to secular shifts in the characteristics of a company. In reality, because managers act independently, there is no one point, or even brief period, in which they collectively decide to eliminate a stock that is leaving their investment style. One by one, they may act quickly, but *as a group* they remove such stocks from their portfolios gradually.

How can an index reflect this reality? One way would be to divide the index into 12 equally sized subcomponents, each associated with a month of the year. If Stock A had a market capitalization of $12 billion, for example, each of the 12 subcomponents would contain $1 billion of Stock A. Every month, the subcomponent associated with that month would be opened up, analyzed, and reconstituted.

Figure 7.4 shows how this might look, using an imaginary set of indexes being reviewed in May 2002. The index sponsor has opened that month's subcomponent, which was established in May 2001, and analyzed the stocks to determine whether they still meet the index criteria. In May 2001, Stocks A, B, and C were large cap, and Stock D small cap. A year later, Stock C has migrated down to the small-cap category, and Stock D has migrated up to the large-cap category. The subcomponent's ½₂ position in Stock C is moved to the small-cap index, and its ½₂ position in D is moved to the large-cap

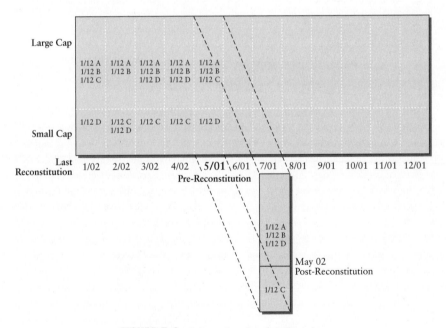

FIGURE 7.4 Managing Stock Migration

index. Adjustments made in the May subcomponent have no effect on the other 11 subcomponents.

This process means that, during any one month, only $\frac{1}{12}$ of a stock's float-adjusted market capitalization would be transferred from one index to another. At a minimum, it would take 12 months for a stock to entirely migrate from one index to another. During this transition period, the stock might be in two indexes, but the weights in the large- and small-cap indexes would be complementary. A particular stock might have $\frac{7}{12}$ of its weight in the large-cap index and $\frac{5}{12}$ in the small-cap index.

This migration process more closely reflects how active managers invest. First, they do not as a herd pile into, or out of a stock as it crosses a certain threshold. Instead, they collectively wade into and out of a position. An index that followed the same process would not only be a better benchmark, it would also benefit index fund investors by significantly reducing turnover and allowing the portfolio to be repositioned in a more orderly fashion, significantly reducing the fund's transaction costs with the monthly reconstitutions. The index itself would have lower embedded transaction costs, which would enhance long-term results.

Most indexes currently lead to significant transaction costs when securities are added or subtracted. The cost of style integrity is disproportionately high for small-cap indexes, which have recently had annual turnover as high as 35 percent to 45 percent.

MAJOR GLOBAL AND U.S. EQUITY INDEX PROVIDERS
Steven A. Schoenfeld and John Spence

As an introduction to the major global equity index families used in the United States and worldwide, this sidebar provides a brief, somewhat opinionated overview of the firms and their best-known flagship products (listed alphabetically). As so much of the discussion about index methodology and index products in the book revolves around both the construction methodology and business objectives of index providers, it is important to know the players in this dynamic field.

A more detailed description of each index family, in the words of key executives of the index vendors, is provided in this book's E-ppendix, available at www.ActiveIndexInvesting.com. A list of these entries appears in the "Guide to the E-ppendix," which starts on page 649. IndexUniverse.com also has a section called "Index Research," which includes substantial information on various index families and benchmarks. We couldn't possibly include all the index providers operating in the United States, let alone worldwide, so we must apologize for any omissions, which are likely rectified in the following chapters and in the book's web site. Both www.ActiveIndexInvesting.com and IndexUniverse.com strive to maintain updated information about global index vendors and their benchmarks.

Dow Jones Indexes

Charles Henry Dow, founder and first editor of the *Wall Street Journal,* developed the Dow Jones Industrial Average (DJIA) in 1896. It became the most widely quoted indicator of the U.S. stock market— not just within the United States, but also around the world. Today, the Dow is made up of 30 American companies representing major industries. Although the DJIA enjoys a rich tradition and enduring popularity, most investment professionals don't consider it a true measure of the U.S. economy because it contains only 30 industrial stocks and the index is price-weighted. In price-weighted indexes, a company with a small market capitalization but a high stock price can affect index performance more than larger companies with cheaper shares.

The editors of the *Wall Street Journal* select the components of the industrial average. Taking a broad view of what industrial means, they look for substantial companies with a history of successful growth and wide interest among investors. It is a subjective judgment, not a quantitative one. The components of the DJIA are not changed often because the *Journal* editors believe that stability of composition enhances the trust that many people have placed in it. The most frequent reason for changing a stock is that something is happening to one of the components, such as being acquired. Whenever one stock is changed, the rest are reviewed.

For many years, Dow Jones refused to license its industrial average as the basis of any investment products, such as mutual funds, futures, or options. In 1982, the company successfully went to court to stop the Chicago Board of Trade from trading a futures contract based on the average. But some 15 years later, the company's leaders became convinced that experience with such products along with safeguards designed by regulators and the exchanges made the time right to consider licensing their indexes. In June 1997, Dow Jones granted licenses to the Chicago Board of Trade for futures on the Dow, the Chicago Board Options Exchange for options on the Dow, and the American

(Continued)

Stock Exchange for an exchange-traded fund commonly known as "Diamonds" (ticker: DIA).

Dow Jones maintains a broad array of international blue-chip, total market, and style indexes, and together with partner STOXX Limited manages a family of European equity benchmarks. Dow Jones also has corporate bond and REIT indexes, and in partnership with AIG, a commodities index. A number of these indexes are used for ETFs and index derivatives trading in the United States, Europe, and Asia.

FTSE International

London-based FTSE (Financial Times Stock Exchange) is best known for its U.K. and global indexes. The FTSE 100, with its broader FTSE All-Share variants, is the recognized index for the British stock market. The FTSE Global Equity Indexes have nine subseries, the best known being the FTSE All-World, which covers 49 different countries and over 2,400 stocks capturing 90 to 95 percent of the investable market capitalization. The index is divided into Developed, Advanced Emerging, and Emerging Market segments, and its "ex-U.K." variant is the dominant benchmark for international equity investing by British investors. The newly broadened FTSE Global Equity Index series goes deeper into the small-cap universe. FTSE calculates over 20,000 indexes daily, including more than 600 real-time indexes.

FTSE has also been an innovator in both the multinational/global index area and the socially responsible benchmark space. The FTSE Multinational Index was the first such *global leader* index, while the FTSE4Good index series has social screens. It also has a series of U.K. and Global bond indexes. FTSE maintains a strong partnership with many local and regional stock and derivative exchanges, collaborating to calculate flagship local indexes as both market indicators and benchmarks for ETF and derivative products. The FTSEuronext series is the latest of such ventures, which also includes calculations for Hong Kong, Taiwan, South Africa, Greece, and China. The later partnership has resulted in the FTSE/Xinhua Indexes, which are benchmarks for Chinese stocks trading globally and in China (both Shanghai/Shenzhen and Hong Kong).

Morningstar Indexes

In 2002, Morningstar, long known for independent investment research, released a family of indexes based on its popular style-box categories. By coming to the market relatively late, Morningstar was able to design an index family that incorporates the current best practices in index construction.

The indexes are free-float, not market capitalization-weighted—which means that a company's weight in an index is based on shares only available for purchase on the open market and excludes shares held, for example, by company insiders and governments (see Chapters 5 and 6).

Morningstar's index family consists of 16 U.S. equity indexes that track the U.S. market by capitalization and investment style using a comprehensive and nonoverlapping approach based on the methodology for the Morningstar style box. The investment style of each individual security is determined by a comprehensive 10-factor methodology that separately measures both the value and growth characteristics of each security, using historical and forward-looking elements. One of the defining characteristics of the indexes is the treatment of the core style for the stocks for which neither growth nor value characteristics dominate. Such stocks merit their own category, allowing them to be treated as a distinct group. Further, it permits value and growth indexes that reflect the accepted definitions of these different approaches to security evaluation and selection. The 16 indexes in the Morningstar Index family serve as building blocks of a diversified portfolio—thus offering a flexible basis for portfolio construction, and ultimately as the basis for ETFs.

MSCI (Morgan Stanley Capital International)

MSCI is the premier provider of international equity indexes, with an estimated 90 percent of international institutional equity assets in the United States benchmarked to MSCI indexes. MSCI offers international investors performance benchmarks for 50 national stock markets as well as regional, sector, industry group, and industry aggregations. MSCI was originally started in 1969 as Capital International Perspective and, in 1986, Morgan Stanley bought a controlling stake in the index provider.

MSCI made several major moves starting in the late 1990s to cement and expand its role as a dominant index provider. In 2001, it adjusted its indexes for free float, which resulted in a large rebalancing and a transition for managers using MSCI benchmarks. Although many analysts feared detrimental index front-running, MSCI ensured

(Continued)

a smoother transition by spacing the float adjustment in two phases over the course of an entire year.

In 1999, MSCI, in collaboration with Standard & Poor's, introduced the Global Industry Classification Standard (GICS). The GICS is designed to assist the investment research and management process for financial professionals worldwide by providing highly granular and accurate security classification.

The MSCI EAFE (Europe, Australasia, Far East) is perhaps the most recognized broad index for international equities, and is the benchmark of choice for many international managers. However, the index came under attack in the 1990s because active managers were able to trounce the index by underweighting Japan. In 2001, MSCI expanded the index coverage by increasing the target market representation of its indexes from 60 percent to 85 percent coverage of the relevant market on a free-float basis. This expanded coverage should make the MSCI EAFE a more difficult target to best for active managers (see Chapters 3, 6, and 9).

In late 2002, MSCI entered the U.S. index market with a set of equity benchmarks tracking various sectors of the American stock market. The indexes have been well received, and Vanguard, the large retail index fund firm, licensed the indexes shortly after their release and has transitioned the majority of their U.S. index funds to the new benchmarks, as well as launching a broad series of ETFs based on the U.S. indexes.

MSCI entered the alternative asset class benchmark area in 2002, bringing its hedge fund indexes to the market and has expanded its fixed-income index offerings as well.

Nasdaq Indexes

The Nasdaq Stock Market, which is run by the National Association of Securities Dealers, is the largest electronic stock exchange in the world. Most investors are familiar with the Nasdaq-100 index; the benchmark is commonly used to take the pulse of U.S. technology stocks. The Nasdaq-100 Trading Stock "cubes" (ticker: QQQ) are by far the highest traded ETFs tied to any stock index and were extremely volatile since their launch in 1999. The index consists of the largest domestic and international nonfinancial companies listed on the tech-heavy Nasdaq by market capitalization. The slightly less volatile Nasdaq Composite Index, another commonly cited equity benchmark, contains around 4,000 securities, and now also has an

ETF tied to it (ticker: ONEQ). In the 1970s, the exchange introduced its first indexes based on economic sectors such as banks and industrials, and it has an expanding range of sector indexes.

NYSE Indexes (New York Stock Exchange)

The Big Board established the NYSE Composite Index in 1966 to reflect the performance of all the common stocks listed on the exchange. The NYSE Composite represents over 80 percent of the total market capitalization of all publicly traded companies in the United States. In January 2003, the NYSE reintroduced the index under a new rule-based and transparent methodology; for example, the index moved from a full market cap weighting to a float-adjusted cap weighting that accounted for only those shares available for trading. With the rise of exchanged-traded funds, the NYSE introduced four additional proprietary benchmarks in June 2002. The NYSE U.S. 100 Index tracks the top 100 NYSE-listed U.S. stocks. The NYSE International 100 Index measures the performance of the largest 100 NYSE-listed non-U.S. stocks. The NYSE World Leaders Index includes all the components in the NYSE U.S. 100 and International 100 Indexes. The NYSE TMT (technology, media, telecom) Index tracks the performance of the largest 100 NYSE-listed U.S. and non-U.S. companies in those sectors. ETFs based on the NYSE composite (ticker; NYC) and the NYSE 100 (ticker: NY) were launched in spring 2004.

Russell Indexes

Russell introduced its family of indexes in 1984. Most investors are familiar with the Russell 2000 index, which measures the performance of U.S. small-cap companies. More than $214 billion is invested in funds modeling Russell's U.S. indexes, and more than $1 trillion in funds is benchmarked against the global family of Russell indexes, including a complete series of Russell-based iShares ETFs listed on the American Stock Exchange. Listed futures on the Russell 2000 and 1000 trade at the Chicago Mercantile Exchange and the New York Board of Trade, respectively.

The Russell indexes are objective, transparent, and rules-based. Russell's total stock market index, the Russell 3000, simply includes the largest 3,000 U.S. companies based on total market capitalization, representing approximately 98 percent of the investable U.S. equity

(Continued)

market. The large-cap Russell 1000 is the top 1,000 largest companies, while the Russell 2000 contains the remaining and smaller 2,000 securities. These indexes are rebalanced only once a year in June.

Russell manages a set of style indexes across market capitalizations—the methodology incorporates nonlinear probability algorithms for stock style classification, using price-to-book ratios. Additionally, Russell maintains a family of benchmarks measuring the Japanese stock market.

Standard & Poor's

Standard & Poor's introduced and maintains the most visible and widely used index for investment professionals: the S&P 500. Although the S&P 500 is often mistakenly thought of as representing the largest 500 companies in the United States, the benchmark is actually a representative sample of the U.S. economy. The S&P 500 represents about 80 percent of the total value of the American market and is used by more than 90 percent of U.S. money managers and pension plan sponsors, while an estimated $1 trillion is indexed to the S&P 500. First introduced in 1928 with just 90 stocks, it was later expanded to include 500 companies in 1950.

An eight-person committee decides which stocks enter and leave the index, so the index methodology includes a measure of subjectivity as opposed to a rules-based index. This has both advantages and disadvantages that are discussed in Chapter 6. S&P 500-based index funds experienced huge asset growth in the bull market of the 1990s as the public became increasingly aware of the overwhelming number of U.S. mutual funds that failed to beat the index over longer time periods. S&P 500-based futures and options (and OTC swaps) are the most widely followed and traded index-based derivative products.

In 1999, S&P, in collaboration with MSCI, introduced the Global Industry Classification Standard (GICS). The GICS is designed to ease the investment research and management process for financial professionals worldwide by providing the rapidly updated and detailed security classification.

Standard & Poor's also maintains a flagship mid-cap index, the S&P 400, and a small-cap benchmark, the S&P 600, which are aggregated with the S&P 500 to form the S&P 1500 Composite index. S&P has also assumed management of what is now known as the S&P/Citigroup indexes, which includes a float-adjusted U.S. equity index, addressed in a sidebar in Chapter 8. As discussed in the following chapters, S&P also has a broad and steadily expanding family of global/international indexes and broad benchmarks, as well as benchmarks tracking ADRs, commodities, credit, municipal bonds, and most recently, hedge funds. Standard & Poor's Hedge Fund Indexes were the first benchmarks to have a U.S.-domiciled, publicly available index fund based on them.

Wilshire

The Wilshire 5000 is the most recognized yardstick for the broad U.S. economy, hence the title "broad market" index. This benchmark includes all U.S.-based securities with readily available price data. The Wilshire 5000 has actually become a misnomer, since it holds well over 5,000 stocks, reflecting the growth in stock issuance since its introduction in 1974. In 1983, the Wilshire 4500 Index was created by removing the 500 stocks in the S&P 500 from the Wilshire 5000. Often called an "extended market" index, many mid- and small-cap fund managers use the index as their benchmark.

Wilshire also offers style (growth and value) subset indexes for its large-, mid-, and small-cap benchmarks. Originally dubbed the Quantum Style Indexes, they were launched in 1996 by separating the Wilshire 5000 into four capitalization groups (large, small, mid, and micro), and then dividing the large-, small-, and mid-cap issues by capitalization equally into growth and value indexes. Growth and value are defined by looking at two factors: price-to-book ratio and projected price-to-earnings ratio. Additionally, Wilshire manages a "Target" index series with more concentrated versions of its style indexes, and stronger growth and value characteristics. Finally, Wilshire offers a family of real estate indexes, which includes a popular REIT index.

CONCLUSION

To create relevant benchmarks for actively managed investments, our frame of reference should be the active managers themselves. It is these managers, not investment theory, who define *growth* and *value, small cap* and *large cap*. With indexes that mimic the thought processes of active managers, investors would have better tools for evaluating the performance of professional managers, helping them to make smarter decisions about their portfolio allocation. Consultants and researchers would also have better tools for attributing a portfolio performance to the returns of different investment styles.

A widespread misconception is that indexing works in large caps, but not in "inefficient" sectors such as small caps. At times, this conclusion appears to be supported by the data. But the data's real lesson is that we're measuring managers with the wrong yardsticks. With better benchmarks, outperforming—or underperforming—an index would no longer be a matter of holding stocks from a different universe. Performance would reflect the success of a manager's stock selections within the appropriate universe. Although it is unlikely that large numbers of active managers could boast of index-beating performance, even over short periods, these better indexes could in fact be a boon to talented active managers. Their relative success could be attributed to skill, not dismissed as an artifact of faulty benchmark construction.

CHAPTER 8

U.S. Equity Benchmarks— Broad-Cap, Size, and Style Indexes

Slicing and Dicing the U.S. Equity Market

Gardner Platt, Brad Pope, and Chad Rakvin

_____ Editor's Note _____

Although there are many ways to segment markets when measuring their movement, the only acceptable choices are the ones that are intuitive to investors and are derived from empirical evidence. In discussing the development of the style segments and the construction of indexes to measure the market, Gardner Platt, Brad Pope, and Chad Rakvin point out that investors and index providers define indexes and applications of style in many ways. They then discuss the challenges in developing benchmarks for these segments where such differences exist. The chapter also includes a comprehensive overview and assessment of broad-cap U.S. equity benchmarks, using the framework for assessment ("seven key criteria") established in Chapter 6. The authors rank six of the most popular broad-cap and large-cap indexes along these criteria. As with the chapters following this one, some of the data and assessments might be dated by the time of publication, and readers are encouraged to check for updates—or to submit comments— on www.ActiveIndexInvesting.com.

_____

This chapter is partly adapted and synthesized from several BGI *Investment Insights* publications that were written by some/all of the authors.

Gauging market behavior is notoriously difficult because there are thousands of market indexes representing every conceivable country, asset class, and investment style. This abundance reflects the explosive growth of the investment industry and suggests a healthy emphasis on quantifying investment results and processes. The downside is that differentiation among the many indexes also becomes more difficult.

In this chapter, we focus on indexes for slicing and dicing the world's largest stock market—the U.S. equity market. We outline the characteristics of a good index and clarify the choices that are available to investors. Although there are infinite ways to benchmark market performance and benchmark providers have segmented the market ever more finely, few indexes are widely recognized. The indexes that the investment community favors are often based on market capitalization size, sector/industry, country, and style. By *style,* we are referring to growth and value indexes, which have become increasingly popular. Still, the core of index usage continues to be broad capitalization-weighted indexes including (in descending order of number of stocks included) the Wilshire 5000, Dow Jones U.S. Total Market Index, Russell 3000, and S&P SuperComposite1500. (The new MSCI U.S. indexes and the rebranded S&P/Citigroup U.S. indexes are discussed in sidebars within this chapter.) Because many investors and investment managers use the large-capitalization Russell 1000 and S&P 500 indexes to represent the market, we have included them although they are not truly broad-capitalization.[1]

In addition to the "four key uses" discussed in Chapter 5 (gauge of sentiment, performance measurement, basis for index products, and asset allocation), domestic flagship indexes are also heavily used for style and size segmentation within the market. We provide a solid overview of this rapidly growing area.

Style Investing

In recent years, growth and value criteria have emerged as additional measures of the market. Interestingly, although growth and value are readily accepted as valid measures, there is almost no consensus on what constitutes these measures or how to construct style benchmarks. This makes choosing a benchmark especially difficult. Even the most general definitions of style are subject to debate. Does value refer to companies attractive at a specific point in time or to companies with a high dividend yield? Does growth translate into a valuation based on estimated future earning potential or some other growth factor? Later in this chapter, we address the common definitions of growth and value and discuss the evolution of the available indexes.

Market Capitalization-Weighted Indexes— The Widely Accepted Norm

As discussed in earlier chapters, market capitalization (cap) weighting is the central organizing principle of good index construction. Simply put, market capitalization's magic is that it moves with the market because market cap is a stock's share price multiplied by the number of shares outstanding. As a stock rises in an index, its weight grows accordingly and automatically. There is no need for the frequent and expensive rebalancing associated with most other weighting schemes.

Market cap weighting is also the only weighting scheme consistent with a buy-and-hold strategy. Ignoring dividends, a market cap-weighted index of all securities would never need to be rebalanced. Of course, investors wouldn't want to ignore dividends, nor is an index available that constitutes all securities. However, owning all the securities in a market cap-weighted index will greatly reduce the amount of portfolio turnover necessary to capture the index's return. In contrast, indexes that are not cap-weighted require constant rebalancing due to ordinary changes in the prices of stocks. Turnover results in transaction costs, and transaction costs result in forgone returns.

WHAT CHARACTERISTICS ARE DESIRABLE IN AN INDEX?

As previous chapters illustrate, indexes are useful as benchmarks for active management, as the basis for index funds, and as proxies for asset classes in asset allocation. Ideally, investors should choose an index that can serve all three purposes simultaneously. When selecting an index for one or more of these purposes, investors must consider all the characteristics of the index and determine which one meets their needs. No broad-cap U.S. equity index is perfect, so (as with most choices) trade-offs are involved.

How do you choose among the competing alternatives? In addition to market capitalization-weighting, which is a prerequisite of a good index, the following *seven key criteria* are useful in identifying an acceptable benchmark for U.S. equities (the logic supporting this framework is discussed in detail in Chapter 6):[2]

1. Completeness.
2. Investability.
3. Objective, published rules.
4. Accurate and complete data.
5. Acceptance by investors.

6. Availability of derivatives and other tradable products.
7. Low turnover and related transaction costs.

We cover each criterion in depth, and later in the chapter, we rank the indexes when we examine the trade-offs in the context of the U.S. indexes under consideration. We now examine four of the "five inherent trade-offs" introduced in Chapter 6.

Completeness versus Investability

From a purely theoretical standpoint, the ideal index includes every security in an asset class. No one knows exactly how many stocks there are in the United States, but the Wilshire 5000 (so named because it was originally composed of 5,000 stocks) contained 5,512 stocks as of May 30, 2003. Thus it includes more issues than any other widely distributed U.S. equity index.[3] However, many of the smaller stocks in the Wilshire 5000 are illiquid, and investors can have a difficult time trading them. Thus, no full-replication index fund has ever been constructed for the Wilshire 5000.

For these reasons, a somewhat less broad index may be more investable. By an investable index, we mean that the investor can buy and sell the stocks in the index and a closely tracking portfolio can be constructed without incurring high transaction or market impact costs, or unusual delays due to a stock's illiquidity. Accessibility is an important characteristic. An index is accessible to investors to the extent it is the basis for existing index funds and exchange-traded funds (ETFs). Access to the index through derivatives (futures and options) also is desirable, but less important than access through index funds and ETFs.

Because the Russell 3000 index, containing 3,000 stocks, specifically excludes the smallest and most illiquid issues, all or nearly all of its capitalization can be held efficiently through full replication. This index is the broadest of the widely distributed indexes that exclude illiquid, hard-to-trade stocks. Narrower U.S. equity indexes that are still considered broad-cap (e.g., the Dow Jones U.S. Total Market Index and the S&P 1500) also are investable.

Reconstitution Frequency versus Turnover

Reconstitution, the periodic process of deciding which stocks to include in the index, is a source of costly turnover for investors because the manager must trade to keep pace with the index. Because reconstitution enables an index to track accurately the asset class it is designed to represent, there is a trade-off between accuracy and trading cost.

Turnover due to reconstitution is a major concern for managers of small-cap and style indexes, where companies with a large weight in the index are constantly crossing the size or style boundaries. For this reason, the index providers of size and style indexes tend to reconstitute them at regular and somewhat infrequent intervals, such as quarterly or annually.

Reconstitution-related transaction costs are primarily a burden for small-cap, mid-cap, and style-specific indexes. Turnover is costly whatever its source or volume, and a cost advantage accrues to indexes with less of it.

Rebalancing Frequency versus Turnover

Rebalancing, which is different from reconstitution, is the adjusting of stock weights in the index for changes in the number of shares outstanding. While this process gets much less press, it is vitally important to index viability. A theoretically ideal index continuously updates the number of shares that a company has issued, but there is a trade-off: The investor must rebalance to reflect these changes, imposing transaction costs and thus a drain on returns. Therefore, index providers typically decide on a prearranged schedule for updating outstanding shares.

Objective Rules versus Judgment

Some indexes are constructed using reasonably objective rules, whereas others are constructed using judgment. The advantage of objective rules is that any investor with access to the relevant data can predict, more or less accurately, which stocks will be added to and deleted from the index. This enables investors to trade in anticipation of (instead of reacting to) additions and deletions, and in general to manage index replication in an orderly and efficient manner.

The subjective selection of stocks for an index enables the index provider to achieve certain traits that cannot be attained with transparent objective rules. Index providers that create judgment-based indexes claim this is desirable. Standard & Poor's, which uses a committee format to select stocks for its S&P 500 and S&P 1500 indexes, asserts that its indexes are superior in stability, accurate representation of the industry distribution of the economy, and other attributes. The S&P indexes can achieve these traits specifically because the index construction staff need not act mechanically in selecting and removing stocks. They can deliberately construct an index with the desired characteristics. Thus, there is a trade-off between the clarity and predictability of a rule-based index and the flexibility of a judgment-based index.

CHOOSING AN INDEX

The criteria of general acceptance for choosing an index depends somewhat on whether the index is to be used as a benchmark for active management, as a portfolio (index fund), or as a proxy for an asset class in asset allocation. As noted earlier, however, the best index is one that can be used for all three purposes simultaneously.

Selecting an Asset Class Proxy

Some investors want the broadest possible index (i.e., the Wilshire 5000) because they want the theoretically ideal market portfolio. Breadth, however, should not be the sole deciding factor. All true broad-cap indexes have essentially the same historical and expected returns, as well as risk and correlation characteristics. Given this, other criteria are more important. Investors should favor an index with the longest and most accurate history, as well as other features (e.g., style and size subindexes) that are important in their approach to studying asset classes.

The selected index, of course, should be representative of the asset class it is intended to represent. How often do you hear "the market was up today" and not know whether this means the DJIA, S&P 500, or the Russell 3000? Often the daily, monthly, and annual return differences between these indexes are large. The S&P 500 is not a broad-cap index and should not be used as a proxy for the full spectrum of U.S. stocks. You must ask yourself, "What do I mean when I say 'the market'?"

FLOAT ADJUSTMENT

As discussed in Chapters 5 and 6, an index should represent a viable investment alternative and should therefore be investable. Simply put, you should be able to manage a portfolio with returns that are very close to the index return. To better represent the shares available for purchase by the public, some index providers remove closely held and illiquid shares when calculating a company's number of shares outstanding. Known as *float adjustment,* this makes an index more useful as a benchmark and as the basis for an index fund. Typically, investors cannot buy shares held by founders, directors, employees, other corporations, and governmental bodies. The larger the proportion of illiquid and closely held stock, the more difficult it is for an investor to obtain a full market-cap proportion.[4]

A closely related criterion is the exclusion of illiquid issues. Just as it is difficult to track an index that includes stocks with a limited float, it is also difficult to track an index that includes thousands of small, illiquid issues. While the illiquid issues in the Wilshire 5000 but not in other indexes such as the Russell 3000 and Dow Jones U.S. Total Market index are individually small, the large number of such stocks causes them to add up to a significant amount of capitalization. Thus, we counsel investors to use indexes constructed to capture the U.S. equity market while trading off the costs of illiquid securities. This is done with construction guidelines and a conscious liquidity screen.

DEFINING STYLE

For years researchers have explored the characterization of stocks along style lines. At the most basic level, style is broken into growth and value. Yet there is still debate on what constitutes growth and value (see Chapter 7). Research has made great strides in validating these styles. Modern Portfolio Theory (MPT) introduced the concept of investing in terms of the relationship between risk and return in efficient markets. Others developed asset-pricing models using factors to help define the risk/return relationship. Quantitative factors designed to capture growth/value characteristics soon evolved. Also, as the need to analyze different investment manager styles increased, so did the need for viable benchmarks to measure style. Eventually, the newly developed style indexes began to transform from measurement tools to investment vehicles.

During the 1970s, there was great success in quantifying the relationship between risk, return, and the market. The research focus on style came to a head with the work of Eugene Fama and Kenneth French. During the early 1990s, Fama and French constructed a model to explain return differentials using already accepted factors. For CAPM, beta (ß) worked well during the time period leading up to Sharpe's work; but from 1963 to 1990 the relationship was not clear. Instead Fama and French found size and book-to-market ratios (inverse of P/B) as having the most powerful explanatory powers of returns. They looked at returns from 1924 to 1990 (they had first looked at 1963 to 1990, then 1941 to 1990, finally going back to 1924 in response to criticism, and found the results still held). They found a strong correlation between ß and size, but when these two factors were separated, size alone showed the relationship with return. There was a negative relationship between size and return—smaller stocks returned more than larger stocks.

As part of their analysis, they also looked at earning/price ratio (E/P), leverage, and book-to-market (inverse of price-to-book) ratios as return factors. Fama and French found a positive relationship between book-to-market and return. Value stocks seemingly outperformed growth stocks as measured by book-to-market. Their results showed that book-to-market was more effective at explaining returns than size and, in fact, when combined with size, rendered other factors (e.g., E/P) redundant. Book-to-market became a highly important measure of style. Although their results continue to be debated, they solidified the central themes of investing along size and style. The correspondent indexes soon followed suit.

Yet the debate over the definitions of value and growth rages on. As the name suggests, value represents companies that are attractive because their intrinsic value—as defined by book value or liquidation value—is above the value defined by the market. In contrast to value, growth represents companies with above-average earnings growth and potential for above-average growth in the future. As mentioned, there are several ways to interpret style investing. Since this poses a problem for the consistency of index development, it becomes increasingly important to uncover the differences.

THE AVAILABLE BROAD MARKET INDEXES

Of the broad-cap indexes, the Wilshire 5000 was the first to be constructed. It was designed to capture the return and wealth behavior of the entire U.S. market portfolio, not as the basis for an index fund—thus its relative lack of investability. The Russell indexes, which came later and were constructed for performance evaluation instead of specifically for indexing, are nevertheless well adapted to index-fund management. The Russell 2000 came to be, and still is, dominant in the small-cap segment of the market. It was in existence in the 1980s when a strong need for such an index first arose. All the Russell indexes are float-adjusted and are well supported with clear construction rules and readily available data.

Realizing that it had the oldest and best-known brand name in market averages but no market cap-weighted index that investors could use to build an index fund or derivative contract, Dow Jones & Company recently introduced its suite of global indexes. These include the Dow Jones U.S. Total Market Index, which was initiated in February 2000.

The S&P 1500, another relative newcomer, was constructed by adding the S&P MidCap 400 and the S&P SmallCap 600 to the S&P 500.

The major index providers today all have established style indexes fairly recently. Russell first created style indexes based on the Russell 1000 in the 1980s but did not develop its current style methodology until 1993. S&P followed suit in the early 1990s with a series of indexes. It wasn't until 1997 that Dow Jones added its growth and value benchmarks, while Wilshire developed style indexes as recently as 1996. Although MSCI launched a series of growth and value indexes in 1997, they were little used, and the methodology was completely revamped in 2003.

MORGAN STANLEY CAPITAL INTERNATIONAL'S
NEW U.S. EQUITY INDEX FAMILY
Eric Brandhorst

MSCI has incorporated several attractive features into the construction methodology of its new U.S. equity benchmarks targeted at U.S. domestic investors, which were introduced in early 2003. As discussed in Chapters 5 and 6, the benefits of different index features are largely a matter of investor preferences and the intended use of the benchmark. MSCI has created a series of U.S. benchmarks that can meet many investors' benchmark needs. The new U.S. equity indexes reflect both the accumulated experience of MSCI as an index provider, and the fact that MSCI was able to respond to the strengths and weaknesses of the well-established U.S. benchmarks analyzed in this chapter.

A Representation of the Market Portfolio

The MSCI U.S. equity benchmarks capture the important basic features in a benchmark that aims to represent the broad market portfolio:

- Capitalization-weighted.
- Float-adjusted.
- Exhaustive (except for the "tail" of the capitalization distribution).
- Objective and transparent.

The breakdown of the capitalization segments reflects generally accepted measures of large-cap, mid-cap, and small-cap stocks. In addition, the distinct micro-cap segment allows investors to evaluate liquidity issues and determine whether this segment plays a role in either the broad-market portfolio or a small-cap portfolio. The elimination of the tail (beyond 5,000 securities) of the equity universe avoids a part of the market that often provides little in market representation but can introduce liquidity issues.

Costs

MSCI is conscious that its actions can influence the wealth of passive investors who use its indexes as investment benchmarks. The successful manner in which MSCI handled its significant 2001–2002 global index methodology enhancements (the move to float adjustment and capitalization extension discussed in Chapter 9) speaks to this sensitivity. This appreciation for the wealth give-up related to index providers' actions also is apparent in features of the new MSCI U.S. indexes:

(Continued)

- Buffer zones between capitalization segments to reduce turnover.
- Buffer zones between style segments to reduce turnover.
- Elimination of the tail of the equity universe capitalization distribution.
- Distinct segmentation of a micro-cap segment where liquidity can be a concern.

At this stage, the MSCI U.S. benchmarks may provide investors some cost advantages in that they will likely not be used by investors representing a material percentage of outstanding capitalization. As a result, at least initially, the MSCI indexes may avoid some of the costs associated with index changes (additions, deletions, reconstitution, etc.) when a material pool of assets implements the index changes at more or less the same time.

Style Definition

MSCI's style definition is an area where the new MSCI methodology is unique. The main feature is the use of independent dimensions for evaluating the extent to which a security has growth or value characteristics. Within each dimension, MSCI uses a multifactor approach in determining the relative strength of both the growth and value dimensions. The multifactor analysis strays a bit from a purely objective form of analysis, however, with its use of forecasted earnings per share (EPS) in both the growth and value dimensions.

As discussed throughout Part Two, selection of a suitable benchmark is an important decision for investors. The new MSCI U.S. equity indexes give investors another benchmark family to consider when making their index-based equity allocation decisions.

More information on the MSCI indexes is available at IndexUniverse.com or www.msci.com. ETFs on many of these indexes were launched in January 2004, and information on them is available at IndexUniverse.com and www.Vanguard.com.

This analysis was originally published by State Street Global Advisors (SSgA) in September 2002. Data used reflects the index and market levels at that time. The information contained herein does not constitute investment advice and it should not be relied on as such. It should not be considered a solicitation to buy or an offer to sell a security. It does not take into account any investor's particular investment objectives, strategies, tax status, or investment horizon. We encourage you to consult your tax or financial advisor. Past performance is no guarantee of future results. The views expressed are the views of Eric Brandhorst only through the period ended September 24, 2002, and are subject to change based on market and other conditions. The complete original version is available in the book's E-ppendix at www.ActiveIndexInvesting.com as well as at SSgA's web site www.ssga.com.

Index providers do not assign growth/value designations to companies at the broad market level. Instead, they first start with capitalization indexes and then segment these indexes into style indexes. The S&P 500 growth index is not created by determining the securities in the S&P 500 that fall into the S&P 1500 growth index. If style were determined at the broad market level, the growth indexes would be biased toward large-cap stocks, and value indexes would be biased toward small-cap stocks. This becomes increasingly important when considering that the investment decision is usually made along the lines of both size and style. In fact, style indexes at the broad market level have gained much less attention than at the size level.

Creating the Capitalization Indexes

Although there is consensus that defining an index along size parameters is valuable, the definition of size can be subjective. While the concept of market capitalization is straightforward, each index provider differs on how to distinguish between large-, mid-, and small-capitalization. Table 8.1 outlines the methodology for each major index provider (see note at end of chapter).

TABLE 8.1   Size (Cap Range) Index Construction Rules

Provider	Large	Mid	Small
S&P	Committee selection of 500 industry-leading companies.	Committee selection of 400 companies. Generally within range of $1 billion to $5 billion.	Committee selection of 600 companies. Generally within range of $3 to $4 million to $1 billion.
S&P/Citigroup U.S.	Primary Market Index (PMI) represents top 80% of total index market cap.		Extended Market Index (EMI) represents bottom 20% of total index market cap.
Russell	Top 200 companies by market cap at reconstitution date.	Next 800 companies (ranked 201 to 1000 by market cap).	Next 2000 companies (ranked 1001 to 3000 by market cap).
Dow Jones	Top 70% of adjusted market cap.	Next 20% of adjusted cap (70%–90%).	Next 5% after re-sorting by cap and turnover (90%–95%).
Wilshire	Top 750 companies by market cap.	500 companies ranked 501 to 1000. Combination of Large and Small.	Next 1750 after Large cap (ranked 751 to 2500).

Source: Barclays Global Investors' Index Research Group and Global Index Strategies. Information current as of December 2003.

Creating the Style Indexes—Split versus Exclusive Constituents

Although each methodology has its roots in the research mentioned earlier, S&P, Russell, Dow Jones, and Wilshire define their growth and value indexes differently. The only common threads are to assign style at the capitalization level and to use P/B ratios. The indexes differ on what other factors are used, and how stocks are assigned according to the factors.

One of the biggest debates surrounding style indexes is how to classify the style of a particular stock. Should each name be classified 100 percent as growth or value, split between growth and value, or excluded altogether? The following list outlines the primary argument for each choice:

- *Exclusive classification.* In the investing world, it is much easier to describe stocks as being either growth or value. When looking at top performers and index contributors, companies that appear in both growth and value indexes tend to create confusion.
- *Split classification.* In actuality, stocks are moving from one classification to another. Splitting companies reflects this transition and limits turnover (names aren't suddenly jumping from one style index to another). This also increases the selection universe for active managers.
- *Neutral classification.* Style indexes and funds should be true to their style and effectively capture return differences. Stocks that don't have strong growth or value characteristics should not be forced into a style designation. Although this limits the index's completeness, it creates a true style index and limits turnover. Stocks migrating from growth to value will not immediately move from one index to another (see Table 8.2).

SELECTING AN INDEX

In selecting an index, investors should start by determining their investment goals and evaluating how well a particular index matches these goals. Each index has distinct advantages and disadvantages, and only through understanding the indexes can investors make informed decisions. Several criteria determine the effectiveness of an index:

- Investability—liquidity and name availability.
- Turnover, transaction costs, and clear methodology.
- Investor acceptance, data availability, funds, and derivatives.

In the following subsections, we explore these criteria and rank the various indexes. The rankings are by index family and consolidate the rankings

TABLE 8.2   Style Index Construction Rules

Provider	Split or Exclusive Classification	Sum up to Broad Market	Methodology	Factors
S&P	Exclusive	Yes	Basic	P/B
S&P/Citigroup U.S.	Exclusive	Yes	Multifaceted Separate factors for growth and value	Growth: Trailing EPS growth Trailing sales growth Internal growth rate Trailing BV growth Average annual EPS growth ROE ROA Dividend payout Long-term debt to equity Projected EPS growth
				Value: Trailing EPS growth Trailing BV growth Trailing sales growth Cash flow Dividend yield
Russell	Split	Yes	Multifaceted	P/B IBES long-term growth estimate
Dow Jones	Exclusive	No	Multifaceted	P/B Projected P/E Projected EPS growth Trailing P/E Trailing EPS growth Dividend yield
Wilshire	Exclusive	No	Basic	P/B Projected P/E

Note: BV = Book value; EPS = Earnings per share; P/B = Price to book ratio; P/E = Price to earnings ratio; ROA = Return on assets; and ROE = Return on equity.
Source: Barclays Global Investors' Index Research Group and Global Index Strategies.

STANDARD & POOR'S/CITIGROUP U.S. INDEX—
A NEW ADDITION TO THE U.S. EQUITY INDEX UNIVERSE
Melinda Chu

Standard & Poor's added a new family of indexes to its existing index offerings in late 2003 to complement its well-recognized series of U.S. indexes, including the S&P 500 and S&P MidCap 400. The former Citigroup indexes (previously the Salomon Smith Barney indexes) are known for their breadth of coverage, comprehensive database, and complete history.

The S&P/Citigroup U.S. index is a broad market, rules-based, free-float-adjusted index with history dating back to 1989. It is a good complement to the existing S&P U.S. index offerings. The S&P 500, S&P MidCap 400, and S&P SmallCap 600 indexes, which together combine to form the S&P Composite 1500, are highly recognized tradable indexes. In particular, the S&P 500 is the underlying basis for the most highly traded futures contract, and the largest ETF, known as the SPDR (Standard & Poor's Depository Receipt, ticker: SPY). These indexes are representative proxies for the U.S. equities market and are maintained by the Standard & Poor's Index Committee.

The Broad Market Index

With the new S&P/Citigroup U.S. index, Standard & Poor's now offers a choice of broad-based indexes for the U.S. market:

- The *S&P 500* is the world's most widely used index and represents about 80 percent of the total market.
- The *S&P Composite 1500* offers 90 percent coverage and has started to gain acceptance as a broad market benchmark among the larger plan sponsors.
- The *S&P/Citigroup U.S.* index covers 97 percent of the market, is free-float-adjusted, and follows a simple, objective, rules-based methodology.

The S&P/Citigroup U.S. index is reconstituted once a year. All companies with a market capitalization greater than $100 million are included in the index, and all companies with a capitalization less than $75 million are removed from the index. This minimum size criterion means the index is all-inclusive, while avoiding many small companies that are often associated with liquidity issues.

> The S&P/Citigroup U.S. index is referred to as the Broad Market Index (BMI). This index is further broken into large-cap and small-cap segments referred to as the Primary Market Index (PMI), representing the top 80 percent of capitalization; and the Extended Market Index (EMI), representing the bottom 20 percent.
>
> ### Turnover
>
> Index turnover is a major cost factor for index-based investors. As discussed in Chapters 5 and 6, investors must make a trade-off between choosing an index for low turnover or an index that is reconstituted frequently to reflect the market.
>
> The S&P Committee-based indexes are reconstituted on an as-needed basis throughout the year. As they are fixed-number indexes, a new addition replaces every removal. For the S&P/Citigroup indexes, reconstitution takes place once a year. The indexes do not use fixed numbers and so do not replace removals throughout the year from mergers, acquisitions, or delistings. Setting a market-cap buffer zone for inclusion ($100 mil) and exclusion ($75 mil) reduces turnover.
>
> ### Style
>
> The S&P/Citigroup indexes, in their earlier incarnations, were the first to develop a multifaceted approach to evaluating style by looking at different factors for growth and value. The S&P/Citigroup Growth & Value indexes adopt a multifactor approach. In total, the S&P/Citigroup style indexes incorporate three growth factors and four value factors.

for the broad-cap and style indexes. All ratings are assessed on a scale of 1 to 5, with 5 as the highest rating. Ratings are intended to be from the investor's perspective, where investors include individuals and institutional investors (defined contribution plans, defined-benefit pension plans, endowments, foundations, and mutual funds).

Investability—Liquidity and Name Availability

It is important that any index represent an investable set of constituents. And an index should also represent a viable investment alternative. As noted in Chapter 6, there is a trade-off between completeness and investability (see Table 8.3).

TABLE 8.3   Investability Rating

Provider	Rating	Comments
S&P	4	Specific liquidity screen and fewer, carefully selected names. Do not float-adjust shares.
S&P/Citigroup U.S.	–	No liquidity screen but shares adjusted for free float. Avoids many illiquid smaller issues by setting a minimum size criterion of $100 million at time of inclusion.
Russell	3	No liquidity screens and the broadest universe, including smaller hard-to-trade names.
Dow Jones	4	Specific liquidity screen; float-adjust shares. More companies than S&P, but investability shouldn't be an issue.
Wilshire	3	No liquidity screens and a broad universe. Do not float-adjust shares.

Source: Barclays Global Investors' Index Research Group and Global Index Strategies. There is no rating for S&P/Citigroup U.S. indexes because of the authors' non-inclusion of the benchmarks in their earlier studies.

Turnover, Transaction Costs, and Clear Methodology

Turnover and the resulting transaction costs become increasingly important as the market is divided into smaller and smaller segments. Capturing small market segments creates a more concentrated constituent base in indexes. This means that events affecting turnover or transaction costs have greater impact. Each index provider has its own methods for limiting turnover. Indexes should be objective measures of a specific asset class, so clear published rules are necessary. Index methodologies can and do change, but they should remain as stable as possible; and providers should state the process used to achieve that stability. Once they establish their methodology, they should publish it and make it available to the public. It is essential that investors understand the index, how it is created, and what it measures (see Table 8.4).

Investor Acceptance, Data Availability, Funds, and Derivatives

Acceptance of an index by the investment world is an important factor. Wide use of an index leads to constant evaluation and validation of an index provider's methodology as well as the availability of investment vehicles. Major requirements of acceptance are readily available data, reliability, and

TABLE 8.4   Turnover and *T*-Cost Rating

Provider	Rating	Comments
S&P	4	Low turnover for S&P 500 and S&P 1500. Style indexes rebalanced semiannually. Exclusive style membership increases turnover of style indexes. Clear style methodology. Judgmental security selection.
S&P/Citigroup U.S.	–	Rebalances annually. Stocks are included if greater than $100 million and removed if less than $75 million. This size buffer helps smooth turnover. Simple, clear, objective rules.
Russell	4	Rebalance occurs once a year along with all other changes—minimizes turnover. Transition can be gradual because 30% of names are split between growth and value. No liquidity screens but float-adjusted. Objective, published rules for all indexes.
Dow Jones	4	Rebalances quarterly. Specific turnover rules at the style and capitalization levels help reduce turnover but complicate transparency.
Wilshire	3	Rebalances once a year. No liquidity screens so high *T*-cost names included. Names are 100% classified and can shift completely. No float adjustment or specific liquidity screens. Rules clear and inclusive.

Source: Barclays Global Investors' Index Research Group.

as much history as possible. Without supporting data, there cannot be a meaningful index evaluation. Additionally, the discussion of investability becomes less relevant if investment vehicles are inadequate. A greater number of financial products can bring higher visibility to the index and more liquidity to index names as well as contribute to a complete and efficient market. If more alternatives are available for investing in an index (via funds, ETFs, derivatives), it helps assure proper pricing (see Table 8.5).

Editor's note: In an effort to enter the market as a U.S. "domestic" index provider (as opposed to their strong position as a U.S. equity benchmark for non-U.S. investors), MSCI began calculating and maintaining a series of comprehensive U.S. equity indexes in December 2002. Limited history and data availability precludes us from making a complete assessment of these indexes along the seven key criteria used in this book.

TABLE 8.5   Investor Acceptance, Data Availability, Funds, and Derivatives

Index	Rating	Comments
S&P	5	Indexes are widely used; data available; extensive financial products available.
S&P/Citigroup U.S.	N/A	Rebranded to S&P/Citigroup in 2003. Extensive data available back to 1989, from Citigroup predecessor Salomon Smith Barney.
Russell	4	Indexes are widely used. Data available; numerous financial products, especially ETFs.
Dow Jones	3	Not widely accepted; style indexes relatively new. Data available; numerous financial products, especially ETFs.
Wilshire	2	Wilshire 5000 broadly used but not other indexes. Data available; few financial products available, limited to Wilshire 5000 and Wilshire 4500.

Source: Barclays Global Investors' Index Research Group.

Among the characteristics of the index series are the following:

- Float-adjusted shares.
- Quarterly rebalancing (2 full reconstitutions and 2 partial recons, with sophisticated buffers to limit turnover).
- Semiannual style rebalancing based on 5 variables for growth and 3 variables for value (and a framework to bring them together with no overlap).
- Names with split style classification.

The sidebars within this chapter provides basic information on the indexes. For more information on the new MSCI U.S. Equity Indexes as well as the Morningstar indexes for the U.S. Market, please go to IndexUniverse.com, www.msci.com, www.morningstar.com, or www.vanguard.com.

CONCLUSION

As discussed in Chapter 6, there is no one perfect index, particularly if an investor seeks to blend size and style within a single benchmark family. Perfection needs to be measured against specific preferences and often mutually exclusive trade-offs. In this chapter, we have explained the characteristics that an investor should seek in an index. We have outlined the trade-offs necessary in index selection. Last, the chapter ended with an overview of relative rankings for each index provider along important selection criteria. The proper selection of a benchmark begins with investors who understand their objectives. Once investors understand what they want to accomplish and their investment philosophy, this chapter can provide the framework for deciding the appropriate benchmark. Our hope is that this information will make it easier for readers to select the optimal indexes for their needs.

NOTES

1. Additional broad-capitalization indexes have been introduced or rebranded since mid-2003, and are not featured in the scope of analysis of this chapter. They are featured in sidebars, and IndexUniverse.com provides more information on these relatively new index series.
2. As well as numerous other microlevel considerations, discussed in the sidebar "Don't Stop at Seven" in Chapter 6.
3. The contents of the Wilshire 5000 are not the totality of U.S. publicly traded securities. Standard & Poor's maintains an internal equity database, but not an index. As of June 30, 2003, the database contained 8,467 U.S. common issues (including NYSE, ASE, NASDAQ National Market, and NASDAQ small-cap issues), plus 1,540 ADRs and foreign stocks traded in the United States, for a total of 10,007 common stocks. Dow Jones's internal database, of which its U.S. Total Market Index represents 95 percent by capitalization, contained 6,314 stocks as of June 30, 2003.
4. See Steven A. Schoenfeld, Peter Handley, and Binu George, "International Equity Benchmarks for U.S. Investors—Assessing the Alternatives, Contemplating the Tradeoffs," *Investment Insights* (San Francisco: Barclays Global Investors, December 2000). The authors point out that there is a trade-off here, too: An index that makes precise float adjustments and keeps them up to date will experience higher turnover (and thus higher transaction costs) than a full-float index.

CHAPTER 9

International/Global Equity Benchmarks for North American Investors

Steven A. Schoenfeld and Robert Ginis

_____ Editor's Note _____

This chapter addresses the evolution of international equity benchmarks in the context of the changing face of a global stock market brought on by the rise and acceptance of emerging markets, by the growth of international investing by institutional and individual investors, and by cross-border mergers and acquisitions that have increased integration across countries and sectors. The heightened profile of global markets and the explosion of choice in international benchmarks mean that North American investors need additional perspective and data to align their international equity framework with the new framework of global equity markets. Rob Ginis and I address how key international index providers make benchmark construction decisions, how these indexes measure up within the framework of the Seven Key Criteria of a good benchmark (detailed in Chapter 6), and the nuances of using style and size breakdowns with international indexes. There is also some discussion of the relevance of transition costs in switching benchmarks for index-based portfolios. This chapter provides a solid foundation for understanding the challenges of managing international index portfolios, which is thoroughly covered in Chapter 21 within Part Four of the book.

What are the leading international equity benchmarks, and what type of market coverage and construction methodology do they offer? How can investors evaluate and select a benchmark that meets their goals? What transition costs should investors anticipate when switching benchmarks?

In this chapter, we explore how the changing face of global markets has led to the development of dozens of international benchmarks, highlight the features of those benchmarks for North American investors, and discuss the growing importance of style and sector based investing.[1] We also present a framework for evaluating benchmarks and conclude with an overview of transition scenarios between the major benchmarks. Our purpose is to help North American-based investors align their international equity framework with the new shape of world markets in an informed, deliberate way. As we well stress, the benchmark decision, while critical, is only the beginning of the process. For asset owners and their index managers, the real work begins with the implementation of that decision.

THE CHANGING LANDSCAPE OF GLOBAL EQUITY BENCHMARKS

Five events have triggered enormous change within the international benchmark arena: globalization of markets and cross-border investment, the growth of indexing and benchmarking and the increased focus on sector and style indexes, competition within the international index vendor business, the globalization of investment approaches, and finally the globalization and consolidation of trading activity and exchanges. We discuss them in the following sections.

Globalization of Markets and Cross-Border Investment

The recession of 2001–2003 hampered global merger and acquisition activity markedly. However, the surge in worldwide mergers and acquisitions, particularly in Europe and North America in the late 1990s and early 2000s, dramatically blurred the distinction between domestic and foreign companies and stocks, and we anticipate that future economic expansions will continue this trend.

All this raises some interesting questions. Should U.S.-based plan sponsors hold significantly less of BP plc or DaimlerChrysler now that these companies are considered to be European and are no longer in their U.S. equity benchmarks such as the S&P 500 or Russell 3000, despite active trading in the stocks in New York? Should plan sponsors increase their non-U.S. allocations to compensate for this loss of U.S. industry exposure? Similarly, should U.K. investors suddenly hold more BP plc than their entire U.S. equity exposure because its acquisition of Amoco and ARCO doubles its weight in their U.K. domestic benchmark?

The integration and consolidation of exchanges, the growth of multiple stock listings, and around-the-clock trading can make the picture even cloudier. Even though DaimlerChrysler is now considered a German company, it has retained its NYSE listing. Many U.S. investors still trade the stock in New York, and include it in their U.S. portfolios. In such examples, stockholders run an increasing risk of doubling or tripling their stock and sector exposures through the holdings of their active managers. Comprehensive and seamless benchmarks become critically important as tools to mitigate these risks and maintain a precise asset allocation process.

The growing dominance of large multinational companies such as DaimlerChrysler and BP plc has prompted a new alternative in asset allocation. Investors now can dedicate a large, separate allocation to the biggest global companies (and benchmarked to indexes such as S&P's Global 100, Dow Jones's Global Titans, and FTSE's Multinational Index). However, despite a surge of interest in this approach in the late 1990s, few North American or Continental European investors have adapted this structure for their strategic asset allocation policy.

The Growth of Indexing and Benchmarking and the Increased Focus on Sector and Style Indexes

As discussed in Chapter 3, since the 1970s there has been a strong and steady trend in the adoption of indexing as a core strategy in plan sponsors' international equity investment strategies. Simultaneously, there has been a dramatic increase in benchmarking of active managers, as more emphasis has been placed on benchmark-relative performance.

Several statistics demonstrate this increase. As of December 31, 2001, U.S. institutional tax-exempt investors held $1.6 trillion in indexed assets (domestic and global).[2] Of this, over 10 percent ($175B) was held in international equities.[3] Similarly, U.K. fund managers held approximately $540 billion in indexed assets, and Continental European managers had over $90 billion in indexed assets in this same timeframe. We anticipate that the trend toward indexing will continue, which is consistent with the variety of uses of index strategies discussed in Part One.[4]

The growth of assets directly tied to major benchmarks also reflects the virtually universal use of these benchmarks to develop and implement asset allocation policy, and to select and measure investment managers. For every plan sponsor dollar that is formally indexed in international equities, at least four or five dollars are actively managed, but linked to benchmarks. For example, while MSCI estimates that approximately $300 billion is managed in index funds tied to its indexes, it believes that $3 trillion is benchmarked in total.[5]

Thus, as stated in an Institute of Chartered Financial Analysts Research Foundation (now the AIMR Research Foundation) publication, "Plan sponsors must understand the strategic statements implied by that benchmark regarding country, currency, sector, and company exposures."[6] Many participants in the investment industry believe that this risk is a fiduciary duty at least as important as overall asset allocation and performance measurement.[7]

Performance differentials are important contributors to the growth in indexed assets, both in *home markets* and for international investing, whatever the home country of the investor.[8] A careful analysis of the performance data confirms that most active managers who claim stock selection as their expertise are generally adding value only through their incidental country bets.[9] Thoughtful investors question whether such outperformance is likely to persist, particularly if the country factor is diminishing for structural reasons.

Meanwhile, many investors argue that with increasing globalization, sector investing (and, therefore, sector benchmarks) has become more important than country or even regional-based investing. However, asking whether countries or sectors are more important in explaining historic equity returns is not as relevant as developing a framework for incorporating relevant information concerning both sectors and countries. Increasing globalization does indeed suggest a partial erosion of the dominance of the country paradigm in favor of sector-based investing. However, asynchronous business cycles, unique considerations of local domestic market participants, and segmented markets will ensure that both sector and countries remain important.

As already discussed in detail in Part One, institutional use of index strategies has been in a steady growth phase. Figure 9.1 shows the proportion of total institutional equity assets that were indexed in 11 developed markets at the end of 2001. However, retail investment products as well as derivatives usage have also grown dramatically, and all of these factors have increased the importance of understanding the construction methodology of international indexes.

Competition within the International Index Vendor Business

The major index providers have been in competition to achieve a dominant position in global equity benchmarks for well over a decade, but the race heated up considerably in the late 1990s and has continued into the

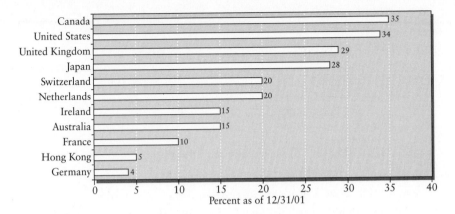

FIGURE 9.1　Index-Managed Assets as a Percentage of Total Equity Assets
Source: Global Asset Study, Watson Wyatt Worldwide, 2002.

mid-2000s. The four leading international index providers are Morgan Stanley Capital International (MSCI), FTSE International (FTSE), Standard & Poor's (S&P) (both their *flagship* series emulating the S&P 500 and the newly rebranded S&P/Citigroup Indexes which were formerly the Salomon Smith Barney Global Equity Indexes), and Dow Jones (DJ).[10] The overall scope of the global index vendor business is highlighted in the sidebar by Schoenfeld and Spence in Chapter 7. See that chapter's E-ppendix entry at www.ActiveIndexInvesting.com and the Index Research section on IndexUniverse.com for more detailed information on these index providers, including a "Web only" sidebar by Hugh Wilson of State Street Global Advisors on global (World *including* the U.S.) equity benchmarks.

Globalization of Investment Approaches

An example of the impact of the globalized investment approaches is the vibrant competition for emerging market benchmark preeminence in the first half of the 1990s. As investors increased their interest and commitments to emerging markets, an intense struggle broke out to provide the dominant emerging market benchmark. The primary competition was between benchmarks provided by IFC and MSCI, with some inroads by Barings (later ING Barings). A significant outcome of this competition—which was heightened by the Asian economic crisis of 1997 and 1998—was the recognition that emerging markets were actually closely linked to developed international markets. All the major index providers now offer seamless benchmarks that incorporate developed markets (including Canada) and emerging markets, an approach that we have termed "integrated international." As further demonstration of the integration of emerging markets into the global equity universe, all three of the major emerging market index families continue to be used as benchmarks. However, they have only survived as subcomponents of seamless, "integrated" global index families—with the IFC indexes having been absorbed by S&P, and the ING Barings indexes acquired and expanded by FTSE.

Globalization and the Consolidation of Trading Activity and Exchanges

As noted, both these issues are blurring the distinction between foreign and domestic companies. This domicile issue has greatly affected the benchmark providers, stretching their ability to classify the nationality of a company, and spurring them to create new global and multinational indexes. For example, FTSE International's practitioner committees have had such difficulty determining various companies' domiciles that they have created a Nationality Subcommittee to focus specifically on the issue.

Globalization is also causing increased concentration within countries; the United States, Canada, and Japan are now the only developed markets without any stocks with a weight of over 10 percent of the national benchmark. As of 2002, fully 12 (of 22) developed markets have over 60 percent of their market capitalization accounted for by just five stocks.[11] This impact on fund-level diversification, exacerbated by tax and regulatory restrictions in some instances, has also increased the demand for new global/multinational indexes, as well as "regulatory-compliant indexes."

THE SEVEN KEY CRITERIA AND FIVE INHERENT TRADE-OFFS IN SELECTING A BENCHMARK

We use the same consistent framework established in Chapter 6 to assess the indexes and help investors evaluate international equity benchmarks.

As a reminder, the seven key criteria of a good index benchmark are:

1. *Completeness.* Does the index accurately reflect the overall investment opportunity set, both in terms of country and company coverage?
2. *Investability.* Does the index include only those securities that foreign institutional investors can purchase?
3. *Clear published rules and governance.* How transparent are the rules that govern the various indexes? Are these rules well established and publicly available?

4. *Accurate and complete data.* For an index to be useful, return data must be accurate, complete, and readily available.
5. *Acceptance by investors.* In general, investors prefer a well-known and widely used index.
6. *Availability of crossing opportunities and derivatives/tradable products.* Indexes that are widely used, especially within pooled investment vehicles, offer potential cost savings because they provide crossing opportunities between large institutional investment managers. And the availability of listed derivative products and ETFs can further benefit asset owners and managers.
7. *Turnover and transaction costs.* All indexes incur a certain amount of annual turnover as they maintain index constituency in line with their stated methodology. In general, the lower the turnover, the fewer rebalancing costs the investors incur, and the easier the index is to track.

These criteria form the core of the comparative analysis of the benchmarks in this chapter. As mentioned in Chapter 6's sidebar, "Don't Stop at Seven," these are not the only criteria that investors may want to consider in choosing a benchmark, and the same considerations apply for the indexes discussed in this chapter.

Furthermore, as asserted in Chapter 6, no single benchmark can fulfill all the criteria listed. Several of the criteria are mutually exclusive and investors should establish their relative preferences for the different features and then select the benchmark that best meets those preferences. To reiterate, the *five inherent trade-offs* are:

1. Completeness versus investability.
2. Reconstitution and rebalancing frequency versus turnover.
3. Potential index effect versus liquidity/crossing opportunities.
4. Precise float adjustment versus transaction costs.
5. Objective and transparent rules versus flexible judgment-based methodology.

Investors should keep these trade-offs in mind when determining the benchmark most appropriate for their needs.

A FRAMEWORK FOR ASSESSMENT AND RATING

How do the various global indexes measure up against the seven key criteria? In this chapter, we discuss the relative strengths and weaknesses of five leading benchmark families and several of their popular variants:

1. MSCI: ACWI ex-U.S. Index, EAFE, World ex-U.S.
2. FTSE: All-World ex-U.S., World Developed ex-North America.
3. S&P/Citigroup Global Equity Indexes (formerly SSB) Broad Market Index (BMI) Global ex-U.S., and Primary Market Index (PMI) EPAC.
4. S&P: Global 1200 Index ex-U.S. (and the S&P ADR Index).
5. Dow Jones: Global ex-U.S.

The tables in the following section define each criterion in more detail and rate each contending index by each criterion. All ratings are assessed on a scale of 1 to 5, with 5 as the highest rating. Ratings are intended to be from the client's perspective, where clients include individual investors, sponsors of defined-contribution retirement plans, and traditional institutional investors (defined-benefit pension plans, endowments, and foundations). We rate each index based on how closely it meets the criterion as described. The data contained in tables and this chapter's E-ppendix (at www.ActiveIndexInvesting.com) was compiled from index vendor information. More information on these indexes, including updates, is available from the "Index Research" section on IndexUniverse.com.

Completeness

The more complete an index—the broader and deeper its coverage—the greater the opportunity set it offers, and the more effectively it represents the investable universe for both index and active managers. And by spreading its allocation among most of the available securities and markets, a comprehensive benchmark maximizes diversification and thereby can reduce risk.

Where the Benchmarks Stand   All the international indexes we analyze here have representation of the world's largest and most liquid equity markets. The FTSE All-World ex-U.S. Index, MSCI All-Country World ex-U.S. Index, and the S&P Citi S&P CITI BMI Global ex-U.S. Index provide the most significant breadth in terms of country coverage, with each including nearly 50 markets. Their extensive coverage across the world's emerging markets separates them from the Dow Jones Global ex-U.S., S&P Global 1200 ex-U.S., and the developed-only benchmarks, which include fewer markets. We provide a single rating for each index series.

A broad international index must not only cover the relevant world of equity markets, but also effectively represent the investment universe within each market. Again, all the indexes treat coverage differently to a greater or lesser degree. Each index aspires to cover a certain proportion of the available market opportunity set known as the *investable market universe*. However, the definitions of this representation can be confusing making direct comparison of the indexes extremely difficult.

TABLE 9.1　Completeness of International Indexes

Index	Number of Countries	Number of Securities	Target Market Cap by Country (%)	Rating
MSCI ACWI ex-U.S.	48	1,741		
MSCI World ex-U.S.	22	1,090	85	4
MSCI EAFE	21	1,007		
FTSE All-World ex-U.S.	46	1,842	90–95	
FTSE World Developed ex-North America	21	1,031	90–95	4
S&P/Citigroup BMI Global ex-U.S.	51	3,918	95	5
S&P/Citigroup PMI EPAC	24	729	80	
S&P Global 1200 ex-U.S.	28	700	70 (by region)	2
Dow Jones Global ex-U.S.	29	3,129	80	3

Source: Index providers, BGI International Equity Strategy Group, Global Index Strategies (data as of 6/30/03).

The variation in the countries in each index, together with differences in stock-level composition, accounts for the underlying variations in the weight of each country across the various index series, as detailed in Table 9.1. Differences that exist in the relative country/regional weightings are principally a result of the investablity adjustments made by each index. This is explained in more detail in the following section.

Investability

An effective benchmark should represent the universe of stocks from which investors can realistically be expected to select their portfolios—the investable universe. It is therefore essential that the stocks in the index are actually tradable both in terms of liquidity and also are available in the proportions in which they are included in the index—or in proportion to their available free-float.

Where the Benchmarks Stand on Float Adjustment　Each index provider has its own approach to adjusting for each security's free-float weight in the index.

Float has become one of the primary technical distinctions between indexes, a crucial factor in discussing and evaluating global benchmarks. And although the initial battle over float may be over, the manner by which it is measured still remains.

As discussed in Chapters 5 and 6, *free-float* refers to the amount of a company's shares outstanding that are available for purchase on the open market at any point in time. Large blocks of stock may be held by governments, private individuals (typically corporate insiders, founders and their families), corporations, or other ownership groups who trade infrequently. These share blocks lower a company's free float for good reason—they are virtually unavailable to the general public. Table 9.2 highlights the distinct

TABLE 9.2 Investability Adjustments of International Indexes

Index	Rating	Availability Adjustments
MSCI ACWI ex-U.S. MSCI World ex-U.S. MSCI EAFE	5	Constituents are float-adjusted for corporate cross ownership, private holdings, government holdings, and foreign ownership restrictions. MSCI uses a banded system for determining the level of float inclusion.
FTSE All-World ex-U.S. FTSE World Developed ex-North America	5	Index constituents are float-adjusted for foreign ownership limits, government holdings, cross-holdings, significant long-term holdings (founders), and employee stock incentive plans. FTSE uses a banded system for determining the level of float inclusion.
S&P/Citigroup BMI Global ex-U.S. S&P/Citigroup PMI EPAC	5	Float is adjusted based on corporate cross-holdings, private holdings, government holdings, and foreign ownership restrictions. S&P/Citigroup attempts to target the exact float levels for inclusion.
S&P Global 1200 ex-U.S.	4	Non-U.S. stocks are float-adjusted for government ownership, corporate cross-holdings, strategic partners, or control groups using an investable weight factor. The U.S. component (S&P 500) is not yet float-adjusted, but liquidity is a consideration in security selection for the index. The S&P 500 will be fully float-adjusted by 2005.
Dow Jones Global ex-U.S.	4	The exclusion of companies occurs if ownership of the stock is not broad based. If foreign ownership restrictions exist, only the available portion of a security is included.

Source: BGI International Equity Strategy Group and Global Index Strategies.

methodologies that the five indexes use to adjust for float; and rate the benchmarks on their outcomes.

Measuring for float is a critical step toward determining how investable a company may be. Equally important to the way float is measured is how an index adjusts for it. Investments are periodically rebalanced as part of regular benchmark revisions, along with the impact of corporate events such as mergers and acquisitions. As mentioned in Chapter 6, benchmarks that calculate float precisely will generally have higher turnover and associated costs than those that use a banding system. Benchmarks such as FTSE (five float bands; increments 15 to 25 percent, 25 to 50 percent, 50 to 75 percent, and 75 to 100 percent) and MSCI (18 float bands at 5 percent increments beginning at 15 percent), which employ bands, may not mirror true float exactly. However, this method also results in less turnover than a benchmark with precise float adjustment, such as S&P/Citigroup. This turnover and associated cost can potentially have direct and material performance implications.

Where the Benchmarks Stand on Liquidity   Some stocks are too illiquid to be reasonably included in a manager's portfolio and therefore should not be included in a benchmark index. Employing a liquidity screen makes the index more representative of the investable universe and ensures that investors can trade without facing prohibitive market impact costs. There can be a limit to the benefit of precision in this adjustment, as too frequent adjustment could cause excessive turnover. The different index vendors adopt varied approaches to liquidity screening.

The ratings in Table 9.3 are based on whether providers have explicit rules to screen out illiquid securities, the likelihood that illiquid securities could become index components, and whether the providers regularly review for liquidity.

Clear, Published Rules and Governance Structure

As discussed in Chapter 6, for an international index (or for that matter, any index) to be truly useful as a benchmark and investment vehicle, index construction rules should be established, transparent, and publicly available. This requirement increases during periods of index reconstitution reviews and when corporate actions occur—especially the frequent cross-border mergers and acquisitions that are common in the developed international markets. Having established rules reduces the risk of interested parties being able to influence an index's constituents. Furthermore, rules that are clear, published, and applied consistently enhance the ability of investment firms to effectively manage their portfolios.

TABLE 9.3   Liquidity of International Indexes

Index	Rating	Liquidity Screening—Vendor Stated Policies
MSCI ACWI ex-U.S. MSCI World ex-U.S. MSCI EAFE	4	No explicit minimum liquidity screen is applied. The index implicitly tends to select the most liquid stocks through its methodology of industry representation—the current target is 85% capitalization. For North America institutional investors, the dominance of the EAFE benchmark for index funds ensures ample crossing opportunities.
FTSE All-World ex-U.S. FTSE World Developed ex-North America	5	Securities that do not turn over at least 0.5% of their shares in issue, after the application of any free-float restrictions, per month for 10 of the 12 months prior to review will not be eligible for inclusion in the indexes. An existing constituent failing to trade at least 0.5% of its shares in issue (after the application of any free-float restrictions) per month for 4 or more of the 12 months prior to review will be removed.
S&P/Citigroup BMI Global ex-U.S. S&P/Citigroup PMI EPAC	4	S&P/Citi's methodology of constituent selection—by minimum size and float—is designed to address illiquid and restricted share capital.
S&P Global 1200 ex-U.S.	5	Stocks are ranked in terms of dollar value traded. This ranking together with float turnover, is analyzed monthly to ensure liquidity requirements are met. By definition, these are larger-cap indexes, and only includes the major emerging markets, which also ensures greater liquidity.
Dow Jones Global ex-U.S.	4	A security must have traded for at least 10 days during the previous quarter. A stock is excluded if its average daily turnover is in the bottom 0.01% of its country's equity market. The European sub-indexes of DJGI are highly liquid, as the DJ EuroSTOXX family has become a dominant benchmark for the EuroZone markets.

Assessment based on data through December 2003.

The general responsiveness of the index vendor's staff and management to the input of major index users (both active and index fund managers) is an additional consideration. Very often, investment managers, especially index fund managers, have significant insight into complex corporate actions and index methodology. Index vendors who listen to the input of index fund managers and derivatives/ETF market makers usually produce better benchmarks and often can minimize the index inclusion effect. [12]

Where the Benchmarks Stand   Generally, extensive rules-based methodologies are available for each index. Most of the providers operate a review committee, designed to maintain and revise policy and construction methodology, but the key differentiation is the level of independence that each attains. More information on the specific rules and governance structure for each of the indexes is available on the providers' web sites, accessible from the "Links" sections in the book's E-ppendix at www.ActiveIndexInvesting.com and the "Index Research" section on IndexUniverse.com.

Accurate and Complete Data

For investors and their managers, monitoring a benchmark requires return data that are accurate, complete, and readily available. Moreover, index information is not free. Index vendors negotiate pricing with asset managers and asset owners, both for the use of their data and for licensing of index products. For much of this chapter, we have evaluated benchmarks from an institutional investor's perspective. In this section, we are adding the perspective of index fund managers and index product users. We admit we are tough customers, but to track a given benchmark accurately, the details matter. Investors and their managers should have access to the following information: price/total/net dividend returns; quality and timely data; and historical returns.

Where the Benchmarks Stand   The historical data available from the index providers vary considerably, from less than a decade for the S&P Global 1200 ex-U.S. to over 30 years for MSCI EAFE. FTSE, S&P/Citi, and DJ Global all have about 15 years of historical data, with a bit longer track record for FTSE. More information is available from the Index Research section of IndexUniverse.com.

Acceptance by Investors

Investors generally prefer a benchmark that is well known in the financial community. This provides a level of comfort in the ongoing integrity of the index and in the ability to make peer group comparisons. Furthermore, academic and proprietary research, which is the foundation for asset allocation studies, generally focuses on established benchmarks to provide helpful and relevant insights for investors.

In addition, initial and ongoing transaction costs are lower for a well-known benchmark because a critical mass of investors using a single index series creates a network effect. This assessment is primarily from the perspective of North American investors. Once crossing and liquidity are derived globally, however, we factor in benchmark usage outside the United States and Canada. An updated rating is available directly from the authors.[13]

Where the Benchmarks Stand   In the United States and Canada, MSCI currently enjoys the lead in this area, having provided international benchmarks for over 30 years, first through EAFE, and more recently through ACWI ex-U.S. The competing index providers all have launched strong marketing efforts in the United States to win or retain market share. To date, MSCI has not been displaced for institutional investors, but S&P is making inroads in the retail/advisor space; and the subcomponents of the S&P 1200 ex-U.S. comprise key local/regional benchmarks such as the S&P Europe 350, S&P/Topix 150 (Japan), and the S&P/TSE 60 (Canada). Finally, S&P's acquisition of the S&P/Citigroup indexes—and the resulting imprimatur of independence—will likely make these former investment-bank run indexes significantly more competitive.

Availability of Crossing Opportunities and Derivatives/Tradable Products

Crossing allows investment managers to match their own clients' buy and sell orders, without incurring the typical costs that those transactions would incur in open markets. The extent of crossing levels depends on the amount of assets that are benchmarked against a particular index and the diversity of the investor types that use it. Ideally, a widely used benchmark creates a virtuous circle of activity by a critical mass of investors, in turn creating the potential for crossing trades. The critical mass for North American-based international assets is currently centered on the MSCI benchmarks. This is also true for Japanese-based international assets, where the MSCI Kokusai index is the primary benchmark for non-Japan developed markets, although FTSE and S&P are well known. In Europe, however, it is more divided, with FTSE dominating U.K.-based assets and Continental Europe-based assets being split between MSCI, FTSE, S&P, and DJ STOXX. Major global investors in large institutional investment arms in Hong Kong, Singapore, and the Gulf tend to use some combination of MSCI and FTSE as their primary benchmarks.

A further benefit of widely accepted benchmarks is the availability and liquidity of index-linked products. Futures can provide a useful cash management tool for managers of index funds when reinvesting dividend income. Until recently, market exposure using futures was based on the highly liquid local stock exchange contracts. However, many new contracts have been created since the index vendors began battling over the development of EuroZone benchmarks in 1998 and 1999. These vary significantly in both liquidity and coverage with the DJ EuroSTOXX 50 being dominant for both derivatives and ETFs.

Where the Benchmarks Stand   It is quite difficult to measure crossing statistics, especially as they vary from fund manager to fund manager, so we will not attempt to do so. There are futures contracts based on two MSCI regional indexes, MSCI Euro and Pan-Euro. While they have been approved by the CFTC they are not currently very liquid. In addition, liquid contracts for MSCI Taiwan and MSCI Singapore trade on the Singapore Exchange, with recently launched MSCI Japan contracts as well. There are also contracts based on FTSE's Eurotop series of indexes and DJ STOXX indexes. The EuroSTOXX 50, the key contract covering the 10 markets of the EuroZone, has attained wide usage and superb liquidity. Within the subcomponents of the S&P Global 1200, CFTC-approved futures contracts are linked to the S&P 500 and S&P/TSX 60. Currently, there are actively traded exchange-traded funds for each region of the S&P Global 1200 except for Asia ex-Japan. The relatively new S&P ADR Index offers exposure to both developed and emerging markets in ADR form. A discussion of the benefits of index-based products on this index is included in the sidebar in Chapter 21. Thus, once an exchange-traded fund is launched, investors will be able to access complete non-U.S. exposure in a single U.S. time-zone traded instrument. There are no specific contracts or products designed around the S&P/Citi's BMI Index. Table 9.4 summarizes the listed product status as of the third quarter of 2003, but of course this is a highly dynamic product set and marketplace. For updates, see the Futures/Options section of IndexUniverse.com.

Turnover of Index Constituents and Transaction Costs

All indexes will incur a certain level of turnover each year to maintain the index components in line with their investment methodology and their goal of effective market representation. Generally speaking, the lower the level of turnover, the lower the portfolio rebalancing costs and the more attainable the performance of index-tracking funds. Indexes that have no fixed limit on

TABLE 9.4   Listed Equity Index Products on International/Global Benchmarks

Listed Products on Major Global Benchmarks	Futures/Options	Exchange-Traded Funds (ETFs)
MSCI	Euro, Pan-Euro Hong Kong, Taiwan, Singapore	iShares MSCI (many were formerly called WEBS) trade in the U.S. on 26 markets/regions
FTSE	Eurotop 100, 300 (plus local, U.K. indexes, i.e., FTSE 100)	iShares FTSE 100 FTSE Eurofirst 80/100
S&P/Citigroup	None	None
S&P Global 1200 Sub-indexes	S&P/TSE 60, S&P/Tokyo 150 (plus S&P 500 in U.S.)	iShares S&P Europe 350, iUnits S&P/TSE 60, iShares S&P/Topix 150, iShares Latin America 40, iShares S&P Global 100, 5 S&P Global Sectors ETFs
DJ/DJ STOXX	STOXX 50, EuroSTOXX 50	iShares EuroSTOXX ETFs (European listed), Global Titans ETF, Fresco ETFs (U.S. listed)

Source: Exchanges, Global Index Strategies, ETFR, Morgan Stanley, and IndexUniverse.com.

the number of stocks and that are all-inclusive in terms of their capitalization range have a small advantage over indexes with a fixed number of securities, with fewer turnover and trading costs.

Where the Benchmarks Stand   Turnover among the indexes ranges from 6.71 percent for the FTSE Developed All-World ex-North America to 11.15 percent for MSCI's ACWI ex-U.S. The higher recent turnover of MSCI is a product of its historically more optimized selection methodology, as well as recent significant changes, and it may not be representative of turnover levels now that MSCI's 2001–2002 methodology evolution and enhancement is complete. Due to the long production process for a book, we have not included complete turnover statistics, but we would be happy to provide them directly upon request.[14]

THE EMERGENCE OF SECTOR AND STYLE INDEXES

As discussed, international investing traditionally has been based along country lines, with traditional active managers aligning themselves along top-down or bottom-up lines to differentiate style. Today, international equity managers are beginning to construct portfolios along sector, size, and style lines, much as they do in their domestic markets, although we do not expect this approach to gain as much acceptance as in domestic markets.

Sector Indexes

While evidence suggests that sector allocation strategies have not yet fully materialized on a global basis, Europe, as a result of the European Monetary Union (EMU), has begun the process of sectors rivalling countries in asset allocation importance. In response to the growing significance of the industry effect, investors are becoming increasingly interested in sector and size indexes for this asset class.

Where the Benchmarks Stand   All the index providers break down their global indexes by sectors and industry subsectors, along with various country and regional indexes. MSCI, S&P/Citi, and FTSE offer size indexes. The FTSE All-World Index has 10 economic groups classified into 39 sectors and 102 subsectors. In February 2000, Dow Jones introduced a new industry classification structure that comprises 10 sectors, 40 industry groups, and 70 subgroups. In August 1999, MSCI and S&P jointly launched a global industry classification system (GICS) that comprises 10 sectors, 23 industry groups, 59 industries, and 123 subindustries.[15] Although the sector and industry groupings are similar, it is difficult to directly compare them because of the variations in classification. All the benchmarks except S&P provide individual country subindexes. The S&P Global 1200 ex-U.S. comprises three country and three regional indexes.

In addition to sector and size subindexes, several index vendors have created new global categories, particularly for large multinational companies. FTSE has its Multinational Index; S&P has launched its Global 100 Index, initially designed for "round-the-world" trading, although only an ETF product has attracted significant interest. Dow Jones calculates its Global Titans Index, which is the basis for several retail mutual funds.

Style Indexes

The most recent area of differentiation between the indexes is the availability and relative quality of style subindexes. The remaining index providers offer value and growth style indexes, but with different methodologies and coverage. In addition, both MSCI and S&P/Citigroup also provide style-based (i.e., value/growth) subindexes for their broad benchmarks.

Where the Benchmarks Stand

Morgan Stanley Capital International (MSCI) In response to investor concerns, MSCI has revised its methodology for growth and value subindexes. Previously, MSCI determined the style of a particular constituent by ranking it in terms of one factor: price/book (p/b) value. A high p/b ranking (relative to the average of the index) would place the constituent in the growth index, and a low p/b would place it in the value index. This relatively simplistic approach has caused investors to question whether it accurately represents growth and value characteristics. Industry trend and investor demand have encouraged MSCI to adopt a more robust methodology going forward. This same framework has been used for the new MSCI US Indexes, which were discussed in the sidebar within Chapter 8.

The new methodology, adopted in the first half of 2003, ranks constituents for inclusion in the value and growth subindexes based on three and five factors, respectively. For value stocks, in addition to the p/b value ratio, MSCI added price to 12 months' forecasted earnings and dividend yield. For growth stocks, the following five variables are now used: long-term forecasted EPS growth rate, 12 months' rolling forecasted EPS growth rate, and current sustainable growth rate (ROE × [1 − payout ratio]), 5 years' historical EPS growth rate, and 5 years' historical sales per share growth rate. These definitions of value and growth are applied globally, with the assumption that value and growth characteristics are sufficiently similar across countries.

All the factors are equally weighted with the exception of one growth factor—to ensure the same importance is given to past and future growth measures. Each security will be represented in either the value or growth index, and any security that is double counted will have its market capitalization split to ensure that the market capitalization across the two style indexes adds up to the market capitalization in the standard index. Value and growth indexes will be determined for each country separately. Each country will be split evenly into the value and growth subcomponents. The value/growth split for each stock will be based on the relative distances of the value and growth score from the origin. For example, if the contribution of a stock's growth score is 80 percent or higher, it will be classified as pure growth (100 percent growth and 0 percent value). If the growth score contribution is between 60 and 80 percent, it will be classified as 65 percent growth, 35 percent value. And, if the growth score contribution ranges between 40 and 60 percent, the classification will be 50 percent growth, 50 percent value. There will be a buffer to reduce the turnover during the rebalances, which are now semiannual, at the end of May and November.

To capture the benefits of these methodology changes, MSCI originally proposed to give more importance to the "performance benchmarking role" during its client consultation period, as opposed to the "strategic asset allocation role" of style indexes. This argues for fully attributing the market capitalization of securities, depicting both value and growth characteristics to the value index and the growth index within each MSCI country index, unless one of the style characteristics clearly dominates (at least 80 percent of a security's style characteristics equates to dominance). Although this index design leads to an overlap between value and growth indexes, MSCI felt it produces style indexes which more accurately reflect the unmanaged representation of value and growth investment processes. In the end, based on input from investors—including the authors of this chapter—MSCI elected to ensure a seamless benchmark family and revert to favoring the strategic allocation role in its new benchmark design. Given the importance of strategic allocation to plan sponsors, the plan sponsor community will undoubtedly accept the change to make this characteristic paramount in the final methodology.

FTSE International (FTSE) The recently released FTSE style methodology aims to strike a balance between providing a stable benchmark for the measurement of performance and a tool for investors to build their strategic allocation framework. The flexibility in the methodology allows for allocating constituents to either growth or value, or proportionally to both. Furthermore, all constituents in the universe (currently developed and advanced emerging, but soon to include all emerging markets) are included in either the growth or value index, or both.

The following factors determine whether to include a stock in the value index: price-to-book ratio, price-to-sales ratio, price-to-cash flow, and dividend yield. The determinants for the growth index are 3-year historical sales growth, 3-year historical earnings-per-share growth, 2-year forward sales estimates, 2-year forward earnings-per-share estimates, and the equity growth rate (defined as ROE × [1 − Payout ratio]). FTSE then defines whether a stock is value or growth by normalizing the data derived from the aforementioned factors to find scores for both value and growth. After normalization, the data for each constituent are averaged to arrive at its particular Overall Style Ranking (OSR). Constituents are ranked according to their respective OSR on a scale of zero to one hundred (0 = High value; 100 = High growth). The cumulative investable market cap is then allocated to either value or growth along the following lines: The bottom 35 percent of adjusted market cap of high-growth stocks is allocated to the growth index at 100 percent; the top 35 percent of adjusted market cap of high-value stocks is allocated to the value index at 100 percent; and the middle 30 percent of adjusted market cap is apportioned across both indexes as 75/25 or 50/50.

The style indexes are implemented at the country level so that rebalancing at each country index equals 50 percent of the investable market capitalization of the underlying country index. After each semiannual rebalancing, value and growth weights are allowed to float. A constituent can appear in both the value and the growth indexes, thus the indexes are *allocative,* as is the approach adopted by MSCI.

The S&P/Citigroup Indexes (Previously the Salomon Smith Barney Indexes)
Standard & Poor's/Citigroup constructs its style indexes from the PMI and EMI indexes of each country, covering the size segment of style in addition to growth and value. Regional growth and value indexes are constructed by merging the corresponding growth and value indexes of the countries comprising each region. This methodology, when originally introduced by SSB, was among the most refined value/growth methodologies at the time.

Three growth and four value variables are used to assess the style of each constituent. For value stocks, these are book-to-price ratio, sales-to-price ratio, cash-flow-to-price ratio, and dividend yield. For growth stocks, the variables are 5-year historical EPS growth rate, 5-year historical sales per share growth rate, and 5-year average annual growth rate (defined as IGR = [ROE] × 1 – Payout ratio).

Cluster analysis is then used, and growth and value scores are calculated to show the relative magnitude of a stock's growth and value characteristics using equally weighted variables. High-growth and low-value stocks are considered to be pure growth; high-value and low-growth stocks are pure value. The remaining stocks' available market value is allocated to each of the indexes according to its growth and value probability weights. The weights are then adjusted so that the constituents of each style index comprise approximately 50 percent of the float capital of the PMI and EMI index within each country and region.

Standard & Poor's Global 1200 Series   S&P doesn't currently offer growth and value indexes for its non-U.S. "flagship" index series. The construction of the S&P 500 growth and value indexes is similar to MSCI's previous methodology of using price-to-book as the sole determinant. As the rest of the index community works to improve and extend its value/growth offerings, we anticipate S&P will follow suit with its Global 1200 ex-U.S. index and its subcomponents.

Dow Jones STOXX   Dow Jones has created separate benchmarks for the EuroZone for both growth and value stocks. They provide broad coverage of their respective style segments (the indexes are derived from the DJ STOXX Total Market Index, which covers 95 percent of European free-float market capitalization), are easy and cost-efficient to replicate, and minimize turnover (or style oscillation) among components.

Dow Jones's multifactor approach uses six criteria to determine inclusion. They include projected earnings growth (based on an expected 3- to 5-year annual increase in operating earnings per share), projected price-to-earnings ratio (based on the closing price at the semiannual review and on mean annual EPS for the next fiscal period), and dividend yield (based on the closing price at the semiannual review and on total dividends declared during the previous 12 months). The remaining factors are price-to-book ratio, trailing earnings growth (based on average annualized EPS growth for the previous 21 quarters), and trailing price-to-earnings ratio (based on the closing price at the semiannual review and on the previous quarter's EPS from continuing operations).

The indexes are reviewed twice annually, in March and September. To minimize turnover, a stock is reclassified only under certain conditions. If a nongrowth stock qualifies as Strong Growth for a single review period, it is reclassified as Growth. Similarly, if a nonvalue stock qualifies as Strong Value, it is reclassified as Value. If a Value stock qualifies as Weak Growth or a Growth stock qualifies as Weak Value, it is reclassified as Neutral. If a Value stock or a Growth stock qualifies as Neutral, it remains classified in its current category. If a Neutral stock qualifies as Weak Growth or Weak Value, it remains classified as Neutral. If for two consecutive periods, any stock qualifies as Value or Growth, it is reclassified into that category. Neutral stocks with a market capitalization of at least 0.5 percent of their size segment total market capitalization are selected as either growth or value stocks, based on the nearest cluster mean. In addition, these indexes can be further segmented in terms of capitalization range: large, mid, and small.

As readers can see from this relatively dense explanation of the different approaches to creating style indexes for international/global benchmarks, understanding the methodology "inside the indexes" is critical to both choosing the appropriate benchmark, and index-based products. Similarly, the definition of size/capitalization ranges can have a material impact on portfolios. Developments in both the style and size subcategories, as well as the broader international indexes, move rapidly within the financial industry, so readers are advised to visit the index providers' web sites, which can be accessed through the E-ppendix at www.ActiveInvesting.com and IndexUniverse.com.

CONCLUSIONS FOR A COMPLEX WORLD

While the theoretical implications of the benchmark decision are important, investors must consider numerous real-world issues in evaluating benchmarks. As is extensively discussed in Part Four (especially in Chapter 21), the ongoing frictional costs of managing international index portfolios can be substantial, and fund managers need to fully understand the indexes and the markets they cover in order to tightly track the indexes. Furthermore, transaction costs are an unavoidable component of index-based portfolio management. Every benchmark scores differently on the metrics of coverage, liquidity, turnover, and acceptance by investors.

Once these complex issues have been addressed, the trade-offs prioritized, and an appropriate benchmark chosen, transitioning to the new benchmark presents its own challenges. Plan sponsors implementing benchmark transitions should work with their brokers, consultants, and/or investment managers to produce a detailed plan before adopting or transitioning to a global benchmark.

There is nothing simple about international benchmarking. Nor is international index investing particularly passive—as Chapters 21 and 23 both highlight. Thus, the multiple choices cannot have easy answers that fit all investors' needs.

Finally, the complexity of the index decision should not be used to ignore or defer a choice. Asset allocation remains the most important investment decision. However, the choice of benchmarks on which to determine the asset allocation is critical, and thus, in effect, becomes almost as important as the allocation determinant itself.

North American investors are participating in a dynamic global equity market environment. An appropriate international policy allocation and benchmark will ensure that asset owners most efficiently capture the return and diversification opportunities that the world beyond domestic borders abundantly provides.

NOTES

1. This chapter draws heavily from two previously published monographs—Steven A. Schoenfeld, Peter Handley, and Binu George, "International Equity Benchmarks for U.S. Investors—Assessing the Alternatives, Contemplating the Trade-offs," *Investment Insights* (San Francisco: Barclays Global Investors, December 2000), and the updated and expanded version, by Steven A. Schoenfeld and Robert Ginis (November 2002). The authors acknowledge the contribution of their former colleagues, as well as that of David Kurapka, who assisted in editing the updated version and contributed to the development of this chapter. Given the rapid pace of developments with global equity benchmarks, the authors take full responsibility for the analysis and assertions in the chapter, and urge readers to seek out updated data and analysis. We recommend this chapter's E-ppendix entry at www.ActiveIndexInvesting.com and IndexUniverse.com as your starting point.
2. Fred Williams, "Still Attractive: Indexing Assets Steady Overall; Some Growth in Foreign Equity," *Pensions & Investments* (March 18, 2002): 32.

3. Charles Williamson, "It Was a Very Good Year: Institutional Money Managers Trounce Stock Market in '01," *Pensions & Investments* (May 27, 2002): 1.

4. Watson Wyatt, "Global Asset Study, Watson Wyatt Worldwide" (2002). Updated figures are cited in Chapter 31 along with predictions for the growth of global indexing.

5. MSCI Newswatch, Morgan Stanley Capital International, New York/Geneva (June 2002): Authors' Note: Most index providers' estimates of indexed and benchmarked assets tend to be exaggerated. An informal tally of the major global index vendors' market share claims result in total figures greater than world equity market capitalization.

6. Stephen Gorman, *The International Equity Commitment,* Research Foundation of the Institute of Chartered Financial Analysts (Charlottesville, VA, 1998) p. 39.

7. Ibid. pp. 39–55.

8. While this chapter focuses on international benchmarks from a North American perspective, the analysis is relevant for all non-domestic investment, whether the home country is the U.K., Japan, or smaller entities such as Singapore, Hong Kong, and Abu Dhabi, where institutional investors naturally take a thoroughly global perspective. This more global approach might also be appropriate for institutions in emerging markets such as Israel, the Czech Republic, or Chile. The "Web-only" sidebar by Hugh Wilson of State Street Global Advisors in this chapter's E-ppendix section at www.ActiveIndexInvesting.com explores most of the benchmarks covered in this chapter from a global perspective, or what we call "the Martian's view of the world's investment opportunity set."

9. *Source:* InterSec data as of December 2002.

10. The competition was *five-way* until the late-2003 assumption of calculation of the former Salomon Smith Barney indexes by Standard & Poor's, which is now integrating these U.S. and international indexes into their broad global benchmark offerings. For a more colorful view on the implications of these developments, see Jim Wiant's "The Inside Scoop" in the *Journal of Indexes* (first and second quarters, 2004), also available at www.IndexUniverse.com.

11. MSCI data as of December 2002.

12. Index vendors have become increasingly aware of the market impact (on stocks and occasionally entire markets) of their index reconstitutions. Therefore, they have solicited input from practitioners on ways to minimize the index inclusion effect and introduce longer notification periods, phase in of changes, parallel implementation, and other innovations in index construction and maintenance (see Chapter 5 and the sidebar within Chapter 6).

13. See www.IndexStrategy.com or www.globalindexstrategies.com for contact information.

14. As noted in the text, index turnover has attenuated since the late 1990s (with its vibrant M&A activity) and early 2000s (with major structural changes to both the MSCI and FTSE indexes due to float adjustment). Authors can be contacted via information in footnote 13.

15. Information on GICS can be obtained at www.MSCI.com and www.standardandpoors.com.

CHAPTER 10

Fixed-Income Benchmarks

Vache Mahseredjian and Mark Friebel

_____ **Editor's Note** _____

Although many investors naturally think of equities when the discussion turns to indexing, benchmarks have a significant role in fixed-income markets, and the use of index-based products has been growing steadily. This chapter discusses the distinctive features of bond markets that drive the requirements for a good fixed-income index. Vache Mahseredjian and Mark Friebel adapt the same framework of analysis of "best practices" in index construction established in Chapter 6 and apply it to the major fixed-income indexes. The authors address two major questions: How much does the choice of indexes matter? and, why and how are bond indexes different from equity indexes? The authors point out that, within a single market, most of the major bond indexes are over 90 percent correlated with each other. Differentiations occur primarily over smaller bond issues, or over a limited number of structures, such as bonds with put or call features, which may be included in one index, but not in another. Therefore, the choice of benchmark index often becomes a decision based on finer points. For the second question, the authors identify four primary differences between fixed-income benchmarks and stock indexes which I believe that readers will find illuminating. The chapter also provides a valuable history of the development of U.S. bond indexes. Although fixed-income indexes are generally well known only among financial professionals, with the advent of bond ETFs in Canada, the United States, and Europe, fixed-income indexes will become increasingly

_____

The terms fixed income and bonds are used interchangeably in this chapter, even though there are important technical differences especially regarding the instruments' terms and duration. The editor and authors request readers' forbearance and believe that this does not detract from the main points made in the chapter.

prominent. I therefore believe that their role within the context of the four key uses of indexes, as described in Chapter 5, will steadily grow.

The chapter ends with a sidebar on commodity indexes, as such this chapter begins Part Two's transition to a discussion of alternative asset class benchmarks and applications of indexes, which continues in Chapter 11.

U ntil relatively recently, the vast majority of investors focused primarily on stocks and had little interest in, or awareness of, bonds. The nightly news and the popular press seldom mentioned the bond market. Occasionally, the yield of a Treasury security would be reported, but there was no discussion of the market's performance. Whereas many investors could quote the level of the Dow Jones Industrial Average, the S&P 500, or the Nasdaq index, and could recite how these indexes performed in recent periods, very few people outside the bond profession were familiar with bond market performance. But that has begun to change. One of the catalysts was *performance*. As Table 10.1 shows, bonds outperformed stocks by a wide margin over the 5 years ending December 2002.

This robust performance was driven by a decline in interest rates to lows not seen in over 40 years. Lower interest rates began to capture the attention of home owners who could now refinance their homes more cheaply. The resulting increase in disposable income fueled greater consumer spending, the sole source of strength in the U.S. economy in recent years.

Another catalyst was an *increase in transparency*. Bonds are traded in an over-the-counter market, not on a physical exchange. This means that trades are conducted over the telephone or via computer terminals linking the buyer and seller. Because no central exchange is involved, the trade information is not widely disseminated. In addition, many bonds don't trade on any given day, resulting in certain sectors that are illiquid and obscure. But this, too, has begun to change. The bond market's natural evolution, prompted by reg-

TABLE 10.1 Total Returns for Periods Ending 12/31/02

Year	Lehman Brothers U.S. Aggregate Bond Index (%)	Wilshire 5000 Index (%)
1	10.27	−20.86
3	10.10	−14.37
5	7.54	−.87
10	7.51	8.74

Data source: Lehman Brothers, Wilshire Associates.

ulatory agencies' desire to promote transparency, has increased the dissemination of information about trades. This will eventually lead to greater liquidity, which in turn will enhance awareness of, and interest in, bonds. And the greater investors' demand for bonds, the greater their need for benchmarks to measure the performance of the managers they have hired. As discussed in previous chapters, this is exactly where indexes come in.

ROLE OF FIXED-INCOME INDEXES

To understand the key role of bond indexes, we must consider three important themes. *First,* human beings are competitive by nature. Within the arena of investing, everyone competes for the highest profits and returns. But it is widely accepted that the key to achieving the highest returns is having superior information and analysis. Therefore, the competition for returns becomes a competition for information.

Second, as mentioned, historically there has been a lack of information and transparency in the bond market. Indexes help fill this void. Their primary role is to define the market by giving it structure. An index can define either a broad market or a narrow segment and can provide critical information—such as price, yield, and duration—on the individual bonds that compose the market. Indexes also describe the market's composition in terms of sector and industry weights, maturity profile, and credit rating distribution. Indexes provide a common ground for discussions about the market. Without an index, how would two people reach agreement on what constitutes the market, either in broad terms (the U.S. bond market) or narrow terms (high-yield bonds rated B)?

Once an index defines a market, it can be used for other purposes, as discussed in Chapter 5. Indexes enable investors to make strategic asset allocation decisions; they provide investment managers with a baseline for constructing portfolios; and they are an objective measure of investment performance. Indexes also help broker/dealers in making trade recommendations to investment managers and in advising bond issuers about popular market sectors. By providing information to all market participants, bond indexes help level the playing field. Indexes make the bond market more efficient by eliminating the information advantage formerly held by a few.

Our *third* main theme is innovation. The need to sustain an advantage being eroded by the dissemination of information drives innovation. Every few years, a new type of security is created that, by virtue of being new, is not in the established indexes. Examples are numerous, but the prototypical example is the development of the mortgage-backed securities (MBS) market in the mid-1980s. Previously, the most popular broad investment grade bond indexes included only government and corporate bonds. The evaluation of the prepayment option embedded in MBS was little understood, and those who had superior information on the composition of the underlying pools of mortgages, as well as superior quantitative tools, were able to generate large profits. As these securities became better understood, they were added to the broad market indexes. In the process, information on pool characteristics and analytics became more widely available, greatly reducing the potential for profit. As mortgage-backed securities became more mainstream, forces of innovation led to the creation of structures such as asset-backed securities (ABS) and commercial mortgage-backed securities (CMBS), and in time these sectors also were absorbed into the established market indexes. The very act of adding a new sector to an index fosters the further development of that new sector because index inclusion brings the sector to the attention of more investors. This leads to greater intermediation between borrowers and lenders.

So we are witnessing a cycle in which the competitive spirit leads to the development of new securities, and as those markets develop and mature, they are absorbed into the broad indexes. In the process, their profit potential declines, and so the competitive drive fuels further innovation. The evolution of bond indexes reflects this innovation and expansion.

WHAT EXACTLY IS A BOND INDEX?

A bond index is nothing more than a collection of bonds. The index is determined by its constituents, which are in turn defined by a set of entry and exit rules. All major U.S. bond indexes are reconstituted on a monthly basis: A set of bonds is defined as constituting the index at the beginning of the month. Most bond index providers apply a rules-based approach to screen and identify index constituents although some index vendors also apply qualitative screens. Most rules-based indexes have constraints on the bond's issuer, structure (maturity, coupon type), rating, and issue size.

Whether index constituents are determined objectively or subjectively by the index provider, index mechanics are remarkably similar. Each bond is assigned a price at the beginning of the period, and this price, along with the bond's starting accrued interest, determines the bond's initial market value. The product of the bond's market value and its principal (or par) amount outstanding determines the total starting market value attributable to that bond as well as the percentage of the total index market value attributable to that bond. The same bonds are valued at the end of the month (with accrued interest to the end of the month), and the product of the ending market value times the ending principal amount (which may have decreased) determines the total ending market value attributable to the specific bond. An adjustment is made to the ending value by adding back any intramonth coupon payments and principal repayments. (Index vendors differ in their treatment of these intramonth cash flows. Lehman Brothers assumes the cash stays uninvested until the end of the month, whereas Citigroup reinvests the cash at an appropriate short-term rate until the end of the month.) Dividing the ending market value by the beginning market value (and then subtracting 1) results in a total return for each bond. A weighted average of these individual bond returns, using the market value percentages calculated at the beginning of the month as weights, provides the total return of the index. At the end of the month, a new set of bonds is identified to compose the index for the following month.

DESIRABLE INDEX CHARACTERISTICS

The *seven key criteria* for a good index that were articulated in Chapter 6 apply to fixed-income benchmarks as well as to stock indexes. We give examples of the relevance of these criteria:

1. *Completeness.* An index should accurately reflect the overall opportunity set within an asset class. All the broad bond benchmarks are rules-based so that any bond that meets the eligibility requirements is included. Typical eligibility requirements for the U.S. market are that a bond must be U.S. dollar-denominated, nonconvertible, publicly issued, have a fixed coupon or one that changes according to a prespecified schedule, have a minimum maturity of 1 year, a minimum issue size, and satisfy credit rating constraints.
2. *Investability.* The bonds in an index should be available for purchase at a reasonable transaction cost. However, as described in Chapter 6, here is an inherent trade-off between completeness and investability. The minimum issue size requirement exists specifically to exclude small issues, which typically are not as liquid. Over time, index providers have raised the minimum issue size requirement to keep current with issuance practices.
3. *Clear published rules.* The index rules should be clear, thorough, and publicly available so that there is no doubt about whether a bond is included, how cash flows from coupons and prepayments are treated, and how the index returns and characteristics (e.g., yield and duration) are calculated.
4. *Accurate and complete data.* Because bonds have historically been traded in an over-the-counter market, there has not been a central storehouse of information, particularly outside the Treasury sector. The index providers themselves have therefore played a vital role in

storing this information, which is of keen interest to investment managers, consultants, and researchers. Some index providers guard historical data more closely than others. Ideally, an index should provide constituent-level historical information on prices and characteristics for each bond; it should also include the index returns and statistics at the aggregate level as well as for subsectors.

Gaining access to accurate prices has always been a challenge in the bond market. In the past, the most accurate prices were available at month end because everyone focuses on monthly returns. (And since price determines characteristics such as yield and duration, month-end characteristics were the most accurate.) With the growth of electronic trading, end-of-day statistics are improving in quality. And with the advent of index-related products such as ETFs (which trade on a stock exchange), real-time data is within reach.

In addition to bond prices and index statistics, the best index providers also provide software that enables investors to analyze individual securities as well as entire portfolios. This software enables investment managers to analyze the risks inherent in a portfolio both on an absolute basis and relative to the index. The software can also do performance attribution, to identify the sources of return. Although such software could be developed in-house or purchased from an independent party, the advantage of using the index provider's software is that the prices and portfolio calculations are identical with those used to maintain the index.

5. *Acceptance by investors.* Investors will accept an index that meets the previously listed criteria. In other words, if an index accurately reflects its market by being complete yet investable, has clear rules, and provides accurate data, it will succeed. In addition, investors are more likely to accept an index if they have a voice in shaping it. As an example, Lehman Brothers conducts roundtable meetings and invites investment managers, consultants, and other market participants to express their opinions on index-related matters. Though less formal, this also serves a similar purpose as the equity index committees described in previous chapters.

6. *Availability of tradable products.* Several investment managers provide index funds designed to track either the broad bond market or specific sectors. As discussed later in this chapter, the broad indexes are so highly correlated, that the choice of index matters relatively little, especially when compared with equity indexes. In the corporate sector (specifically in the high-yield sector), however, the choice of index can have a significant impact on returns. Because the high-yield market is much less liquid than the other sectors of the bond market, this sector most clearly exemplifies the inherent trade-off between completeness

and investability. In fact, several index providers have created liquid high-yield indexes by limiting the number of issues or setting a high minimum issue requirement.

Unlike the S&P 500 and other flagship equity indexes, which have futures and options contracts that track them, no broad bond index has an associated exchange-traded derivative. However, index returns can be achieved through swaps, and various brokers have proprietary products for trading baskets of bonds. And, of course, ETFs are now available on an ever-increasing range of fixed-income market sectors and are discussed in Chapter 22.

7. *Relatively low turnover and transactions costs.* All the major bond indexes are reconstituted on a monthly basis, and turnover arises from bonds entering and exiting the index each month. Bonds that satisfy the entry requirements are added to the index at the month-end following their issue date, so this source of turnover is a function of issuance volume. On the exit side, turnover occurs because a bond's maturity falls below 1 year, it no longer meets the credit rating requirement, or it gets called. Prepayments (i.e., bonds getting called) can be a significant source of turnover in the MBS sector when sharp declines in interest rates lead to high refinancing rates by home owners.

Within the broad, investment-grade indexes, there is no material difference in turnover rates. Turnover only becomes a significant issue in comparing high-yield indexes in their treatment of fallen angels. In the high-yield market, new bonds enter either as a newly issued high-yield bond, or as a fallen angel—a bond originally issued as an investment grade bond that has since been downgraded. Index vendors differ in their treatment of fallen angels—as some allow the bond to enter in the month following its downgrade, whereas others require a "seasoning period," typically 1 to 2 months. But the real issue is neither turnover per se nor the associated transaction costs, but the performance of the fallen angels and their impact on the performance of the overall index.

HISTORY AND OVERVIEW OF U.S. BOND/FIXED-INCOME INDEXES

In the United States, the modern era of bond indexes dates back to the early 1970s, and the indexes maintained by broker/dealers play the predominant role.[1] The passage of ERISA in 1974 had a tremendous impact not only by safeguarding pensions, but also by fostering the growth of the institutional investment management industry, as well as the investment consulting business.[2] These institutional investors and advisors needed benchmarks to define the market and to measure manager performance.

In this environment, the broker/dealers identified a need for bond index information that they were ideally positioned to provide. The lack of a bond exchange meant that there was no accepted measure of the bond market (like the myriad of "flagship" equity indexes discussed in Chapters 5 through 9) and no readily available source of end-of-day prices. The broker/dealers also recognized that they could benefit by offering indexes and providing information because, in the process, they received valuable information in return. It is well recognized that a key part of an institutional bond salesperson's role is to provide information to his or her trading desk on what customers (the investment managers) are thinking and doing. This information is extremely valuable in determining the proprietary positions traders take (the dealer function) and often much more profitable than the bid/ask spread they earn from doing customer trades (the broker function). At the same time, investment managers needed information on the index rules and analytics, so they could construct portfolios that outperformed the index. Bond broker/dealers went into the index business because they realized that becoming the provider of an index meant that instead of having to go to the market to find out what others were thinking, the market would come to them. The important point is not which side benefited most from the relationship—because both sides were better off, as in Adam Smith's "invisible hand"—but that information became broadly disseminated. And indexes were the agent in that information exchange.

The following overview highlights the major bond indexes but does not attempt to provide a comprehensive list of U.S. bond indexes and their construction methodology. In fact, new indexes are being introduced with such frequency that an all-inclusive list could not remain comprehensive for long. In addition, the construction methodology of existing indexes changes periodically, rendering many previously published overviews obsolete. (For example, minimum issue-size requirements increase every few years.) The best sources of information are the broker/dealers and index fund managers themselves. The E-ppendix www.ActiveIndexInvesting.com contains the Internet addresses of the firms that offer a broad set of indexes or products based on these indexes. IndexUniverse.com also provides more background information and the actual links.

Lehman Brothers is the leading provider of U.S. bond indexes, and its flagship index, the U.S. Aggregate Bond Index, is the benchmark that U.S. institutional investors most often use. The other major providers of indexes include Citigroup and Merrill Lynch. All three maintain numerous indexes spanning investment grade and noninvestment grade markets both domestically and globally. JP Morgan offers a more limited number of indexes, but its emerging market bond indexes are the best known in that universe. Other dealers that offer indexes include Goldman Sachs, Morgan Stanley, and CSFB.

In the United States, there are three main measures of the broad U.S. investment-grade bond market. Lehman Brothers has its U.S. Aggregate, Citigroup maintains its Broad Investment Grade (BIG), and Merrill Lynch has its Domestic Master. These indexes employ a modular structure with subindexes that reflect a specific sector. Lehman's U.S. Aggregate Index comprises the following sectors: Treasury, Agency, Credit (consisting of bonds issued by U.S. corporations, as well as U.S. dollar-denominated bonds issued by foreign entities), mortgage-backed securities (MBS), asset-backed securities (ABS), and commercial mortgage-backed securities (CMBS). Table 10.2 shows the sector composition of the Lehman U.S. Aggregate Bond Index as of 12/31/02. Each of these sectors can be further divided into subsidiary indexes based on maturity, credit rating, or subsector. Using these as building blocks, investors can customize indexes to suit their needs. For example, by eliminating bonds that mature in more than 10 years, one can construct the Intermediate Aggregate Index. Similarly, by eliminating bonds rated below A, one arrives at what Lehman calls its Aggregate A+ Index.

The composition of the three firms' broad investment grade bond indexes reflects each provider's index construction methodology, most notably its unique rules for eligibility, index entry, and exit. In addition, each index provider uses proprietary prices to value the constituent bonds, and each uses a different procedure for handling intramonth cash flows. It is no surprise, therefore, that there are material differences in the composition of the indexes in terms of number of issues, market values, sector weights, and descriptive statistics.

Despite these structural differences, the long-term performance of the broad indexes is almost identical. For the 10 years ending 12/31/2002, the annualized returns for Lehman's U.S. Aggregate Index, Citigroup's BIG Index, and Merrill Lynch's Domestic Master Index are 7.51 percent, 7.53 percent, and 7.57 percent, respectively. For the same period, the pairwise correlations

TABLE 10.2 Sector Composition of the Lehman U.S. Aggregate Bond Index

Sector	Weight (%)
Asset-backed securities	1.61
Commercial mortgage-backed securities	2.33
Credit	26.26
Treasury & Agency	34.78
Mortgage-backed securities	35.02

Note: Data as of 12/31/02. Updates available at www.ishares.com and www.lehman.com.

are all in excess of 99.8 percent. A comparison of the major subindexes that make up the broad indexes shows that the three index providers' government and MBS sector returns are similar, whereas the corporate indexes exhibit significant dispersion of return. And the dispersion in returns is even more pronounced among the various high-yield indexes, because in that sector there is less agreement on what constitutes the market, and there is greater variability in pricing.

An interesting index that uses a different approach is the Citigroup U.S. Large Pension Fund (LPF) Baseline Bond Index. This index uses static sector weights—40 percent government bonds, 30 percent collateralized bonds (MBS and ABS), and 30 percent Credit—and has a minimum maturity of 7 years for all non-MBS issues. Because of the minimum maturity requirement, this index has a longer duration than the standard broad market indexes and appeals to pension plans seeking a long duration bond portfolio to match their long-lived liabilities.

FIXED-INCOME INDEX EVOLUTION

The evolution of bond indexes reflects the expansion of the bond market in general, and in particular, the creation of new security structures. This transformation has some similarities to the evolution of international indexes discussed in the previous chapter, particularly in the vital role that benchmark indexes play in defining an evolving asset class.

The bond indexes of the early- to mid-1970s consisted of Treasury and Agency bonds, as well as a few of the most liquid corporate bonds. Until the late 1980s and early 1990s, Lehman Brothers' Government/Corporate Bond Index was the most commonly used benchmark. Then, following the development of the mortgage-backed securities market, Lehman introduced the U.S. Aggregate Index, which consisted of the Government/Corporate Index, plus MBS.[3] Over the years, the Aggregate Index has been expanded to include new sectors/security types as those markets became sufficiently developed. At the end of 1980, the Government sector (consisting of Treasury and Agency bonds) represented 54 percent of the Aggregate Index. By the end of 2002, that percentage had declined to 35 percent. At the end of 1980, 25 percent of the corporate market was rated Aaa by Moody's and only 13 percent was rated Baa; by the end of 2002, Aaa-rated bonds had declined to 10 percent of the Credit market, while Baa-rated bonds increased to 34 percent.

The major index providers devoted most of the past 20 years to expanding coverage of their indexes to encompass as many sectors of the global bond market as possible. In 1999, Lehman introduced its U.S. Universal Index, which attempts to capture the entire U.S. market by including sectors rated below investment grade (e.g., high-yield and emerging-market bonds) in addition to the sectors included in the Aggregate Index.[4] That same year, coincident with the growth in the corporate and collateralized bond markets overseas, Lehman attempted to map the global investment-grade market by introducing its Global Aggregate Index. The corresponding indexes offered by Citigroup and Merrill Lynch are, respectively, the Global Broad Investment Grade (or Global BIG) Index and the Global Master. An even more comprehensive index, encompassing both investment-grade and below-investment-grade bonds globally is Lehman's MultiVerse Index (introduced in 2001), comprising their Universal indexes of the United States, Europe, and Asia.

With the majority of the global bond markets now covered, the most recent trend has been the rise in *constrained* and *liquid* bond indexes. Constrained indexes limit the contribution of any single issuer, while liquid indexes are limited to very large issuers. Three related factors motivated the introduction of these indexes: the significant underperformance of corporate bonds relative to Treasury securities in 1998, 2000, and 2002; the attendant decline in bond market liquidity; and the development of the trading of baskets of bonds. The decline in liquidity began following the Asian crisis and the demise of the hedge fund Long-Term Capital Management in 1998, and reached a low point in the summer of 2002 following a record number of corporate bond downgrades and defaults. The relative underperformance of corporate bonds, combined with reduced liquidity, created demand for well-diversified portfolios and the ability to quickly enter and exit the corporate bond market by trading a basket of bonds. The development of new products such as bond and fixed-income exchange-traded funds (ETFs), which require the ability to value a liquid set of bonds throughout the day, have also created demand for indexes of liquid bonds.

HOW BOND INDEXES DIFFER FROM STOCK INDEXES

There are a variety of key differences between fixed-income benchmarks and stock indexes. We have identified four major ones. The single biggest difference between stock and bond indexes is that there is no widely accepted source of bond prices. Except for the most liquid sectors of the market—Treasuries, MBS, and certain Agency bonds—ascertaining the current price of a bond can be a significant challenge. Even end-of-day prices can vary considerably. The rules for inclusion in a bond index vary from dealer to dealer, so that the constituents in one dealer's index of corporate bonds can be materially different from those in the corporate index of another dealer.

Naturally, these two indexes will generate different returns. However, even if there were complete agreement on which bonds to include, the returns still would not match because each dealer uses its own prices to value the index. This situation will likely improve in the near future. The desire on the part of the Securities and Exchange Commission (SEC) and the National Association of Securities Dealers (NASD) to increase transparency in the corporate bond market has led to the development of the Trade Reporting and Compliance Engine, or TRACE, program. TRACE makes trade information—price and volume—publicly available for thousands of bonds. Though this program is still in its infancy, it is expected to have a profound impact on the bond market. Once the program develops, TRACE could become the accepted source for valuation prices.

Even with complete agreement on prices, different investors can reach different conclusions on the risk characteristics and relative value of bonds with uncertain cash flows. Different prepayment assumptions for MBS can lead to materially different duration and option-adjusted spread calculations. Another difference is that, unlike stocks, bonds have a stated maturity date. Therefore, with the passage of time, a bond's risk characteristics change. These are just two examples of how bond managers have to actively manage the risk of their portfolios relative to their benchmarks.

Another significant difference with stock indexes is that bond indexes can have a fairly high turnover rate. Lehman Brothers estimates that the turnover of its Aggregate Index typically ranges between 30 and 40 percent. The index is reconstituted monthly, and each month a bond can exit because of a downgrade or the passage of time (the time to maturity falls below 1 year). Another source of index turnover is mortgage prepayment. In recent years, as interest rates reached historical lows, the record refinancing rate by home owners led to very fast MBS prepayment rates, resulting in MBS index turnover rates in excess of 50 percent. A final source of index turnover is that new bonds are added each month.

The third important difference between stock and bond indexes is that a given issuer may be represented several times in a bond index, whereas it will typically be counted only once in a stock index. A corporation may issue bonds of varying seniority in the capital structure, as well as different maturities. Therefore, even among the bonds of a single issuer, an investor can select securities with different levels of credit risk and interest rate risk.

A fourth major difference is the rich variety of security structures in the bond market. Unlike the equity indexes, which consist almost exclusively of common stocks (although some indexes include preferred and/or foreign stocks), the broad bond indexes comprise several types of securities. In addition to debentures, there are bonds collateralized by various assets (including residential property, commercial property, credit card receivables, automobiles, manufactured housing, and utility payments) and each has a slightly different structure. The bond market is vibrant and ever expanding, and bond indexes expand to reflect this growth. Because of the multitude of security types, however, no index can fully reflect the market's diversity. For example, bonds whose cash flows are derived from other bonds, such as zero coupon U.S. Treasury securities (STRIPS) and mortgage derivatives (e.g., collateralized mortgage obligations [CMOs], interest only [IOs], principal only [POs]) are not included in indexes. Also not included are floating-rate securities, whose unique characteristics make grouping and classification difficult.

CONCLUSION

Because most fixed-income securities are not traded on a centralized exchange, any discussion of this huge global market would be vague without reference to an index. Bond indexes define the market by giving it structure and a framework for analysis. They bring transparency by providing critical information to all market participants, and in the process, they make the bond market more efficient. And the advent of fixed-income index-based investment vehicles, such as index funds and ETFs, has accelerated this process. Because indexes illuminate the market, it is fair to say that the most opaque, least understood parts of the bond market are those not included in an index.

Bond indexes enable investors to make strategic asset allocation decisions, and they serve as performance benchmarks for investment managers. In reviewing desirable index characteristics, we found that the *seven key criteria* for a good index detailed in Chapter 6 apply equally to bonds as to stocks, despite the major differences between stock indexes and fixed-income benchmarks. We therefore wholeheartedly endorse these criteria as a robust framework for assessing the two primary investable asset classes—stocks and bonds.

The modern era of bond indexes dates back to the early 1970s, when most indexes consisted of government and corporate bonds. Since then, new sectors such as MBS and ABS have been introduced, and bond indexes have expanded to incorporate the new sectors. Although each index provider has its own rules and uses its own prices, there is little difference in returns among the broad, investment-grade bond indexes offered by Lehman Brothers, Merrill Lynch, or Salomon (now Citigroup, as the Salomon Smith Barney indexes were re-branded effective in April 2003 and adopted the Citigroup name). The biggest difference in performance arises in the corporate market, particularly in the high-yield sector.

The efforts of index providers to broaden coverage of their global indexes to new sectors is unending; at the same time, a recent trend has been the rise in liquid indexes. This has been driven partly by demand from investment managers who want narrower indexes more reflective of their actual portfolios in the high-yield sector and also by the introduction of bond fixed-income ETFs in Canada, the United States, and Europe, which require intraday pricing. The lack of accurate pricing information has always been a challenge, particularly for corporate bonds, but the development of the NASD's TRACE program is expected to significantly increase price transparency in the corporate sector.

In closing, bond indexes have played a pivotal role in the development of the fixed-income marketplace. Indexes have provided definition to the market, thereby making the market more comprehensible to investors. This, in turn, has fostered the market's growth. The recent development of fixed-income ETFs around the world—the management of which is discussed in Chapters 22 and 23—has also highlighted the role of bond indexes. In the future, the need for accurate bond indexes will escalate as the continually expanding global bond market increases in complexity.

Editor's Note

Just as fixed-income indexes have helped bring more transparency and a framework for analysis to the bond market, commodity indexes are doing the same for this "real" asset class. With this sidebar, Part Two will now shift to a focus on alternative asset class benchmarks with a discussion of commodity indexes, and continue in the following chapter on Hedge Fund Indexes. A third "alternative" asset class—Real Estate—is covered in Chapter 17, in Part Three, while others are discussed in the book's E-ppendix at www.ActiveIndexInvesting.com.

COMMODITY INDEXES—TAMING A WILD ASSET CLASS
David Burkart and Mark Friebel

Commodities are one of the oldest asset classes, and the related futures markets offer very investable vehicles to gain exposure. Commodities present low to negative correlation with traditional asset classes, strong average returns relative to equities and bonds, and standard deviations comparable to equities. Four main indexes exist: the Goldman Sachs Commodities Index (GSCI), the Commodity Research Bureau Index (CRBI), the Standard & Poor's Commodity Index (SPCI), and the Dow Jones AIG Commodity Index (DJ-AIG). The Commodity Research Bureau Index is the oldest and most widely recognized, but has little following among practitioners because of liquidity issues around its equal-weighted components. Standard & Poor's offers a commodity index that has no gold, while the DJ-AIG index is well established, with both futures and Commodity TRAKRS (Total Return Asset Contracts) available on the benchmark. Goldman Sach's index offers a relatively wide industry following, as measured by volume/open interest on the futures contract, and numerous swaps and derivative notes support it. Also, with five subindexes and coverage of 25 contracts, its breadth is the widest.

As of this writing, there are currently two commodity index-based mutual funds in the United States offered by PIMCO and Oppenheimer, and a number of firms are working on ETF-like products for gold, crude oil, and other commodities. More information on commodity indexes and index products is available in the Gold/Commodities section of IndexUniverse.com.

NOTES

1. Other providers of less commonly used, or specialized, bond indexes include the U.S. Treasury (constant maturity indexes), futures exchanges, investment managers, industry publications, and advisory firms. In addition, in certain sectors where mutual funds play a large role (e.g., municipal bonds and high-yield bonds), the peer group averages maintained by the mutual fund rating firms are sometimes used as benchmarks of performance.
2. ERISA is the abbreviation for Employees Retirement Income Security Act, which was enacted by the U.S. Congress in 1974.
3. Although Lehman introduced the U.S. Aggregate Index in 1986, it was created with 10 years of prior data. Therefore, information on returns, sector weights, and characteristics is available dating back to 1976.
4. The choice of the name Universal is unfortunate, since the index consists only of U.S. dollar-denominated bonds.

CHAPTER 11

Hedge Fund Benchmarks and Asset Allocation

Mark Anson

_____ **Editor's Note** _____

This chapter provides an overview of the burgeoning field of hedge fund performance measurement and benchmarks.[1] It defines the methodology, scope, and limitations of these universes and how investors are increasingly using them for asset allocation. Although many would argue whether these new investable universes are indexes at all, the industry certainly will be using them in the same way that they use equity and fixed-income indexes. In fact, all four of the primary uses of indexes described in Chapter 5 are already being applied with hedge fund benchmarks. Thus, it is vital to understand their construction methodology, relative strengths and weaknesses. Furthermore, hedge fund indexes are beginning to be used as the underlying basis for index funds, and potential investors must understand the attributes of these products. Thus, a sidebar in this chapter describes the rapidly expanding world of investable hedge fund indexes.

From their inception in the 1960s, and during their growth in the 1970s and 1980s, hedge funds were primarily the domain of individuals with high net worth and of some pioneering foundations and endowments including those of Yale and Harvard universities. In the 1990s, however, large institutional investors discovered the benefits of these investments. Endowments were first, followed by corporate and public pension plans.

_____

This chapter represents the insights and opinions of the author and not the author's employer.

As more and more institutional investors entered the hedge fund arena, they demanded many of the same investment parameters from their traditional long-only programs.

Generally, institutional investors using external investment managers have three requirements:

1. A well-defined investment process.
2. Transparency.
3. Relative returns.

This chapter focuses on the last requirement—relative returns. Relative returns are one of the primary reasons for index construction. However, hedge funds strive for absolute returns. Thus, hedge fund indexes actually attempt to define this asset class (which generally is considered beta) by, in effect, measuring alpha, or "excess return."

The chapter first reviews the construction of hedge fund indexes. It is followed by a comparison of hedge fund universes and indexes currently in existence. Third, we consider the selection of hedge fund indexes, and then conclude by looking at the diverse asset allocation outcomes that are derived from different benchmarks.

HEDGE FUNDS AS AN INVESTMENT

Before discussing hedge fund indexes, it is necessary to address a threshold question: Should investors consider hedge funds as part of a diversified portfolio? Considerable research has pursued this issue, and the answer is consistently, *yes*.

As Brown, Goetzmann, and Ibbotson (1999) note, the most interesting feature of the hedge fund industry is that an investment in a hedge fund is almost a "pure bet" on the skill of a specific manager.[2] Hedge fund managers seek out arbitrage or mispricing opportunities in the financial markets using cash and derivative instruments. They tend to take small amounts of market exposure to exploit mispricing opportunities, employing large amounts of leverage to extract the greatest value. The key point is that hedge fund managers pursue investment strategies unfettered by conventional financial market, asset-class benchmarks. Their investment styles are "alpha-driven" instead of "beta-driven." Thus, hedge fund benchmarks are actually measuring alpha, and the relative alpha of these managers, not the beta of a specific asset class.

Table 11.1 shows that hedge funds have favorable risk/return attributes compared with traditional stocks and bonds, at least in the recent past. In

TABLE 11.1   Sharpe Ratios for Hedge
Fund and Capital Market Indexes

Tuna Funds	1.28
Van Hedge	0.59
Hennessee	0.84
MAR	0.77
HFR	0.89
EACM	0.61
Zurich	0.52
Tremont	0.59
S&P Index	0.88
MSCI Equal Weight	0.88
MSCI Asset Weight	0.53
Barclay CTA	0.70
S&P 500	0.36
Russell 1000	0.30
Russell 2000	0.25
10-Year T-bond	0.43

Second Quarter (2003) data/calculations.

the Sharpe ratios for several hedge fund universes/indexes as well as stock market indexes and U.S. Treasury bonds, the hedge fund indexes have higher ratios than either stocks or bonds.

Furthermore, many studies document the diversification benefits of hedge funds. Goldman Sachs and Financial Risk Management (1999, 2000), in two reports covering two time periods (1993–1997 and 1994–1998), investigate the interaction of hedge fund returns with traditional asset classes.[3] In their first study, a portfolio of 60 percent S&P 500, 30 percent Lehman Aggregate Bonds, and 10 percent hedge funds outperformed the Pension Plan Index of 60/40 split of stocks and bonds by 78 basis points, with a reduction in portfolio standard deviation by 31 basis points. In their second study (which included the turbulent year of 1998) the portfolio with hedge funds outperformed the 60/40 Pension Plan Index by 48 basis points, but volatility increased by 14 basis points.

Similar results are found in other studies. Lamm (1999) suggests that hedge funds may act as a cash or fixed-income substitute for a diversified portfolio because of their low volatility and high absolute return.[4] Purcell and Crowley (1999) find that including hedge funds in a diversified portfolio can increase the expected return by as much as 200 basis points.[5] Edwards and Liew (1999) find that an unconstrained optimization including stocks, bonds, and a hedge fund of funds allocates 84 percent to the hedge fund of funds, 7 percent to the S&P 500, and 10 percent to long-term bonds.[6]

Hedge funds in aggregate have consistently demonstrated the ability to add value to a traditional portfolio of stocks and bonds. With respect to the growing number of hedge fund indexes, they currently have three key uses (along the paradigm established in Chapters 5 and 6). First, they serve as a proxy for the hedge fund asset class and thus are an indicator of the alpha delivery of the hedge fund industry. Second, these indexes—or universes—of past performance are the primary tool investors use to determine the appropriate asset allocation to this burgeoning asset class. Third, hedge fund indexes can serve as performance benchmarks to judge the success or failure of individual hedge fund managers or style category. As this chapter will demonstrate, there are many differences among the several hedge fund index products, and like the assessment of equity and fixed-income indexes previously in this part of the book, it is essential to understand those distinctions. And finally, as the sidebar by Hookway and Schoenfeld describes, they are beginning to have the same fourth use—as the basis for investment products—as their equity and fixed-income counterparts. Thus, investable hedge fund indexes and their linked hedge fund index funds are emerging as an alternative to actively managed funds of funds for obtaining the diversifying portfolio effect from varied hedge fund styles and managers.

KEY ISSUES WITH HEDGE FUND INDEX CONSTRUCTION

As of this writing, there are 10 hedge fund indexes warranting discussion, although others are sure to have been created post-writing and pre-publication. (Updates are available on this chapter's E-ppendix entry at www.ActiveIndexInvesting.com.) Each index is based on a different number of hedge funds, ranging from 60 to over 2,000. Most of these indexes use equal-weighted averages, while some use capitalization-weighted indexes. Also, some index providers collect the underlying data themselves, while others allow the hedge fund managers to submit the data. The indexes vary greatly in the number and type of strategies, and the inclusion or exclusion of multistrategy funds, long-only funds, and funds of funds. In addition, some hedge fund indexes include managed futures, whereas others do not. Thus, there are many construction techniques for hedge fund indexes, and the diverse methodologies naturally result in diverse characteristics of these benchmarks.

The Size of the Hedge Fund Universe

A major problem with constructing a hedge fund index is that the size of the total universe of hedge funds is not known with certainty and is constantly evolving. Depending on which report you choose, there are 5,000, 6,000, or 7,000 hedge funds in existence with assets ranging from $500 billion to $1 trillion.[7]

The uncertainty over the true size of the hedge fund industry stems mostly from the lack of regulation and from its being a restricted, disperse, and opaque industry.[8] Hedge funds in the United States are not required to register with the Securities and Exchange Commission (SEC) and are not required to report or publish their performance data.[9] This is in marked contrast to their mutual fund and unit trust counterparts, who must report performance to investors, which is then covered by database providers such as Lipper, Morningstar, and S&P, to name just a few.

Mutual funds are regulated investment companies that must register with the SEC. In addition, investment advisors to mutual funds are required to register with the SEC. In fact, mutual funds are considered public investment companies that issue public securities (mutual fund shares) on a continual basis. Therefore, they are required by law to report and publish their performance numbers to the SEC and the public.

Bing Liang demonstrated the unknown size of the hedge fund universe.[10] He studied the composition of indexes constructed by two well-known providers: TASS and Hedge Fund Research Inc.[11] At the time of his study, there were 1,162 hedge funds in the HFR index and 1,627 hedge funds in the TASS index. He found that only 465 hedge funds were common to both hedge fund indexes. Further, of these 465 common hedge funds, only 154 had data covering the same time period.

Another problem with measuring the size of the hedge fund universe is that the attrition rate for hedge funds is high. Park, Brown, and Goetzmann (1999)[12] and Brown, Goetzmann, and Ibbotson (1999)[13] find that the average life of a hedge fund is 2.5 to 3 years. The short half-life of the average hedge fund may contribute to higher annual turnover for hedge fund index construction.

Perhaps the larger issue is that the hedge fund industry is still a nascent marketplace. More hedge funds are created daily as talented portfolio managers, analysts, and traders leave the traditional world of long-only management for the richer fees of the hedge fund marketplace. The growth of the hedge fund galaxy is not transparent because virtually all hedge funds are created as private enterprises. Thus, the hedge fund universe is not known with certainty, and very little overlap exists between hedge fund index providers.

Data Biases

Several data biases are associated with hedge fund indexes. The first is *survivorship* bias. While this bias is also common in equity mutual fund *universes,* it is generally not a major factor in equity *indexes.* Survivorship bias arises when constructing a hedge fund index today based on hedge funds that have survived the time period of study and are available for index construction. Hedge fund managers that have not survived are excluded from the index construction. This can bias the performance of an index of hedge funds upward, because presumably, the remaining hedge funds survived as a result of their superior performance. This bias is also common with institutional equity managers and mutual fund performance studies.

However, the lack of a uniform regulatory environment for hedge funds creates the opportunity for other data biases that are unique to the hedge fund industry. In addition to survivorship bias, three other biases may affect hedge fund index construction. First, there is *selection* bias. Essentially, because they are unregulated, hedge fund managers have a free option to report their data. They can pick and choose when and with whom to report their data. This approach to reporting may allow a fund to have an artificially high Sharpe ratio and not adequately capture some of the risks that the fund may be taking between arbitrary reporting periods. Selection bias also pushes hedge fund index returns upward because, not surprisingly, it is the better performing hedge fund managers who will exercise their option and report their performance to an index provider.[14]

Closely related to selection bias is *instant history* or *backfill* bias. Instant history bias occurs because once a hedge fund manager begins to report performance to an index provider, the index provider backfills the hedge fund manager's historical performance into the database. Again, because hedge fund managers are more likely to begin reporting their performance after a favorable period, this bias pushes index returns upward.

Last, there is *liquidation* bias. Frequently, hedge fund managers go out of business or shut down an unsuccessful hedge fund. When this happens, these managers stop reporting their performance in advance of the cessation of operations. Several months of poor performance may be lost because hedge fund managers are more concerned with winding down their operations than they are in reporting their performance to an index provider.[15]

In total, these biases can enhance the annual performance of hedge fund indexes by 3 to 4 percent. Since all indexes suffer from these biases, they cannot be diversified away by constructing a portfolio of indexes.[16] Table 11.2 details the size of these biases from several recent studies on hedge funds and hedge fund data collection.

TABLE 11.2 Biases Associated with Hedge Fund Data

Bias	Park, Brown, and Goetzmann, 1999	Brown, Goetzmann, and Ibbotson, 1999	Fung and Hsieh, 2000	Ackermann, McEnally, and Ravenscraft, 1999	Barry, 2003
Survivorship	2.60%	3%	3%	0.01%	3.70%
Selection	1.90%	Not Estimated	Not estimated	No Impact	Not estimated
Instant History	Not Estimated	Not Estimated	1.40%	No Impact	0.40%
Liquidation	Not Estimated	Not Estimated	Not estimated	0.70%	Not estimated
Total	4.50%	3%	4.40%	0.71%	4.10%

Strategy Definition and Style Drift

Strategy definitions can be very difficult for index providers. An index must have enough strategies to capture the broad market for hedge fund returns. Index providers determine their own hedge fund strategy classification system, and this varies from index to index.

A hedge fund manager may go long the stock of a target company subject to a merger bid and short the stock of the acquiring company. The strategy of this hedge fund manager could be classified alternatively as merger arbitrage by one index provider (e.g., HFR), relative value by another index provider (e.g., MSCI), or event driven by still another index provider (e.g., CSFB/Tremont).

To further complicate strategy definition, some hedge fund managers may simply be hard to classify as ongoing concerns because their strategies frequently change over time. Most hedge fund managers are classified according to the disclosure language in their offering documents. However, consider the following language from an actual hedge fund private placement memorandum:

> *Consistent with the General Partner's opportunistic approach, there are no fixed limitations as to specific asset classes invested in by the Partnership. The Partnership is not limited with respect to the types of investment strategies it may employ or the markets or instruments in which it may invest.*

Where should one classify this manager? Relative Value? Global Macro? Just as Diversified? With hedge funds, this type of strategy description is commonplace. The lack of specificity about the manager's strategy may lead to guesswork by index providers. Alternatively, some index providers may leave out a manager because of lack of clarity (e.g., Dow Jones Hedge Fund Strategy Benchmarks—formerly the ZCM Indexes), but this adds another bias to the index by purposely excluding certain types of hedge fund managers. In sum, there is no established format for classifying hedge funds. Each index provider develops its own scheme without concern for consistency with other hedge fund index providers.

Even if an index provider can successfully classify a hedge fund manager's investment strategy, there is the additional problem of strategy drift. Again, because of the opaque and unregulated nature of hedge fund managers, there is no requirement for hedge fund managers to notify an index provider when their investment style has changed (except with some of the newer investable hedge fund indexes such as S&P's SPhinX. The growing field of hedge fund consultants is thus providing an important analytical service in their scrutiny of manager performance and style consistency.

To continue with the example of merger arbitrage managers, the market for mergers declined significantly in the sluggish U.S. economy of the early 2000s. There were simply too few deals to feed all the merger arbitrage manager mouths. Consequently, many of these managers changed their investment focus toward the rising tide of distressed debt deals, which are countercyclical from mergers and acquisitions; or they expanded their investment portfolio to consider other corporate transactions such as spin-offs and recapitalizations. Once a hedge fund manager has been classified as merger arbitrage, all too often the fund will remain in that category despite significant changes in its investment focus, though hedge fund consultants increasingly focus on detecting these style changes.

Investability

One key issue is whether a hedge fund index can be or should be investable. This issue for hedge fund universes is distinct and different from their mutual fund counterparts. Mutual funds are public companies. They can and do continually offer their shares to the public. Capacity issues are virtually nonexistent, although some funds and strategies do close to new money, especially if focused on small cap equities. However, hedge funds generally do have capacity issues as some strategies only work well within certain limits of investment capital. This means that hedge fund managers often refuse further capital when they have achieved a maximum level of assets under management. Consequently, it is difficult for hedge fund indexes to remain investable when the underlying hedge funds close their doors to new investors.

A related issue is whether hedge fund indexes should even be investable. The argument is that an investable index will exclude hedge funds that are closed to new investors and, therefore, will exclude a large section of the hedge fund universe. Most index providers argue that to be truly representative, an index that is a barometer for hedge fund performance should include both open and closed funds. The trade-off, therefore, is between having as broad a representation as possible of hedge fund performance versus having a smaller pool of hedge fund managers that represent the performance that is accessible through investment. It would not be surprising to see the industry evolve rapidly along the same lines that were discussed in previous chapters on equity and fixed-income benchmarks—toward acceptance of both broad total-asset-class indexes and narrower, highly investable/tradable indexes. The former might be used primarily for asset allocation purposes and the latter as the basis of investment products.

DESIGN AND CONSTRUCTION OF THE MAJOR HEDGE FUND INDEXES

This section provides summary information on 10 hedge fund index providers. These indexes vary as to number of hedge fund managers, types of strategies employed, and investability. Table 11.3 summarizes the key attributes of the hedge fund indexes under observation. The author acknowledges that there are several more hedge fund benchmarks that are not included in this chapter.

Fees

All of the hedge fund indexes listed in Table 11.3 calculate hedge fund performance net of fees. However, two issues related to fees can result in different realized performance than that portrayed by a hedge fund index. First, incentive fees, that portion of hedge fund remuneration that is tied to the performance of hedge funds, are normally calculated on a quarterly or annual basis. However, all these indexes provide month-by-month performance. Therefore, on a monthly basis, incentive fees must be estimated and subtracted from performance. The actual fees collected at quarter or year-end may be very different from the monthly estimates.

Second, and somewhat more critical, hedge funds are a form of private investing. Indeed, virtually all hedge funds are structured as private limited partnerships or private limited liability companies. As a consequence, the fee terms of specific investments in hedge funds often are negotiated inconsistently among different investors or across different time periods. The lack of consistency means that the net-of-fees returns earned by one investor may not be what another investor can negotiate. In fact, the more successful hedge fund managers are, the greater is the likelihood that they will increase their fee structure to take advantage of their success. The end result is that index returns may overstate what a new investor can obtain in the hedge fund marketplace.

Several index providers have either offered or licensed investment products tied to the performance of their index, and the field is growing rapidly. The first was Credit Suisse First Boston (CSFB), which in conjunction with the Tremont hedge fund index has offered an investable CSFB/Tremont product tied to the total return of the Tremont hedge fund composite. When first introduced, this product was initially offered for a fee of 1 percent, but competition from other investable hedge fund index products may soon lower this fee. In fact, one of the newest entrants to the field, FTSE, has a licensed series of funds tied to its indexes that charge no incentive fee. The following sidebar by Simon Hookway and Steven Schoenfeld discusses this burgeoning area

TABLE 11.3 Summary of Hedge Fund Indexes

Index Provider	Provides a Single Index	Date Launched	Number of Subindexes	Number of Funds	Includes CTAs	Equal or Asset Weighted	Investable	Net of Fees	Web Sites
EACM	Yes	1996	13	100	No	Equal	Yes	Yes	eacm100@eacm.com
MAR/CISDM*	No	1990	15	2,500	Yes	Median	No	Yes	marhedge.com
Hedge Fund Research	Yes	1994	33	1,400	No	Equal	No	Yes	hedgefundresearch.com
Dow Jones/ Zurich Capital	No	2001	5	60	No	Equal	No	Yes	zindex.com
CSFB/Tremont	Yes	1999	9	383	Yes	Asset	No	Yes	hedgeindex.com
Van Hedge	Yes	1995	14	872	No	Equal	No	Yes	hedgefund.com
Hennessee Group	Yes	1992	23	3,000	No	Equal	No	Yes	hedgefnd.com
Tuna Indexes	Yes	1979	33	2,300	Yes	Equal	No	Yes	hedgefund.net
MSCI	Yes	2002	150	1,500	Yes	Equal and Asset	No	Yes	msci.com
Standard & Poor's	Yes	2002	9	40	Yes	Equal	Yes	Yes	standardandpoors.com

* The data originally compiled by Managed Account Reports was sold to Zurich Capital Markets which, in turn, gifted the database to the Center for International Securities and Derivatives Markets. Data/summary as of January 2004.

THE EXPANDING WORLD OF INVESTABLE HEDGE FUND INDEXES
Simon Hookway and Steven A. Schoenfeld

In response to increasing demands from institutional investors (who desire benchmarks that accurately inform them about real investment risks and rewards) and retail investors (who unfortunately tend to desire simple marketing promises), a whole new generation of investable hedge fund indexes and related tradable products is evolving. As with the broader universes discussed by Mark Anson in the chapter text, there are large differences between index providers in how they select, classify, weight, and rebalance funds. As a result, the picture of the investment universe that emerges when comparing products of competing providers can be very confusing. All hedge fund indexes, whether they belong to the broad measure of market class or the new emerging class of investable indexes, are by their nature "peer group" benchmarks.

As of mid-2003, there were 14 leading providers of hedge fund indexes—many of which are also described within the main chapter. Given the rapid development of this area, please note that more information can be gathered from the links available in the E-ppendix at www.ActiveIndexInvesting.com, and on www.IndexUniverse.com.[a] All hedge fund indexes are built on databases of individual manager returns, and thus all are peer-group benchmarks that suffer from all the usual self-reporting deficiencies and variances associated with such benchmarks. In addition, measurement errors peculiar to hedge funds further undermine related indexes;[b] these are explored later.

Index providers base their indexes on three main databases: TASS Research, Managed Account Reports (MAR), and Hedge Fund Research (HFR), with other databases available principally from Van, Altvest, and Hennessee. Because hedge fund returns are self-reported, none of these databases can be exhaustive (individually or collectively), nor are they mutually exclusive. All the indexes that are built from

[a] A longer version of this sidebar is available in the book's E-ppendix, at www.ActiveIndexInvesting.com. Updates on investable hedge fund index developments will be covered by IndexUniverse.com, as well as data tables and other information. General information about hedge funds and hedge fund indexes is available from "Albourne Village" at www.village.albourne.com.
[b] Specifically survivorship, selection, liquidity, instant history, and self-reporting biases as discussed within this chapter.

these databases take the form of a weighted global composite[c] and a series of substyle indexes. However, because the hedge fund industry is relatively new, terminology has not been standardized,[d] and thus the same strategy can be referred to under multiple different subindex names.

Emerging Investable Hedge Fund Indexes

Given the disappointing performance of traditional asset classes from mid-2000 through mid-2003, the acceptance of hedge funds as a core portfolio holding has gained significant momentum in the early part of the decade. However, serious hurdles to achieving truly broad-based acceptance remain. Many industry surveys reveal the institutional investors' list of concerns when evaluating initial and/or increased allocations to hedge funds and funds of hedge funds. These include lack of transparency, risk control difficulties, lack of understanding (principally due to the confusing performance picture of the investment universe that emerges from the comparison of broad-based indexes noted earlier), lack of regulation, and liquidity issues.

Typically based on data from dedicated managed-account platforms,[e] the new investable indexes aim to confront all these institutional concerns head-on, address most of the academically identified biases in the broader noninvestable indexes, and appeal to retail investors to the extent that they are also associated with household index brand names.

As discussed throughout Part Two, benchmarks for either performance measurement or investment must have key criteria. For hedge fund indexes, the four most important characteristics are:

1. Representativeness.
2. Investability.
3. Transparency.
4. Evolutionary (remaining relevant to asset class).

---

[c] All except MAR, which does not produce a global composite.
[d] At the time of writing, an AIMA project is in progress to establish just such a standard categorization. For more information see Index D in the *AIMA Journal* (September 2003).
[e] Except CSFB/Tremont Investable Index.

(Continued)

The table below indicates the extent to which meeting these requirements involves trade-offs (as discussed for equity indexes in Chapter 6). All the index providers tend to be rule driven (albeit in some cases crudely) and therefore, reasonably transparent.[f] Most, but not all, evolve to the extent that the number of funds they include ebb and flow with the underlying universe. Yet they differ markedly in representation and investability.

Representation versus Investability

Investability	Low	High
Representation		
High	Broad benchmarks	Ideal index position
	Data issues	Ideal for tradable products
	Self-classification	
	Monthly data	
	Fund access issues	
Low	Customized baskets	Quantitative fund of funds
	Not a useful benchmark	Not a useful benchmark

Source: Global Index Strategies.

Not only do the major index providers differ markedly in their selection criteria (e.g., the treatment of funds that are closed to new investment), they also vary in their style classifications, weighting, and schemes. Furthermore, many of the indexes suffer from underlying sources of bias/measurement error (survivorship, selection, self-reporting liquidity, and instant history bias) that cannot be diversified away.

Survivorship biases arise when the underlying database (and hence index) does not include funds that have ceased to exist in its return history. Selection bias is endemic to hedge fund databases and related indexes that rely on managers' self-reports and self-classification (e.g., how to deal with a fund that simply stops reporting its data). Liquidity bias occurs when an index's periodic recomposition fails to recognize and adjust for asymmetrical subscription/

---

[f]However, Van Hedge does not makes its index performances freely available to the public. EACM does not disclose the funds in its indexes.

redemption terms, lock-ins, exit penalties, and a host of other fund-specific investing realities. Instant history bias occurs as a result of "soft-launching" hedge funds. Taken together, Fung and Hseih (2000, 2002); Brown, Goetzmann, and Ibbotson (1999); and others estimate that these biases upwardly bias the historical returns of the TASS database by as much as 3 to 4.5 percent per annum.[g]

In combination, these perceived hurdles and drawbacks[h] have conspired to keep retail and institutional capital largely out of the hedge fund arena. In recognition of these problems, new investable indexes are emerging that recognize the deficiencies of what has gone before. Institutional investors desire benchmarks that accurately inform them about the investment risks they are taking and the rewards they are likely to receive, and retail investors often are influenced by marketing promises and the power of brand names they know and trust. To satisfy both, a new breed of index is emerging that is both representative and investable (i.e., the top right quadrant of the table in this sidebar). Representation is achieved by rigorous quantitative techniques, and investability is assured through qualitative due diligence and suitability testing.

Evolving Tradable Products

The mechanics of the hedge fund world mean that to provide investors with representative, investable, transparent, daily priced indexes, *the index itself has to be an investor in the underlying hedge funds.* This means that the performance of such an investable index can only be derived from the performance of a fund of funds vehicle[i] that invests solely in the designated index constituents.[j] This is a unique role for an index provider and further underscores one of our major points: "Hedge fund indexes" are really a form of transparent, scientifically built manager universes. Important concerns, such as risk

---

[g] See main chapter, especially Table 11.2.
[h] Plus some very real regulatory and asset admissibility issues driven principally by the fact that hedge funds do not have to be listed on any exchange and are largely unregulated.
[i] Except MSCI.
[j] LJH, VAN, and Magnum offer fund of funds vehicles that track their own proprietary indexes with an optimal sample of funds drawn from their respective indexes.

(Continued)

monitoring and control, worries about investment liquidity (to mitigate "blow up" event risk), and fears of inadequate regulation of public fund vehicles have typically driven investable index providers toward having their own dedicated managed account platforms to calculate the related fund of funds structured index.[k]

This is both an elegant and practical solution as well as being, currently, the most successful business model for the index provider and their partners. Index rule structures tend to be transparent and provide for universe representation via exposure to constituent funds that are open to and receiving subscriptions. The fund of funds structure built on managed accounts with the constituent funds ensures, daily, that all exposures are transparently monitored, controlled, and independently valued as well as providing a ready-made investment conduit for interested investors. In addition, these structures eradicate many of the biases that—according to academics— plague the broader, noninvestable indexes.[l]

As of the fourth quarter of 2003, there were five principal investable hedge fund index providers: S&P, HFR, CSFB/Tremont, MSCI, and the Dow Jones Hedge Fund Strategy Benchmarks (formerly Zurich Capital Markets or ZCM). This universe expanded to six with the April 2004 launch of the FTSE Hedge Fund Index. This latter index series comprises one global index, three management style indexes, and eight trading strategy indexes.

Other index tracker products are available from VAN, LJH Global Investments, and Magnum. These products are significantly different in that they are not based on managed accounts and use an optimized sample of funds to track those companies' own proprietary indexes.

All publicly distributed funds and structured products related to tracking the S&P Hedge Fund Index are invested via the "SPhinX" (S&P Hedge Fund Index) product, launched in 2002 and managed by PlusFunds, who hold a global exclusive license to do so. It should be noted that the first mutual fund-like hedge fund index product available

---

[k] Except CSFB/Tremont Investable, which is totally invested in publicly available fund shares.

[l] However, care must be taken when interpreting the investable indexes published pro forma back histories. These all rely on significant assumptions that, inter alia, may well do nothing to mitigate survivorship, selection, liquidity, instant history, and/or self-reporting bias and can be quite material biases, all of which are described in the main chapter.

to U.S. individual investors was launched in 2003 by Rydex Capital Partners, in association with PlusFunds, based on the S&P Hedge Fund Index, and has a pathbreakingly low $25,000 minimum investment. Zurich Capital Markets began life in 2000 with a product specifically tailored to the needs and requirements of the U.S. insurance industry. ZCM offers tracker funds matched to all its indexes which have been rebranded as the Dow Jones Hedge Fund Strategy Benchmarks, and many MAR indexes, too. For some time now, HFR has had an investable index that it made privately available to its institutional clients, but in May 2003 it launched a tradable index that it will license to all interested parties. The first takers have been five investment banks: Lehman Brothers, DRKW, Bear Stearns, Barclays Capital, and Deutsche Bank. Finally, all 12 of the previously mentioned FTSE Hedge index series will be available as individually listed share classes, in a fund of fund products managed by MSS Fund Management Ltd.

Of the leading investable index providers, the only one not to be structured as a managed account platform is the CSFB/Tremont Investable Index. Credit Suisse Asset Management holds the exclusive license to track the CSFB/Tremont Investable Index and launched this product in August 2003. CSFB will also continue to offer hedge index participation shares (HIPS) and sector index participation shares (SIPS) on its original CSFB/Tremont Hedge Fund Index. As of this writing, MSCI is the only investable index provider to have launched an index that is not based on a fund of funds vehicle. MSCI's product is essentially constructed by reweighting some of the funds that are already on the SocGen Lyxor managed account platform.

As the first of investable index providers encouraged the construction of tradable products for investors, and those products succeeded in gathering funds for related distributors and asset managers, the main global index providers have inexorably moved to produce their own investable hedge fund indexes. Although the number of investable hedge fund indexes is likely to increase, those that will attract investors' interest over the long run will be those with a known global brand, transparent methodology, clear investment objectives, and a delivery mechanism that produces superior risk and return diversification benefits. We believe that the competition in this field, like that witnessed in the global equity index arena, will result in both better indexes *and* more transparency for investors.

and raises some important issues about the economics of the index providers and fund structures.

Turnover

Most of the turnover in hedge fund indexes tends to be onesided. That is, the index composite grows as new hedge funds enter the marketplace and report their performance to the index provider. However, some hedge funds go out of business or close their fund to new investors and cease reporting their returns. This can lead to several of the data biases presented in Table 11.2. In sum, turnover tends to be low, with more hedge fund returns added to the composite over time.

A more interesting point is whether the hedge fund index has a constant number of hedge funds similar to equity index construction (e.g., the S&P 500 and the Russell 1000). Certain index providers such as EACM and Zurich Capital contain a fixed number of hedge funds similar to their equity index counterparts. However, other hedge fund index providers grow their index constituent base as more hedge funds are created. Hedge fund indexes that maintain a constant number of hedge funds are more "index-like," whereas the other hedge fund index providers attempt to capture the expanding hedge fund universe.

It is a matter of debate which type of hedge fund index is better. Index providers that maintain a constant number of hedge funds in the index may provide a more consistent benchmark for performance measurement. However, indexes that grow as the hedge fund universe expands might be a better choice in asset allocation studies because they capture the broader risk and return characteristics of the hedge fund marketplace.

Performance

Figure 11.1 demonstrates the historical performance of the 10 indexes.[17] The most striking observation is that the risk/return performance of the 10 indexes varies significantly. The highest return is associated with the Tuna funds (average annual return of 16.35 percent) and the lowest associated with MSCI (7.62 percent). Also, the standard deviation of annual returns ranges from 14 percent (Van Hedge) to 3 percent for the S&P Hedge Fund Index.

We also include as an additional reference, the risk and return of the S&P 500, the Russell 1000 and 2000 stock indexes, 10-year U.S. Treasury Bonds, and the Barclay CTA Index (managed futures index).[18] The U.S. Treasury Bonds and managed futures offer about the same risk and return

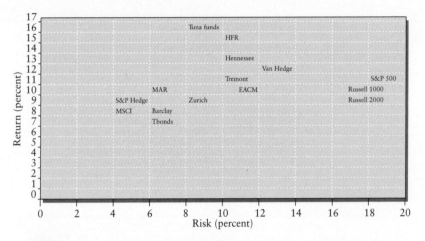

FIGURE 11.1 Risk and Return of Hedge Fund and Equity Market Indexes
Note: Location of index name is the approximate risk/return point.

relationship, with modest returns but low volatility. We include Treasury bonds to provide a low risk/low return alternative to stocks, and we include the Barclay CTA Index because some of the hedge fund indexes include managed futures, whereas others exclude this hedge fund subclass. All three of the stock indexes appear as outliers on this chart with average returns of 9 percent to 11 percent, but with volatility significantly higher than that for the hedge fund indexes, at 19 percent to 20 percent.

Figure 11.1 underscores our earlier comments regarding the diversity of index construction and the fact that the size of the hedge fund universe is not known with certainty. Further, the wide range of historical risk/return performance carries over to the hedge fund subindexes. In Figure 11.2, we present the historical risk/return profile for equity long/short indexes.[19] If anything, there is even more variability in this category.

All these attributes mean that investors choosing a hedge fund composite index or subindex must ensure that the chosen index is representative of their hedge fund investment program. For example, using the Zurich long/short equity hedge index to measure the performance of a program that more closely resembles the economic parameters of the MSCI long/short equity hedge index could lead to inaccurate conclusions about the program's performance.

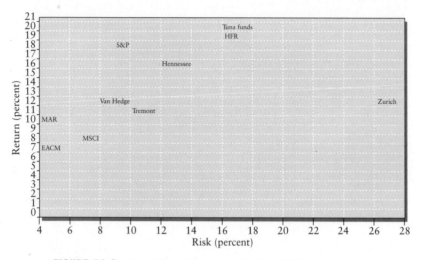

FIGURE 11.2 Long/Short Equity Hedge Fund Subindexes
Note: Location of index name is the approximate risk/return point.

CORRELATION ACROSS HEDGE FUND INDEXES AND STOCK INDEXES

Table 11.4 presents a table of correlation measures between the hedge fund indexes and the stock indexes. We also include the Barclay CTA Index to represent the managed futures asset class that is excluded from approximately half of the hedge fund indexes. We omit the S&P Hedge Fund Index and the MSCI Hedge Fund Index from this analysis because of their shorter, pro forma track records.

The variability of historical risk/return profiles is demonstrated in the correlation coefficients between the different hedge fund indexes. The coefficients range from a high of 0.98 (Tuna funds/HFR) to a low of 0.67 (Tremont/Zurich). Most of the correlation coefficients are in the range of 0.8 to 0.9. Compared with equity stock indexes, these correlations are low; the correlation between the S&P 500 and the Russell 1000 stock indexes is 0.99 although the correlation between the S&P 500 and the Russell 2000 is only about 0.75. Similarly, the previous chapter highlighted the very high (more than 0.98) correlation between major fixed-income indexes. This simply underscores that the hedge fund universe is truly not known with certainty and while certain indexes may capture similar parts of the universe, there is still a wider variation among hedge fund index returns than among equity index returns. The hedge fund indexes are much more highly correlated with

TABLE 11.4 Correlation Coefficients between Hedge Fund Indexes and Stock Indexes

	Tuna Agg	Van Hedge	Hennessee	MAR	HFR	DJ/ Zurich	Tremont	EACM	S&P 500	Russell 1000	Russell 2000	Barclay
Tuna Agg	1.000											
Van Hedge	0.968	1.000										
Hennessee	0.983	0.986	1.000									
MAR	0.869	0.812	0.895	1.000								
HFR	0.980	0.982	0.992	0.882	1.000							
DJ (Zurich)	0.935	0.952	0.959	0.818	0.919	1.000						
Tremont	0.842	0.777	0.842	0.927	0.877	0.673	1.000					
EACM	0.933	0.973	0.971	0.856	0.953	0.951	0.776	1.000				
S&P 500	0.681	0.520	0.542	0.455	0.578	0.454	0.575	0.383	1.000			
Russell 1000	0.695	0.532	0.556	0.477	0.591	0.470	0.589	0.401	0.999	1.000		
Russell 2000	0.883	0.793	0.858	0.861	0.873	0.765	0.870	0.717	0.744	0.753	1.000	
Barclay CTA	-0.501	-0.625	-0.575	-0.292	-0.549	-0.664	-0.174	-0.537	-0.099	-0.093	-0.454	1.000

Second quarter (2003) data/calculations.

small-cap stocks (represented by the Russell 2000) than with large-cap (S&P 500) or large/mid-cap stocks (Russell 1000).[20]

It is also noteworthy that the Barclay CTA composite index is negatively correlated with both hedge fund and stock indexes. For hedge fund indexes, a large component of these strategies includes convergent, or arbitrage, managers who engage in arbitrage trades where they expect the prices of two securities to converge over time. These strategies are known as short volatility or convergent trading. Managed futures strategies tend to be long volatility trades, however, or divergent trading. As a result, it appears that managed futures (which trade in a huge variety of asset classes) make a good diversifying agent for other hedge fund styles.

CAPITALIZATION/ASSET WEIGHTED VERSUS EQUAL WEIGHTED INDEXES

In contrast to the discussion of best practices of index construction in Chapters 6 and 7, hedge fund indexes are unique in that cap-weighted might not be the best approach. A capitalization/asset-weighted index is susceptible to disproportionate representation from large funds that have a very large gain or loss in any given time period. Additionally, an asset-weighted index can be distorted by errors in reporting by larger funds. Further, some of the largest funds choose not to report their data to public databases, and it may be difficult to interpret an asset-weighted index return that does not include some of the larger hedge funds.

Equal weighting has the advantage of not favoring large funds or hedge fund strategies that attract a lot of capital (like global macro or relative value). Investors may be prone to chasing either returns or the latest hedge fund "flavor of the year." This can distort a market capitalization index because the flows of capital will influence the returns of a market-cap index. Most hedge fund index providers argue that fully reflecting all strategies requires that a hedge fund index be equally weighted.

Nevertheless, there are two worthwhile arguments for a capitalization/asset-weighted hedge fund index. First, smaller hedge funds can transact with a smaller market impact. An asset-weighted index would more accurately reflect the full market impact from the hedge fund universe as it conducts its transactions. This is all the more important for hedge fund managers because of the high portfolio turnover associated with their frequent and opportunistic trading patterns.

Second, most other asset classes are benchmarked against capitalization-weighted indexes. As discussed in previous chapters, the S&P 500, Russell 1000, and MSCI EAFE are all cap-weighted equity indexes. This is relevant because large institutional investors use these cap-weighted indexes in their asset allocation decisions. Therefore, some investors believe that to compare on an equal basis, hedge fund indexes would ideally be cap-weighted when used for asset allocation decisions. That being said, it still may not be a practical approach given the differences of this unique asset class; dilemma underscores the reality that "hedge fund indexes are different" and really are more like performance universes in an equity or bond asset class.

INDEX DIVERSIFICATION

The size of the 10 hedge fund indexes under comparison varies from 60 funds to over 2,000. Most index providers have a single composite index with the exception of MAR and Zurich Capital. However, MAR provides a fund of funds median index that acts as a proxy for its total universe, while Zurich Capital does not. Each index provider constructs several subindexes to track the performance of specific hedge fund strategies more closely.

But what is the right size for an index? Do 60 funds offer sufficient diversification to mitigate the idiosyncratic risk of individual managers? Two studies have examined the issue of the proper diversification level for hedge funds. Henker (1999) finds that the majority of idiosyncratic risk associated with equity long/short hedge funds can be diversified away with as little as 10 funds, while most of the risk is diversified away with about 20 funds.[21] Similarly, Park and Staum (1999) find that about 95 percent of hedge fund's idiosyncratic risk can be diversified away with about 20 hedge funds.[22]

Another question is, how many hedge funds are necessary in an investment program to produce a sufficiently high correlation with a chosen hedge fund index? This is important since hedge fund indexes may be used for asset allocation purposes, and the resulting hedge fund investment program should meet the expectations of the asset allocation study. Lhabitant and Learned (2002) examine several hedge fund strategies and find that an investment program of 20 hedge funds captures 80 percent to 90 percent of the correlation with the chosen hedge fund index.[23]

ASSET ALLOCATION WITH HEDGE FUND INDEXES

As noted, a hedge fund index can be used for asset allocation studies. Asset allocation studies are used to determine the target weights in a diversified portfolio to allocate across individual asset classes. In this example, we seek to find the allocation that might be made to hedge funds using different hedge fund indexes. Asset allocation studies attempt to create the optimal portfolio that provides the greatest utility to the investor.

When presented with various outcomes of portfolio return and volatility, an investor will choose the portfolio that provides the greatest expected utility. The issue we examine is whether the addition of hedge funds to a portfolio of stocks and bonds will increase an investor's expected utility beyond that obtained with only stocks and bonds.

Many researchers have used the following equation to determine the target allocation level across individual asset classes:[24]

$$E(U_i) = E(R_\rho) - A_i \sigma^2(R_\rho)$$

where $E(U_i)$ = Expected utility of the i-th investor
$E(R_\rho)$ = Expected return of the portfolio $\Sigma_i w_i E(R_i)$
$\sigma^2(R_\rho)$ = Variance of the portfolio returns $\Sigma_i \Sigma_j w_i w_j \sigma_i \sigma_j \rho_{ij}$
A_i = Measure of relative risk aversion for the i-th investor
w_i and w_j = Portfolio weights of the i-th and j-th asset classes
σ_i and σ_j = Volatilities of the i-th and j-th asset classes
ρ_{ij} = Correlation coefficient between the i-th and j-th asset classes

The expected utility in this equation may be viewed as the expected return on the investor's portfolio minus a risk penalty. The risk penalty is equal to the risk of the portfolio multiplied by the investor's relative risk aversion. This is another way to say that the equation is simply a risk-adjusted expected rate of return for the portfolio, where the adjustment depends on the level of an investor's particular risk aversion.

The equation which is based on the mean and variance, does not include the higher moments of the return distribution such as skew and kurtosis. Two comments are necessary. First, incorporating higher moments into a utility function can lead to the countereconomic results of increasing marginal utility.[25] Second, the impact of skew or kurtosis for an asset class should have a lesser impact within a diversified portfolio.

Whether we call the equation the expected utility or the risk-adjusted return, solving this function requires quadratic programming because solving for E(U) involves both squared terms (the individual asset variances) as well as multiplicative terms (the covariances of the various asset classes). The important point is that quadratic solutions recognize that the risk of the portfolio depends on the interactions among the asset classes.

There are two problems with determining the exact asset allocation for hedge funds. First, utility functions are hard to define in terms of all the factors that affect investors' behavior. Second, even if a utility function could be specified for each investor, these functions would be as varied and as different as the investors they attempt to describe. Consequently, asset allocation and expected utility will be unique for each investor.

Instead of trying to describe the unique benefits of hedge funds for every investor, we develop a simple scale to measure risk aversion. An asset allocation study should consider how tolerance for risk can affect an investor's behavior. In this asset allocation example, we specifically incorporate investors' risk preferences into their investment decisions by maximizing expected utility as the objective function, with the level of risk aversion incorporated in the equation.

In this example, we consider three levels of investor risk aversion: low, moderate, and high. At low risk aversion, the investor is driven to maximize total return instead of reducing risk. At the moderate level of risk aversion, risk reduction becomes a more important factor. Last, at a high level of risk aversion, reducing risk becomes more important than maximizing total return. As the level of risk aversion increases, portfolio volatility becomes a greater concern in the investor's utility function, and the investor will seek greater diversification to manage risk.

We use four hedge fund indexes that have data back to 1990: Tuna Aggregate, HFRI FOF index, Hennessee Index, and CISDM/MAR Index. It is important to have as long a historical track record as possible when conducting asset allocation studies, because in any short time period (e.g., 5 years) the relationships among asset classes can become distorted.[26] We include the S&P 500 to represent stock market exposure, 10-year Treasury bonds to represent bond market exposure, high-yield bonds to represent credit exposure, and 1-year Treasury bills to represent cash. Our objective is to mix these asset classes together according to the preceding equation, to determine the optimal asset allocation to hedge funds.

A constrained optimization program is run to solve the equation at each level of risk aversion.[27] In Table 11.5, we present the results for each hedge fund index.

At low levels of risk aversion, the allocation to hedge funds is as high as 87 percent for the low risk-averse investor using the Tuna Aggregate index. However, as the investor's level of risk aversion increases, the amount allocated to hedge funds declines. The reason is that these asset classes have less than perfect correlation with each other. By diversifying across asset classes, investors can reduce the volatility of their investment portfolio. This volatility-dampening effect has greater usefulness as the level of risk aversion increases.

Similar results are found for HFRI, Hennessee, and the CISDM/MAR indexes. Smaller amounts are allocated to hedge funds as risk aversion grows. The reason so much is allocated to hedge funds at a low level of risk

TABLE 11.5 Asset Allocation with Different Hedge Fund Indexes

Risk Aversion	Hedge Fund	10-Year T-Bond	S&P 500	1-Year T-Bill	High Yield	Expected Utility	Sharpe Ratio
Tuna Aggregate							
Low	0.87	0.13	0	0	0	0.1200	1.190
Moderate	0.66	0.34	0	0	0	0.0950	1.250
High	0.46	0.24	0	0.30	0	0.0790	1.200
HFRI Fund of Funds Index							
Low	0.62	0.38	0	0	0	0.0944	0.880
Moderate	0.36	0.25	0	0.39	0	0.0730	0.845
High	0.25	0.15	0	0.60	0	0.0648	0.781
Hennessee Index							
Low	0.61	0.39	0	0	0	0.0900	0.840
Moderate	0.38	0.30	0	0.32	0	0.0700	0.789
High	0.25	0.18	0	0.57	0	0.0616	0.696
CISDM/MAR Index							
Low	0.66	0.33	0.01	0	0	0.0790	0.690
Moderate	0.46	0.24	0	0.30	0	0.0660	0.659
High	0.32	0.14	0	0.54	0	0.0600	0.590

aversion is that the four hedge fund indexes have a very favorable historical risk and return trade-off—high levels of return with low to moderate levels of volatility.

There is a very wide range of allocations to hedge funds depending on the hedge fund index selected and the investor's level of risk aversion. Allocation levels range from 25 percent to 87 percent. *Such a wide range of results would not be expected for a homogenous asset class.* This simply highlights that the hedge fund universe is unknowable—each index has its own methods of construction resulting in very little overlap with other available hedge fund indexes.

Therefore, if a hedge fund index is to be used for asset allocation purposes, the investor must select an index that reflects the economic parameters of the hedge fund program being implemented. Otherwise, an asset allocation study may produce unusual results that must be used with care.

As a practical matter, most large institutional investors would not allocate more than 25 percent of their investment portfolio to hedge funds. In fact, most public pension funds have a less than 5 percent allocation to hedge funds, and many place a specific asset allocation limit on hedge fund investing in the 1 percent to 10 percent range. Therefore, many of the allocation examples presented in Table 11.5 might be beyond an explicit asset allocation constraint.

CONCLUSION

As discussed in previous chapters of Part Two, benchmarks serve several vital roles. First, they provide a yardstick for measuring performance of an asset class. Second, they measure the skill of an individual portfolio manager. Third, indexes are used in asset allocation studies to determine how much to allocate among broad asset classes. And finally, benchmarks can be the basis for investable products. As investors' interest in hedge funds continues to grow, they will require hedge fund portfolios. These will need to be built in one of three ways: (1) with the assistance of specialized hedge fund consultants; (2) with funds of funds; or possibly, (3) with investable hedge fund index products, which *at minimum,* provide a diverse, relatively objective, and transparent portfolio of hedge funds.

Investors now have a wide variety of hedge funds indexes or universes to choose from—and this number is likely to grow.[28] Unfortunately, the construction of hedge fund indexes lacks consistency.

This lack of consistency creates two distinct problems. First, given the large range of performance among the hedge fund indexes, investment managers who invest in hedge funds can significantly outperform or underperform their bogey by the choice of hedge fund index. Second, asset allocation studies that are driven by the risk/return trade-off of different asset classes may over- or underallocate to hedge fund investments based on the simple choice of hedge fund index. Some variability among hedge fund indexes is desirable, but too much can result in misleading asset allocation decisions. Last, all these indexes suffer from several data biases that can boost returns by 3 percent to 4 percent.

This lack of consistency is a serious problem, but one can expect some of the same phenomenon of competition between index providers—described in previous chapters of this part of the book—to improve both methodology and transparency of hedge fund indexes. This process will inevitably benefit investors.

The world of hedge fund performance measurement and indexes is still maturing. There are many indexes to choose from, each with its own strengths and weaknesses. Also, the consistency among hedge fund indexes is considerably less than that for equity or fixed-income indexes. Perhaps the best way to choose a hedge fund index is to first state the risk and return objectives of the hedge fund investment program. With this as their guide, investors can then make an informed benchmark selection. And regardless of the benchmark chosen, hedge fund indexes are increasingly vital tools for building and monitoring portfolios in this dynamic asset class.

NOTES

1. An earlier, shorter version of this chapter appeared as "Hedge Fund Indexes—Benchmarking the Hedge Fund Marketplace" in the *Journal of Indexes* (third quarter, 2003). It can be accessed via the archive feature on IndexUniverse.com.
2. Stephen J. Brown, William N. Goetzmann, and Roger G. Ibbotson, "Offshore Hedge Funds: Survival and Performance, 1989–95," *Journal of Business,* vol. 72, no. 1 (1999): 91–117.
3. Goldman Sachs & Co., and Financial Risk Management Ltd., "The Hedge Fund 'Industry' and Absolute Return Funds," *Journal of Alternative Investments* (Spring 1999).
4. R. McFall Lamm Jr., "Portfolios of Alternative Assets: Why Not 100 Percent Hedge Funds?" *Journal of Investing* (Winter 1999): 87–97.
5. David Purcell and Paul Crowley, "The Reality of Hedge Funds," *Journal of Investing* (Fall 1999): 26–44.
6. Franklin Edwards and Jimmy Liew, "Hedge Funds versus Managed Futures as Asset Classes," *Journal of Derivatives* (Summer 1999).
7. See Daniel Collins, "Alternative Vehicles Open to Retail," *Futures* (December 1, 2002); Robert Clow, "Investors Pile into Alternative Fund Strategies," *Financial Times* (April 30, 2002); Robert Clow, "Hedge Fund Data Are No More Than a Rough Guide," *Financial Times* (March 14, 2002); and Matt Kelly, "Chipping Away at Hedge Funds," *Boston Business Journal* (December 13, 2002).
8. This unregulated nature, at least in the United States, may soon end. SEC Commissioner Roel Campos recently stated that several regulations are being considered including registration of hedge funds and hedge fund managers, as well as restrictions on short-selling and hedge funds' ability to leverage their portfolios.
9. The one exception is managed futures funds. This subclass of the hedge fund industry is managed by commodity trading advisors and commodity pool operations. CTAs and CPOs must register their hedge funds with the Commodity Futures Trading Commission and publish the performance results.
10. Bing Liang, "Hedge Funds: The Living and the Dead," *Journal of Financial and Quantitative Analysis* (2001).
11. The Tass database is now used by the joint venture of CSFB/Tremont Advisors.
12. James Park, Stephen Brown, and William Goetzmann, "Performance Benchmarks and Survivorship Bias for Hedge Fund and Commodity Trading Advisors," *Hedge Fund News* (August 1999).
13. See note 2.

14. A contrary argument can be made for selection bias: Successful hedge fund managers choose not to report their data to hedge fund index providers because they have no need to attract additional assets. Both situations contribute to the bias.

15. The flip side to liquidation bias is *participation* bias. This bias may occur for successful hedge fund managers who close their fund and stop reporting results because they no longer need to attract new capital.

16. William Fung and David Hsieh, "Performance Characteristics of Hedge Funds and Commodity Funds: Natural versus Spurious Biases," *Journal of Financial and Quantitative Analysis,* vol. 35 (2000).

17. For Zurich Capital—now the Dow Jones Hedge Fund Strategy Benchmarks—we used the average performance across its five subindexes, and for MAR/CISDM, we used the performance of its Fund of Funds Index. Data for S&P and MSCI are based on pro forma performance prior to 2002.

18. The Barclay CTA Index is a composite of all Commodity Trading Advisors in the Barclay CTA database that have at least 4 years of performance data. About 300 CTA managers are included in the index, and the index is equally weighted. CTA trading styles are a subset of the hedge fund marketplace and are often referred to as "Managed Futures." Readers should note that this index does not have an "s" at the end of its name and has no affiliation with Barclays Bank or Barclays Global Investors.

19. Equity long/short hedge fund subindexes are also referred to as equity hedge (HFR and EACM), long/short hedged (Tuna funds), and market neutral long/short (MAR and Van Hedge).

20. I am indebted to Matt Moran of the Chicago Board Options Exchange for pointing out this difference in correlations to me.

21. Thomas Henker, "Naïve Diversification for Hedge Funds," *Journal of Alternative Assets* (Winter 1998).

22. James Park and Jeremy Staum, "Fund of Funds Diversification: How Much Is Enough?" *Journal of Alternative Assets* (Winter 1998).

23. Francois-Serge Lhabitant and Michelle Learned, "Hedge Fund Diversification: How Much Is Enough?" *Journal of Alternative Investments* (Winter 2002).

24. See Philippe Jorion, "Risk Management Lessons Learned from Long-Term Capital Management," Working Paper (2000); Richard Grinold, and Ronald Kahn, *Active Portfolio Management* (New York: McGraw Hill, 2000); William Sharpe, "Asset Allocation," in *Managing Investment Portfolios: A Dynamic Process,* eds. John Maginn and Donald Tuttle (Warren, Gorham and Lamber, 1990); and Mark Anson, "Maximizing Expected Utility with Commodity Futures," *Journal of Portfolio Management* (Summer 1999).

25. See Pierre-Yves Moix, "The Measurement of Market Risk" (PhD dissertation, University of St. Gallen, 2000). Increasing marginal utility would mean that the more an investor invests in hedge funds, the greater the utility. There is no point of saturation. This would lead to an even higher allocation to hedge funds than shown in Figure 11.1.

26. For an example of this, see Mark Anson, "Maximizing Utility with Private Equity," *Journal of Investing* (2001).

27. To solve the utility maximization equation, we program an optimization as follows:

    Maximize $E(U) = \Sigma_i w_i E(R_i) - A_i \Sigma_i \Sigma_j w_i w_j \sigma_i \sigma_j \rho_{ij}$

    Subject to the constraints $\Sigma w_i = 1$, and $0 \leq w_i \leq 1$.

28. Readers can consult publications like *MAR Hedge* and *Institutional Investor's Alpha*, as well as online resources such as IndexUniverse.com to stay abreast of rapidly moving hedge fund index developments. Direct links to the web sites of many of the hedge fund index providers are available on IndexUniverse.com. Whenever possible the author and/or editor will submit updates to this chapter's E-ppendix entry at www.ActiveIndexInvesting.com (also accessible via IndexUniverse.com).

CHAPTER 12

Using Indexes as Analytical Tools

Viewing Changes in the World's Stock Markets through the Benchmarks

Mark Sladkus

_____ Editor's Note _____

In this chapter, Mark Sladkus shows us that indexes not only help us assess stock market movements, but also capture and reflect what we as a society have lived through in both economic and political terms. In Chapter 5, we detailed the four uses of indexes—and this chapter focuses primarily on two of the uses, namely, indexes as a gauge of market sentiment (and relative sector and market values), and the use of indexes as an asset allocation tool. Broad market capitalization-weighted equity benchmarks such as the MSCI Indexes, published since 1968, can be a reference for observing the evolution of markets and much more. These and other benchmarks are designed and maintained to reflect the underlying industrial and macroeconomic structure and evolution of the world's markets.

This chapter reveals the utility of benchmarks for analyzing global markets as a whole, and the trends within markets. Examples of the rise and fall of markets and sectors are provided throughout. The dramatic fall of the Soviet Union and rise of emerging markets is described in the text and in the country and regional indexes that these momentous changes spawned. And how many investors remember that energy stocks were the bubble sector in the late 1970s and early 1980s, representing over 30 percent of the S&P 500 at one point in 1980? Mark also blends in valuable history of the development of index-based investment products (one of the other of the four uses of indexes). For readers who are relatively new to the field of finance and investing, it also serves as a superb history lesson of a full generation of market evolution.[1]

As noted in Chapter 5, indexes can be constructed and used for many investment purposes. Indexes that are broad-based and market cap-weighted are typically referred to as benchmarks. They represent an important subset of the world of indexes that can measure performance and attribution of returns. They also are helpful research tools for determining asset allocation. Another common use is as investment vehicles (e.g., as exchange-listed products).

Broad market cap-weighted equity benchmarks such as the MSCI Indexes, which have been published since 1968, are used as a reference to observe the evolution of markets. Because these and other benchmarks are designed and maintained to reflect the structure and progression of the markets, analyzing these indexes often provides a snapshot of changes in the world's economy such as trends in markets, economies, and commodities. When coupled with fundamental data, such as valuation ratios, specific investment strategies can be explored. For example, an investor may wish to test the usefulness of a value-oriented strategy that invests in low price/book value securities. A 10-year study based on MSCI historical valuation data (1981 through 1990) demonstrates that, regardless of the significant accounting differences across countries and sectors, investments in low price/book value securities have performed better on average than investments in the higher price/book value securities.[2]

History over the past four decades illustrates how indexes provide such a snapshot of world economic changes. Countries have been created and split apart, political systems have changed, markets have evolved and are devolving. Among currencies, there have been fixed exchange rates, floating rates, dirty float, and dollar pegged. An important new currency—the Euro—was created. Industries have exploded, in both the positive and the negative senses of the word. Using the MSCI Indexes, we can look at snapshots of history to illustrate the relative importance of a country's equity markets, the comparative importance of their publicly traded industries, the extremes of valuations that have occurred within countries and across global sectors, and their willingness to accept foreign investors.

THE EARLY YEARS

As previously mentioned, the MSCI Indexes were created in 1968, and were originally known as Capital International Perspective. To place this in historical perspective, in 1968 Czechoslovakia was being invaded by Russia, China was in the midst of the Cultural Revolution, and Neil Armstrong was about to look back at Earth as he walked on the moon. It was a notable period in world history.

At that time, the philosophy behind the MSCI Indexes was to consistently represent the evolution of an unmanaged portfolio consisting of all equity securities. This philosophy remains the same today even though the methodology has been adjusted to reflect changes in the liquidity and float of the world's markets, the constraints imposed on nondomestic investors, and the dramatic increase in the availability of information. Enormous changes have ensued in the subsequent 30 years. Restrictions on equity investing are still present, but they are less frequent and of a different nature; exchange controls have been essentially lifted, although the recent turmoil in Argentina reminds us that sometimes liberalizations get reversed; and information on the cross-holding of companies, while not fully transparent, is more available than in the past. The indexes have evolved to dynamically reflect these changing characteristics of the markets. Part of the evolution of indexes has been to ensure that they stay relevant to their growing uses. The increasing kinds of financial instruments based on indexes and the growth in the use of index funds have implications for how best to implement corporate actions.

In 1968, the market capitalization of the world outside North America was only \$191 billion, roughly the size of IBM or the country of Finland in 2002, as is visible in Table 12.1. At the time, the biggest market after the United Kingdom was not Japan, but Germany. The European Union (EU) was then known as the Common Market with only 6 members and its total market capitalization was only \$65 billion. The United States represented about 65 percent of the world's equity market capitalization, while Japan was arguably an emerging market. Against this backdrop, it may seem natural that from an investment standpoint the United States was insular. At the time, only a small handful of U.S. institutions were investing in non-U.S. equity markets.

THE EARLY 1970s: CURRENCY TURMOIL

Moving up the historical time line, turbulent economic times occurred globally, and for the United States politically. Among the market events, during August 1971, the United States had suspended convertibility into gold on its way to abandoning convertibility in 1973. Perhaps it was brave that Wells Fargo, the predecessor to today's Barclays Global Investors (BGI) had launched the first index fund. As discussed in Chapter 2, it was a domestic index fund tied to an equally weighted New York Stock Exchange (NYSE)

TABLE 12.1   Market Coverage of Capital
International Indexes

Country	December 31, 1967 Estimated Market Capitalization ($Billions)
Germany	24.1
France	16.5
Italy	10.5
Netherlands	10
Belgium/Luxembourg	4.6
E.E.C. (Common Market)	65.7
United Kingdom	66.1
Switzerland	8
Spain	5.6
Sweden	4.1
Denmark	0.7
Austria	0.7
Norway	0.5
Europe	151.4
Australia	15.5
Japan	23.9
Europe, Australia, and Japan	190.8

Note: The MSCI Indexes were originally called Capital International Perspective. Morgan Stanley bought into the enterprise in 1986.
Source: MSCI.

index. By December 1971, the Smithsonian agreement led to a revaluation of currencies relative to the dollar, marking the end of Bretton Woods. In 1972, the EMU, often referred to as "the Snake," was formed, which would be the forerunner to the European Monetary System (created in 1979), leading eventually to the European currency unit (ECU), and today's Euro.

Looking back in time from the start of 1975, the equity markets were reflecting the turmoil in the currency markets. The prior year, 1974, had been a terrible year with many markets down 50 percent or more. The MSCI World Index sank almost 28 percent in 1975, and investors still could not buy an index fund tied to international equities. This would not become available until the end of the decade.

TABLE 12.2 Largest Companies outside North America in 1975

Company Name	Country	US$MM	(%)	April 1975 Country Total US$MM	(%)	January 1970 Country Total Industry Group
Telefonica Nacional	Spain	4,952	15	1,575	10	Telecommunications
Royal Dutch	Netherlands	4,774	30	5,318	42	Energy
British Petroleum	United Kingdom	3,673	5	4,624	6	Energy
Shell Transport and Trading	United Kingdom	3,416	4	4,856	6	Energy
Siemens	Germany	3,313	6	1,386	4	Electrical and electronics
Daimler Benz	Germany	3,074	5	1,759	5	Automobiles
Imperial Chemical	United Kingdom	2,820	4	3,038	3	Chemicals
Banco Central	Spain	2,457	8	708	4	Banking
Iberduero	Spain	2,445	8	1,014	6	Utilities
Nestle	Switzerland	2,305	13	1,101	9	Food and household products

Source: MSCI.

From today's perspective, most investors would be surprised to learn that in 1975, 3 out of the top 10 non-U.S. companies were Spanish firms. In those days, Spain had a very protected economy (Franco was alive until the end of 1975), and this allowed local utilities and other monopolies or oligopolies to prosper (see Table 12.2).

From an investor's standpoint, the MSCI World, representative of the global investment opportunity set, now had 18 countries plus South African gold mines. Gold mines, which were added to the World Index at the end of 1974, would seem today to be a curious addition but, in fact, they were a significant percentage of the equity capitalization at the time representing over 3 percent of the opportunities outside the United States. Gold mine shares in South Africa, both when they were introduced and for much of the next 10 years, represented an investment opportunity larger than many countries including Hong Kong, Sweden, Singapore, Belgium, Denmark, and Italy. By the end of the period, the biggest market outside the United States was Japan. As visible in Figure 12.1, its size was roughly the same as the United Kingdom, Germany, and Spain—the largest three European countries—combined.

Indexes can be particularly useful if they chart not just performance but also the relative attractiveness of a market sector or entire asset class. Valuation ratios are a means of comparing countries (or sectors) to one another as well as to themselves over time. Reviewing performance, the returns for the preceding 5 years of the 1970s were disappointing, with the World Index down over 20 percent since the beginning of the decade. In contrast

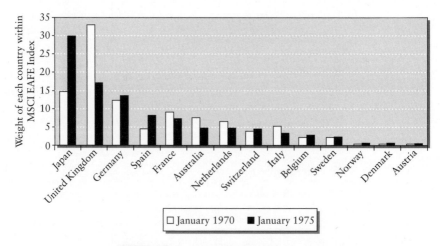

FIGURE 12.1 EAFE Weights: Rising Sun

to the present period (early 2000s) where markets have also dropped severely, valuation measures at that time seem very inexpensive. As shown in Table 12.3, at the end of 1974 the World P/E stood at 7.7, the United States at 8.1, and Japan at 14. In contrast, P/E ratios at year-end 2002 were World 23.2, United States 22.6, and Japan having negative P/E ratio due to its economic distress. Price to Book Value (P/BV), another important measure, showed similar results. The P/BV for the United States was 1.17 versus 2.6 at the end of 2002. At the end of this period, the nation experienced the OPEC oil embargo and the ongoing turmoil associated with Watergate, which had started in 1973. With the benefit of 30 years hindsight, buying at these low valuations would have truly been the "allocation of a generation."

THE LATE 1970s: ENERGY DOMINATES

Moving forward six years to the end of the decade, 1979 saw the start of war in Afghanistan, Margaret Thatcher come to power, and the world went through the dramatic energy shocks associated with the ripple effects of the

TABLE 12.3 Country Returns 1970 to 1975: Poor Market Performance and Low Valuations

Country	Performance	P/E
Australia	−59.6	6.4
United Kingdom	−57.1	3.1
Netherlands	−47.9	5
Italy	−44.7	NA
France	−37.7	5.9
Switzerland	−37.6	6.3
Germany	−32	9.7
United States	−29.3	8.1
Canada	−4.3	6.8
Singapore	17.8	8.7
Hong Kong	19.6	6.4
Spain	35.4	NA
Japan	48.6	14
World	**−21.8**	7.7

Source: MSCI.

OPEC oil embargo of 1973. From this historical perspective, it should not be surprising that Norway, Canada, and Australia—all commodity-rich countries—were three of the top four performers, as visible in Table 12.4.

The other market that was a top performer in 1979 was Hong Kong, which was up 80 percent. Hong Kong, in fact, was now the best performing market for the decade. No, the island was not sitting on oil or gold reserves. Hong Kong's rise in 1979 was partially due to an easing of tensions with China, precipitated by then Prime Minister Margaret Thatcher's visit to Beijing and Deng Xiaoping's statement that Hong Kong can "rest at ease." These two events helped propel the Hong Kong market and increased Hong Kong's weight in EAFE to 3 percent.

The performance of industries and sectors also highlighted the significance of the energy price and supply dislocations at the turn of the decade. Commodities were the top performers with Gold Mines, Non Ferrous Metals, Energy, and Energy Equipment & Services all showing major increases. Industries such as Tires, Autos, Steel, and Airlines that were large consumers of energy suffered the most.

Oil and energy seemed to be the place to be back then, with astronomical predictions for the price of oil and gasoline in the future. Much as technology grew to become a large portion of the equity capitalization in the late 1990s, energy grew to such a level that it represented over 30 percent of the S&P 500 Index toward the end of 1980. That 30 percent U.S. share

TABLE 12.4   1980 Reflections: Energy and Commodities Dominate

	Percent Return
Norway	170
Canada	48
Australia	43
Gold Mines	149
Non Ferrous Metals	52
Energy	49
Energy Equipment and Services	43
Tires and Rubber	−20
Automobiles	−13
Steel	−13
Airlines	−11

Source: MSCI.

TABLE 12.5 Largest Companies outside North America—1980

Company Name	Country	October 1980 US$Mil	Country Total (%)	January 1970 US$Mil	Country Total (%)	Industry Group
British Petroleum	United Kingdom	19,252	9	4,624	10	Energy sources
Royal Dutch Petroleum	Netherlands	13,262	51	5,318	42	Energy sources
Shell Transport & Trading	United Kingdom	12,423	6	4,856	6	Energy sources
General Electric	United Kingdom	7,613	4	1,565	2	Electrical and electronics
Toyota Motor	Japan	6,933	2	805	2	Automobiles
ELF Aquitaine SNEA	France	5,885	10	641	3	Energy sources
Broken Hill Prop	Australia	5,677	10	2,635	8	Energy sources
Siemens	Germany	5,477	7	1,386	4	Electrical and electronics
Nissan Motor	Japan	5,170	2	400	1	Automobiles
Matsushita Electric Industrial	Japan	4,919	1	1,673	4	Appliances and household durable

Source: MSCI.

contrasts with a weight of 6 percent today (early 2003). Not unexpectedly, if you look at the top 10 companies outside North America in 1980, 5 out of 10 were energy companies (see Table 12.5).

As we saw in Figure 12.1, the major change in country weights during the late 1970s was Japan's continued rise, despite its economy being heavily dependent on energy imports. The U.S. market lagged other markets as EAFE increased 70 percent from 1976 to the end of the decade versus the rise of 12 percent for the MSCI U.S. Index (see Figure 12.2).

State Street Global Advisors (SSGA) launched the first international index fund for U.S. investors in 1979, tracking the MSCI EAFE Index. Vanguard had launched its first indexed mutual fund 3 years earlier, a domestic fund based on the S&P 500. It took a few more years for Vanguard to offer international index funds—starting with MSCI Europe and MSCI Pacific-based funds in the mid-1980s. Index funds were also launched on domestic indexes outside the United States, with the United Kingdom taking the lead, followed quickly by Australia, Canada, and Japan. The first stock index futures contract was also a few years away. That contract, launched on the Kansas City Board of Trade in early 1982, was tied to the Value Line Composite Index. It was followed by the Chicago Mercantile Exchange's (CME's) hugely successful S&P 500 index futures (see Chapter 14 for more details on the global proliferation of index-based investments, including stock index futures, which are also discussed in Chapter 25).

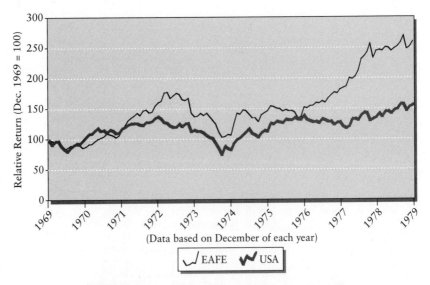

(Data based on December of each year)

EAFE   USA

FIGURE 12.2   EAFE and United States, 1970–1980

1980s JAPAN: THE SUN RISES

U.S. President Reagan was sworn in for the second time in 1985, while Gorbachev assumed power in the Soviet Union. It was also the start of a remarkable surge in Japan's stock market. For the year, Japan was up over 43 percent, contributing to the increase in the World Index, up almost 42 percent and EAFE, up almost 57 percent. By the end of 1987, 5 out of the top 10 banks in the world were Japanese, and all of the top 10 companies outside North America were Japanese (see Table 12.6).

The following year, 1986, the Japanese market doubled, and by April 1987, the Japanese market, for the first time, exceeded the size of the United States in market-capitalization. By the end of 1987, the Japanese market had increased an additional 43 percent. In 1988, the year that the first President Bush beat Michael Dukakis and Benazir Bhutto came to power in Pakistan, Japan's torrid growth in its equity market continued with a 36 percent increase. Many investors became increasingly uncomfortable with Japan's weight in EAFE and MSCI World, viewing its ascension as a market bubble, but it continued its relentless rise for another year. At its height at the end of the decade, Japan's equity market cap (the value of all the publicly listed equities) was 50 percent bigger than that of the United States! Only 10 years earlier it was merely one-third the size of the United States. Looking at the MSCI valuation ratios provides a

TABLE 12.6 Largest Companies outside North America in 1987

Company	Market Capitalization ($Billions)
NTT	305
Tokyo Electric Power	57
Sumitumo Bank	52
Daichi Kangyo Bank	50
Fuji Bank	50
Nomura Securities	46
Mitsubishi Bank	44
Industrial Bank of Japan	43
Sanwa Bank	39
Toyota	36

Source: MSCI.

valuable perspective on this unsustainable situation. By the peak of the market, the P/E of MSCI Japan was 51.9 versus a U.S. P/E of 14.1. A lot has been written about the comparison of Japanese P/E ratios with those of other countries. A discussion of this issue is far beyond the scope of this chapter. Nonetheless, those worried about Japan's increasing market at the end of the decade could note from the valuation of MSCI's indexes that the average premium of Japan's P/E relative to the United States had increased to roughly 180 percent during the 1980s versus a premium of only 50 percent for the prior decade.

To provide investors with an alternative, non-market-weighted approach, which more and more asset owners and fund managers were demanding, MCSI launched a series of GDP weighted indexes. *(Editor's note: Asset managers also created "Japan-lite" benchmarks from the FTSE index series.)* These allowed investors to lower Japan's weight without necessarily making an explicit active decision (albeit the decision to move away from market cap-weights indeed was an active one; see Chapter 18). Other investors worked with their managers to design custom strategies whereby Japan's weight would be cut by some fixed percentage, such as 50 percent. Ultimately, Japan's weight in EAFE exceeded 60 percent in September 1987 and stayed above that level for the next two years reaching a high of almost 65 percent in late 1989. A GDP-weighted approach allowed investors to cut the weight roughly in half as shown in Figure 12.3, where the darker bars represent the GDP weights, and the lighter bars represent capitalization weights. The reduction of Japan's weight through this approach is

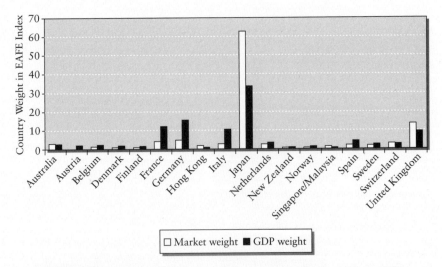

FIGURE 12.3   MSCI EAFE Market Cap and GDP Weights, July 1, 1988

quite dramatic, and the adoption of custom benchmarks served many investors well.

Many investors believed that Japan's high weight was caused partly by the low available free-float of many of its largest companies, and the high degree of cross-ownership, especially of its then mega-cap banks. The lack of float adjustment in the MSCI and FTSE benchmarks and the distortions it caused in Japan and elsewhere are discussed in detail in Chapters 3 and 9. Japan does have a lower float, but its relatively transparent disclosure of this information relative to other countries gave some investors a distorted view. While Japan's float is somewhat lower than that of other countries (65 percent on average versus 75 percent for EAFE), many countries (e.g., Italy and Belgium) had lower average float than Japan's. The reduction in Japan's float was more visible in part because corporate cross-ownership reduced the availability of shares. Other countries had even lower float but the shares tied up were in family hands and therefore not as widely disclosed. Regardless of the added distortion of low float, at the end of the day, Japan's market was a bubble pure and simple.

JAPAN IN THE 1990s: THE SUN SETS

At the very end of the 1980s, Japan's stock market ran out of steam, as did its economy shortly thereafter. After a small rise in 1989, Japan's market fell 36 percent the following year. As of this writing, in early 2003, more than a decade later, Japan seems stuck in a deflationary cycle with zero percent interest rates, increasing unemployment, and seemingly a lack of policy options to turn things around. As visible in Figure 12.4, Japan's weight in the World Index has plummeted, falling to 21 percent at the end of 2002 compared with its peak of 65 percent (as shown in Figure 12.3). All other country weights increased, in many cases doubling, to make up for Japan's relative decline.

On a GDP-weighted basis, Japan's fall has caused a reversal. As mentioned, some investors switched to a GDP-weighted approach to EAFE to lower Japan's weight. By late 1997–early 1998, the weighting equalized: The weight of Japan in EAFE was the same using a market cap-weighted or GDP-weighted approach. It was at this point that many investors who had adapted a GDP-weighted approach shifted back to cap weighting. Today, as illustrated in Figure 12.5, a GDP-weighted approach would increase the weight for Japan to 31 from 21 percent.

By the late 1990s, most large institutional index fund managers had worked with their pension fund clients to normalize their EAFE GDP and other nonmarket cap strategies back to a market cap approach. Since inception, EAFE GDP ended up outperforming a market cap-weighted approach by approximately 1 percent per year over 32 years. This performance

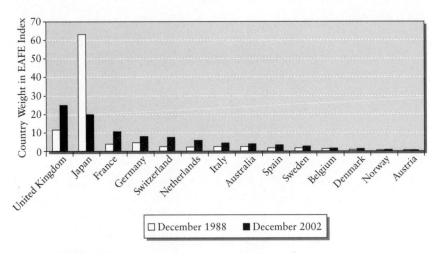

FIGURE 12.4   EAFE Weights: Burst Bubble, Less Concentration

difference was probably a combination of the underweighting of Japan during its decline as well as the rebalancing effect (Chapters 18 and 28 discuss the benefits of rebalancing). Those managers still following a GDP-weighted version of EAFE would have a much higher weight in Germany at the end of 2002 (11.9 percent versus market cap weight of 5.8 percent) and a much lower weight in the United Kingdom (11.4 percent versus 27.7 percent).

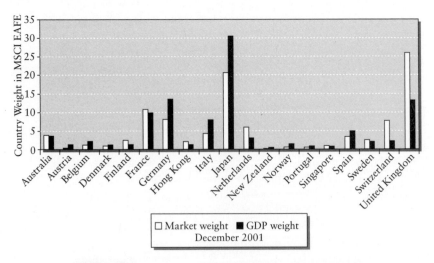

FIGURE 12.5   MSCI EAFE Market Cap and GDP Weights

THE FALL OF THE SOVIET UNION AND THE RISE OF EMERGING MARKETS

In the late 1980s, a series of political events dramatically changed the investor landscape. These events began with the fall of the Berlin Wall (November 1989) leading to the coup in the Soviet Union (August 1991), and the eventual end of the Soviet Union and of the Cold War. This presaged a time when many countries that previously had none or insignificant equity markets opened up, allowing global investors to benefit from a more diverse universe of economies. As countries moved toward a market economy, capital markets matured and stock exchanges were opened. Institutional and retail funds (both open- and closed-end) were launched to capitalize on these new and exciting investment opportunities. These funds were single-country, regional, and global. The investment thesis promulgated was that investing in these markets would be beneficial due to the risk reduction associated with diversification. Some also speculated that the emerging markets, particularly those that were coming out of decades of economic mismanagement and State planning under Communism, would grow at a faster rate than those of the larger and more established markets. Some active managers argued that categorizing emerging markets as a separate asset class would allow them to add value (alpha), as there were many under-researched opportunities. And while the bulk of new money being put into these markets took the active approach, emerging market indexation got started as well. Investors who wanted to get lower cost and efficient exposure to these emerging markets had a choice of some country and regional index funds by the early 1990s.[3]

Starting in 1988, MSCI added emerging countries such as Hungary and Poland to its coverage. Over time, as these countries became investable to nondomestic investors and as their liquidity and depth developed, MSCI shifted them into an investable series of indexes, the first emerging markets series created from the standpoint of the nondomestic investor. Looking back at countries entering (and, to a lesser extent, exiting), the investable series of indexes provides a story line to markets relaxing or tightening restrictions or moving from emerging to developed status. Although the definition of when a market becomes "open" to nondomestic investors is subject to different interpretations, the number of open equity markets around the world expanded from 31 in 1988 to 47 by 1998.

New listings surged as the performance of these markets rose. From 1987 through mid-1994, all emerging markets (both open and closed), as measured by MSCI EMG, increased 265 percent in U.S. dollars. Over the same period, the approximate capitalization of emerging markets rose from $184 billion to $1.3 trillion U.S. dollars—a sevenfold increase. The difference incorporates the entry of public and private sector companies, as well as corporate actions and new equity capital raised by companies already listed. Other index providers, notably the World Bank's IFC affiliate, launched a series of indexes designed to capture the frontier markets that, while not traditionally considered open, may in certain cases be investable to nondomestic investors. In early 2003, there were 49 developed and emerging countries in the MSCI All Country World Index Free (ACWIF) of which 26 would be considered emerging markets that are investable to nondomestic investors. As an example of how established both emerging markets and EM indexation has become, in April 2003, almost exactly 10 years after the launch of the IFC Investable indexes, the first ETF tracking a global emerging market index was launched—the iShares MSCI Emerging Market fund.

EUROPE: ENLARGING THE UNION

The concept of Europe as a community sharing certain common institutions was a long time in the making. The first treaty following World War II was actually the Treaty Establishing the European Coal and Steel Community. The six founding members initially focused their attention on the creation of a common market in coal and steel.

The opportunities for equity investing in Europe were at one time limited. Eventually foreign exchange controls were relaxed, government stakes were partially unwound, and restrictions on nondomestic investors were reduced. More of an equity culture developed. As one measure of the increased interest and greater supply of equities, Europe's market cap as a percentage of GDP grew significantly. Between 1985 and 1995, GDP as a percentage of market cap rose from 69 to 122 in the United Kingdom, from 34 to 74 in the Netherlands, from 10 to 35 in Finland, and from 13 to 32 in France. The market for European equities was further expanded following the addition of the Czech Republic, Hungary, and Poland.

Over time, Europe strove for greater integration though treaties that fostered economic and political coordination. The Maastricht Treaty in February 1992, which brought the European Union into existence, helped prod European companies to compete on a Pan-European and global level. Maastricht pushed European governments toward privatizing sectors that had previously been government owned. Large telecommunication companies were listed on the stock exchanges for the first time and grew to become a significant part of the opportunity set. In 1992, telecoms made up only 5 percent of MSCI Europe compared with 11 percent at the beginning of 1999, at the launch of the Euro. With the creation of the Euro, integration moved to a new level. Among other things, this provided the fiscal and monetary discipline that allowed several European countries to thrive. For investors, one of the implications of the Maastricht Treaty was a change in fiscal and monetary requirements that forced discipline on European policymakers. This discipline, among other factors, led MSCI to upgrade the status of Portugal (December 1997) and Greece (May 2001) to the developed markets and their well-known aggregate benchmarks, such as EAFE and Kokusai.[4]

As the country of domicile became less important, investors in Europe also started to focus more on sector investing. Today, certain investors avail themselves of products such as index futures and ETFs to make sector bets in Europe, treating it as a single country (more information on index products is provided in Part Three). Local indexes for European countries became less important as many investors looked for a pan-Euro or pan-Europe approach. This also led to the introduction of new index providers such as STOXX, a joint venture of European exchanges and Dow Jones & Company. In fact, the DJ EuroSTOXX 50 has become the dominant trading index for futures/options and ETFs.

INDUSTRIES "CHANGE PLACES" IN A NEW BUBBLE

In any broad market cap-weighted index, an investor's exposure to various industry segments will increase and contract with the industry segment's relative importance. As previously discussed, energy grew to become 30 percent of the S&P 500 in the late 1980s, before shrinking drastically. By the end of 1999, at the height of the technology and Internet boom, the exposure in a global portfolio to software, hardware, and telecom was almost 33 percent of the World (see Figure 12.6). That was up from 11.6 percent 5 years earlier. Following the bust in technology, the weight of the same three tech-telecom sectors today (early 2003) is only 16 percent.

Although by the end of 2002, the MSCI World Index had fallen 50 percent from its all-time high in early 2000, and sectors such as IT and Telecommunications have fallen over 75 percent, valuations were still expensive by some measures. For example, the P/E of MSCI World at the end of 2002 was 23.2. With a long-term average P/E of 17.8, one could argue that prices are still vulnerable. By contrast, other valuation measures could lead one to different conclusions. The P/BV at the end of 2002 was 2.1, which is identical to MSCI's long-term historical P/BV average. Investors in early 2003 saw value at this equilibrium point, as global markets made a major bottom coincident with the start of U.S. military action in Iraq in March 2003.

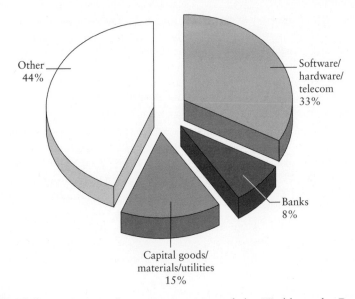

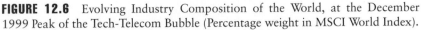

FIGURE 12.6 Evolving Industry Composition of the World, at the December 1999 Peak of the Tech-Telecom Bubble (Percentage weight in MSCI World Index).

CONCLUSION: INDEXES REVEAL BOTH THE PAST AND THE FUTURE

Just as our world has changed dramatically in geopolitical terms since the late 1960s, indexes have reflected the spectacular transformation of the world's economy and capital markets. Instead of Czechoslovakia (now the Czech Republic and Slovakia) being invaded by Russia, both the invader and the Czech Republic are now members of the MSCI EM index, as is China. China in fact has a company, China Telecom, that ranks among the largest companies in the world.

So in some sense, we have come full circle. Thirty years from now, when we reflect back to the beginning of the millennium, will we be looking back at today's flash points or basket cases that later went on to thrive? Will the United States continue to represent more than half the opportunity set for global investors? Or will economic growth in Asian developed and emerging markets reduce the U.S. weight considerably?

Will the instability of the economy in Argentina, for example, be viewed in retrospect as a buying opportunity? (Chapter 18 has some ideas on this.) Will peace finally come to regions such as the Middle East and enable further development of equity markets? Only time will tell the outcome . . . but the benchmark will reveal the story, and will allow future generations of portfolio managers and analysts to gain insight into market trends, valuations, and sector, country, and regional performance.

NOTES

1. For those who want to see one view of where the global investing story goes, I suggest a look at the world of extraterrestrial indexes in 2016, provided in the "For Fun" section of the book's E-ppendix at www.ActiveIndexInvesting.com.
2. Barton Biggs, "Ben Graham Would Be Proud," Morgan Stanley *Investment Perspectives* (New York, April 19, 1993).
3. The first global emerging market index fund was launched in a joint venture between the World Bank's International Finance Corporation (IFC) and SSGA in 1993 and was based on the IFC Investable EM Index, followed the next year by an emerging market index mutual fund from Vanguard tracking a modified MSCI EM index.
4. Editor's Note: Other global index families, such as FTSE and the predecessor to today's S&P/Citigroup indexes also *graduated* these markets to developed market status in the same general timeframe.

CHAPTER 13

Socially Responsible Investment and Index Benchmarks

Peter Wall

_____ **Editor's Note** _____

This chapter offers a comprehensive overview of the concepts of socially responsible investing and corporate social responsibility. It looks at some of the factors reinforcing the rise of Socially Responsible Indexes and propelling these investments into mainstream portfolios around the world. In sync with the theme of this book, Peter Wall makes the case that passive investment strategies in the SRI field may be the most active investment decision one could ever make. The chapter is supplemented by a sidebar on the important topic of Corporate Governance and its implications for index-based investing. Readers will note that this critical area of investing remains unresolved for indexing, and that further research and product development are still needed. Finally, readers will get a sense of the myriad types of SRI indexes and investment products, with supplemental information in this chapter's E-ppendix entry at www.ActiveIndexInvesting.com.

The author would like to thank Craig Greaves for his research support and many contributions, particularly concerning the case studies. I would also like to thank Nizam Hamid, head of Deutsche Bank's Global Portfolio, Index, and Futures Research for bringing his fine report to our attention (see Nizam Hamid and Yvonne Sandford, "Are SRI Indices Responsible?" Deutsche Bank AG, Pan-European Portfolio, Index and Futures Research, October 2002) and Jayn Harding, FTSE's director of CSR, for her comments. Despite the contributions of others, any faults and flaws of this chapter are solely those of the author.

During the first few years of the new millennium, world financial markets struggled with dramatic declines in stock values, the sudden bankruptcies of corporate giants, and a deep and growing loss of public confidence in company management, auditors, investment bankers, fund managers, and "the system" at large. The phrases *improved corporate governance* and *corporate responsibility* are everywhere, and all sides are searching for ways to give them meaning in practice.

This widespread concern about corporate governance found a kindred spirit in the Socially Responsible Investment (SRI) community, which had been growing independently across the world during the 1990s. This community, which seeks to improve the world while improving financial returns on investment, sees the private sector's cooperation as fundamental to improving global climate and environment and meeting society's broader long-term needs. And in response, many companies more fully recognize their roles and responsibilities toward stakeholders communities with many diverse interests.

Surely then, it is appropriate to examine the concept and practice of SRI and its obverse concept, Corporate Social Responsibility (CSR). This chapter offers a brief overview of the concepts of socially responsible investing and corporate social responsibility, looks at factors reinforcing the rise of SRI into mainstream portfolio investment around the world, and then focuses on leading SRI benchmarks. This review explains why a passive investment strategy in the SRI field may be among the most active investment decisions one could ever make.

WHAT DOES "SOCIALLY RESPONSIBLE INVESTING" MEAN?

For many people, the term *socially responsible investing,* or SRI, stirs up visions of wild-eyed activists who seek to change the world by using small investments to intervene in "bad companies." The goal is to get these companies to change their business practices to ones that the activists favor. Likewise, these investors hope they can promote the business of "good companies." Often, the activist investor does not seem to have any concern about investing for profit; certainly it is not a top priority.

From the perspective of many pension plans, their fiduciary responsibilities preclude using plan funds for any purpose other than for maximizing economic benefits to plan participants. Pension plans have tended to avoid SRIs on the principle that it may preclude investments in good, legitimate business opportunities, which in turn can reduce returns, diminish portfolio diversification opportunities, and correspondingly increase portfolio risk. For public employee pension plans, Socially Responsible Investing sometimes becomes a catch phrase that politicians and others employ to force an allocation of pension fund money to their favorite social works projects. In the worst case, such investments can pork barrel projects that are financially unviable and practically guarantee losses to the pension fund.

Both perceptions of SRI, while having some validity in fact, overlook what SRI can and should be. The Social Investment Forum, the leading U.S. association of SRI practitioners, defines SRI as "an investment process that considers the social and environmental consequences of investments, both positive and negative, within the context of rigorous financial analysis. It is a process of identifying and investing in companies that meet certain baseline standards or criteria of Corporate Social Responsibility (CSR) and is increasingly practiced internationally."[1]

The concepts of ownership and shareowners must be considered. Robert A. G. Monks, the well-known corporate governance activist and fund manager, identifies types of shareowners in his book, *The New Global Investors*.[2] He reminds us that "shareowners" range from short sellers, day traders, and arbitrageurs with investment horizons of days, if not minutes, to pension plans and other institutional types that measure time horizons in decades and have investment portfolios that cover almost every asset class. He identifies pension plans, in particular the world's major funded plans, as "the new global investors," which by dint of their diversification needs, expanding asset bases, and overall participation in the economic globalization process, are virtually compelled to own a growing piece of everything on the planet.

In these circumstances, pension plans and institutional investors can no longer "vote their shares by trading," simply because there are no alternative places to put the assets. From this perspective, long-term shareholders of all types have a fiduciary obligation to engage company management and assure that the long-term interests of their beneficiaries are met. In many respects, it is not even a choice. Monks reminds us that it may be too narrow a definition of fiduciary responsibility to limit it to meeting the future financial needs of beneficiaries, when the same beneficiaries would put a clean environment and broadly defined social welfare among their goals for themselves and their posterity. According to this argument, pension plans and other institutional investors (bondholders and shareowners) have an obligation to press for corporate social responsibility just as they advocate good corporate governance. Thus, CSR is intrinsic to good corporate governance.

THE PRACTICE OF SOCIALLY RESPONSIBLE INVESTING

Some commentators have made the analogy that SRI is akin to "style investing" policies—such as size, sector, value, growth, among others—where the investors are seeking companies with commonly held features and actively excluding companies without those features.

Within the general category of socially responsible investing, it is useful to distinguish three principal motives, or investment policies. The implementation of these policies typically starts with fundamental financial analysis, as with any portfolio, unless the investor selects a pure passive/index-replicating strategy.

The three general policies are:

1. *Religious or faith-based investment policies.* These were the earliest forms of SRI and remain prominent today with Christian denominational and Islamic principled funds, where strongly held religious beliefs determine the eligible investment opportunities.
2. *Sustainable business practice policies.* Under this mandate, investors choose companies based on their evaluation of the companies' abilities to sustain profitable operations. Profits by companies that harm the environment, their employees, or their communities and stakeholders, will not be considered sustainable and quite apart from their negative contributions to society, will not be good long-term investments.
3. *Corporate social responsibility policies.* Such policies dictate investors' evaluation of companies based on how they meet a broad range of investor-set criteria such as environmental impact, employee relations, and community and stakeholder relations. Company financial performance and outlook are separate from the CSR review process.

In addition, numerous other "public policy" based screens and approaches may be used. Some of these screens may isolate a single country or market, or may be pursued under a global investment mandate.

SOCIALLY RESPONSIBLE INVESTING—
THE PORTFOLIO PERFORMANCE ISSUE

As noted, SRI strategies will be adopted only if the strategies are seen in general to have good odds of beating alternative strategies. Fiduciaries have concerns over adopting SRI screens or strategies, and the performance outlook is key. In considering an SRI strategy, actual portfolio performance results can help the decision process, as can the results of SRI indexes with reasonable histories.

Most studies of SRI portfolios and simulations show that there has been minimal impact on performance returns from pursuing SRI strategies, either positive or negative. Most studies conclude that investors in U.S. and international equities could have pursued passive SRI strategies based on broad SRI benchmarks without sacrificing returns achievable on diversified equity portfolios in the same types of securities, over the review periods.[3]

The Social Investment Forum awarded its 2002 Moskowitz Prize for SRI research to the paper, "International Evidence on Ethical Mutual Fund Performance." The authors conclude that after adjusting for risk and controlling for investment style using multifactor review parameters there seems, on average, to be no statistical significance in returns between SRI funds and conventional equity funds.[4]

More recent information suggests SRI-screened mutual funds have provided investors above-average returns over the near- and mid-term past, albeit with a short timespan. According to a report from Lipper, over the five-year period ending September 12, 2002, the socially responsible equity funds it tracks had +0.47 percent total return, compared with a −0.1 percent return for U.S. diversified equity funds, and had about a 30 basis point lower loss for the year 2002 to date. The SRI-screened fixed-income funds were also reported to have performed in line with their peers for the past year and three-year perspectives.

Results from the SRI international equities series FTSE4Good demonstrate similar return patterns for recent periods. In Table 13.1, spreads of the returns to a FTSE4Good benchmark index (Global, U.S., Europe, and U.K. indexes) are compared with those of its universe index (the FTSE World Index and the country/regional series), as of the end of September 2002.

Although the results are period sensitive, the five-year returns are significantly better than those of their universe in three of the four instances.

Outside the regions described in Table 13.1, contrasting relative performance has been experienced in Canada and Japan. Canadian equities demonstrate a similar SRI index/market index performance relationship, whereas the results for Japanese SRI funds and benchmarks are, at best, inconclusive.

TABLE 13.1   Performance Relative to Benchmark Universe

FTSE4Good Index	1 Month (%)	3 Months (%)	12 Months (%)	2 Years (%)	5 Years (%)
Global (in US$)	−0.6	−1.6	−1.8	−2.3	+2.3
United States (in US$)	+0.6	−0.5	+0.2	−1.4	+0.3
Europe (in Euros)	−0.9	−0.4	−3.8	−3.1	−1.3
United Kingdom (in GBP)	0.0	0.0	−2.2	0.0	+0.6

Note: FTSE4Good Indexes—Relative Performance, Cumulative Spread to FTSE World Index Universe, as of September 30, 2002.
Source: FTSE.

In Canada, the Jantzi Social Index (JSI), produced by Michael Jantzi Research Associates Inc., is a socially screened, market capitalization-weighted index of 60 Canadian common stocks, modeled on the S&P/TSX 60 index. From the JSI's inception on January 1, 2000, through October 31, 2002, it has outperformed its S&P/TSX 60 comparator by over 400 basis points, and the S&P/TSX Composite (formerly the TSE 300 Index) by 46 basis points.

Japan currently has a relatively small amount of assets-under-management (AUM) in SRI-related funds.[5] The first, the Nikko Eco Fund, was launched in August 1999. There are now 11 SRI-related funds in Japan, listed in Table 13.2. Three general sets of policies underlying SRI investments—"religious or faith-based investment policies," "sustainable business practices," and "corporate social responsibility"—were summarized earlier. Religious and faith-based criteria have not been used in managing SRI funds in Japan, only sustainable and corporate socially responsible policies. Although SRI funds are often termed ECO funds in Japan, separate screens for both profitability and environmental friendliness appear to be used in several funds such as the Nikko Eco Fund and the Sumitomo-Mitsui fund (the latter is an "Eco Balance" fund). As such, these funds would fall within the corporate social responsibility approach discussed earlier in this chapter.

The returns on the funds, shown in Table 13.2 over the most recent Japanese fiscal year March 31, 2002 to March 29, 2003, were in the negative 25 percent to 30 percent range. This dismal performance is roughly in line with the negative 26 percent return on the Nikkei 225 and Topix indexes over the same period, though as noted earlier, these widely used market indexes may be inappropriate for the SRI-related funds.[6] The Nikko Eco Fund holds roughly 100 stocks compared with 1,300-odd stocks in the Topix index, and the universe for the fund is broader than that of the Nikkei 225 and Topix indexes. To meet the need for SRI benchmarks, the NPO Public Resource Center and Morningstar have recently designed a set of SRI Indexes for Japan. Time will tell whether this and other SRI indexes will achieve performance that is similar to their equivalent in Europe and North America.

Portfolio performance and the pros and cons of SRI portfolios in this regard is sure to be an ongoing topic of research and discussion for many years to come, and as the near-universal investment industry disclaimer goes, "past performance is no guarantee of future returns."

BENCHMARK DECISIONS AND SRI INDEXES

Selecting a portfolio's benchmark based on closely shared asset allocation, performance, and risk characteristics is fundamental to any investment

TABLE 13.2 Socially Responsible Investment Funds and Relative Performance in Japan

Fund Name	Fund Manager	Investment Focus	Inception Date	Net Asset (in 100 million yen)	1-Year Return (%) (Mar 2002– Mar 2003) (TOPIX −26.4%)
Nikko Eco Fund	Nikko Asset Management	Japan	08/1999	337.96	−27.4
Green open	SOMPO JAPAN Asset Management	Japan	09/1999	66.58	−26.2
Eco Fund	DIAM Asset Management	Japan	10/1999	42.62	−29.0
Eco Japan	UBS Asset Management	Japan	10/1999	36.21	−27.9
Eco partners	UJF Partners Asset Management	Japan	01/2000	24.46	−26.6
SRI Fund	Asahi Life Asset Management	Japan	09/2000	38.29	−26.3
Eco Balance	Sumitomo Mitsui Asset Management	Japan	10/2000	11.35	−13.2
Global sustainability	Nikko Asset Management	International	11/2000	7.92	−23.8
Global sustainability (without Exchange hedge)	Nikko Asset Management	International	11/2000	12.98	−21.5
Global Eco Growth	DAIWA SB Investment	International	06/2001	24.03	−20.8
Total AUM				640.62	

Source: Keiko Negishi (Tokyo Keizai University) and Mutsumi Sakai (Obirin University).

strategy, and critical to a passive strategy. For SRI strategies, benchmark selection usually means two things.

One, the portfolio will be reviewed against a standard index or commonly accepted investment "hurdle rate." In most instances in U.S. SRI equities, this would be the S&P 500, Russell 2000, or some other mainstream U.S. equities index. The portfolio returns cannot be allowed to lag the hurdle benchmark's returns for any extended period. In such instances, the investors would just as well invest their assets in the hurdle benchmark and "do good" with the excess money earned on "done well."

Second, as noted, SRI portfolios vary widely in content, often having widely differing stock, sector, industry, or country allocations. The best comparator benchmark may require that overlays or screens be put on mainstream benchmarks, so companies are treated roughly from the same perspectives. Other indexes screen from the bottom up, and go outside the standard benchmarks for stock and security selection. The very nature of SRI portfolios, with their sometime unique asset emphases, makes selection of a meaningful benchmark index important to properly evaluating how a manager may be doing. A number of specialized benchmark consultants can assist asset owners in navigating these complex index selection and performance attribution issues.

SRI INDEXES—NEW STANDARDS IN MEASURING PERFORMANCE

The inclusion of a hurdle rate is a critical way to demonstrate ERISA/fiduciary prudence when pursuing an explicit SRI strategy. Over time, though, formal SRI benchmarks have evolved and are gaining acceptance in their own right. These benchmarks can serve as reference points for undertaking research and conducting investment strategies, as well as for evaluating fund manager performance.

Table 13.3 lists the principal SRI benchmarks for common investment targets and notes the web sites that provide information about the benchmarks. These and other SRI benchmarks will play an increasingly important role as the investment community at large faces the demand to deploy more assets in SRI opportunities.

Still, a passive SRI strategy has unique challenges. What Monks calls "the ominous significance of indexing"—the common practice of indexes that leaves considerations of companies' SRI and CSR qualities out of constituent inclusion qualifications—may cause index funds to abdicate a degree of ownership responsibility.[7] The FTSE All-World Index has no screens that keep out stocks of tobacco companies, or producers of nuclear power or weapons systems. Any SRI strategy that chose to replicate the FTSE All-World Index would have to include stocks it preferred to avoid, or understand why portfolio returns, tracking error, and other portfolio results would not fit the benchmark well.

Investors in SRI-indexed strategies in commingled accounts should also be sure they can reconcile matters concerning voting proxies with the

TABLE 13.3 Leading Global and Regional SRI Indexes

Index Name	Target Coverage	Selection Universe	Initiated	Web Site
Dow Jones Sustainability World Index	World	Dow Jones Global Indexes	September 1999	www.Sustainability-index.com
FTSE4Good Global Index (& FTSE4Good Global 100)	World	FTSE All-World Index Developed Markets	July 2001	www.FTSE4Good.com
Ethibel Sustainability Index Global	World	S&P Global 1200	June 2002	www.ethibel.org
ASPI Eurozone	Europe/Eurozone	Dow Jones Euro STOXX	July 2001	www.arese-sa.com
Dow Jones STOXX/EURO STOXX Sustainability Index	Pan-Europe & Eurozone	Dow Jones STOXX 600	October 2001	www.STOXX.com
Ethibel Sustainability Index Europe	Europe	S&P Europe 350	June 2002	www.ethibel.org
FTSE4Good Europe (& FTSE4Good Europe 50)	Europe (developed markets)	FTSE All-World Index Developed Europe	July 2001	www.FTSE4Good.com
Jantzi Social Index	Canada	S&P/TSX Composite	Jan. 2001	www.mrja-jsi.com
Calvert Social Index	USA	Largest 1,000 listed US companies	April 2000	www.calvertgroup.com
Domini 400 Social Index	USA	NYSE, NASDAQ & AMEX listed companies	1990	www.domini.com
KLD Broad Market Social Index	USA	Russell 3000	Jan. 2001	www.kld.com
KLD Nasdaq Social Index	USA	Nasdaq Composite	Jan. 2001	www.kld.com
FTSE4Good USA index	USA	FTSE All-World USA Index	July 2001	www.FTSE4Good.com

Sources: Deutsche Bank AG, Pan-European Portfolio, Index & Futures Research report, "Are SRI Indices Responsible?" October 2002, Global Index Strategies.

INDEXING AND CORPORATE GOVERNANCE

Steven A. Schoenfeld and Stephen Wallenstein

The financial scandals of 2001–2002 changed the face of the American corporate regime. Media critics, financial advisors, and investors alike labeled failing corporations victims of poor corporate governance. The government responded quickly, enacting the Sarbanes-Oxley Act of 2002, and the NYSE and NASDAQ substantially reformed their listing standards. The act and ensuing regulations mandated director independence—especially in the auditing, nominating, and compensation committees—and overall financial transparency.

Concurrently, organizations such as Institutional Shareholder Services (ISS), Standard & Poor's, and the Investors Responsibility Research Center (IRRC) began ranking corporations for good corporate governance. The ISS Corporate Governance Quotient (CGQ) rates over 5,000 American corporations primarily according to eight core criteria: (1) board of directors, (2) auditors, (3) charter and bylaw provisions, (4) laws of the state of incorporation, (5) executive and director compensation, (6) qualitative factors, (7) ownership, and (8) director education. Ideally, the CGQ assists investors in evaluating both the independence and quality of corporate boards and the effect of governance on corporate performance. Similar services are available from the IRRC and other independent assessment firms.

Institutional investors—broadly defined to include pension funds, foundations and endowments, and institutional investors such as mutual funds and ETFs—own or control over 50 percent of all of the equity of American corporations. Institutional holdings could give major pension funds, mutual funds, hedge funds, and investment banks a stranglehold over corporate governance. Yet, only a select few institutional investors systematically act on the belief that shareholder involvement results in greater long-term corporate value.

Prior to the passage of the Employees Retirement Income Security Act of 1974 (ERISA), private pension funds invested solely in the debt market. ERISA expanded the common law prudent man standard, allowing for the evaluation of a manager's performance based on portfolio performance, not just individual investment performance. Under ERISA, pension fund managers maintain various fiduciary duties with their stockholders, including the duty to actively monitor where doing so promotes fund investments. Yet, despite private pensions' large equity holdings, most managers traditionally have not used their voting power to promote good corporate governance. This inertia results from a combination of a belief that shareholders are traders and not owners, as well as potential conflicts of interest in generating investment banking and asset management business from portfolio companies.

Some, notably the California Public Employees Retirement System (CalPERS), have overseen their long-term investments' management to provide shareholder gains. CalPERS employs eight staff members specifically to monitor companies and vote proxies. Hermes Investment Management, a U.K. asset manager linked to the BT Pension Fund, is a very activist shareowner and employs 47 people to monitor companies and vote proxies. In part, this disparity in staffing may reflect the U.K.'s generally greater emphasis on SRI issues and compliance, which require staff with skills outside traditional corporate governance issues. It may also reveal something about the lesser importance given to Corporate Social Responsibility (CSR) by even leading American institutional investors. TIAA-CREF, the largest private pension system in the United States, with assets of approximately $275 billion, has actively utilized shareholder powers to ensure better corporate governance. TIAA-CREF managers believe institutional stockholder corporate governance programs produce better shareholder outcomes. Both formally and informally, those managers have worked to ensure corporate director independence and financial transparency. Sometimes TIAA-CREF managers have been forced to fight antishareholder provisions, such as the "dead hand pill," and egregious corporate executive compensation. More often, managers have worked with corporate management to better protect TIAA-CREF's investments.

The Council of Institutional Investors (CII) was set up in 1985 by leading U.S. public pension funds to coordinate the pursuit of their interests with government, the securities industry, and money management industry. Today it brings together public, corporate, and Taft-Hartley pension plans, foundations, endowments, and mutual funds. Corporate governance is an important theme in much of the work of the CII.

In contrast to the varied history of private pension funds, active and index mutual funds have generally avoided using their institutional holdings to promote good corporate governance. The vast majority of mutual funds either rubber stamp management decisions or sell their investments in poorly managed companies. Few active managers maintain investments long enough to compel improved decision making. Consequently, most mutual funds' short-term strategies provide no

(Continued)

long-term incentives to improve the corporate governance regime. Index-based mutual funds and ETFs as long-term passive holders face a particular quandary—and also a responsibility—with regard to corporate governance.

Index-based mutual funds, and particularly ETFs, provide few if any inducements to improvements in American corporate governance. As of yet, we believe ETF managers have not utilized their voting rights to monitor management (the exception being Vanguard, whose ETFs are actually a share class of their index mutual funds). Currently, all available ETFs are predominantly based on indexes, which select constituent stocks/bonds for many reasons (as described elsewhere in this part of the book), but not (at least yet) for their CSR characteristics. Thus there may be little motivation for ETF management and ETF shareowners to vote individual company proxies. If the security is in the index, it usually must be in the ETF portfolio, optimization techniques aside (discussed in Chapter 19). In addition, the research and engagement processes necessary to apply pressure for good company governance add costs that detract from the ability of ETFs to achieve index-like returns. This is not to say that index-based mutual funds don't take their proxy voting seriously. The major index mutual funds do have rigorous proxy-voting guidelines, and these are generally publicly available.[a] To take the concept further, James Bicksler, in an article in the *Journal of Indexes*, stresses that index funds, in contrast to active investors, have long-term investment horizons and do not have the option of selling individual stocks. As a result, Bicksler posits that index funds should find activist corporate governance strategies even more compelling as a return-enhancing tool.[b] This claim obviously needs to be supported with substantial research, and backtesting such an approach would pose significant challenges and pitfalls, but we believe it would be a worthy endeavor.

In the final analysis, important questions persist. Do institutional investors, many of whom disregard their voting rights, benefit from corporate governance, and consequently, stressing corporate governance in their index-based investing? Are corporate governance and long-term shareholder gains inherently linked? Moreover, even if they

---

[a] For example, Vanguard's proxy voting policies are available at www.vanguard.com/web/corpcontent/CorpAboutVanguard ProxyVoting.html.
[b] James Bicksler, "The Value of Good Corporate Governance," *Journal of Indexes,* second quarter, 2003.

are, do positive and negative corporate governance ratings equally predict long-term shareholder value? The results are unclear and worthy of further research. Even assuming a link between good corporate governance and shareholder value, some of the current metrics may be less useful than advertised. Critics point out that the "check-the-box" type ratings may disregard some of the subtleties of corporate governance and thereby inflate the ratings of some companies. For example, director independence may hide deep on-paper informal connections between directors and management.

Anecdotal evidence suggests that poor governance does undermine shareholder value. Director-management relationships and conflicts of interest transactions contributed in great part to the Adelphia and Enron collapses. Yet, armed with a seemingly independent board and a then-accredited auditor, Enron may have scored well on the CGQ. Consequently, while a low CGQ rating may accurately predict poor shareholder returns, a high CGQ rating may not necessarily be correlated with future shareholder returns. Similarly, Standard & Poor's research findings on best practices in corporate transparency and disclosure could provide insights to produce a systematic approach to weighting portfolios with a strong corporate governance tilt.[c] We believe that this is an important area for further research, and the Duke Global Capital Markets Center hopes to play an active role in exploring the implications.

[c] S&P produced a research paper on T&D that focuses on 98 disclosure items grouped into categories of ownership, financial transparency/disclosure, and corporate board/management structures and processes (George Dallas and Sandeep Patel, "Transparency and Disclosure: Overview of Methodology and Study Results," Standard & Poor's, New York, October 16, 2002). We believe that like ISS' CCQ, this data could be used to develop systematically developed index weightings reflecting slight portfolio tilts, which could appeal to certain types of investors. Duke's Global Capital Market Center, in collaboration with Global Index Strategies, is currently exploring this robust research area. In a major step forward in this field, in early 2004, FTSE announced the development of a Corporate Governance-screened Index, utilizing ISS' CGQ Factors. For updates, see www.IndexUniverse.com.

degree of passivity they can accept. There may be some momentum of change in this area, at least on the corporate governance front, as discussed by Stephen Wallenstein and Steven Schoenfeld in the sidebar within this chapter.

The construction and publication of SRI indexes in formats similar to the standard benchmarks and the widespread acceptance of the standards for identifying SRI-eligible constituents now make it easier to measure, observe, and choose index strategies for SRI portfolios.

As might be expected, construction of SRI indexes has blended the evolution of standard benchmark construction (market cap-weighting, free-float adjusted, liquidity-screened, sector/industry balanced, etc.) with a variety of SRI philosophies on company and stock selection. The three selection methods used are commonly known as industry exclusions, uniform screens (screen in or out), and "best of class."

Industry exclusions were the earliest and most intuitive SRI actions. These generally arose from the religious or "faith-based" communities and are commonly used today. In this method, entire industries such as producers and distributors of weapons, tobacco, alcohol, pornography, nuclear energy, and other businesses are deemed socially irresponsible and ineligible for investment. Industry exclusions are still common to most SRI portfolios and benchmarks, but the method is often too coarse to evaluate the corporate social responsibility qualities of companies in general.

Screen-in and screen-out strategies have their drawbacks in theory and practice. In theory, screen-out is not the best answer to a principal purpose of SRI—to produce change. Not investing in a screened-out company is a denial that investors need to do anything about the reasons the company got screened out in the first place. The theory and practice of *engagement,* where investors bring management and other shareholders' attention to SRI issues, is a reaction to this theoretical flaw.

From a practical viewpoint, screening, especially for traits indicating corporate social responsibility, involves extensive data gathering and interpretation skills. As a result, it can be costly and slow to offer updates. Further, screens and filters are often specified in terms that lead to comparisons of companies across very different business sectors based on common but inappropriate standards. For example, it may be unreasonable to compare a technology service company's environmental policies, practices, and impacts with those of an oil and gas company. This in turn leads to a a tendency for screened portfolios and benchmarks to lack diversification. Strict application of screen results has caused some SRI funds to have unintended sector and size biases—overweighting the relatively clean (so we all thought!) tech, media, and telecom stocks vis-à-vis those stocks' weights in a standard benchmark like the S&P 500. Investors thus need to work closely with their consultants and index managers to fully understand (and potentially offset) these unintended bets.

The problems of strictly applied screens have led many SRI investors to consider another stock selection approach, generally called *best of class*. Often used in conjunction with exclusion lists and an engagement process, the best-of-class approach sets screens at the broad sector level and invests in those companies that best meet CSR criteria. Increasingly, the fund manager's CSR specialist also contacts these companies to start the engagement process for improving the firm's overall performance. The best-of-class approach with the engagement overlay has found some appeal because it encourages activist engagement and heightened oversight, and provides additional portfolio diversification flexibility.

FUTURE DEVELOPMENTS IN SRI AND OTHER SCREENED INDEXES

The future possibilities for SRI-screened portfolios and indexes seem virtually unlimited. Factors such as improving stock, bond, and company databases, cheap computing power, and most importantly, efforts such as the Global Reporting Initiative which aims to expand company sensitivity to SRI issues and improve corporate reporting, all suggest that SRI strategies can become much more targeted in the future.

Customization of hurdle benchmarks and even standard SRI benchmarks will allow the launching of new indexes and financial products. SRI research bodies like the Investor Responsibility Research Center (IRRC) are adding new services such as corporate governance and terror/proliferation-screening tools that may feed into stock indexes.[8] (See the sidebar within this chapter for more on this area.)

It is also easy to contemplate the application of SRI-screens to corporate fixed-income and money-market instruments. By combining SRI criteria with credit rating factors, individual instruments and securities pools can be evaluated and packaged on combined SRI/credit-rated bases.

In fact, the debate today about the importance of good corporate governance is sure to bring SRI more into the mainstream of investment considerations across the financial practices landscape. Screening companies for SRI characteristics also is seen as adding some element of risk management. One Islamic fund manager credited the Islamic restrictions on investing in highly leveraged companies (because of *Shariah* prohibitions on debt and interest) for getting the fund out of Worldcom before its collapse.

Indexation techniques will surely play an important part in SRI development on a broad scale, and hence indexes designed to meet SRI criteria will be vital to process. For SRI investors, "knowing their benchmark" will be even more important than ever.

NOTES

1. Social Investment Forum, *2001 Report on Socially Responsible Investing Trends in the United States* (Washington, DC: November 28, 2001), pp. 4–5.
2. Robert A. G. Monks, "Shareholder Activism—A Reality Check," presentation from conference, *Bottom Line 2001: The Future of Fiduciary Responsibility* (San Francisco, April 2001).
3. Auke Plantinga, Bert Scholtens, and Nanne Brunia, "Exposure to Socially Responsible Investing of Mutual Funds in the Euronext Markets," *Journal of Performance Measurement* (Spring 2002): 40–48. This article also cites earlier research efforts, which generally conclude "the returns of socially responsible investment portfolios are not much different from those of comparable investments."
4. Robert Bauer, Roger Otten, and Kees C. G. Koadijk, "International Evidence on Ethical Mutual Fund Performance and Investment Style," Moskowitz Prize winner (The Netherlands: Maastricht, 2002).
5. These two paragraphs on Japanese SRI and the related table were developed for the editor by Professor Keiko Negishi (Tokyo Keizai University) and Professor Mutsumi Sakai (Obirin University), with the enthusiastic collaboration of Professor Terry Marsh (Haas School of Business/UC Berkeley).
6. It would certainly be inappropriate for the Sumitomo Mitsui Eco Balance Fund which, as a balanced fund, held roughly 50 percent of its AUM in bonds at the end of March 2003.
7. Robert A. G. Monks, *The New Global Investors* (Oxford: Capstone Publishing Ltd., 2001), pp. 182–183. Elsewhere, he notes that owners of index funds often are not permitted to vote their proxy statements, which is a practical hindrance to effective SRI practice via passive funds. The sidebar on Corporate Governance and Indexing discusses some approaches for index funds to follow. Also, it should be noted that index-based separately managed accounts, as discussed in detail in Chapter 24, *do* enable investors to implement their own social/policy screens, and may, in fact, be an optimal vehicle for developing a variety of customized portfolios.
8. For more information on tools to screen portfolios for companies with business exposure to countries which are designated as state-sponsors of terrorism, see www.conflictsecurities.com. For updates on general SRI indexes and index products, see IndexUniverse.com.

Three

The Ever-Expanding Variety and Flexibility of Index Products

Steven A. Schoenfeld

This part of the book focuses entirely on one of the *four key uses* of indexes described in Chapter 5—their use as the underlying basis for investment products. The next five chapters collectively provide an overview of the broad range of index-based products in a variety of forms (funds, derivatives, etc.) and, increasingly, on most investable asset classes. There is a heavy emphasis on equity products, but there is some coverage of fixed income and alternative asset classes, including a full chapter on real estate index products. (Other alternative index products, such as commodity and hedge fund indexes, were introduced in Part Two, while fixed income index products are covered within Part Four's chapter on managing bond index portfolios.)

To fully explore the subject of index-based products around the world would require an entire book in itself. But my goal in assembling these chapters is to give you an overview of the types of investable index products, with a strong emphasis on the considerable variants to "plain vanilla" indexing. You will discover that there are many different investment objectives for index products—tight tracking, "index alpha," other types of enhanced indexing, tax optimization, and leveraged long or short exposure, whether via listed derivatives or specialized funds. And then there are the vast array of

OTC index derivatives. Clearly this area is complex and ever-growing, but we've got to start somewhere!

And where we start is Chapter 14, "The Wide World of Index Products: Building Blocks for an Efficient Portfolio," which provides an introduction to the index product family that continues to expand to meet different investor needs. This chapter, by Joy Yang of AXA Rosenberg and your editor of this book, covers the breadth and depth of index products, the basic metrics of performance assessment, and the purpose they serve as building blocks of an efficient portfolio. Consistent with the theme introduced in the beginning of the book, this chapter demonstrates by example why index investing involves so much more than passive investing, and that the latter is simply one subcategory of indexing. Three sidebars are included within this extensive chapter—one defining tracking error and the information ratio and the other two focusing on the growth of indexing within two large emerging markets.

After gaining an understanding of the broad range of index products, Chapter 15 focuses on one of the fastest growing—and least understood—areas of indexing, "Enhanced Indexing: Adding Index Alpha in a Disciplined, Risk-Controlled Manner" describes the skills and resources required to implement successful enhanced index strategies. Joy Yang and I guide you through a discussion of "index plus" portfolios—constructed solely with securities, as well as derivative-based strategies, two broad categories that add alpha by taking advantage of capital market imperfections and index methodology idiosyncrasies. To maintain a successful strategy with a positive and high information ratio, the manager must be able to identify the opportunities, diversify risk by diversifying the source of alpha, and keep costs down. A streamlined version of this chapter was published in the *Journal of Indexes* (Fourth Quarter, 2003) and has already generated substantial debate within the investment community regarding the appropriate way to define enhanced indexing.

From enhanced indexing, we move to another exciting and rapidly growing area of indexing—exchange-traded funds (ETFs) which were introduced in Part One and discussed in Chapter 14. In Chapter 16, "Exchange-Traded Funds: A Flexible and Efficient Investment Tool," Yigal Jhirad, Omer Ozkul, and David Qian of Morgan Stanley provide a comprehensive overview of the dynamic field of ETFs, with a focus on U.S.-listed products. They explain the product structure and the variety of uses and users of the products. The chapter also provides case studies of applications of ETFs by a variety of institutional investors.

A sidebar on fixed income ETFs provided in this chapter, "Fixed Income ETFs in Europe: A Revolution for European Bond Investors" by Elizabeth Para, which explores how the ETF structure provides efficiency and transparency in Europe, and gives some general fixed-income index product

chp 16 → chp 23

background. Chapter 16 provides an essential introduction to ETFs and should be read before moving on to the detailed chapter on managing ETF (Chapter 23). It also provides a good foundation for Chapter 18 and for Part Five, which discusses sophisticated uses of ETFs for both institutions and individual investors.

In recent years, a variety of indexes and index products have been developed for alternative asset classes such as commodities, real estate, and hedge funds. While some would argue that these asset classes are "un-indexable" the reality is quite different.

The availability of index benchmarks and investment products based on those indexes is, in fact, considerable, and serve to better define the opportunity set for investors as well as increase transparency of the asset class. In Chapter 17, "Indexing Real Estate," Jim Keagy, a real estate investment veteran, makes the case for indexing real estate. In the process, he sheds some light on the benefits of including the asset class in portfolios. The chapter provides an overview on *real estate investment trusts* (REITs), which form the basis of publicly traded real estate investments. REITs are the primary constituents of most real estate indexes. It describes some of the benchmarks and products available to investors and shows how some institutional investors use indexed real estate products in their portfolios. You will find that much of the same logic that undergirds the case for indexing stocks and bonds is also present for real estate.

Chapter 18, "Active Indexing: Sophisticated Strategies with Index Vehicles," is all about combining the efficiency and transparency of index portfolios with an infinite variety of allocation approaches. In this chapter, your editor, Robert Ginis of Global Index Strategies, and Niklas Nordenfelt of Wells Fargo Bank look at different potential index weighting schemes, both within asset classes and in multi-asset class strategies, and assess the benefits of these approaches. A detailed example of the rationale and structure of an alternatively weighted approach to emerging market indexing is included. This chapter provides an essential foundation for the concept of "portfolios of indexes" and highlights how investors can be "as active as they want to be" using index products.

Two important sidebars in this chapter illustrate how some of the largest and most sophisticated institutional investors use index strategies. The first, "Creating Value through Style Index Strategies: How Illinois SURS Neutralized and International Equity Growth Bias with a Value Index Fund," is written by John Krimmel of the Illinois State University Retirement System. It provides an excellent case study of risk budgeting in action, through his plan's addressing a major risk hole with a value-oriented international index strategy. The second sidebar, "How Do Active Managers Use Index Products?" is an interview with Aje Saigal of the Government of

Singapore Investment Corporation. He describes how Southeast Asia's most sophisticated institutional investor uses index strategies—funds, ETFs, and derivatives—to maintain targeted exposure to the world's capital markets.

Finally, there are two web-only sidebars to supplement Part Three in the book's E-ppendix at www.ActiveIndexInvesting.com. The first, "Hedge Fund Indexing: A Square Peg in a Round Hole?" by Adele Kohler of State Street Global Advisors (SSgA), provides a skeptical view of the utility of investment products based on hedge fund indexes. This assessment provides some contrast to the sidebar on the same topic within Chapter 11. The second, which supplements Chapter 18, is an essay entitled "The Active Index Strategist," which shows how investors and traders can implement technical market signals, using ETFs and index futures and options. This essay by the editor provides an expanded framework for understanding how indexing is "anything but passive" and how individual investors and their advisors can actively use index products to construct and manage optimal portfolios.

By the end of Part Three, you will have a solid understanding of the full range of index-based products being used around the world. The book's supporting web sites—ActiveIndexInvesting.com and IndexUniverse.com—will have much more information on new index products as they are developed and provide links to the sites of various product and service firms. The knowledge gained from Part Three will increase your appreciation of the in-depth treatment of the *art and science of managing index portfolios* covered in Part Four.

CHAPTER 14

The Wide World of Index Products

Building Blocks for an Efficient Portfolio

Steven A. Schoenfeld and Joy Yang

_____ Editor's Note _____

The range and scope of index-based products is immense and is growing every year. This chapter—one of the longest in the book—sets the stage for both this part of the book, as well as for Parts Four and Five which describe the management and use of index-based products in detail. Thus, this chapter can serve as a foundation for readers new to the world of indexing, but also serves as a useful overview of the breadth and depth of index-based investment products for industry professionals. It introduces key concepts and linkages to the time line of benchmark and product development from the 1970s through 2004 provided in the introduction to Part One and also in Chapter 31. The chapter covers a broad range of financial products based on equity, fixed-income, and alternative indexes and provides key background on the products for readers new to the subject. We also show the global scope of the industry with examples from several countries, including two sidebars on the development of indexing in Brazil and China, which is supplemented by the "International Indexing" section on IndexUniverse.com.

In addition to standard index-based products, this chapter touches on innovative index products such as leveraged/inverse index funds and index-based separate accounts. Finally, as indexing is a highly dynamic industry, the odds are certain that further product innovation will have arrived even by the time this chapter is published. Further and more up-to-date information is available in the book's E-ppendix at www.ActiveIndexInvesting.com.

Since the launch of the first institutional index funds in 1971–1973, and the first index mutual fund in 1976 (both discussed in Chapter 2), index investment strategies, funds, and products have grown exponentially. This expansion has been so dramatic that there is really no single measure to encompass it, even if data could be kept up-to-date. The industry cites information on institutional and retail indexed assets under management (AUM) in the United States and, less accurately, globally. Since the early 2000s, it has been equally important to track the number of exchange-traded funds listed worldwide and the growth of their assets. This latter subject is tackled in Chapters 16 and 31. Similarly, index providers often articulate AUM figures of the benchmarked assets to various indexes—but these are notoriously inaccurate.[1] Finally, it is almost impossible to track over-the-counter (OTC) index derivatives, such as swaps and customized structured products, though some licensees (notably S&P and MSCI) try to keep track of the "notional value" of such products outstanding.

The bottom line is that it is difficult to express in a single measure the growth and stock (outstanding assets, real + notional) of all index products worldwide. But it is *very* easy to state that the growth and proliferation have been dramatic. And it is important, particularly in a book such as this, to provide a broad overview of index products and some of the ways investors use them.

An important caveat is in order at the outset: The goal of this chapter is *not* to provide exhaustive or comprehensive coverage—to some extent, that is the ambition of Part Three in its entirety. Much more detail is available in subsequent chapters of the book, in this chapter's E-ppendix entry at ActiveIndexInvesting.com, on IndexUnivese.com, and in the articles, data, presentations, and links on both web sites. Furthermore, you are encouraged to submit updates (and, if needed, corrections) to ActiveIndexInvesting.com.

INDEX FUNDS, INDEX DERIVATIVES, AND EXCHANGE-TRADED FUNDS

Although providing an overview of the ever-evolving world of index products is a difficult task, it is essential background for readers of this book, as subsequent chapters assume a knowledge base of these products and their uses. Thus, we try to link the already-acquired background from Parts One and Two, and build the foundation from there. By design, we occasionally flip back and forth between the products and their uses.

Academic theory demonstrates that all investors seek the most efficient portfolio and that the most efficient one an investor can hold is a broad-based market portfolio. This theory holds true for all investors, whether institutional or retail, taxable or tax-exempt. Investment managers are evaluated based on their performance against such a broad-based market index. *Tracking error* (TE) is most often used to denote the difference between the performance of the portfolio versus the benchmark index. *Information ratio* (IR) is most often used to evaluate the return a portfolio achieves against the risk the portfolio takes on. Index management against a broad-based index fulfills the dual objectives of achieving the most efficient portfolio with its goal of zero tracking error, and consequently zero information ratio. This part of the book describes products that minimize TE and often have specific IR goals. Part Four of the book then goes into great depth on the portfolio management techniques required to achieve these objectives. We have also provided detailed and formal definitions in the accompanying sidebar.

Index-based investment management serves multiple functions. They can be used as the main investment strategy or as part of a larger portfolio strategy. An index portfolio can be set up in an asset allocation framework and facilitate dynamic life cycle funds. Moreover, index management can be used to execute complicated trading strategies or to complete transition plans. A broad-based index can be broken down into defined building block components to fulfill the requirements of the different scenarios. In turn, each subcomponent can be tailored to the specific needs of the investors, whether they are institutional or retail, taxable or tax-exempt. These subcomponents can also be mixed and matched between passive and active managers to complete the larger portfolio strategy. As such, a broad-based index strategy can be suitable for all investors. Part Five goes into substantial detail on how investors use index products. However, we provide a short summary here:

- *Core and satellite strategies* involve combining index funds with highly focused actively managed mandates. The core index funds provide low-risk diversification and cost effectiveness. The satellite funds can consist of other more or less risky assets to add value above their relevant benchmark.
- *Asset allocation strategies* set tactical and strategic objectives on what is the optimal percentage to invest among different asset classes. Rebalancing to optimal objectives must often be weighed against the costs and frequencies of rebalancing. An index fund can be used as a precise and low-cost vehicle to maintain tighter and timelier tactical and strategic allocations. Chapter 18 and several chapters in Part Five discuss these uses extensively.
- *Life cycle strategies* seek different investment goals at each stage over a specified period. The stages usually shift from growth strategies into capital preservation strategies as the cycle completes. Index funds provide a cost-effective way to manage these shifts from one stage to the next with minimal disruption on performance targets. More details are provided in Chapter 18.

DEFINITIONS OF KEY INDEXATION/QUANTITATIVE FINANCE TERMINOLOGY

Tracking error (TE) is the annualized standard deviation (SD) of the difference between the portfolio's return r_p and the benchmark return r_B.

$$TE = SD \{r_p - r_B\}$$

Another way of defining TE is "a method of calculating the normalized deviation between portfolio returns and the benchmark index." All other factors being equal, low tracking error is considered the primary goal of index-based investment management.

Information ratio (IR) is a ratio of annualized residual return to residual risk. Residual return θ_p is the portfolio return independent of the benchmark. It is the difference between the portfolio's return r_p and beta $ß_p$ times the benchmark return r_B.

$$\theta_p = r_p - ß_p \times r_B$$

Residual risk is the annualized standard deviation of the residual return.

$$SD \{\theta_p\}$$

Investors generally seek active managers with the highest information ratios. However, the objective is different for indexation. In general, information ratio can be stated as follows:

$$IR = \frac{\theta_p}{SD} \{\theta_p\}$$

For index-based portfolio managers, $ß_p = 1$ and $r_p = r_B$, thus $\theta_p = 0$ and $IR = 0$.

"Index Plus" and Enhanced Index portfolio managers aim to achieve a positive Information Ratio.

- *Complex trading strategies* can increase risks or hedge risks in a portfolio transaction depending on the objective. Index funds within a complex trading strategy can facilitate liquidity, mask flows, or provide low-cost alternatives. Similarly, the use of index derivatives can also facilitate rapid transactions.
- *Transition strategies* help preserve portfolio value in the complicated process of transferring assets to new managers, new strategies, or new asset classes. The goal is to use low-cost trading techniques and technological advantages to realize substantial savings for clients. Index funds are ideally suited for cost-effective liquid vehicles to complete or manage large transitions. These strategies are discussed in both Part Four and Part Five.

CONTINUED PRODUCT AND APPLICATION INNOVATION

As discussed in Chapters 1 and 3, index products have proliferated dramatically in type, quantity, and geographic scope. While many of the first products were developed and launched in the United States, other innovations occurred elsewhere. For example, OTC index product innovations were often more advanced in the European market because of regulatory differences. Similarly, the structural predecessors for both WEBS (now iShares) and Merrill Lynch's HOLDRs were first developed in the European market. Single stock futures were developed in Australia long before they were implemented in the United States. That being said, as the largest and most diverse market for index-based products, developments in the United States can still be considered a leading indicator for index product growth elsewhere in the world.

Other background documentation on the history and growth of index-based products is provided on www.IndexUniverse.com, as well as the archives of both the *Journal of Indexes* and the *Exchange Traded Fund Report (ETFR),* which are accessible from IndexUniverse.com.

THE DRIVERS OF INDEX PRODUCT INNOVATION

As befits the dynamic and competitive financial services industry, innovation in index products is constant. The sources and drivers of innovative product development are multifaceted, and the interplay between the players is a key part of the process. We have identified *five drivers,* which we describe in the following subsections. All of them are affected by evolving asset class segmentation within the industry, which is itself driven by many of the same players, as well as by investment consultants (e.g., style, size, sectors, regional subdivisions). In assessing the forces influencing the industry, it is helpful to know and appreciate the unique but interrelated roles of these key players.

Index Portfolio Managers (Buy Side)

Index-based fund managers, many of which also have robust active-management capabilities, will develop new index products to meet client demand and adjust to trends in product/asset class segmentation. As style segmentation (value/growth) has grown in popularity, index managers have introduced value/growth variants of popular asset class strategies. The launch of European sector-based index funds and ETFs after the launch of the Eurozone in 1999 is another example of innovation by index portfolio managers.

Index Providers

Index vendors aim to meet the needs of their asset manager and asset owner clients as well as their exchange partners by constructing appropriate benchmark and index products. They also face a very competitive environment—most major regions and markets have at least three and often four or more index providers competing for market share. The growth of ETFs in the early 2000s has only further intensified the competition. Thus, index providers must follow trends in markets (e.g., segmentation of asset classes by consultants), respond to clients for standard and custom indexes, seek input from the industry through their advisory boards, and respond to competitive moves. This process inevitably leads to improvement in construction methodology (discussed extensively in Part Two) and to new twists in benchmark design. The rapid launch of new pan-European benchmarks by Dow Jones STOXX, FTSE, and MSCI in the late 1990s was an example of index providers both leading change and reacting to competition (at the time, many called it the "European Benchmark Battle"). The innovative "FTSE 4Good" series (discussed in Chapter 13) and the efforts by Dow Jones, S&P, and FTSE to develop global and multinational index products—in collaboration with exchanges, asset managers, and consultants—also demonstrate this dynamic at work. More recently, the aggressive moves by S&P, MSCI, Dow Jones, and FTSE into the field of hedge fund indexes (discussed in Chapter 11) show how index providers can lead the consolidation and institutionalization of nascent asset classes by providing transparent and reputable benchmarks.

End-User Needs

Asset owners often identify needs that lead to index product innovation. The managers sometimes develop the product exclusively; other times, they work in conjunction with index providers. When a critical mass of such needs surfaces, standardized products result. Some examples of this driver at work include the development of "Japan Lite" strategies in the late 1980s/early

1990s (also discussed in Chapters 9 and 12). Asset owners, concerned about the high weight of Japan within benchmarks like MSCI EAFE, asked their managers to structurally underweight Japan, usually by 50 percent. As these needs were consolidated, asset managers asked for official benchmarks from MSCI, which eventually began publishing an "EAFE Lite" index, reflecting the 50 percent reduction in Japan's weight. GDP-weighting of EAFE was another asset owner-driven solution to the Japan problem that eventually resulted in standardized index products. Similarly, in the late 1990s, as U.S. states were engaged in legal action with tobacco companies, many public pension plan boards mandated that plans divest from tobacco stocks. Thus, asset owners initially asked their active and index managers to divest, and index managers required custom ex-tobacco benchmarks, from the index providers.

Investment Banks/Brokers (Sell Side)

Investment banks and brokers initially had most of their involvement with indexing as a counterparty to index fund managers, and thus had a significant role in the development of program trading techniques to facilitate *informationless* trades.[2] As index assets grew, and particularly following the launch of stock index futures and options in the early 1980s, major brokers such as Goldman Sachs, Merrill Lynch, and Morgan Stanley developed specialized index trading and research groups that tracked index changes, made markets in index derivatives, and facilitated program trades and trades that linked the cash and futures markets. In the late 1980s, brokers worked with asset managers and consultants to establish "portfolio insurance" strategies for asset owners. This strategy did not work out particularly well during the October 1987 stock market crash, and in the aftermath, portfolio insurance was discredited.[3] Many investment banks and brokers have driven product innovation as well. The first emerging market index derivative products were created by Bankers Trust in 1994 when they issued three series of warrants linked to the performance of IFC Investable Indexes for Poland, Hungary, and the Czech Republic, and it serves as a classic example of the sell-side partnering with an index provider (in this case the International Finance Corporation/World Bank) to meet investor demand for efficient access via an index-based product.

One of the best examples of broker-led index product innovation, in the early 1990s, is the Morgan Stanley launch of OPALS (Optimized Portfolios As Listed Securities). These were essentially packaged program trades, designed to track MSCI country and regional indexes. The OPALS received a nominal listing on the Luxembourg Stock Exchange. These products became the foundation for the AMEX-listed WEBS (World Equity Benchmark Securities), which were launched in March 1996 for 17 countries. These 17 WEBS were rebranded as part of BGI's iShares MSCI Series in mid-2000, and they continue to have the strong support of Morgan Stanley. See Chapters 16 and 23 for more background on what we affectionately call "the iShares formerly known as WEBS," given both of our involvement in the development and management of these products.

Commercial banks are also involved in developing and distributing structured index-based products. A recent example would be Citigroup's Safety First Investments Principal-Protected Trust Certificates, which track U.S. equity indexes.

Even though the marketplace tends to prefer independent index calculators, investment banks and brokers have also become index providers, particularly in market niches where they have strengths. Examples are Lehman and CSFB in fixed-income Indexes, Goldman Sachs in commodity, fixed income, and specialized sector indexes, and Morgan Stanley in a variety of niches, but primarily through its majority ownership of MSCI.

Exchanges

In the early years of indexing, stock exchanges were developing the systems and technology to handle program trading to accommodate index funds. In the 1980s, exchanges worldwide focused primarily on developing derivative products on brand-name indexes, such as the S&P 100 options on the CBOE, Nikkei Stock Average Futures at the Osaka and Singapore exchanges, and FTSE futures on the London Stock Exchange. Since the 1990s, and especially since the start of the new millennium, exchanges have become actively involved in index product development, particularly in the ETF area, which in many ways the exchanges pioneered and nurtured (notably the TSE in Canada and the AMEX in the United States). There is also an increasing tendency for exchanges to joint-venture index development and calculation with global index vendors such as S&P, Dow Jones, and FTSE, and then license or create products on those indexes.

In emerging markets such as Brazil, South Africa, Taiwan, and Israel, exchanges are intricately involved in product development, often developing and calculating indexes that are used for listed derivatives and ETFs trading on their own exchanges, and encouraging new product development within their financial community. See the International Indexing section of IndexUniverse.com for a variety of current examples.

EQUITY INDEX FUNDS—INDEXES, VEHICLES, AND MANAGEMENT TECHNIQUES

To the extent that institutional versus retail and taxable versus tax-exempt investors have different requirements and face disparate restrictions, they will seek distinct broad-based index products. Institutional, individual, tax-able, and nontaxable investors have differing holding periods, face divergent restrictions and limits on tradable assets, have different borrowing or lending rates, have different tax liabilities, and negotiate different commissions and fees. All these affect assumptions for the optimal broad-based index portfolio and contribute to the proliferation of many broad-based indexes and products indexed to those indexes. Diverse and flexible vehicles and instruments provide investors a multitude of options to achieve their investment goals. This section shows the wealth and depth of index products offerings and management techniques but is not intended to be a comprehensive listing.

In the dynamic global markets, views of the appropriate building blocks within the board-based index are constantly changing. Index-based portfolios can be created based on global or local indexes, style, size, or sector indexes through "standard customized" indexes or other customized-weighting approaches. Chapter 18, which covers *active indexing,* goes into more detail on this portfolio of indexes approach.

Index-based equity portfolios can be constructed on the following types of standard and custom indexes:

- *Market-capitalization indexes* weight stocks within a country or region and countries within a region by their market capitalization. Subcomponent indexes can be defined based on market capitalization to determine large- versus mid- versus small-capitalization indexes.
- *Regional/country indexes* produce subcomponent indexes based on regions or countries or groupings of countries.
- *Sectors/industries indexes* use global industry classification to define index subcomponents into sectors, industries groups, industries, and/or subindustries.
- *Local exchange indexes* allow investors access to local markets and provide the basis of traded derivatives. Several firms have created index-based portfolios that track these local indexes, such as the FTSE 100 in the United Kingdom and the Topix Index in Japan. The numerous links to global stock and derivative exchanges provided at www.IndexUniverse.com are a source of further information on these indexes.
- *Currency-based indexes* reflect the performance of the particular currency. They can be used to hedge an index against a currency exposure or attribute the performance of an index to a currency factor.
- *"Stage of market development" indexes* group countries into developed or emerging markets by their growth of industrialization, level of national income, market liberalization, and/or capital market development. The World Bank uses gross domestic product (GDP) as a measure

to classify countries. More refined strategies for global investing can be built on this framework.

- *Style indexes* classify broad-based indexes by growth or value, where growth companies seek capital appreciation as their primary goal, and value companies are securities whose current market values are undervalued relative to their fair value.

Readers can refer back to Part Two for more background on index construction methodology.

As discussed extensively in Part Two, issues on maintaining index subcomponents arise around complexities in defining the investable universe. How does one define growth versus value? How do definitions evolve for new industries and sectors? What are the identifiers for overlaps and graduations between subcomponents (small-cap versus mid-cap versus large-cap, emerging versus developed markets)? What should be done with components that do not neatly fit within the definitions (the miscellaneous category)? Different subcomponents can be combined to further define new subcomponents, providing a wealth of index permutations.

The following are variants of equity indexes:

- *Price indexes* measure market performance through adjusted share price changes.
- *Total return indexes* measure market performance, using price performance including income impact.
- *GDP indexes* weight countries or regions by gross domestic product instead of by market capitalization. In many instances, a country's GDP weight can be significantly different from its market capitalization weight.
- *Hedged indexes* neutralize the index against a specified currency exposure.
- *"Free" or investable versus "nonfree" indexes* account for accessibility and restrictions for foreign investors. The index integrates foreign ownership or trading restrictions to reflect true liquidity and market from a foreign investor perspective.[4]

ADR indexes track U.S. stock exchange-listed Depositary Receipts and/or U.S. *global shares* issued by non-U.S. companies. The U.S. listing provides the transparency, disclosure, and liquidity that U.S. investors desire. With few exceptions, U.S. stock exchange-listed Depositary Receipts are subject to SEC registration, disclosure, and reporting requirements under the Securities Act of 1933 and the Securities Exchange Act of 1934. ADR Indexes are also discussed in Chapters 9 and 21.

Screened indexes, and custom variants thereof, are proliferating and focus on a particular market segment. Chapter 13 provides detailed information on the philosophy undergirding many of these indexes and discusses their construction methodology. The line between the benchmark index and an investment strategy is blurred in the cases where the socially-screened index is customized to the an investor's specific preferences. The following indexes integrate personal values with social and environmental concerns into investment management:

- *Socially responsible indexes* track companies with good records of corporate social responsibility using criteria based on social, economic, environmental, and corporate governance factors.
- *Green indexes* track companies based on corporate environment performance and practices.
- *Ex-sin indexes* exclude or screen out companies dealing in industries such as tobacco, alcohol, gaming, pornography, or arms. And while no "sin" index has been constructed, there are those who posit that investing in a basket of sin stocks might have a contrarian investment appeal.
- *Religious-oriented indexes* track religious-compliant companies, or companies that do not violate specific religious principles. For example, the Dow Jones Islamic Index was introduced in 1999 in response to investors seeking Shari'ah-compliant stocks. There are a variety of other Islamic indexes, as well as a variety of custom indexes that adhere to other religious beliefs.

The connection from benchmark indexes to investment vehicles is a holistic one—and a somewhat circular link. If widely accepted benchmark indexes didn't exist, index products could not develop. But in many ways, investable index products help to enshrine a benchmark as it becomes a true alternative to active management in a particular asset class or subasset class. Perhaps the best example of this "chicken and egg" phenomenon comes from the early 1990s when portfolio investment in emerging stock markets was gaining acceptance. Institutional investors wanted an investable benchmark for the nascent asset class that reflected the true investment universe. Entities such as MSCI, the International Finance Corporation affiliate of the World Bank, and Barings (later ING Barings), responded with investable indexes. But to sufficiently demonstrate the indexes' investability—and their legitimacy as performance benchmarks—emerging market (EM) index funds needed to be created. This development occurred in 1993–1994, starting with institutional index funds, but soon expanding to retail EM index funds. And despite volatility and occasional crises, both emerging markets as an asset class, and EM indexes as benchmarks for performance measurement and investment vehicles—including exchange-traded funds (ETFs)—have become an established asset category. Having broadly-recognized and accepted *investable* benchmarks was a key part of the process (and also happened to be the catalyst that brought these two authors together professionally).

As U.S. equities are only 50 percent of world equities, and world equities comprise less than half of total world investable wealth, extending beyond U.S. equities demonstrates the power of diversification. Extending beyond equities to other asset classes—bonds, bills, real estate, metals, and so on—further expands the diversification principle. New indexes are introduced to meet the specific needs of investors, and new vehicles are created to capture the benefits and value of the available indexes.

Nontraditional index-managed assets are becoming increasingly accessible to retail investors through the explosion of ETFs. Indexed ETFs combine features of both funds and securities while providing investors with tax efficiency as well as real-time trading opportunities. Indexed ETFs provide the trading features of a security and offer the diversified exposure of an entire index within a single trade. International ETFs enable foreign investors to overcome the operational challenges of investing in local equity markets. As of October 31, 2003, 271 ETFs were listed across 28 exchanges with total assets of over $185 billion.[5] Today, with a single transaction in MSCI EAFE iShares (EFA), an investor can track a broad index strategy that may otherwise require over 1,000 individual stock transactions traded in over 21 countries with multiple currency transactions and settlements operations. Even more powerful, emerging market ETFs and index funds from Vanguard and BGI's iShares provide efficient, cost-effective exposure to over 25 emerging stock markets, saving investors enormous operational and legal complexity of accessing these markets. ETFs can offer the small retail investor the same efficiencies and cost benefits that large institutional investors traditionally have obtained. For institutional investors, ETFs increase the flexibility and provide an alternative option in managing their tactical strategies. For taxable investors, ETFs allow shareholders to bypass taxable events within a fund by redeeming shares for securities versus cash. More details on the efficiency of the ETF structure are provided in Chapter 16.

Alongside the proliferation of indexed investment vehicles is the growth in acceptance of varied index management techniques. "Indexing is anything but passive . . ." Although index investing is commonly referred to as passive management, index investing and passive investing are two distinct portfolio management techniques with emphasis on different objectives. With general index investing, the focus is on replicating index returns through the most efficient route, bounded by costs and risks with some degree of active techniques to compensate for investing costs. In pure passive management, the focus is on reducing costs and risks using the index as a reference point for a broad-market portfolio. True passive management contains costs by reducing turnover and minimizing transactions. It uses opportunistic cash flows and times market liquidity to manage index events. Passive management reduces complexities through a buy-and-hold strategy, and to the extent that published indexes represent a subset of the target market, this strategy will *always* incur tracking error to the reference index. However, investors who opt for a "pure passive" approach understand this tradeoff of tracking error (TE) versus "wealth erosion." More details on these techniques and the inherent trade-offs are discussed in Chapter 19 as well as other chapters in Part Four.

Just as passive index management steps down the process and complexities, enhanced index management builds up on the process and adds to its complexities. High information ratios and low tracking errors characterize this space that straddles the spectrum between index and active management. Using the low-risk diversified structure of index funds, enhanced indexing adds value distinct from traditional fundamental active management to provide risk-controlled diversified alpha alternatives. Enhanced indexing is extensively discussed in the following chapter.

INDEX PRODUCTS AROUND THE WORLD

One asset class for indexing represents approximately 50 percent of global equity market capitalization: non-U.S. stocks. International equities is actually a standard asset class, but it has taken a long time to get there. Index investing internationally has evolved from serving only sophisticated U.S. institutional investors to being open to U.S. retail investors, and increasingly to institutional and retail investors abroad. Still a nascent industry in most parts of the world, indexing has begun to gain steam, particularly in Europe, and increasingly in Asia. Indexes and index products are now available in most emerging markets. But China? In a country that many are looking to for rapid economic growth, there has only been a mutual fund industry since 1997, but already China has a half-dozen index funds. See the accompanying sidebar for more details on China's nascent indexing industry and another sidebar covering indexing in Brazil later in the chapter. You can also review Table 14.1 for an overview of the breadth and depth of index products around the world. Table 14.1 aims to be comprehensive, but indexing is a dynamic field, and thus it may already be obsolete. Readers are urged to consult the International Indexing section on IndexUniverse.com for updates, as well as this chapter's E-ppendix on www.ActiveIndexInvesting.com for updates.

TABLE 14.1   Equity Index Products around the World

Index Products	Index Funds	ETFs	Index Futures	Index Options	OTC Index Derivatives	Options/SSFs on ETFs
United States	x	x	x	x	x	x
Canada	x	x	x	x	x	
United Kingdom	x	x	x	x	x	
Eurozone	x	x	x	x	x	x
Eurozone countries	x	x	x	x	x	
Sweden	x	x	x	x	x	
Switzerland	x	x	x	x	x	
Japan	x	x				
Australia	x	x	x	x	x	NA
Hong Kong	x	x	x	Illiquid	x	
New Zealand	x		x	x	x	
Brazil	x		x	x	x	x
Korea	x	x	x			
Israel	x	x	Illiquid	x	x	
S. Africa	x	x	x		x	
India	x	x	x			

Source: ETFR, Morgan Stanley, Global Index Strategies LLC, Goldman Sachs Group, *Journal of Indexes,* and *Futures* magazine. See IndexUniverse.com for updates on stock index products listed around the world.

ENHANCED EQUITY INDEX FUNDS

Enhanced Index strategies operate within an index-based framework having a clearly defined benchmark and management that is sensitive to TE, but takes small bets with the goal of outperforming the benchmark index. Strategies can be built around domestic benchmarks, like the S&BP 500 or Japan's TOPIX, or on regional or global strategies, based on benchmarks like MSCI ACWI or FTSE All World. Well-managed enhanced index funds provide slight, but consistent outperformance with minimal additional risk (measured by TE), thus producing attractive information ratios. In a risk-budgeting framework, as discussed in Chapters 1, 3, 26, and 30, enhanced indexing adds substantial value. This is a major reason the approach has grown dramatically in acceptance globally in the past few years.[6] But this category of fund is often misunderstood and inappropriately characterized, particularly regarding the boundary line between enhanced indexing and risk-controlled active. This distinction, and a thorough explanation of the

INDEXING IN CHINA
Yi Zheng

Index funds have found a burgeoning new market in China, which many consider the world's fastest developing capital market. By the third quarter of 2003, China had developed six index funds using several benchmarks and fund structures. The new funds are drawing interest and assets from both Chinese institutional investors and retail investors.

In a little over a month in the summer of 2003, China's Boshi Fund Management Company raised about RMB 5.1 B (US$614 million at the official exchange rate) for its newly launched Boshi Yufu index fund. It has been the largest initial public offering for a mutual fund in China. This equity index fund, formally launched on August 26, 2003, was the recipient of attention from Chinese private investors, whose investments accounted for 61 percent of the total capital raised. It is the first index fund benchmarked to the FTSE/Xinhua China A200 index, which tracks the 200 largest firms listed on both the Shanghai and Shenzhen stock exchanges. As noted in Chapter 7, FTSE/Xinhua is a Hong Kong incorporated joint venture between FTSE and Xinhua Financial Network in China. It has a range of broad benchmarks and investable subsets geared for both local and international investors. The Boshi Yufu Index Fund is the first index fund encompassing both the Shanghai and Shenzhen exchanges. Compared with other index funds that are indexed to just one of the two stock exchanges, many observers think the Boshi Yufu fund offers more complete coverage of China's stock markets.

Many of China's first index funds used the Shanghai Stock Exchange's Shanghai SE 180 Index as the benchmark. China's very first index fund, Huaan Fund Management Company's Huaan ShangZheng 180 index fund, was funded by RMB 3.1 Bil. (US$373 million) raised from October 18, 2002, to November 8, 2002. The fund invested in at least 120 stocks listed in the Shanghai Stock Exchange's (SSE), Shanghai SE 180 index, with the rest in the Chinese bond market (thus it is actually a balanced index fund). Early in 2003, China's Tiantong Fund Management launched another RMB 2 Bil. (US$241 million), Tiantong 180 index fund, which was raised from February 10, 2003, to March 3, 2003, and also tracks the SSE's SE 180 index. It is also a balanced fund and will invest at least 20 percent of its capital in bonds.

(Continued)

The first index fund tracking the Shenzhen Stock Exchange 100 (SZSE 100) is the Rongtong Fund Management Company's first stock index fund and was founded on August 26, 2003. China's Full-goal Fund Management Company is working with the Beijing-based CITIC Securities Company to develop a stock index fund to track the CITIC Composite Stock Index. The CITIC Composite Index, developed by CITIC Securities Company in 2000, includes only the A-share stocks that have the largest market capital and best liquidity in each industry. The market capital of CITIC Composite Index accounts for 60 percent of total market capital in China's Shanghai and Shenzhen A-share markets.

Innovation is not limited to equity indexing. In August 2003, Changsheng Fund Management Company started raising a Changsheng CITIC bond index fund, the first bond index fund that is indexed to CITIC's China Total Bond Index. Further bond index products are expected to be launched in the coming years.

In China's burgeoning mutual fund industry—started only in 1997—index funds are the latest attempt at innovation, but clearly not the last. In terms of performance, index funds have held their own against comparable investment funds available in China. More funds, including ETFs, will be launched in the coming years; both the Shenzhen and the Shanghai Stock Exchanges have implemented major feasibility studies on the required operating and regulatory environment needed for a successful ETF market.[a] Furthermore, international investors can access Chinese securities through China oriented index funds available in Hong Kong, and sometime in 2004, through a NYSE-listed ETF based on the FTSE /Xinhua China 25 Index.[b]

---

[a] "ETFs—An Ideal Financial Instrument for Index Tracking Fund," *Shenzhen Stock Exchange Research Report, Shanghai Securities Journal* (August 2002); and "Study on Launching ETFs in China," *Shanghai Stock Exchange Research Report, Shanghai Securities Journal* (April 2003).

[b] A shorter version of this sidebar originally appeared as "Index Funds Make Strong Debut in China" on IndexUniverse.com, in October 2003. The article is available in archive on www.IndexUniverse.com and in the book's E-ppendix on www.ActiveIndexInvesting.com.

various investment strategies employed to deliver enhanced returns, is provided in Chapter 15.

FIXED-INCOME INDEX PRODUCTS

As Chapter 10 details, fixed-income benchmarks are every bit as sophisticated and nuanced as equity indexes. Yet the growth of strategies for fixed-income indexing has lagged substantially that of equity indexing, partly because of the immense equity bull market in the late 1990s, and partly because in the past, active fixed-income managers could consistently beat standard bond benchmarks by taking duration or out-of-index bets. However, just as over the long term, the "arithmetic of active management" always results in a performance edge to indexing, this has become the case in fixed-income investing as well. There has been substantial growth of both institutional and retail commitments to bond and shorter term fixed-income indexing. All major institutional index managers have fixed-income offerings, and the giant of retail index funds, Vanguard, has a full range of taxable intermediate and long-term bond index funds. The launch in 2002 of fixed-income ETFs in the United States has also substantially contributed to this growth.

Chapter 22 and the sidebar in Chapter 16 describe some popular fixed-income index products. More information can be accessed on IndexUniverse.com.

ALTERNATIVE ASSET CLASS INDEX PRODUCTS

The following short descriptions highlight some alternative index products that have gained favor with investors. Many are discussed in more detail elsewhere in the book.

Real Estate Index Funds Based on REIT Indexes

Although technically REITs (real estate investment trusts) and REIT Indexes are considered equities, most investors treat them as an alternative asset class, both because of their exposure to real estate, their distinct legal and income distribution structure, and because of their proven low correlation to equity markets and indexes. Many REIT Index products are available to investors. There are large REIT portfolios, REIT mutual funds, and REIT ETFs, and investors ranging from large institutional to individual retail investors are now easily able to invest in REIT index funds. Chapter 17 provides a comprehensive overview of this important extension of indexing to a hybrid asset class that has substantial risk-reducing potential for investors' portfolios.

Commodities

Another alternative asset class that continues to gain popularity is commodity investing. Commodity indexes generally aim to reflect broad trends in key industrial commodities by calculating a benchmark based on listed commodity futures contracts. As with equity and fixed-income indexes, they use various methodologies to construct the indexes. As mentioned in the sidebar in Chapter 10, the most popular commodity indexes are the Commodity Research Bureau's CRB Index, the Goldman Sachs Commodity Index (GSCI), the AIG-Dow Jones Commodity Index, and the S&P Commodity Index. The first two indexes have reasonably liquid listed futures contracts, which help asset managers construct other index products on the benchmarks. Several large asset managers offer GSCI-based strategies, either as futures-based portfolios or structured products. Two retail commodity index funds are also available in the United States, managed by Oppenheimer Funds and PIMCO.

Hedge Funds

At the end of the 1990s, few hedge fund indexes existed, let alone products based on them. In June 2003, Rydex Funds launched the industry's first retail/public "Hedge Fund Index Fund," the Rydex SPhinX Fund, based on the Standard & Poor's Hedge Fund Index (S&P HFI). The S&P HFI is an investable benchmark reflecting the performance of a select group of hedge fund managers. They pursue investment programs that represent the full range of major strategies employed by hedge funds. Chapter 11 and the sidebar on investable hedge fund index products in the chapter provide more information on hedge fund indexes and products based on them. The Rydex SPhinX Fund is a fund of hedge funds (FoHFs) that tracks the returns of the S&P HFI, and thus allows eligible investors to participate in the investment programs of multiple hedge fund strategies. Aside from the fund's sophisticated structuring, its real motivation is that (like index funds for other asset classes) relatively small investors gain transparency and clarity about what is in their fund. This is especially valuable for the usually opaque world of hedge fund investing. For a complete review of the available hedge fund indexes, see Chapter 11, and the web-only sidebar in this chapter's E-ppendix entry.

Other asset classes, such as Private Equity, Venture Capital, and even Art have nascent benchmark indexes, but have not yet reached a level of critical mass to generate index products. Somewhat similarly, many indexes exist for what we call "nonasset" classes such as U.S. equity volatility

(VIX), hypothetical S&P 500 index buy/write option strategy (the CBOE's BXM, the S&P 500 Buy-Write Index), and Wine (Bordeaux Index) that serve an economic purpose (and in the case of the latter, also provide olfactory and inebriating satisfaction).[7]

Finally, a huge cross-section of indexes are used in measuring economic trends and activity, many of which are key financial variables for retirement plans, corporate planning, and government spending. Perhaps the best known is the Consumer Price Index (CPI), which is used to adjust thousands of variables for inflation. In 2004, the Chicago Mercantile Exchange is launching futures on the CPI, an entirely new type of tradable index product area.

INDEX-BASED DERIVATIVES

Listed futures/options, index swaps, and other OTC derivatives stock index futures originated in the United States, but they have proliferated around the world. Initially a vehicle for speculation and hedging (and the ill-fated "portfolio insurance" strategies), they have evolved into liquid, efficient, and indispensable tools for a wide range of industry participants. In February 1982, the Kansas City Board of Trade launched futures on the Value Line Index, followed two months later by the launch of S&P 500 index futures at the Chicago Mercantile Exchange.[8] Stock index options also began trading in the United States in the early 1980s, with robust trading on the Chicago Board Options Exchange (CBOE), the American Stock Exchange (AMEX), the Pacific Stock Exchange (PSE), and the Philadelphia Stock Exchange (PHLX).

Since then, no major global equity market could be without a corresponding stock index future (or in the case of major markets, multiple competing local and regional products), and this proliferation has since spread to the emerging markets. Currency and commodity indexes also have corresponding futures. Chapter 25, by Joanne Hill and Barbara Mueller, discusses stock index futures and options in substantial detail. Index swaps and other OTC structured products are discussed in detail in Chapters 25 and 27.

SYNTHETIC INDEX FUNDS AND INDEX-BASED STRUCTURED PRODUCTS

Synthetic index funds do not invest directly in stocks. They may use derivatives to enable investors to realize the return of the index for a specified period. Were it not for the development of index derivatives, they would not be possible. In general, these funds are developed and managed by the major institutional index fund managers, such as State Street Global Advisors, Barclays Global Investors, Northern Trust Global Investments, and Mellon Capital. Global broker-dealers can also assist internally-managed pension funds construct these synthetic portfolios. They can provide investors an alternative vehicle to gain exposure to a particular asset and bypass regulations and restrictions that may be imposed on holding the assets directly. They can also alter the tax impact of particular asset exposures since income distributions of synthetic index funds are usually considered ordinary income instead of capital gains.

The New Hybrids

Leveraged and inverse index mutual funds have gained assets, particularly at the more active, leveraged retail side of the market, though some institutional investors implement leveraged and short techniques as well. Three mutual fund companies have been prominent in this area: Rydex, ProFunds, and Potomac Funds. All three welcome traders into their funds, and Rydex provides for the intraday entry and exit from its funds. At the time of publication, ProFunds had filed with the SEC for the launch of leveraged and inverse ETFs as well. Table 14.2 summarizes some of Rydex and ProFunds (the two larger companies of the three) leveraged, inverse, and sector fund offerings. Updates can be accessed through links to the fund managers on IndexUniverse.com.

TABLE 14.2   Leveraged and Inverse Index Mutual Funds

Type of Fund and Index	Rydex	ProFunds
Leveraged S&P 500	x	x
Leveraged Nasdaq 100	x	x
Inverse S&P 500	x	x
Inverse Nasdaq	x	x
Leveraged S&P MidCap 400	x	x
Sector Funds	x	x
Leveraged U.S. SmallCap	x	x
International/Regional Index	x	x

Sources: Rydexfunds.com, ProFunds.com, IndexUniverse.com, and Global Index Strategies. See the E-ppendix and IndexUniverse.com for links to a full listing of innovative leveraged and inverse index funds.

Guaranteed Index Products and Index-Linked Notes

Many products guarantee some level of absolute return, or even guarantee some small premium over the index return. The insurance industry, in particular, has some interesting structures for such funds, which play on the unique asset/liability spread and tax situation of the insurance products. There are also index-linked, principal-protected products that are set up as equity-linked certificates and guarantee certain levels of returns. Many of these products are listed on stock exchanges, both in developed markets and in certain advanced emerging markets.

OTHER AVAILABLE INDEX PRODUCTS

- *Index-based stock baskets.* These involve a form dollar-denominated, "slimmed-down" indexing to provide direct ownership of smaller baskets of stocks by the investor (e.g., an "S&P 20" to track S&P 500). Baskets like this are available from discount portfolio companies such as FolioFN. E*Trade had a similar facility, but closed it in 2003.
- *Risk-controlled index funds.* Many of these funds sprang up in the wake of the recent market turmoil, although one, the Gateway Index Fund, has been in existence for over 10 years. They use trading strategies that minimize risk, such as the fund using covered-call writing and protective put purchases. The previously-mentioned CBOE BXM Index provides a similar risk-return profile. Other index-based products, such as structured notes, have a similar risk-return profile, but with more predetermined payoff patterns.
- *Index-based separate accounts.* This is a fast-growing area of investing, though it traditionally has focused almost exclusively on actively managed investing. Separate accounts are set up for high-net-worth clients and are customized around the client's overall financial holdings and liabilities. They allow for direct, tailored control of the investment portfolio.

  Chapter 24 discusses the sophistication of the management of these products, and both Chapters 24 and 27 highlight the tangible benefits of index-based separate accounts for taxable investors.
- *Options and Single Stock Futures (SSFs) on ETFs.* The latest generation of index products involves index derivatives based on index derivatives; this allows for better risk control strategies and greater investment leverage and flexibility. As this is a new area, applications are still being developed. Good background pieces are available from exchanges and in various journals.[9]

INDEX INVESTING IN BRAZIL
Stephen Wallenstein and Steven A. Schoenfeld

Brazil has one of the most vibrant financial markets in the world. Its stock and futures exchanges are ranked among the most liquid in terms of contract volume and dollar amount and provide a wide range of financial products.

The country's stock market dramatically evolved during the 1990s. The total market capitalization jumped from a mere 3.5 percent of GDP in 1990 to 37 percent of GDP in 2002. This growth reflected an augmented interest by the global financial community based on the increased stability of the economy and the liberalized regulation of foreign investment in stocks as shown in the table that follows. This has improved the quality and variety of services provided by the different market participants. For example, the number of mutual funds increased from 184 in 1990 to 4,424 in 2002.

Brazil's Market in Perspective

Key Brazilian Market Facts (2002)	Market Rank
BOVESPA (Stock Exchange)	2nd in trading volume in Latin America 1st in market cap in Latin America
BM&F (Futures Exchange)	10th in the world in terms of trading volume
Economy	13th largest GDP in the world 14th globally in foreign investment inflows

Source: Duke Global Capital Markets Center.

Brazilian Index Products

Brazil's financial market uses index products in ways similar to that in many developed markets. Two types of products are based on indexes: derivatives and mutual funds. They are principally structured around the IBOVESPA or IBX (both indexes of the *Bolsa de Valores de São Paulo*—São Paulo Stock Exchange—whose stylized acronym

The authors thank Eduardo Haiama for his research assistance in preparing this review of index investing in Brazil.

is BOVESPA) and range from futures, options on futures, and swaps, to equity index funds. These products are generally focused on stocks, since other markets (e.g., corporate bonds) are illiquid.

The main stock indexes produced to track the Brazilian market are as follows (their correlations are provided in the table that follows):

- IBOVESPA (the BOVESPA Index) is the most important stock index comprising 80 percent of total trading volume.
- IBX includes the top 100 most traded stocks.
- IGC comprises stocks whose companies are listed in Level I or II of corporate governance.

Correlations between Brazilian Indexes

	IBVSP (%)	IBX (%)	IGC (%)
IBOVESPA		85	82
IBX	85		91
IGC	82	91	

Note: Correlations based on daily returns since 2000 (for IBVSP and IBX) and 2001 (for IGC).
Source: BOVESPA and Duke Global Capital Markets Center.

BOVESPA is planning to launch new benchmarks for index products (options and futures) to fulfill perceived market demand. The IBrX-50 Index covers the 50 most traded stocks on the exchange and is easier to replicate than the IBX.

Index Funds

The table "Equity Mutual Funds in Brazil" represents a breakdown of equity mutual funds, showing the importance of IBOVESPA and IBX index-based products in this market. As of spring 2003, there were 53 index-tracking mutual funds in Brazil. Interestingly, *all* major asset management firms in the country currently offer index funds—there are no violent "active versus index" debates among the major financial

(Continued)

firms. (A similar situation exists within the Israeli capital market.) And benchmark awareness is high. As shown in the following table, the percentage of funds that passively tracks the market, combined with actively managed funds that use those indexes as benchmarks, is 47.9 percent in terms of assets under management and 69.5 percent in terms of number of funds.

Equity Mutual Funds in Brazil (Open-Ended)

	Data as of May 2003		
Types of Funds	Total Assets (US$ Millions)	% of Total Assets	Number of Funds
Equity Funds			
IBOVESPA	201.99	3.80	44
IBX	100.51	1.89	9
Passive funds that track	302.50	5.70	53
IBOVESPA	1,752.80	33.01	224
IBX	487.85	9.19	71
Active funds that seek to outperform	2,240.65	42.20	295
Others*	2,766.13	52.10	153
Total	$5,309.28	100.00%	501

Others includes active funds with different benchmarks and funds with other investment strategies.
Source: ANBID–Consolidated Report—Net Assets, May 2003, Duke Global Capital Markets Center.

Derivatives

IBOVESPA (the BOVESPA index) is currently the only index traded on Bolsa de Mercantil e Futuros (BM&F) in the form of futures, options on futures, and swaps. It is the most active index in the Brazilian market and serves as proxy in most mutual funds (see the following table). Since correlations are high and demand for other indexes is low, there are few economic incentives to introduce products based on the other two indexes.

Trading Volume on IBOVESPA Index Products at BM&F in 2002

Type	US$ Millions
Futures	66,756
Options on futures	96
Flexible options on IBOVESPA*	5,838
Total	72,690

*Flexible options are products that can have some parameters defined by the counterparties similar to OTC options.
Source: BM&F.

Financial Turbulence and the Brazilian Index Futures Markets

Since a peak in 1997, the futures market has shrunk in dollar volume, albeit from extremely high levels (see the table at the top of page 274). The severe financial crisis that affected the country throughout in 1998, and the devaluation of the Brazilian Real in early 1999 (and again in 2002) contributed to this decline. In mid-2003, the number of traded contracts had started recovering from the sharp drop. Like liquid index futures markets in developed markets, the value traded of the index derivative is substantially higher than the value traded in the underlying cash market (usually 50 percent more) and has remained so for almost a decade. This is a clear indicator of a healthy equity derivatives market.

(Continued)

Annual Traded Volumes of Future and Spot Markets
of IBOVESPA

Year	Traded Futures[a]		Spot Market In US$ Millions
	In 000s of Contracts	Value Traded in US$ Millions	
1997	14,915	438,050	191,092
1998	9,927	244,669	139,971
1999	5,552	105,127	85,500
2000	7,000	190,375	101,730
2001	5,152	97,377	65,261
2002	5,232	66,756	41,297
2003[b]	3,003	35,240	20,816

[a] Index reference: IBOVESPA.
[b] Through June 2003—actual, not annualized number.
Source: BOVESPA and BM&F.

Indexing's Future in Brazil

In the next few years, index-based investing and trading is likely to grow as a result of structural changes and trends in the financial-market. Hedge funds continue to be established in Brazil and will drive demand for derivative instruments. Greater equity investments by individual investors will lead to increased demand for equity funds, including index funds and derivatives. Financial innovation also should continue—many Brazilian institutions are familiar with the iShares MSCI Brazil fund (EWZ) trading in the United States and hope to introduce local ETFs in the near future.

The Brazilian stock market—and economy—is expected to grow considerably over the foreseeable future. This will increase the demand for index-based products for hedging, benchmarking active or passive strategies, and building diversified portfolios. Global market participants are certain to want to pay attention to this dynamic environment.

The sidebar on pages 270–274 reviews the state of indexing in Brazil, a country that exemplifies the burgeoning growth of indexing around the world. The essay will open your eyes to the advanced state of indexing in this dynamic market—and the potential for index products in other, more advanced emerging markets such as Mexico, South Africa, Israel, Korea, and Taiwan. You can also learn more about index investing outside the

United States in Chapter 31 and in the international indexing section of IndexUniverse.com.

TOWARD THE CONTINUED EXPANSION OF INDEXING

As discussed in Part One, indexing experienced strong secular growth during the U.S. and global bull market of the late 1990s, and to many investors' surprise, this growth continued during the devastating bear market of the early 2000s. In fact, it was during these suboptimal investment conditions that the efficiency, flexibility, and transparency of index-based products proved their utility to many investors.

What trends are likely to develop and grow in the coming years? This question is explored in detail in Chapter 31, but the following paragraphs provide a brief summary.

There will be continued growth of use and acceptance of index strategies worldwide, both in the developed markets of Europe, Japan, and Australasia and in the developing world, as demonstrated with the examples of China and Brazil. There will also be continued strong growth of index products in India, the Middle East, emerging Asia, and Latin America. In fact, since we wrote the first draft of this chapter, new equity index products were launch in Korea, India, Israel, and China. To keep up-to-date with the rapidly evolving index trends worldwide, we recommend regular visits to the "International Indexing" area of IndexUniverse.com.

Some other near and long-term trends that are evident now and will continue to grow are exchange-traded funds and derivatives based on ETFs worldwide, as well as future index derivatives products to meet the demands of investors. There will be continuing growth of the risk-controlled area of enhanced indexing, which has expanded dramatically and is poised to capture greater assets from the traditional active approach, particularly in the institutional investing area. Our next chapter focuses on this robust area.

Finally, do not be surprised to see a continuing expansion of indexing into new asset classes. Not long ago, style or even international investing seemed a stretch for indexing. Now, as was discussed in Chapter 11, indexes have entered even into the previously veiled world of hedge funds, bringing greater transparency to this market—and starting some of the same debates witnessed in the equity investing world when benchmarks first were systematically introduced. In the future, indexes will go wherever investors go, with a wide variety of innovative products tracking them, shorting them, hedging against them, and trying to boost their returns with leverage.

Despite the considerable innovation we have covered in this chapter, it cannot be overemphasized that we have just scratched the surface. Subsequent chapters go into more detail on the attributes and uses of index products. But beyond anticipation for these chapters, the most important fact readers should keep in mind is that when it comes to innovation in index products—to quote Bachman Turner Overdrive—"You ain't seen nothin' yet . . ."

NOTES

1. One of the authors of this chapter conducted some research on the market-share global equity benchmarks in late 2000 at the height of one of the occasional benchmark wars between different index vendors. This investigation showed that the sum of each of the index vendors' claimed market share of benchmarked assets was very close to total world equity market capitalization. This would hardly be credible, given that a large percentage of local equity assets are not benchmarked to the global index benchmarks.

2. See William W. Janke, "The Development of Structured Portfolio Management: A Contextual View," in *Quantitative International Investing*, ed. Brian Bruce (Chicago: Probus Publishing Company, 1990), pp. 153–181.

3. See *The October 1987 Market Break—A Report by the Division of Market Regulation—U.S. SEC* (Washington, DC: U.S. SEC, February 1988), see Chapter 3 in particular.

4. "Unfree" was an insider term adapted by many in the investment community in the 1990s as a result of MSCI's decision to name their investable emerging market index series as "Free." This nomenclature was unfortunate given the sensitivity of certain emerging market governments with spotty human rights records.

5. Deborah Fuhr, "Exchange-Traded Funds Global Summary as of October 31, 2003," Morgan Stanley Equity Research. Updates to this research and other data is available at IndexUniverse.com.

6. See, for example, "Indexers' Growth Continues; U.S. assets near $1.6 Trillion" *Pensions & Investments* (September 15, 2003); and "Dial R for Enhanced," *Investments & Pensions Europe* (June 2002).

7. For more information on Volatility options and futures and the BXM index see www.CBOE.com. For more information on Bordeaux Wine Futures, see www.EuroNext.com.

8. An excellent history of the development and growth of stock index futures is provided in Bob Tamarkin, *The MERC: the Emergence of a Global Financial Powerhouse* (New York: HarperCollins, 1993), see especially pp. 272–280.

9. One of the best overviews on the potentials for ETF derivatives is Sheldon Gao and Heather Bell, "A New Dimension of ETF Investing: ETF Derivatives" in Institutional Investor's *ETFs II: New Approaches and Global Outreach*, ed. Brian Bruce (September 2003).

CHAPTER 15

Enhanced Indexing

Adding Index Alpha in a Disciplined, Risk-Controlled Manner

Steven A. Schoenfeld and Joy Yang

_____ **Editor's Note** _____

Enhanced indexing (EI) is a major offshoot of the immense variety of index-based strategies and products described in Chapter 14. The goal of enhanced indexation is to slightly outperform the benchmark with minimal additional risk, thus achieving a high information ratio. Few areas of investment management are as misunderstood (and often misclassified) as enhanced indexing. For an investment approach that stresses precision, this is rather ironic. Yet despite this hindrance, enhanced investing has been growing dramatically around the world, particularly in the bearish early years of the new century.

This chapter reviews the different types of enhanced indexing. It also refines the definition of enhanced index, and proposes a new segmentation between true enhanced index strategies and risk-controlled active approaches (which commonly get tossed into the "enhanced indexing" category). An important sidebar explores the key question of whether enhanced indexing really works. And if so, which type of investor is it suitable for? A clearer, more precise definition of both areas will benefit asset owners and investment managers by pinpointing more appropriate performance universes and comparisons. The logic and value of these approaches can lead to more growth in both areas while clarifying the best ways to measure the services provided by risk-controlled active managers.

A shorter version of this article originally appeared in the *Journal of Indexes* (fourth quarter, 2003).

ENHANCED INDEXING COMES OF AGE—BUT THE DEFINITION GETS BLURRED IN THE PROCESS

The steady and accelerating growth of enhanced indexing products is partly the result of both disappointing active manager performance and increasing allocation to index-based strategies as a core component of overall equity allocation. At the end of June 2003, over $325 billion was allocated to enhanced index strategies (in all asset classes) by U.S. institutional tax-exempt investors—approximately 20 percent of all index-based assets.[1] Even more impressive has been the steady growth of the approach among the largest and most sophisticated investors. Among the top 200 U.S. defined benefit pension plans, enhanced equity index strategy assets grew by 66 percent from September 1999 to September 2003—despite this period's difficult market environment and negative returns.[2] Furthermore, it is not just fund managers but also asset owners who are adapting this approach. Norges Bank Investment Management—an arm of Norway's government that oversees management of the State Petroleum Fund—initially used only external index managers. In early 2000, however, they brought a substantial amount in-house. The fund was built to approximately €7 billion Euro by the end of 2001 and is being managed in an enhanced index framework.[3]

The investment management industry generally defines enhanced index strategies as *investment approaches that aim to outperform a benchmark index within predetermined risk and return parameters.* This definition leaves a lot of room for interpretation, and investors who ask investment managers, plan sponsors, and consultants to explain the term are likely to get a wide range of answers. Should the enhanced indexing designation— which drives numerous plan sponsor searches—encompass traditional, fundamental active techniques that have been toned down with risk controls? Or should the industry dig deeper into how the alpha is produced? This would create the complexity of more segmentation between enhanced indexing and risk-controlled active, yet yield greater clarity of definitions for both approaches.

As investment professionals who have both worked in all three areas— "pure" indexing, enhanced indexation, and quantitative risk-controlled active techniques—we aim to explore this subject in a novel way and propose some paths toward more clarity of definitions. In this chapter, we appropriately classify the EI space that lies between index and risk-controlled active in the risk spectrum. This classification encompasses a granular segmentation of alpha, with subdefinitions for *index alpha, active alpha,* and even *tax alpha.* We then identify the different types of enhanced index strategies (using our proposed definition).

CLASSIFYING ENHANCED INDEXING ON THE PASSIVE-ACTIVE SPECTRUM

Enhanced indexing has two basic goals in relation to active management and passive management. Enhanced indexing seeks to outperform the index while maintaining the risk characteristics of the index. The first objective, to outperform the index, requires a robust and stable alpha that is consistent over different investment cycles and sustainable over time. The second objective, risk containment, naturally constrains the first objective to a relatively modest level of excess returns, especially when compared with traditional active strategies. The industry's generally accepted definition of an enhanced index fund is as a strategy that seeks to outperform an index benchmark by less than around 1.5 percent, and aims to achieve this with tracking error of less than 3 percent, usually lower. Enhanced indexing is often considered to be a superior form of investing because it leads to more consistent performance with minimal turnover and low transaction costs. Managed properly, it also provides higher information ratios, as discussed below. The combination of active and index management draws on the best of both investment strategies. Enhanced indexing requires the skills needed to identify and maintain alphas combined with the expertise required to understand the index. The resulting benefit of the nexus between active and index techniques in successful enhanced index strategies is the potential for high information ratios.

As detailed in Chapter 14, the information ratio summarizes the risk and return properties of an active portfolio to access performance relative to a benchmark. It can distinguish between the skilled portfolio manager, who achieves outperformance with relatively little risk, from the "cowboy" portfolio manager, who achieves outperformance through very high-risk strategies.[4] It can also differentiate between strategies that have the opportunity to achieve greater outperformance relative to a benchmark by exanining the number of bets it takes away from the benchmark. Mathematically, the information ratio is the ratio of expected residual return to residual risk. By definition, the benchmark portfolio and the risk-free portfolio have an information ratio of 0. Through empirical evidence presented by Grinold and Kahn, investors can use information ratios to assess skill and consistency of active (and enhanced) managers. In their framework, an information ratio of 0.50 is "good," 0.75 is "very good," and 1.00 is "exceptional."[5] All investors seek the highest information ratio possible, and all portfolio managers seek to maximize the information ratio. Given its low-risk (low tracking error) characteristics, enhanced indexing has a natural potential for high information ratios. However, the magnitude of the deviation in a portfolio's return away from the underlying benchmark is directly related to the number and size of the bets the manager makes, whether through stock selection, synthetic derivative exposures, or fixed-income duration bets.

However, as noted above, the industry has been vague, and often "all over the map," in defining enhanced indexing. The following notable definitions all have some validity and acceptance within the industry:

- Richard Ennis, founder of a well-respected investment consulting firm, stated "Enhanced indexing is nothing more than active management— pure and simple. It is highly risk controlled. It is an active product that comes with a benchmark built in."[6]
- A feature article on enhanced indexing in *Global Pensions* came up with this inconclusive definition, which certainly fits the all-over-the-map description: "A strategy with a tracking error of between 25 and 200 basis points is normally described as enhanced indexation, although some would place it between 75 and 150 basis points or put a ceiling on it of 100 basis points."[7]
- John Loftus of Pacific Investment Management Company (PIMCO) took a similar approach—but at least was rigorous in his categories and his logic. He proposed general categories—indexed, enhanced index, and active—based on expected alpha, predicted tracking error, and information ratios, as delineated in Table 15.1.[8]
- Ron Kahn of Barclays Global Investors defined it as follows: "Enhanced Indexing incorporates aspects of both indexing and active management to outperform an index benchmark. As with active management, it seeks investment ideas that will provide an extra boost to the portfolio. However, it builds on the foundation established by index fund managers by delivering on promises of risk management with greater predictability of consistent returns."[9]

Though the investment industry seems prepared to accept definitions based on past IR (information ratio) performance, return/risk, or aspirational

TABLE 15.1   One Definition of Enchanced Indexing

	Indexing (BPs)	Enhanced Index (BPs)	Active Management (BPs)
Expected alpha	0	50–200	>200
Tracking error	0–20	50–200	>400
Information ratio	0	0.5–2.0	<0.5

Source: John Loftus—PIMCO.

return/risk targets, we believe that ranges of expected alpha and risk should not define enhanced indexing. Figure 15.1 graphically illustrates the industry's current position on enhanced index strategies. On the left end of the spectrum is passive (or index-based) management, on the other end, to the right, is traditional active management. We define passive management as a portfolio technique constructed to match the assets and activity of an index with the objective of replicating the index return.[10] We define active management as a portfolio technique that takes explicit bets away from the index (therefore adding risk) with the objective of outperforming the index/generating alpha. Enhanced indexing (labeled EI in the diagram) lies relatively close to passive strategies and falls within the linear spectrum between passive and active strategies. There is currently no industry agreement on where exactly enhanced indexing begins and ends. Furthermore, the much misunderstood risk-controlled active (labeled RCA on this and the subsequent figure) approach falls just to the right of EI, and given the confusion about where EI falls on the spectrum, the distinction is often blurred between EI and RCA— or sometimes obscures RCA completely.

More appropriate would be a definition based on the *actual investment techniques the manager employs,* not the expected results (which investors should know may not be a reliable indicator of future performance). In some ways, this is similar to the convention of defining active managers as value or growth managers. Thus, we propose the following *functional, descriptive definitions for both approaches.* They appropriately distinguish between enhanced indexing and risk-controlled active (as well as fundamental, traditional active) techniques.

Enhanced Indexing employs technical and structural strategies in the capital market to systematically deliver outperformance of benchmarks with minimal additional risk/tracking error. "Index Alpha" can be created by trading index changes aggressively, blending cash and derivative market exposures, harvesting tax-arbitrage or tax-loss harvesting, or actually going outside the target asset class to exploit inefficiencies in other markets.

In contrast, "Active Alpha" refers to many of the low expected alpha/ low predicted tracking error strategies that currently get lumped into the enhanced index category as risk-controlled active. We propose the following

| Passive | EI | EI/"RCA" | Traditional Active |

Increasing risk

FIGURE 15.1 Current Definitional Framework for Enhanced Indexing

definition: *Risk Controlled Active strategies employ fundamental equity analysis (whether quantitative or traditional) to outperform the asset class with tight, benchmark-linked risk controls,* and aim to consistently deliver high information ratios. Some firms in the industry refer to these approaches as "Structured Active," which is equally appropriate.

This approach clearly segments the two distinct investment approaches and expands their definitions by focusing on *how* the alpha is created, not just the aspirational alpha levels (ex ante or ex post). Our proposed definition of enhanced index would revise the current two-dimensional illustration of enhanced indexing (portrayed in Figure 15.1) with the diagram shown in Figure 15.2. Employing strategies outside the equity framework broadens the active-risk spectrum into a multidimensional spectrum. By adding value over the benchmark return to enhance the investment, managers move away from the passive strategy point along the risk dimension as well as the asset class opportunity—including synthetic equity exposure ("Synthetic" in Figure 15.2), fixed-income duration bets ("Fixed income" in Figure 15.2), and option overwriting and other derivative strategies ("Derivatives" in Figure 15.2). This shift of perspective opens up the opportunity set for enhanced index strategies and enables increased information ratios. However, EI opportunities are not limitless; they are bounded by the cap on the outperformance target moving right along the spectrum. This EI space is both similar to and differentiated from low-risk active management in its objective to control risk by replicating specific characteristics of the benchmark. As such, it controls unintended bets against the index. However, RCA generally seeks *fundamental* sources of alpha through quantitative means, whereas EI seeks what we call "technical" and/or "capital market alpha"—often outside the asset class of the index benchmark on which the investment strategy is based. Both risk target and alpha delivery delineate the boundary between enhanced

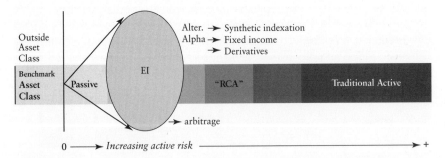

FIGURE 15.2 Proposed "Expanded and Segmented" Definitional Boundaries for Enhanced Index and Risk-Controlled Active Management

index management, risk-controlled active (RCA), and traditional active management, also portrayed in Figure 15.2. The broader search for technical/capital market alpha leads enhanced indexers into the outer reaches of the oval extension in the figure. In contrast, the RCA approaches stay within the asset class spectrum, and fall further along the risk spectrum, moving closer to Traditional Active.

The one weakness of this diagram is that it still relies on a spectrum approach in defining the active risk levels. In fact, using our *functional* definitions, which focus on how the alpha is created, it is quite possible for an aggressive enhanced index strategy to have higher risk/return targets or performance than a low-risk RCA strategy. Several institutional managers offer standard and/or custom low-risk RCA strategies for both domestic and international equities. Some of these lower risk structured active approaches exhibit lower tracking error than aggressive enhanced index strategies.

It is imperative for the industry to move toward greater definitional clarity. It may not occur exactly along the lines proposed in this chapter, but moving in this direction makes sense. As enhanced indexing/risk-controlled active strategies proliferate and grow in assets, the industry inevitably will slice and dice the category, and we should end up with a more precise definition. Although the industry is unlikely to suddenly adapt to this proposed narrower definition of enhanced indexing, it is worthy of consideration. The rest of this chapter focuses on describing and explaining the types of enhanced indexing that fall within this narrower definition.

DEFINING THE TYPES OF ENHANCED INDEX STRATEGIES AND THEIR RELATIVE ATTRIBUTES

Using our more precise definition, sources of properly defined enhanced indexing strategies fall under two broad categories: securities-based strategies and derivatives-based strategies. Each method exploits a different form of capital market imperfection and inefficiency. Some approaches take advantage of index methodology idiosyncrasies and/or capital market inefficiencies. The following subsections detail the variations within these broader categories.

Securities-Based Enhanced Indexing Strategies

Securities-based strategies rely on a diversified portfolio of stocks to replicate the risk characteristics of the index, and they exploit alpha through relative value mispricings or event-driven opportunities. In a relative value situation, alpha source comes from temporary price deviations between two securities with an established relationship or historic correlation. These include convertibles arbitrage, pairs arbitrage, and dividend enhancement. Event-driven opportunities arise from corporate restructuring situations (e.g., mergers and acquisitions, share offerings) and index changes (e.g., adds and deletes within index reconstitutions). As index managers tend to hold broad portfolios and need to track hundreds—if not thousands—of securities, they are well positioned to capitalize on these opportunities.

Constructing a securities-based enhanced index portfolio involves identifying the appropriate alpha sources and choosing a technique to control tracking error relative to the benchmark. The majority of the portfolio is constructed to replicate the index. A portion is then devoted to achieving alpha by overweighting or underweighting the sources of alpha. The core replication can be achieved through a full replication of the index. Alternatively, indexlike returns can be achieved through an optimization method to match the risk characteristics of the index. The alpha can be overlaid or integrated with the core position through the optimization technique with a tilt toward the alpha sources. Portfolio risk can be contained through diversifying the sources of alpha or neutralizing the overweights and underweights by index risk characteristics. Table 15.2 summarizes the various stock-based approaches to enhanced indexing, including the theoretical basis for a technique, the trading strategy, and the potential risks (there are no free lunches in the marketplace).

Several firms, particularly those with large index management operations or capabilities, have developed "Index Plus" strategies based on implementing a more aggressive approach to index changes and corporate actions. While linked to "best practices" of index portfolio management, these strategies allow portfolio managers to take a predetermined amount of additional risk around structural changes in the markets and thus incrementally add index alpha. Several large plan sponsors with in-house indexing capabilities follow similar strategies. Part Four provides considerable insight into the intricacies of simply tracking benchmark indexes—which should give readers a healthy dose of respect for both index and enhanced index managers.

Another type of securities-based enhancement is based on tax-loss harvesting (available for taxable investors) or dividend tilts (for tax-exempt investors). Taxable investors gain a tangible benefit if managers can systematically generate tax losses while maintaining a portfolio's tracking.[11] Conversely, tax-exempt investors have a slightly higher preference for dividends, as they are not taxed on this income. Thus, an index-based portfolio that slightly tilts toward higher dividends can have appeal. The first enhanced index strategy, developed by Wells Fargo Investment Advisors in 1979, took this exact approach.[12]

TABLE 15.2 Stock-Based Enhanced Index Strategies

Securities-Based Alpha	Theory	Trading Strategy	Risks
Convertible arbitrage	Equity-linked securities issued by same company will converge in relative price/value.	Sell the stock. Buy the convertible.	Interest rate, credit, tracking error.
Pairs arbitrage	Mean reversion—two positively correlated securities with temporary deviations will ultimately revert back to normal relationship.	Sell relatively overvalued stock. Buy relatively undervalued stock.	Breakdown in fundamental established relationship or historic correlation.
Dividend enhancement	Differential dividend treaties between countries result in differential asset valuations for investors.	Sell stock to a tax-advantaged investor. Buy instrument that maintains exposure in the sold stock. Share tax pickup.	Tax/regulatory changes, credit, execution, tracking.
Mergers and acquisitions	Empirically, a spread is typically observed between the market price of the target company and the offer value of the stock. This spread theoretically reflects the risk associated with the completion of the M&A.	Sell the relative overvalued stock (the acquirer). Buy the relative undervalued stock (target).	Deal breakup, regulatory intervention, index action and timing.
Share offerings	If an IPO or privatization is likely to be in high demand, and an index inclusion will be treated in a unique way, manager could add value by buying the new offering prior to index inclusion.	Buy stock at offering, hedging any additional market exposure. Use lower acquisition price to add return once stock is included in index.	Fall off in demand, unexpected market moves.
Index add/delete	Imbalances in supply and demand create short-term pricing pressures that cause adds to outperform and deletes to underperform the index around adjustment date.	Buy/sell stocks in alignment with anticipated trading flows.	Anticipated trading flow and resulting price impact does not materialize; unintended bets in offsetting trade, stock-specific risks.

supply ↑ in "delete"
dd ↑ in "add"

(continued)

TABLE 15.2   *(Continued)*

Securities-Based Alpha	Theory	Trading Strategy	Risks
Tax-loss harvesting (for taxable accounts)	As an index strategy is agnostic as to alpha potential for individual stocks, systematic tax-loss harvesting and substitution with stocks with similar factor exposure will deliver incremental after-tax outperformance, with relatively small additional tracking error.	Sell stocks in sectors/cap-ranges that have experienced losses in given period. Sell only when tax-loss benefit to client exceeds *T*-cost of sell + substitute buy by 3× or more. Replace with securities with similar factor risk (size, sector).	Strategy works best with portfolios substantially smaller than full-replication. Thus initial portfolio construction and choice of substitute stocks can create significant tracking error, and PTE estimates may not be as accurate.
Portfolio tilt toward high dividend-yielding stocks	Generally suitable for tax-exempt investors such as pension plans. Tilting portfolio toward higher yielding stocks, while aiming for similar tracking to benchmark.	Conduct dividend screen and establish hurdle for overweighting high-dividend stocks. Implement with extensive optimization to minimize tracking error to untilted benchmark.	Higher tracking error than standard index portfolio. Potential changes in corporate dividend payout raions. Potential changes in governmentt tax policies.

Source: Global Index Strategies LLC.

When defined in our proposed framework, securities-based enhanced indexing is based on capital market inefficiencies and not generally a fundamental alpha-target for each security. We call this *index alpha* in that much of the outperformance of the index strategy is based on a more risk-seeking profile around trading index changes. Although index providers have become much more attuned to the potential market impact of their changes, major index rebalances and reconstitutions will continue to provide opportunities (and risk) for index and enhanced index fund managers. The following sidebar highlights some of the past and ongoing areas of opportunity for delivering index alpha.

Complexities in maintaining a securities-based portfolio increase with complexity of the index itself, the asset class (e.g., U.S. versus international equities), and the number of multiple alpha sources. At a minimum, it requires the same expertise and infrastructure of index-based management. In addition, many of the resources and research expertise of active management are necessary to maintain and monitor the alpha sources. Furthermore, risk

INDEX ALPHA OPPORTUNITIES
Steven A. Schoenfeld and Joy Yang

When defined in our proposed framework, securities-based enhanced indexing reflect capital market inefficiencies and not a fundamental alpha target for each security. Some of the recent opportunities included the following market events (many of which are described in detail in Parts Two and Four, and in the Index Research area of www.IndexUniverse.com):

- 2001/2002 MSCI Free-Float Reconstitution.
- 2001 FTSE Free Float Reconstitution.
- S&P and Russell Indexes—historical performance of additions versus deletions.
- Royal Dutch (NL) versus Shell (U.K.) spread.
- Japanese banking consolidation—2001 Mizuho multicompany merger.
- 1999 Vodaphone/Mannesman cross-border acquisition.
- NTT/NTT DoCoMo—opportunity set of names outside benchmark.
- July 2002 S&P 500 removal of Dutch and Canadian companies.

Looking forward, one can anticipate future areas of opportunity for index alpha in some, if not all, of the following scenarios:

- Major weighting changes of stocks due to privatization and/or increase in investability factors for certain industries (e.g., aviation, broadcast media, defense).
- Evolution of the S&P 500, S&P 400, and S&P 600 to a float-adjusted weighting methodology.
- Other one-time structural changes for major index families.
- International equity dividend tilt trades during dividend season—especially in European equities.
- Graduation of advanced-emerging markets (e.g., Korea, Taiwan, Israel, Poland, Mexico) into developed market benchmarks such as MSCI EAFE and FTSE All World.
- Increase in weighting of Taiwan in major benchmarks due to relaxation of QFII (qualified foreign institutional investor) status.
- Major cross-border mergers of large index constituents, especially if stocks are in both local "flagship' indexes (e.g., FTSE 100 or S&P 500) and major global benchmarks (e.g., DJGI/MSCI/FTSE/S&P Citigroup).

analytics are critical to understanding, monitoring, and controlling biases relative to the benchmark.

Derivatives-Based Enhanced Index Strategies

A derivatives-based approach to enhanced indexation replicates index performance through synthetic vehicles derived from the underlying index such as futures, options, swaps, and other exchange-traded vehicles. Although we don't categorize ETFs as derivatives, the arbitrage activity between ETFs, the underlying baskets of securities, and the growing number of derivatives on ETFs is closer in form to derivatives-based strategies than to stock-based strategies. (Details on the mechanics of this vital relationship are provided in Chapters 16, 23, and 25.) Derivative-based approaches can simplify the complexities involved in maintaining securities-based strategies. Like stock-based EI approaches, however, they also can increase risk and tracking error relative to the benchmark.

Table 15.3 provides an overview of the primary derivative instruments used derivatives-based EI strategies. As the range of instruments grows, the opportunities for a variety of arbitrage trades can grow. It should be noted that ETFs are not derivatives, but the creation/redemptions mechanism can be used to capture mispricing—in fact, this mechanism is what keeps ETFs trading in line with their underlying index (see Chapters 16 and 23 for more information).

An index arbitrage strategy is based on the arbitrage relationship between the index derivative and the underlying constituents of the index. Switching between futures and the securities in the underlying index typically achieves this process. When the futures are overvalued, sell rich futures and replicate the underlying index; when futures are undervalued, buy cheap futures, invest cash, and sell the underlying index. Moreover, long and short positions index options can be combined to replicate the index while simultaneously profiting from the mispriced options. For example, a futures-based strategy can take advantage of richness or cheapness in the quarterly roll cycle by moving in the opposite direction as the prevailing street sentiment. As noted previously and in Table 15.3, the availability of ETFs and options on ETFs expand the arbitrage opportunity set to another instrument and, perhaps more importantly, expands these strategies to substantially more indexes and subindexes (see the comparison in Table 25.1).

An extension of the aforementioned strategy is to hold long positions in the derivative to obtain the underlying index returns. Thereafter, the available cash (after margin requirements are met) is transported to a strategy to generate additional returns. To achieve optimal index outperformance, these strategies must cover the costs of the derivative positions as well as any

TABLE 15.3 Derivatives Instruments for Derivatives-Based Enhanced Indexing Approaches

Derivatives-Based Vehicles	Definition	Risks and Costs
Futures	A standardized, transferable, exchange-traded contract that requires delivery of a commodity, bond, currency, or stock index, at a specified price, on a specified future date.	Futures mispricing, expiration—futures have an expiration date every 3 months which requires selling and buying contracts that may be mispriced, fees, cash management risk, liquidity risk.
Options	The right, but not the obligation, to buy (for a call option) or sell (for a put option) a specific amount of a given stock, commodity, currency, index, or debt, at a specified price (the strike price) during a specified period of time.	Credit risks associated with OTC instruments, expiration risk, cash management risk, liquidity risks, exit risk, volatility risk.
Swaps	An exchange of streams of payments over time according to specified terms. As index-based managers are naturally long stocks, they act as a natural buyer of index returns from swap counterparties.	Credit/counterparty risks, expiration risk, exit risk, volatility risk. Tracking risk possible if mismatch between index underlying swap and portfolio benchmark.
ETFs and ETF derivatives	Authorized participants in ETFs can arbitrage between the ETF and the creation baskets of the funds. Options and futures on ETFs have proliferated since 2001 and are usually settled into the physical ETF, which open up further arbitrage opportunities. Options and single stock futures on ETFs have expanded the arbitrage opportunities.	As with futures and options, occasional small price discrepancies often develop between related instruments. Enhanced indexers are natural participants in this area, as they are "naturally long" the index returns, and thus may not need to hedge a cheap long index situation.

Note: ETFs are *not* derivative instruments although, like individual stocks, they can serve as the underlying for options and single stock futures.
Source: Global Index Strategies LLC.

tracking error and exceed the implied interest rate used in calculating the fair value of the derivative.

Portfolio managers have been using options as a performance-enhancing tool since listed options became available in the mid-1970s. However, the introduction of index options in the early 1980s and the ability to combine options strategies with a futures-based indexing strategy provide a robust tool kit to enhance returns. Since 1992, First Quadrant has offered an enhanced indexing strategy that combines these two techniques. The key to successful implementation of options strategies for enhancement is to have diverse techniques and a deep experience set to determine when one approach would be more likely to succeed.

Finally, several large quantitative asset managers use index options to enhance returns or, in some cases, dampen volatility. Four common options-based strategies that are used in enhanced index strategies are detailed in Table 15.4. It should be noted that volatility-dampening strategies can also be used to transform the investment objective of the fund—for example, targeting a lower beta relationship with the market. The Gateway Fund is one such mutual fund, and Chapter 31 discusses "variable beta" portfolios.

TABLE 15.4 Common Options-Based Strategies for Enhanced Indexing

Option Strategies	Implementation	Risks and Costs
Call writing	Out of the money call options (on stocks or indexes) are sold; profits generated through time decay.	Need to accurately assess volatility. Can have drawdowns/performance impact when the option is exercised, placing a cap on upside returns.
Strangle/straddle selling	Simultaneous sale of put and call options (strangle is at current market levels; straddle is sale of put and call with out-of-the-money strike prices).	High losses possible during volatile markets. Full market cycle returns can be inconsistent.
Sell options/ hedge with futures	Generate income/enhancement through sale of puts and calls (stock or index options); hedge market exposure dynamically with futures.	Gap risk, precise trading required. High T-costs. Potential benchmark mismatch.
Sell options/ buy options	Market neutral; simultaneous purchase and sale of put and call options—benefiting from varying decay rates of this portfolio of options.	Tends to underperform during steady, trending markets.

Source: Global Index Strategies, LLC, First Quadrant LP[a] and PIMCO.[b]
[a] Miller, Todd and Timothy Meckel, "How to Improve Your Indexed Portfolio," *First Quadrant Investment Management Reflections*, Number 5, 1998.
[b] Loftus, John, "Enhanced Equity Indexing," *Perspectives on Equity Indexing* (New Hope, PA: Frank J. Fabozzi Associates, 2000), pp. 92–93

Another approach that some index fund managers with large international equity index assets have used extensively is index total return swaps. In many markets, due to unique local supply/demand elements, it is possible for index fund managers to receive a premium over the index return. During the late 1990s, it was common for swap pricing to yield 500 basis points or more over the index, particularly for certain Asian developed and emerging markets. The best opportunities appear only occasionally, and as Chapter 21 discusses, portfolio managers need to be alert to a myriad of factors in order to capture the performance advantages for their funds.

As with securities-based strategies, managers can employ a market-neutral derivatives-based strategy by combining options according to realized or implied volatility in the underlying index. These strategies exploit the mispricing of options or temporary deviations of options from their relative fair values. These strategies carry exposure to movements in the price of the underlying index.

Alpha-transport strategies can be ported to any strategy and do not need to maintain an equity link. These strategies can be implemented in many forms, from a simple enhanced cash fund to more complicated hedge fund techniques. Increasingly, pension plan sponsors and other large institutional investors seek pure alpha exposure in whatever approach meets their needs, and get their strategic asset class exposure through passive or quasi-passive vehicles. The challenge for asset managers of the future increasingly will be that of finding the right blend of alpha and beta, and the beta component will likely come from index and/or enhanced index strategies. This new paradigm is explored in Chapters 30 and 31, but it is important to note that enhanced index strategies are one of the few disciplines that can suitably provide both the beta—asset class return—exposure, and the alpha for this rapidly evolving framework for institutional investors.

Derivatives-based strategies usually increase portfolio risk, introduce credit risk, and may lower the information ratio. They also add additional operational complexities (e.g., the cash and derivatives may have different trading hours). All these elements must be weighed against the benefits of the index alpha they can potentially deliver. Furthermore, as with securities-based enhanced indexing, derivatives-based indexing requires substantial investment in portfolio management resources (people and systems).

REFINED DEFINITIONS WILL DRIVE GROWTH IN ENHANCED INDEXING

As noted previously in the chapter, what consultants and managers alike often cubbyhole as enhanced indexing, is actually not EI; but is risk-controlled

DOES ENHANCED INDEXING WORK?
Steven A. Schoenfeld and Joy Yang

The academic research on publicly available enhanced index funds is sparse, but two studies on U.S. mutual funds—generally based on the S&P 500—have concluded that less than half of such strategies outperform their benchmark, mainly due to high transaction costs and higher expenses.[a] A more current exercise reached similar conclusions—tracking only securities-based S&P 500-based enhanced index mutual funds through a "basket" representing approximately $8 billion in assets under management. The period from January 1990 through August 2003 produced an average monthly alpha of 0.4 (0.004 percent) basis point (bp) before fees, but this was eroded to negative 7.4 bps per month −.074 percent/month) after fees were incorporated into the returns. The study also determined that the distribution of alphas were normally distributed around the mean—just as we've seen with traditional active managers.[b] Furthermore, during the full year of 2003, the average enhanced index fund in this same sample underperformed the benchmark net-of-fees, and only in the third quarter did more than half of the managers outperform.[c]

A much wider range of enhanced index strategies is available to institutional investors such as corporate and public pension funds, foundations, and endowments. Furthermore, several large asset owners/pension funds manage large amounts of index-based assets in-house, and a few have chosen to develop enhanced index capabilities, with some success.

These institutional-quality strategies generally have lower costs and therefore have a better chance of outperforming their benchmarks. Anecdotal evidence and data from major investment consultants

---

[a] Block (2002); Riepe and Zils (1997) cited from Adam Schwartz, *Enhanced Index Fund Viability,* doctoral dissertation (Princeton, NJ: Princeton University, April 2003), p. 20, provided by Professor Burton Malkiel.
[b] Ingid Tiernens, "Focus: When Do Enhanced Indexation Managers Add Alpha?" in *Quantitative Insights—Goldman Sachs Equity Derivatives Strategy* (New York; October 15, 2003), pp. 3–6. It is important to repeat that this study only included securities-based enhanced index strategies. Derivatives-based strategies were not included in the study.
[c] Ingrid Tierens, *Quantitative Insights—Goldman Sachs Equity Derivatives Strategy* (New York; February 12, 2004), p. 18.

show that institutional enhanced index products have delivered on their performance promise—consistent outperformance with low levels of additional risk—generating high information ratios.[d]

Now we can be accused of reverting back to a definition that we attacked. But since consultants and the industry remain entrenched in the "old school" broader definition of the category, we have to use the data that are available. An example of the performance from enhanced indexing/risk-controlled active is available in our favorite asset class—international equity. Analyzing institutional non-U.S. equity for U.S. tax-exempt investors, using the Wilshire Mentor database, we found that over both five- and 10-year periods, enhanced index/risk-controlled active managers delivered on the performance promise of beating their EAFE benchmark. The median manager outperformed by over 1 percent annualized in the 5-year time frame, and almost 3 percent in the 10-year time frame (although some of the factors discussed in Chapter 3 were at play in the early 1990s).[e] More significantly, the information ratios of top performers—using Grinold and Kahn's definitions—are exceptional, with five-year annualized IRs between 0.36 and 1.47, and 10-year annualized IRs between 0.69 and 1.19.

A summary of academic research on enhanced indexing was inconclusive at best. In the two most comprehensive studies of U.S. large-cap equity strategies benchmarked to the S&P 500, neither sample group consistently beat their benchmark, and the sample groups displayed higher tracking error (and thus lower IRs).[f] In general, the cause was more frequent trading and higher expenses. (Does this sound like the "arithmetic of active management" of a certain Nobel Prize winner?)

We also conducted a review of Morningstar Principia Pro data and found both the data and the results truly "all over the map." The category included both equity and balanced funds, and really only demonstrated the need for more refined definitions of this strategy category.

Some products of specific firms *have* produced steady outperformance. First Quadrant's various derivative-based enhancement strategies have regularly produced annualized *index alpha* of over 150 bps

---

[d] Callan Associates, "Enhanced Indexing: In Search of a Free Lunch?" (1999).
[e] Wilshire Mentor Database—EAFE Universe (third quarter, 2003).
[f] Adam Schwartz, *Enhanced Index Fund Viability*, doctoral dissertation for Prof. Burton Malkiel (Princeton, NJ: Princeton University, April 2003).

(Continued)

on top of an S&P 500 strategy. Similarly, BGI's Global Equity Index-Plus strategies have produced in excess of 50 bp of *index alpha* over global benchmarks, but do not yet have a sufficient track record to demonstrate sustainability of this index alpha.

As mentioned in the chapter's main text, Norges Bank Investment Management initially used only external index managers for the State Petroleum Fund, but in early 2000, they brought a substantial amount in-house.[g] They now pursue an enhanced index approach by gathering input from both their sell-side brokers and their remaining buy-side index managers.

In the arena of taxable investment for high-net-worth individuals, firms have consistently delivered tax alpha using systematic tax-loss harvesting to produce superior after-tax returns. Historical backtests of 25 years or more demonstrate that these active tax-loss-harvesting strategies can deliver 75 to 125 bps of tax alpha per year.[h] Some of the firms offering these strategies for individuals are Parametric Portfolio Associates, Advisor Partners, The Aperio Group, State Street Global Advisors, Northern Trust, Active Index Advisors, and the aforementioned First Quadrant. The strategy that one of the authors was responsible for during 2003 produced over 400 bps of after-tax alpha (portfolio performance—S&P 500 after-tax benchmark). For certain types of taxable investors, these strategies can be particularly efficient core investments, and they are discussed in Chapters 24 and 27.

Across the range of product types, the verdict on whether enhanced indexing can consistently work as promised is not clear—we need better definitions and more data to really know the answer. But it is encouraging that sell-side researchers are now tracking enhanced index mutual funds. Furthermore, there is at least one major structural advantage that makes this approach more compelling—at least for institutional investors. It goes back to an original argument for indexing: lower costs. Unlike traditional active strategies, most institutional pricing structures rely extensively on incentive fees—you don't pay extra unless the enhanced strategy delivers on its promise of low-risk alpha.

---

[g] "Petroleum Fund's Active Indexing," *Investment & Pensions Europe* (July/August 2002), p. 67.

[h] See, for example, Christopher G. Luck, "Tax-Advantaged Investing," in First Quadrant's *Investment Management Reflections,* no. 4 (2000).

active (or structured active). We have made the case for a more refined terminology—and hopefully this chapter will spark further debate on the subject. But even before the definition issue is resolved, innovation in this space will continue and probably accelerate. And as the number of such strategies and the assets under management grow, the continual search for new sources of *index alpha* will become that much more aggressive.

The beauty of enhanced indexing is that techniques can and will evolve as new market inefficiencies develop, whether in the underlying equity market, in the listed and OTC derivatives markets, with the growth of ETFs and ETF derivatives, or even in the fixed-income market. And these capital market opportunities will be uncovered by varied players in this space—index fund managers who see opportunity lying just beyond the mandate of their index-tracking funds, active managers who will increasingly be expected to adhere to rigorous risk parameters, hedge funds that will continue to target index changes and dividend season, and the broker-dealers who both service all these actors and have proprietary trading desks on the other side of their shops.[13]

Diversification is as vital in an investor's overall policy mix and manager line as it is within portfolios. Enhanced index strategies provide a source of *index alpha* that is neither targeted or produced by traditional active managers, nor by most risk-controlled active strategies. We believe that this element, combined with better segmentation of categories, will drive focused innovation.

With the product spectrum precisely defined, as we have proposed, the question remains whether an optimal mix of strategies can coexist along the spectrum. This optimization approach looks at the combination of managers essentially as a portfolio that should have desirable risk and return characteristics in aggregate, instead of assessing one manager at a time. The goal of this optimization exercise is to maximize the portfolio's expected alpha while controlling its active risk. Enhanced indexing fits perfectly into this mix, as there generally should be no overlap between enhanced indexing and traditional active sources of alphas.

Through this risk-budgeting approach, an enhanced index strategy can be combined with a blend of core index exposure (to reduce active risk) or risk-controlled active and traditional active to add value and heighten returns. And increasingly, this spectrum approach will be available for most major asset classes.

Just as the industry's future is no longer a simple debate between index and active techniques, our proposal to segment and apply more precise definitions for both enhanced indexing and risk-controlled active is not designed to spur another debate. It is about ensuring that the investor chooses the appropriate mix of each of these approaches to achieve the optimal results for their portfolio.

NOTES

1. "Top Index Managers," *Pensions & Investments* (September 15, 2003): 16.
2. "Indexed Assets Roar Back to Cover 2 Years of Decline," *Pensions & Investments* (January 26, 2004): 31–35.
3. "Petroleum Fund's Active Indexing," *Investment & Pensions Europe* (July/August 2002): 67.
4. Which, of course, have significant potential to underperform.
5. Richard Grinold and Ronald Kahn, *Active Portfolio Management* (Chicago: Probus Publishing, 1995), pp. 93–94.
6. As quoted in the *Future of Investment Management,* ICFA Continuing Education—Association for Investment Management and Research (Charlottesville, VA, 1998), p. 23.
7. Shona Cronin, "Enhanced Indexation," *Global Pensions* (September 2002): 29.
8. John Loftus, "Enhanced Equity Indexing," *Perspectives on Equity Indexing* (New Hope, PA: Frank J. Fabozzi Associates, 2000), pp. 83–84.
9. Ron Kahn, "Passive Plus," *Plan Sponsor* (June 2001): 44.
10. Ideally, even a "pure" index manager will track the index after costs, which in reality means slightly outperforming the index, which has no frictional costs or management fees. See Chapters 19, 20, and 21 for insight and examples of this challenge.
11. The investment process of generating tax alpha is discussed in Chapter 24 as well as in other sources available on the book's E-ppendix at www.IndexUniverse .com.
12. There has been a resurgence of interest in these dividend tilt types of strategies since the U.S. federal dividend tax rate reductions in May 2003 created expectations that companies would increase their dividends.
13. As more market participants enter this arena, it raises the question of the sustainability of index alpha opportunities in a competitive and increasingly efficient global market. As the stock of EI assets grows, will competition for the "nickels and dimes" become self-defeating? One way to attenuate this will be through expanding EI applications deeper into small-cap and international equities, and into new asset classes. This chapter has focused on enhanced equity indexing, with an emphasis on major developed markets with a full range of ETFs and derivative products. In the not-too-distant future, it is likely that we will see more enhanced index approaches for emerging equity markets, as well as dramatic growth in enhanced fixed-income indexing.

CHAPTER 16

Exchange-Traded Funds

A Flexible and Efficient Investment Tool

Yigal Jhirad, Omer Ozkul, and David Qian

_____ Editor's Note _____

Exchange-traded funds have dramatically expanded the scope of indexing and brought the benefits of index products to a broad range of new users who apply them in a myriad of ways. This chapter provides a comprehensive overview of the rapidly growing field of exchange-traded funds (ETFs), with a focus primarily on U.S.-listed, equity-based products. A sidebar on fixed-income ETFs in Europe helps provide coverage of this additional asset class and developments in other dynamic regions. If space and time permitted, I would have also included an entire additional chapter on ETF developments around the world. Although some overview of this subject was provided in Chapter 14, a more comprehensive treatment was not possible—especially given the rapid developments in this field. For background information and updates on international ETF developments, see the ETF and International Indexing sections on IndexUniverse.com.

In this chapter, Yigal Jhirad, Omer Ozkul, and David Qian of Morgan Stanley provide some vital background on the history of ETFs, going deeper

---

This material reflects only the personal views of the authors and does not reflect the views of their employer, Morgan Stanley & Company. The information in this chapter is not and should not be construed to be legal, tax, accounting, or other advice. The information was collected from publicly available sources that the authors believe to be reliable. No representation is made as to the accuracy, reliability, or completeness of the information in this chapter. This material was compiled solely for educational purposes and is not an offer or solicitation of an offer to buy or sell any security or financial instrument.

than the discussions in Chapters 1, 2, and 31, particularly in the history of "OPALS," a predecessor to WEBS, which pioneered the 1940 Act structure for ETFs, as well as the use of optimized portfolios—both features which became fundamental elements of subsequent ETF launches. (WEBS were branded as iShares MSCI series in 2000.) The authors fully explain the ETF product structure as well as the uses and users of the products. The chapter includes a description of the two types of ETF structures and the grantor trust structure used by HOLDRs. Several illuminating tables and figures shed light on complex but vital mechanics of the ETF "creation/redemption" process and the role of the "Authorized Participants" (APs) in the asset gathering and trading of ETFs. They briefly compare ETFs with alternative sources of index exposure (this topic is explored further in Chapter 25, which also fully reviews the broader choices between different index products for institutional investors). The chapter also provides several case studies of applications of ETFs by institutional users. The authors and I would like to thank William Miller of Morgan Stanley for his support for the development of this chapter, and for his suggestions and contributions to its final realization.

Exchange-traded funds (ETFs) are exchange-listed, equity securities backed by a basket of stocks from which they derive their value. Unlike closed-end funds, the basket of securities can be expanded as demand for the product increases. ETFs are designed to track country, sector, industry, style, and fixed-income indexes. In North America, market coverage of ETFs includes indexes from Standard & Poor's, Dow Jones, Frank Russell, Morgan Stanley Capital International, Merrill Lynch, and Lehman Brothers. ETFs are listed on recognized securities exchanges globally. We include within the broad category of U.S. listed ETFs not only products organized as registered open-ended funds or unit investment trusts (UITs) but also ETFs organized as grantor trusts (e.g., Merrill Lynch's HOLDRs product). HOLDRs (Holding Company Depository Receipts) are not based on traditional indexes. They consist of a static basket of stocks selected to track a particular subsector of the market such as Broadband or Biotech, and are not registered funds regulated by the Securities and Exchange Commission (SEC), under the Investment Company Act of 1940. However, they are generally treated as ETFs by investors, and they are included in the data tables within the chapter.

A SHORT HISTORY OF EXCHANGE-TRADED FUNDS

The Standard & Poor's Depository Receipts (SPDRs) introduced in 1993 by the American Stock Exchange (AMEX) became the first exchange-traded fund that was listed on an organized securities exchange in the United States.

The objective behind the SPDRs was to fully replicate the S&P 500. The firm of Leland, O'Brien and Rubinstein (LOR) did important product structuring and legal work for their "SuperShares" vehicle, and this effort provided the foundation and some key precedents for the SPDRs.[1] Concurrently, in 1993 Morgan Stanley launched[2] an index-linked note product called OPALS (Optimized Portfolios as Listed Securities) that was listed in Luxembourg. The OPALS provided economics similar to those provided by ETFs and were designed around MSCI's global indexes, discussed in detail in Chapters 9 and 12. The premise behind OPALS was that instead of including every stock that made up the index, a basket of liquid stocks would be constructed to closely track the target index. These two structures—fully replicated baskets and optimized baskets—would become a dominant feature of ETFs. The most important contribution of OPALS to the overall thinking about index investment was its dependency on optimization to achieve index tracking within designated ranges. This tool was incorporated into an ETF in March 1996 when Morgan Stanley and Barclays Global Investors launched World Equity Benchmark Shares (WEBS) on the AMEX. This launch occurred simultaneously with a competing international equity ETF series—Country-Baskets. This series, which tracked the Financial Times Stock Exchange (FTSE) indexes was sponsored by Deutsche Bank and was listed on the New York Stock Exchange (NYSE).[3]

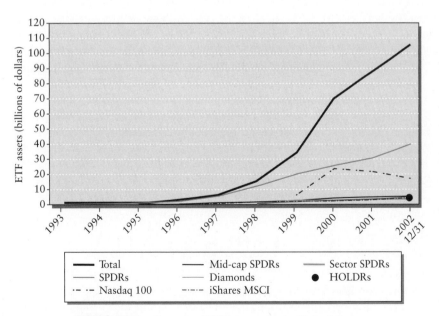

FIGURE 16.1   Growth of ETF Assets in the United States

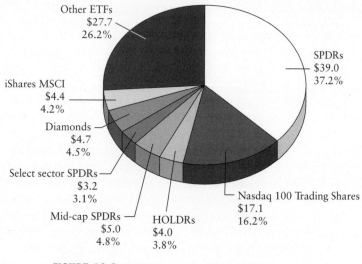

FIGURE 16.2   Segmentation of U.S. ETF Assets
Source: Morgan Stanley. (Data as of the end of 2002)

The development and growth of ETFs continued steadily throughout the 1990s, especially toward the end of the decade. Figure 16.1 highlights the growth of U.S.-listed ETF assets over the past 10 years. In 1999, the popular Nasdaq 100 Tracking Stock (QQQ) was launched, also for trading on AMEX. As of year-end 2002, ETFs listed on U.S. exchanges had over $105 billion under management (updated information on U.S. and global ETF assets can be found in the book's E-ppendix at www.ActiveIndexInvesting.com, or at www.IndexUniverse.com).

Exchange-traded funds were created in the early and mid-1990s to facilitate trading of indexed-based portfolios in an environment where index investing gained popularity. Their flexibility for a variety of uses and users has dramatically expanded their growth. Figure 16.2 highlights the segmentation of assets under management for some of the U.S. ETF markets, and updated information is available on www.IndexUniverse.com.

ANATOMY OF AN EXCHANGE-TRADED FUND

As previously discussed, ETFs are funds or unit investment trusts that bundle stocks or bonds to provide exposure to a basket or index in a single security. ETFs trade on exchanges like stocks and can be bought and sold at any time

TABLE 16.1 Operating Structures for Exchange-Traded Funds

ETF Structure	Description
Managed investment companies	These have the flexibility to fully replicate an index or to use an optimized basket. Typically, many funds formed in this manner do not fully replicate the target index. Instead, they include a subset of the index's constituent securities with weights that are optimized to track the index. Examples of this structure are the iShares MSCI tracking funds.
Unit investment trusts	These structures must fully replicate the index they are designed to track. Examples include S&P 500 SPDRs (SPY) and the Nasdaq 100 Index Tracking Fund (QQQ).
Grantor trusts	The Merrill Lynch HOLDRs, an example of a grantor trust, and are not based on traditional indexes. They consist of a static basket of stocks selected to track a particular subsector of the market such as Broadband or Biotech. These are not registered funds, regulated by the Securities and Exchange Commission (SEC), under the Investment Company Act of 1940.

during the trading day. They can be sold short, margined,[4] or loaned, and are exempt from the uptick rule with some exceptions.[5] ETFs have three main operating and legal structures, which are portrayed in Table 16.1.

FEATURES OF EXCHANGE-TRADED FUNDS

Five of the many distinct features of ETFs are highlighted here. Some other features are discussed in Chapters 23, 25, and 31.

The first key feature is *operational simplicity*. With a single trade, an investor can gain exposure to thousands of stocks (e.g., the Russell 3000 iShares). One settlement, with one booking entry, results in exposure to a diversified portfolio. Most ETFs are registered investment companies that are backed by securities held in the trust or management company. ETFs are redeemable through authorized broker-dealers (subject to a minimum size restriction), usually on an in-kind basis. ETF shares may be created—subject to minimum size restrictions—through authorized broker-dealers by transfer of the securities comprising the underlying portfolio and a cash component (subject to a creation fee). This differs from a closed-end fund, which has no such provisions. Thus, while closed-end funds may trade for long periods away from their fair value or their underlying securities, ETFs will tend to trade over the long run at the perceived value of the underlying securities.

Second, ETFs offer investors important *liquidity enhancement and cost reduction* benefits. Certain ETFs are designed to track particular benchmarks with a subset of companies in the benchmark. By properly diversifying and using optimization techniques, the underlying assets efficiently track the desired benchmark. The ability to select the stocks to include in the portfolio (within specified parameters) allows managers to enhance the liquidity of the underlying portfolio by excluding the more illiquid names. Also, managers have the flexibility to determine whether to respond to index composition changes, which may reduce cost.

Third, ETFs enable *close tracking relative to a benchmark*. Products such as the S&P 500 SPDRs, iShares S&P 500, and the Nasdaq 100 Tracking Stock Fund provide full replication of an index. These ETFs closely match the underlying index, and additions and deletions to these indexes flow through to these ETFs. As a result, tracking risk is relatively low. Other ETFs use sampling methodologies to reduce costs in less liquid market segments, yet they still achieve close tracking. The various portfolio management approaches to tracking indexes are discussed in Part Four with a focus on ETFs in Chapter 23.

Fourth, *ETFs may be a useful tool to monitor and adjust off-hour market exposure.* Currently, many ETFs trade during U.S. trading hours even though their underlying assets trade in markets that are closed for all or part of the U.S. trading day. In these cases, the ETF acts as an off-hour price discovery mechanism that allows investors to trade in closed markets. A good example is the iShares MSCI Japan (EWJ), which often acts as a proxy and/or leading indicator for Japanese equities, supplementing the role of the Nikkei Stock Average futures listed at the Chicago Mercantile Exchange.

Fifth, the *tax efficiencies of ETFs are compelling for many investors.* For a managed investment company or a unit investment trust, the fund typically incurs a tax liability when it sells shares and realizes a capital gain. However, two aspects of an ETF lighten the overall tax burden. First, investors who want to sell an ETF may do this through the secondary market. Since they do not have to rely on the ETF for liquidity (as would be the case for a mutual fund), the sales by investors do not result in the portfolio's liquidation by the fund.[6] *Second, to the extent that investors want to redeem shares, in most cases the redemptions would be executed through "in kind" exchanges by the ETF for a portion of its underlying shares.*[7] A redemption effected in kind permits the ETF fund manager to transfer shares that have the lowest cost basis (highest liability), thereby reducing the overall potential tax liability of the fund. The mechanics and uses of this benefit are discussed in more detail in Parts Four and Five.

MARKET PARTICIPANTS AND ETF MANAGEMENT

Exchange-traded funds are managed by a fund manager or trustee who ensures that the fund owns the appropriate securities that make up the ETF.[8] They are responsible for ensuring that any necessary adjustments to the fund are made. Chapter 23 describes the intricacies of ETF portfolio management in more detail (and the book's Glossary provides definitions of key ETF-related terminology sprinkled throughout this chapter and elsewhere in the book). The custodian, either directly or through subcustodians, generally has physical custody of the stocks that comprise the ETF. Authorized Participants (APs) are broker-dealers with the ability to create and redeem ETFs.

To create an ETF, the AP needs to deliver a specified portfolio of underlying stocks and bonds or cash that make up the ETF to the trustee, distributor, or transfer agent. The reverse takes place at redemption. The AP delivers ETF shares and receives a basket of stocks and cash that make up the ETF. Currently, a number of ETFs are created and redeemed on an in-kind basis; some ETFs, however (e.g., iShares MSCI Taiwan), may only be created and redeemed on a cash basis. Figure 16.3 highlights the roles that a full-service AP plays in the ETF creation/redemption and trading process.

Should the ETF trade out of line with its net asset value, an arbitrage opportunity exists. For example, if the SPY (S&P 500 ETF) is trading above the net asset value of its component stocks, an arbitrageur could sell short the SPY and purchase the underlying securities until the ETF's price is consistent with its underlying value. The sell pressure on the ETF and the buy pressure on the component stocks would eventually bring their prices in line subject to creation and other fees. Figure 16.4 provides a graphic illustration of this complex but vital element of the ETF structure.

USES OF EXCHANGE-TRADED FUNDS

Index Tracking

The objective of many exchange-traded funds is generally to give exposure to an index of stocks or bonds. Certain factors, such as fees and expenses, corporate actions (mergers, acquisitions), differences in trading hours between the ETFs and its underlying assets, and changes to the underlying indexes, may introduce tracking error relative to the benchmark. However,

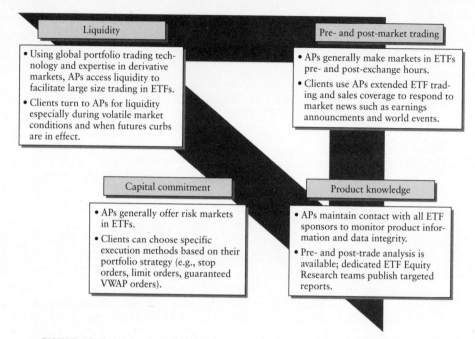

Liquidity
- Using global portfolio trading technology and expertise in derivative markets, APs access liquidity to facilitate large size trading in ETFs.
- Clients turn to APs for liquidity especially during volatile market conditions and when futures curbs are in effect.

Pre- and post-market trading
- APs generally make markets in ETFs pre- and post-exchange hours.
- Clients use APs extended ETF trading and sales coverage to respond to market news such as earnings announcments and world events.

Capital commitment
- APs generally offer risk markets in ETFs.
- Clients can choose specific execution methods based on their portfolio strategy (e.g., stop orders, limit orders, guaranteed VWAP orders).

Product knowledge
- APs maintain contact with all ETF sponsors to monitor product information and data integrity.
- Pre- and post-trade analysis is available; dedicated ETF Equity Research teams publish targeted reports.

FIGURE 16.3   ETFs and the Role of a Full-Service Authorized Participant (AP)

an investor may find that the ETF's ease of use and efficient management of index changes offset these risks.

As an example of tracking the S&P 500 index, we look at three alternatives: ETFs, a basket of the 500 constituent stocks, or S&P 500 index futures. In Table 16.2, we compare factors such as the cost of implementation and maintenance considerations. *(Editor's note: A similar comparison, also including index swaps, is included within Chapter 25.)*

The ETFs that track the S&P 500 (SPY and IVV) have generally proven to be competitively priced and simple to maintain and trade. In a stock portfolio, the investor needs to manage index changes and corporate actions. Futures involve margin requirements and may have unknown rollover costs. Additionally, futures have a minimum trade size based on their contract size. Investors need to choose the best alternative for their particular objectives and timeframes.

Aside from the broad market index-based ETFs such as the S&P 500 SPDRs (Ticker: SPY) and the Nasdaq 100 Index Tracking Fund (Ticker: QQQ), many ETFs track country, sector, style, and size indexes. For example, to track certain international indexes, iShares based on MSCI country benchmarks are available. Brazil (EWZ) or Hong Kong (EWH) are examples of this type of iShares. Two possible ETFs for tracking a sector such as

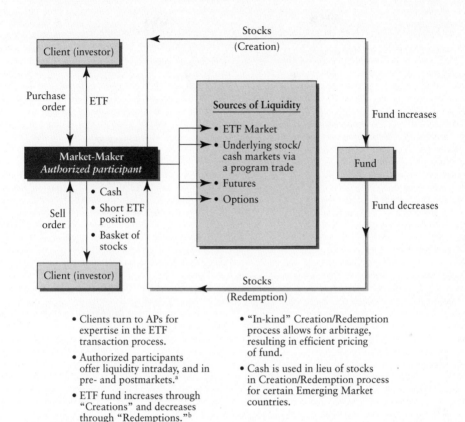

FIGURE 16.4 ETF Transaction Process: Mechanics of "In-Kind" Creation/Redemption

technology are the DJ U.S. Technology iShare (IYW) and Technology sector SPDR (XLK).

Several key factors are associated with using ETFs for index tracking:

■ *Investment strategy.* Two types of investment strategies are used to track indexes: replication and representative sampling.

—*Replication.* ETFs that use the replication strategy attempt to closely track their underlying indexes by holding nearly all the index stocks in approximately the same weightings as their underlying benchmarks. Most ETFs with broad-based benchmarks, such as the iShare Russell

TABLE 16.2   Alternative Methods to Track the S&P 500 Index—Stock Portfolio, Index Futures, ETFs

Investment Vehicle	Investment Description	Commissions Cost (BPs)	Highlights/ Considerations
Stocks	Invest in a total of 500 stocks	10	Must manage corporate actions
			Must manage index changes
			Low holding costs—only pay trade commissions
Index futures portfolio	Invest in S&P 500 futures	0.3	Positions may need to be rolled
			Contracts can trade expensive or cheap
			Leveraged instrument
			Requires daily margin administration
			Least expensive T-cost for short-term positions
			Can be used to accumulate positions
ETFs	Invest in S&P 500 SPDRs/iShares (SPY/IVV)	3	Can be used to accumulate positions
			Commission not economical for short holding periods
			If held longer duration, expense ratios may become a consideration
			Simple operational structure
			Dividend reinvestment/ payout may be an issue

Note: Assumes a commission of 3 cents per share on stocks and $7.50 on futures.
Source: Morgan Stanley Quantitative Strategy.

1000, S&P 500 SPDR, or the Nasdaq 100 Index Tracking Stock (QQQ), adopt the replication investment strategy.

—*Representative sampling.* The representative sampling strategy involves holding a sample of stocks with similar fundamental and liquidity characteristics, market capitalization, and industry weightings as the underlying index. The representative strategy generally is used when full replication of the underlying index is difficult. The iShares MSCI series is an example of ETFs that use this strategy.

In general, funds that employ the representative sampling strategy tend to have more tracking risk than funds using the replication strategy. Part Four discusses the trade-offs of various index portfolio management approaches for ETFs and other index-based investment products in great detail.

■ *Portfolio rebalancing.* Since many ETFs employ a replication strategy, the underlying portfolios have to be rebalanced in accordance to changes in the underlying index. For example, the Nasdaq 100 Fund (QQQ) rebalances the portfolio at least once a month unless a significant change in the index requires immediate attention. Significant changes would include additions or deletions of a security in the index. In these cases, adjustments would have to occur within three business days before or after the day the change is scheduled to occur. A delay in replication may increase the tracking error of the ETF portfolio.

Since index rebalances are implemented by the trustee, the ETF holder does not need to initiate transactions to get back in line with the index. As discussed in Chapter 5, these transactions may be significant for some indexes such as the Frank Russell annual rebalances at the end of June each year. In July 2002, the Russell 2000 index had turnover of 25.3 percent. The Russell 1000 Value and Growth indexes experienced over 10 percent turnover. Since the trustee manages index changes and transactions, the holder of IWM, an ETF that tracks the Russell 2000, need not make any trades as a result of the rebalance to continue tracking the Russell 2000.

■ *Composition guidelines.* Many of the ETFs include guidelines for the composition of the portfolios. These provisions allow the fund manager flexibility in responding to corporate actions to best replicate the performance of the underlying. For example, iShares MSCI only require the investment of 90 percent of its total assets in the stocks of its underlying index. The other 10 percent may be in other stocks, cash and cash equivalents, futures contracts, options on futures contracts, options, and swaps related to the underlying index. This may affect tracking risk since only a minimum of 90 percent of the assets must be directly invested in the underlying stocks. *(Editor's note: In practice, international equity ETF portfolio managers do not utilize this flexibility and focus the portfolio in stocks. See Chapter 23 for more insight into this issue.)*

■ *Dividend payout.* The dividends earned by the exchange-traded funds are paid out in different ways. In the case of iShares ETFs, dividends are immediately reinvested into the fund. Other ETFs may hold the dividends in noninterest-bearing accounts and pay them out periodically. For example, the S&P 500 SPDR and Nasdaq 100 Tracking Stock (QQQ) funds pay out quarterly cash dividends on the last business day of April, July, October, and January. The dividend payout policies of an ETF may affect the tracking of the ETF fund to its underlying benchmark.

■ *Trading hours.* ETFs based on foreign indexes may have tracking risk. U.S. exchange-traded funds trade during the American and New York Stock Exchange hours, whereas the underlying portfolios trade in the local markets. There is lag between the close in the local markets and the close in the United States. As a result of the lag, the ETF's return in the United States may differ from the underlying portfolio's return on the same day. This may increase the short-term tracking risk of the ETF to the underlying index; however, a longer-term perspective should mitigate this lag.

The vast majority of listed ETFs have historically exhibited relatively low tracking risk. However, the actual tracking risk going forward may be lower or higher depending on the implementation of the fund manager.

In summary, ETFs can be used to track markets and sectors. Some key sources of tracking risks are the ETF's investment strategy, rebalance frequency, composition guidelines, dividend payout schedules, and trading hours.

GAINING EXPOSURE TO GLOBAL MARKETS

ETFs can provide efficient exposure to international markets. In particular, iShares MSCI Series provide access to equity markets in more than 20 developed and emerging market countries, such as Japan and Brazil (products based on other indexes are mentioned next). The previously mentioned iShares MSCI Japan (EWJ), whose underlying portfolio tracks the MSCI Japan index, allows investors to obtain the return on a diversified basket of Japanese equities. The MSCI-based iShares may also be used to gain exposure to emerging market countries such as Taiwan, Korea, and Brazil.

In addition, iShares are available on multimarket international indexes. Investors seeking exposure to Europe have a broad range of products to choose from. Investors could use the iShares MSCI EMU (EZU), iShares S&P Europe 350 (IEV), Vanguard VIPERS Europe (based on the MSCI Europe index), Fresco DJ EuroStoxx 50 (FEZ), or the Fresco DJ Stoxx 50 (FEU).

Investors seeking to gain exposure to MSCI EAFE can purchase the iShares EFA that tracks MSCI EAFE with approximately 25 bps of tracking risk.[9] Table 16.3 compares this ETF strategy with alternative ones that involve futures and a portfolio of stocks. One can see the pros/cons and trade-offs, but also the simplicity that regional ETFs provide.

TABLE 16.3 Comparing Alternatives to Achieve International Equity Exposure

Investment Vehicle (Benchmark)	Tracking Risk to MSCI EAFE (%)	Country Capitalization Coverage of EAFE (%)	RT Commissions (bps)	Other Costs (bps)	Total Cost (bps)	Expiration	Minimum Roundlot Size	Short Exposure	Investment Description	Summary of Key Features
Stocks	0–2.00	100.0	18	36	54	None	$5–20mm	Yes (in most markets)	Invest in up to 1,000 local stocks across EAFE countries	Low tracking risk versus index Multiple stock settlements Requires local custodial relationships Must manage corporate actions and index changes Broad investor eligibility
ADRs	3–7.00	100.0	54	—	54	None	$5–10mm	Yes	Invest in a total of up to 173 American depository receipts	Higher tracking risk to index Less liquid than underlying stocks, but ADRs can be created or redeemed for a fee Trade at different hours than local underlying stocks; may result in differences in tracking Broad investor eligibility

(continued)

TABLE 16.3 *(Continued)*

Investment Vehicle (Benchmark)	Tracking Risk to MSCI EAFE (%)	Country Capitalization Coverage of EAFE (%)	RT Commissions (bps)	Other Costs (bps)	Total Cost (bps)	Expiration	Minimum Roundlot Size	Short Exposure	Investment Description	Summary of Key Features
iShares MSCI EAFE	0.19	98.9	10	35	45	None	N/A	Yes	1 security	Low tracking risk versus index 1 security to track MSCI EAFE Gives exposure to 17 countries Incremental securities lending revenue Traded in U.S. dollars during U.S. market hours
Developed markets 100 ADR BLDRS	4–8.00	95.4	20	30	50	None	N/A	Yes	1 security	1 security to track MSCI EAFE Gives exposure to 16 countries Incremental securities lending revenue Traded in U.S. dollars during U.S. market hours

Index futures portfolio	1–2.00	99.7	17	1–15	18–32	Quarterly/ monthly	$500k	Yes	Invest in a portfolio of up to 5 CFTC approved futures	Higher tracking risk versus index Low explicit costs Positions must be rolled periodically Variable roll costs Leverage possible Daily margin administration
Swaps and structured products	0.00	100.0	10–20	10–35 (long) 35–110 (short)	20–55 (long) 45–130 (short)	Flexible	$5mm	Yes	Total return equity swap, forward, 144A note or warrant that guarantees MSCI EAFE performance	Must be eligible contract participant (swaps) or "qualified institutional investor" under U.S. Securities Act of 1933, Rule 144A Customized terms (collateral, reset frequency, term) leverage possible Net dividends paid out or reinvested

Since April 2003, investors have been able to get efficient exposure to a broad-based emerging market index, MSCI EMF, with the iShares MSCI EMF fund (EMM). The Vanguard Group has also launched ETF share classes on its MSCI-based international index funds, comprising European, Pacific, and emerging market funds. A comprehensive listing of all international equity ETFs is available on www.IndexUniverse.com.

An important contrast with domestic equity ETFs is that not all MSCI-based iShares closely track their respective benchmarks, in part because of diversification requirements set forth in IRS rules and other U.S. regulations. One of the IRS requirements is that the weight of any one constituent of the underlying portfolios cannot exceed 25 percent at the time of a rebalance. Tracking errors may result due to weighting mismatches between the iShare and its benchmark index. This issue is described further in Chapter 23.

MSCI-based iShares generally are not managed in a manner that fully replicates their MSCI benchmarks. The international iShares portfolio managers at Barclays Global Investors often employ optimization and sampling techniques that include only a subset of the stocks in the benchmark for tracking purposes. As of January 1, 2003, 284 stocks were underlying the iShares MSCI Japan, while the MSCI Japan Index contains 319 names. In other instances, the number of stocks underlying an MSCI iShares is greater than in the MSCI benchmark that the iShares seeks to track. These deviations occur more readily in smaller markets such as Belgium (whose MSCI iShares has 19 names versus 17 names in the MSCI Belgium Index). Chapter 23 provides more details on portfolio construction of these international equity ETFs, and it can be assumed that portfolio managers at other ETF sponsors such as SSGA and Vanguard use similar approaches.

Editor's Note

While this chapter focuses extensively on ETFs tracking equity indexes, the structural advantages of ETFs are equally valuable for fixed income and other asset classes. The following sidebar discusses the relevance and value of fixed income ETFs for the European market, although these same features apply to the U.S. and Canadian markets. I include the following sidebar as a way to expand the coverage of this chapter to another asset class and geographical region.

FIXED-INCOME ETFs IN EUROPE:
A REVOLUTION FOR EUROPEAN BOND INVESTORS
Elizabeth Para

ETFs made their first appearances in Europe in 2000. Since then, well over 100 ETFs have been launched in Europe, with assets under management of around $11 billion. Until 2003, however, all these ETFs tracked equity indexes.

Spring 2003 saw the launch of fixed-income ETFs in Europe. First off the mark was Indexchange, which launched *eb.rexx*, a German government bond ETF. Shortly thereafter, iShares launched € Liquid Corporates, the first corporate bond ETF to be made available to European investors.

As discussed throughout, ETFs are well entrenched as tools for equity exposure. But can fixed-income ETFs replicate the success of equity ETFs?

Indications from North America are positive. Canada has a well-developed fixed-income ETF market. In the U.S. market, where fixed-income ETFs were launched in mid-2002, these ETFs got off to a solid start, gathering over $5 billion in assets in their first 18 months. In Europe, the € Liquid Corporates ETF, after only a few months, was already the third largest ETF trading. What has driven this success?

Like their equity counterparts, fixed-income ETFs bring many new benefits and efficiencies to the bond market:

- As index tracking strategies, they deliver market exposure and returns.
- ETFs offer investors diversified exposure to a market.
- Bond ETFs allow investors and traders to access the market portfolio in a market where program trades are not common practice, and index futures do not exist. (As there are currently no futures contracts on credit markets, fixed-income ETFs fill a genuine gap in the market.)
- ETFs are competitively priced on exchanges and by multiple market makers, on an OTC basis, which minimizes price discrimination between investors.
- ETF portfolio holdings are transparent and objectively selected to deliver a market index's return.
- Many ETFs are based on liquid indexes to efficiently facilitate large institutional-size trades.

(Continued)

Like equity ETFs, fixed-income ETFs can be used by institutional and retail investors for the following investment strategies:

- Instant market exposure for cash flows.
- Hedging.
- Sector rotation/asset allocation.
- Long/short strategies—spread trades.
- Buy and hold positions.
- Transition tool.
- Core/satellite investment strategies.

Trading of fixed-income ETFs can be executed either directly with a market maker in over-the-counter transactions, or on exchange, through any broker. Large institutional investors are likely to continue to trade over-the-counter, through their usual dealers, at least in the initial stages. Smaller institutions and individuals can trade on exchange in the same way that they would trade an individual equity.

The positive reception of fixed-income ETFs in Canada and the United States and early indications from recent European product launches demonstrate that there is strong demand for these products.

As investors become familiar with the benefits of fixed-income ETFs, at least as much demand is likely as we have seen for equity ETFs. In Europe, one can expect to see application of fixed-income ETFs in place of the OTC derivative-based products that are currently available to bond investors. Potentially, fixed-income ETFs could eclipse equity market ETFs because they represent true innovation in the fixed-income arena, give investors access to greater price transparency and competition, and provide a new and efficient way of accessing credit markets.

A list of fixed-income ETFs in markets of the United States, Canada, and Europe is provided in the E-ppendix, available at www.activeindexinvesting.com and at www.IndexUniverse.com.

Managing Cash Levels and Index Change Management

ETFs can be a tool to manage cash inflows and redemptions for a fund. They are a feasible alternative to index futures for gaining desirable market exposure and equitizing cash that will eventually be invested into stock. Though index futures require little commission costs to trade, using ETFs may be more cost-effective or beneficial in some situations. One example is when the incoming cash flows being equitized are too small to use futures. One standard S&P 500 e-mini futures contract has a nominal value of over $50,000, whereas an S&P 500 SPDR (SPY) or S&P 500 iShare (IVV) can be purchased at approximately $110 per share (as of Q4 2003).

An important situation for using an ETF is when a futures contract does not exist for the required index exposure. No futures are currently traded on the S&P 600 Small Cap Index, but the index exposure can be obtained by purchasing S&P Small Cap iShares (IJR). The ETFs essentially bring efficient index exposure to more discrete slices of the equity market than would be possible (or practical) with listed futures or options. This element is also highlighted in Chapter 25. ETFs may also be preferred for long-term holdings because futures must be rolled over periodically and incur additional rollover risk and transaction costs.

Exchange-traded funds may also be used to manage cash inflows, index changes, and fund redemptions. Managers of portfolios that are indexed to S&P 500 might keep a small portion of their portfolios in S&P 500 SPDRs (SPY). This approach is particularly useful for pension plans with internally-managed index funds. These managers generally rebalance their portfolios at least once a quarter to correspond to the S&P quarterly shares changes. But often, they have to make changes to the portfolios more frequently because of ongoing changes to the S&P 500 index. In the case of the addition of Simon Property Group (SPG) and deletion of Conexant (CNXT) from the S&P 500 index, as detailed in Table 16.4, the manager of a $100 million S&P 500 index fund would have had to purchase up to $69,279 worth of SPG.

The manager can purchase SPG with cash by setting aside enough cash. But cash that is set aside produces tracking error with respect to the S&P 500 index unless there is an overlay of S&P 500 futures. The manager who sets aside no cash needs to sell a slice of this fund to raise enough money to purchase SPG at the appropriate benchmark weighting. This leads to a transaction involving hundreds of stocks and their settlements. Of course, the manager may instead hold some S&P SPDRs in the portfolio and can sell the SPDRs to raise the cash necessary to purchase SPG, again taking advantage of ETFs' "one-trade" characteristic. Similarly, where selling a large name that has been deleted from the index produces a cash surplus, it can be invested into the SPDRs until the next scheduled rebalance for the fund—when the stocks are purchased and the SPDRs are sold. Thus, index-based ETFs can help make the job of other index fund managers easier.

The following sections highlight a variety of applications of ETFs for active investment strategies. These approaches are consistent with the *Active Indexing* concepts described in Chapter 18. We focus more heavily on U.S. equity strategies, while Chapter 18 goes into more detail on international equity strategies for both developed and emerging markets.

TABLE 16.4 Using ETFs for Portfolio Management—Index Changes

S&P 500 Index Adjustment (Add/Delete)		
Name	SIMON PROP GRP	CONEXANT SYS STK
Symbol	SPG.N	CNXT.O
Price	35.88	3.30
New benchmark shares	176,037,000	0
Adjustment type	Addition	Deletion
Annoucement date	Wednesday, 06/21/2006	Wednesday, 06/21/2006
Effective date (at the close)	Monday, 06/26/2006	Monday, 06/26/2006
Classification		
S&P industry	Real estate investment trusts	Technology hardware and equipment
S&P sector	Financials	Information technology
S&P value/growth	Value	Value
Buy/Sell List		
Old weight	0.00%	0.01%
New weight	0.07%	0.00%
Old shares in a 100 MM$ basket	—	2,837
New shares in a 100 MM$ basket	1,931	
Buy/sell	1,931 Buy	2,837 Sell

Sector Rotation Strategies

In this section, we focus on the application of ETFs to sector rotation strategies. The availability of sector-specific ETFs (e.g., Sector SPDRs, as well as iShares on the Dow Jones U.S. indexes and VIPERS on the MSCI U.S. indexes) and the ability to trade ETFs like a stock are advantageous for implementing sector tilts as part of an overall portfolio strategy.

An example that uses sector SPDRs illustrates the feasibility of using ETFs for sector rotation. One important technical note is that SPDRs are restricted from having more than 25 percent of the fund's assets invested in a single security, and from having the sum of all securities in the fund with a weighting of more than 5 percent exceed 50 percent of the fund's total assets.[10] These restrictions may mean that SPDRs may not replicate exactly the S&P's GICS (Global Industry Classification Standard) sectors.[11] The constituents of the S&P's Telecommunications Services Sector and Information Technology Sector are combined in the Technology Select Sector SPDR (ticker XLK).

As a starting point, Select Sector SPDRs can be used to create a sector-neutral basket to track the S&P 500. *(Editor's note: Similar strategies can be developed using the iShares Dow Jones U.S. sector index products, or the Vanguard VIPERS products tracking the MSCI U.S. sector indexes.)*

Table 16.5 highlights a basket of sector SPDRs, constructed to track the S&P 500 with approximately 50 basis points (bps) of tracking error. This table also provides the ticker symbols for all of the Select Sector SPDRs.

TABLE 16.5   Tracking the S&P 500 with Sector SPDRs—Neutral Sector Weights as a Starting Point for Industry Tilts

Ticker	Sector Representation	Neutral Portfolio Weight (%)
XLY	Consumer discretionary	13.34
XLP	Consumer staples	9.18
XLE	Energy	5.76
XLF	Financials	20.65
XLV	Health care	14.71
XLI	Industrials	11.32
XLK	Information technology and telecommunications	19.43
XLB	Materials	2.76
XLU	Utilities	2.87

Source: Morgan Stanley.

These weights could then be modified to gain or reduce exposure to certain sectors. Investors seeking greater exposure to the Financials sectors could make the XLF account for 25 percent of their SPDR basket as opposed to 20.65 percent. Dynamic *sector rotation* strategies continuously adjust the overweight/underweight of sectors. Similar approaches can be applied between cap-ranges, styles, or country weights, and are discussed later, as well as in Chapter 18.

ETFs can also be used to hedge actively-managed equity portfolios. Since they are generally exempt from the uptick rule (with certain exceptions in the case of HOLDRs), an ETF can be shorted at any time.[12] Given the breadth of ETFs and their index characteristics, a portfolio of ETFs can be constructed to track a wide range of portfolios. A portfolio that is made up of S&P 500 stocks can be hedged by shorting the SPY. Alternatively, if a portfolio does not match an ETF, it may be possible to combine ETFs that will optimize tracking the portfolio. Let's say an active manager specializes in both finance and tech companies. A combination of XLF and XLK may be used to develop a hedge position for the portfolio.

Implementing Long/Short Strategies Using ETFs

Long/short strategies that can be implemented with ETFs include the following:

- Size, style, and country strategy implementation.
- Modification of portfolio exposure.

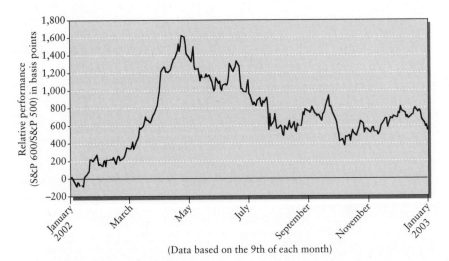

(Data based on the 9th of each month)

FIGURE 16.5   S&P Small Cap Outperforming S&P Large Cap (2002)

Size- and style-based strategies can be easily implemented using ETFs. If a portfolio manager believes that S&P small-cap companies will outperform large-cap companies, the manager can use ETFs to position the portfolio to reflect expectations. This is a type of *Active Indexing* discussed in Chapters 18 and 31. Shorting S&P 500 SPDR (SPY) and going long S&P 600 Small Cap iShares (IJR) establishes the position. The outperformance of the S&P 600 Small Cap versus the S&P 500 during 2002 can be seen in Figure 16.5. A long IJR/short SPY ETF strategy could have been used to capture this return.

Similarly, ETFs can also be used for active style-based strategies. ETFs that replicate value and growth indexes are available, so if a manager believes that value is going to outperform growth, Russell 1000 Growth iShares (IWF) could be sold and Russell 1000 Value iShares (IWD) could be bought. The outperformance of Russell 1000 Value versus Growth from January 9, 2002, to January 9, 2003, can be seen in Figure 16.6. Again, ETFs based on these indexes could have been used to capture these return differentials.

For international equities, investors can use MSCI and S&P Global iShares to implement country strategies that will achieve their investment goals. Chapter 18 and the accompanying web-only sidebar by Schoenfeld discuss these applications. For example, investors can choose to long MSCI Japan iShares and short MSCI U.K. iShares if they believe that stocks in Japan will outperform equities in the United Kingdom. This entire strategy requires only four trades: two to establish the long/short position and two more trades to unwind it. With the availability of regional ETFs, investors can make similar relative performance trades on Europe versus Pacific Rim

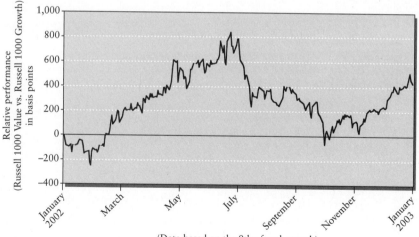

(Data based on the 9th of each month)

FIGURE 16.6 Russell Large Cap Value Outperforming Russell Large Cap Growth (2002)

(EZU versus EPP) or Emerging Markets versus Developed Markets (EEM versus EFA). ETFs can also be used to hedge market exposure. For example, the iShares MSCI EAFE can be used to hedge overall international equity exposure.

Investors can take advantage of their ability to short these ETFs (even on downticks) to establish a hedge. The ultimate advantage of ETFs in long and short strategies is their breadth of coverage, liquidity, and simplicity of implementation.

THE RANGE OF USERS OF ETFs—AND WHAT THEY DO WITH THEM

Institutional investors including mutual funds, pension funds, foundations and endowments, hedge funds, and insurance companies, as well as individual investors, use ETFs. Figure 16.7 graphically summarizes some common applications by these investors using ETFs. The diagram is designed to show the big picture of why users find ETFs so attractive.

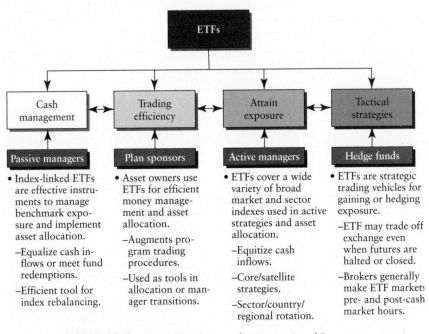

FIGURE 16.7   Flexible Solutions for Institutional Investors

The following examples describe some institutional uses of ETFs and are based on actual client activity:

- *Cash management.* A public pension fund uses iShares MSCI EAFE (EFA) to provide intramonth liquidity to the (international) portfolio. A large fund manager in Sweden managing a EuroStoxx 50 Index fund uses ETFs to invest cash flows by using the EuroStoxx 50 ETF trading in Europe. The manager purchases ETFs to minimize cash drag. Once the holding in the ETF has reached approximately 4 percent of the portfolio, the manager will sell the ETF and buy shares.
- *Sector allocation.* A large asset manager, who developed a European sector allocation strategy, uses ETFs trading in Europe to track MSCI Europe sectors. This decision was driven by the lack of available European sector futures contracts and limited back office capacity to handle program trades.
- *International exposure.* Many types of investors use ETFs to gain exposure to markets that would be difficult to invest in directly such as Korea, Taiwan, and Brazil. As discussed, the iShares MSCI ETFs trading in the United States allow investors to gain exposure to these markets without the need to apply for or have "qualified foreign investor status." Investors also avoid having to deal with potential settlement issues, which may arise when buying local shares. Along these lines, several U.S. public pension funds have used iShares MSCI Taiwan to gain exposure to Taiwan.
- *Hedging.* The manager of an Asian hedge fund wanted to hedge the technology exposure in his fund. Based on his correlation analysis, he found that the NASDAQ 100 index would be a good hedge. Shorting the NASDAQ 100 ETF (QQQ) is cost-effective relative to shorting a basket of shares because the investor only has to deal in one share that is liquid and less expensive to borrow than many technology stocks.

CONCLUSION . . . AND THE BEGINNING

Exchange-traded funds have become mainstream investment management tools with a wide user base that ranges from institutional clients to individual investors. And their application has expanded to additional asset classes. In 2002, ETFs based on fixed-income indexes were introduced to the United States and have met with substantial success. Bond ETFs were launched in Europe in 2003; the sidebar by Elizabeth Para in this chapter describes this development. A key use of fixed-income ETFs has been to facilitate asset allocation trades.[13] Steven Schoenfeld's concluding chapter (Chapter 31) discusses the probability of continued expansion of the ETF vehicle into more asset classes, including commodities and currencies, and the advent of what he calls "quasi-active" ETFs. He also takes a long-term view of the future of indexing in general.

Another area of product expansion has been in ETF options and single stock futures on ETF. These options and futures trade on the AMEX, CBOE, NQLX, OneChicago, and other exchanges, and are based on the underlying ETFs. They generally feature physical settlement, which helps provide a unique tool for risk management of index exposure. Chapter 31 discusses the wide implications of this development.

Although this chapter has focused on ETFs that are listed and trading in the U.S. market, a broad range of ETFs are available globally.[14] By mid-2003, more than 130 ETFs were trading outside the United States. The area is at least as dynamic as that in the United States, and other chapters in the book (especially Chapters 1 and 31) discuss these trends. From our perspective, ETFs have provided an enormously valuable tool for investors to efficiently and flexibly gain exposure to markets and sectors, and their use will only continue to grow in the coming years. Thus, we must conclude that we are really only at the beginning of even greater applications and development of ETFs.

NOTES

1. In fact, the LOR SuperTrust and its Index SuperUnit component was actually listed a month before the SPDR, in December 1992, but were discontinued about a year later.
2. On a Reg. S basis only (for non-U.S. investors).
3. CountryBaskets relied on some of the same LOR technology and resources that helped launch the SuperShares in 1992. Deutsche Bank withdrew support for the CountryBaskets in 1997, giving the WEBS, which were rebranded as "iShares MSCI Series" in 2000, a de facto monopoly on international equity ETFs until SSGA launched their StreetTracks and the 2004 launch of Vanguard's three international equity VIPERS. See IndexUniverse.com for updates on new ETF product launches.
4. But not, subject to very limited holding period exceptions, by authorized participants as a result of limitations imposed by the U.S. Securities and Exchange Commission in their interpretation of Rule 11(d)(1) of the Securities Exchange Act of 1934.
5. Provided that the securities can be borrowed and affirmative determination does apply. It must be determined whether the client is long or short prior to the trade. The HOLDRs are an exception and may not be shorted on a downtick.

6. Which would generally give rise to a taxable event.
7. Subject to applicable minimums and through an authorized participant.
8. Except for HOLDRs, which are not "managed."
9. iShares MSCI EAFE are issued by a different iShares fund series than the other ETF portfolios that track MSCI indexes. The EAFE portfolio is included in the same ETF series that issues IVV and U.S. indexed products.
10. Because it is structured in a manner to avoid double taxation and thus is subject to Subchapter M of the Internal Revenue Code.
11. The GICS methodology was jointly developed by S&P and MSCI. More information is available from their web sites, which can be accessed via IndexUniverse.com.
12. See note 5.
13. A good overview of U.S. listed fixed-income ETFs is provided in "Taking Stock of Bonds: ETFs Reach the Fixed Income Markets" in Institutional Investor's *ETFs II—New Approaches and Global Outreach*, ed. Brian Bruce (Institutional Investor Guides, September 2003). Available from www.iiguides.com.
14. A number of investor restrictions apply, and ETFs listed outside the United States generally are not available for purchase by U.S. persons. More information on non-U.S. listed ETFs is available on www.IndexUniverse.com and in the book's E-ppendix, at www.ActiveIndexInvesting.com.

CHAPTER 17

Indexing Real Estate

James S. Keagy

_____Editor's Note_____

Several indexes and index products have been developed for alternative asset classes such as commodities, real estate, and hedge funds. Although some would argue that these asset classes are "unindexable," these alternative benchmarks, and investment products based on those indexes serve to better define the opportunity set for investors as well as increase transparency of the asset class. In this chapter, real estate investment veteran Jim Keagy makes the case for indexing real estate and in the process sheds some light on the benefits of including the asset class in portfolios. He provides an overview on real estate investment trusts (REITs), which form the basis of publicly traded real estate investments. REITs are the primary constituents of most real estate indexes. He describes some of the benchmarks and products available to investors and shows how institutional investors use indexed real estate products in their portfolios. Much of the same logic that undergirds the case for indexing stocks and bonds is also relevant for real estate, and REIT index products are among the most efficient ways to get exposure to this diversifying asset class.

As previous chapters make clear, indexing equities and fixed income offers considerable advantages for an investor, but is it practical to index an asset class like real estate, which is illiquid (it takes months to buy or sell a property)? Some would also argue that it is less efficient than equities or fixed income. In fact, thanks to the emergence of index funds that track the major real estate investment trust indexes, as well as real estate investment trust (REIT) exchange-traded funds, indexing real estate is not only possible, but it is a smart approach to owning real estate for individuals and institutions alike.

Before discussing indexed real estate investing, however, it is helpful to look at why one should consider investing in real estate in the first place, what methods are available for investing in real estate, and why REITs or real estate stocks are an attractive alternative.

WHY INVEST IN REAL ESTATE?

The benefits of owning real estate are income, capital appreciation, inflation protection, and a low correlation with other asset classes.

Real estate is a huge, yet largely untapped, asset class. In the United States alone, the institutional-grade real estate market is valued at some $5 trillion, compared with roughly $7 trillion for the U.S. fixed-income market, and $16 trillion for the U.S. equity market. Real estate represents 7.2 percent of U.S. Gross Domestic Product (GDP), making it one of the largest sectors of the economy. Many institutional investors have discovered the performance benefits of real estate, but today only about 5 percent of institutional portfolios are held in real estate assets, when these assets represent about 50 percent of U.S. (and global) wealth. The potential for real estate to contribute to the performance of a multi-asset class portfolio is significant and well understood, both from a returns standpoint and a risk-reduction standpoint, lifting an investor's efficient frontier (discussed in Chapter 3).

Modern portfolio theory suggests that investors should hold a wide variety of asset classes in proportion to their capitalization in the economy, including real estate. Interestingly, about 50 percent of pension plan sponsors have lacked the resources to include real estate in their portfolios in any meaningful way. By underweighting real estate, investors are missing an important diversification opportunity, thereby lowering their expected risk-adjusted returns.

Real estate has a low correlation with equities and fixed-income securities, as demonstrated in a 2001 study by Ibbotson Associates. The correlation advantage holds true whether the real estate is held in private equity interests or in REITs.

Because REITs are real estate stocks, one might wonder whether they behave more like real estate or like stocks. And if they are indeed stocks, does a portfolio already have adequate REIT exposure if it invests in a broad U.S. benchmark like the Wilshire 5000? An updated study by Ibbotson in 2003 suggests that REITs share the distinct characteristics of real estate, with low correlations to other equities. For example, the 10-year correlation (at mid-2003) of the Morgan Stanley REIT index with Russell 3000 stock returns is only 0.36.

In addition to the diversification advantage, owning real estate has three important economic benefits: income, appreciation, and inflation protection. With REITs, much of the return is paid currently in dividends, which helps pension funds pay current liabilities, and this suits many investors better than a "hope certificate" for future appreciation. The average REIT paid a 7 percent cash yield in 2002, more than four times the dividend yield on the S&P 500.

REITs also offer the potential for capital appreciation, and total returns of real estate have been impressive relative to other asset classes. As of the printing of this book, REITs outperformed the Russell 3000 (a good proxy for the U.S. market) and the Lehman Aggregate (the U.S. bond market) on a 1-, 3-, 5-, and 10-year basis. Whereas in 2000 through 2002, U.S. equities had their worst performance since the Great Depression, REITs turned in their best performance ever with double-digit returns.[1]

Real estate can also act as a hedge against inflation. Why? Property values—like the prices of other hard assets—have historically kept pace with general price inflation, especially in periods of prolonged inflationary pressure (e.g., much of the 1970s). Additionally, most commercial leases are indexed to the current inflation rate, locking in real returns during periods of inflation. Rental rates increase automatically with the Consumer Price Index (CPI) in these leases, and operating expense increases are also passed through to the tenant, effectively locking in a "real" return for the landlord. (It is worth noting that other types of equities also can be an inflation hedge if an inflationary environment allows companies to raise prices.)

HOW TO INVEST IN REAL ESTATE

The investment merits of real estate are compelling. What, then, is the best way to invest? Investing in real estate may seem easy. After all, even a novice can tell a good building from a bad one, and the right side of town from the wrong one, right? Wrong. Any experienced investor will tell you that such decisions are not so simple, and that real estate is anything but an armchair investment.

Choosing the most effective way to gain exposure to the asset class is key, particularly for investors with limited capital or oversight capability. Institutional investors can opt for private equity investments (available through real estate investment advisors) or securitized real estate, most commonly organized as REITs. While the best solution depends on the investor's return objectives, risk profile, and resources, REITs offer some important advantages over private equity investments (see the sidebar "What's in a REIT?").

The real estate capital market can be divided into four quadrants, as illustrated in Figure 17.1. Each quadrant has different risk and liquidity characteristics, and each one appeals to different kinds of investors.

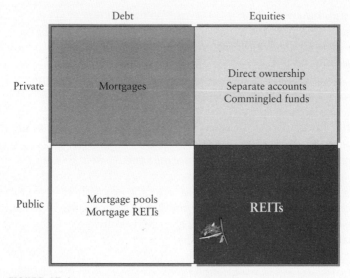

FIGURE 17.1 The Four Quadrants of Real Estate Capital Markets

Until recently, institutional investors confined themselves to the private equity quadrant (upper right). Banks and insurance companies participate in the two debt quadrants, as they represent the traditional sources of debt financing. In the public debt quadrant, investors of all sizes are indirectly financing real estate when they invest in pools of mortgage-backed securities. The public equity quadrant, composed mostly of REITs, is a viable option for both institutional and individual investors.

Private equity real estate is challenging, and pension funds often complain that it represents the 5 percent of their portfolio that consumes 95 percent of their time. It is illiquid, difficult to value, and it is people- and capital-intensive. Many pension funds avoid real estate altogether because of a poor prior experience, often around a property that they bought at the top of a market cycle and could not sell. Too much exposure to a single market (e.g., Silicon Valley in 2000) or type of property (e.g., office buildings) has been the downfall of many investors.

A successful real estate investment requires skillful management, leasing expertise, and local market insight. And, contrary to the old adage that the three most important things about real estate are location, location, and location, even the best locations in the world won't turn a profit if you overpay for them, or overleverage, underlease, or mismanage them.

A better formula for real estate success is to invest in the right properties, with the right people, at the right prices. Property, people, and price are the three key components of a successful strategy. Getting all three of these components right is more difficult than it might seem, and missing any one of them can easily result in losses.

First, properties of obvious quality, like stocks with a high P/E, will always be more expensive, but only an expert will know whether they are a smart investment. These are referred to by institutional investors as "core" or Class A property holdings. If they are not overpriced, Class A properties can be a good growth play. Second, properties of lesser quality can still be great investments if an owner has the capital and the expertise to turn them around—a value play. These are often referred to as "value-added" holdings.

One should not underestimate the importance of professional management, from both an acquisitions and an operations standpoint. Every investment starts with a valuation analysis, followed by a financial structuring decision (how much leverage to use, and how to structure the debt). Then there is leasing, property management, ongoing maintenance, and refurbishment. If the market softens or a tenant experiences financial difficulty, a skilled asset management team can make the difference between repositioning an asset and losing it in foreclosure.

Another secret to successful real estate investing is diversification. Yet, while the principles of diversification are essential for other asset classes, it is surprising how few real estate investors pay much heed to it. Whether assets are held privately or in REITs, diversification across property types and geographic markets helps. A well-diversified portfolio, with professional management, is the best approach to strong real estate returns.

But creating a truly diversified real estate portfolio is costly and difficult for even the largest institutional investors. Real estate assets are expensive and "lumpy." A typical property of institutional quality can easily cost $25 million or more (a regional mall will set you back well over $100 million). There are five basic types of real estate that investors should consider holding (apartments, office, retail, industrial, and hotels), and there are 30 geographic markets of institutional quality in the United States. If you want to build a portfolio with only one property of each type in each geographic market, you would need to acquire 150 properties at a cost of $3.75 billion. Figure 17.2 illustrates the complexity of the diversification problem, showing seven different approaches to the asset class with varying degrees of risk and potential reward.

Because real estate is so management intensive, overseeing a geographically diversified portfolio would be extremely challenging, as property management and leasing expertise is generally a local business and would be needed in each local market. Only a few of the largest pension funds such as CalPERS (California Public Employees Retirement System) and General Motors have the resources to manage a broadly diverse portfolio. For everyone else, a fully diversified private equity portfolio is simply out of reach.

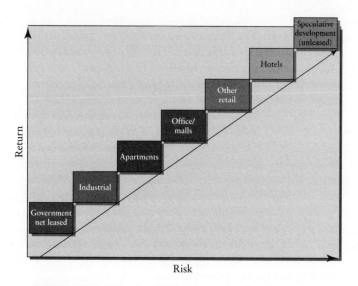

FIGURE 17.2   The Real Estate Risk-Reward Continuum

With REIT index funds and exchange-traded funds (ETFs), however, a diversified real estate strategy is available to even the smallest investors. As with equities and fixed income, an indexed approach provides exposure to the entire asset class (i.e., to the entire Risk-Reward Continiuum portrayed in Figure 17.2), at market prices, and with REITs you get skilled management talent along with investment-grade properties.

The Case for REITs

REITs squarely address the shortcomings of private equity real estate investments. They offer liquidity, diversification, and professional management. They solve the equation of investing in the right property, with the right people, at the right price in one investment.

For most investors, REITs are simply better packaging for owning real estate than other vehicles. There is no difference in the physical quality of the underlying assets between REITs and private equity vehicles. Surprisingly, despite all the benefits of REITs, they hold only about 10 percent of the U.S. investment-grade real estate market, which is considerably less than the percentage of securitization in other countries. This is one reason the REIT market is expected to continue to attract capital in the United States.

REITs typically have focused investment strategies, concentrating on one property type such as apartments and/or a geographic area. The result is that they bring deep expertise in the acquisition and management of a particular type of real estate portfolio. Equity Office Properties is currently the largest owner of office buildings in the United States, and Equity Residential is the largest owner of apartments. Both companies target only certain markets for investment, and they actively work to achieve economies of scale and pricing power in those markets.

While private equity programs have been criticized for going anywhere and paying any price to do a deal, REITs have done a good job of maintaining their focus, and the investment community rewards a disciplined investment strategy. Every REIT company is a specialist, and Wall Street demands that they maintain their edge in their chosen niche, or their stock price.

Another advantage of REITs is the alignment of interests between shareholders and management. Typically, the executives who manage the portfolio are also major holders of the REIT shares, so their interests are perfectly aligned with other investors. When you invest in a REIT, you typically receive not only an ownership interest in a portfolio of real estate, but also an interest in the management company that runs the properties. Private equity vehicles, usually set up as partnerships, rarely offer the same alignment, and advisors have been criticized for being more motivated by the fees they collect than by the value they create in the underlying portfolio.

REITs also bring a corporate governance and financial reporting advantage. Because REITs trade on the major stock exchanges, they are subject to the same Securities and Exchange Commission reporting requirements as other publicly traded companies. Private partnerships are not required to provide the same level of reporting or transparency.

REITs have a valuation advantage over private equity, in terms of both convenience and accuracy. Valuing privately held real estate assets has always been an imperfect science. The process depends on backward-looking appraisals, which means there is a lag effect. Because of the analytical work and expense of commercial appraisals, most institutional investors only take a close look at private equity valuations every 1 to 3 years. Because securitized property is traded and valued on an exchange, investors have an indication of value on a real-time basis.

Liquidity is another advantage. The liquidity afforded by the public market makes trading securitized real estate assets considerably easier than trading privately held properties. Many REITs qualify as large- and mid-cap securities and enjoy high daily trading volumes. Small-cap and particularly micro-cap REITs may pose some degree of illiquidity, but no more so than privately held real estate portfolios.

A final advantage to owning REITs is the ease of oversight. Private equity investments are accompanied by constant demands of tenants, capital outlay decisions (Shall we expand for a new anchor tenant? Shall we renovate?),

WHAT'S IN A REIT?

REITs, or real estate investment trusts, are publicly traded companies that own and operate commercial real estate as their primary business. They can be thought of as real estate stocks. There are over 300 REITs in the United States, about 180 of which are publicly traded.

REITs can be divided into three categories: equity REITs, which own and operate commercial properties; mortgage REITs, which provide financing for commercial and residential properties; and hybrid REITs (a combination of the first two types). Equity REITs, comprising more than 90 percent of the REIT market, generate earnings from the rental income received on their holdings and capital gains from the sale of properties. REITs are a convenient way for all types of investors to gain exposure to a diverse set of real estate holdings, across property types and geographic markets.

Operating as a REIT is a voluntary election under the U.S. Internal Revenue Code for qualifying real estate companies. On the surface, REITs look much like the real estate equivalent of a stock mutual fund. They invest in a portfolio of properties, and they lease and manage the properties for the benefit of shareholders. Many REITs follow a focused investment strategy, such as apartments in the Western United States, whereas others pursue a broader mandate. Unlike mutual funds of corporate stocks, however, REIT earnings are not taxed at the corporate level. Most corporations experience double taxation; earnings are taxed once at the corporate level and then again at the individual level when investors pay ordinary income tax on dividends.

In exchange for this favorable tax treatment, REITs are subject to additional regulation: At least 75 percent of total income must be derived from real property, at least 75 percent of assets must be qualifying real estate assets, and at least 90 percent of earnings must be distributed to shareholders annually. For investors, these added requirements have led to annual dividend yields of 5 to 7 percent, which compares favorably to the current returns on other stocks and many fixed-income securities.

Real estate companies that do not elect to operate as a REIT are often referred to as real estate operating companies, or REOCs, and are close relatives to REITs. REOCs are organized as C corporations for tax purposes and are not required to distribute earnings, but they do not enjoy the tax-exempt status of REITs. Starwood Hotels is an example of a REOC. Some real estate operators prefer the flexibility to retain earnings, particularly in capital-intensive businesses like hotels. The Wilshire Real Estate Securities Index includes REOCs as well as REITs, whereas the Morgan Stanley REIT index purely comprises only REITs.

and myriad financial issues (Is it time to sell or refinance?). With REITs, these concerns are handled by experts, the REIT management company working on behalf of the shareholders.

Are there any disadvantages to REITs? One disadvantage is that an investor has no control over the properties that are bought and sold. If you disagree with management, however, you can "vote with your feet" and sell your shares.

Another disadvantage is the perception that share prices are more volatile than private equity prices. Watching a real estate portfolio swing in value on a daily basis is disconcerting for some investors, especially if they are accustomed to the slow and less informative process of appraisals every few years. REIT stock prices capture news about the financial markets and respond quickly. It is important to understand that the stock market also influences private equity values, but the valuation process makes it difficult to see how values have changed until the property is appraised or, better, ultimately sold.

A final drawback might be that because REITs are so efficient, they take some of the fun out of investment management. Private equity real estate will always play a role in institutional portfolios because it is interesting to manage, even if some investors lack the resources to manage it properly.

INDEXING WITH REITs: AN EFFICIENT STRUCTURE FOR REAL ESTATE INVESTING

The notion of indexing real estate is considered heresy to traditional real estate investors. They argue that real estate as an asset class is inherently inefficient and that direct ownership with the assistance of a knowledgeable local partner can capture value in any market. Real estate is the last domain for active managers and entrepreneurs.

But are real estate markets really that inefficient? Markets and properties of institutional quality are becoming increasingly efficient with time. For the 30 or so geographical markets that matter to institutional investors in the United States, there is ever-more efficient information about properties and tenants. When a building is sold or a lease is signed, everyone in the market knows the terms. Indeed, the leases of major tenants approach the transparency of some fixed-income securities. (A Wal-Mart lease in New York is like a Wal-Mart lease in California, subject to nuances in local real estate laws.) Yes, local market players may have an edge in their backyard, but they also lack the skill and resources to invest objectively in other markets when their backyard is overbuilt or otherwise out of favor.

Sharpe's "Arithmetic of Active Management," detailed in Chapter 2 and cited in subsequent chapters, can be applied to real estate securities just as it has been to managers of conventional stocks and bonds. The overall market return is simply the average of all managers, active and passive, skilled and not so skilled. And after fees and transactions costs, which are substantial in this sector, the average manager will underperform the market average. An indexed real estate strategy, on average, will, therefore, generate a higher long-term return than an active one.

It is important not to confuse indexing real estate to a passive real estate strategy. Every REIT holds and actively manages a portfolio of properties through a skilled, hands-on, and financially motivated management team. REIT management teams are seldom passive, buy and hold investors. *Owning an indexed REIT portfolio is equivalent to owning a fund of actively managed real estate assets.*

The only thing passive about an indexed approach is that the shares in each company are held at their market cap weight, which takes the risk out of guessing which REITs to over- or underweight. An indexed REIT portfolio offers the benefits of both indexing and active management, and the active management comes in at the property level where it can make the most difference. In this way, it has similarities to the hedge fund index funds described in the sidebar in Chapter 11.

Indexing reduces the risks and costs of real estate investing. The same benefits achieved by indexing equity and fixed-income investments—broad market exposure at a low cost—can be achieved by indexing real estate securities.

Indexed REIT funds also provide investors with manager style diversification. One REIT may create value by refurbishing older buildings (a value strategy), whereas another might focus on acquiring blue-chip office properties (more of a growth strategy). Indexing gives investors exposure to a range of management styles, instead of concentrating on just one style.

Investment management costs are also more favorable for REIT index funds. Traditional real estate advisors might charge 100 basis points (bps) plus incentive fees, whereas REIT index funds typically charge 20 to 50 bps. REIT exchange-traded funds charge 30 to 65 bps, or about one-third of private equity and REIT mutual funds.

Indexed REITs can be a perfect complement to a private equity portfolio. Many institutional investors have long been committed to real estate as an asset class (4 to 8 percent is a typical allocation), but they have struggled to meet their allocation targets. Finding the right property in the right market at the right time is an elusive challenge. REITs can fill in the gap, either permanently or as a temporary "parking place" for capital while an investor is in between private equity deals. Because REIT stocks can be purchased in any amount, they are appropriate for big and small investors alike.

Indexed REITs are a convenient way for investors to acquire exposure to a diverse set of real estate holdings, across property types and geographic markets. This is virtually impossible to accomplish through a private equity strategy for all but the largest institutions. Performance tracking is also easily obtained through REITs, as they are valued daily in the equity markets. As with closed-end stock and bond mutual funds, REITs may trade at a premium or discount to their net asset value. Because of the liquidity and other advantages of the REIT structure, it is logical for REITs to often trade at a premium.

If only investors had indexed real estate in the late 1980s and early 1990s, perhaps they would not have found 30 percent of their assets tied up in a half-vacant shopping center in Houston or an illiquid commingled fund interest in the Sears Tower with 25 percent vacancy. Today, an indexed REIT strategy affords broad market exposure without the oversight headaches of a private equity strategy.

THE MAJOR REAL ESTATE INDEXES

The REIT market is well represented by indexes. In some ways, it is actually over-indexed in relation to the $200 billion market capitalization of the REIT universe, as the following list of the major indexes shows:

- NAREIT Index.
- Wilshire Real Estate Securities Index.
- Morgan Stanley REIT Index.
- Dow Jones Real Estate Index.
- Cohen & Steers Realty Majors Index.

Links to the index vendor's web sites are available in the book's E-ppendix at www.ActiveIndexInvesting.com or on IndexUniverse.com. It provides profiles for the major real estate indexes such as this one for the Wilshire index:

The Wilshire Real Estate Securities Index lists 94 commercial equity companies, 88 of which are REITs and 6 of which are REOCs (real estate operating companies). The index is capitalization weighted—with a market cap of approximately $194 billion as of 12/31/03—and it is rebalanced monthly. Among other criteria, companies included in the index must have a market capitalization of at least $100 million, and share liquidity comparable to industry standards.

Several investment firms now offer indexed real estate/REIT products. For example, Barclays Global Investors (BGI) and State Street Global Advisors (SSgA) both offer institutional REIT index funds, both for defined benefit plans and for defined contribution (401(k)) plans. BGI's U.S. Real Estate Securities Index Fund is a portfolio of 99 publicly traded REITs and REOCs designed to track the Wilshire Real Estate Securities Index. Covering the five main institutional property types—office, industrial, multifamily, hotels, and retail—in major markets throughout the United States, the fund includes the same REITs and REOCs as the Wilshire Index. SSgA's institutional products also track the Wilshire Real Estate Index.

There are three ETFs that hold REITs available in the United States. As discussed in Chapters 14 and 16, ETFs are open-end index funds that trade like stocks. The iShares Cohen & Steers Realty Majors fund (ticker ICF) tracks an index of 30 large-cap REITs. BGI's iShares Dow Jones U.S. Real Estate Index ETF (IYR) tracks the returns of 71 REITs and 4 REOCs in the Dow Jones U.S. Real Estate Index. SSgA's StreetTracks Wilshire Real Estate Index ETF (RWR) tracks the previously mentioned Wilshire index. The Vanguard Group offers a very popular REIT Index Fund with over $4 billion in assets that tracks the Morgan Stanley REIT Index and has an ultra low expense ratio of 27 bps.

Managing REIT stocks requires many of the same skills used in the more traditional securities markets. Investors should expect the same attention to cost and risk controls that they get from their equity and fixed-income managers. Because REIT stocks are securities, they should be managed by an advisor with extensive equities trading expertise. Traditional real estate advisors, who may bring bricks-and-mortar experience, will lack this expertise, especially if they treat REITs as a sideline operation.

The State Universities Retirement System of Illinois, a seasoned real estate investor (see sidebar in Chapter 18 on one of their innovative strategies to international indexing) recognized this connection explicitly when they chose an indexed approach for the core component of their publicly traded real estate portfolio. Because of the availability of REIT Index mutual funds and ETFs, smaller institutions, financial advisors, and individual investors can benefit from the same approach followed by Illinois and other large pension plans.

CONCLUSION—THE RIGHT TIME FOR REITs?

During the early to mid 2000s, in the face of low expected returns for stocks and bonds, many institutional investors increased their real estate allocations. Some consider an indexed REIT strategy as a complement for their less liquid real estate holdings. Others are attracted to the high current returns and potential for long-term appreciation. Although it is nearly impossible to successfully time the market, it is important to consider both capital market factors and real estate fundamentals when evaluating a REIT investment.

When stock market prices declined to historically low levels in early 2003, REITs held their value despite the weak economy. Some investors saw real estate as a safe harbor from more volatile markets. Real estate values are a function of rental income and capitalization rates. Rental income, because it is tied to a portfolio of leases, is not as volatile as say sales revenues in other publicly traded companies. Capitalization rates, which represent the required return on capital from commercial real estate, have remained low, consistent with fixed-income securities. Low capitalization rates have, in turn, kept property values high.

Despite three consecutive years of negative performance in U.S. equities during 2000 to 2002, the REIT market delivered impressive returns. For the 5 years ending December 2003, the Wilshire Real Estate Index returned 14.12 percent annually compared with 6.62 percent for the Lehman Aggregate bond index, and −1.05 percent for the Russell 3000 Index. In fact, as of December 31, 2003, REITs outperformed both bonds and other equities on a 1-, 3-, 5-, and 10-year basis.

Real estate fundamentals, or the supply of and demand for property, vary greatly from submarket to submarket and by property type. Oversupply has generally been the biggest problem facing real estate investors. Developers and lenders now have better information about markets and have become more disciplined about adding to supply. Many communities have put growth constraints in place to deter overbuilding.

In terms of demand, the local economy—particularly job growth— is a key driver of demand in every geographic market. The demand for office space is directly tied to jobs. The demand for apartments is also tied to household formation and interest rates, because low interest rates mean more people can afford to purchase homes. Shopping center performance is tied to the health of the local economy, and retail leases typically have a percent-of-sales rental clause. Hotel demand is tied to tourism. Hence, an investment in REITs can capture expected improvement in local economies.

REITs are gaining acceptance by noninstitutional investors and are making their way into 401(k) plans. Whereas, real estate has long been a staple for defined benefit plans, it is gradually being embraced for defined contribution plans for the same reasons: income, appreciation, diversification, and hedge against inflation. A major retailer just added REITs to its menu of 401(k) options to provide employees with a diversification opportunity away from traditional stocks and bonds. REITs are also being added as an asset class to "life cycle" funds that offer diversified portfolios with varying degrees of risk depending on an employee's expected year of retirement.

Real estate has often been called an *alternative* asset class. With the diversification benefits of real estate investing, and the ease, convenience, and lower costs of index-based real estate products, it is rapidly becoming an *essential* core asset class that belongs in most investors' portfolios. Chapter 30 provides some specific examples of how to integrate REIT index products into an overall investment strategy.

NOTE

1. Refer to www.NAREIT.com for an up-to-date look at REIT performance and correlations relative to other asset classes. IndexUniverse.com has complete data on the various REIT index funds and ETFs available to investors.

CHAPTER 18

Active Indexing

Sophisticated Strategies with Index Vehicles

Steven A. Schoenfeld, Robert Ginis, and Niklas Nordenfelt

_____ **Editor's Note** _____

The term passive investing, which is commonly used to refer to indexing, is truly the oxymoron of the investment management industry. No investment activity is passive, and as subsequent chapters in Part Four will demonstrate, managing an index fund is a complex and active endeavor. Another popular misconception is that "indexing guarantees mediocrity." The reality is far from it, and in fact, aside from the long-term track record of indexing in out-performing traditional active managers (discussed in Part One), this chapter demonstrates that the use of index products within an actively-managed approach can often achieve better results than an active approach that doesn't utilize index products.

*But what is **active indexing?** As discussed in Chapter 1, the term has multiple meanings—enough to name a book and a chapter on the concept. As an adjective, it can describe the way in which the art and science of indexing is "anything but passive." But, as also discussed in Chapter 1, in the form of a noun, active indexing can be defined as an investment approach that uses the tools and/or objectives of indexing to efficiently provide an alternative risk-return profile from that of the index. It is not always about producing alpha—it could be about maximizing the efficiency of an asset allocation de-cision. But it is definitely not "plain vanilla" indexing, nor is it passive.*

This chapter describes how single asset class or style/sector/size index funds—as efficient as they may be—are only the starting point for index-based investing. Modular index funds can be used as implementation vehicles for sound investment strategies and, in fact, may well be the most efficient vehicle for any investment strategy. And with the availability of ETFs on virtually any index and sub-index, some strategies that were previously designed for institutional investors (including several discussed in this chapter) can now be implemented by almost any type of investor. Index products' three primary advantages—low cost, transparency, and precision of return— allow investors to create strategies without major slippage between strategy design, implementation, and achieved performance. And the same three advantages make performance attribution of the strategy a relatively straightforward exercise.

Thus, even though the management of "traditional" index funds is far from a passive endeavor (and this will be extensively explored in Part Four), active indexing means taking the index investment process several steps further. It can develop index-based portfolios that deliver specific value by the following three robust methods: (1) actively allocating between sector, size, style, or country/regional index portfolios (some of the examples provided in Chapter 16 introduced readers to these concepts); (2) using index products to plug "risk holes" in an investment strategy or overall strategic asset allocation; or (3) actively customizing the portfolio within an index benchmark framework.[1] These alternative indexing and weighting approaches deliver value in several ways and are discussed here. I have emphasized emerging market equity strategies in this chapter, partly because my co-authors and I have significant experience in this area, but also because these volatile markets are surprisingly (to some!) appropriate for "active index" strategies.

To further illustrate the sophisticated, active use of index products, the chapter includes two sidebars featuring the perspective and experience of large institutional investors. The first, by John Krimmel of the Illinois State Universities Retirement System (IllSURS), provides an excellent case study of how indexing helps facilitate risk budgeting, through his plan's avoidance of a major risk hole with a value-oriented international index strategy (this concept was originally covered in Chapter 3). The second sidebar, an interview with Aje Saigal of the Government of Singapore Investment Corporation (GSIC), highlights how the globally-oriented and actively-managed GSIC uses index-based strategies and products for Tactical Asset Allocation and as a core implementation vehicle for both efficient and inefficient asset classes.

I hope that this chapter serves to broaden readers' understanding of how investors can be "as active as they want to be" with index-based strategies. The examples and case studies are not designed to be comprehensive, but illustrative of the virtually infinite flexibility of the potential applications of the ever-expanding range of index products and techniques described in this part of the book (Part Three).

This chapter illustrates sophisticated index-based strategies used by institutional investors and applicable in an individual context, ranging from the lowest risk strategies to others that take on as much risk as investor appetite can digest. There are *unlimited* approaches to using index vehicles, and this chapter does not attempt to cover even half of the potential uses. However, index-based portfolios are the ideal starting point to tailor customized portfolios for investors' unique needs and preferences, and this chapter will demonstrate a myriad of ways to make it happen.

Many studies have shown that the most important decision a pension plan sponsor makes is the policy allocation decision.[2] This also applies to the individual investor, for whom policy is the *investment strategy*. Just as the pension plan sponsor must carefully determine the overall allocation strategy, an individual investor should focus on choosing an investment strategy instead of spending excessive time on stock research.[3]

This chapter includes a detailed example of a real-world *active index* application that has been developed both at large institutional managers as well as boutique investment advisors. This approach is consistent with the sector and style rotation strategies using ETFs first highlighted in Chapter 16. Our goal is to show the enormous range of strategies that can be constructed with index-based portfolios, and thus set the context for Part Four, which provides a unique insight into the index portfolio management process.

USING INDEX PRODUCTS TO PLUG RISK HOLES IN A PORTFOLIO/STRATEGY

All active investment decisions—be it in individual securities, sectors, or countries—should be in areas where the investor has insight. For example, an investor who is unfamiliar with the technology sector and the companies that compose it should obviously not be day-trading technology stocks. Similarly, an investment plan or policy benchmarked to a broad index, such as the Wilshire 5000 or Russell 3000, should not take on unintended over/underweights to sectors or styles. However, this often happens, even among sophisticated investors and investment plans. Many institutional investors inadvertently overweight growth stocks because their collection of externally managed active managers may (in aggregate) be biased toward the same growth stocks. These unintended bets are not trivial, and can have serious consequences for the portfolio.

More often than not, these "nondecisions" drive the success or failure of investment plans. To take a basic example, if the investment plan is overweight growth stocks and value stocks outperform growth stocks, the plan is likely to underperform its benchmark regardless of the stock-picking

CREATING VALUE THROUGH STYLE INDEX STRATEGIES— HOW ILLINOIS SURS NEUTRALIZED AN INTERNATIONAL EQUITY GROWTH BIAS WITH A VALUE INDEX FUND

John Krimmel

As many chapters and sidebars in this book illustrate, indexing can play vital roles for large institutional investors. It can be a core component of an allocation to an asset class, a tool for efficient exposure to sectors and/or cap ranges, or a vehicle to plug risk holes in an overall strategic policy mix.

Plan sponsors are paying closer attention to growth and value investing in their international portfolios. In the fall of 2001, my colleagues and I at the State Universities Retirement System of Illinois (Ill-SURS) analyzed the plan's international exposure. By combining the indexed portion of the portfolio with the actively managed side, we discovered the portfolio had taken on a strong growth bias. Paying attention to style is increasingly important in one's international portfolio. We detected a growth bias in our plan that we had not intended in our overall strategic asset allocation.

We consulted with our index fund manager to get a clear picture of the different international style indexes. Working with their international index strategists, we assessed the benchmark offerings from the major index providers. Eventually, that discussion led the pension plan to transition $400 million in assets to a newly created MSCI (Morgan Stanley Capital International) EAFE (Europe Australasia Far East) Value Index strategy. In the summer of 2002, we transitioned an additional $45 million to this EAFE Value Fund from an actively managed international fund.

In addition to helping the Illinois Universities plan devise the right strategy and choose the appropriate benchmark, our portfolio manager made sure the transition occurred as smoothly and cost-effectively as possible. To reduce risk, we also neutralized our currency exposure through the transition period and invested that cash. All in all, we were able to make this large strategy and style transition in a cost-effective manner, and more importantly, plugged a significant *risk hole* in our overall portfolio, which paid off handsomely when value outperformed growth in the 2001/2002 timeframe.

prowess of the external managers. Index funds are ideal solutions to plug these holes in investment plans. For the plan's overweight growth stocks, it can invest the appropriate amount into a value index strategy and thereby neutralize the undesired style bet. This approach is as useful for international as domestic equity strategies, as described in the sidebar by John Krimmel, which provides the perspective of a major U.S. pension fund.

Investors who have a set of strategies or funds that are underweight energy stocks can invest the appropriate amount into an energy index fund (e.g., there are a variety of ETFs based on the energy sector) and neutralize the unintended sector bets. A similar approach can be used for capitalization ranges (e.g., large, mid, or small cap) or style (as described in the example in the previous sidebar).

Most individual investors have far less stringent constraints on their investments and many do not benchmark their investments to any benchmark or index. Similarly, many investors do not diversify sufficiently, and often their holdings are concentrated in one or just a handful of securities. Though these investors may not be tied to a benchmark, such investment programs are risky and in strong need of diversification. Completion strategies, *whether index-based* or *enhanced index* are investment programs in which 30 to 50 stocks are purchased such that the combination of the existing position(s) with the additional securities creates an index-like exposure. They are usually implemented in a *separate account* framework (see Chapter 24).[4] Furthermore, such a strategy can also take advantage of tax-loss harvesting by selling stocks with capital gain losses and replacing them with similar securities thereby preserving the investment style (e.g., large-cap index).

Corporations often face the same kind of situation, either in their pension plan, or for their beneficiaries in defined contribution retirement plans. For example, an oil company's pension plan that holds a large position in its own stock is highly exposed to the performance of both the company's stock and the energy sector in general. The reason is that its stock has a relatively high correlation with the performance of other oil company stocks. Once again, indexing strategies can help solve such situations. Investing in an index strategy "ex-their industry" (i.e., *ex*cluding oil stocks) assures diversification across all sectors and places far less reliance on its own performance and that of the oil sector.

SOPHISTICATED METHODS TO ENHANCE PERFORMANCE, CONTROL RISK, AND LOWER COSTS

Investors and portfolio managers can use index vehicles to enhance performance, control risks, and lower costs. The notion that indexing somehow limits an investor to mediocre returns is a tremendous fallacy. In this case, we are discussing the use of index vehicles and not just investment plans designed to track an index. The choices are virtually limitless.

If designed appropriately, combinations of a cash/fixed income position and index derivative contracts such as an S&P 500 futures contract result in a synthetic index fund tracking the S&P 500. If an investor holds the equivalent cash (and invests it in a Treasury bill) as the notional value of the futures contract, then the performance of the futures contract and the interest earned on the invested cash will match that of the S&P 500 index.[5] Chapter 15 discusses derivative-based enhanced index strategies that use stock index futures.

Index futures contracts can be used to increase beta (or leverage) to the market. Since the beta (sensitivity of one instrument relative to another) of the S&P 500 is essentially 1.0 with the U.S. market,[6] investors—through the purchase of futures contracts—can decide their level of exposure to the market. Similarly, shorting futures contracts can help reduce risk or overall exposure (beta) to the market's fluctuations.

As discussed in Chapters 14 and 16, exchange-traded funds (ETFs) based on indexes also provide extremely useful vehicles for creative investment strategies. Buying an ETF on margin is effectively the same as buying a futures contract because investors get index-like exposure at a desired beta/leverage level. Just as with a futures contract, the amount of collateral or underlying cash that the ETF is equitizing determines the leverage to the market. If investors desire more leverage, then they put up the minimum collateral required for the margin position. If no leverage is desired, they simply buy the ETF with cash.

As discussed in previous chapters—as well as in Part Five—ETFs are available in a plethora of choices, ranging from broad market indexes to the smaller, more defined indexes such as styles, sectors, and countries. Exchange-traded funds are ideal vehicles for active overlays (see Chapters 16 and 25). For example, an investment plan benchmarked to a global index (e.g., MSCI World) could make active country bets by investing the majority of the money in an MSCI World index fund and then adding small overweights in specific markets via individual ETF country funds. For example, if an investor has insight into the British stock market, and believes that the United Kingdom will outperform (underperform) the rest of the world, they could buy (sell) the U.K. ETF to position the country as an overweight (underweight) in the overall plan. Similarly, investors who are fully invested in the U.S. market but wary of the tech sector could simply short one of the many ETFs based on a technology index while maintaining a long position in an ETF based on the total market such as Vanguard VIPER Total Market Fund (Wilshire 5000) or the iShares Russell 3000 fund.[7]

THE IMPORTANCE OF THE ALLOCATION

As stated at the outset, investment returns are driven more by the asset allocation (or investment policy) decision than by the funds or stocks chosen within the asset classes. A 1986 article by Brinson, Hood, and Beebower proved that 94 percent of the variability of performance was attributable to the investment policy. Although this number has been challenged, a more recent study by Surz, Stevens, and Wimer concluded that the policy decision explains actual returns experienced even *more* closely than previously believed. In their 1999 article, they found that the investment policy accounted for 104 percent of the total return for mutual funds (and 99 percent of the pension funds in the study).[8] This means that outside the benchmark decision, actions such as timing, stock selection, and fees *detracted* from the performance. These two studies and a subsequent one that combined their data set are discussed in more detail in Chapter 30.

These studies show that it is crucial to make the appropriate policy/strategic allocation decision first and foremost. The choice of stocks and/or actively managed funds within the asset class has generally detracted from total return. Therefore, investors should expend more attention and energy on determining an investment strategy and less time on choosing managers. In fact, the cited evidence strongly suggests that after determining the investment strategy, investors would improve results by simply choosing index products that track the asset classes within the strategy.

Sophisticated institutional investors have long recognized this: They focus their energies on where they believe they can add value, and where they don't have the skill or resources, they take an index-based approach. They know that getting exposure is the most important factor. Chapter 30 goes further with this line of reasoning and proposes some universal axioms to guide investors.

Global investors are often the most keenly aware of this, as they are relatively free from the home country bias that can cloud the vision of more domestically oriented investors. One of the most sophisticated, globally oriented investors is the Government of Singapore Investment Corporation (GSIC)—the entity that manages the island republic's substantial portfolio investment and retirement funds.[9] In the following sidebar, the Government of Singapore Investment Corporation's Aje Saigal explains how and why index-based investing is an indispensable component of an active investment strategy. The interview describes how GSIC effectively uses index products for both asset allocation shifts between markets/asset classes, and for efficient core exposure for both developed and emerging equity markets.

HOW DO ACTIVE MANAGERS USE INDEX PRODUCTS?— AN INTERVIEW WITH AJE SAIGAL

The Government of Singapore Investment Corporation is one of the largest asset managers in the world. Its portfolio of over US$100 billion is invested in equities and fixed-income markets globally, in both developed and emerging markets. Aje Saigal, Director of Investment Policy and Strategy, offers his insights into how GSIC manages its equity portfolio.

Would you describe GSIC's investment style and how it has evolved?

We are global investors, using the MSCI World equity index as our benchmark. We actively invest in all major as well as emerging markets. Our equity team consists of about 25 portfolio managers who are encouraged to develop their own style bias when picking stocks in each of their regions. The more experienced managers in this team are also given sector and global portfolios to manage. To fill the gaps in the styles of our internal portfolio managers, we engage external managers with strong orientation in those styles.

In addition to the portfolio managers, we have built a separate equity research capability to provide objective analysis of companies. Our research analysts are assigned to six global sector groups and manage research portfolios.

What challenges do you face managing such a large portfolio, and how do index-based products help you overcome them?

GSIC's size and reputation offer both benefits and challenges. Thanks to our size, we often get to meet the management of companies, as well as the top analysts who cover them.

However, like some U.S. pension funds, our size sometimes makes it difficult for us to make asset allocation changes in a timely and cost-efficient manner, due to market impact costs and other factors. To minimize such costs, we use index funds/portfolios; exchange-traded funds (ETFs) that have good liquidity; and index derivatives such as stock index futures.

How do you manage the risk of your equity portfolio?

We seek to minimize the overall risk of our portfolio through a high degree of diversification and low style bias. We use different approaches in different markets. In the more efficient and developed markets like the

United States, a significant part of the portfolios is indexed. In the less efficient Asian markets outside Japan, we use mainly an active, stock-picking approach. In some emerging markets outside Asia, where we do not have sufficient knowledge or familiarity, we hold a passive core and a few individual stocks spotted by the global sector analysts. This allows us to spend our risk budget in markets where our active management can consistently add alpha.

ALTERNATIVELY WEIGHTED INDEX STRATEGIES

Index-based vehicles are extremely efficient for implementing many alternative weighting approaches to indexing, whether a custom-weighted benchmark, or an active strategy (see Chapters 1, 12, and 14 for some examples). In this chapter, we focus extensively on international equities, as this is our area of greater experience, but the variety of approaches is just as extensive for U.S. equities, as was portrayed in Chapter 16, and is lightly discussed here.

Domestic Equities

As a short overview, index funds and ETFs are ideal for sector and style rotation strategies. These approaches are common with active managers using fundamental signals and have been implemented for years by investors who time entry and exit of sector mutual funds such as the Fidelity Select Sector series and the ProFunds and Rydex sector index funds. Similarly, many active managers pursue style-rotation strategies, attempting to time trends of when value or growth styles are likely to outperform. They can do this within a specific cap range (i.e., rotating between large-cap value and large-cap growth) or across style and size (i.e., rotating from small-cap growth into mid-cap value).

Implementing domestic size, style, or sector rotation strategies with index vehicles, either driven by fundamental signals, or with quantitative rules similar to the structured-tiered approach described later in this chapter can yield a pure exposure to the signals, without noise from active risk within the sector, cap range, or style portfolio. As mentioned above, Chapter 16 provided several excellent examples of these types of applications.

International Equities

For more than 30 years, institutional investors have debated their international allocation strategy. Instead of investing aligned with the straightforward market cap, which weights each country by the size of their relative market capitalization, institutional investors have looked for alternative weighting schemes. The calculation of country capitalization, with its quirks and inefficiencies, has been the primary driver for this effort.

As discussed in Chapters 9 and 12, until 2001 the predominant international index provider, MSCI, did not adjust the market cap to reflect the actual free float, or the amount available to investors. This fact, combined with the Japanese equity bubble, which drove Japan's weight in the MSCI EAFE index to over 60 percent, rightly led investors to consider alternative weighting methodologies that might better diversify their international investments.

The following strategies are some of the more popular alternatives. These are country allocation strategies as opposed to the segmented strategies for single markets (discussed for U.S. equities) such as sectors, size, and value/growth.

Capitalization-Weighted Strategies   The market capitalization of individual securities represents the collective wisdom of all investors on a global scale. Capitalization-weighted strategies can be sliced as finely as an investor desires. A global strategy can invest according to the cap-weights of the countries. Single country strategies invest according to the cap-weights of the securities within the country, whereas a sector strategy invests according to the cap-weights of the securities within the sector. The common denominator in any of these and other strategies is that the relative market capitalization determines the asset weights (whether for securities or countries).

To some, this may seem simplistic and lacking in investment insight; however, cap-weighted strategies are appealing on many fronts. The core benefit of the capitalization-weighted multimarket index is similar to the case made in Chapter 5 for capitalization single market indexes, namely; low cost and turnover, good relative liquidity, self-rebalancing, and theoretical soundness—as cap-weighting is consistent with the Capital Asset Pricing Model (CAPM). However, the problem with market cap-weighted strategies is that they may create highly concentrated portfolios when one country outperforms the other markets. As discussed in Chapter 12, Japan's strong performance in the 1980s led it to become (at its peak in 1989) 65 percent of MSCI EAFE's overall capitalization. As a result, market cap-weighted strategies often incur higher risks from country concentration and the lack of diversification across markets. In addition, flaws in the calculation of the true market cap (or free float) may lead to distorted weights causing liquidity issues for large institutional investors. Thus, investors developed alternatively-weighted strategies such as "EAFE Lite" and GDP-weighted EAFE to address this distortion. EAFE-Lite was discussed in Chapter 12, and GDP-weighted strategies are discussed next.

The U.S. market has experienced similar distortions with the rise and fall of sectors during major market and economic trends (e.g., energy stocks in 1979 and technology in 1998 to 2000), Emerging markets had their share of roller-coaster rides in the late 1990s, including very high weights in Mexico, Malaysia, South Africa, and Korea. The colorful history of the rise and fall of countries and sectors within the benchmarks is detailed in Chapter 12.

Equal Weighting   Perhaps the first—and intuitive—shift from a cap-weighted approach is an equal-weighted strategy. As the name suggests, this strategy simply weights the countries equally. For example, for an investable universe of 20 developed market countries, each country would have an equal allocation of 5 percent in the overall portfolio.

The primary benefit is that it eliminates country concentration issues. Equally weighting markets is the simplest and most effective way to assure that the performance of one or a small handful of countries does not unduly affect a portfolio's return. Another benefit is that the weighting scheme sets up the possibility of capturing mean reversion (discussed later in the chapter) across markets.

A significant downside to an equal-weighted strategy, however, is that an investor implicitly makes relatively large bets on small and illiquid markets. This is especially true for large pension plans with sizable allocations to the emerging markets asset class. Moreover, a significant allocation to smaller markets would require considerable ongoing costs for rebalancing that would erode the total return of such a strategy.

Excluding the smaller markets and limiting investments to the larger more liquid countries would eliminate much of the ongoing transaction costs, but it would do so at the expense of diversification. Smaller markets may have liquidity constraints, but they provide diversification benefits and potential for enhanced returns. Finally, any equal-weighted strategy creates unintended regional and sector bets relative to a capitalization-weighted benchmark. While an equal-weighted strategy may minimize country concentration risks, paradoxically it may create security concentration issues since a few securities dominate several small markets.

GDP Weighting   Weighting countries by their relative size of gross domestic product (GDP) has been a popular alternative for many years. Although there is no real theoretical reason to support GDP weights, the existence of a GDP benchmark (calculated by MSCI) has increased their legitimacy. Mark Sladkus provides background on the development of MSCI's GDP-weighted indexes in Chapter 12. An appealing aspect of these indexes is that the weights are relatively stable because GDPs do not change much over the years. In fact, changes in exchange rates have been the most significant drivers for changes in the GDP figures and weights. As a result, a GDP weighting scheme is similar to an equal weighting scheme in that investors can capture mean reversion by selling the best-performing markets and buying the worst-performing markets as the strategy is reset annually to the GDP weights.

Furthermore, this approach alleviates some of the liquidity issues of equal weighting as the smaller markets tend to have smaller GDPs and therefore smaller weights in the strategy. However, the lack of theoretical support for using a GDP-weighted strategy has limited its appeal. The bulk of the appeal has been as a justification for limiting Japan's weight when Japan made up such a large portion of the cap-weighted benchmark. By 2002, Japan's weight had fallen to about 20 percent of EAFE and there was a noticeable decline in the desire to further limit its weight. As a result, there has been little demand for new GDP-weighted strategies; instead there has been a return to the more traditional cap-weight approaches.

While GDP weighting had a solid logic and gained some popularity for developed equity markets, GDP weights in emerging stock markets would generally be completely misaligned with the realities of market size and structure. Liquidity is poor in countries like China and India, which would have huge weights relative to liquidity, due to the size of their economies. Thus, there has been little demand for GDP-weighted emerging market indexes, and with the exception of a few regional portfolios, to the best of our knowledge, few have been created.

Liquidity-Tiered Weighting   Liquidity-tiered strategies are essentially a more sophisticated variant of equal-weighted strategies. Countries are weighted equally within multiple tiers. Based on market liquidity, the countries are grouped into tiers by similar liquidity and then equally weighted within the tiers.

The primary advantage of this approach is that it answers the biggest drawback of equal-weighted strategies, which give large weights to small, illiquid markets. In liquidity-tiered strategies, those countries are grouped in the bottom tier at lower weights than the countries in the top tiers. The other advantage is that the prospects for capturing mean reversion remain because markets are rebalanced periodically to their preset weights. Again, the winners are sold and the losers bought. It should be noted that this approach requires significant discretion in determining which countries should be grouped together, what weight should be assigned to each tier, and how frequently the countries should be rebalanced.

Structured-Tiered Strategies (Mean-Reversion Capture)[10]   This strategy is different from the liquidity-tiered strategy in that it places countries into tiers based on more than just one factor and aims to capture the *structural* characteristics of individual markets. These characteristics form the basis for the strategic allocation decision, with an expectation that there will be tactical rebalancing to "capture mean reversion" as well as a regular review of the tiers. The objective of the strategic allocation is to create a weighting structure that segments markets into groups with similar, long-term expectations. Such approaches can be applied in a variety of global equity strategies, and for both developed and emerging markets. The strategy we developed and managed at Barclays Global Investors from 1999 to 2002 used five factors—market capitalization, stage of development, portfolio risk, liquidity/transaction costs, and operational risk.[11] Table 18.1 highlights how countries ranked within this framework in mid-2002, with an emphasis on the highest and lowest scores. The sidebar, "Capturing Mean Reversion in Emerging Markets," provides some more detail and context on the rationale and potential of this strategy for emerging stock markets.

It should be noted that these factor scores are dynamic, and need to be re-evaluated on a regular basis. Unlike many *quant-active* strategies, there is a high degree of subjectivity and fundamental knowledge of the markets that plays a role in determining scores, especially at the margin. Finally, experience has shown us that the rebalancing process and mean-reversion capture strategies are most effective when quantitative rules and qualitative market knowledge are combined. This is discussed further under "Portfolio Construction."

Next we highlight the five factors we developed for a structured-tiered international equity strategy.

TABLE 18.1 Scoring of Emerging Markets by Factors (Partial View)

Market Capitalization	Stage of Development	Portfolio Risk	Liquidity/ *T*-Costs	Operational Risks
High Scores				
Korea	Mexico	Philippines	Israel	Korea
Taiwan	Hungary	Chile	Korea	Thailand
South Africa	Israel	Poland	Brazil	Turkey
Low Scores				
Pakistan	Indonesia	Russia	Venezuela	Russia
Colombia	Pakistan	Indonesia	Jordan	Venezuela
Venezuela	Philippines	Turkey	Peru	India

Note: As of June 30, 2002.
Source: BGI International Equity Strategy Group.

Market Capitalization   The market capitalization factor anchors the strategy to the underlying benchmark and thereby controls for relative risk (variance versus the benchmark). The markets are scored based on their size; however, since the strategy aims to capture mean reversion, size is measured not by the current market capitalization, but by trailing average market capitalization. With this system, the markets that have risen (or fallen) substantially in recent months will be scored lower (or higher) than if based on the most recent market capitalization. Consistent with the overall contrarian objectives, the strategy in effect gives less weight to recent outperformers and more weight to recent underperformers, but in a relatively risk-constrained manner. In times when large markets outperform, the performance of the strategy may underperform vis-à-vis a capitalization-weighted benchmark. However, market history has shown that, time and time again, performance trends come to an abrupt end, and while the secular trend may remain strong, the cyclical trend suggests an inevitable downturn.

Stage of Development   This factor rewards countries showing convergence to developed market norms and overweight markets that are expected to outperform on a relative basis. Countries that converge economically, socially, and politically with developed market countries are more likely to create pro-business environments. The inputs for this factor include membership in economic and/or free-trade organizations (EMU, EU, NAFTA, OECD, to name a few), Standard & Poor's sovereign credit ratings, and corporate governance scores from several independent sources. The inputs directly address peer pressure to conform (membership), the treatment of lenders (sovereign scores), and equity shareholders (corporate governance) and effectively indicate a country's commitment to positively evolve its business and economic environment, all of which we believe impacts long-term performance.

Portfolio Risk   A primary goal of the strategy is to control for absolute portfolio risk. Overweighting (underweighting) markets that have low volatility (high volatility) and low correlation (high correlation) to the other markets will lower the strategy's overall risk characteristics. The inputs for this factor are the volatility of the markets (as measured by standard deviation of returns) and the pairwise correlation of market as measured by the correlation of a market with other markets.

Since this factor directly addresses risk, constructing a portfolio on this factor alone should result in significantly lower standard deviation than a capitalization-weighted benchmark. Back-tested results confirm this objective—the annualized standard deviation (over the period January 1997 to April 2002) of this single-factor portfolio was only 12.9 percent, far less than the emerging market index's annualized standard deviation of 28.0 percent.[12]

Liquidity/Transaction Costs Trading in emerging markets can expose investors to significant transaction costs, as illiquid securities are more expensive to trade. This factor seeks to avoid excessive trading in expensive markets that would quickly degrade the performance of the strategy. Using data provided by brokers, and many years of experience in trading these markets, we estimate the liquidity of the markets and the transaction costs broken down by commissions, taxes, and bid/ask spreads.

The strategy benefits significantly from the ability of this factor to segment countries such that the overweighted markets are typically the ones with lower transaction costs and higher liquidity.

Operational Risk Operational procedures and the regulatory and capital market infrastructure are indicative of the commitment to capital markets development. It is important to "watch what they do, not what they say." Furthermore, investors should avoid overexposure to investments in stock markets where they may experience difficulties with and/or delays in the free movement of capital. As a result, this final factor, operational risk, addresses the practicality of investing in emerging markets by penalizing (through a low score) markets for trading and settlement risks. Operational risk scores are calculated from data obtained from local and global custodial relationships and index vendors such as S&P/IFC and MSCI (see Table 18.1).

Portfolio Construction Summing the individual factor scores results in a natural clustering of scores. The countries are equally weighted within each tier (the particular strategy described previously uses five tiers) to allow the strategy to maximally exploit mean reversion. The weight given to each tier is dependent on how many countries are in the cluster and the relative average score of the cluster. If the average score of one cluster (or tier) is twice that of the next cluster (or tier), the weights of the countries within that tier would be about twice as high as the countries within the next tier.

Equally weighting the countries within each tier sets the framework for capturing mean reversion. The target weight within each tier becomes the fair-value basis against which markets are measured. The long-run expected returns of each market within the tier should be relatively similar. Therefore, as markets deviate from the target weight, they are either bought (if the weight has dipped substantially below the target weight) or sold (if the weight has risen well above the target weight). In this way, markets that have become cheap on a relative basis are bought, and vice versa.

The use of low-cost, well-diversified index funds as the implementation vehicles minimizes the transaction costs and assures proper stock-level diversification and exposure to each of the markets.

We consider the structured-tiered approach as the evolutionary successor to liquidity tiering. Whereas the latter strategies characterize markets by liquidity and typically sets somewhat arbitrary fixed weights for the tiers, the structured-tiered approach uses a more rigorous method in determining "like" countries for the groupings and a systematic determination of the appropriate tier weight. The preceding example is just one approach that has proven successful both in performance and in generating institutional appeal.[13] The concept can be used to create structured-tiered strategies based on different factors and for different markets. Some ideas along this dimension are discussed in Chapter 30. Ultimately, investor insights into markets drive decisions and should be incorporated into any method. The process itself merely provides the guardrails for disciplined real-time investment decisions, transaction cost containment, and the framework for capturing mean reversion and improved risk/return trade-offs.

Tactical Strategies and Strategic Approaches

Tactical Asset Allocation   Tactical asset allocation (TAA) strategies can be used on a stand-alone basis or as a complement to long-term strategic asset allocation (SAA). As discussed, the overwhelming evidence is that the strategic allocation is the most important investment decision, but, a tactical asset allocation strategy can work as an active strategy to take advantage of the shorter-term opportunities in global capital markets.

TAA strategies generally focus on the concept of *market segmentation,* in which investors in different markets react differently to information. Market segmentation leads to different asset classes (e.g., stocks, bonds, and cash) being priced on differing assumptions. TAA strategies look for relative mispricing across the asset classes and can be combined with the strategic allocation to tilt the overall portfolio toward/away from one or several asset classes.

The TAA process involves determining expected return and risk for each asset class. The expected return for equities can be derived by a dividend discount model. Most sophisticated TAA managers use multiple inputs in deriving the expected return. The expected return of bonds is generally based on the prevailing yields on long-term Treasury bonds, whereas the cash return is simply the cash yield.

Predicting risk (or volatility) can be equally complicated. Generally, managers look at past data (priced movements in equity and bond prices) and infuse expectations based on their insights into the individual asset classes and real-time market conditions. They use mean-variance optimizers to determine allocation among stocks, bonds, and cash. Mean-variance optimizers optimize expected return for a given risk tolerance.

CAPTURING MEAN REVERSION IN EMERGING MARKETS
Steven A. Schoenfeld, Robert Ginis, and Niklas Nordenfelt

A key component of fixed-weight strategies (be they equal weighted, liquidity tiered, or structured tiered) is that they need to be periodically rebalanced back to strategy weights. This adds expense, but it also provides an opportunity to capture mean reversion across the markets. Uncorrelated (but similar), highly volatile assets offer optimal opportunities to capture mean reversion. If the long-run expected returns are similar, a strategy (absent transaction costs) that exploits the cross-sectional volatility around the mean (in this case, the average return of the markets) will outperform a capitalization-weighted strategy and can also dampen portfolio volatility. This technique has relevance for the variety of alternatively-weighted country strategies discussed, such as equal-weighted, liquidity-tiered or structured-tiered.

Contrary to popular perception, emerging markets are not highly correlated, particularly across diverse regions. While the market crisis, commonly known as the "Asian Contagion" of 1997/1998, popularized the theory that emerging markets behave as a single risk category, the dispersion in returns across the emerging markets is, in fact, significantly greater than that of the developed markets. Even during the 1997/1998 period, Greece (an emerging market country at that time) was the top-performing market in the world, though most investors focused on the greater than 80 percent losses in the Southeast Asian markets. The five-year pairwise correlation among emerging markets countries is 0.31 versus 0.47 for the developed market countries.[*]

While globalization, through synchronized monetary policies and growing trade links, may have increased the prevalence of global (instead of regional or national) business cycles, other factors are likely to push correlations back down and closer to historical levels. In the developed markets, the comparative advantages of some countries (e.g., United Kingdom's media and banking sectors, Germany's auto industries, Switzerland's pharmaceuticals, Finland's and Sweden's technology and paper products companies) and exclusively local

---

[*] Five-year observation (January 1999 through December 2003). *Source:* Global Index Strategies LLC, calculated with MSCI "Free" (investable) country index returns.

(Continued)

events (e.g., a political or banking crisis) will ensure the persistence of different cycles and divergent market performance. This is even more true in the emerging markets where these differences are much more prevalent. There are substantially fewer trade links across the markets, far greater omparative advantages (e.g., technology in Korea and Taiwan; natural resources in Russia and Venezuela) and truly idiosyncratic shocks and crises (e.g., the political crises in Turkey and the currency crisis in Argentina).

The annualized volatility among the individual developed market countries is typically around 20 percent, with a range from 25 percent to about 15 percent. The volatility among the emerging market countries is much greater with an average of about 40 percent. (The MSCI Emerging Markets Index or S&P/IFC Emerging Market Indexes are considerably less volatile because they benefit from the low correlations across markets.)

Market Structure Provides Opportunities for Adding Alpha

Here are a few examples to highlight the opportunities for capturing mean reversion in these volatile and weakly correlated markets:

- After reaching its high in December 1994, Korea fell 86 percent through December 1997. In fact, Korea fell 67 percent in 1997 alone. In 1998 and 1999, the market rebounded by 141 percent and 92 percent, respectively.
- From August 1996 to August 1998, Thailand fell a whopping 90 percent. The market rallied 185 percent over the following 10 months.
- The Russian market fell 92 percent in a 1-year period from September 1997 to September 1998. The market then rebounded 363 percent over the next 18 months and 702 percent from the low to June 2002.
- From November 1998 to January 1999, the Brazilian market fell 42 percent and subsequently rallied by 126 percent over the next 11 months.
- Mexico fell 68 percent over a 4-month period in 1994/1995 and then came back with a 203 percent return over the next 30 months.
- From its high in early 2000, Argentina fell 84 percent by the end of June 2002. This was followed by a phenomenal recovery in the final quarter of 2002 and the first three quarters of 2003. For this latter period, it was the world's best-performing stock market, with a gain of over 80 percent.

> This volatility leads to opportunities that require highly disciplined tactical decisions. Fixed-weight strategies buy into markets that have fallen relative to other markets, and they sell those markets that have risen. Ultimately, capturing mean reversion requires making contrarian trading decisions that run against the prevailing market sentiment and counter to the majority of managers. As discussed in Chapter 30, it greatly facilitates implementing a contrarian trade if portfolio managers have a rigorous set of rules to guide the rebalancing—and to help fight the tendency to go along with the crowd. And the most efficient and transparent approach to capture the mean reversion dynamic is with index-based products.

Since TAA strategies make large swing bets on top of the strategic allocation, and these are based on the macro capital markets' pricing environment, it is critical to make the bets with no slippage relative to the asset classes and their assumptions for risk and return. Index funds assure that the TAA bets are implemented without error from active stock or bond selection. Active security selection could have the impact of negating the value added from the TAA process, which carefully assesses the relative value between the asset classes. The TAA strategy takes advantage of that relative value, or mispricing across asset classes, and therefore requires vehicles that more or less perfectly represent the asset classes being measured.

Furthermore, since TAA strategies are active by nature and require frequent trading to respond to changing market environments, they need cheap trading vehicles. Institutional index funds, futures contracts, and index-based ETFs provide the liquidity and ease to accommodate the trading activity. Many institutional TAA strategies can be adapted to individual investor strategies using ETFs. Synthetic TAA strategies, such as an overlay using futures contracts, also use equity index futures and interest rate futures as implementation vehicles. One can also say that the availability of index products has helped facilitate the growth of these strategies.

Strategic Asset Allocation (with Systematic Rebalancing) Implementing a strategic investment policy with index products is another key application of active indexing. Many institutional investors get their core asset class exposure through low cost index strategies. The approaches of the Government of Singapore Investment Corporation (GSIC) and Illinois State University Retirement System (IllSURS) highlighted in this chapter, and the three institutions highlighted in Chapter 26 provide robust examples of this technique in practice. The same techniques are available to retail investors, usually through financial advisors. These approaches go by a variety of names and brands, depending on provider and client. We call them *Multiasset Class Strategies,* but they are sometimes known as *Multiple Style Portfolios* (discussed in Chapter 24). As with the above-mentioned TAA strategies, the most efficient implementation is via index products, as discussed in Chapter 30.

"Life-Cycle" Strategies—Evolving Portfolios for Changing Objectives and Time Horizons   Investors have different risk tolerances in different stages of their lives. They can afford more risk and therefore should be more aggressive investors in the earlier part of their lives, and more conservative in later years. There are time-targeted strategies that can automatically fulfill this stage-of-life evolution of investment goals, and at least a half-dozen firms offer packaged "Life Cycle" strategies.[14]

These stage-of-life products are time-decaying strategies designed for investors' complete lifetimes, with different degrees of risk aversion at distinct stages of their working life. The most efficient way to implement these strategies is to use index funds because it is more important to get the allocation correct than stock selection. The use of index products as components assures that investors do not incur active management risk. The overall design of the strategy—a slowly evolving strategic allocation that is optimized for the changing risk profile of an investor's age—already incorporates the appropriate risk level. Therefore, the use of active funds for specific asset class exposure would simply add additional risk, namely active management risk, which tends to detract from value.

For example, in a study of mutual fund returns conducted in 2001 found that that the standard deviation of equity mutual fund returns around the year's mean return was 21.1 percent during 1999. The difference between the stock and bond asset-class returns was 22.8 percent.[15] The use of actively managed funds to proxy the asset classes within the defined strategic allocation could create such large deviations from the expected asset class return that it might compromise the work put into defining the strategic allocation.

Choosing several actively managed funds essentially creates an expensive index fund. The actively managed funds may end up creating indexlike portfolios (when aggregated) at the expense of active management—higher fees, higher turnover, and transaction costs.[16]

Therefore, whether investors buy a packaged time-targeted strategy or build such a strategy by themselves, it is substantially cheaper to trade index slices than individual securities. Furthermore, the transparency of index products makes it easier to focus on the key active decisions. Chapter 30 provides some ideas for do-it-yourself investors in establishing their strategic allocation, and provides several alternative sources for "starting point" allocations.

CONCLUSION

Investing in index funds is simply the most efficient starting point—or default option—to gain exposure to either broad asset classes or narrower slices of markets or regions. The ability to actively manage "portfolios of indexes" (i.e., portfolios of index products such as funds, ETFs, or even index derivatives) is thus the most effective way to actively seek the optimal return profile relative to risk, whether the objective is pure alpha seeking or attenuating risk.

As discussed in Part One, and again in Part Five, choosing which index to invest in and deciding the allocation to each asset class benchmark are by far the most important investment decisions. And, as this and previous chapters have explained, these decisions require just as much IQ—investment quotient—and skill as that of traditional active management (or of choosing active managers). The only difference is that the outcome has a greater chance for long-term investment success when index products are used as a foundation for a portfolio.

Both "within benchmark" and "across benchmark," index portfolio management can be infinitely customized and decidedly active. The most sophisticated investors and asset managers use one or more of these techniques. As discussed in Chapters 30 and 31, the growth of ETFs and index derivatives will further extend and accelerate these approaches and applications and will make the benefits of *active indexing* increasingly accessible for individual investors. Part Five will describe the path to such success.

NOTES

1. In the context of this chapter, the term *active* is best understood as "nonpassive," that is, not static within the investment strategy, whether capitalization-weighted, or nonstatic. This contrasts with other usage of the term, particularly in Part Four, where the index portfolio management process is described in detail, and decidedly proven to be anything but passive.
2. See Gary P. Brinson, Gilbert Beebower, and L. Randolph Hood, "Determinants of Portfolio Performance," *Financial Analysts Journal* (July/August 1986); and Roger G. Ibbotson and Paul D. Kaplan, "Does Asset Allocation Policy Explain 40, 90, or 100 Percent of Performance?" *Financial Analysts Journal,* vol. 56 (January/February 2000), and the discussion on this topic in Chapters 1, 2, 3, 26, 28, and 30.
3. This latter point—particularly as it applies to individual investors—is explored further in Chapter 30.
4. Separate account programs can be implemented with active or index managers. However, index-based separate account strategies are ideally suited for completion portfolios, as the tracking variance is more easily measured and managed.

5. In reality, such a strategy is complicated to set up and generally requires the assistance of professional investment managers. In addition, the pricing of the futures contract may not exactly match that of the underlying index at any given time resulting in slightly different performance results from the index itself.

6. The S&P 500 represents most (about 70 percent) of the U.S. equity market. Therefore, the sensitivity (beta) of the price movement in the U.S. market to the price movement of the S&P 500 is close to 1, meaning that for each 1 percent increase (decrease) in the U.S. market, the S&P 500 responds with a corresponding 1 percent increase (decrease).

7. IndexUniverse.com and the book's E-ppendix includes a feature on how investors and traders can use ETFs to implement tactical market signals (with the first piece originally published as "The Active Index Strategist" on IndexUniverse.com in January 2004).

8. Dale H. Stevens, Ronald J. Surz, and Mark E. Wimer, "The Importance of Investment Policy," *Journal of Investing*, vol. 8, no. 4 (Winter 1999): 80–85.

9. GSIC does not manage Singapore's foreign reserve assets—this is done by the Monetary Authority of Singapore.

10. The structured-tiered approach to international equities described in this chapter was originally developed by the authors and their colleagues at Barclays Global Investors during the mid- to late-1990s. The approach was initially applied to emerging markets, as discussed. Using a different methodology, it was subsequently extended to developed international markets. The authors have since left Barclays, and thus this strategy description reflects the portfolio construction work conducted at the time, with some updated concepts that are independent of any current Barclays emerging market strategy. A further evolution of this approach—with updated factors and country scores—was provided in the excerpt of this chapter that was published in the July/August 2004 (2nd Quarter) issue of *The Journal of Indexes*.

11. The logic behind focusing our investment insights on the country factors in emerging markets was discussed in Steven A. Schoenfeld, "Emerging Markets— Which Strategy Works Best," *Canadian Investment Review*, vol. 13, no. 2 (Summer 2000): 39–40.

12. By design and by definition, this factor is dynamic, and it must be continually reevaluated (as do all the other factors). This dynamic market/portfolio evaluation process further underscores the *active indexing* nature of this strategy.

13. As of mid-2003, the major index-based institutionally oriented firms have well over $5 billion in such strategies, primarily in emerging markets.

14. The authors worked extensively with BGI's product offering of this type— "LifePath," which targets a specific retirement year such as 2030 and evolves the asset mix of the strategy over time.

15. Barton Waring, Lee Harbert, and Larry Siegel, "It's 11 P.M.—Do You Know Where Your Employees' Assets Are?" *BGI Investment Insights* (October 2001).

16. These realities have not prevented mutual fund companies from offering actively managed age-targeted funds, but it is hard to imagine that the higher costs and risks of active management will pay off in these structures.

Four

Managing Index Funds
It's Anything but Passive!

Steven A. Schoenfeld

This section of the book provides a unique insider's perspective into the art and science of managing index funds, much of it never-before detailed in print. Written by seasoned index fund managers—all of whom I am pleased to have called colleagues at some time in the past 10 years—these chapters describe the fundamental concepts and techniques of equity and fixed income index managers in minimizing costs, controlling risk, generating "index alpha" (not always an oxymoron!), and minimizing tracking error. The section also provides insight into the complex and unique challenges of managing the multiple dimensions of risks in less-efficient parts of the U.S. stock market, within fixed-income portfolios, in international equities, and in emerging markets.

Some of the themes in Part Four are at the heart of why I embarked on the book project back in 2001. For example, in numerous meetings with experienced financial professionals I would be asked during a discussion about management fees, "How hard is it to manage an index fund—don't you just buy all the stocks in the index and hold them?" I would then describe a few few complex index changes and this would occasionally achieve some understanding of the skills required to manage index strategies. After reading the six chapters in Part Four, I believe that readers will have a much greater appreciation of both the art and science of index portfolio management.

In the first chapter of this section, Kevin Maeda and I provide an overview of how index portfolio management is anything but passive, and detail the fundamental index portfolio management techniques that are used by most index fund managers. Portions of this chapter are adapted from lectures that I delivered at Duke University's Fuqua School of Business and University of California at Berkeley's Haas School of Business between 2002 and 2004. The chapter also provides some key definitions and explanations of terms used throughout this part of the book. A sidebar by James Creighton, chief investment officer of Northern Trust Global Investments, is a provocative examination of the challenges of trading index changes.

How difficult can it be to manage assets in the world's most efficient and liquid market? As noted previously, many are tempted to think that it is a comparatively easy task. Truth is, the depth and breadth of the U.S. market brings a multitude of complexities and challenges. In Chapter 20, "The Unique Challenges of U.S. Equity Index Management," current and former members of BGI's U.S. equity index portfolio management team take us through how they handle the complexities they face, such as corporate actions, stringent tracking error tolerances, multiple choices of indexes, their trading strategies in a highly efficient market, and their use of derivatives in the management process.

Delivering performance in international indexing requires many of the same skills as in U.S. equities, but often requires a unique focus on a myriad of different factors. In Chapter 21, some of my former international equity index portfolio management colleagues and I detail the key challenges to deliver performance in both developed and emerging equity markets. The complexities of multiple time zones, market conventions, and regulatory factors are described, as well as detailed examples of trading strategies and cross-border corporate actions. The sidebar, "ADRs and ADR Indexes: Great Taste, Less Filling," by Kevin Maeda and myself, focuses on an alternative to the complexities of local securities in foreign markets.

In "Managing Fixed-Income Index Funds," Elizabeth Para and Partha-Dasgupta explain how fixed income indexing differs substantially from equity indexing. Chapter 22 details several nonderivative and derivative based methods of creating an index tracking fixed income portfolio and why these methods have won over active investors. They then evaluate each of these methods and examine their advantages and disadvantages, and market circumstances under which each method is practicable. A short discussion of bond ETFs is also included.

In Chapter 23, two ETF portfolio managers at BGI in San Francisco, Lisa Chen and Patrick O'Connor, provide insight on what it takes to manage an ETF portfolio, and how it is different from managing traditional index funds. Having worked closely with both authors—in the trenches of

ETF launches and index rebalancings, as well as on the development of this chapter—I can assure readers that they will get a unique and valuable insider perspective of what it takes to manage ETFs. This detailed chapter addresses virtually every possible question you may have about the intricacies of managing ETFs from portfolio management strategies that focus on cost control to regulatory guidelines, tax harvesting strategies, and turning a portfolio of stocks into a share of ETF. The information in the chapter links closely with the overview of ETFs provided in Chapter 16.

Chapter 24 explores one of the newest, but potentially most value-creating areas of indexing—the management of index-based separate accounts for individual investors. The case for using these approaches, which are now offered by numerous firms offering a full range of benchmarks, is quite strong, and the logic is developed in the chapters by Mark Adams, Kevin Maeda, and the editor. We describe the key challenges of tracking benchmarks within the constraints of relatively small individual accounts, especially when customization is applied. The concept of "Tax Alpha" is also fully explained and explored, and readers will gain an appreciation of the power of index-based strategies to deliver better solutions to individual investors in high tax brackets.

Despite the length of these chapters—and the scope of Part Four of the book—the coverage is far from comprehensive, and it has a heavy U.S.-based perspective. For example, I would have liked to have an entire chapter on various trading approaches, especially agency and principal portfolio trading. A chapter on managing domestic Japanese or European equities would have added to the coverage as well. More references to the importance of the risk management and compliance functions would have also been relevant. Similarly, the important area of *securities lending,* which often provides significant value-added for both asset owners and index fund managers, is also only briefly discussed in Chapters 19, 21, and 26 within Part Five. Finally, the dynamic field of *transition management,* within which index managers often play an integral role, is not included. Many of these topics are also discussed in the book's E-ppendix at www.ActiveIndexInvesting.com.

My purpose in raising these examples is not to denigrate the chapters that follow, but to stress that even their level of detail merely opens the door for readers to understand the depth and breadth of the index portfolio management field. And this brings me full circle, back to the primary motivation for engaging in this immense book project; to demonstrate that indexing is a very active endeavor. As you start digging into the chapters, I am confident that you will agree with this view.

CHAPTER 19

Fundamental Index Portfolio Management Techniques

Steven A. Schoenfeld and Kevin Maeda

_____ Editor's Note _____

This chapter explains how index portfolio management is "anything but passive" and details the fundamental index portfolio management techniques that most index fund managers use. It sets the stage for subsequent chapters in Part Four that explore index portfolio management in an unprecedented level of detail. Portions of this chapter are adapted from lectures that I have delivered at Duke University's Fuqua School of Business and the Haas School of Business at the University of California–Berkeley. Readers should gain a foundation in the techniques of indexing as well as an appreciation of the art and science of managing index-based portfolios. We also provide key definitions and explanations of index portfolio management terms used throughout Part Four (which are supplemented by the book's Glossary, with an unabridged version available at www.ActiveIndexInvesting.com). Partly due to the background of the authors, much of the focus of this chapter is on equity index portfolio management, even though some of the principles are relevant to fixed-income indexing, which is covered in detail in Chapter 22.

As noted in the introduction to Part Four, this chapter also includes a provocative sidebar by James Creighton of Northern Trust Global Investments on the challenges of trading index changes. He addresses some of the same issues as Larry Siegel's sidebar in Chapter 5, but from the perspective of

The authors gratefully acknowledge the substantial contribution to an earlier draft by Jonathan Cohen, who was a strategist at Northern Trust Global Investments at the time. John Spence also assisted in the development of this chapter, particularly some of the more complex graphics.

an index fund manager. I should note that his view is far from a consensus position in the index industry—and I count myself among those who don't fully subscribe to his views. In my opinion, the "wealth erosion" discussed in the sidebar is primarily a factor in the major flagship indexes such as the S&P 500 and the Russell 2000, which have a huge and visible asset base tracking them. Broader-based indexes and less-followed benchmarks tend not to experience this phenomenon. But this point of view and the general debate over the index effect, covered in Part Two, only further demonstrate that indexing is a vibrant, dynamic field.

Several years ago, a prominent business newspaper related a conversation in which an investor told a Vanguard index fund manager, "A monkey could run an index fund."[1] Similarly, many sophisticated industry veterans view index funds as a commodity-like product that should be differentiated only by how low they can negotiate the management fees. Something in our industry went desperately wrong. Somehow, the investment community created the myth that index-based investing is driven by computers, that anyone can manage an index fund, that nothing changes in indexing investing, and that indexing is a commodity business. These mammoth misconceptions caused us to contemplate the scope of investment talent required for proper management of index portfolios, as well as the intellectual and financial resources that must be dedicated to preserving and creating wealth for our clients. This chapter debunks the fallacies and hopefully replaces them with a deep understanding and appreciation for the multiple layers of sophisticated and quite active investment activity performed by index portfolio managers. It also underscores the tangible value that professional portfolio management delivers for investors in index products.

As discussed in Chapter 14, index management has as its primary objective the performance tracking of an underlying index, such as the S&P 500 or MSCI EAFE. However, benchmark indexes are ultimately calculated without the frictional costs of transacting in the capital markets. The steps and factors that index managers must focus on to achieve their goal are index knowledge, portfolio construction, ongoing management, and trading. Index portfolio managers are also at the center of a broader operational process that requires constant diligence and involvement in trading, settlement, client flows, and holding databases. In addition, the portfolio management function involves substantial interface with other functions within and beyond the asset management firm. Figure 19.1 portrays these big-picture responsibilities, dividing the functions into four broad quadrants, although many functions are interrelated (and as readers will see in Figure 19.2, quite dynamic).

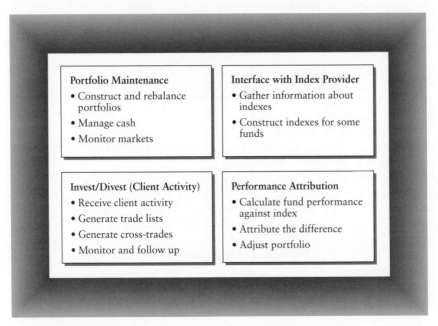

FIGURE 19.1 Index Portfolio Management: The Big Picture Responsibilities
Source: Global Index Strategies LLC.

A successful index manager will produce a portfolio whose performance replicates that of the index, within a few basis points, while minimizing the deadweight costs that produce negative tracking error. Within the index management process, portfolio managers have to make myriad decisions every day, including what to trade, when to trade, and how to trade in achieving their clients' goals.

An index manager may choose to accommodate cash flow by trading stock index futures, by using exchange-traded funds (ETFs), or by trading a basket of the underlying securities. To maintain performance close to the index, however, an index manager must make the precise allocation to each of these investment vehicles and be correct virtually 100 percent of the time. We think you will see that index management is *anything but passive*.

SEEMINGLY SIMPLE, BUT COMPLEX IN REALITY

On the surface, the objective of index management seems straightforward and uncomplicated: Replicate the performance of an index. An index is a

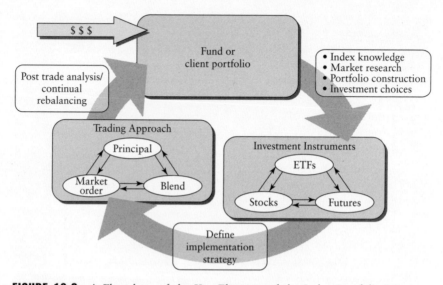

FIGURE 19.2 A Flowchart of the Key Elements of the Index Portfolio Management Process
Source: Global Index Strategies LLC.

theoretical construct that attempts to represent a particular asset class (e.g., large-cap U.S. stocks, global developed markets, the European credit market). In principle, to effectively create and manage an index portfolio, the manager only needs to buy all the securities in the relevant benchmark at their correct weightings and hold them until the benchmark changes. Sounds simple enough.

However, closer inspection of the index portfolio management process yields a very different reality. At minimum, replicating the performance of a benchmark is challenging because index providers do not factor in transaction costs in their return calculation methodologies. For many asset classes, transaction costs can be significant. The question, then, is how do index managers overcome the friction of transaction costs while still tracking the index closely?

The answer lies in the sophistication of the management process. It has multiple objectives: tracking the index; minimizing transaction costs; and potentially looking to enhance value through thoughtful implementation techniques or by bundling ancillary services, such as securities lending.

Tracking the index is the simplest of these objectives, when assessed in a vacuum. Sophisticated portfolio management and risk control tools allow us to determine the precise amount of each security to buy or sell, whether the index has 200 or 6,000 securities. However, we would never dare to actually take the results of this portfolio management output and implement it blindly. Indexing is part art, part science; the trade list is just a starting point—the output of raw science and technology.

The art involves determining how and what part of the trade list should actually be executed to achieve the objectives. The answer to this question comes from careful, real-time analysis of the relevant market along such dimensions as liquidity (or lack thereof), market impact, and risk exposures. When factoring in these hurdles, we formulate an execution strategy that maximizes the expected return to our clients by minimizing the impact of transaction costs and risk. As we develop strategies to avoid implementation costs, it is possible to steer execution around the distortions caused by *non-index* investors intent on beating the index at its own game.

How? By way of example, non-indexers, such as active managers, hedge funds, and the proprietary desks of brokerage firms (let's group them together for our analysis and call them "speculative investors"), may look to trade ahead of anticipated index investor flows. Index providers, of course, make public changes to their indexes (most commonly, we think of the periodic additions and deletions to the S&P 500 or the annual reconstitution to the Russell benchmarks). Speculative investors, with the benefit of this free potentially market-moving information provided by the index providers, assess the impact that they believe index managers will cause and trade in such a way as to exploit that information. This supply/demand situation was first introduced in Chapter 5. A typical case would be when a hedge fund or proprietary desk buys a large block of stock before it is added to the S&P 500 index, knowing that index managers' flows at the effective date of the index change will allow them to unwind their positions. But index managers are familiar with these strategies, can anticipate the actions of speculators, and beat them at their own game in a highly risk-efficient manner.

The preceding example demonstrates that the index portfolio management process requires active, thoughtful development of implementation strategies, based on a continually changing mix of market participants and market environments. But it also oversimplifies what we do as portfolio managers, because the process sounds iterative. In fact, it is dynamic: All the actions are being analyzed and undertaken simultaneously. The results can make the difference between lagging the benchmark, precisely matching it, or in some cases actually outperforming it by a few basis points. Should investors care if the difference between the most rote index management process and the most creative can be expressed in hundredths of a percentage point? Of course they should.

Figure 19.2 portrays a stylized view—a kind of flowchart—of the index investment process. The cycle of index portfolio management in fact, never ends; it demands constant activity and daily interface with the markets, clients, and operations.

Another major issue for consideration is the investment process being used. As previously mentioned, index management is part art, part science. The science comes from the tools, such as portfolio management systems, risk optimizers, trade list generators, and trade order routing tools. These tools not only vary substantially from firm to firm, but also can be changed, substituted, or rebuilt regularly within the firm. In fact, continued innovation and business success in the industry require constant evolution, and most firms have system developers permanently attached to the portfolio management groups. The art comes from the unique ways that each portfolio manager and portfolio management team will use these tools to achieve their objectives, blending it with deep market and benchmark knowledge and an understanding of client objectives.

There are also diverse portfolio management techniques, and most index portfolio managers have capability in more than one approach. These four techniques are described in the following sections.

FULL INDEX REPLICATION

The goal of *full replication* is to minimize the differences between the portfolio and the index by holding all the stocks in the portfolio at their index weights. Full replication is a literal approach to indexing and is why indexing is often considered simple (a monkey could manage a portfolio using this approach).

Although in theory full replication appears relatively simple, there are numerous challenges in practice. First, not all funds/portfolios are large enough to fully replicate an index. Large institutional indexers generally try to create perfect slices of their flagship index funds, but smaller index portfolios may be unable to manage their portfolios using this approach and may opt for one of the methods described later in this chapter. Second, broad flagship indexes around the world generally have several hundred, and often several thousand, stocks (e.g., the Russell 3000, MSCI Kokusai & EAFE, FTSE All-World, or S&P/Citigroup Broad Market Index). Trading, maintaining data, and following corporate actions and index changes require intense dedication of resources and scale. Finally, full replication is an anachronism in the index business: The hidden costs of indexing often require us to use hybrid strategies that achieve the same tight risk constraints as full replication, but without mechanistically trading every single stock misweighted relative to its index weight. Chapters 20 and 21, immediately following this chapter, provide examples of full replication in U.S. large-cap and international equities.

Determining the acceptable trade-off between trading every miniscule misweight for an unknown improvement in tracking versus the relatively quantifiable trading costs requires exceptional judgment. But even if you work out all that, you may think full replication is a slam-dunk as long as you have a sufficiently large portfolio. But one shouldn't be so easily fooled. This assumes a key, but false, belief—that indexes are truly replicable. They decidedly are not.

Indexes assume—or at least are calculated with—zero trading costs. But trading a portfolio costs money, not just in execution, but in operating costs to produce trade lists, execute them, settle them, record and account for them, and so on. These operating costs are traditionally either charged to the accounts or billed as fees.

Beyond fees, other less obvious factors also are not fully replicable. Most indexes make their changes effective after the close on a particular day. What this means is that they add, delete, or adjust shares using the closing prices, but with no market impact. But large institutional investors may be trading two, three, or even one hundred times (as in emerging markets) average trading volume. There simply is not enough market liquidity to support such large trades, thus necessitating other trading strategies and hence tracking error.

Another feature of indexes that make them not fully replicable is in the timing and treatment of corporate actions of index constituents. Investors may get non-index securities as part of a corporate action. In such cases, the indexes assume that the investor receives the cash value by using either an intrinsic price or the price of the security on the first day it trades. In the case of non-U.S. securities, however, it may take days or even weeks before settlement of the new security allows the stock to be sold. Additionally, intrinsic prices (a security's theoretical value if the parts equal the whole) often are not equal to actual value once the securities trade.

The reinvestment of dividends is another complex—and historically contentious—issue. For example, because the payment dates for international dividends have different lag times, MSCI used a method known as *dividend smoothing* to calculate its total returns for over 30 years. Instead of using actual dividends to calculate total returns on a monthly basis, MSCI used one-twelfth of the past year's dividend yield. This created three nonreplicable problems. First, their dividend yield lagged the actual yield, but even if it didn't, there would still be a difference because dividends do not flow one-twelfth per month in actuality. Second, MSCI assumed there was no cash drag, but from an accounting point of view, there is a cash drag effect between the time the dividends go "ex" and the time they are invested. Third, MSCI applies Luxembourg tax rates to the dividends, which will be different for every investor in any other country. While this last issue remains (and is now relatively well understood), the other two issues have been resolved, as MSCI shifted to including dividends at or near "ex-date" in the 2001–2002 timeframe.

As should now be evident, full index replication is not as trivial as it seems. For the reasons described earlier, index managers may choose other strategies, depending on the circumstances, or blend several strategies.

STRATIFIED SAMPLING (LINEAR OPTIMIZATION)

Stratified sampling breaks an index into its factor components using a matrix. The matrix in two dimensions might include capitalization along the Y-axis and industry along the X-axis. This approach has the advantage of simplicity. Stocks are selected from each stratum so that the portfolio has the same proportion in each "bucket" as the underlying index.

Sampling is simple to understand, yet complicated to construct. As with full replication, it isn't a trivial task. One sampling technique may be to select a cross-section of securities from an index based on industry sector and market capitalization. Table 19.1 shows the pattern of a filling in a two-dimensional sampling matrix. Sounds and looks simple enough, right?

So what makes sampling complicated then? Well, as soon as you begin constructing a sampling method, you will find that you have more questions than answers. First, how do you determine what the sectors should be? You could use those defined by the GICS (Global Industry Classification Standard) codes. But you still need to decide whether to use the sector, industry group, industry, or subindustry codes. Next, how do you decide how many groupings to use for the market capitalizations and what the breakpoints will be? Will you use fixed levels, floating levels, or have bounds? Or perhaps break them down by the number of stocks instead? What portfolio

TABLE 19.1 Stratified Sampling Process (Partial, Stylized View)

	Industry Group			
	A	B	I	J
Capitalization decile 1	1A	1B	1I	1J
Capitalization decile 2	2A	2B	2I	2J
Capitalization decile 9	9A	9B	9I	9J
Capitalization decile 10	10A	10B	10I	10J

Note: Stylized table, reflecting use of S&P/MSCI Global Industry Classification's (GIC) ten industry groupings.

size should you choose? How should you allocate your stocks to each sector and market cap?

Let's say the portfolio manager works out all these issues. Other issues remain. How do you decide which stocks to choose in each stratum? Do you start by selecting the largest, smallest, median, every second or third stock, or make a random selection? What about the second stock in the stratum? Or the third? And once you select the desired stocks, how should you weight each of them? If you cap-weight them, the large stocks will dominate the small ones, making the latter insignificant in the portfolio and creating a large-cap bias. If you equal-weight them, their weights will fall out of line with your target very quickly. Again, another investment question without an easy answer.

Assuming you haven't given up yet on creating a sampling methodology, there are still more challenges—managing such a portfolio on an ongoing basis. What happens if the securities that were your original choices fall out of line and are no longer a true cross-sectional representation? Because you are not fully replicating, the stocks you are holding may slip into different strata. Corporate actions and index changes will also push your target portfolio out of line. Aligning objective guidelines to manage robust portfolios is a fine art. Managers must track an index with subjective judgment about the best ways to execute such goals.

Here's an example of a sampling technique for the S&P 500 that will help answer some of the previous questions. Using the ten GICS sector codes, we choose a portfolio size of 50 stocks and allocate them based on the prorated ratio of sector stocks in the index. We divide each sector in quartiles so there are 40 strata.

Now we begin selecting stocks in each sector, based on their allocation. The first stock chosen is the largest in the first quartile. If a second stock is chosen, we select the median in the second quartile. If there are still more to be chosen, we choose the median in the third and fourth quartiles. If a more stocks are required, we'll start with the next closest to the median in the fourth quartile, then third, and second. Then we'll choose the next largest stock in the first quartile. This process continues across all sectors.

Next, we cap-weight the stocks within each quartile. Finally, we calculate a portfolio weight based on the cap-weight of the stock within the quartile times the quartile weight (usually 25 percent, but more on this later) times the sector weight. But, what if there are only two or three stocks in a sector? Then you don't have representation in all quartiles. So perhaps you decide to weight them equally based on the number of quartiles filled. How do you determine which stocks should go into each quartile, especially since you will always have some falling on the breakpoints? Again, this produces more questions than answers once you dig deep enough.

This set of rules isn't necessarily the best for all situations, but it at least shows the complexity in developing a solid methodology before implementing a sampling strategy. Often, for stratified sampling to work optimally, index managers will add several factors to control risk. Thus, this involves moving beyond the two-dimensional matrix to a multidimensional matrix. Fixed-income indexers generally use three-dimensional matrices for their sampling techniques, and Chapter 22 portrays an example of this approach.

SAMPLED OPTIMIZATION (QUADRATIC OPTIMIZATION)

Another way to create an index-tracking portfolio without holding all the constituent stocks is through optimization. This approach uses computer models that measure the historical interrelationship of several risk factors to glean how the mix of these factors impacts security movements. Most of the pioneering work on optimizers was conducted in academia, with a disproportionate amount done at University of California–Berkeley. Optimizers quantify the covariances of one security to every other security in the index along these factor lines. Therefore, it can construct a portfolio that has the lowest expected tracking error—also known as *active risk*—given a set of parameters supplied by the portfolio manager. Optimizers are powerful and flexible tools in risk management and have many applications beyond index management, particularly in developing asset allocation strategies. Certain types of portfolios must be optimized, especially total market portfolios like the Wilshire 5000 (which has well over 5,000 names).[2]

Like stratified sampling, optimization attempts to minimize expected tracking error in a portfolio, given that all of the stocks in the index cannot be held in the portfolio. *A key difference between optimization and stratified sampling is that optimization relies on the extent to which historical security interrelationships (covariances) will remain predictive and static in the future.* The reality is that covariances change constantly, though sometimes in undetectable ways. However, an optimizer might not capture a shock to a covariance matrix, which could include either a change in the behavior of one stock or a more systematic effect such as a general near-term rise in market volatility. In fact, this problem was the cause of poor performance for many managers in the months leading up to and following the technology market apex of March 2000. Another factor to keep in mind with estimation errors in optimization is the inverse relationship between the magnitude of the expected mistracking and the severity of the understatement. For relatively large predicted tracking errors (PTE) (say the 2 to 3 percent range) this understatement is rarely a problem. However, for tight TE estimates (of the 0.10 to 0.30 percent range) the realized tracking error is frequently double the PTE.[3] In contrast, stratified sampling is more simplistic, but does not have a historical bias inherent in its approach.

BLENDED APPROACHES

The best index management processes are often a blend of the most desirable attributes of all these strategies. The premise of full replication—owning all the index securities in their correct weights—is the starting point onto which managers can overlay both optimization and sampling approaches. These cutting-edge strategies balance the seemingly mutually exclusive goals of minimizing risk while minimizing transaction costs. There are many possible blended combinations, but highlighting just two of them will provide adequate examples.

The first combines full replication and optimization. This is a popular approach for broad-capitalization *total market* indexes like the Wilshire 5000 or the Russell 3000. The large-cap component of the benchmark is fully replicated, either within a single fund, or in a stand-alone fund.[4] A second hybrid approach combines stratified sampling and quadratic optimization, which could be called *stratified optimization*. Stratified sampling is used for the core stocks in the portfolio with optimization for the noncore stocks.

It is important to understand the size and magnitude of the hurdles that index manager's face along the road to precise tracking. As discussed, index management would be simple indeed if all the manager had to do was buy a basket of securities and hold them indefinitely. Index portfolios change frequently as a function of changes by index providers (which are generally made to reflect changing realities in the markets), corporate actions, and primary market issuance.

The methodologies that index providers employ to maintain their indexes affect index managers significantly because they serve as a road map for when and how to make changes in investor portfolios. The growth of indexed assets has exacerbated the impact of both indexers and speculators, potentially resulting in short-term price distortions that can affect investor portfolios. These distortions are the hidden costs of indexing, not directly observable in an index investor's returns. They are opportunity costs driven by investors' increasing demand for precise performance replication. As index portfolio managers, we spend an increasing amount of our time and intellectual energy assessing the potential impact of different implementation strategies.

Furthermore, since this information is publicly available, speculators try to exploit it to their advantage. If we, as indexers, demanded to know exactly when large active managers or hedge funds were going to place their trades, we would be laughed at. But somehow, the idea that the world should know when indexers are going to trade (in some cases tens of billions of dollars) is acceptable. Something seems awry here! Luckily, many in the industry are developing solutions—both from the portfolio management side, and from the index provider side. Even the Securities and Exchange Commission has made public comments on the topic.[5]

MANAGING INDEX CHANGES

Index changes refer to the way index providers add and delete stocks from their indexes. This topic was discussed from a benchmark and market microstructure perspective in Chapter 5. For example, the S&P 500 is maintained by Standard & Poor's, which has a committee that meets privately to assess the extent to which the index represents the U.S. large capitalization market. Based on their subjective assessment, S&P will add and delete stocks throughout the year. In contrast the Russell indexes are rebalanced annually on June 30 as a function of objective criteria, yet are still subject to an annual "Russell Mania," as discussed in the sidebar of Chapter 5, as well as discussions in Chapters 21 and the sidebar in Chapter 23. Still other index providers (MSCI, Wilshire, Dow Jones) use different methodologies in maintaining and rebalancing their indexes.

Flagship indexes with highly visible reconstitutions (the ones that get a lot of focus, heat, and press) probably need to be traded differently. This is a frequent topic of discussion within the indexing community and as noted in the introduction to the chapter, generates a diversity of views. The following sidebar provides a provocative perspective from the head of a major index fund management group.

In addition to adding and deleting securities to/from an index, securities are updated to reflect changes in shares outstanding and float adjustments. Every index does this differently to avoid unnecessary turnover, which means that the shares outstanding may not match across index vendors or reflect the real world. This isn't necessarily a bad thing, but it may have unintended consequences.

For example, to align their ADR Index with their Global 1200 index, S&P temporarily decreased the shares outstanding on Alumina Limited on June 20, 2003, and increased them back to nearly their original level on June 30, 2003. While this was largely due to changes in reconstituting the Asia Pacific region in the Global 1200, it still demonstrates that the methodology that index vendors use for changes to shares outstanding and float factors may have undesirable real-world effects on index managers.[6]

If you were trying to track the index as closely as possible, you would sell down Alumina and buy a slice of the rest of the index. Ten days later, you

MANAGING THE TRUE COSTS OF INDEX STRATEGIES
James Creighton

The costs associated with indexing have traditionally been considered to be commissions, spreads, market impact, and fees associated with asset management and custody. As discussed in Part One, these low costs are a major part of the attraction of indexing. However, the expansion of indexing and the impact of this growth on the trading of index changes has resulted in another cost that is seldom discussed by plan sponsors and other investors. This is the *wealth erosion* effect for index investors that occurs around index changes in the major brand-name indexes. This wealth erosion is significant and dominates all other costs associated with flagship-benchmark index investing in the United States.

As noted in Part One, index investing had a slow takeoff. As long as indexing was a small part of the investment markets, it attracted little attention from other market participants. Trading related to index funds was for some time a negligible part of total securities trading in the capital markets.

Growth was further fueled by the increasing awareness that the majority of active managers did not beat the index in many parts of the market, and certainly not in the critical large-cap part of the market. Moreover, although active management costs were high, both in terms of fees and trading costs, the expenses associated with index funds were very low, particularly on the trading side.

The growing use of index funds ultimately led to changes in behavior of other market participants. It is not hard to see why this happened. It is estimated now that close to 15 percent of the total market capitalization of the S&P 500 is indexed. Moreover, approximately 25 percent of the U.S. equity assets of institutional investors are indexed. These numbers continue to grow in other developed markets as well, including Japan, the United Kingdom, Canada, Australia, and parts of Europe.

The Goal of Indexing and the Impact of Growth

The growth of indexing has altered the behavior of other investors in the market and this in turn has affected index investors.

In the early years of indexing, the goal was simple—match the index return. This was the goal because of the academic conclusions

(Continued)

mentioned earlier and because the majority of active managers could not beat the index. Index managers expended a great deal of energy creating approaches to duplicate index returns. The methodology of indexing may seem routine now, but that was not always the case. Sampling methods had to give way to full replication and sophisticated optimizers. Managers had to design techniques and the supporting infrastructure for trading baskets of securities, market on close orders, and so on. Having put forth considerable effort and money over many years to build the infrastructure to duplicate index returns at low cost, index managers were properly proud of this achievement. The development of new techniques then tended to slow down, if not stop.

In the meantime, other market participants were observing the growing volume of index trades around index changes. Moreover, as noted in the sidebar in Chapter 5, the trades were often predictable. If a stock was to be added to the index at 4 P.M. on Thursday, then market participants could count on a significant volume of buy or sell orders for the stock at the appointed time. Trading index changes has become a way for proprietary trading desks within the broker/dealers, hedge fund managers, and other nimble market participants to enrich themselves at the expense of index investors. The price movement that others induce by trading index changes has raised a new issue for index investors—wealth erosion.

The explicit costs of indexing represent just a small percentage of the total costs of indexing. Explicit costs are things like commissions, spreads, manager fees, and custodial costs. The largest economic cost of indexing, however, is now associated with the loss of wealth around index changes. The huge volume of trades that need to be executed around index changes today overwhelms natural liquidity in the market and induces a marked volume-driven impact on prices. As discussed in Chapter 5 and in this chapter, there is no lack of market participants trying to take advantage of this situation to earn money at the expense of index investors.

The Concept of Wealth Erosion

When an index change is announced, it becomes known to all market participants. In the terminology of Game Theory, it becomes *common knowledge* and anyone can use it to formulate profitable trading strategies.

In a game, a player who can depend on the predictable behavior of another can use that information to formulate winning strategies.

In the trading of index changes, other market participants have been able to rely on indexers to bring a large volume of trades to the market on the appointed date and at the appointed hour to execute at the add/delete price. Buying a stock to be added to the index in advance of the inclusion date and selling it to an indexer at the add date at a higher price is an obvious way to make money at the expense of index investors.

When indexing started over 30 years ago, the sums involved were small and index changes had little meaningful impact on market behavior. As indexing has grown and the sums to be traded around flagship index changes have increased, other market participants have been able to extract wealth from index investors' predictable behavior and the sheer volume of shares traded around those changes. To put this in a charitable light, there is a cost to providing liquidity at a point in time now required by the enormous sums that are indexed. In the case of index changes, the cost of immediate liquidity for huge volumes is high.

Quantifying Wealth Erosion

Calculating the dollar value of wealth erosion is a complex problem. To get an initial estimate, we assumed the wealth erosion was equal to the difference in price from the preannouncement price to the add price, adjusted for market movement. Other methodologies could be used. We then simply looked at the volume of shares purchased by indexers at the add price. This yields an estimate of $23.3 billion since 1990 to the end of 2002 for S&P 500 adds. This equates to approximately 15 basis points per annum without considering the cost of deletes and certain other costs, such as the impact of investors who try to accumulate positions in stocks likely to be added to the index prior to announcement.

Mitigating Wealth Erosion

One way to address the wealth erosion issue is to construct index methodologies that help to minimize the opportunity to game index changes. Chapters 5 and 6 address this topic. But, as discussed in this chapter, portfolio managers also have ways to mitigate the wealth erosion effect for flagship indexes.

First, do not make your trades entirely predictable to other market participants. To the extent that there is uncertainty about how

(Continued)

indexers will trade, other market participants will be less inclined to try to take advantage of the trade.

Second, index changes are an information-based game, and thus you need to "play the game." In such games, the player with better information should be able to devise winning strategies to use against other players. The key information that other market participants have is knowing that indexers must acquire a large amount of stock, which can be estimated, and knowing approximately when the stock will be acquired. On the other hand, only the indexers know exactly when and how they will trade. In this game, a certain amount of wealth loss to nonindexers is almost certain. However, the indexers have sufficient information to mitigate the erosion of wealth and to trade the index change at a better average price than the index add/delete price. Given the information available to the index and nonindex players, neither side should completely dominate the other. However, if all you strive for as an index investor is to get the add/delete price, then in essence you are allowing the other players in the game to dominate and to maximize wealth erosion.

For index fund managers to trade an index change in a way that mitigates wealth erosion, they must analyze the way an index change is likely to trade. Once this is understood—including the various risks associated with the trade—it is possible to devise a trading strategy to mitigate the loss of wealth in a risk-controlled way.

Finally, large investors in index strategies should have explicit discussions with their index manager about these issues. Managers who do not know what the investor expects usually will err on the side of reproducing exactly the index return. This is likely to result in high wealth erosion.

would sell off the slice you just bought and buy Alumina back. Although this would provide one with better tracking, you would also pick up unnecessary trading costs and capital gains.

In addition to known shares outstanding and adjustment factor changes, index vendors often make unannounced changes that show up in daily data loads, but not until after the change has taken place. Needless to say, this makes it extremely difficult to keep up with an index. Portfolio managers do not have the leisure of going back in time to trade.

8

CORPORATE ACTIONS

Corporate actions most commonly include rights offerings, cash/stock elections (i.e., voluntary dividend reinvestment plans), stock buyback offers, and tender offers. Again, each index vendor handles these differently. Some assume that you always take the cash offer, even if it is not in the best economic interest of the portfolio.

A portfolio manager must understand how the index reflects such corporate actions and consciously decide not only how to respond, but when. Additionally, the manager must determine when to react with a response that differs from the way the index is likely to reflect such actions.

For example, a portfolio manager may choose to receive stock for a cash/stock election because it is a better economic value, whereas the index may assume that all investors choose the cash option. Now the portfolio is overweighted in that security. Eventually, the security settles, and the portfolio manager may decide to sell the security to bring its weight in line in the index. At some point in the future, the index decides to update the shares outstanding to reflect the increase in shares as a result of those subscribing to stock rather than cash. Again, the portfolio manager must decide whether to give chase in this cat-and-mouse game. The situation with initial public offerings (IPOs) and privatizations can be similar. The addition of Yahoo! to the S&P 500, which is discussed in a sidebar within Chapter 5, provides a particularly dramatic example of the index change game.

TRADING TECHNIQUES AND TRADING COST MINIMIZATION

Index managers are faced with a constantly changing array of choices in the portfolio management process. The strategies to maintain our portfolios are a function of the type of trade and the investor's objective. Index changes are information-based trades since they involve many market participants who all have different objectives. These are trades where the implicit cost—including market impact and opportunity cost—eclipses the explicit (commission) cost. In contrast, cash flows are anonymous trades, without an information premium.[7] In either case, determining the best strategy for implementation requires a unique focus on the divergent goals of minimizing risk and cost. To be successful, index managers rely on trading strategies.

Index managers are on a never-ending quest to find the deepest sources of liquidity in the market for implementing their strategies. We seek liquidity from both typical and atypical sources, and we have at our disposal sophisticated trading platforms to accomplish this goal. We look for liquidity among three major sources: internal crossing, external crossing, and traditional market or agency trades with brokers that have strong execution capabilities. Each of these sources has different benefits and costs that need to be actively managed to be successful.

Internal crossing is a basic way to implement risk-controlled index trades. An internal cross aggregates all the trades at a particular index manager, in-house. An index manager can have multiple portfolios, all of which are trading in overlapping asset classes. Instead of paying a broker to implement these trades, an index manager can use an internal cross to match trades from all the trade lists in a pro rata fashion (i.e., so all clients enjoy the benefits of the cross equally). Cross-trading has a role in index management because it effectively reduces explicit cost. However, it does not address implicit cost and therefore must be used strategically in concert with other strategies.

External Crossing Networks (ECNs) and Alternative Trading Systems (ATSs) can help provide anonymous, inexpensive liquidity. There are many different platforms in this area, some of which generate their own cross based on the closing price on a particular exchange, and match off orders on a pro rata basis. Others, however, act as price discovery mechanisms in their own right, offering another liquidity source to actively implement trading strategies.

Finally, while internal and external crossing have received significant attention recently, the role of the broker has not diminished in importance. To the contrary, as implicit costs have grown exponentially relative to explicit costs (which have generally contracted in recent years), index managers have increasingly focused on developing active trading strategies. Active trading refers to our need to develop strategies that not only avoid commissions and market impact, but that also consider the impact of opportunity cost.

In a typical index change (e.g., an addition to the S&P 500 index), index managers, hedge funds, long-only active managers, and the proprietary desks of brokerage firms can significantly affect the underlying security. If index managers trade on the effective date of the index change—for example, through an internal cross—they may avoid explicit cost, but they may then bear potentially major opportunity cost since the closing price on the effective date is often the worst price at which to trade. Index managers have developed complex strategies that precisely blend the right mix of active trading with risk minimization to avoid the opportunity cost in such events. These often work extremely well, enabling managers to add slight value on the index change. But as the previous sidebar hints, this is not always the case, and there is some controversy about this approach.

THE VISIBLE AND HIDDEN IQ OF INDEX FUND MANAGERS

Portfolio managers possess several additional areas of deep "investment quotient" (IQ). These skills and experience are described in detail in the following five chapters, but to lay the groundwork, they are highlighted here in several broad categories. Readers will note that these areas of required "IQ" correspond with many of the functions portrayed in Figures 19.1 and 19.2.

Cash Flows in and out of the Portfolio

Whether because of client contributions/redemptions, or the need to reinvest dividends, index portfolio managers must continually buy and sell slices of their portfolio. This is a critical element of portfolio managers' jobs, and the firms that are skilled in this area can provide substantial value to their clients, using cash flows to smooth the implementation of minor portfolio rebalances.

Index/Benchmark and Market Structure Knowledge

Index portfolio managers (PMs) need to understand the methodology and maintenance of the benchmarks that they are tracking. Quite often, managers know the index better than the index providers themselves. Many PMs have taught index providers how to handle complex corporate actions, especially in cross-border mergers. This actually makes sense: Portfolio managers interact with local and global brokers and custodians on a daily basis, and therefore tend to know the underlying market and individual securities better.

This market microstructure knowledge of portfolio management teams is leveraged by the resources of many global firms that have offices in the regions for global investment. The subsequent chapters in Part Four discuss this knowledge base as well as the extra challenges of managing ETFs, with robust examples from U.S. and international equity and bond markets.

Risk Management

While almost all investment firms have dedicated risk management and compliance groups, very often index portfolio managers are on the "front lines" of managing the myriad risks associated with the investment process. The subsequent chapters in Part Four cover many of these risks, with real-world examples for a variety of asset classes. Risk management generally focuses on two broad areas—*operational risk* and *investment risk*. While portfolio

managers will be constantly managing the investment risk, they cannot ignore operational risk, especially when performance is measured in fractions
of basis points. When dealing with the overall operational environment of
cross-border investing (described in detail in Chapter 21), systems risk, or
the operational elements of trading and settlement, the challenges are considerable, and portfolio managers must be attuned and alert to risk management in all of their activities.[8] Furthermore, in addition to "traditional"
parameters of investment risk, index portfolio managers must also often
contend with complex portfolio transition issues as well as index vendor
data risks. Many of these additional investment risks are described in the following chapters.

Gaining Incremental Returns from Securities Lending

Securities lending is an important source of income for institutional index
funds and can contribute to steady *index alpha* for portfolios. A team within
an asset management firm usually handles securities lending, but portfolio
managers need to collaborate tightly with their counterparts who arrange the
lending programs with external counterparties. The value-added strategies
and benefits of securities lending are discussed a bit further in Chapters 21
and 26 and distinctions between different approaches and providers can
make a significant difference in overall index portfolio performance.

Bifocals Needed—Broad Perspective and Detail Orientation

Skilled index portfolio managers have a wide field of vision—but one that
also dives deep into almost microscopic levels of detail. They know the total
investment and operations environment, which enables them to manage
complex portfolios in an efficient and scalable manner. This includes the
cash and derivative markets, trade and order operations, and the "plumb-
ing" of settlement, order deadlines, client flows, and the overall objectives
and expectations of clients. Index portfolio managers also must be aware of
the need to efficiently use resources. As discussed in Chapter 3, index funds
are generally priced quite cheaply, so cost-control (for the firm) is an integral part of an index portfolio manager's job. Similarly, portfolio managers
must be comfortable with technology. Systems are constantly evolving, and
often different systems are in place to track the portfolio, benchmark indexes, and trading flows. Often, portfolio managers work hand-in-hand
with systems developers and programmers, and will be constantly testing
new applications.

Figure 19.3 provides a granular illustration of the issues, information, and transaction processing flows that institutional index portfolio management entails. And good index PMs understand all of the details.

DELIVERING PREDICTABLE INDEX FUND PERFORMANCE—THERE IS NO FREE LUNCH

Just like the key trade-offs in the choice of benchmarks discussed in Chapter 6, index portfolio management has different approaches, techniques, and trade-offs for different objectives and fund/product structures. The concept of "Perfection Impossible" has resonance for the index investment process—as with benchmark selection, the question continuously needs to be asked: perfect for what objective?

A multibillion-dollar institutional comingled domestic large-cap equity fund will be managed in a very different way from an institutional emerging

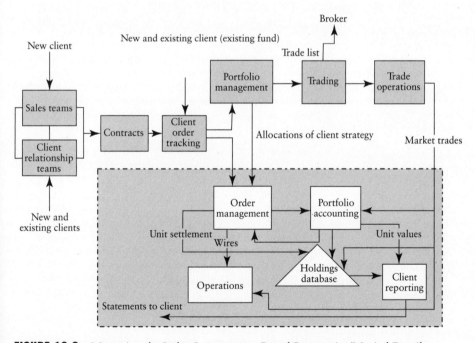

FIGURE 19.3 Managing the Index Investment—Broad Perspective/Myriad Details
Source: Barclays Global Investors; Global Index Strategies; Northern Trust Global Investments.

markets strategy, even at the same firm. Similarly, even the largest fixed-income index mandate is unlikely to be managed in a full replication approach. The regulatory and operational requirements of mutual funds and ETFs involve techniques that differ from those used for institutional products, even when they are tracking the same benchmark. Finally, customized index strategies—whether institutional portfolios, index mutual funds, or individual investor SMAs (separately managed accounts)—take unique approaches that are in sharp contrast to standard, flagship index funds.

Portfolio managers for each of the above-mentioned strategies will make investment decisions that reflect the trade-offs between tracking error (which generally can be reduced with a greater number of securities) and the costs of both acquiring the securities as well as maintaining the portfolio. We hope that this chapter has helped to illustrate the objectives and nuances of index portfolio management so that readers now understand these tradeoffs.

The next five chapters in Part Four explore all these nuances—and more—and provide detailed, asset-class specific, and/or product-specific examples of index portfolio management techniques and challenges. After a thorough reading, few investors will be able to credibly call index portfolio management passive—or claim that it is anywhere close to the simple, "even a monkey can do it" perception quoted at the start of this chapter.

NOTES

1. Michael Siconolfi and Robert McGough, "Equaling S&P Results Can Be More Difficult Than It Appears," *Wall Street Journal* (January 28, 1997).
2. A detailed look at management of a Wilshire 5000 index portfolio is provided in Julia K. Bonafede, "The Wilshire 5000 Total Market Index—The Logistics behind Managing the U.S. Stock Market," *Journal of Indexes* (third quarter, 2003). Available from the archive of www.IndexUniverse.com.
3. George U. Sauter, "Medium and Small-Capitalization Indexing," in *Perspectives on Equity Indexing: Professional Perspectives on Indexing,* 2nd ed., ed. Frank J. Fabozzi (New Hope, PA: Frank Fabozzi Associates, 2000), pp. 135–150. This chapter has an informative discussion of the trade-offs between optimization and sampling, and the impact of low liquidity in small capitalization stocks.
4. For example, many firms break the Wilshire 5000 into a "top 500" component that essentially is a fully replicating S&P 500 index fund, and an "extended" 4500, which will be optimized. For more details see the *Journal of Indexes* article, cited in note 2.
5. SEC Chief Economist, Larry Harris, in a speech at an indexing conference in September 2003, proposed potential solutions to attenuate the market impact of major index changes. This includes phasing-in of changes and longer-lead times. Some of the tactics used by index fund managers during the major MSCI

and FTSE structural index changes in the 2000–2002 period (discussed in Chapter 21) could be relevant for future index changes.

6. S&P's "Global 1200" series is discussed in Chapter 9. The S&P ADR Index is discussed in a sidebar in Chapter 21.

7. An excellent discussion by William Fouse on the origins of portfolio trading can be found in "Ignorance to Awareness to Denial to Acceptance," in *Perspectives on Equity Indexing*, 2nd ed., Fabozzi.

8. For a complete description of both *operational* and *investment* risks that confront index portfolio managers, see Steven Schoenfeld, "The Multiple Dimensions of Global Equity Risk Management," in *Global Investment Risk Management*, ed. Ezra Zask (New York: McGraw-Hill, 2000), pp. 45–65.

CHAPTER 20

The Unique Challenges of U.S. Equity Index Management

Amy Schioldager, Will Hahn, Ed Hoyt, and Jane Leung

_____ Editor's Note _____

This chapter, written by current and former members of a team of U.S. equity portfolio managers from the world's largest index fund manager, provides insight into the challenges and nuances of tracking well-known benchmarks.[1] As stated in Chapter 19, while many users of index funds believe that managing index-based portfolios is relatively easy, the reality is quite different. This chapter delves deeper into the process, illustrating the complexities of handling corporate actions, major index reconstitutions, and client requirements. The use of stock index futures in portfolio management is also described. Index management requires a thorough knowledge of benchmarks and their construction methodologies, and an understanding of disciplined trading approaches. The chapter provides an important foundation for understanding the challenges of tracking the same U.S. equity indexes with different vehicles like ETFs and Separate Accounts, covered in Chapters 23 and 24, respectively. Readers should be amazed by the investment knowledge and dedication that index portfolio managers possess and will have a newfound respect for the science and art of managing U.S equity index funds.

As the previous chapter stressed, managing index funds is anything but passive. But we are often asked: How difficult can it be to manage indexed assets in just one market? Unlike some of the markets discussed in Chapters 19, 21, 22, and 23, the U.S. equity market has standardized procedures, no currency/exchange rate issues, and seemingly unlimited liquidity. On the surface, it appears to be a very friendly market for index managers. But this is an oversimplification that fails to account for the depth and breadth of the underlying components of the U.S. equity market. This market has layers of complexity that heighten the challenges of managing U.S. indexed assets. Some of the difficulties include:

- Challenges of scale and scope.
- Management of multiple indexes with multiple index rebalancings and development of appropriate trading strategies.
- Developed, complex, and liquid derivative markets, including futures.
- Stringent tracking error tolerances among investors.

COVERAGE

The United States is only one of the world's markets, but it currently represents about 50 percent of the world's equity (market capitalization), and its exchanges list more than half of the world's securities. For example, the New York Stock Exchange and Nasdaq Composite Indexes as of December 31, 2002, listed 2,077 and 3,550 securities, respectively, for a total of 5,627 traded and recognized securities covering 99 percent of the U.S. market. The Wilshire 5000 actually contains 5,667 constituents and is one of the broadest U.S. equity benchmarks. When you add in over-the-counter (OTC) and other exchanges, the total number of U.S. securities passes the 8,000 mark. For comparison, as of December 31, 2002, the MSCI All-World ex U.S. had approximately 1,763 constituents covering of the world outside the United States. *(Editor's note: There are thousands of smaller securities outside of those benchmarks especially in larger emerging markets like India.)*

Using the MSCI All-Country World Index (ACWI) as a framework for global capitalization, we find that the United States represented 53.71 percent of the world's total market capitalization as of December 31, 2002. The United Kingdom (11.02 percent) and Japan (8.39 percent) were the next two largest in terms of total market capitalization (see Table 20.1). *(Editor's note: Although the data may be dated at the time of publication, the authors' point is still completely relevant.)*

SCALE AND VOLUME

The United States is often considered the most efficient and most liquid stock market in the world today. The common definition of liquidity is the degree to which an asset or security can be bought or sold in the market without affecting the asset's price. Furthermore, liquidity and overall market efficiency can be gauged by trading volume, the number of institutional investors, and

TABLE 20.1   Investable Market Capitalization of Major World Equity Markets in U.S. Dollars

Country	Total ($)	Percentage
United States	7,146,046,779,628	53.71
United Kingdom	1,466,644,293,916	11.02
Japan	1,115,914,534,991	8.39
France	497,577,348,321	3.74
Switzerland	436,404,666,222	3.28

Source: Morgan Stanley Capital International, December 2002.

the diversity of investors in the market (we use the number of open-ended mutual funds as a proxy). As detailed in Table 20.2 the U.S. market is the leader in all these metrics.

What inferences can we draw from these simple metrics applied across the four largest markets? The United States has the greatest number and percentage of sophisticated institutional investors, 10-fold more trading volume per day, and the most open-ended mutual funds. Combine these figures with 50 percent of the world's market cap and around half of the world's equities, and the United States is undoubtedly the most competitive, efficient, and liquid market in the world.

DIVERSITY

For international equities, there are currently two primary index providers used by U.S. institutional investors: MSCI and FTSE, with MSCI far and away the leader in global benchmarks. In the U.S. domestic market, in

TABLE 20.2   Liquidity Metrics for Major World Stock Markets

Country	Number of Institutional Investors/ Percentage of Market Cap	Number of Open-Ended Funds (9/30/2001)	U.S. Dollar Equivalent Value-Traded (Daily Average in Millions)
United States	>1,300/>50	8,300	69,121
United Kingdom	~100/~12	1,961	6,744
Japan	~100/~6.5	2,744	5,465
France	~481/~5	7,473	4,292

Source: 2002 Mutual Fund Fact Book, Investment Company Institute.

addition to the sheer number of securities, there is little consensus concerning the best benchmarks, and there is also a penchant to slice and dice each index into component benchmarks. In Part Two, particularly Chapters 5 and 6, readers can find detailed information and background about U.S. equity benchmark indexes. For illustrative purposes, however, consider that the U.S. market is often divided by the following benchmarks, benchmark modules, and custom screens:

- Overall Benchmark Index Framework:
  —Standard & Poor's, Wilshire, Russell, Dow Jones, and MSCI.
- Style:
  —Growth, value, and sometimes "core."
- Size:
  —Large, mid, small.
  —Microcap and macrocap.
- Sector:
  —Industry-specific slices and subsectors.
- Screens:
  —"Standardized"[2] (e.g., ex-Tobacco, Socially Responsible, Islamic).
  —Newer, policy and/or investment oriented (e.g., corporate governance, bankruptcy, ex-terror/proliferation).
  —Custom screens: Social, political, and other stock/sector specific.

The permutations of benchmarks and substyle benchmarks, combined with the specialized client needs and requests unique to the U.S. market, are enough to make statisticians quit their day job. To make matters even more complex, the benchmark providers do not agree on the optimal rules and methodologies (Chapters 5, 6, and 7 go into far more detail on this subject). However, just consider the radically different treatment of a simple capital market event—a delisted or nonpricing stock, as shown in Table 20.3.

Which is the best pricing option? From the index fund manager's perspective, the MSCI deletion price of zero is easy to beat. As a fair market practitioner, Russell's new pricing policy provides a fair means for managers to track the index.

THE FINAL ELEMENT OF COMPLEXITY: THE HUGE NUMBER OF CORPORATE ACTIONS AND INDEX CHANGES

As mentioned in the previous chapter, index portfolio managers must react to a myriad of corporate and index developments. The total numbers for

TABLE 20.3   Examples of Index Methodology Approaches for Nonpriced Stocks

Index Provider	Rule for Nonpricing Assets
Wilshire	Delete at last price after one day of not pricing.
Russell	Delete at the last price on the first day the security begins to trade over the counter (as of January 2002). Prior to January 2002, it was the price at the time of delisting (generally the same last price that Wilshire would utilize).
Dow Jones	One cent (US$0.01) subject to10 days of nontrading, trading suspension, and/or ongoing bankruptcy proceedings.
MSCI	Delete at the smallest market incremental (essentially zero) value after a MSCI discretionary number of days of not pricing, suspended, bankruptcy, and so on.
S&P	Generally ends to avoid the issue by deleting companies for "lack of representation" at early signs of potential company failure.

Source: BGI U.S. Equity Portfolio Management.

corporate actions and index changes are not well documented. For comparison, however, we can look at a few common corporate actions, and from there make some general assumptions about the overall number of changes. The data in Table 20.4 come from a BGI data consolidation/cleansing database for all corporate action information. The numbers from calendar year 2001 reveal the scale and complexity of the U.S. marketplace, especially in comparison to a variety of international markets.

First, all of the 31 common types of corporate actions take place in the United States. We have a vibrant capital market—and a lot of eager investment bankers and lawyers. If you take away cash/stock and cash dividends, the United States accounted for 533 of 724 corporate actions for the calendar year 2001. From the perspective of a U.S. equity index manager, you then have up to five different index vendors who are likely to treat the corporate action in subtly different ways. For example, all five major index vendors will treat a spin-off differently. Lastly, you have to ask which and how many entities participate in each major corporate action, such as the following players:

- Mutual funds, hedge funds, and the rest of the sophisticated institutional investors.
- Market timers and retail investors.
- Index managers.

TABLE 20.4 2001 Global Corporate Actions by Type of Event

Event Name	Australia	Canada	Japan	Netherlands	Korea	United Kingdom	United States	Grand Total
Cash/stock election	187	473		51		198	14	1,058
Cash dividends	814	889	3,825	656	358	1,344	9,839	21,863
Class action							31	31
CUSIP name change						1	20	21
Information	1	2		2		1	23	37
Merger		3	1		3	1	105	117
Other dividend	3	2		1			86	131
Spin-off							14	18
Stock dividend	2				5		51	71
Stock split		2	5		2	1	55	81
Tender offer	3	11	1		1		147	176
Grand total	1,019	1,382	3,832	711	370	1,554	10,386	23,645

Source: BGI Security Universe Maintenance System (SUMS).

TRADING STRATEGIES FOR INDEX CHANGES

It's important to plan an appropriate trading strategy when thinking about index changes. A fundamental premise is that markets are efficient. Indexers (and investment advisors as a whole) don't have privileged information that isn't made public to all investors. Index vendors release index change information to everyone at the same time. For example, the Standard & Poor's web site publishes constituent changes for all S&P indexes four times each day. Anyone can log on to the web site and view this information at the predetermined times. Assuming everyone has the same information, it becomes even more critical to devise a trading strategy that, among other things, takes into account the expected index demand.

Investment managers consider many variables when devising trading strategy: macroeconomic events, sector, index demand, migrations, and risk. Some of them are discussed next.

Macroeconomic events include the timing of the release of federal economic indicators. Examples are the Consumer Price Index (CPI), Consumer Confidence, Purchasing Price Index (PPI), housing starts, gross domestic product (GDP), unemployment numbers, and Federal Open Market Committee (FOMC). Although there are numerous economic indicators (see whitehouse.gov./fsbr/esbr), some may affect stock prices more than others. An index change for a stock in the finance industry could be affected by an FOMC announcement about interest rate changes. Retail trade announcements could affect price movement on stocks in the retail sector. Announcements related to inventories could affect technology and manufacturing firms. It's important to know in which sector an individual stock belongs, as well as the types of announcements that could influence that sector. Additionally, it is worthwhile to know the release date of economic indicators when planning index change strategies.

Another factor to consider, which is similar to macroeconomic events, is earning announcements. It's imperative to be aware of announcements specific to index change stocks, and to a lesser degree the announcements of all other stocks in the broader sector. Even the soundest index change strategy can fall to pieces if an earnings announcement goes against it.

Sectors, macroeconomic events, and earnings announcements can also affect individual stocks. It won't come as a surprise that knowing the sector and the implications of certain sectors is critical in planning index change strategy. In the late 1990s, telecom, media, and technology (TMT stocks) were booming. The price movement was much more volatile for these sectors than for a relatively sedate sector like consumer durables. Some sectors tend to be more cyclical than others, so keeping this in mind can help when devising a well-informed trading plan.

Sophisticated index managers also spend time ascertaining the total demand of the index change. This is viewed in terms of index demand versus total demand. Total demand would take into account active strategies and other nonindex funds (e.g., sector funds). Index demand, on the other hand, takes into account only those investors that will likely have a specific benchmark. The benchmark would be the effective date of the index change. Typically, index events occur at the closing market price of the effective date. By knowing the amount of indexed assets under management tied to a particular benchmark, managers can calculate the index demand. From there, they can ascertain the expected trading activity and/or volume surrounding the market close on the effective date. By viewing historical volume against expected volume, they can get an idea of liquidity and possible price movement, given the liquidity constraints.

Lastly, tied in with expected volume is understanding where the stock is coming from or where it is headed: Is it a migration from another index? S&P 500 changes can be migrations from or to the adjacent mid-cap index, the S&P 400. This may help in understanding liquidity needs and in determining whether there is another side to the trade. *(Editor's note: In addition, large index fund managers such as BGI, SSgA, Northern Trust, and Vanguard, who manage portfolios for all the indexes impacted by these migrations often have both an informational and trading cost advantage. Only they know exactly how much of each stock will move between their various strategies [e.g., large-cap S&P 500 and mid-cap S&P 400 strategies], and they can implement cost-free crossing between funds.)*

The overall trading strategy will take into account all the preceding variables. Even in the index change environment, however, the market is still considered efficient. The information that is available to a large indexer is the same information that is available to the general public. Our expertise in devising trading strategies is a result of our taking all known information into account and combining that intelligence with our experience of trading in the U.S. marketplace. Portfolio management and trading work together to devise large index change trades.

We use a Value at Risk (VAR) calculation to understand the risk that is undertaken. All our portfolios have a predetermined risk budget; tracking error tolerance and trading strategies are designed to fit the appropriate risk budget. A standard fully-replicating commingled fund is expected to have a smaller risk budget than an optimized separate client account. Risk budgets for U.S. index portfolios may vary from less than 2 to over 25 basis points (0.02 percent to 0.25 percent).

Another aspect of trading U.S. equity index changes is the size of the funds that we are trading. Because we have significant assets under management, confidentiality and discreet trading are essential to prevent detrimental "front-running" by outsiders. We work very closely with our broker counterparts to ensure privacy and, wherever possible, devise appropriate strategies to minimize market impact.

STOCK INDEX FUTURES IN DOMESTIC EQUITY MANAGEMENT

Derivatives instruments such as index futures and options play an important role in the management process. Because derivative instruments derive their prices from an underlying asset, portfolio managers can potentially use derivative instruments to gain exposure to a particular asset on which the derivative is based (see discussion on stock index futures in Chapters 14 and 25). It is their use as a cost-effective tool to gain short-term exposure to assets that makes derivatives particularly valuable to index portfolio managers.

Most portfolios have cash-flow activities such as client redemptions subscriptions, and fees and expenses that make it impossible for managers to remain fully invested in equities at all times. A certain level of cash or a cash-like instrument must remain in the account to handle short-term liquidity needs. Even if managers could invest all the cash, it might not be cost-effective from an operational or trading perspective to constantly trade small amounts of securities.

Another problem related to cash management stems from dividends. There is often a substantial lag between when dividends are declared and when they are actually paid. In calculating index returns, however, the dividends are deemed received and reinvested on the ex-date. (Ex-dividend date refers to the last day of trading when the seller, not the buyer, of a stock is entitled to the most recently announced dividend payment. The date set by the NYSE and followed by other exchanges is usually two days before the record date. The record date is the date by which the shareholder must officially own the relevant shares to receive the dividend from the company declaring.) Unless portfolio managers invest the accrued dividends, they run the risk of not matching the index return (tracking error). Accrued dividends or any cash accruals are mere accounting balances and do not represent actual cash on hand. Derivatives allow portfolio managers to receive equity returns on the cash and cash accruals that cannot be immediately invested in securities.

The most commonly used derivative instrument in the index portfolio management world is the stock index future. These contracts are an agreement between parties to deliver and receive underlying index names at a future date for a specified amount. Index futures contracts have the added benefit of being standardized; the size of each contract and the delivery date are prespecified. The futures are also traded actively on an exchange, which means that parties can get in and out of their obligations quickly. An index manager who manages a fund to an S&P 500 Index can take a long position (buy the futures contracts, or agree to take delivery of the index at a future date) in an S&P 500 Index futures contract equal to the amount of cash in the fund. In practice, no physical assets change hands. Only the net value of the contract is exchanged between parties daily in a process called *mark-to-market*. It is important to distinguish between futures price and futures value. The current S&P 500 Index price level may be say, 1200. A futures *price*, or the delivery price agreed to by the parties, may be 1210. If the S&P 500 Index subsequently rises to 1210, the *value* of owning a futures contract should rise by 10, since the owner of the contract will pay a fixed price at a future date for an index that has now increased in price by 10. The return on the futures position plus the interest return on the cash position should equal the return on the index.

There is no guarantee that the futures price will change in lockstep with the underlying index price. However, the theoretical futures pricing and the principle of arbitrage closely enforce this one-to-one for relationship. *(Editor's note: Chapter 25 provides some basic principles on the pricing of stock index futures and options.)*

Although the theoretical prices of futures and the principle of nonarbitrage are beyond the scope of this chapter, it is sufficient to say that the price of the future depends on assumptions about the short-term interest rate and the index's dividend yield. Any changes in the assumptions, along with market liquidity or other transactions costs, may cause the return on the futures to deviate from the returns on an underlying index. The term "basis risk" is used broadly to describe the risk that the futures price does not track the underlying index. The term is also applied to the mistracking present in using futures of one index as a proxy to track another index. Using futures contracts of the shortest maturity may arguably reduce basis risk since it reduces any uncertainties about interest rate and dividend yield. It may, however, subject the portfolio to more frequent cost of rolling the futures forward, or costs associated with closing out the position at or near the expiration and buying a contract of a later date. Portfolio managers must always bear in mind the risk associated with futures and the relative size of the future position when assessing the benefits of using futures to obtain synthetic index returns.

TRACKING ERROR

As discussed in Chapter 14, tracking error is best described as the deviation of fund performance from index or benchmark performance. The benchmark is an objective measure that is specified within the client investment guidelines. Predicted tracking error for any given index strategy depends on several elements, including characteristics such as size, risk, and liquidity, as well as whether the strategy is fully replicating or optimized. Tracking error tolerance describes the bounds within which tracking error is deemed acceptable in a portfolio.

Tracking error tolerance is an important concept in the overall management of index portfolios, as it aids both the client and portfolio manager. This tolerance is defined in the investment guidelines and depends on the index strategy and nature of the client's risk appetite. Clients use the performance of the portfolio, or tracking error, to measure a portfolio manager's skill in managing the portfolio against a benchmark. Additionally, performance measurement allows clients to analyze a particular strategy against an overall asset allocation. Likewise, portfolio managers use tracking error to check that the management of the strategy is working as they anticipate, and also to detect any potential systematic biases that might exist.

A Different Measure of Tracking Success for Different Benchmarks

Understanding how a portfolio's predicted tracking error (PTE) affects performance is straightforward. For example, a fund with a predicted tracking error of 0.20 percent will earn the index return, plus or minus 0.20 percent, 67 percent of the time. But as mentioned in the previous chapter, there are different definitions of "perfection" for index portfolio mangers, depending on the benchmark being tracked (and the asset category and fund type). Even for institutional comingled funds, different benchmarks will require a tradeoff between tracking and costs/risks that results in varied PTE. As visible in Figure 20.1 fully replicating funds such as those benchmarked to the S&P 500 Index have fairly tight tracking tolerances, anywhere from 0.01 to 0.001 percent. Optimized funds managed against the Russell 2000 Index are expected to have approximately 0.10 to 0.25 percent annual predicted tracking error. Socially screened funds—which are both optimized and will have tracking bias inherent in their exclusion of numerous stocks—may have annual predicted tracking error of 40 to 50 basis points for "standard customized indexes" or even 1 percent or more for client-specific custom benchmarks.

Tracking error has many components: the cost of liquidity, basis risk, security and sector misweights, rounding, transaction costs, index changes, and securities lending. These factors may introduce either positive or negative tracking error and, as such, it is necessary to understand how they can affect the overall performance of the strategy.[3]

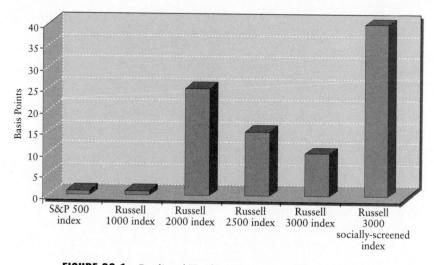

FIGURE 20.1   Predicted Tracking Error for Different Indexes
Source: BGI U.S. Equity Management.

The cost of liquidity refers to the mistracking caused by holding either unequitized cash or cash equitized by futures. Cash "drag" or "pop" is the negative or positive tracking error introduced to the portfolio by unequitized cash. Holding cash in an upwardly moving market will create negative cash drag in the portfolio. Likewise, holding cash when the market is down creates a cash pop in the portfolio.

Basis risk can occur in portfolios that use futures to equitize cash. While this reduces the tracking error due to cash drag or pop, holding futures can cause tracking error if the futures simply trade away from the index closing price or create an imperfect hedge to the underlying index. In S&P 500 index funds, portfolio managers are likely to hold S&P 500 futures contracts to equitize cash. In this case, the performance of the futures contracts should perform in line with the securities in the fund. However, in funds with no corresponding futures contracts to the underlying index, mistracking may occur from holding futures. In funds benchmarked to the Russell 2000 Value Index, portfolio managers will likely hold Russell 2000 contracts as the closest proxy, due to the lack of a Russell 2000 Value futures contract. Doing so, however, has introduced growth exposure to the fund. Further illustrating the imperfect nature of this hedge, the predicted tracking error between the Russell 2000 Value Index and the Russell 2000 Index is approximately 4 percent. In other words, this hedge is certain to cause some degree of mistracking, depending on the growth component. Portfolio managers need to carefully navigate these tradeoffs.

Security misweights can also factor into the tracking error of domestic index funds, particularly optimized ones. Index portfolio managers use risk models developed by companies such as Barra, Northfield, or Qrantal to determine the specific securities and industries, as well as their respective weights, in the fund. A fund with a larger risk appetite may have greater security and industry misweights, as determined by the optimization model. However, this deviation from the benchmark due to security sampling will certainly introduce tracking error in any given period. Over the long term, though, performance should revert to the mean.

Certain sectors within the small-cap universe sometimes cause unintentional biases. According to some risk models, banks will continually be underweighted and optimized out of the portfolio because most of the banks in the small-cap universe tend to be regional ones that do not trade often. Sectors with such characteristics may be unintentionally biased in the portfolio because of the volume and liquidity constraints that optimization models use to screen out undesirable stocks. Portfolio managers seek to reduce such biases when they occur.

As an example of how even the smallest factors can impact performance, the *rounding effect* is random and tends to revert over time, but can have a noticeable monthly impact on performance and tracking. Some portfolios record unit values using two digits, whereas others may record it using six digits. Table 20.5 shows the return improvement using six-decimal unit values versus two-decimal ones. This underscores the point made in Chapter 19 about how index portfolio managers mush both have a broad perspective and rigorous focus on detail.

Finally, transaction costs will certainly affect tracking because the index is calculated without any transaction costs. As discussed in Chapters 14 and 19, in the real world, index-based investors bear the cost of commissions, bid/ask spreads, and market impact. These costs can be minimized through skillful management, but alas not avoided entirely.

TABLE 20.5 "The Devil's in the Details": The Rounding Effect in Index Fund Management

	2-Digit Unit Value	6-Digit Unit Value	Difference
01/31/02	8.33	8.327489	0.002511
02/28/02	7.79	7.794795	0.004795
Return	−6.48%	−6.40%	+0.08%

Source: Barclays Global Investors.

Positive Tracking—Working for *Index Alpha*

Just as there are sources of negative tracking, there also are sources of positive tracking. Portfolio management expertise, as well as the manager's close interaction with other groups such as trading desks and investment strategy and research, can add tremendous value to an index fund. At index additions and deletions, "smart trading" can certainly create value in a portfolio by, among other things, reducing market impact and keeping transaction costs down. Additionally, analysis of corporate mergers and acquisitions helps portfolio managers understand the implications of, and opportunities associated with this type of activity.

Annual and quarterly index reconstitutions provide an excellent occasion for adding value to portfolios through careful analysis, robust research, and nimble trading. Whenever available, securities lending can provide additional income and thus improve overall positive performance in the portfolio. This latter source of performance is more likely in small cap portfolios, and is a major value-add in international portfolios, as discussed in Chapters 21 and 26.

CONCLUSION

Managing index-based portfolios in the U.S. equity market is a challenging and complex investment process. The sheer number and diversity of investors, funds, money managers, benchmarks, corporate actions, and index changes all raise the bar. As money managers, we love this challenge and appreciate the opportunity to manage money in the largest and most efficient market in the world.

We have mostly described the challenges of managing large, institutional funds and strategies tracking U.S equity indexes. Chapters 23 and 24 discuss the unique challenges of managing exchange-traded funds and separate accounts that track some of the same benchmark indexes. These portfolio managers must be aware of additional nuances and undertake different trade-offs to meet their products' unique investment objectives. In these chapters you will note the "different definitions of perfection" that are used for these products.

As portfolio managers, it is our professional and fiduciary responsibility to ensure minimal disruption in the trades that we create, and to deliver index-tracking performance in line with our clients' expectations. Managing index portfolios requires a unique talent, diligent and painstaking attention to detail, and a continual focus on objectives. Despite the conventional wisdom described in the previous chapter that managing U.S. equity index portfolios is a relatively easy and straightforward endeavor, we believe this chapter has added more evidence to prove the opposite: Indexing in the U.S. equity market requires enormous skill and creativity.

NOTES

1. Two of the authors are no longer employed with Barclays Global Investors, but the views reflect the approach and techniques used by BGI at the time of the chapter's writing.
2. While the concept of a "Standardized" Custom Index might sound like an oxymoron, within the world of large institutional tax-exempt investment, key screening criteria have developed (and evolve), and thus a critical mass of asset owners would request similar screening approaches. This is similar to the "standardized" alternative weights for the EAFE Index discussed in Chapter 12.
3. A more detailed discussion of tracking error choices and tradeoffs facing U.S. index portfolio mangers—including some of the pros and cons of stratified sampling, quadratic optimization, and hybrid approaches—can be found in Julia Bonafede, "The Wilshire 5000 Total Market Index: The Logistics Behind Managing the U.S. Stock Market," in *Journal of Indexes* (third quarter, 2003) pp. 8–17, also available from the archives section on www.IndexUniverse.com.

CHAPTER 21

Delivering Performance in International Equity Indexing

Eleanor de Freitas, Robert Ginis,Creighton Jue,
Tom McCutchen, Steven A. Schoenfeld,
and Amy Whitelaw

_____ **Editor's Note** _____

*Delivering performance in international index strategies requires many of
the same skills used in U.S. equities as well as an additional focus on factors
that are not a consideration when investing in one's home market. In this
chapter, some of my former international equity index portfolio management colleagues and I detail the key challenges of delivering performance in
both developed international and emerging equity markets. For readers not
familiar with the asset class, Chapter 9 provides a framework for understanding the range of international equities covered in the major global
benchmarks and Chapter 12 provides an historical perspective on the evolution of this asset class. The complexities of multiple time zones, market conventions, and regulatory factors are described. Detailed examples of trading
strategies and cross-border corporate actions are included as well as a sidebar on ADRs and ADR-based index portfolios. An explanation of both
agency and principle trading is included. And what would a chapter co-
written by former colleagues be without some international market "war
stories." (More graphic details are provided in the book's E-ppendix on
www.ActiveIndexInvesting.com.)*

The original conceptualization for this chapter occurred when all the authors were
colleagues in the Global Index and Markets Group at Barclays Global Investors in San
Francisco. Kevin Maeda (coauthor of ADR Index sidebar) was also a member of the
international equity group at BGI in the mid/late 1990s. The authors thank Christina
Polischuk for her very helpful edits and suggestions for this chapter.

The recipe for success in international equity index investment calls for the careful combination of many ingredients. It begins with the same issues faced by the domestic index investor. These are multiplied by opportunities and risks in 21 to 50 unique markets and further complicated by more than eight time zones. To this, add an array of currencies, and for the finishing touches, introduce restrictions levied on the foreign investor. These complexities and challenges are what makes international indexing so complex, interesting and, at times, quite exciting. And by the end of this chapter, we are certain that readers will agree that it is anything but boring!

WHAT MAKES A GOOD INTERNATIONAL EQUITY BENCHMARK?

Over the past decade, benchmarks have become an increasingly essential tool for evaluating and judging performance across international markets. A truly valuable global benchmark should provide a neutral and accurate reflection of the investment universe from which an international investor can realistically select holdings or draw comparisons. As discussed in Part Two, particularly in Chapters 6 and 9, for an international index to achieve this effectively, it must at minimum be:

1. *Complete.* The index should represent the entire investment opportunity set at both the country and company level.
2. *Investable.* Securities included must be truly attainable and adjustments must be made to reflect situations where shares are unavailable to certain or all investors.
3. *Transparent.* Index methodology should be defined and consistent across all markets.

A benchmark should also be able to stand the test of time, adequately reflecting the current conditions and requirements of an ever-changing investment landscape.

Does the Choice of Benchmark Matter?

As awareness and interest in global investment heightened, the late 1990s witnessed a sudden increase the international benchmarks available to investors. The four leading global index providers are Morgan Stanley Capital International (MSCI), FTSE International (FTSE), Dow Jones, Standard & Poor's Global 1200 series, and their S&P/Citigroup (formerly Salomon Smith Barney) Global Equity Indexes. Most global index managers offer products based on at least one of these indexes for their institutional clients in North America.[1] The importance of index selection and the key criteria used to evaluate the benchmarks are highlighted in Chapter 9.

As Chapters 19 and 20 indicate, the crucial decision of selecting an appropriate benchmark is just the beginning of the index investment process. Indexes are frictionless constructs, whereas index-based funds face the real world of complex markets and their varied costs and risks. As with domestic indexers, for international index managers, the work really starts when they must implement that decision.

THE CHALLENGES OF INTERNATIONAL EQUITY MANAGEMENT

Achieving the benchmark return may seem simple enough in theory, but even if assets are held in the requisite index weights, an international portfolio can still suffer performance variance from its benchmark. Variance creeps in as a function of the complexities of dealing in international markets. Everything from fund valuation to market closing mechanisms, corporate actions, and market settlement cycles can add to the challenge of matching index performance.

Pricing Methodology

Is valuing an international portfolio really that difficult? It depends on whether you are trying to value the portfolio to track a benchmark or simply to reflect current market conditions. The secret to valuing a portfolio to track an index is to use the same pricing sources as the benchmark. In the United States, pricing is fairly consistent across sources, so the exact source may not matter. In non-U.S. markets, pricing discrepancies can arise between sources, and identifying the appropriate information supplier becomes an issue.

Price variation is largely an offshoot of the closing mechanisms encountered within each market and the assumptions about which price best reflects closing value. Some markets have multiple closes, some have closing auctions, some simply have a last tick—all of which add to the variation in interpretation of the correct closing price. And this only covers the local equity price. Once you throw different exchange rate interpretations into the equation, it is easy to recognize the importance of consistent pricing methodologies. No matter how talented a portfolio manager may be, the use of anything other than benchmark prices to value a fund will cause the fund's performance to vary from the benchmark. When viewed across time, the mistracking effect tends to smooth out, but performance for any particular period will almost certainly differ.

Corporate Actions

As with any single country portfolio (examples regarding the U.S. market are supplied in Chapter 20), an international portfolio will experience corporate actions requiring the portfolio manager to elect one of the options the company puts forth. For benchmark purposes, index providers will assume a particular option is chosen. U.S.-based investors tracking a domestic index often take for granted the ability to replicate the benchmark by electing the same option as the benchmark assumption. When the same investors step across international boundaries, a whole new set of complexities may arise.

Non-local investors are sometimes excluded from electing certain options, or restricted from participating altogether. For example, matching benchmark performance on a rights issuance is normally straightforward, but when foreigners are explicitly restricted from exercising their rights, parallel performance is not guaranteed for the international investor. Typically, if the rights are "in the money," a benchmark will assume an increase to the number of shares outstanding for the company on the ex-date of the offering. The benchmark will then include the incremental shares outstanding into the benchmark at the discounted offering price. A restricted investor, who must instead trade in the market to purchase the new shares, is at a disadvantage. Luckily the majority of corporate actions are free from restrictions, but for the ones that are encumbered, investors must give particular attention to understanding the implications of the restrictions and devising an appropriate solution.

Settlement Cycles

The length of security settlement cycle is a risk area that has been addressed across the world, more vigorously in some countries than in others. It is on settlement day that cash and securities change hands. As the delay between trade execution and asset delivery increases, the risk of default increases as well. To lower settlement risk, the United States changed its equity settlement cycle in 1995 from a trade date plus five (T+5) to a T+3 cycle. Many other developed countries were either already T+3 or followed suit shortly thereafter.

Settlement cycles are very important to portfolio managers because they define when cash must be available to pay for "buy" trades, or when cash will be available from "sell" trades. In an environment where settlement dates coincide, funding decisions for an equity portfolio rebalance are a nonissue. Currently, out of the 23 developed countries, as defined by

Morgan Stanley Capital Investment (MSCI), all but two countries have a standard T+3 settlement cycle. Germany and Hong Kong are the outliers with T+2 settlement cycles. This has helped minimize the number of funding decisions made by portfolio managers working in this environment. Nevertheless, net purchases of Germany and Hong Kong still create funding mismatches requiring ingenuity on the part of the portfolio manager. Many countries may be settled long or short at a funding cost. Yet, in some countries, flexibility around the settlement cycle is not an option, as the sidebar "A Difficult One to Settle" describes.

If emerging markets are included within an equity rebalance transaction, the funding solution becomes increasingly complicated. To sell South Africa to purchase Taiwan, a 5-day funding difference needs to be covered. Although cash and securities change hands with a settlement date of T+1 in Taiwan, the Taiwanese market demands all funding cash be available to deliver from a trading account on the actual trading day (T). South Africa settles T+5, meaning cash will not be available until 5 days too late. It is no wonder that nondedicated emerging market managers have turned to exchange-traded funds (ETFs) to access many emerging markets (including the two in this example).

A DIFFICULT ONE TO SETTLE

With cash flow often operating on a settlement cycle dictated by the business days of a market other than that in which you are invested, international equity trade settlement can present a real stumbling block. Even when the funding schedule is equal in length to the cycle of the investment universe, problems can arise from time to time. If a U.S.-domiciled fund with a T+3 cycle (the common and longest trade cycle in developed markets) needed to raise cash at April month-end (in 2003) from investments in Greece, the managers would have had a problem. Although it would have been possible to execute the trades in line with the redemption on April 30, because of a Greek holiday on May 1, those trades would not settle until May 7. The cash, however, had to be delivered in line with the T+3 cycle of the U.S. client on May 6. In many markets, short settlement would have been an option, but it is not permitted in Greece. Consequently, the only way to avoid overdrawing the account was to trade early or late and, unfortunately, away from the benchmark. These kinds of scenarios are not unusual for an international portfolio manager, and we must navigate the challenge with creative solutions.

The 23-Hour Workday

Time is a constant challenge for the international portfolio manager. The developed markets alone span at least eight time zones, and for investors diversifying further, the emerging equity markets introduce an additional four to five zones. This presents an array of problems, the most obvious of which is the length of the "International Trading Day." The first Pacific market opens while most of New York is beginning to tackle the rush hour (after their working day) and the U.S. West Coast has just finished their lunch (also on the previous day). Essentially, there is just one hour in any day when no equity market is open. Consequently, managing international assets with the same flexibility and information provided by the domestic market would be a job with a 23-hour workday, as described in the sidebar "Not Enough Hours in the Day."

In reality, most international equity managers do not spend the entire day in the office (despite what they might lead you to believe). Since time travel is not yet a viable option, time zones present the following issues:

- *Information.* The linchpin of quality investment management is information, particularly for index funds. Key information pertaining to the benchmark and assets held is usually provided by a source located in a different time zone. Often, this can lead to delays in accessing essential information making it difficult to act in a timely fashion. With index funds scrutinized to the basis point (bp) of tracking error, such delays can result in significant performance effects.
- *Implementation.* The ability to effect investment decisions immediately is not a luxury afforded to the international investor. Whatever the trading motivation, once trades have been decided on, their execution may be impossible if few (or no) markets are open. This delay frequently occurs and can lead to serious portfolio/benchmark gap risk.
- *Holidays.* There are many holidays that the domestic and international markets do not share; this heightens the two preceding problems. Anyone who has ever tried to buy a "slice of EAFE" on December 26 knows what a problem this presents.

Foreign Currency Requirements

The most obvious addition to the investment equation for the international equity manager is foreign currency. For the majority of securities around the world, trading and settlement is conducted in the currency of the local market. This introduces a further set of unique challenges and risks to confront, and an extra variable to affect performance.

NOT ENOUGH HOURS IN THE DAY

In the Northern Hemisphere's winter months, there really are "not enough hours in the day" to manage a truly global portfolio. As the last markets close in the Americas, the New Zealand stock exchange has already started trading for the next trading day. If emerging markets are included in a portfolio, a number of markets trade on either Saturday or Sunday (or both). Some of these markets with dual-listed high-tech stocks—notably Israel—can in fact be leading indicators of major market openings on Monday, as they react first to news that breaks after Friday's close in the Western Hemisphere. The following diagram illustrates the international equity indexer's view of the world's time zones and helps explain why many of us have an arcane knowledge of the exact time in Tokyo, Mumbai, Tel Aviv, Frankfurt, and São Paulo.

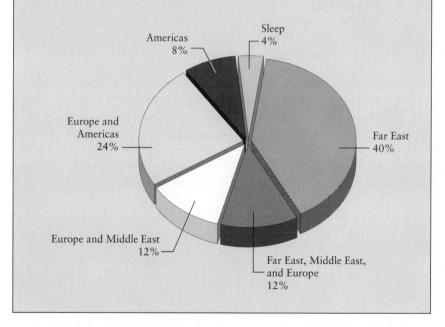

Currency Risks and Restrictions

In contrast to securities, foreign currencies trade around the clock and transactions can be executed even if the underlying equity market is closed. Like equity transactions, however, the settlement of currency is complicated by varying cycle lengths and local holidays and, therefore, requires careful

consideration. As the penalties incurred for overdrafts in many foreign currencies can be particularly high (far greater than a corresponding negative
balance in US$), there is often little room for error.

A range of factors has led many emerging market economies to impose
currency repatriation rules to govern foreign exchange transactions. In these
markets, it is effectively impossible to execute currency trades without providing evidence of an associated investment in the local equity market. This
severely limits execution control and flexibility because completed equity
trades must often be confirmed before the currency trading process can
begin. In a wide range of emerging markets—from Brazil to Zimbabwe—
these restrictions sometimes become even more severe.[2] However, few situations were as complex and politically charged as Malaysia's imposition of
capital controls in 1998, discussed in the following sidebar.

The Benchmark Rate

An international equity portfolio, indexed or otherwise, holds securities
denominated in the local currency of different countries. To value such a

---

MALAYSIA CURRENCY CONTROLS: INDEXERS LEAD WITH SOLUTIONS
Steven A. Schoenfeld

In a sharp reversal of four decades of liberalization, on September 1,
1998, Malaysia shocked the international community in the midst of
the Asian financial crisis by imposing onerous capital controls. These
restrictions were combined with heated rhetoric from Malaysia's
prime minister, who blamed foreign "speculators" for his country's
problems. He sharply restricted investors' ability to repatriate their
Malaysian equity investments, fixed the exchange rate for Ringgit at
RM3.80/US$, banned offshore trading of Malaysian currency and se-
curities, and required local assets to remain in local currency.

For international index portfolio managers, critical implications
stemmed from this event and required risk management in several dimensions. At Barclays Global Investors (BGI), my colleagues and I
worked simultaneously with our brokers and custodians to understand the rapidly changing situation. We helped our clients understand the ramifications and options, and we gave input to the major
index providers on the "least bad" solutions for treatment of the securities markets and the Ringgit exchange rate. As Malaysia was

dropped from the major developed and emerging market benchmarks like MSCI and Financial Times Stock Exchange (FTSE) (and was deemed an impaired market for the investable emerging market benchmarks), we created "carve out" portfolio solutions for clients who wanted to separate their frozen Malaysian assets from their core international portfolios. We also participated in conference calls with industry bodies and U.S. regulators, and established policies for the fair value pricing of our "WEBS Malaysia" (now iShares MSCI Malaysia) exchange-traded fund, whose Amex-traded price became a major price discovery mechanism for the industry.

Finally, we initiated efforts to establish a dialogue with Malaysian regulatory, exchange, and government officials to help them alleviate the situation they had created for foreign portfolio investors. This led to two personal visits to Kuala Lumpur for in-person discussion with the authorities, as well as with brokers and our local sub-custodian. Whether this helped alleviate the situation, even slightly, may never be determinable, but the visits certainly helped us develop solutions for our clients, and enabled us to update them on the very latest developments regarding their Malaysian investments.

More colorful information about the Malaysian Capital Controls Crisis is provided in the web-only sidebar, "Managing Political and Financial Risk in International Index Funds from B–Z—Brazil, Malaysia, Russia and Zimbabwe 1997–2001" by Steven A. Schoenfeld and Robert Ginis. It is available in the book's E-ppendix at www.ActiveIndexInvesting.com, also accessible via IndexUniverse.com. The site also includes some highlights of Prime Minister Mahathir's rantings against foreign investors in its "FOR FUN" section.

collection of stocks on a level plain, their prices must be converted into a single base currency. The question for investors is—at what exchange rate should the conversion take place? With foreign currency essentially trading around the clock, there is no "end of day" for the market and subsequently, no obvious closing price. As with any asset, the objective is to reflect what the currency would be worth in the market—the rate at which the investor could sell it. The most suitable rate will always be debated, but work has been done to set a standard for index calculation, investment management, and portfolio valuation.

For funds closely tracking an index, both foreign currency valuation and execution targets should be determined by the exchange rate applied to the index. In most cases, this is a rate cut at a single point in time and more often

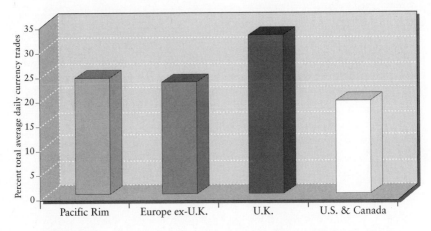

FIGURE 21.1 Foreign Exchange Turnover by Region (Daily Averages)

than not is the WM/Reuters Closing Spots Rates,™ which uses 16:00 (4 P.M.) London time as the reference point. The rationale for this time is that it reflects the peak trading period for the London and New York foreign currency markets and captures data contributions on a fully global basis. This peak in foreign exchange trading (and therefore liquidity) is apparent in Figure 21.1, especially if one aggregates the Europe ex-U.K. and U.K. figures, which tend to reflect the same liquidity pool. And in a way, the fact that major benchmarks use the 16:00 GMT close reinforces this concentration of liquidity, as fund managers will direct their order flow to this timeframe.

INVESTMENT RESTRICTIONS AND RISKS

The investment restrictions placed on nondomestic investors contribute heavily to the complexity of tracking an international benchmark. A fund that invests across several countries must deal with numerous restrictions including structural restrictions applied by each country into which a fund invests, restrictions applied by the country where the fund is registered, and restrictions that individual companies may impose on their own shares. These limitations often make it impossible to replicate the target benchmark perfectly, thus requiring the investment manager to devise a strategy that will allow the fund to track as close as possible with the minimal amount of risk. American Depository Receipts (ADRs) and Global Shares, which are discussed in a sidebar later in this chapter, can help navigate around some restrictions, but usually, portfolio managers have to swim among the sharks in the local waters.

Foreign Ownership Limits

Several countries, particularly in Asia, impose foreign ownership limits (FOL) on companies domiciled in their markets. For indexers, this can become a real obstacle, regardless of whether the index recognizes such limits.

For companies with FOL restrictions, a limited supply of stock is available to all foreign investors, usually represented as a percentage of shares outstanding. Once this limit is reached, foreign investors are unable to purchase additional shares. If a company has reached its FOL limit and a fund sells its shares, the fund would not be able to repurchase the shares until the foreign ownership level drops back below the limits.[3] The sidebar, "The No-Fly Zone" provides a useful illustration of this investment challenge for index managers.

Foreign ownership limits present two sets of index tracking issues. The first problem arises when the fund is unable to purchase shares when a fund inflow or an index rebalance trigger a need. The second may arise when the fund needs to sell shares because of a redemption. In this case, the portfolio

---

THE NO-FLY ZONE: RYANAIR INVESTMENT RESTRICTION

Ryanair is an Irish-domiciled airline company that imposes a foreign ownership limit restriction on its stock. The restriction sets a maximum permitted number of shares that non-European Union domiciled investors may own. The restriction is invoked at the discretion of the company's board of directors so that the company may "continue to hold or enjoy the benefit of any license, permit, consent or privilege which it holds or enjoys and which enables it to carry on business as an air carrier." The limit is set to a level at which the company feels will comply with the regulatory agencies that govern it. In this case, to satisfy non-EU investor demand, the company has issued a separate class of shares (ADS shares) for foreign investors. U.S. investors may invest in these ADS shares in the form of ADRs on the U.S. exchange.

manager must decide between short-term and long-term tracking errors. If overweight shares are immediately sold, the portfolio may not be able to repurchase the shares, potentially underweighting the name in the future. Alternatively, the portfolio manager may decide to overweight the name and not sell the shares. This could result in tracking error, but mitigates the potential inability to acquire more shares as future contributions flow into the fund.

Requirement for CFTC-Recognized Index Futures Contracts

The U.S. Commodity Futures Trading Commission (CFTC), through a "no-action" letter process, has the authority to essentially approve which non-U.S. stock index futures contracts U.S. investors can use. For a multi-market international index fund, tracking issues typically arise out of restrictions on futures contracts that need to be traded to equitize cash and accrual positions. Most major stock index contracts have been approved by the CFTC, but several key markets have not signed information-sharing agreements with the regulator and are thus off limits. Contracts covering more than 20 percent of the benchmark capitalization have not been approved for funds that attempt to track a developed international market index (not including the United States). For example, the Swiss index futures contract is not approved. In some instances, the restriction may force the fund to purchase contracts of another index as a proxy to hedge uninvested cash and accruals even though the contract of the underlying benchmark exists. A complete list of CFTC-approved index futures contracts is provided in this chapter's E-ppendix entry, available at www.ActiveIndexInvesting.com, which is also accessible through the IndexUniverse.com site.

Participation Restrictions

From time to time, there are corporate actions that restrict certain investors from participation. These restrictions are levied at the option of the offering company. The most common limitation for U.S.-based funds is the *qualified institutional buyer* (QIB) status restriction. Offering companies also impose other restrictions that are usually based on the domicile of the investor.

U.S. institutional investors are often subject to participation restrictions based on their QIB status. The U.S. regulations for an investment company define a QIB as an entity that has $100 million in other assets (unaffiliated with the entity). In many corporate actions, tenders or share offerings are available only to QIBs. The motivation behind the restriction is to ensure that companies not listed on the U.S. exchanges meet the U.S regulatory requirements. Funds and portfolios that do not meet QIB or any other requirements imposed by the offering company may find that tracking an index presents a real challenge.

INDEX REBALANCING AND RECONSTITUTION

As discussed in the previous two chapters, the majority of activity in an index portfolio is driven by changes in the underlying benchmark. These changes fall into two broad categories:

1. *Structural reviews.* A periodic review of constituents.
2. *Event-driven changes.* Implemented as they occur including mergers and acquisitions, initial public offerings (IPOs), changes in shares outstanding, foreign ownership limits, and more recently, adjustments for free float.

The periodic index rebalances are designed to ensure that the index reflects the current market environment. With the MSCI indexes, although such reviews usually occur on a quarterly basis, individual countries within the global universe may only be evaluated annually. These reviews often result in the addition of new securities, the deletion of some existing stocks, and changes in free-float estimates.

Any event-related changes are publicly announced and implemented as they occur with the exception of free float or share changes. To qualify for prenotification, these changes usually must be above a certain size or level of impact to the index. These ad hoc market- or corporate-action driven modifications contribute a fairly noticeable portion of aggregate annual index turnover, and managers need to be alert for them.

The treatment of corporate actions from one country to another can be unique. A host of different accounting and investment standards across the many international markets makes every event seem distinctive. The following sidebar on a Japanese natural resources merger illustrates this point.

Of all the events previously mentioned, the least attention is paid to the effect of postnotified changes. This occurs when the index provider actually

A JAPANESE MERGER

Japan Energy Corporation merged with Nippon Mining & Metals to form Nippon Mining Holdings in September 2002. The last trading day for Japan Energy and Nippon Mining & Metals was to be September 18, 2002, but Nippon Mining Holdings would not commence trading until September 26, 2002. As a result, most indexes maintained Japan Energy at its September 18 closing price until September 26. At that point, it was deleted and Nippon Mining Holdings was added, its price adjusted to reflect the terms of the merger. Index-based managers had to maneuver nimbly around this complex corporate action while minimizing risk to the portfolio.

informs clients of a change in index constituents and/or weights *ex-post facto*. (This frequently occurs for certain U.S. indexes as well.) These changes, in isolation, usually require a much smaller rebalance but they are by far the most frequent adjustment for many international indexes. For tightly constrained index portfolios, the principal risk from such changes is implementation shortfall. The general time zone and settlement-related implementation lag associated with international equity investment heightens this risk.

TRADING AND PORTFOLIO CONSTRUCTION

As mentioned at the outset, the primary hurdle for the successful management of an equity index portfolio—international or otherwise—is matching a friction-free benchmark. An index is not subject to adjustments to reflect the costs of the trading activity required for every rebalance of its constituents. As a result, the index manager is playing catch-up before the race even begins.

For the international index portfolio manager, the practicalities and costs associated with trading can present a particularly high hurdle. Several factors, from taxes to liquidity, contribute to this phenomenon, with each market presenting its own challenges. In the United Kingdom, the largest and most liquid market outside the United States, every buy transaction is subject to a stamp duty of 0.5 percent. In other markets, low liquidity is a

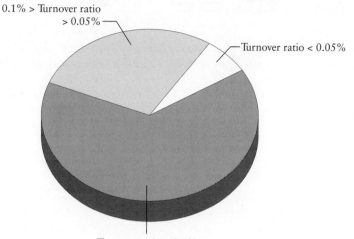

0.1% > Turnover ratio
> 0.05%

Turnover ratio < 0.05%

Turnover ratio > 0.1%

FIGURE 21.2   Weight in Developed Market Index versus Turnover

constant impediment to accurate tracking. As illustrated in Figure 21.2, some 26 percent of a global developed market equity index is represented by countries that trade (or turn over) less than 0.1 percent (10 bp) of their available market capitalization on an average day.[4] This is about half the relative liquidity of the U.S. market, which itself has some liquidity challenges, as discussed in Chapter 20.

Although index providers try to address many of the factors that limit practical investment, they only go so far and cannot always adequately reflect the true constraints investors face, regardless of size or domicile. Their task is further complicated because one simple rule cannot account for all the idiosyncrasies of international markets. Consequently, many obstacles can still impede the efficient trading of an international equity index portfolio.

The first step in tackling these issues is through shrewd portfolio construction. For example, an alternative, more liquid, or less restrictive share class can be held in place of a troublesome stock. It is possible to minimize the impact of costs systematically, but often at the expense of tracking. This illustrates the classic tradeoff described in the previous two chapters. In trying to find an appropriate balance between tracking error and costs, it is impossible to eliminate every trading challenge: Investors must confront these difficulties head-on.

International Trading Impediments

Cultural diversity transcends the interactions between people of various countries. A global portfolio manager knows all too well that cultural nuances spill over into international markets. In each country in which an international portfolio manager and trader transact, they face the difficulty of understanding the culture in which the market mechanisms originated. No two countries have the same market mechanisms or characteristics, and the trading patterns are as varied as the cuisine.

Liquidity Issues

Market liquidity plays an important role in executing trades with ease. For international markets, there is the added complexity of trading across 20 and sometimes as many as 45 markets. What is known as *natural liquidity* or the pairing of buyers with sellers contributes to lower transaction costs. In contrast, artificial liquidity or liquidity created by specialists, broker/dealers, or other intermediaries contributes to higher transaction costs. For an index fund manager, the lack of liquidity also leads to slippage from a benchmark or an inability to achieve a desired result without a significant cost. Although well-constructed indexes attempt to adapt to the trading limitations of certain markets, changing market conditions and liquidity environments can lead to unexpected illiquidity. A comparison of transaction costs of the U.S. market and international markets illustrates this point. To execute a one-way, $133 million trade in U.S. stocks included in the S&P/Citigroup Global Equity Indexes' (formerly Salomon Smith Barney's) Primary Market Index (PMI), the total cost including bid/ask spread and volatility cost is 24 bps.[5] To execute in any other developed market, the costs would range from 23 bps to 76 bps (the highest being Ireland). In emerging markets, the weighted average cost inclusive of bid/ask spread and volatility impact cost is 135 bps. These latter costs—from the third quarter of 2003—are illustrated in Table 21.1. Liquidity or lack thereof can be costly and presents a tremendous headwind for international index fund/ETF managers to overcome.

Market Mechanisms/Transparency

Understanding a benchmark's pricing methodology is crucial not only to fund valuation, but also to understand the risk surrounding trade execution. Trading away from benchmark prices introduces tracking error from the benchmark that in turn will directly affect the fund performance. With

TABLE 21.1 Total Transaction Costs

Market	Total Cost In Basic Points	Market	Total Cost In Basic Points
Argentina	157	Taiwan	37
Brazil	69	Thailand	122
Colombia	98	Hungary	56
Chile	78	Poland	120
Mexico	89	Russia	135
Peru	117	Egypt	84
Venezuela	297	Israel	29
China	64	Jordan	59
Indonesia	69	Morocco	54
India	42	South Africa	18
Malaysia	62	Turkey	118
Pakistan	27	Weighted average	
Philippines	83	cost	135

Note: Total trading costs = Commissions, bid/ask spread, volatility/ market impact.
Source: Citgroup (Salomon Smith Barney) and Standard & Poor's, based on a slice of the S&P/Citigroup PMI Emerging Market Index, Q3 2003.

various and unique market mechanisms, trading an international portfolio can be challenging. One would think the difficult market mechanisms would only be encountered in emerging markets. However, developed markets also pose their own fair share of challenges.

Many international markets trade electronically and, therefore, display the depth of the market only up to a certain point. Otherwise stated, electronic books display how much size is on either the bid or the ask price of the market. In these markets, transparency allows buyers and sellers to make informed decisions about the fair price for stocks. Certain markets, however, have limited access to the order book, further obfuscating large orders that may wait in the wings.

Price Limits

Many markets have mechanisms by which significant market movement will cause temporary trading halts or complete cessation of trading, whether in individual stocks or the market as a whole. These are typically well-known published thresholds, but in some markets, governments or other regulatory bodies may intervene and change these levels on an ad hoc basis. In Taiwan, the price limits are set at ± 7.5 percent of the previous day's close. In times of market turbulence (especially falling markets), as was the case in late summer/early fall of 2000, the Ministry of Finance in Taiwan would indiscriminately change the price limits to ± 3.5 percent. The government was trying to protect individual or retail investors from suffering significant losses—similar to actions taken by the Japanese government in a vain effort to prop up their stock market in the early/mid 1990s. For the foreign investor—index or active—this could translate into an incomplete order that ran the risk of being unexecuted for several days.

Prematching Cash

To limit overall cash drag, index managers, both domestic and international, maintain very small cash reserves. We sell securities to raise the cash to buy other securities. For most markets, no proof is required to show the manager has the cash on hand to fund purchases. In the case of Taiwan, cash (in the form of Taiwan dollars) must be in a custodian account in advance of security purchases.[6] An additional complication is that the brokers who are trading on behalf of an index manager must confirm with the custodian that the Taiwan dollars are available in the client account. For dollar-neutral trades—where no additional cash inflow is available from client contributions—the broker only needs to verify that the securities to be sold are available. In the past, this process resulted in some creative assistance from brokers; for example, they might place an unauthorized call to custodians and check for cash balances in client accounts. This latter challenge has been eliminated, but the prematching of cash can still prove problematic if the custodian and broker are not able to communicate in a timely manner. An index manager is dependent on prematching to execute trades.

The Challenge of "Market on Close"

Many developed markets do not have an auction to match off buyers and sellers at a final price for the day. In this case, different countries use various calculations to derive a market-on-close price. *Market-on-close* mechanisms create anomalous pricing if they are not auction-based or do not allow sufficient time for buyers and sellers to match closing activity effectively. Currently, exchanges in 13 of the 16 developed European countries conduct a closing auction. Some of the most complex developed-market closing mechanisms exist in Hong Kong, New Zealand, Canada, Denmark, Finland, and

Norway. Also, despite the presence in the other markets of an auction mechanism at the close, many participants have observed significant increased volatility around the close. In New Zealand, the market closes at a random time during the last five minutes of the trading session. The last price traded prior to the close is used as an official close. This makes it nearly impossible to guarantee completion at the closing level for the entire index. For the other markets, there is no auction.

With the MSCI index series, the official close is the price of the last trade prior to the close of the exchange for the day. In the flurry of last-minute and close activity, this benchmark can present a significant challenge for traders and portfolio managers. Large imbalances at the close test an auction's efficiency. In many markets, price limits and time extensions support the closing auction. Once a price limit is reached, time extensions give market participants sufficient time to react and offset imbalances. However, if imbalances are not resolved even with time extensions and stocks continue to breach their price limits, stocks may fail to close for the day. In Japan, stocks do not close in 2 to 2.5 percent of the MSCI Japan index stocks on any given day. For the broader Topix index, this incomplete close can impact up to 5 percent of constituent stocks. And this is for normal trading days—on month-ends and on benchmark change days, the number of "unclosed" stocks can be even more dramatic with between 15 and 25 percent of the stocks in the indexes failing to close. Portfolio managers and their traders need to monitor the markets in great detail to execute trades for rebalancing or to accommodate client flows.

The Greek stock market poses another unique challenge—so much so that many investors have questioned its 2001 "graduation" to developed market status as it entered the European Monetary Union (EMU). Its closing mechanism is the volume-weighted average price (VWAP) for the last 10 percent of the day's volume (that approach is difficult to write or say, let alone trade on!). Even with accurate studies of volume distributions over time, traders must use their skill to try to achieve this challenging closing mechanism. For an index manager, the inability to achieve the market-on-close convention can contribute to real-world slippage and/or tracking error versus the benchmark. In addition, significant imbalanced activity around the close can lead to high volatility and significant trading costs. Research by JP MorganChase notes that in Europe, ". . . the average move from the last traded price to the close is 30 basis points (bps). 30 bps is almost twice the average spread and 20 percent of the average open to close return" of a stock.[7] Figure 21.3 graphically presents this data and reinforces the point made in the previous chapter that "the devil is in the details" for index portfolio managers.

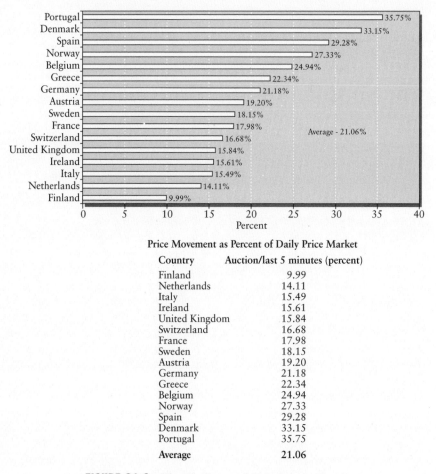

Price Movement as Percent of Daily Price Market

Country	Auction/last 5 minutes (percent)
Finland	9.99
Netherlands	14.11
Italy	15.49
Ireland	15.61
United Kingdom	15.84
Switzerland	16.68
France	17.98
Sweden	18.15
Austria	19.20
Germany	21.18
Greece	22.34
Belgium	24.94
Norway	27.33
Spain	29.28
Denmark	33.15
Portugal	35.75
Average	**21.06**

FIGURE 21.3   The Challenge of "Market on Close"
Data Source: JP MorganChase, March 2003.

PRINCIPAL TRADES

For both index and active investors, principal trades are a tool for mitigating and transferring benchmark risk from an investment manager to a sell-side brokerage firm. A *principal trade* is a transaction in which a broker acts as the counterparty and commits capital for the investor. For this service, the investor pays a risk premium, and the risk that is the difference between the trade execution and market close is transferred to the brokerage firm. However, not all markets allow principal trading. The reasons for these restrictions vary by market. There is a strong correlation between difficulty of execution and the lack of principal trading. Greece, Poland, Taiwan, Korea, Brazil, Peru, Portugal, Colombia, Mexico, and Venezuela all restrict principal trading, thus eliminating some of the tools that would ease the participation of large institutional investors.

Because some Asian market officials and regulators fear that short selling will cause market weakness or will be used to manipulate markets, they do not allow shorting. Korea and Taiwan do not permit either buy-side or sell-side firms to short stocks. In other cases, the exchanges themselves serve as the counterparty to all trades. Therefore, all trades must be transacted on the exchange on an *agency* basis.[8] This situation can also help create opportunities for portfolio managers in these markets—synthetic securities lending in Korea and Taiwan is a way to add incremental return to the portfolio.

ACHIEVING BEST EXECUTION WITH CROSS-BORDER PORTFOLIO MANAGEMENT CONSTRAINTS

Best execution refers to the implementation of trade strategy. Traders must always be mindful of achieving the best execution at the best price with the least amount of risk. The broader the trading array, the more easily a trader can "hide its hand" from the market. Brokers who execute international orders must be highly price competitive, financially sound, and on the leading edge in developing new cost-saving trading techniques. In the absence of other constraints, the trader would carve a portfolio manager's multicountry trade list into as many pieces as necessary to take advantage of brokers' strengths. However, in the international context, many constraints do exist. Dollar neutrality, cash constraints, and client restrictions impose limitations on a trader's ability to achieve best execution. These are all critical areas for the index portfolio manager to be involved in, even as a trading desk might be implementing the trades.

Similarly, portfolio managers must help decide which brokers are best suited to execute transactions in various markets. Brokers' market share, market memberships, and trading expertise are further delineated for global portfolios that include emerging markets and developed markets. Many brokers have gained market share through mergers and acquisitions, but few brokers have consistent capabilities across all global markets. Trading execution may be less optimal if a global trade list cannot be parsed into various regions or countries.

Monitoring Multiple Markets

Monitoring executions in more than one market can be problematic. Even in the age of electronic trading capabilities, not all markets have transparency and efficiency of executions printing immediately in the market. This is typically encountered in the international trading arena. Therefore, time delays in prints result in time delays for reporting or additional trading decisions. If real-time decisions need to be made, a 24-hour trading desk is necessary. If any decisions require input from a portfolio manager, this could result in waking a portfolio manager in the middle of the night. Dealing in 40 or more culturally diverse markets greatly multiplies the dynamic nature of equity markets.

One of the ways that many international equity investors (index and active) are able to bypass some of the numerous complexities and constraints of global markets is to use ADRs and Global Shares. While there is no free lunch in investing, using ADRs (and possibly tracking an ADR index instead of the broad fully replicating MSCI EAFE and FTSE World portfolios commonly used for institutional index funds) provides substantial advantages, especially for narrower portfolios. The following sidebar illustrates some of the benefits of international investing with ADRs and the brave new world of ADR index portfolios.

ADRs AND ADR INDEXES: GREAT TASTE, LESS FILLING
Kevin Maeda and Steven A. Schoenfeld

What if you could get the flavor of the international markets without all the calories and heartburn?

Using American Depository Receipts (ADRs) allows an investor to do just that. ADRs are U.S. equity securities representing a specified number of shares in a non-U.S. domiciled company. They typically trade on a U.S. exchange or over-the-counter (OTC) and are an easy vehicle for international exposure. Global Depository Receipts (GDRs) are similar to ADRs, except that they are issued and offered for sale in more than one country.

So what's so special about ADRs? ADRs allow an investor to obtain foreign exposure, but because ADRs trade in the U.S. markets just like any other U.S. stock, many of the problems associated with investing in equities outside the United States disappear.[a] With ADRs, the investor/portfolio manager does not need to execute expensive currency trades for settlement, can avoid foreign taxes and the often

---

[a] Detailed information on ADRs is available from the web sites of major ADR custody banks, which are listed in the book's E-ppendix, accessible via www.IndexUniverse.com.

cumbersome tax reclaims process, does not have an issue with trade settlement or settlement timing mismatches, need not worry about foreign restrictions on corporate actions or reaching foreign ownership limits, and avoids high foreign commission rates. An additional plus is that the manager no longer needs to worry about the "23-hour workday" and can get a good night's sleep.

This is great! So why doesn't someone build an index with ADRs? Actually, ADR indexes do exist, but they are still in their infancy stage. Bank of New York has a series of ADR Indexes, with coverage of European, Asian, and emerging markets and has ETFs listed on Nasdaq that track them. S&P has developed an ADR index based on the non-U.S. stocks from their Global 1200 index (this latter benchmark is discussed in Chapter 9). The S&P ADR index comprises 267 companies[b] that are a subset of the Global 1200 allowing an investor to easily and cost-effectively gain exposure to the international markets. In July 2003, Active Index Advisors launched the world's first index product tracking to the S&P ADR index. Much as we liked being first, we do not believe that the firm will be alone for long!

---

[b] As of September 2003. Updates of index information are available at IndexUniverse.com and at index provider sites, www.adrbny.com and www .standardandpoors.com.

ACHIEVING TOTAL PERFORMANCE MANAGEMENT

How does one track multicountry benchmarks with close to 1,000 stocks and myriad operational and transaction cost hurdles within just a few basis points and add index alpha in the process? By looking for every opportunity to add value to the portfolio. Some of the ways that happens are described in this section.

Tax Differentials and Reclaims

When we explain variance between benchmark returns and portfolio returns to clients, they are often surprised by the variance that can arise from basic index assumptions about income. It is entirely possible to track a benchmark on price performance, yet have a simple dividend throw tracking out the window. An index is a purely synthetic representation of market conditions based on a set of rules. Certain rules may be enacted to simplify calculations, yet not reflect the true nature of market events. Two key assumptions can introduce this type of error into the equation—income timing and tax treatment.

Income timing revolves around when income is accrued for the benchmark versus when it is accrued for the portfolio. From a practical point of view, a fund must account for dividend flows when they are effective in the market (ex-date). The fund experiences the benefit of the income in line with market-dictated timing. In contrast, the index rules can sometimes make different assumptions about the timing of income.

Similarly, index rules surrounding tax rates on dividend income can also profoundly affect an international portfolio's ability to track its benchmark. For a U.S. investor holding domestic securities benchmarked to a domestic index, the only complication that can arise from index tax assumptions is whether the index supplies only a gross income return number or applies a tax to dividend income and supplies a net income return number. Certainly this difference in rules can create a gap in performance between the benchmark index and the actual index fund. The same "net/gross" question still applies, but what exactly does net income mean? Net income is dependent on the perspective of the investor. In the international arena, investors of different nationalities may achieve different tax treatment for the same dividend/income item. Tax treaties between countries define whether an investor pays a country's statutory rate on dividends or can reclaim a portion of the tax value withheld.

An index that calculates a net income return number must decide which tax rate applies to dividends within each country it covers. No matter the rate implemented, there will always be a real-world portfolio with a different set of actual rates. Depending on whether the index assumes a tax rate that is more or less advantageous than the actual rate, the investor may incur underperformance or outperformance relative to the benchmark.

Reclaiming taxes withheld, however, is not a passive process. Local agencies are rarely eager to give up revenues. Each country will have its own process for reclaims, and the correct paperwork must be filed. Some countries require more documentation than others to prove ownership of securities over dividend cycles. A clear understanding of local and international tax laws is necessary to secure the most benefit for an investor and implement the reclaim process effectively.

The Use of Global Index Futures

Chapters 19 and 20 highlighted the important role of stock index futures in fund management, and the mechanics of these vital tools are described in detail in Chapter 25. Their use is particularly valuable in gaining exposure to securities on cash balances (from dividends or other accruals) that do not represent actual cash at hand. As most indexes consider dividends received and reinvested on ex-date, any portfolio not investing accrued dividends will incur tracking error. Since such cash cannot be invested directly into securities, equity exposure can only be gained through a derivative product—most commonly a futures contract.

The stock index futures available in each market are usually limited to one or two products linked to a local (often exchange-calculated) index. Once liquidity and any restrictions regarding investment in such vehicles are factored in, the actual, practical index futures investment opportunities can become fairly limited (as highlighted in the section above, Investment Restrictions and Risks). For those markets with liquid and unrestricted futures, the underlying index to which the future is linked still differs significantly from the index the portfolio must track. This is frequently the case for the global equity benchmarks that most institutional funds track, as shown in Table 21.2. Readers will note that the local indexes and the futures based on them generally track the FTSE global indexes with less tracking error.

The tracking differentials between the available futures and the actual portfolio benchmark somewhat limit their effectiveness for gaining immediate exposure to stocks and managing short-term liquidity requirements. In terms of dividends and other accruals, this is a burden the portfolio just has to bear. The level of performance mistracking indicated earlier is in many instances more desirable than having it entirely unequitized.

The performance impact of a mistracking future is heightened in many international markets by an extended time lag between the ex-date and payment date of dividends. For example, a fund attempting to track either FTSE or MSCI Japan would have a large accrual position after the large dividend ex-dates in March and September of each year (Japan's dividend season). If the fund is restricted to holding CFTC-approved futures, the only way to gain market exposure on this position is through Topix, Nikkei 225, or Nikkei 300 contracts. (While there is a futures contract

TABLE 21.2 Futures Tracking and Mistracking: Standard Deviation of Weekly Returns versus Local Flagship Index (%)

	Australia	France	Germany	Hong Kong	Japan	United Kingdom
Local index	S&P ASX 200	CAC 40	DAX	Hang Seng	Topix	FTSE 100
Versus MSCI	1.59	1.48	1.65	1.48	1.45	1.12
Versus FTSE	0.52	0.48	0.68	0.97	0.33	0.25

Source: BGI International Equity Strategy, February 2003.

based on the MSCI Japan index—and it is approved for U.S. investors—it is not sufficiently liquid.) Since none of these futures track the fund benchmark closely and accruals can represent a fairly large proportion of the fund, there is likely to be some impact on performance. As the time that dividends remain as accruals lengthen (which could sometimes be over three months), potential for mistracking increases.

Securities Lending

As discussed in previous chapters, with the variety of potentially negative consequences of frictional costs from managing a real-world portfolio, index managers try to add value—*index alpha*—wherever possible. Securities lending is a method managers can use to enhance performance. In the domestic environment, borrowing of securities may be motivated by purely speculative forces, corporate action arbitrage, or facilitation of settlement to name a few drivers. An international equity portfolio benefits from yet another major source of demand, related to the differential in tax treatment between investors of different nationalities. As stated, international tax treaties give some investors a right to a greater portion of dividends than others. When dividends go ex, a portfolio that has loaned its securities to a borrower with a preferential tax treatment can share in part of the borrower's beneficial tax status by charging higher premiums for what is essentially a free tax-arbitrage play. Some of these techniques—and more aggressive variants—are also used in enhanced index strategies, and are covered in Chapter 15.

These sources of demand to borrow securities can be worth 15 bp per year or more in incremental return for an international equity portfolio, and depending on how the income is split, can usually more than pay the investment management fee for institutional clients. (Chapter 26 discusses the importance of securities lending for asset owners.) As noted in the previous chapter, this level of added returns from international equity securities lending is significantly more than for U.S. equities, and is the primary way that international index funds for institutional investors regularly beat their benchmark.

CONCLUSION

In any language, international indexing is decidedly "anything but passive." Mastering the intricacies of a single market well enough to track an index closely takes time and experience. As described in Chapters 19 and 20, an index-based portfolio manager must make intelligent decisions about trading in a constantly fluid environment and must have a solid understanding of benchmark behavior. These same factors extend to an international portfolio. However, on leaving the "home market," new layers of complexity enter the picture. Each new market added to a portfolio brings with it different nuances in trading, corporate actions, participant restrictions, and informational time delays, all of which can potentially create benchmark mistracking. These additional factors increase the challenge of delivering performance and controlling the risks presented when managing an international index fund. As stated at the onset of this chapter, we hope you now agree with us that international indexing is a very active investment activity—and rarely boring.

NOTES

1. The major institutional index fund managers generally offer index-based strategies on at least two of these indexes. For example, as of the writing of this chapter, BGI offered commingled strategies for MSCI and FTSE, SSgA for MSCI, FTSE and S&P/Citigroup, and Northern Trust offers both MSCI and FTSE based funds. See Chapter 9 for a more detailed review of these international equity benchmarks.
2. See this chapter's web-only sidebar "Managing Political and Financial Risk in International Index Funds from B–Z—Brazil, Malaysia, Indonesia, Russia, Zimbabwe 1997—2000" by Steven A. Schoenfeld and Robert Ginis, on the book's E-ppendix, at www.activeindexinvesting.com or on www.IndexUniverse.com.
3. If there is demand to buy shares when the ownership levels are hit, buyers go into a queue and there is a chronological order of priority. Hence, if a fund sells its shares and needs to repurchase at a later date, its order is placed at the end of the queue.
4. What the index defines as "investable."
5. As first mentioned in Part Two, Standard & Poor's assumed management of these indexes in late 2003. The indexes were renamed S&P/Citigroup Global Equity Indices.
6. We hope that readers do not think we are singling out Taiwan for criticism. Taiwan, however, is one of the best examples of a highly attractive market with onerous restrictions. While the government of Taiwan has legitimate policy reasons for its capital and currency controls, relaxing some of these restrictions would greatly improve their market efficiency. For this reason, many alternative ways of accessing Taiwanese equities have developed—ADRs and ETFs, as well as liquid Taiwan Stock Index Futures listed in Singapore.
7. Andrew Freyre-Sanders, "European Closing Prices," *JP Morgan Chase Global Index and Derivatives Strategy* (London: February 2003).
8. *Agency* means that the broker takes no principal risk, acting as the "agent" for the fund manager in execution of the trading orders. This does not mean that the broker doesn't seek best execution, especially if he or she wants repeat business from their customer.

CHAPTER 22

Managing Fixed-Income Index Funds

Elizabeth Para and Partha Dasgupta

_____ **Editor's Note** _____

In this chapter, the authors explain how fixed-income indexing differs substantially from equity indexing. Because much of the book is equity index focused, they begin with an overview of the rationale for fixed-income indexing. They detail several non-derivative and derivative based methods of creating an index-tracking fixed-income portfolio and why these methods have won over active investors. The authors then evaluate each of these methods and their advantages and disadvantages, and market circumstances under which each method is practicable. A discussion of European bond ETFs is also included. Substantial information on North American fixed-income ETFs is available on IndexUniverse.com. Because the authors are London-based, they focus much of their efforts on U.K., European, and global fixed-income. This chapter has a decidedly non-U.S. perspective that gives readers an appreciation of the truly global nature of indexing.

THE GROWTH AND PREVALENCE OF INDEXED STRATEGIES IN FIXED-INCOME MARKETS

Over the past decade, indexing fixed-income portfolios has become a popular strategy among institutional investors. As noted earlier in the book, index-based funds (including nonequity investments) have grown from less than 0.2 percent of externally managed U.S. tax-exempt institutional assets in 1975 to 13.1 percent in 1996.[1] By 2001, as visible in Table 22.1, in the United States and United Kingdom, 23 percent and 29 percent of institutional equity

TABLE 22.1   Equity and Fixed-Income Indexing: Market Penetration Compared

	Mandates in Indexed Strategies (%)	
	Total Equity	Total Fixed-Income
United States	23.0	<5.0
Canada	35.0	20.0
Australia	6.4	6.0
United Kingdom	29.0	<5.0
Germany	4.0	—
Switzerland	20.0	15.0
Netherlands	15.0	5.5
Ireland	15.0	15.0
Japan	27.7	22.8
Hong Kong	5.0	—

Source: Watson Wyatt, year-end 2001.

portfolios, respectively, were indexed.[2] This trend toward indexing is expected to continue given the atmosphere of pension funds reducing their risk exposure, and some recent underperformance by high-profile active fund managers. Furthermore, in markets such as Germany and Hong Kong, one could expect general secular growth in both equity and fixed income indexing.

Several factors have contributed to the growth of index strategies in fixed-income markets. Across markets, bond issuance by nongovernment issuers has been growing, and nongovernment bonds, or credit, have claimed an increasing proportion of the bond market. The growth of credit markets has added to the complexity and expense of active management strategies, and each year investors must research a growing number of credit bond issuers. In Europe, the introduction of the Euro in 1999 created a major new bond market from 12 formerly fractured domestic markets, which is on track to rival the U.S. bond market in size. Whereas previously, a Dutch investor, for example, primarily invested in domestic Dutch government and credit bonds, the advent of the Euro required investors to have knowledge of a much broader range of issuers domiciled across the EuroZone. This encouraged many investors to choose indexed strategies. Another factor that has favored the growth of indexed strategies in bond markets has been the convergence of global government bond yields during the late 1990s and early 2000s. This convergence has made the task of earning excess returns to active management a more difficult objective.

Fixed-income indexed strategies have been increasingly used by investors because they offer several advantages over traditional active bond management. They are fivefold, and discussed next.

Performance

Similar to the empirical story told for equities in Part One, the average actively managed fixed-income fund in the United States, EuroZone, and United Kingdom has consistently underperformed the benchmark market index significantly, after fees, according to empirical studies, as portrayed in Figures 22.1 through 22.3 on this and following pages. Naturally, Figure 22.3 on Euro-Zone relative performance, has a short timeframe, as the Euro only came into existence in 1999.

Lower Cost

Fixed-income indexed strategies have lower cost in a number of dimensions: lower management fees, which can be attributed to the fact that indexed strategies are less costly to manage than traditional active strategies, and lower security turnover.

Security turnover is a drag on portfolio performance because with each purchase or sale of a security, the investor pays away the bid/ask spread. In

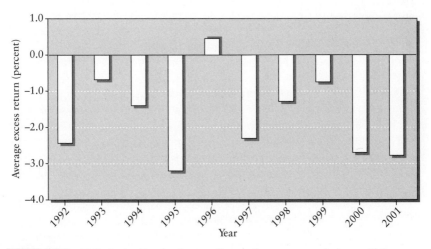

FIGURE 22.1 U.S. Active Funds: Average Excess Return versus Lehman U.S. Aggregate Index
Source: Barclays Global Investors.

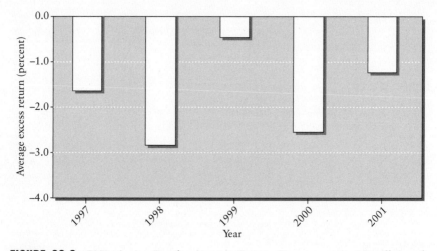

FIGURE 22.2   U.K. Active Funds: Average Excess Return versus Merrill Lynch
Sterling Broad Index
Source: Barclays Global Investors.

bond markets, transaction costs can be significant, depending on the liquidity
of the specific market and security. Table 22.2 outlines how the cost
of transacting in various bonds can vary from a relatively small cost, on a
U.S. Treasury bond, to a significant consideration, on some of the less liquid
Euro corporate bonds.

The turnover of an indexed portfolio, with limited its cash flows,
should be very close to the turnover of the benchmark index, which is relatively low and stable.

A traditionally managed active bond portfolio that seeks opportunities
to outperform an index by buying securities expected to increase in value
and then selling the securities to realize the profit will typically have a much
higher turnover ratio than the benchmark index. An active strategy would
need to take into account turnover and transaction costs to overcome this
shortcoming. This becomes especially important in fixed-income markets,
where transaction costs can be prohibitive on particular issues.

Indexed portfolios are also less expensive to manage because they invest in the benchmark securities, without taking any view on those securities. Therefore, an indexed strategy does not incur the cost of security and
issuer research. Consider, for example, the U.S. Credit market, with 7,000
issues in the benchmark Lehman U.S. Aggregate Index. It is apparent how
significant that saving can be.

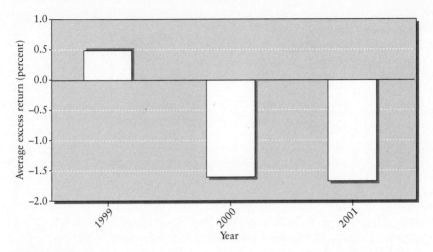

FIGURE 22.3   European (EuroZone) Active Bond Funds: Average Excess Return versus Benchmark
Source: Barclays Global Investors.

Greater Portfolio Diversification Equals Lower Risk

Empirically, indexed portfolios tend to hold more securities than traditional actively managed funds. This allows them to better diversify away nonsystematic, or security-specific risk. Bond investors are sensitive to issuer specific event risk—namely default on bond obligations, or other negative credit

TABLE 22.2   Bond Transaction Costs

Type of Bond	Average Bid/Ask Spread	Cost to Trade Nominal Amount $/€ 10 Million of Bonds
Most Liquid		
U.S. Treasury 10-year benchmark bond	1/32nd	$10mm × (1/32)/100 = $3,125
Euro government 10-year bond	0.02–0.05%	€10mm × 0.04% = €4,000
Liquid euro corporate bond	0.10%	€10mm × 0.10% = €10,000
Least Liquid		
Less liquid euro corporate bond	0.75%	€10mm × 0.75% = €75,000

Note that bonds are price in percentage of face value terms, so a price of 100.04 actually means, 100.04 percent of face value.
Source: Barclays Global Investors, Sharmin Mossaca-Rahmani, *Bond Index Funds* (New York: McGraw-Hill Education, 1990).

events, so diversifying issuer and issue exposure within a fixed-income port-folio is especially important.

A bond investor does not participate in the upside of the issuer's prof-itability, but relies heavily on the probability of a company not going into default in order to guarantee payment on fixed-bond obligations. If a com-pany defaults, a bondholder receives nothing, but for holding this risk, a bondholder does not receive any participation in the upside potential for company profitability. Therefore, a bond investor is heavily exposed to de-fault risk, and the interests of the equity and bond holders can be opposed, with equity holders being incentivized to leverage a company to the maxi-mum extent in order to increase growth and profit, and bond holders being interested in the minimum leverage possible, to reduce the risk of default. Consider a bond portfolio that holds 20 bonds in equal proportion and earns 4 percent per annum yield. If one of those bonds were to default, as-suming a recovery value of 0, the 5 percent capital loss to the portfolio would wipe out more than the 4 percent coupon yield being earned by the portfolio. This illustrates the fact that diversification of issuer exposure within a bond portfolio is especially important.

The greater the number of benchmark securities that a portfolio holds, the lower its expected tracking error versus benchmark is. Therefore, within an indexed strategy, a portfolio manager will aim to hold as broad a swathe of the benchmark as is practical.

Greater Investor Control over Investment Decisions

Because indexed-portfolio management is a very rule-based process, the in-vestor has greater control over what types of investments are held in his or her portfolio, and how investment decisions are taken. He or she is less ex-posed to the subjective views of an individual portfolio manager. Within a traditional actively managed bond portfolio, a portfolio manager has the freedom to expose the investor to whatever degree of issuer exposure and is-suer concentration that he or she deems appropriate, and to credit risk (for example, investments in high yield bonds) and interest rate risk that he or she deems appropriate, within the specific risk concentration limits and any other restrictions in place.

Lower Manager Selection Risk

As with equity indexing, the objective of an indexed strategy is to match benchmark returns, and the process used to achieve this is extremely objec-tive. Therefore, an indexed strategy's performance is generally immunized against individual portfolio manager turnover. In a more traditional active management framework, given the sheer number of bond issues and the multidimensional risk exposures managed within a bond portfolio, different individuals may manage a portfolio in very different ways. When the portfolio manager responsible for historic performance leaves a firm or when portfolio management duties are delegated to another individual portfolio manager, fund performance of a traditional active fund can change significantly.

INDEX-BASED FIXED-INCOME FUND MANAGEMENT METHODOLOGY

As discussed in Chapter 19, there are several methods of creating an index-tracking portfolio. The major non-derivative-based methodologies are similar to those used for equity indexing, namely *Full Replication, Factor-Based Optimization* (or Quadratic Optimization), and *Stratified Sampling*. Derivative-based solutions include the use of futures, credit derivatives, and index total return swaps. As with equities, each of these methods has its advantages and disadvantages, and each is best applicable in various market circumstances and for different investment structures.

Full Replication

Full Replication involves holding each of an index's constituent bonds in exactly the same proportion as the index. At each index rebalance, the index-tracking portfolio is also rebalanced to maintain the same proportional exposure to each bond as the index. Full Replication minimizes the risk of tracking error versus the index to the greatest degree practicable, and from that perspective, is the most desirable index-tracking methodology.

Full Replication is not always practical in bond markets, though, and certainly less so than for broad equity indexes. In order for a portfolio to fully replicate an index, the portfolio must be of sufficient size to invest in each of the constituent bonds in the correct proportions. Therefore, the number of constituent securities in an index directly bears upon a portfolio's ability to fully replicate the index. If the index is small enough, for example, the FTSE U.K. Gilt All stocks index, which is comprised of only 30 bonds, then a portfolio need only gain exposure to 30 issues to fully replicate the index. The same task is impossible for a portfolio attempting to track the Lehman U.S. Aggregate Index, which is comprised of over 7,000 bonds. A portfolio manager must also bear in mind that, not only do bonds trade in minimum size increments (usually $1,000 increments or greater), but to gain tight, competitive pricing on a bond, one often must trade in institutional sized blocs ($1 million to $100 million, depending on the particular bond).

Furthermore, for a portfolio to invest in all of an index's constituents, each of those bonds must be liquid and available in the market. In bond markets, not all issues trade every day. In fact, many bond issues are purchased by retail and other accounts at issuance, and are held until maturity, becoming unavailable in the market for trading. Therefore, many issues that are large enough to be included in a bond index will not be liquid. Furthermore, the OTC nature of the bond market makes it impossible to know who holds specific bond issues, what the average daily trading volume is, or even to gain reliable information on what the bid-and-ask spread on a particular bond issue is, as this might vary from market maker to market maker. The fallout of this is that bond indices cannot always be fully replicated the way many equity indices can, and liquid bond indices are better candidates for full replication than broader indices.

Factor-Based Optimization

Factor-Based Optimization, a quantitative approach to analyzing risk exposures, can be used when a specific portfolio is not large enough to fully replicate the benchmark it is meant to track. As in equity index optimization, risk factors are identified, which may cause the portfolio to differ in characteristics and performance from the index. However, the factors are quite different than those in equity models. These factors are likely to be currency, duration, sector, quality, yield curve, liquidity, and issuer exposure measures. A linear objective function and constraints are then constructed, using linear regression, where tracking error is a function of the risk factors, and the portfolio is constrained by predetermined limits on these risk factors. For example, constraints can be set on the tolerance for issuer exposure mismatch, or tolerance for duration mismatch. This objective function is then minimized (i.e., minimize tracking error), subject to the constraints.

Factor-Based Optimization is a sampling technique, but unlike Stratified Sampling, the solution of the optimization process is unique. Any fund manager using the optimization process, with the same inputs, will end up with the same optimal, sampled portfolio. The advantage of this process is that it is totally quantitative and objective.

While a reasonably successful technique in equity markets, Factor-Based Optimization is not normally practical in fixed-income markets. Several of the risk factors, for example liquidity, are not easily quantifiable. Liquidity constraints also make optimization models difficult to implement in real markets, where often the optimal bond selected from the index universe is simply not available in sufficient size (or at all) in the market, whereas de-signing constraints that would optimize a portfolio subject to bond issue availability and liquidity is too complex a model to be robust.

Stratified Sampling

For fixed income portfolios, Stratified Sampling is the next preferred index-ing methodology after Full Replication. While it allows sampling errors to increase the expected tracking error versus the index above that of a fully replicated portfolio, it is generally the more practical solution in bond mar-kets, where issues can be too numerous and liquidity is often too great a con-straint to allow Full Replication.

Given the multiple dimensions of risk within a bond portfolio (currency, credit, sector, issuer, maturity/yield curve, liquidity), sampling and risk con-trol are complex processes. The solution is to stratify, or divide an index into manageable risk buckets. *(Editor's note: Readers should notice that unlike two-dimensional Stratified Sampling for equity indexing described in Chap-ter 19, bond indexing usually is multidimensional.)*

The benchmark index is generally subdivided according to the follow-ing six risk characteristics:

1. Currency.
2. Maturity.
3. Credit rating.
4. Sector (or country for government bond portfolios).
5. Liquidity.
6. Issuer.

The most complex case is a multicurrency index, the Citigroup (formerly Salomon) WorldBIG, for example. A multicurrency index is first subdivided by currency. Currency is normally the greatest risk factor in an international fixed-income portfolio (see Table 22.3).

Each currency group is now treated like a separate subindex. Within each currency group, the subindex is stratified by the various dimensions of risk, as portrayed in Figure 22.4.

This approach turns the complex task of matching multidimensional risk into a more manageable risk buckets. Figure 22.4 illustrates how the index has been "sliced and diced" into cells, each cell defined by maturity, credit rating, and sector. The highlighted cell contains all of the index bonds that fall between 7 and 10 years maturity, AA credit rating, in the financial sector. (In practice, credit rating and sector are often even more finely spec-ified. For example, AA3, investment bank subsector.)

TABLE 22.3 Citigroup[a] World Broad Investment Grade
Index—Market Capitalization and Weights, October 2003

	Market Cap (US$ Billions)	Weight (%)	Number of Issues
U.S. dollar	7,174	44.57	2,283
Euro	5,256	32.80	1,429
Japanese yen	2,520	15.72	226
British pound	596	3.72	218
Canadian dollar	185	1.15	28
Danish kroner	101	0.63	11
Swiss franc	63	0.39	18
Swedish kroner	75	0.47	8
Polish	34	0.21	17
Australian dollar	30	0.19	9
Norweigan kroner	23	0.14	5

[a] Formerly Salomon Smith Barney.

Basic characteristics are calculated for each cell:

1. Average yield.
2. Average duration.
3. Average option adjusted spread.
4. Average convexity.
5. Number of bonds.
6. Number of issuers.
7. Liquidity.
8. Weight of cell within the index.

A cell may contain 50 bonds, for example, but for the reasons discussed earlier, it may be impractical to invest in all 50. Therefore, the portfolio manager might sample 10 bonds out of the 50 in this cell, with the objective of creating a sampled cell of 10 bonds with the same characteristics as the parent cell. The characteristics are calculated for this sampled cell to ensure that this is true, within tolerance.

When sampling, special consideration is paid to liquidity and issuer diversification. It is important to match the cells liquidity exposure when sampling, because less liquid bonds carry higher yields (the liquidity premium), and a portfolio that invested only in the most liquid bonds would, over longer time periods, be expected to underperform an index that included less liquid

Credit Portfolio: Government Bond Portfolio:

Maturity   Maturity
credit rating   country
sector

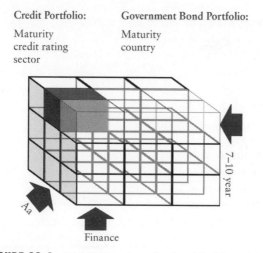

FIGURE 22.4   Risk Dimensions for Stratified Sampling

issues. Issuer exposure that closely matches the benchmark is also essential, to ensure that the sampled portfolio's performance will respond in a similar proportion to issuer specific events, such as a credit up or downgrade.

Once each cell is sampled, the sample cells are put back together into the sampled bond portfolio. This sampled portfolio must be stress tested against different moves in the yield curve, to ensure that it will react in the same proportion as the index itself. Figure 22.5 shows the results of such a stress test.

The ability to break an index down into key risk components and to analyze and index and portfolio according to multidimensional risk criteria is the key to indexed portfolio management. Therefore, just like in equity indexing, a large investment in powerful portfolio analysis systems is essential, confirming why index fund management is a scale business.

TRACKING ERROR

The number of bonds that a sampled portfolio holds is directly determined by the size of the portfolio. A portfolio of $1 billion, in practice, can be diversified over many more issues and can be fine-tuned to match the risk characteristics of the benchmark index to a far greater extent than a smaller portfolio. Bonds often trade in minimum size increments, usually above $1,000. Larger trade sizes also often attract more favorable, institutional pricing, reducing the drag of transaction costs to the portfolio.

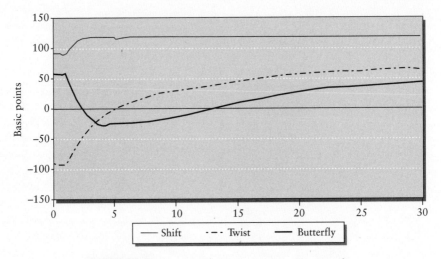

FIGURE 22.5 Stratified Sampling Stress Test Results

The more bonds that a portfolio can efficiently hold, while bearing in mind that small trade sizes can result in unfavorable pricing in bond markets, the lower the tracking error of the portfolio should be versus the benchmark.

If you were to map the relationship between the number of bonds in a portfolio and the expected tracking error versus index, the relationship would look like that depicted in Figure 22.6. As the number of bonds held increases, the portfolio is better able to match the risk factors that create performance differences between the portfolio and the index. These risk factors, *in order of importance,* are: currency, duration, sector, quality, yield curve, liquidity, and issuer exposure.

In the example depicted in Figure 22.6, we have an index that contains 800 bonds. Holding 10 bonds, the portfolio would be expected to track the 800-bond index with a rather wide tracking error, in the order of 60 or 70 basis points (bps) per annum. If the number of bonds in the portfolio is increased to 100, the tracking error quickly falls to a more attractive 20 to 25 bps. With more bonds in the portfolio, the fund manager also has more flexibility to match index risk characteristics within the portfolio, such as currency, duration, sector, quality, and yield curve. The tracking error in a credit portfolio drops very dramatically as the first 50 to 100 bonds are added to the portfolio because the portfolio manager is better able to match index issuer exposure within the sampled portfolio, ensuring that the portfolio will respond in the same way to issuer-specific events as the benchmark index.

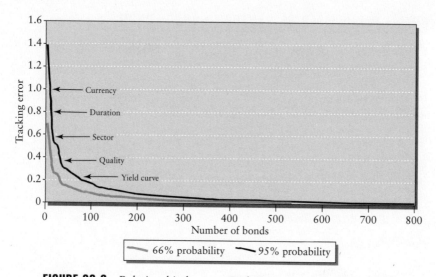

FIGURE 22.6 Relationship between Risk Factors and Tracking Error

BOND FUTURES

Bond futures can also be used as a substitute for government bonds in indexing strategies. For example, consider a portfolio whose objective is to track the performance of a U.S. government bond index with a duration of 5 years. Futures contracts are available in a number of maturities/durations, and thus can be used to match index duration. The portfolio can hold a combination of 5- and 10-year U.S. Treasury bond futures, such that the weighted average duration of the two futures positions is also 5 years. Some futures contracts, like U.S. Treasury futures and German Bund Futures, are more liquid than government bonds, facilitating large trades more easily. Their characteristic liquidity and tight bid/ask spreads make synthetic bond indexing portfolios based on futures a very cost effective alternative. Futures are also operationally tax efficient compared to bonds that are subject to withholding tax, such as Japanese and Swiss government bonds.

In a market shock scenario as well, futures, as the more liquid instrument, may be the best (and sometimes only) way to obtain bond market exposure. A disadvantage of using futures as a substitute for bonds is that there is always some tracking error (basis) between the government bond being simulated and the futures contract itself. Also, futures contracts are currently available mainly on government bonds, so it is not yet possible to use them as a substitute for credit bonds.

CREDIT DERIVATIVES OR SYNTHETIC BOND FUNDS

Credit derivatives can be used to track credit and emerging market debt. In some markets, for example the European credit market, the credit default swap (CDS) market for many issuers is more liquid than the underlying bond market because CDSs can be based on a wider range of debt, including tradable loans and letters of credit. Within a portfolio, CDSs are held to gain credit exposure, while a high quality, AAA rated bond is held to match duration. Holding CDSs introduces new types of risk to the portfolio, however, such as counterparty risk. Furthermore, like futures, there is a varying basis between CDSs and the underlying bonds being tracked.

Index Total Return Swaps

Index swaps agree to pay out a total return exactly matching the return of a specific index. This gives the investor zero tracking error relative to the benchmark, less any transaction costs. Unfortunately, transaction costs, at present, tend to be quite substantial. Because the counterparty receiving fixed payments and paying index returns must hedge its exposure, total return swaps transfer the responsibility for creating an index-tracking portfolio to this counterparty. Index total return swaps have several disadvantages, the major disadvantage being that they are not very liquid. If an investor wants to enter into a total return swap based on a Citigroup index, he is unlikely to find any counterparty for that swap, other than Citigroup.

Furthermore, index swaps are difficult to hedge. While index swaps transfer responsibility for hedging index returns to the swap writer, the cost of that hedging is reflected in the bid/ask spread of the swap. If a particular swap is actively traded, then a dealer can hedge his obligation to pay index returns by entering into an equal and opposite transaction with another party to receive index returns. For less liquid index swaps, the only way the dealer can hedge the swap is with a bond portfolio designed to track the index's return. Because index swaps guarantee the index return, the risk of tracking error is built into the swap price. In addition, because swap dealers are not specialized managers of index-tracking funds, you can safely assume that they are unlikely to be able to build a bond portfolio which will efficiently track an index's performance with minimized tracking error. Therefore, the cost of a total return index swap will be greater than the management fee on an index-tracking bond portfolio.

Swap agreements expose the portfolio to counterparty risk. Index swaps are normally written for fixed term, and being fairly illiquid, are difficult to amend. For example, if an investor enters into a two-year index swap, and at some later date the portfolio's mandate changes, it is not easy or inexpensive to cancel the swap or shorten its term. Because index swaps are so illiquid, they trade at a very wide bid/ask spread relative to indexed portfolio management fees from an established indexed fund manager.

OTC Index-Tracking Notes

Index-tracking notes are special purpose vehicles whose return is linked to an underlying portfolio of bonds. Examples of index-tracking notes are Tracers from Morgan Stanley, Trains™ from Lehman Brothers, and JECIs from JP Morgan. Underlying each of these notes is a static portfolio of bonds or CDSs that, like a managed index-tracking bond portfolio, is constructed to track an index. The tracking error achieved by OTC index tracking notes versus a broad market index, however, tends to be much wider than a managed indexed portfolio, because of the limited number of bonds in the underlying portfolio (normally 30 to 100 bonds or CDSs), and the static nature of the portfolios, versus a dynamically managed bond portfolio.

Because the notes are based on static bond portfolios, as the index rebalances over time, the performance of the note tends to deviate from the index over longer periods. Therefore, a new series of notes is produced periodically (usually quarterly, semi-annually or annually), and investors must undertake the administratively cumbersome roll from the old note series into the new note series. The notes do offer investors greater ability to quickly trade in and out of a market, in one single trade, however, and the ability to short trade a market.

EXCHANGE-TRADED FUNDS

Most institutional and retail investors gain exposure to index-tracking strategies through indexed funds, which can be structured as pooled/comingled funds, with many distinct investors, or as segregated accounts, managed exclusively for one client. Derivative strategies can also offer investors an index-tracking return profile. There are also relatively new (to bond markets), innovative investment tools, called exchange-traded funds (ETFs), that have recently been introduced to fixed-income markets. They are expanding the alternatives for both end-investors and portfolio managers.

Bond ETFs combine the tradability of futures and OTC index-tracking notes, with the low tracking error of a dynamically managed bond portfolio. They thus advance the state of the art for many elements of the bond market.

Fixed-income ETFs have the following attractive features:

■ Allow investors and traders to buy or sell a market index in one trade, through one security.

■ Combine the benefits of futures and funds into a new investment vehicle.

■ Can be traded on an exchange or OTC.

■ Track a market index, giving investors market exposure, market risk, and market return.

■ Are completely transparent, as constituent securities and weights are published daily.

■ Have a low expense ratio.

■ Have multiple market makers, ensuring competitive pricing and liquidity.

For more details on the power and flexibility of these instruments, see the sidebar on fixed income ETFs, in Chapter 16 and the additional feature on European Corporate Bond ETFs in the E-ppendix, at www.ActiveIndexInvesting.com accessible via IndexUniverse.com.

INDEX REBALANCES

Bond indices typically rebalance monthly, although rebalance frequency can be anywhere from daily (FTSE U.K. Government Gilt index) to quarterly (€ liquid indices). When an index rebalances, the universe of possible bonds is reevaluated against the inclusion criteria of the index. Bonds may drop out, or fall in weight, due to falling below the minimum maturity, being downgraded below the minimum credit rating, issuer buybacks, embedded call option exercise, default, and so on. New bonds enter the index to reflect new issuance in the market, bonds upgraded above the minimum credit rating, issue size increases, and so on.

The bulk of an index-based bond portfolio's trades will take place around index rebalance dates, which are generally at or close to month/quarter end. Bonds that have fallen out of the index are sold from the portfolio, and bonds that are new entrants to the index are purchased for the portfolio. In a sampled portfolio, the new index is sliced and diced into multidimensional risk buckets, and the characteristics of the existing portfolio are evaluated against the new, rebalanced index. The portfolio will then be rebalanced when and as much as necessary, to bring the portfolio's characteristics back into line with that of the rebalanced index.

A portfolio is also rebalanced, compared, and stress tested against the index when there are cash flows in or out of the fund, and when there are events that will foreseeably change the index once it is rebalanced. For example, consider a new bond that is issued on August 15. The portfolio manager may be able to forecast, based on the index rules, that this new bond will enter the index on August 30, when the index rebalances, but liquidity and availability in the new issue may be best around the issuance date, when bond dealers have plenty of inventory to sell. Therefore, in the interest of incurring lower transaction costs and ensuring that he or she can purchase the number of bonds needed, the portfolio manager may choose to buy the bonds at issuance, anticipating that the bond will enter the index at the next rebalance. The tradeoff against the benefits of trading at new issuance is that the portfolio is opening itself up to some increased risk of tracking error versus the index, which will not include the new bond for another two weeks.

COST MINIMIZATION

As with stock index funds, transaction costs are both a detractor from absolute portfolio returns, as well as a source of negative tracking error, causing an indexed portfolio to consistently underperform any benchmark index that does not take into account transaction costs. (Most benchmarks do not.) As discussed earlier in the chapter, transaction costs in bond markets can be prohibitively high. Therefore, it is important to minimize the costs of all trading.

Cost management often involves a trade-off with respect to tracking performance in other ways though. For example, a skillful fund manager must manage the trade off between the higher trading cost of less liquid bonds and the lower yields and risk of increased tracking error caused by holding only the liquid bonds in an index. Consider portfolio A constructed entirely of reasonably liquid bonds with an average bid/ask spread on those bonds of 10 bps and an average yield of 5 percent. Compare this to portfolio B constructed entirely of less liquid issues with an average yield of 6 percent, but an average bid/ask spread of 90 bps. If portfolio turnover is high, then portfolio B will underperform A. If security turnover is low, then portfolio B, with its higher yield, should outperform portfolio A, assuming all other variables remain unchanged. Realistically, a portfolio manager will select a mix of liquid and less liquid bonds within one portfolio and will try to limit trading activities to the more liquid issues, insofar as possible, to avoid paying wider bid/ask spreads.

Larger trade sizes can attract more competitive pricing, but if a portfolio manager holds significantly fewer issues in an attempt to minimize trading costs, he or she also increases the expected tracking error of the portfolio. All trading decisions within the portfolio must therefore be made according to the joint objective of minimizing tracking error, and minimizing cost. Turnover should be minimized to avoid paying transaction costs. Where trading is necessary, cost minimization techniques can be used. For example, cash flows in and out of the fund should be used to the maximum

lance the portfolio. Cash flows that are reinvested or divested
tfolio simultaneously with an index rebalance are most efficient.
nd is being sold by one portfolio and purchased by another
e same fund management company, then, where permitted, the
managers can engage in what is called *crossing*. Crossing involves
ties or portfolios trading at mid-market, allowing the bid/ask spread
oorne by each portfolio, rather than trading in the open market twice
ncurring the full bid/ask spread. In an OTC market, like bond markets,
re prices are not transparent, market knowledge, size, and clout are im-
rtant, too. Not everyone receives the same price for the same bond.
arger, more powerful investors can receive more favorable bond pricing,
and maintain more relationships with brokers, giving them access to more
competitive prices.

PORTFOLIO CONSTRUCTION

Sampling errors will occur in all sampled portfolios, because sampling
implies that the portfolio is not exposed to every bond in the index, and
usually, not every issuer either. Therefore, not all security-specific or issuer-
specific returns will be reflected in a sampled portfolio's returns. For example, exposure to a bond that is not in the benchmark index, or an overweight
exposure to an issuer, relative to the index, can result in significant underperformance versus benchmark in the event of a downgrade, default, or other
issuer-specific events.

Furthermore, when constructing a sampled portfolio, it is not always
possible to match all of the index's risk characteristics exactly. For example,
the bond portfolio manager may aim to match index characteristics within
preset tolerances, as displayed in Table 22.4.

TABLE 22.4   Index Tolerances

Characteristic	Benchmark	Sampled Portfolio Tolerance
Weight	1.79	± 0.05
Average duration	6.62	± 0.05
Average yield	5.88	± 0.05
Average OAS	77	± 5
Number of bonds	16	4
Number of issuers	12	4

Thus, by nature, a sampled portfolio is always subject to tracking-error risk. A portfolio manager can minimize the expected tracking error by minimizing risk characteristic mismatches between the index and the sampled portfolio to the extent possible, given constraints such as portfolio size.

Transaction costs, which can be significant—or even prohibitive—in bond markets, are always a negative contributor to tracking error. Part of the job of an index portfolio manager is to make up for the deadweight cost of trading. The three challenges and opportunities highlighted below provide further insight into the bond index portfolio management process.

Taxes and Tax Reclaims

Several countries impose coupon income withholding tax (e.g., Japanese government bonds), and transaction taxes (e.g., each transaction in a Swiss bond incurs a tax charge). Income withholding and other forms of tax cause negative tracking error, because bond indices do not take their effect into account. Tax reclaims, because they occur with a lag, then contribute to positive tracking error.

Pricing Differences

Index valuations and fund net asset value (NAV) depends on the price source used. In the OTC bond market, with little price transparency, one source's price for an individual bond can vary widely from another price source. Unlike an exchange-traded equity market, there is no agreed-upon closing price for even the most liquid bonds.

Trades in index securities do not always take place at the same level as the index price for that security. The timing of index prices, versus the timing of portfolio trades, is one major contributor to this. A fund will not necessarily execute all of its trades at 3 P.M., just because this is when its benchmark index is priced. Holiday period illiquidity and other factors can also contribute to difficulty in matching index prices. Because cash holdings within the portfolio earn nothing, or a very low money market rate, cash holdings within a portfolio create tracking errors, and need to be carefully managed.

Securities Lending

As in equity indexing, securities lending is a positive contributor to tracking error. Lending revenues within a portfolio can be significant if the portfolio holds less liquid bonds, where market participants have bid up the rate at which one can borrow a bond, in order to access limited liquidity. For example, a portfolio may be able to lend a sought-after but small corporate bond issue in the Euro market at premium over the rate at which it would lend a liquid benchmark government. This is similar to the higher securities lending demand for small-cap equities.

RISK CONTROL WITHIN INDEXED PORTFOLIOS

Within an indexed portfolio, the primary task is to match the benchmark index's risk characteristics within the portfolio to deliver performance which mirrors that of the benchmark. But there are numerous additional risk dimensions, in addition to currency, duration, sector, quality, and yield curve, which need to be addressed within the portfolio management process. We highlight six of them below.

Issuer Risk

If issuer exposure within the portfolio is close to issuer weights within the index, the portfolio should mirror the index's performance with respect to issuer-specific events, such as a downgrade or default. Because most bond indices are market capitalization weighted, however, they can hold large exposures to major bond issuers, who can be some of the most leveraged companies in the investment universe. An investor may choose to impose issuer concentration limits to offset this risk, at the expense of higher tracking error.

Credit Risk

Lower rated bonds are considered to have a higher probability of default than higher rated bonds, and compensate for this added risk through higher yields (credit risk premium). An investor may choose to limit his exposure to credit risk by stipulating a minimum credit rating, or minimum average credit rating for the portfolio, for example U.S. investment grade bonds, excluding BBB-rated bonds. In this case, the benchmark being tracked is customized, for example, to Lehman U.S. Aggregate, ex-BBB.

Interest Rate Risk

Within an indexed portfolio, as long as the portfolio's exposure along the yield curve matches that of the benchmark index, the portfolio should mirror the performance of the index under various changes of shape to the yield curve. The longer the duration of a bond is, however, the greater the resulting price volatility will be, with respect to a shift up or down in yields. An investor may be seeking to match short- or long-term liabilities, and, for that reason, may wish to decrease or increase his portfolio's duration, by investing only in the short end of the curve, or the long end of the curve, respectively. In this case, the benchmark index can be customized, for example, to € Sovereign 1 to 5 years Bond Index, or a U.S. Treasury 15-year plus index.

Counterparty Risk

Counterparty risk is the risk that the entity on the other side of an investment instrument, like a swap, for example, fails to deliver on its payment obligations. To protect against counterparty risk, an investor can stipulate a minimum credit rating for any trading counterparty, and a maximum counterparty exposure limit within a portfolio.

Volatility Risk

As interest rates move up and down, bond portfolios with longer durations will be more sensitive to interest rate volatility than shorter duration portfolios. To protect against interest rate volatility, an investor can stipulate a maximum portfolio duration, or select a shorter duration benchmark index.

Reinvestment and Prepayment Risk

Bonds purchased in a high interest rate environment lock in high yields for a portfolio, until they are sold. For example, if an investor purchases a bond at par, with an annual yield of 5 percent, he will earn an annual yield of 5 percent per annum for as long as he holds the bond, regardless of whether interest rates are going up or down (ignoring capital gains/losses and mark to market valuation of portfolio holdings). As coupons are paid, however, he will have to re-invest at current interest rates. If rates have risen, he will be able to re-invest his coupon income in bond markets at more favorable rates, but if rates have fallen, the available re-investment opportunities will be less favorable.

In the context of an index-tracking portfolio, if a bond falls out of the index, and the portfolio manager needs to sell her position in that issue, she will realize any capital gains or losses on the portfolio, but she will also face re-investment risk, as she must re-invest the money at current market rates. Mortgage-Backed Securities (MBSs) are extremely sensitive to re-investment risk, because people prepay their mortgages when rates are falling in order to take advantage of opportunities to re-finance their mortgages at more favorable rates. The holder of an MBS, however, when it comes to re-investing these prepayments, also faces lower interest rate opportunities for investment.

CONCLUSION

Indexed fund strategies have grown in popularity over the past two decades, due to the underperformance of the average active fund manager, low management fees, greater diversification, lower risk (relative to benchmark), and the transparent nature of index strategies. While theoretically, index-tracking portfolio management methodology is straightforward and easy to comprehend, the process requires a major investment in systems that can analyze the risk characteristics of a sampled portfolio versus its benchmark index in order to manage efficiently and minimize operational error, making indexed fund management a scale business. A similarly large commitment of well-trained human resources is also needed. The indexing process in bond markets is significantly differentiated from equity-indexed fund management, where illiquidity, the sheer breadth of issues in a typical fixed-income benchmark, and the nontransparent nature of the OTC bond markets present significant challenges.

Therefore, while fixed-income indexed fund management is often deceptively referred to as *passive bond management*. In fact, indexed-bond management—like its equity-indexing counterpart—is a truly *active* investment management process.

NOTES

1. "25 Years of Indexing: An Analysis of the Costs and Benefits." Study published by PricewaterhouseCoopers and Barclays Global Investors, July 1998.
2. Watson Wyatt, Annual Survey, 2001.

Managing Exchange-Traded Funds

Lisa Chen and Patrick O'Connor

Editor's Note

In this chapter, the authors, two portfolio managers at Barclays Global Investors (BGI), provide insight into what it takes to manage an exchange-traded fund (ETF) portfolio and how it's different from managing "traditional" index mutual funds. This chapter addresses virtually all possible questions you may have about the intricacies of ETFs, from portfolio management strategies focusing on cost control to regulatory and compliance guidelines to tax-loss harvesting strategies. It also picks up where Chapter 16 left off, namely, showing how the creation process turns a portfolio of stocks into ETF shares. Absorbing this chapter, along with Chapters 16 and 25, will give readers a comprehensive understanding of ETFs.

This is a behind-the-scenes look at all of the detailed work involved in ETF portfolio management. Insightful examples are given for both domestic and international equity ETFs, although there is no treatment of fixed income ETFs. The authors also cover the treatment of index reconstitutions on specific index families on which BGI's iShares track, including details of how BGI handled the major Morgan Stanley Capital Investment (MSCI) index changes discussed in Chapters 5 and 9.

The chapter also includes a first-person viewpoint of what portfolio managers go through during a major index reconstitution—particularly when other things are not going exactly right. I am sure that readers will gain an appreciation for the continuous multi-tasking of index fund managers.

The authors and editor would like to acknowledge and thank Lois Towers, Scott Balentine, David Lenik, and Lance Kinkead for their thorough review and thoughtful comments on this chapter. Their support in the critical area of compliance is part of what helps make ETFs the efficient and powerful investment tools that they are.

During the 1990s, bull markets and expanding economies piqued retail investor interest in investing. With the pervasion of market information and investment advice into daily life, investing became a subject widely discussed with investors comparing hot mutual funds at cocktail parties. Armed with increasingly sophisticated investment knowledge, more individuals felt comfortable choosing stocks and funds.

But as investors were becoming more investment savvy, many traditional investment products were no longer fulfilling investors' needs. This combined with the continuing realization and acceptance that indexing should be part of any portfolio and a complement to an active investment strategy has created a positive backdrop for the introduction of ETFs. The result has been an explosion of ETFs available to retail and institutional investors alike. As discussed in Chapter 16, these products contain many improvements over traditional mutual funds and are attractive because they offer flexible, cost-effective, and tax efficient solutions for a variety of investment and trading strategies.

THE GLOBAL SCOPE OF EXCHANGE-TRADED FUNDS

At the end of 2003, there were 281 primary ETF listings on 28 exchanges around the world, with assets totaling $211 billion, according to data collected by Morgan Stanley.[1] Much of the asset growth has been during the 2000 to 2003 period, with over 70 percent of assets concentrated in the United States. Pockets of substantial ETF assets also exist in Europe, Canada, and Japan, and product innovation is occurring around the world.

With more than 20 ETF managers/sponsors around the world, only a few are global players. They include Barclays Global Investors with iShares and iUnits; State Street Global Advisors with Standard & Poor's Depositary Receipts (SPDRs), streetTRACKS and DIAMONDS; and Merrill Lynch with their Holding Company Depositary Receipts (HOLDRs; which are not truly ETFs, as discussed in Chapter 16). Large U.S.-only ETF players include the Bank of New York with the QQQ's and Midcap SPDR, and Vanguard with their ever-expanding VIPERS series.

Canada was the first country to introduce ETFs with the original TIPS/HIPS products in 1989. These products were Index Participation Units based on the TSE 35 Index and TSE 100 Index, later merging into the S&P/TSE 60 iUnits (i60) ETF in March 2000 and managed by Barclays Global Investors. In November 2000, BGI Canada was the first firm to offer fixed-income ETFs.

The first successful U.S. ETF began trading in January 1993 and was named S&P Depository Receipts (SPDRs) or *Spiders,* tracking the S&P 500 Index. It was developed by the American Stock Exchange (AMEX) and is managed by State Street Global Advisors (SSgA). It is currently the largest

U.S. ETF by assets. To date, the AMEX has dominated the market for primary ETF listings in the United States. In July 2001, the New York Stock Exchange (NYSE) cross-listed three major ETFs: the Nasdaq-100 Index Tracking Stock (QQQ), SPDRs (SPY), and Dow Jones Industrial Average ETF DIAMONDS (DIA) and the NYSE has expanded its primary listings in 2003 and 2004. The largest ETF provider of funds in the United States is BGI, with over 80 fund offerings. The firm has been in the U.S. ETF market since 1996 when 17 World Equity Benchmark Shares (WEBS) funds were brought to market, tracking MSCI single country indexes. As discussed in Chapter 16, this was a joint effort between Morgan Stanley and BGI, and built on the success of Morgan Stanley's OPALS. In May 2000, BGI renamed their ETFs as iShares and expanded the product line with more international and domestic ETFs that track popular indexes such as S&P, Russell, and Dow Jones, as well as fixed income ETFs.

Europe has also experienced substantial growth in ETF assets and funds. A significant number of ETFs are cross-traded throughout Europe, which splits the ETF liquidity among numerous trading platforms. The proliferation of similar products across Europe is a direct result of the differing tax and regulatory regimes that currently exist. Still, the dominant European ETF exchange platforms are the DeutscheBoerse XTF and the Euronext NextTrack, which combined have over 85 percent of European ETF market share as of February 2003. To date, the most popular ETFs in Europe have been the European country ETFs the DAX EX and the CAC40 Master Unit, and the regional Euro zone ETF, the Dow Jones EuroSTOXX 50.

In Japan, the three largest retail brokerages, Nomura, Daiwa, and Nikko, have each launched ETF families, many based on the same benchmarks. As such, it remains to be seen which products will gain traction in the long term. Finally, ETFs have started proliferating in emerging markets—more information on this is discussed in Chapter 31 and in the book's E-ppendix.

THE BASIC NUTS AND BOLTS OF MANAGING EXCHANGE-TRADED FUNDS

What is an ETF? As described in Chapters 14 and 16, an ETF is a convenient, liquid instrument providing exposure to a specific benchmark. ETFs can be structured in a variety of ways and employ various strategies. The recent explosive asset growth in ETFs highlights that ETFs appear to be successful in meeting investor needs.

ETFs are used for numerous purposes, including asset allocation, cash equitization, index/portfolio realancing, hedging, transition management, and portfolio completion strategies. ETFs are recognized as being efficient investment vehicles for gaining index exposure (style, market capitalization, sector, and country), easily traded and settled, transparent in their holdings, low cost, and tax efficient.

A unit of an equity ETF represents a block or basket of individual shares, usually 50,000 or 100,000 shares. Each unit is comprised of a basket of securities and a cash component. The securities represent a slice of the underlying index. The cash component reflects various cash items within the fund, including dividend accruals, cash receivables, and cash being substituted for a security in the basket.

Distinguishable features of ETFs include their underlying liquidity, tax efficiency, and lack of persistent premiums or discounts to their net asset values (NAV), which are discussed next.

ETF LIQUIDITY

Individual stock liquidity is measured by analyzing the average daily volume of that security over a specified period. Sophisticated investors and traders, however, understand that the *relevant indicator of an ETF's liquidity is the liquidity of its underlying security constituents.* As daily market supply and demand for the ETFs change, ETFs can be created or redeemed through trading and delivering the underlying security constituents to create shares in a unique process explained later in this chapter. Even the less frequently traded ETFs are quoted continuously by their specialists and typically experience 25,000 bids and offers during a trading day.

As an example, consider the iShares Goldman Sachs Software Index Fund (ticker: IGV), a fund that holds large capitalization names like Oracle and Microsoft. Since it started trading on July 13, 2001, IGV had an average daily volume of 15,083 shares through November 12, 2001. On November 13, 2001, Goldman Sachs hosted a software industry conference, generating interest in software stocks. IGV traded over 1.2 million shares (a dollar-volume of almost $51 million) on that same day. Throughout the day, the specialist maintained a bid/ask spread of $.16 (or 38 basis points). At 12:52 A.M./ET, the specialist showed a market of $42.44 bid and $42.60 ask. At the same minute, the specialist traded a block of 400,000 shares in between the spread at $42.48. The market after the trade moved up slightly to $42.46 bid/$42.61 ask, demonstrating that the ETF is indeed as liquid as the underlying stocks.

REGULATORY AND TAX BACKGROUND—
A VITAL ELEMENT OF THE ETF STRUCTURE
AND ITS MANAGEMENT

ETFs, like mutual funds, are governed by the requirements of federal securities laws, state securities and corporate laws, federal and state tax laws, regulations enacted by self-regulatory organizations and by rules established by the Securities and Exchange Commission (SEC) and the Internal Revenue Service (IRS). ETFs are generally governed by the Investment Company Act of 1940 and regulated by the SEC and the IRS. The IRS ensures that the fund meets specific portfolio guidelines in order to qualify for special tax treatment as a regulated investment company (RIC).

Following is a brief description of some of the regulatory constraints and investment objectives that affect the management of ETFs registered with the SEC.

The Single Issuer Rule

The SEC single issuer rule states that the combined share classes of a single issuer may not exceed 25 percent of the fund's net asset value. This test is conducted every fiscal quarter end for a fund and must be passed subject to a 30-day grace period after the quarter end.

Diversification Tests

Both the SEC and the IRS have established rigorous requirements for mutual funds. Among the statutes are those related to the diversification of fund holdings. For example, a "diversified" mutual fund is one whose portfolio, on a daily basis, has no more than 25 percent of its total assets in issuers that represent more than 5 percent of such assets. In addition, a diversified fund cannot have a single issuer that represents more than 25 percent of total assets. If the fund cannot satisfy these criteria, it must describe itself in its prospectus and Statement of Additional Information (SAI) as "nondiversified."

Only funds that have described themselves as diversified are subject to these daily requirements. All non-diversified mutual funds must comply with IRS asset diversification requirements at their quarter-end. Although a 30-day grace period to correct asset diversification imbalances is available under IRS regulations, corrective action sales may also work against a fund's investment strategy since it may force the disposal of securities that the fund would otherwise wish to hold. Transactions made for the purpose of regulatory compliance may introduce *tracking error* into the performance of index ETFs (see the sidebar "Managing ETFs for Regulatory Compliance").

Required Distributions—Capital Gains and Dividend Income

As a regulated investment company under IRS Subchapter M regulation, mutual funds and ETFs are required to meet certain distribution requirements to

---

MANAGING ETFs FOR REGULATORY COMPLIANCE

The iShares Dow Jones Telecommunications Index Fund (ticker IYZ) provides an example of the impact of IRS regulations on the daily management of an ETF. The Dow Jones Telecommunication index does not meet the IRS single issuer or asset diversification requirements and is therefore a noncompliant benchmark. However, in order to maintain the fund's investment company status and minimize tax inefficiency (i.e., any capital gains that could be generated through open-market trades), a portfolio manager may choose to structure the iShares Dow Jones Telecommunications Index Fund in such a way that it continually complies with the diversification tests applicable only at quarter-end. Consequently, there is a need to analyze the variance between the performance of the fund relative to the index—or tracking error—that is a direct outcome of the fund not being able to fully replicate the benchmark and having misweighted holdings. The portfolio manager has various tools that can analyze risk and assist in determining the optimal portfolio composition while minimizing tracking error. The portfolio manager's challenge for funds based on concentrated indexes with few benchmark constituents, such as the Dow Jones Telecommunication index, is to balance the need to minimize tracking error while meeting regulatory requirements.

---

qualify for special tax treatment. At least 90 percent of net taxable income must be distributed to shareholders annually. Such income items include dividends, interest, and short-term capital gains. Additionally, 1940 Act ETFs must comply with the 1940 Act Excise Tax regulation that is calculated beginning in November of the current fiscal year through October 31 of the following calendar year and requires the distribution of at least 98 percent of income earned during this period.

Prospectus and Statement of Additional Information Requirements

The investment objectives, strategies, and risk associated with achieving the objectives, and fundamental and non-fundamental policies of ETFs and mutual funds are described in their prospectuses and SAIs. The principal investment strategies section of the iShares Trust ETFs prospectus, for example, requires that all the funds invest at least 90 percent of their assets in securities that are represented in the funds' *underlying index*. The industry concentration policy for each fund states that no fund will concentrate (i.e., hold 25 percent or more of its total assets) in a particular industry or group of industries except that a fund will concentrate in the securities of industries to approximately the same extent as its underlying index is concentrated. The SAI also describes the constraints on activities such as borrowing, securities lending, investment in other mutual funds, and the use of derivatives.

IN-KIND MECHANISM

Traditional open-end mutual funds that need to satisfy shareholder redemption requests usually do so by raising cash through the sale of portfolio securities and distributing cash to the shareholder. These transactions may result in capital gains that are then distributed to the fund's remaining shareholders. By contrast, ETFs are redeemable directly from a fund by market makers, large investors, and institutions only in large blocks of securities called *creation units*. Creation units consist of multiple shares of an iShares fund that are acquired or redeemed principally *in-kind* for a portfolio or *basket* of securities. This mechanism is graphically portrayed in Figure 16.4 in Part Three of the book. The in-kind mechanism of exchanging a basket of securities for shares of the ETF is inherently tax efficient insofar as it enables a fund to fulfill redemption requests without having to raise cash through capital market transactions of ETF portfolio securities.

Premiums and Discounts to the Net Asset Values

A premium or discount occurs when the ETF share price trades consistently away from NAV. When the fund's market price trades below NAV, the fund is considered to be trading at a discount. When the fund's market price is trading above NAV, the fund is considered to be trading at a premium. If either situation were to persist with an ETF, an arbitrage opportunity exists for eligible market participants to act through the creation/redemption mechanism to profit from the discrepancy, restoring equilibrium to the two prices. For example, in the case where a fund is at a discount, a market maker could buy shares at the discounted market price and redeem these shares through the primary creation redemption process receiving the higher NAV value of the underlying securities. With fewer ETF shares now in the market, the ETF share price would be expected to move higher. Because of the primary creation/redemption process, described in Chapter 16, substantial ETF premiums and discounts are not expected to persist for long periods of time.

Figure 23.1 illustrates the distribution of daily premiums or discounts to NAV of the iShares MSCI EAFE (ticker EFA) ETF, managed by BGI. This U.S-listed international ETF is benchmarked to the MSCI EAFE Index, consisting of about 1000 stocks in 21 developed countries. As shown, the daily premium/discount for this international ETF appears to be neither significant nor persistently biased over its lifetime.

Note that this is not the case for closed-end mutual funds, which were initially considered a competitor to ETFs. Due to the creation/redemption mechanism, ETFs contain an inherent advantage over closed-end funds. Since closed-end funds are unable to create/redeem new shares, many have historically experienced substantial and persistent discounts or premiums to NAV, making them a less attractive investment vehicle.

How Does the Market Know Exchange-Traded Funds Trade at Net Asset Value?

The indicated optimized portfolio value (IOPV) is an estimation of a fund's NAV. Based on the Portfolio Composition File (PCF) securities and the estimated cash component, the resulting IOPV value is published on Bloomberg and other quotation services and priced throughout the day in 15-second intervals, providing market makers and investors with an estimation of NAV.

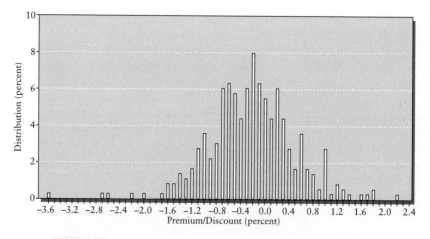

FIGURE 23.1 Distribution of Daily Premium/Discount for EFA Data from EFA inception (August 17, 2001 to January 31, 2003). *Source:* Barclays Global Investors.

The PCF defines the securities and share amounts needed to create or redeem one unit of activity for each ETF fund. In addition to securities is the estimated cash component that must be delivered or received representing cash, accruals, and other items not part of the PCF.

The accuracy of the IOPV is dependent on the accuracy of the PCF as well as the estimated cash component. Any inaccuracies and IOPV pricing is compromised with resulting consequences to those trading the ETF in the market. Pricing discrepancies are perceived almost immediately, since the product is valued real time for trading by multiple parties.

Occasionally, securities are valued in the cash component. By being valued in the cash component, the security's value (previous day's close) remains static throughout the trading day as opposed to being priced in the PCF, which updates for any security price movements as long as the local market for that security is open.

Whenever possible, the ETF's portfolio managers attempts to minimize the value of securities in the estimated cash component. Reasons for excluding securities from the PCF and valuing them in the estimated cash component include halted securities or those awaiting settlement from a particular corporate action. Corporate actions may also result in receipt of odd lots or nonindex securities that do not fit, in the case of odd lots, or belong in the PCF and therefore, must be valued in cash until they can be sold out of the fund. Valuing securities in the cash component tends to occur with more frequency in international funds given the increased complexity of corporate actions and market round lot conventions.

MANAGING AN ETF PORTFOLIO IS *HYPER*ACTIVE

Not all portfolio managers are created equal. Some managers like to pick stocks; some like to pick sectors; some like to track benchmarks. All use their skills to achieve a similar goal—to provide a return consistent with fund guidelines. The preferred method for managing an ETF portfolio is indexing. That is, tracking an index by owning all the benchmark stocks at similar benchmark weights. *(Editor's note: At least for the first dozen years of the structure. See Chapter 31 for some predictions about the future of ETFs.)*

Most U.S. equity iShares fully replicate their respective indexes, including the larger indexes such as the Russell 3000 Index. Because most U.S. stocks are fairly liquid, the preference is for most benchmark names to be represented in an iShares fund. However, a small number of U.S. Dow Jones benchmarks fail a 1940 Act compliance test and are therefore optimized. Almost all international equity iShares are currently optimized. This is largely due to the indexes tracked, many of which have securities that represent a large percentage of the index leading to Single Issuer and 5/50 and 5/25 problems.

Managing Cash

At BGI, daily cash projections are received each morning from an external fund accountant, Investors Bank and Trust. These projections include trades through the previous day and project three business days out by settlement. Spendable cash is managed to be approximately 10 to 30 basis points (bps) for international iShares funds, with even tighter tracking iShares funds kept closer to 10 bps (or less). Domestic iShares funds hold an average of 3 bps. Foreign exchange trades are executed through BGI's internal currency desk and managed on a fund-by-fund basis with sufficient balances held in both local and U.S. dollar currencies. U.S. dollar balances are needed since all U.S.-based iShares pay fund expenses and distributions in U.S. dollars.

MAJOR INDEX RECONSTITUTIONS AND REBALANCES

As discussed in Part Two and in Chapters 19, 20, and 21, as the composition of equity markets change, index providers attempt to reflect such changes in their market indexes. Periodically, index providers such as Russell, Standard & Poor's, Dow Jones, and MSCI make changes to their indexes to reflect developments in the equity markets due to structural market changes and corporate activity. Some of these changes are referred to as *reconstitutions*. As the term implies, reconstitutions refresh an index, ensuring that an index stays current with the market it is intended to represent.

Reconstitutions present a variety of complexities for portfolio managers. Some indexes are reconstituted continuously, meaning that there are no set dates for changes, rather adjustments occur as events in the market occur. For instance, when a company in the index is acquired, the acquired company is deleted from the index and the new company is added. Often these changes are associated with the sometimes-significant price movements of the companies involved.

Other indexes are revised on preset dates. Companies that are acquired or cease to trade may be deleted between reconstitution dates but no replacements may occur concurrently. Instead, the index is completely revised to reflect all changes on the predetermined date such as on a quarterly calendar basis.

The Russell Reconstitution

The Russell Reconstitution has been the hallmark of index changes followed by the entire investment community and business media. As discussed in Chapters 5 and 20, each June, Russell reconstitutes their entire index family—the Russell 3000, Russell 2000, Russell 1000, and the respective Russell Growth and Value Indexes. Russell ranks all qualifying companies in the U.S. equity market-by-market capitalization. All companies are included as long as they trade over one dollar, are U.S. incorporated stocks, and trade on a major exchange or NASDAQ.

Once the universe is determined, Russell draws a line at the 3000th security. Everything above is considered to be the Russell 3000 and everything below is excluded. The Russell 1000 Index is the largest 1000 companies of the Russell 3000, with the remainder making up the Russell 2000 Index. But the Russell 2000 is better known, more widely followed, and historically has more assets tied to it (despite it being a small cap index).

Currently, iShares have the only U.S.-listed ETFs benchmarked to Russell indexes. iShares funds are managed to minimize the impact of the Russell Reconstitution and safely navigate the often-volatile market associated with this event. The various Russell iShares are managed with the intent to deliver index performance during the reconstitution without having an adverse market effect. Throughout the Russell Reconstitution, BGI portfolio managers have successfully minimized capital gains while tracking the benchmark.

As one of the largest institutional asset managers, iShares trades are often combined with BGI's commingled index funds for trading to minimize cost and market impact. In addition, BGI is able to conduct internal crossing between its funds including domestic iShares that can further reduce transaction costs. For example, in 2001, U.S. iShares participated in BGI's Russell Reconstitution cross, crossing 53 percent of all BGI market trades, which totaled $448 million in value and 18.4 million shares.

_____ **Editor's Note** _____

The need for intraday liquidity, combined with high expected tax efficiency, present unique challenges for ETF portfolio managers. For things to run smoothly, different teams must react quickly and work together to overcome unexpected challenges and glitches that inevitably surface along the way. While this process generally goes smoothly from a client's perspective, it is not always an easy time for portfolio managers, as the sidebar titled "A Day in the Life of an ETF Portfolio Manager" colorfully illustrates.)

A DAY IN THE LIFE OF AN ETF PORTFOLIO MANAGER
Patrick O'Connor

The time is 11:30 A.M. PST and I watch stock prices dance across the screen on the Bloomberg quote machine. One is apt to be a little nervous with a billion-dollar trade on the line. I habitually check to see how small-cap stocks are trading. Today is the last trading day in June, or more precisely, the day of the Russell Reconstitution—the day that Frank Russell Company rebalances its entire family of benchmarks to reflect America's top 3,000 stocks by market capitalization. Simply put, today is the busiest trading day of the year for domestic equity indexers.

In preparation for the event, my team stayed late into the previous night, creating trade lists and formulating implementation strategies. This is the first year that iShares Russell funds are going through a significant rebalance trade, having launched the 12 iShares Russell funds only a year earlier. Investors who are long iShares are counting on our team to take them through the reconstitution with minimal capital gains and acceptable tracking relative to the benchmark. In a more dramatic example, the Russell 2000 growth fund is trading over 40 percent of the entire fund in a single day!

At 11:55 A.M. I get up from the Bloomberg terminal to see first-hand how our traders are coping. The last hour of trading is when things can get interesting. I find universal agitation on the desk.

"The Nasdaq computer is down," someone says. Down? How can that be? There are frantic calls to several brokers trying to get color on the situation, and impact to market on close (MOC) trades. No firm answers are forthcoming, just more confusion and uncertainty. Calls to the Nasdaq are not picked up. Bloomberg flashes up that the order routing system for MOC orders will not function for the close. My heart skips a beat. We have hundreds of millions on the line with the Nasdaq and it fails? Didn't we survive the whole Y2K thing? Isn't there a tech hotline? *Can't someone just reboot?*

As the minutes tick by, I begin to realize that several trade lists are looking like they won't trade at all. I scurry back to our portfolio management team that is huddled around a Bloomberg terminal praying for that one scrolling news line saying that we are back in business. More minutes pass.

"Nasdaq to reopen!" finally appears on the screen.

A collective cheer bursts forth from everyone in the office. We still have time with 15 minutes to close. But as quickly as the wind raised us up, it leaves our sails as quickly. "Nasdaq down again." The massive order flow once again crashes the system. It's beginning to feel like a bad episode of *The Twilight Zone.*

We could leave trades unexecuted and trade them on Monday, exposing our funds to risk that stocks won't open where they closed—the funds would mistrack their benchmarks if this happened.

With just minutes to go until the close, Nasdaq comes back online, but not in time to complete trading. In an unprecedented move, Nasdaq decides to keep its trading doors open an extra hour to ensure all orders are executed. I have just been through the portfolio manager's equivalent of Scotty saving the *Enterprise* for Captain Kirk. We executed the trades, survived the Nasdaq meltdown, and kept pace with our Russell benchmarks.

MSCI GLOBAL INDEXES AND FLOAT ADJUSTMENT

As described in Chapters 9 and 12, MSCI has been the preeminent benchmark provider for U.S. institutions investing in markets outside North America. Despite its popularity, the benchmark needed a methodology update, as discussed in Chapter 9. In the 2000 to 2002 timeframe, MSCI conducted its largest index reconstitution to date—in fact, it was the largest index change ever. The main driver behind the changes was to improve its methodology in constructing its international indexes.

With the MSCI Reconstitution, the changes took place in two stages with the first half occurring on November 30, 2001, and the second on May 31, 2002. All changes were preannounced in May 2001. At that time, MSCI also began publishing the new Provisional indexes in addition to the Standard, or old, set of MSCI indexes.

The most significant changes included a move to free float methodology. With the new MSCI indexes, only those shares available to the investing public are included in a company's shares outstanding weight calculation, rounded to the nearest 5 percent band. The second most significant change was the increase in free-float market cap representation from 60 percent to 85 percent.

The prolonged period of implementation allowed investors to move to the new indexes over a year-long period. The end result of these changes was a stronger, more comprehensive international index series that better reflects investor reality.

BGI iShares Implementation to Provisional Indexes

The international iShares funds were rebalanced to the Provisional indexes in June 2001, thus providing investors a set of tools to manage to Provisional exposure within the time they desired. The broad-based iShares MSCI EAFE Fund, which began trading in August 2001, was launched to track the new Provisional EAFE benchmark. As of this writing, it is the only ETF product of its kind for diversified total developed international exposure.

STANDARD AND POOR'S INDEX REBALANCES

Standard and Poor's (S&P) conducts two major types of rebalances during the year: semi-annual growth and value rebalances, and quarterly share change rebalances. For each of its indexes (Large-Cap, Mid-Cap, and Small-Cap), S&P offers additional indexes, for growth stocks and another series for value stocks (S&P/Barra series—discussed in Chapter 7). As determined by Barra for the S&P style indexes, price-to-book value is the main criteria in determining whether a company is a growth or value stock. Companies with high price-to-book values are placed in the S&P/Barra growth indexes and those with low price-to-book are represented in the S&P/Barra value indexes. Each company can only be in the growth or value index, the sum of both indexes equaling the full index.

S&P changes the market capitalization of its constituents as a company changes its outstanding shares. When a company issues shares of 5 percent or more, S&P will reflect the increase immediately in its capitalization calculation and increasing the weight of that stock in its benchmark. For companies that issue shares below 5 percent of its outstanding shares, S&P waits until its quarterly calendar rebalance to reflect these changes. As portfolio managers, we must navigate these major transitions.

ACTIVE MANAGEMENT OF ETFs FOR TAX EFFICIENCY

Because all portfolio capital gains must be passed through to investors, BGI and other ETF managers strive to minimize and, wherever possible, eliminate capital gains. As discussed in Chapters 14 and 16, the structure of ETFs assists this goal by providing a tax-efficient structure. In addition, BGI portfolio managers analyze every corporate action, index delete, and rebalance trade as well as other opportunities to minimize capital gains. Three key elements of this effort are described next.

Tax Lot Accounting Method

Tax lot accounting, managed by the iShares' fund accountants, Investors Bank & Trust, aids the ETFs in achieving tax efficiency. Tax lot accounting refers to when a security position is partially *sold out* of an iShares fund. In this case the highest cost basis tax lot is used. Conversely, when a security is *redeemed* out of the fund, the lowest cost basis tax is used. Since *in-kinds* are not considered taxable, this allows the fund to minimize potential capital gains.

Corporate Action Analysis

The Portfolio Management team actively analyzes every corporate action for tax implications. Gains and losses by securities across all iShares funds are determined and a strategy is developed. For example, Portfolio Management may choose to sell a name thus harvesting losses to offset against future gains.

Tax-Harvesting Strategy

Portfolio Management harvests capital losses by deleting securities that have been removed from index or by managing the fund with an optimized strategy that generates losses without significantly impacting tracking. For example, a name that has a substantially reduced weight in a fund often will have large unrealized losses. Portfolio Management may reduce the weight of this name by selling off most or all of the holding, thus harvesting losses within an acceptable level of tracking error. Once the IRS wash-sale period has elapsed (i.e., 30 calendar days), the position is bought back and brought to benchmark weight.

When losses of the fund are at a sufficient level, ETF portfolio managers will be selective about invoking tax-harvesting strategies at the risk of mistracking, similar to the previous chapters' discussion of the tradeoffs portfolio managers make when juggling costs and tracking error.

PERFORMANCE OBJECTIVES AND TRACKING THE BENCHMARK INDEX

Similar to a traditional index fund, the success of an ETF product depends on its ability to track a particular benchmark. Benchmark indexes are generally chosen to represent a specific mandate such as domestic large cap stocks. Tracking means the fund seeks to match as closely as possible the performance of the benchmark securities with the securities it holds in the fund, as described earlier in the book. Any deviation in relative performance is called *mistracking* or *tracking error.*

Since ETFs can and are bought long and sold short by a variety of market participants discussed in Chapter 16, tracking to the benchmark is extremely important. When used for hedging strategies, any consistent outperformance will hurt holders using the product for short reasons, while any persistent underperformance hurts the long side.[2] While tracking an index sounds simple, in reality, there are a number of factors challenging a portfolio manager's ability to track a benchmark.

At the same time, a corresponding goal is to achieve tax-efficient performance. This goal is extremely important given that tax efficiency is one of the key benefits of ETFs. Due to the in-kind mechanism and tendency of lower portfolio turnover, ETFs should generally prove to be tax-efficient instruments. As noted earlier, Portfolio Management has several tools at its disposal to manage the tax aspects of ETFs.

Portfolio Management Challenges—Replication versus Optimization

As discussed in Chapter 19, replication translates into holding all of the underlying securities in an index, while optimization entails choosing and holding fewer securities than the index by using a sampling, quantitative-based or model-driven solution. Whether a fund follows a replicating or an optimizing strategy is generally dictated by the concentration or depth of the underlying benchmark it tracks and overall market size. Having a greater number of securities creates a more diversified index with fewer concentration issues. Such an index can be replicated more easily by funds, resulting in the funds tracking closely the index and having few, if any, 1940 Act issues. Some countries' market capitalizations are relatively small and spread out between very few companies. In instances like Belgium and Austria, for example, optimization must be followed, resulting in greater levels of mistracking.

Liquidity

Since liquidity of the ETF derives from the liquidity of the underlying securities, having a portfolio made up of securities that are easily tradable is important. For international equities, if the index contains illiquid securities, then the fund could represent those securities with their U.S. American

Depository Receipts (ADR) equivalents, closest ADR alternatives, or in the extreme case, optimized out of the fund completely. The action selected is one in which tracking error and liquidity and premium/discount spreads are considered acceptable.

In-Kind Deliverability

As discussed in Chapter 21, some countries' market regulations do not allow for the free delivery of securities on which the in-kind mechanism is based. They include Greece, Taiwan, Malaysia, Brazil, and South Korea. If in-kinds are not permitted by law, a single country fund becomes a *cash creation* ETF in which cash, and not securities, is received and delivered with any creation and redemption activity. Securities are then traded as regular market trades and the normal in-kind tax advantages are not applicable in this situation. The country or securities may be optimized or represented by a U.S. ADR equivalent or closest alternative if the impact on the fund is minimal. These alternatives introduce possible tracking error and thus liquidity and spreads are scrutinized closely. The challenges of investing in many of these markets are discussed in further detail in Chapter 21.

1940 Act Regulation

The 1940 Act diversification requirements—as outlined earlier in the chapter—may limit a fund's ability to fully replicate its index, causing misweights in the portfolio, and therefore, increases tracking error. The challenge for portfolio management is to be in compliance with the 1940 Act when necessary yet have a fund that tracks the benchmark as closely as possible. As discussed in Chapters 19, 20, and 21, there are inevitable tradeoffs, and one constraint is often achieved at the expense of the other.

Round-Lot Management

In markets such as Singapore, Hong Kong, and Japan, market conventions dictate that trading occur in predefined minimum board lots or round lots. While most trading occurs in round lot sizes, the index may dictate that the PCF should involve some odd lot size trading. The challenge becomes maintaining round lots at the PCF level while still maintaining acceptable tracking to the index.

As mentioned, close tracking is of paramount importance to ETFs' success. U.S. mutual fund compliance regulations, market trading conventions, and index construction methodology all affect a fund's performance relative to the benchmark it attempts to track. In addition, security misweights in

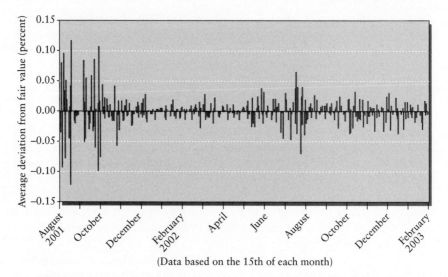

(Data based on the 15th of each month)

FIGURE 23.2   EFA Daily Residual Return: August 2001 to January 2003
Source: Barclays Global Investors.

the case of optimization, corporate actions, trading commissions/costs, cash, management fees and so on also affect a fund's relative performance. Portfolio managers must overcome these challenges to have a fund that tracks within an acceptable range.

As Figures 23.2 and 23.3 illustrate, daily tracking on the iShares MSCI EAFE Fund (ticker EFA) fund has for the most part been well under 5 bps since the fund's inception in August 2001, despite the myriad of operational and investment challenges detailed above and in Chapter 21.

TURNING A PORTFOLIO INTO A STOCK

In addition to portfolio management challenges, ETFs require a unique daily operational process. As mentioned in Chapter 16, Authorized Participants (APs) wishing to create/redeem units will deliver a slice of the fund in return for issued ETF shares. For specialists to make a market for the ETF, they require the ETF basket to approximate the NAV calculation. Portfolio Management defines the composition of the fund security slice daily after taking into consideration multiple factors explained next. This basket slice together with a cash component forms the basis for both the IOPV calculation and the portfolio composition file (or PCF, which is described next).

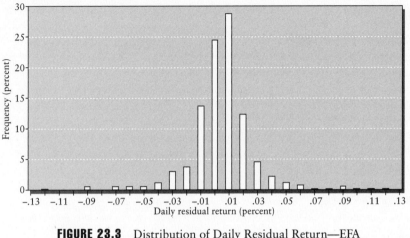

FIGURE 23.3   Distribution of Daily Residual Return—EFA
Inception to January 31, 2003.
Source: Barclays Global Investors.

Basket Considerations

For U.S. equity ETFs trading on American exchanges, it is critical that the basket reflect the fund when the market opens for several key reasons. As discussed in Chapter 16, every fund has a specialist firm responsible for making a market in each ETF. The basket forms the foundation of the IOPV, calculated by the specialists to approximate NAV. The basket is also used by authorized participants on a daily basis if they plan to create or redeem units of the underlying fund through the in-kind mechanism. Both specialists and authorized participants need to have a basket that accurately reflects the fund in order to ensure it is being priced as close as possible to the fund's NAV. Any discrepancy between the two could lead to problems of IOPV pricing, in addition to incorrect delivery or receipt of assets into and out of the fund.

Creating the Portfolio Composition File

The PCF contains the baskets for managed ETFs including domestic equity, international equity, and fixed income. Each basket defines the number of shares of each security and the cash component that comprise one unit (usually 50,000 shares) for each respective ETF. The creation of each basket requires several steps at the end of *each day*. They are as discussed next.

Basket Names   How do fund securities get into the basket? Unless specifically identified by Portfolio Management as a *nonbasket* item, all portfolio securities are considered part of the basket. Referred to as "cutting the basket," the basket is created by taking total fund holdings and dividing by the number of units outstanding for the ETF, incorporating round lot considerations. For a fully replicating fund with round lots of 1, a basket equals a simple slice of the fund proportional to how many units are outstanding and mirrors the underlying index. For optimized funds with round lots of up to 1,000, the basket will not exactly mirror the underlying index. All shares in the basket are adjusted for any corporate actions going effective at the market open the following day.

Non-Basket Names   Nonbasket items represent securities in the fund that are not included by Portfolio Management to be in the basket. Rather, they are excluded from the basket, calculated a cash value based on latest market prices and included in the cash amount associated with each ETF. Such securities may not be deliverable due to suspended trading or corporate events. They could be nonindex securities the fund has received from a corporate action, but not yet sold. Additionally they could be securities tendered and awaiting receipt due to merger and acquisition activity.

Adding Cash   The cash component reflects actual cash in the fund, dividend accruals, and the value of any nonbasket items and odd lots. Odd lots being residuals of security holdings not fitting into the basket due to round lot trading requirements. Total calculated cash is divided by units outstanding to arrive at a cash component per basket. This, along with basket securities, is required for each creation/redemption unit.

Valuation   Each basket of securities plus cash must equal the NAV per unit. Otherwise, if either the basket or cash calculation is incorrect, the fund will experience adverse pricing ramifications the following day when it begins trading. IOPV will not be a true indication of NAV nor of one unit of creation/redemption activity. ETF portfolio managers check this calculation against NAV daily to ensure accuracy of both components before the PCF is sent to be processed for the marketplace.

Sending It to the Marketplace

After confirming the necessary ETF checks and valuations, the final step is to electronically transmit the PCF file to the National Securities Clearing Corporation (NSCC). The NSCC is responsible for processing and distributing all ETF PCFs to market participants and relevant parties who subscribe to this service. Before each day's market open all ETF PCFs are made available and contain the securities and cash necessary for one unit of each respective ETF. The market now possesses the critical information with which to price and buy and sell all U.S. equity ETFs.

SECONDARY MARKET TRADING

Specialist firms are authorized by stock exchanges to provide and enhance the liquidity of securities and ETFs. Generally, a specialist firm employs a minimum number of trading professionals to make markets, manage the firm's inventory risk, and trade for its own account. Under an exchange system, the exchange selects one specialist firm to manage one stock. Consequently, the exchange can transfer the stock to another specialist if the original specialist is unable to maintain a fair and orderly market. Similarly, authorized participants (APs) will be actively participating in the creation/redemption process and secondary market, as described in Chapter 16 and portrayed in Figure 16.3..

"Making the Market" for ETFs

ETF specialists are constantly monitoring the designated indexes, underlying baskets of stocks, and various comparable futures products and any other alternatives. The specialist for the iShares S&P 500 ETF (Ticker IVV), for example, is Spear Leeds, who will watch the price relationship between S&P 500 futures, the iShares S&P 500 ETF, the S&P 500 index, and the underlying physical securities when determining the correct price for SPY, another ETF that tracks the S&P 500.

Whereas order-flow in an individual stock mainly dictates pricing movements in that security, an ETF's value is determined by its underlying basket of equities. So the ever-changing basket of stock prices in the underlying indexes dictate how often the specialist firms have to update their trading markets for their particular ETF. An ETF may not trade for hours, but the specialist is committed continually to updating their quote. This ensures accurate pricing and, more importantly to the specialist firm, the ability to avoid being arbitraged against—the opportunistic buying and selling of two assets that are similar, but present different market prices.

ETFs THAT HAVE AN UNDERLYING PORTFOLIO TRADING IN A DIFFERENT TIME ZONE

Because of the in-kind arbitrage mechanism, the market price of an ETF should generally trade close to its NAV per share. In addition, both should be close to the IOPV given it is simply a slice of the fund together with an estimated cash component to arrive at an "indicated" value of NAV per share. In reality, various factors affect the market price of an ETF such that differences occur between these three values. These differences increase dramatically with international ETFs given differing closing times in local versus U.S. markets, foreign exchange effects, local market holidays, and foreign government intervention. Even though the original international ETFs, WEBS (now part of the iShares international series), were launched in March 1996, yet there is still a lot of confusion on this topic. We hope that this short discussion clarifies this phenomenon.

U.S. Equity ETFs Trading in the U.S. Marketplace—Fully-Open Market

When the underlying securities, futures, alternative instruments, or funds are trading during the same hours and in the same currency as the ETF (e.g., Russell 2000 iShares Listed on AMEX), the market price of the ETF should closely reflect the IOPV and the NAV per share. Small differences may exist due to secondary demand or supply issues and normal factors affecting market maker spreads (ability to hedge, etc.); however, if these differences become too large, the creation/redemption opportunity exists in which to arbitrage away these differences. As mentioned earlier, when nonbasket items and odd lots are valued in the estimated cash component, differences between the IOPV and NAV can occur; although in reality, this is rare.

Partially Open—International ETFs Trading in the U.S. Market

In this case, the underlying foreign equity market(s) closes partway through the U.S. trading day of the exchange where the ETF (e.g., MSCI U.K. listed on AMEX) is trading. The introduction of nonconcurrent trading hours in addition to foreign exchange contribute to differences between NAV, IOPV, and market price. IOPV reflects movements in the underlying securities market as long as the local market is open. Once the local market closes, share price continues to trade, affected by information released during U.S. market hours and may move away from NAV and IOPV. To the extent that U.S. ADRs are contained in the portfolio as opposed to the underlying securities, IOPV will move as well. Known as *price discovery*, the market price reflects expectation and market sentiment as to where the underlying market may open the following day.

Bloomberg updates the IOPV in 15-second intervals with their latest foreign exchange rate. This is in contrast to, in the case of iShares, NAV that uses a fixed foreign exchange rate (the Reuters/WM 4 P.M. London spot rate) to value the funds. The presence of differing foreign exchange rates thus introduces differences in IOPV to NAV throughout the trading day. In the case of a country like South Korea where foreign exchange does not trade offshore, IOPV will not be updated for foreign exchange changes and, therefore, does not contribute to IOPV NAV differences. The occurrence of local market holidays on days where the U.S. market is open serves to aggravate any pricing differences between NAV, IOPV, and market price for U.S. trading ETFs. In addition, foreign government intervention, for example, actions by Malaysia barring repatriation in 1998 can also cause persistent deviations in these values. Chapter 21 includes a discussion of the extreme challenges faced in Malaysia for international indexers.

CONCLUSION

We hope that this chapter has provided substantial insight into the process of managing ETFs. In a way, even given as much detail as we have provided, we have just scratched the surface. And as more firms offer a variety of ETFs— some with quite novel structures—there will be further innovation in the ETF portfolio management process. We hope that it is apparent that the ETF portfolio management combines most elements of traditional index portfolio management with additional layers of operational, regulatory, and real-time market challenges. And we're sure you don't see *anything* passive about this endeavor.

NOTES

1. For more up-to-date information on ETF product developments, assets under management, and volume, see the ETF section on IndexUniverse.com. For information on the many benchmarks on which ETFs are based—including news on index reconstitutions and index changes—see the Index Research sections on IndexUniverse.com.
2. *Editor's note:* The use of ETFs as capital market instruments by a variety of players is a key distinction from traditional index mutual funds, and therefore ETF sponsors and their portfolio managers may have a *disincentive* to produce "excessive" *index alpha* as it would harm investors who are short the ETF.

CHAPTER 24

Index-Based Separately Managed Accounts

Delivering on the Performance Promise

Mark Adams, Kevin Maeda, and Steven A. Schoenfeld

_____ **Editor's Note** _____

This chapter provides background information and insight on a relatively new and small area of indexing that has enormous potential to provide the benefits of indexing in the most appropriate structure for taxable high-net-worth individuals. Whereas previous chapters have discussed at length the many tax benefits of index funds and exchange-traded funds (ETFs) (i.e., the way that indexing is tax-efficient and doesn't generate as much of a tax bite as active strategies), this chapter focuses on an indexing technique that takes the benefits even further. The chapter starts with an overview of the structure and features of separately managed accounts, and makes a persuasive case for index-based separate accounts. As mentioned in Chapter 15, professionally managed index-based separate accounts are actually a form of enhanced indexing and can outperform benchmark indexes after-tax. They also can be intricately customized to each investor's unique economic situation, tax status, pre-existing holdings, and even social preferences. Chapter 27 in Part Five provides a robust comparison of the optimal index-based vehicles for taxable investors which reinforces the case for index-based separate accounts.

The authors would like to acknowledge the assistance of Charles Nance, who helped with an earlier draft of this chapter, Tamara Dyer, who assisted with the graphics and tables, and John Spence, who helped edit several later drafts.

479

This chapter provides the essential foundation to understand the potential for index-based separate accounts, and the intricacies of managing them for optimal performance and what I called tax alpha, in Chapter 15 (and here). Customized, index-based separate accounts are available from about 10 firms in the United States, but they have historically been uneconomical for managers to deliver to clients investing less than $500,000.[1] However, innovations in technology, the proliferation of ETFs, and the ever-increasing recognition of the case for indexing have brought this capability to a wider audience. This chapter explores the rationale for index-based separate accounts and provides details on the science and art of managing portfolios to deliver on the promise of these strategies.

Since the late 1990s, separately managed accounts (SMAs) have become the investment product of choice for affluent and emerging affluent investors. Although traditional active managers (stock pickers) currently dominate these programs, index-based strategies are slowly but steadily growing. Despite this growth, individuals' use of index-based strategies in SMAs is significantly lower than their use by larger and more sophisticated institutional investors. Only 1 percent of separately managed accounts is invested in index-based strategies, as opposed to over 20 percent of institutional assets and more than 10 percent of mutual fund assets. This disparity is not entirely surprising, given the history and background of the separate account market. But it is a disparity that is sure to narrow, as the SMA market and its products continue to evolve. Index-based strategies, combined with the active tax management and customization that individual investors can find only in separate accounts, will play a key role in this evolution.

HISTORY AND BACKGROUND

The term *managed account* or SMAs is used to describe most types of fee-based advisory programs available from broker/dealers or Registered Investment Advisors (RIAs). More familiarly known as *wrap accounts,* they have been a major segment of the industry and are dominated by a handful of large wirehouses. Individually or separately managed accounts refer to individually, directly owned portfolios, usually managed by an institutional-level investment manager and promising individual tax management and customization. Managed accounts got started in the mid-1970s, soon after the appearance of the first index funds, but index-based SMAs only began to gain substantial assets and recognition in the early 2000s. As of year-end

2002, the SMA consultant wrap business had approximately $400 billion under management, but that figure is expected to double by the end of the decade.[2]

In the past few years, despite a bearish market environment, assets in these accounts have increased dramatically in response to demand and the entrance of new players in the market, both on the sponsor and money manager side. From 1996 through 2002, assets increased at over 20 percent annually, on a year-to-year percentage basis, from just over $100 billion in 1996 to the aforementioned $400 billion in 2002.[3]

The first separately managed account was created in 1976 at EF Hutton Investment Management, who, for the most part, monopolized this business into the mid-1980s. Growth was slow during this period as the infrastructure was immature and SMAs, by their nature, are operationally intensive. In this first SMA program, EF Hutton (the sponsor) acted simply as the introducing broker, custodian, and trade executor. The money managers within the program were the record keepers and interfaced directly with the clients. The money managers were also free to set their own fees and minimum account sizes.

This changed, however, when EF Hutton introduced its Select Managers program in 1987. This was the beginning of the true, modern "wrap" or separately managed account business. Before long, EF Hutton's success spawned many imitators as most of the major wirehouses followed EF Hutton with their own programs.

The key to the success of this new SMA business was that the sponsor (the broker) assumed most of the responsibilities heretofore belonging to the money manager. The sponsor assumed the fiduciary responsibility for the money managers, the record-keeping responsibility, and all the client service and reporting responsibilities. The money manager became, essentially, a subadvisor of the sponsor. This structure, and the economies of scale it engendered, allowed both minimum account sizes and fees to shrink, making these products more accessible and less expensive. Growth of assets under management remained at or near 30 percent a year until the early 2000s bear market slowed it temporarily.

Industry Concentration

The SMA industry is characterized by a high degree of concentration on both the sponsor/brokerage side and the money management side. Over 70 percent of SMA assets are with the big five wirehouses (Citigroup's Smith Barney, Merrill Lynch, Morgan Stanley, UBS, and Wachovia). In turn, some 50 percent of those assets are concentrated in just two wirehouses: Smith Barney and Merrill Lynch. However, the wirehouse share of this market is slowly declining as more and more alternative sponsors and RIAs enter the market.

The concentration is also substantial on the money management side. Almost 35 percent of SMA assets are placed with the top 10 money managers. Again, this share is slowly eroding as more institutional and mutual fund managers enter the SMA market.

Choice of Investments—Active versus Indexed

Given its deep roots in traditional brokerage, it is no surprise that traditional active management products dominate the SMA business. As is visible in Figure 24.1, in 2003, while index-based investing comprised over 20 percent of institutional invested assets and over 10 percent of mutual fund invested assets, a remarkably small 1 percent of assets in SMAs was invested in index-based products.

To many in the indexing community, this is an astounding statistic. Given the long-term relative performance record of indexing discussed throughout Parts One and Five, combined with the inherent tax-efficiency of indexing and its affluent, tax-sensitive investor base, one would think that *more* assets of SMAs than of institutional or mutual funds should be invested in index-based strategies. Again, this may be a by-product of SMAs' brokerage roots with their emphasis on traditional active strategies based on stock picking.

THE LOGIC OF SEPARATELY MANAGED ACCOUNTS

What is the reason for the rapid growth in separately managed accounts in recent years? On the demand side, the bull market of the 1990s created a large class of affluent and emerging affluent investors. These investors are likely to be more knowledgeable about investments and more demanding of

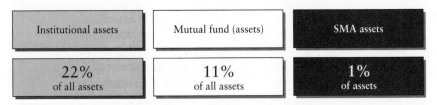

FIGURE 24.1 Indexing in Institutional Investing, Mutual Funds, and SMAs
Source: Pensions & Investments, Investment Company Institute, Money Management Institute.

them as well. They are increasingly aware of the many shortcomings of mutual funds, especially in the areas of customization and tax management.

On the supply side, driven by technology and process improvements, both the account fees and account minimums have decreased, making separate accounts available to more and more investors. In years past, account minimums were typically $500,000 or more. Today, minimums of $100,000 or less are not uncommon.

Disenchantment with mutual funds is fueling the demand for SMAs. Whereas mutual funds have provided many opportunities for the average individual investor, they present problems for investors who want to have more control of their investments and the attendant tax consequences. This was the case even before the mutual fund pricing and trading scandals burst on the scene in 2003. The perceived disadvantages of mutual funds relative to SMAs include the following five shortcomings:[4]

1. *No direct ownership.* Mutual funds by definition are jointly owned, commingled vehicles. The actions of some investors affect all the other investors. This lack of control, particularly of withdrawals, can influence portfolio results.
2. *No transparency.* Mutual fund holdings are only available every six months, so it is difficult if not impossible to know what is in the fund.
3. *No customization.* A mutual fund is a one-size-fits-all product. While a myriad of mutual funds slice and dice the market in a variety of ways, an investor cannot restrict the mutual fund from holding certain securities or sectors.
4. *No tax manageability.* Since there is no direct ownership, individual investors do not own the cost basis of individual issues within a mutual fund. This makes it difficult and cumbersome to harvest taxable losses to offset gains either within or outside the portfolio. Additionally, the required distribution of gains earned in mutual funds can trigger tax liabilities for investors and for some investors who may not have experienced the benefit of that gain.
5. *Cash funding.* Mutual funds can only be funded with cash. If an investor holds securities, those securities must be liquidated to fund a mutual fund account. By selling the securities, an investor creates a tax-realization event that could have adverse tax implications.

THE PROMISE OF SEPARATELY MANAGED ACCOUNTS

Separately managed accounts *promise* to be all five things that mutual fund are not:

1. *Direct ownership*. Separately managed accounts are individually owned investment products—the investor owns the cost basis of the stocks or other securities in the portfolio.
2. *Transparency*. Separately managed account holdings are available at any time on request.
3. *Customizability*. SMAs are completely customizable; the investor has the ability to exclude or include sectors and or stocks for any reason.
4. *Tax-manageability*. SMAs can be actively tax-managed to increase after-tax returns.
5. *Cash or security funding*. SMAs can be funded with cash, securities, or a combination thereof. If funded with securities, the transition can be managed on an individual basis to minimize the tax impact.

Many of those promises of separately managed accounts remain just that—promises, not reality. Most separate accounts are not extensively customized and are not tax-managed to any significant degree. Another reason is that managing thousands of separate accounts is difficult enough. Managing thousands of separate accounts with individual customization and active tax management is nearly impossible for many money managers. Thus, what most investors who use the SMA as their investment vehicle receive is not a truly customized investment strategy for their particular circumstances, but an investment strategy customized for the masses.

DELIVERING ON THE PROMISE: ADAPTING INDEX-BASED INVESTING FOR SEPARATELY MANAGED ACCOUNTS

Index-based separate account strategies and the technology and infrastructure supporting them are ideal for delivering on the promise of separately managed accounts. However, tight tracking error with respect to the benchmark—a key feature normally associated with and expected with indexing in the larger, commingled funds described in Chapters 20 and 21—must be modified. The constraints in managing a small, tax-managed, separate portfolio that may be customized around investor preferences require increasing the range of acceptable tracking error. Less rigorous tracking error must be acknowledged and targeted to accomplish other important features of the portfolio such as transparency, customization, and tax sensitivity and management. In other words, to deliver on the SMA's promise of customization and active tax management, *it may be necessary to accept a higher tracking error.*

Let's briefly review the basics of index portfolio management in the context of indexing for the separately managed account structure.

Core Investment Management Process for Building and Managing Index-Based Separately Managed Accounts

As discussed in Chapter 19, managing an index-based portfolio involves two major processes: (1) buying the initial portfolio and (2) managing the portfolio on an ongoing basis. At a glance, building an index-based portfolio sounds very simple. You buy securities in the same weight as the index; but on closer inspection, this is not a trivial task, especially for smaller accounts. Because of the large number of securities in most indexes, only huge accounts (typically institutional, including mutual finds and large ETFs) can fully replicate the index. This leads to the question of how best to achieve index representation. Anything less than full replication introduces tracking error, or active risk, into the portfolio. Various portfolio construction methods are available in managing index-based portfolios.

Choosing the Index Approach—Replication, Sampling, and Optimization

When constructing any index-tracking portfolio, SMA or otherwise, there are three possible approaches: full replication, sampling, and optimization. These were discussed at length in Chapter 19, but we discuss the pros and cons as they apply to SMAs here.

Full replication is simply holding all, or substantially all, of the securities in an index with the same weights as the index. This technique is most appropriate in a tax-free setting with a very large asset base. While a properly managed, fully replicating portfolio will invariably track the index very closely, there are several drawbacks, especially for the SMA market.

The first drawback is the mathematics of applying a fully replicating strategy to relatively small amounts of money. To gain exposure to each stock, very small positions would invariably need to be held. Indeed, for a large enough index and small amount of money, no exposure may be possible without fractional shares. Trading costs are another drawback. The potentially large number of securities held, and the potential number of trades required to keep the portfolio in balance after share adjustments and corporate actions, would necessitate constant small trades. While the investor may not be especially sensitive to this, the program sponsor/broker may be. The administrative and operational costs are prohibitively high for full replication in an SMA, and few, if any, SMA sponsors will offer such a product unless the fees and assets are sufficiently large to make them profitable.

Finally, and most importantly, full replication does not offer the degree of freedom necessary to deliver the customization and tax management that investors desire in their separate accounts. For an index-based, actively tax-managed strategy, full-replication is a poor choice. As soon as securities are sold to realize losses, the portfolio will not be fully replicating and may have extremely large style or sector biases. For example, if technology were in a down market, the manager might end up selling all or most of the technology stocks to realize losses. These stocks could not be bought back into the portfolio for at least 30 days without violating the wash sale rules first mentioned in the previous chapter and thus negating the losses just realized. For at least 30 days, the portfolio would be ex-technology, introducing additional active risk versus the benchmark.

The *sampling* technique involves taking a strategic sampling of securities from an index to achieve a level of risk similar to the index, but with fewer securities. A common approach is to sample by sector and weight proportionally to the index. Other risk factors such as capitalization, yield, or growth/value classifications may be taken into consideration when constructing a portfolio. This technique alleviates some of the problems with replication, but the trade-off is greater tracking error. For the average SMA account of about $200,000, this technique has great appeal despite the potentially elevated tracking error. It is easier to understand, more transparent than optimization, and more manageable than full replication. Additionally, sampling lends itself well to a tax-managed account. Unlike full optimization, sampling only a portion of the index allows for sufficient replacement stocks when loss-harvesting securities in the portfolio.

As discussed in Chapter 19, a quadratic *optimization* model may also be used to build an index-based SMA product. This technique attempts to match the risk profile of a selected index as closely as possible. This method has the advantage of potentially lower tracking error for a given number of securities. However, optimization is not very transparent, nor easy to understand for those not familiar with modern portfolio theory. It requires the use of an optimization software package available from such firms as Barra, Quantal, or Northfield. In cases of portfolio customization, optimization can be useful in quantifying and managing risk. On the downside, third-party optimization software does not always offer easy scalability and integration into an investment manager's existing process and systems. This can create a significant burden when managing hundreds or thousands of separate accounts that must be individually optimized.

Managing the Portfolio for Index Tracking and Cost-Minimization

The management of these indexed-based strategies is anything but passive. Arguably, managing a customized, tax-managed account involves as much (if not more) skill as managing the typical active strategy available in the

SMA world. The following paragraphs detail some of the portfolio management considerations in delivering value to the SMA investor.

Once the initial portfolio is constructed, managing it on an ongoing basis presents additional challenges. Portfolio managers must determine how much cash to hold for liquidity, how to respond to corporate actions, how and when to rebalance or tax-loss harvest, how to handle contributions and redemptions, and how to transition existing portfolios. Portfolio managers must also consider operational processes and limitations, and understand the nuances of index construction to minimize active risk while maximizing benefits to the client.

Holding too much cash causes the performance of the portfolio to diverge from the performance of the index, also known as "cash drag." Holding too little cash may require unwanted trading, realization of capital gains, and poorer after-tax performance. To reduce the issues with cash drag, some or all of the cash may be equitized by investing in a market proxy such as exchange-traded funds or futures contracts.

There is no single rule for how to best respond to voluntary corporate actions. It is generally best to respond to achieve the most "advantageous economic benefit"; a seemingly simple and straightforward task. However, this also is not as clear-cut as it may initially sound. Managers must consider that their responses may cause tracking error, additional turnover, or significant operational difficulties, which could result in higher costs, which in turn may eventually need to be passed on to the clients. Thus, in every response to voluntary corporate actions, managers need to consider all these factors before deciding on the best course of action.

Non-fully-replicating portfolios will move out of line with the index. Even portfolios that are fully replicating will fall out of line since the indexes make periodic changes to reflect new securities, mergers, bankruptcies, shares outstanding, and so on. This necessitates rebalancing. But when should a manager rebalance? Again, as discussed in previous chapters, there is a trade-off between the frequency of rebalancing and the level of acceptable active risk. Ideally, managers should rebalance when the benefits exceed the attendant transactions costs, but in index-based SMAs, they must make a judgment call on relatively known trading costs versus the unknown benefit of improved future tracking. The addition of tax management adds another dimension to this decision. Rebalancing may result in capital gains that would negatively impact after-tax performance.

Once the manager determines *when* to rebalance, what follows is the more difficult question of *how* to rebalance, especially when using a non-optimized, index-based, tax-managed strategy. If you, as a manager, sell a stock but want to maintain a similar active risk profile, you could replace it with a stock closest in expected behavior (e.g., similar industry and size);

this seems simple enough. But what if you are selling a very large security, say 35 percent of an industry sector, and the next closest replacement stock in that sector only has a 5 percent index weight? Should you overweight the new stock by sevenfold? Or should you buy more than one security as a replacement? Should you force a rebalance again in 31 days to repurchase the loss-harvested stock? What if the temporary replacement stocks are in such a large gain that they would wipe out the benefits of the losses just harvested? These difficult questions must be addressed. There is no right answer for every situation, as every client places different utility on tracking error versus tax benefit. Tax-aware optimizers from Barra or Northfield are available to help answer this question.

Client flows also require the portfolio manager to actively engage in the best course of action, particularly for large redemptions. As an account decreases in size, it may no longer be large enough to hold the complete target portfolio in the appropriate weights. The portfolio manager would need to determine which stocks should be liquidated to minimize taxes while best maintaining the integrity of the portfolio's strategy. As with rebalances, there is a trade-off between managing the portfolio's active risk with known transaction and tax costs.

Customization

The direct ownership of stock in SMAs allows for consideration of the investor's entire financial picture when constructing a portfolio. In this truly customized portfolio, specific securities or entire sectors can be modified to accommodate an investor's preexisting positions, risk tolerance, or social preferences. While modifications such as these will invariably affect the tracking of the portfolio relative to the index, many find the benefit of customization more important.

Existing exposures may include other securities held outside the portfolio or through employment. An investor may work for a technology company and own stock options in the company. Using a holistic approach, the investor may want to avoid additional exposure to the technology sector. Or, as portrayed in Figure 24.2, an investor who already has a core stock holding in the health care industry—perhaps due to an inheritance of stock—can invest in a large-cap strategy that excludes the entire sector.

Index-based SMAs, because of their individual stock ownership, allow infinite customization for an investor's social concerns or preferences. These restrictions may seek to exclude tobacco, gaming, or alcohol stocks from a portfolio. The extensive discussion of socially responsible investing and benchmarks in Chapter 13 describes how large institutions can take a customized, activist approach to their indexing. While individuals have

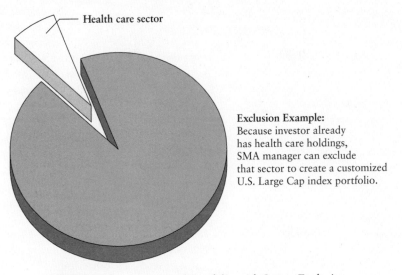

Health care sector

Exclusion Example:
Because investor already
has health care holdings,
SMA manager can exclude
that sector to create a customized
U.S. Large Cap index portfolio.

FIGURE 24.2 Customized Portfolio with Sector Exclusion

access to socially responsible index funds, their views must be aligned with that of the fund. In contrast, with an index-based SMA, individuals have the same flexibility as institutions to act on their specific concerns, whether it be environmental, corporate governance-oriented, religious, or even political.

ACTIVE TAX MANAGEMENT

The Jobs and Growth Tax Relief Reconciliation Act of 2003 allows for qualified dividends and long-term capital gains to be taxed at a maximum of 15 percent from 2003 through 2008. Short-term capital gains are taxed at a maximum of 35 percent. While this is an improvement over the prior rates, taxes still dramatically reduce investors' real return both before and post liquidation. The longer an investor defers paying taxes, the greater the benefit. Active tax management makes this possible.

Active tax management is one of the most appealing benefits of an index based SMA. Owning the individual securities in a portfolio makes it possible to control when capital gains and losses are realized. This has benefits for ongoing portfolio management, and can also be used in establishing a client portfolio, through a tax-managed transition (see the *Tax-Managed Transitions* sidebar).

TAX-MANAGED TRANSITIONS

With an SMA, it is possible to transition an existing position in a tax-efficient manner. In the example in this box, a cash investment of $100,000 was made in a new SMA portfolio along with an existing position with a market value of $30,000 (cost basis $10,000). The investor may either liquidate the existing position and pay the taxes of $7,500 (assuming a tax rate of 35 percent on a gain of $20,000), or build a portfolio with the cash investment and harvest losses to offset the unrealized capital gains.

For simplicity in this example, we are assuming the overall value of the portfolio stays flat for a three-year period. We then assume that enough losses are generated over the next three years to completely offset the unrealized gain of the existing position. At the end of three years, the existing position has been completely sold, but we have deferred $7,800 in taxes. Notice that as losses are harvested, the cost basis of the portfolio drops.

	New SMA Investment $100,000 ($)	Existing Position $30,000 ($)	Cost Basis $110,000 ($)	Unreal G/L $20,000 ($)	Losses Harvested ($)
End year 1			103,000	13,000	−7,000
End year 2			96,000	6,000	−7,000
End year 3			90,000	0	−6,000

Even the most basic techniques of tax management require a manager to utilize tax lot accounting. Using HIFO (highest cost basis in, first out) when liquidating can minimize the impact of taxes. Avoiding short-term gains is another simple technique. A large percentage of the benefits of active tax management can be realized by combining two strategies, described below.

Tax-Loss Matching

Tax-loss matching is accomplished by incurring an offsetting realized loss whenever the portfolio incurs a capital gain. Although this technique is much easier to implement than aggressive loss harvesting, the after-tax benefits may be diminished compared with those of a loss-harvesting program.

Tax-Loss Harvesting

Loss harvesting involves actively selling securities below their cost basis to realize capital losses. This technique can increase after-tax returns by allowing the investor to offset current and future capital gains inside and outside the portfolio. The power of loss harvesting comes in the deferral of the tax. When a loss is incurred in a portfolio, the cost basis of the portfolio drops by the amount of the loss incurred.

As an example, assume an investor has an original cost basis of $100,000 in a portfolio and has harvested $10,000 in losses. After reinvestment of the proceeds for the loss sales, the new cost basis would be $90,000. If the portfolio appreciated 10 percent from the initial value in both the portfolio using loss harvesting and the portfolio not using loss harvesting, the terminal value would be $110,000. The portfolio using loss harvesting would have $20,000 in capital gains at liquidation, while the non-loss-harvesting portfolio would have $10,000 in gains. The difference is that the loss-harvesting portfolio deferred $10,000 in gains until the time of liquidation. The longer taxes can be deferred, the greater the capital base to invest and generate additional return. Thus, while the tax liability does not go away, it is deferred with the potential to add return on the portion of funds that would have otherwise been sent to the government.

A loss-harvesting program within an SMA should be both aggressive and reasonable in terms of trading. One may argue that losses should be harvested anytime the tax-benefit of the loss outweighs the cost of the trade. This can create additional operational burdens due to the potentially high trading activity. Quarterly loss harvesting can achieve much of the same benefit with less turnover than harvesting as the opportunities present themselves (other trigger-based rules may be used as well). In an index-based SMA, it is important to reinvest proceeds immediately after loss harvesting, to avoid the cash drag on the portfolio. To avoid wash-sale rules, proceeds may not be invested in the same security for at least 30 days, but proceeds may be invested in securities with a similar risk profile to minimize the impact on the portfolio. Loss harvesting also presents an opportunity to rebalance the portfolio (e.g., in a sampled portfolio, a manager could invest the proceeds in industry sectors underweighted relative to the benchmark index).

Capital losses can be used to offset capital gains incurred during the year or in future years using capital loss carryforwards. Loss-harvesting opportunities are more prevalent in the early years of a portfolio, and it is important to harvest losses aggressively during that period. Prices of stocks within the portfolio will be closer to their original cost basis in the early years, increasing the odds of owning stocks with unrealized capital losses. After several years, fewer stocks are likely to have unrealized capital gains and the portfolio may experience lockup. Loss harvesting is a powerful technique in maximizing the after-tax returns of an index-based SMA. Numerous studies have shown that loss harvesting can consistently add anywhere from 25 to 75 basis points annually of after-tax return, and many portfolio track records have substantially exceeded this performance.[5] This extra return is gained from deferring capital gains offset by losses generated from tax-loss harvesting.

Delivering on the Index-Based Separately Managed Accounts Promise

Like institutional index funds and ETFs, managing index-based SMAs is *anything but passive*. While they aren't active in the sense of requiring traditional security research, analysis, and stock-picking skills, they need more attention than just following the index. Index-based SMAs require a sensitive balance between minimizing tracking error for relatively small account sizes while using a limited number of securities. Additionally, portfolio managers must take great care to use active tax-management strategies that maximize the benefits of tax-loss harvesting while maintaining portfolio integrity and risk control.

USES OF INDEX-BASED SEPARATELY MANAGED ACCOUNTS

The flexibility and simplicity inherent in index-based strategies make them ideal investment strategies for the investor in separate accounts. These strategies are similar to their institutional counterparts but may be even more critical for the individual investor, and are consistent with the philosophy articulated throughout the book. We highlight two of them here, but they are described in more detail in Part Five.

Core-Satellite Strategy

One of the most important strategies is the *core-satellite* approach, or "core and explore," as it is popularly known. The concept is simple: An indexed-based portfolio provides a stable, efficient core around which traditional active managers take satellite positions. This practice has become almost the standard among large pension funds and other institutional investors. It is not yet commonplace within the SMA world, but is rapidly gaining traction with fee-based independent advisors, as described in Chapter 28. Index-based portfolios provide stable, cost-efficient exposure to key core benchmarks, while satellite actively managed portfolios exploit opportunities in less-efficient market segments. This strategy provides important benefits to the taxable investor:

■ *Adds value.* Indexing provides consistent benchmark-like performance that provides the base from which carefully selected active managers offer the opportunity to outperform the benchmark.
■ *Lower costs.* As discussed in previous chapters, index-based strategies generally have lower expense ratios than actively managed funds, both from lower fees and lower portfolio turnover.
■ *Lower taxes.* An actively tax-managed index-based portfolio can harvest losses that can be used to offset the gains from the active managers—increasing after-tax returns.
■ *Risk control.* A core-satellite strategy lets investors budget and control risk more effectively. If one thinks of risk as something you can budget, then a core-satellite approach (discussed in more detail in Chapters 28 and 30) lets you "spend" your risk budget more effectively.

Completion Portfolio

Another strategy that was first seen in the institutional investor arena is the *completion* or residual portfolio. The concept is that in any investment program put together with several active investment managers, there are inevitably overlaps and gaps in the overall asset allocation—whether an overweight in growth stocks, or large-cap value. As discussed in Chapter 18, an index-based portfolio is an ideal vehicle to use to offset any overlaps and fill in any gaps in a strategic or tactical allocation.

Even a carefully selected group of active managers may still leave investors with gaps in their asset allocation or overall investment plan. For example, active managers may be concentrated in large-capitalization stocks, leaving the small-cap area underinvested. In this case, a small-cap index strategy may be used to plug the *risk hole* in the overall plan. The completion portfolio can therefore improve the investor's asset allocation. A completion portfolio provides simple and efficient exposure to parts of the market that may be missing with an active-only investment plan.

THE FUTURE OF INDEX-BASED SEPARATELY MANAGED ACCOUNTS

While as of this writing in the fourth quarter of 2003, index-based SMAs have captured only about one percent of the approximately $450 billion wrap account business, this market share undoubtedly will grow. The investment logic of indexing is just as relevant in the SMA marketplace as it is to the institutional or mutual fund market. Given that industry's promise to its clients is to deliver institutional quality management, it is surprising that it has not gained more traction to-date. Index-based separately managed accounts have the potential to provide individual investors with the best of both worlds—the wisdom of indexing combined with the power of customization and active tax management. Tax management creates tax alpha that investors can realize each year at tax season. Investors and their advisors can no longer ignore this value proposition.

As discussed by Mark Zurack in Chapter 27, there are clear advantages for high-net-worth investors to prefer an index-based separate account over traditional mutual funds and even ETFs. And as Michael Chasnoff highlights in Chapter 28, more advisors are adapting the core-satellite allocation approach—index-based customized tax-managed core portfolios are exactly the type of product that should be at the center of such approaches. Chapter 30 provides some examples of how such overall strategies can be constructed.

Finally, rigorous performance measurement—and the transparency that comes with it—are finally coming to the separately managed account industry. Both Morningstar and S&P are developing manager databases for these financial products. Thus, it is inevitable that more accurate style categorization and greater use of benchmarks will occur. From the early history of indexing's growth in both the institutional arena in the 1980s and the mutual fund marketplace in the 1990s, as described in Part One, we know that rigorous benchmarking is the first step toward greater use of index products.

Product integration within the financial services industry will also drive growth of index-based SMAs. "Tax-managed core" (a.k.a. index-based) strategies are now available on the two largest managed account programs sponsored by Merrill Lynch and Citigroup/Smith Barney. Major brokers and advisors are also developing the capabilities for unified managed accounts. The two first examples introduced to the industry are Citigroup/Smith Barney's Integrated Investment Solutions and Lincoln Financial Services' LincSolutions platforms. These enable the seamless combination of SMAs with ETFs, mutual funds, and other investment vehicles such as hedge funds. This integration will spur growth of multiple style accounts and other multiasset class strategies (see Chapters 18 and 30). The customization capabilities and tax-efficient attributes of index-based separate accounts will logically place them at the core of these integrated approaches that hold so much promise for investors.

NOTES

1. The first widely available index-based separate accounts were developed by Parametric Portfolio Associates (www.paraport.com), but the trust/high net worth arms of both State Street Global Advisors and Northern Trust Global Investors have been managing such strategies for a similar amount of time.
2. Industry estimates project the decade-end figure at well over $1 trillion, but we prefer to be conservative in our expectations.
3. Source: Cerulli Associates Inc. Cerulli's year-end 2003 estimate was just under $500 billion.
4. Chapter 29, an excerpt from *The Great Mutual Fund Trap* highlights other shortcomings of mutual funds, though for a full exposé, we recommend reading the entire book (New York: Broadway Books, 2002).
5. Robert Arnott and Robert Jeffrey, "Is Your Alpha Big Enough to Cover Its Taxes?" *Journal of Portfolio Management* (Spring 1993); and Robert Arnott, Andrew Berkin, and Jin Ye, "Loss Harvesting: What's It Worth to the Taxable Investor?" *First Quadrant Investment Management Reflections,* no. 1 (2001).

Pulling It All Together

How to Use Index Products to Build an Efficient, Risk-Controlled Investment Strategy

Steven A. Schoenfeld

In Part Three of the book, readers learned about the breadth of various index products and strategies. In Part Four, a detailed discussion of the art and science of managing index-based portfolios was provided. In Part Five of the book, we now look at how the most sophisticated investors in the world use index products as a key element of their investment strategy. As with the previous parts of the book, readers will see that there is nothing passive about the ways in which many investors deploy index-based approaches. This introductory section includes contributions and the perspective of major pension funds and other asset-owning institutions, global broker-dealers, financial advisors, and authors with a focus on individual investors' needs. In addition, the seven chapters of Part Five—and how they connect with other parts of the book—are summarized.

In Chapter 25, Joanne Hill and Barbara Mueller of the Goldman Sachs Group explore how an institutional investor can choose among the ever-growing variety of index-based investment strategies and products—with a focus on the products that investors can directly employ in the markets.

Like the authors of Chapter 16, they give readers the perspective of institutional brokers who provide advice and execution services to a wide range of investors—from pension plans to mutual fund managers to hedge funds. The chapter explores the key decision criteria for different types of users (tax-exempt plans, active managers, hedge funds, etc.) and looks at the pros and cons of use of each type of directly accessed index vehicle—among them index funds, exchange-traded funds (ETFs), futures, over the counter (OTC) swaps, and structured products. Thus, they cover four out of five of the primary choices for investors (with the following chapter covering the other option, namely use of externally or internally managed institutional index funds). As discussed earlier, this chapter also contains three valuable sidebars on the "pricing essentials" of index futures, ETFs, and index options.

In Chapter 26, "How and Why Large Pension Plans Use Index-Based Strategies as Their Core Investments," Nancy Calkins of the Washington State Investment Board (WSIB) looks at the ways that pension plans use index funds—whether as a core holding complemented by active satellite portfolios or with actively managed portfolios playing the lead role and index funds filling the gaps and reducing risk. It also depicts some of the ways that index funds can be used as building blocks to create active portfolios. Nancy notes that market volatility in the early 2000s has caused some pension plan assets to fall and liabilities to rise. Although there are no easy solutions to these situations, being cognizant of the pension plan's risk exposure, understanding the asset/liability characteristics, and maintaining a long-term perspective will assist in the development of a structure that fits the plan's needs. Clearly, index funds, with the flexibility they bring, will continue to play an important role in the structure of each pension plan.

The chapter also provides insight into how pension plans measure the value-added elements of institutional index fund managers—which helps them determine which ones to hire when mandates are put up for bid.

The three general ways plan sponsors can have securities-based index strategies are:

1. Commingled funds.
2. Separate accounts.
3. Internally managed funds.

Nancy explores the pros and cons of each approach, and thus when combined with the analysis in Chapter 25, through these opening chapters, readers will understand the full array of index products and how to make the choices of receiving index-based investment returns.

In addition to Nancy's extensive chapter, this part of the book includes two informative sidebars on other large institutions' use of index strategies and how they both correspond and differ from WSIB's approach. The first, *The State of Oregon's Blend of Index, Enhanced Index, and Active Equity Strategies* by Mike Mueller of the Oregon Treasury, shows how this large fund skillfully blends index, enhanced index, and active approaches to maximize performance and minimize risk for the fund. The second, *The Background and Logic of the Japan's Pension Fund Association's Use of Index Strategies,* is written by Yasuchika Asaoka, the PFA's Executive Director and a thought-leader within Japan's investment community. This chapter and sidebars should expand readers' insight on how institutional investors use index funds as part of their overall investment strategy.

In Chapter 27, "Tax-Efficient Indexation," Mark Zurack, a former partner at Goldman Sachs who now teaches at Columbia University, details the trade-offs and choices an investor faces when adding tax considerations into the index-based investment equation. It builds on the knowledge gained in Part Three, Chapters 25, and 26, and highlights how indexing is most efficient for tax-sensitive investment and also how with some strategies one can even add *tax alpha,* as first explored in Chapters 14 and 24.

The next chapter, "Indexing for Advisors: A Sophisticated Strategy for Professional Investment Advisors and Their Clients," provides the framework for advisors and investors to develop and implement an intelligent investment program through index strategies. This chapter begins the shift in focus of Part Five more toward the investing needs of individual investors. Michael Chasnoff—who heads a financial advisory firm that assists high net worth investors with their investments—concludes that it is a sensible framework for establishing long-term investment strategies that take into account the investment objective, investment time-horizon, and a realistic expectation of securities markets over the long-run. A sidebar within this chapter by Joyce Franklin of JLFranklin Wealth Management discusses the way advisors can use ETFs to minimize taxation in their clients' portfolios.

Chapter 29, "Indexing for Individual Investors," is an edited excerpt from the book *The Great Mutual Fund Trap,* which was recently published in paperback. This chapter further shifts the focus of Part Five toward individual investors, and how they can emulate the successful approaches used by larger and more sophisticated investors. The authors, Greg Baer and Gary Gensler, both former senior U.S. Treasury officials, recount the many traps that sensible people seem to fall into when it comes to making investment decisions. The book was originally published in 2002 and was quite prescient about numerous issues that were to become factors in the mutual fund scandals that surfaced in 2003. With insightful statistics and humorous anecdotes, they remind individual investors that past performance really isn't indicative of future performance; that paying front loads and back loads defies common sense; and that while index investing may be less fun, it can certainly be more profitable—as U.S. civil servants participating in the government's Thrift Savings Plan know very well.

Chapter 30, "Indexing at the Core: The Four Key Axioms of Long-Term Investment Success," is in some ways the editor's *investment manifesto,* applying the experience of major institutional investors and my own two decades of investment experience. This chapter highlights some of the key macro concepts of investing, and how index product can be used to implement them. These four key concepts—which I call Axioms—are:

1. Determining an appropriate and diversified asset allocation.
2. Using risk-budgeting to determine appropriate manager/strategy allocation.
3. Disciplined rebalancing.
4. Explicit and implicit cost control—the one thing you can always control.

The chapter includes an overview of best practices in investing (not just for indexing) with extensive references to more detailed information on practical implementation issues, including ideas on how to access the best index-based strategies and products. The overarching goal of the chapter is to distill the lessons of the most sophisticated investors and provide insight for financial advisors and individual investors to achieve the subheading of the book's title, namely, to *maximize portfolio performance and minimize risk through global index strategies.* It also includes three notional model portfolios as an example for self-directed investors who might want to build their own portfolio with indexing at the core.

Finally, the book's concluding chapter, "The Future of Indexing: The Revolution Has Just Begun!," summarizes the key themes of the book, and provides some bold predictions for the future of indexing in world markets.[1] One of the major themes that I try to convey in this chapter is that the innovation and dynamism that has driven so much progress in the field of indexing in its first thirty years is still very much at work. All of the "drivers of innovation" described in Chapter 14 continue to work in overdrive. In many ways, the investment community has only just begun to fully apply the enormous potential of indexing, and this chapter takes a big picture approach to predict future growth for a variety of index products and some of the directions that we might see in their use.

Part Five of the book is entitled "Pulling It All Together: How to Use Index Products to Build an Efficient, Risk-Controlled Investment Strategy" because it aims to consolidate the themes and knowledge already explored in Parts One through Four of the book and demonstrate the ways in which sophisticated investors apply the flexibility of indexing. I hope that readers will find useful, actionable examples and insight that will be applicable to their own investment challenges. Thus, we start Part Five with a core chapter, Chapter 25, one that provides substantial fundamental information and sophisticated analysis.

NOTE

1. Although unique to the book, this chapter draws extensively on several previously published articles. A shorter, ETF-focused version of this chapter was published in *Institutional Investor's* Fall 2003 "ETFs II—New Approaches and Global Outreach" (see www.iiguides.com). Other parts of the chapter were adapted and enhanced from an article entitled "The Future of Tradeable Index Products" published in Hebrew in *HaBorsa*, the monthly publication of the Tel Aviv Stock Exchange. Finally, several other elements of the chapter were based on nonproprietary research and analysis conducted for one of the author's consulting clients in Q4 2003 and Q1 2004.

CHAPTER **25**

Choosing among Index Vehicles

How Does an Institutional Investor Select an Investment Product?

Joanne Hill and Barbara Mueller

_____ **Editor's Note** _____

As discussed in the introduction to Part Five, to start this section the authors provide an essential overview of the factors determining an investor's choice of index products, and the pros and cons of various instruments and strategies. Their analysis focuses on the choices available to institutional investors—pension funds, active and index mutual fund managers, global asset allocators, hedge funds, and proprietary trading desks, with an emphasis on strategies deployed directly in the capital markets. Although there are really five choices for a large investor, Joanne and Barbara's focus is on four of them—with the assessment of using internal or external index portfolio managers covered extensively by Nancy Calkins in Chapter 26. Even though not all of these instruments and strategies are available or appropriate for all types of investors, it should be useful for readers to understand the broadest range of choices. Furthermore, even with a more limited choice, much of the decision process regarding investment vehicles would be similar for sophisticated financial advisors or individuals.

As readers might expect, the decision process employed involves trade-offs—different index vehicles and techniques have varied benefits and costs, and this helps determine which index product is right for any given purpose. The authors conclude that—similar to the choice of benchmarks discussed in Chapter 6—there is no one best solution for all situations. In fact, a mix or range of index products are commonly used by institutional investors and the differences among the products provide valuable choices as well as additional arbitrage opportunities for investors.

Readers will find that while there is a degree of repetition with some other chapters in the book, Chapter 25 also supplements and enhances readers' understanding of the topic. In particular, there is some overlap with the coverage in Chapters 14, 15, and 16 of various index and enhanced index strategies, and the overview of ETFs in Chapter 16. However, this chapter integrates the coverage of the vehicles with a specific assessment of the pros and cons of the alternatives. Finally, the chapter includes three useful sidebars on the pricing essentials for index futures, ETFs, and index swaps. I am sure that readers will find this to be an invaluable chapter, one that can be a foundation for understanding the nuances of the primary index vehicles.

There are many ways to capture index returns without buying (or shorting) a stock portfolio that tracks a benchmark. This book identifies five ways to own index returns; namely, securities-based index-tracking portfolios, index futures, exchange-traded funds (ETFs), index swaps, and index options. The latter four—index futures, ETFs, index swaps, and index options—all play a crucial role in a variety of investment strategies, including index replication, enhanced indexing, traditional active management, and leveraged strategies favored by hedge funds. These four ways are the focus of this chapter, which focuses only on equity index products, although most of the issues discussed are relevant for other asset classes. Investors often prefer these index products for their liquidity, pricing, and ease of entry and exit relative to a direct investment in a traditional index fund or stock portfolio. In this chapter, we first describe some of the most important properties of stock index futures, ETFs, equity index swaps, and index options and then summarize features to be considered when selecting the best vehicle to achieve an investment objective.

FIVE WAYS TO OWN EQUITY INDEX RETURNS

Even though the products differ in important ways, each provides the economic equivalent of investing in a index-tracking basket of stocks. Figure 25.1, "Five Ways to Own Equity Index Returns," shows the elements of index return delivered by five different products: physical stock portfolios, equity index futures, exchange-traded funds, index swaps, and index options. Although the total returns for each product are similar, the cash flows that result from each investment are quite different and are represented by

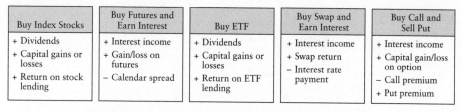

Buy Index Stocks	Buy Futures and Earn Interest	Buy ETF	Buy Swap and Earn Interest	Buy Call and Sell Put
+ Dividends	+ Interest income	+ Dividends	+ Interest income	+ Interest income
+ Capital gains or losses	+ Gain/loss on futures	+ Capital gains or losses	+ Swap return	+ Capital gain/loss on option
+ Return on stock lending	− Calendar spread	+ Return on ETF lending	− Interest rate payment	− Call premium
				+ Put premium

FIGURE 25.1   Five Ways to Own Equity Index Returns

the "+" and "−" signs within the boxes. This has significant implications for many investment strategies and may affect transaction costs, tax efficiency, and leverage.

Part Four of the book focused heavily on the types of institutional index funds (managed by major institutional asset managers). As discussed in the Editor's Note, this chapter focuses primarily on the types of index exposure that are available directly in the capital markets, usually facilitated by a broker-dealer such as our firm. Chapter 26 includes further discussion of the distinguishing features and advantages of institutional comingled index funds which pension plans, foundations, and endowments acquire directly from large index fund management firms. This chapter now goes into detail on the latter four of these five ways to achieve index returns, which we have numbered from 1 to 4.

1. SYNTHETIC INDEXING WITH FUTURES

As discussed in Chapters 14 and 20, equity index futures are often used to generate synthetic index returns. Consider the case of an investment manager who needs $100 million of S&P 500 index exposure. Rather than buying stocks, the manager may buy S&P 500 futures contracts. With the index level at 1000 and a multiplier of $250 for the large S&P 500 contracts listed on the Chicago Mercantile Exchange (CME), the manager needs 400 contracts to get $100 million of index exposure.[1]

No actual payment is required to establish the futures position, but the futures exchanges require that a performance bond or initial margin in the form of cash or U.S. Treasury bills be posted with the clearing broker, who in turn posts the margin with the exchange. Although initial margin requirements are periodically adjusted, they typically represent 5 percent to 10 percent of the notional value of a futures position. Since futures are marked-to-market daily, the holder's futures account also receives daily cash profits and must have cash deposited to cover any day-to-day losses.

Because the manager has not used the $90 to $95 million that remains after satisfying margin requirements for the futures, the manager can invest this in another instrument. To match index returns, the manager must earn interest equal to or higher than the interest rate implied in the futures price, as described in the sidebar titled "Futures Pricing Essentials." The synthetic returns generated from this investment should be very similar to the total returns of the S&P 500 Index. If the manager decided to maintain the synthetic index exposure longer than the three-month life of an S&P 500 futures contract, the position would be rolled forward by closing out the initial position and initiating a position in the next contract, usually by trading the calendar spread. Over any period, the synthetic return can be calculated as:

$$\text{Synthetic return (percent)} = \frac{(\text{Change in futures level} + \text{Interest income} - \text{Calendar spread})}{\text{Index level at start of period} \times 100}$$

While holding the futures, the manager can experience tracking risk between the actual index and the synthetic index fund due to deviations of the futures contract from its fair value at interim performance measurement points and mismatches between interest income and the interest rate implied by the futures prices.

Figure 25.2 shows how S&P 500 futures have traded relative to fair value based on daily closing futures levels over the five years ending December 2002. Because futures trade 15 minutes beyond the close of the stock

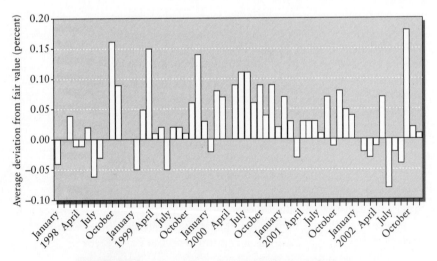

FIGURE 25.2   Mispricing of S&P 500 Futures Contract
Source: Goldman Sachs.

FUTURES PRICING ESSENTIALS

Whereas the owner of a stock portfolio earns income in the form of dividends and experiences capital gains or losses, the owner of futures contract does not receive dividends and has a built-in capital gain or loss from the futures basis, which is calculated as the difference between the futures level and the level of its corresponding index. Although the actual future's basis fluctuates due to the supply and demand for futures at any point, the theoretical or "fair" future's basis can be calculated as the difference between future's fair value and the index, as follows:

$$\text{Fair basis}_t = \text{Fair value}_t - \text{Index}_t = \text{(Expected interest income}$$
$$- \text{Expected dividend} - \text{Expected stock lending}$$
$$\text{proceeds) from } t_s \text{ to } T_s, \text{ expressed in index points}$$

where t_s = Settlement day for stock purchased on day t
T_s = Settlement day for stocks sold on the future's expiration date

A future's fair value is the price at which a futures position is economically equivalent to an investment in an index stock portfolio held over the same period. Because a stock index futures contract is a commitment to transact at a point in the future, the fair futures price is not equal to the current price of the stock portfolio (or index). For a seller of stocks to be indifferent between receiving the transaction proceeds now or at a future date, the buyer must pay the appropriate interest on the amount owed until expiration. On the other hand, the seller continues to receive dividends and any proceeds from lending stock until the transaction is completed. This means that the fair value for a futures contract is equal to the current price of a stock portfolio (or index) plus interest income minus dividends and stock loan proceeds until expiration. When futures trade at fair value, both buyer and seller should be indifferent between an immediate stock transaction and exchanging a futures contract for settlement at a later date.

When futures prices move out of line with their fair value, there may be an arbitrage opportunity, depending on the costs of executing the arbitrage trade. If futures are trading below fair value, or "cheap," arbitrageurs may buy futures and sell stocks to capture the futures basis. When futures trade above fair value, or "rich," arbitrageurs may

(Continued)

sell futures and buy stocks. Because futures prices converge to the value of the index on expiration by definition, the profit can be locked-in on any positions held to expiration. If the futures become even more mispriced, a profit can be realized by closing the position at market prices, but holding the contracts to expiration guarantees a profit equal to the actual basis minus any costs of trading.

In fact, fair value is better expressed as a range rather than a single value, where the width of this fair value range is driven by the cost of arbitrage. The width of this band can vary greatly, depending on the cost of trading stocks and futures, and the degree of difficulty in executing simultaneous transactions in stocks and futures. Because shorting stocks requires borrowing the securities, while shorting futures does not, transaction costs are typically not equal for both sides of the arbitrage transaction. In addition, because the interest rates, dividends, and stock loan proceeds that will prevail through the expiration date can't be predicted with perfect certainty, different investors may calculate different fair values.

Fair value band (Max) = Fair value + Cost of buying stocks and
                        selling futures + Execution timing risk
                        premium

Fair value band (Min) = Fair value − Cost of borrowing stocks
                        (shorting) and buying futures − Execution
                        timing risk premium

There is a second source of mispricing for futures contracts. Since futures expire, investors who desire to hold index positions beyond the expiration date must *roll* into a new contract, executing what is called a *calendar spread trade*. For example, if an investor is long June 2003 S&P 500 futures and wishes to maintain index exposure, he or she must sell the June future and buy the September future, usually in a single calendar spread transaction. The spread, or difference between the prices of these two contracts, can also trade away from the fair spread, which is calculated as the difference between the fair values for each contract.

markets, there is a timing differential in the performance of futures versus the underlying stock index. When stock or macro news announcements are made during this 15-minute interval, the futures reflect market moves that will not be reflected in the stock market until the next day. When calculating daily mispricing or comparing daily performance, this tends to exaggerate the differences between the futures and stocks, although these only reflect timing differences and are not true mispricing.

Because of the "noise" that results from the difference in closing times, the CME now marks futures settlement prices at fair value at month-end. Although these month-end marks do not indicate where futures can be traded, they minimize the transient fluctuations in futures mispricing for performance measurement purposes. Since trading flows are often concentrated around month-end, supply and demand imbalances may temporarily push futures more than usually rich or cheap versus fair value. The mispricing is often reversed in the next period and so increases the performance deviations for both periods; however, arbitrage and the convergence of futures to the index price at expiration will keep pushing the futures back toward fair value.

When investors roll stock index positions in order to maintain index exposure beyond the date of the futures expiration, they may experience mispricing of the calendar spread, which can introduce deviations in performance relative to the index. The longer the position is held, the more times the investor must roll and the more important the calendar spread mispricing becomes relative to initial mispricing. Figure 25.3 shows the

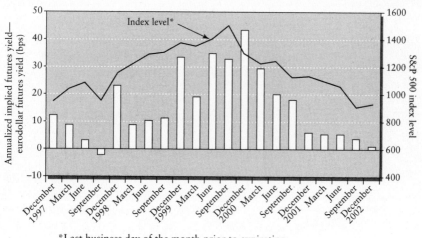

*Last business day of the month prior to expiration.

FIGURE 25.3   S&P 500 Futures Calendar Spread Mispricing

range of mispricing for the S&P 500 calendar spread, calculated on an annualized basis for the five years ending December 2002. As visible in the figure, during the period of the strongest bull market returns many investors aggressively bought futures to gain exposure to the market and many portfolio managers bought futures to "equitize" any cash balances in order to avoid missing out on the high equity returns. This led to persistent excess demand for long futures positions, pushing up the mispricing of S&P 500 calendar spreads during the 2000/2001 period to about 20 basis points (bps) to 45 bps over the fair spread. This premium subsequently declined, and since 2002, there now appears to be a more balanced demand and supply for index exposure via S&P 500 futures.

Futures Liquidity

One of the greatest advantages of stock index futures is their deep liquidity; in the United States the notional value traded in futures frequently exceeds that of the stock market. Greater liquidity tends to decrease the market impact of a trade, reducing the transaction costs for entry and exit. Futures tend to become more liquid in periods when investors are focused on geopolitical or economic events, and in declining markets. This occurs because investors have a greater desire to adjust their market exposure, and the futures market offers an efficient way to do so. Short positions are also easier to establish with futures since there is no need to borrow stock and, unlike stocks, futures may be sold short without waiting for an uptick (although the same is true for ETFs). Figure 25.4 shows the average daily volume of U.S.-listed stock index futures as a percentage of the value-traded of U.S. stock volume. For most years, futures volume represents more than 100 percent of stock volume, but during the late 1990s and very early 2000s stock volume increased more rapidly than futures volume as investors concentrated on stock-picking and technology exposure rather than the index exposure provided through futures.

With over a 20-year history of floor trading for index futures, a significant shift to electronic trading is occurring in the U.S. stock index futures volume in the United States grew 73 percent in contract terms in 2001, and another 50 percent in 2002. Much of this growth has been in the electronically traded "e-mini" contracts—traded on the CME's Globex platform.

S&P 500 futures are the most liquid equity futures contracts in the world, in part because of the wide acceptance of the S&P 500 index as a proxy for market exposure. The dollar value of trading in S&P 500 futures averaged about $43 billion per day during 2002, accounting for 79 percent of the index futures activity in the United States and 44 percent of the world's total stock index futures trading volume. Although equity index futures first

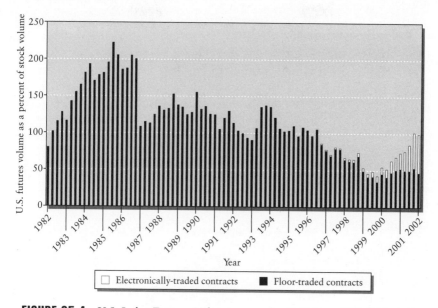

FIGURE 25.4   U.S. Index Futures Volume versus Stock Volume (Value-Traded)

traded in the United States (starting in 1982), as discussed in Chapter 14, there are now liquid futures contracts for most of the world's major markets. The most liquid index futures contract outside the United States during 2002 was the EuroSTOXX 50 contract, which traded a value of US$9 billion per day and represents some of the largest capitalization stocks in the EuroZone. Figure 25.5 shows the distribution of stock index futures activity in the major regions of the world as of the end of 2002. As in the United States, futures volume is high relative to stock volume in many international markets—and this has become a general indicator of overall equity market liquidity.

The wide selection of global futures contracts and the liquidity and leverage they provide has spurred the development of a number of strategies that use futures to overlay cash or indexed stock portfolios to enhance return. These include global-asset allocation strategies that use futures to establish long or short positions in equity markets according to quantitative models. Futures are now an established part of the equity trading markets globally and the most widely used product for managing broad equity market exposure on the part of both investors and equity dealers. Futures markets are often the first to react to key events and are recognized as the centers of price discovery for very active markets. Figure 25.6 shows the ratio of index futures volume to stock volume for some of the major international equity indexes in Europe and the Pacific.[2]

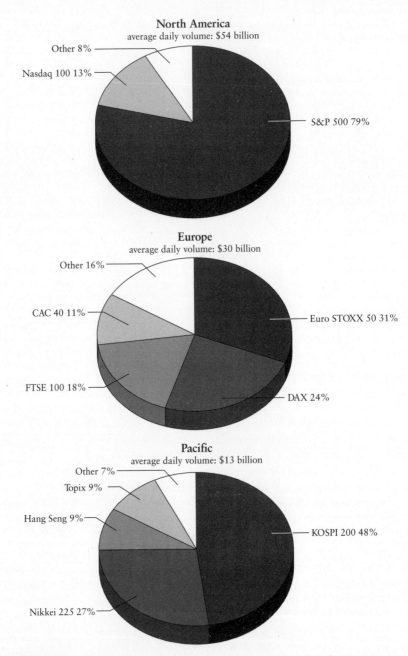

FIGURE 25.5 Trading Activity in Major Index Futures Markets by Region (End-2002)
Source: Goldman Sachs.

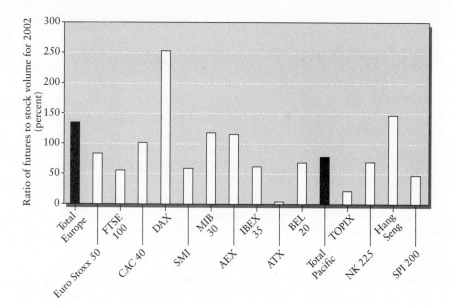

FIGURE 25.6 Ratio of Index Futures Volume to Stock Market Volume (End-2002)

Transaction Costs for Futures

Since index futures positions need to be, in effect, turned over 100 percent each quarter, it is important to consider the trading costs of a synthetic index strategy. The costs for establishing a futures position include commissions and market impact. Futures commissions are typically much lower than those for a comparable investment in a stock portfolio. Although commission rates vary, we estimate that commissions on an S&P 500 futures trade are currently about ¹⁄₁₀ the commissions for an equivalent S&P 500 stock portfolio trade. Market impact is the second element of initial transaction costs. This cost is defined as the amount that the market moves as a result of the trade, even if prices were unchanged by other factors. Market impact varies over time and in response to market conditions, but is typically somewhat lower for futures when compared with the stocks in an underlying basket.

The holding costs for futures are different from those of stocks. Each time a futures contract is rolled, the investor pays commissions and experiences some market impact. In addition, the investor has on-going risk that the calendar spread trades away from fair value. When trading rich, this is an additional cost for a long futures position and a benefit for a short position.

The reverse is true when the calendar spread trades cheap. Historically, the richness or cheapness of calendar spreads for many futures contracts has persisted over multiple market cycles. For example, over the 12 months ending in December 2002, the S&P 500 closing calendar spread averaged 5 bps rich, with a range of 0 bps to 6 bps.

As discussed in Part Four of the book, a stock-based index fund has some holding costs as well. Stock portfolios that track indexes need to be rebalanced periodically to follow index changes and must reinvest dividends, while futures automatically reflect the changes. Over the past five years, the average annual turnover of the S&P 500 has been 6 percent and the annual dividend yield was about 2 percent. Rebalancing and reinvesting activities for stock portfolios would typically incur commission and market impact costs.

Other Important Considerations

An advantage of futures is that they allow for greater leverage than does a stock portfolio. In the United States, the requirement for stocks falls under the Fed's Regulation T, which typically requires 50 percent margin while futures margin is usually 5 percent to 10 percent. This means that futures can be used very effectively in overlay and asset allocation strategies. Frequently, in these strategies, the investor has a core portfolio that is combined with dollar-neutral long and short positions designed to overweight and underweight countries or asset classes based on a fundamental view.

For U.S. investors to directly buy or sell international equity futures, the futures contracts must receive a "no action" letter from the Commodities Futures TradingCommission. As discussed in Chapter 21, contracts that do not have this de-facto approval will have limited access for U.S.-based investors. Another aspect to international index investing with futures is the management of the currency exposure. To illustrate the issue, consider the case where a U.S.-based investor owns S&P 500 exposure by being long S&P 500 futures along with a position in U.S. Treasury bills. The investor wants to shift half of his holding into EuroSTOXX 50 futures and the other half into Topix futures in order to invest in Eurozone and Japanese equities. If he sells his S&P 500 futures and buys EuroSTOXX 50 and Topix futures, he will only have to put up a small proportion of his position as margin in euros or yen. The rest of his funds still retain exposure to U.S. dollars. Therefore, if he wished to replicate a position in these international indexes, he might capture euro and yen currency exposure using currency forwards of futures covering the notional amount of the international futures. In this way, his position will deliver returns similar to those achieved by an investor who would sell a portfolio of S&P 500 stocks and shift into EuroSTOXX 50 or

Topix stocks at the prevailing exchange rates. If the investor wished to invest outside the United States on a currency-hedged basis, he would not buy foreign currency exposure, but would instead sell foreign currency forward in an amount equal to any cash put up for initial margin against the international futures.

The relatively low-cost, high-liquidity, high-leverage features of index futures make them especially useful for some of the following investment strategies:

- Equitizing cash.
- Tightening benchmark tracking.
- Enhancing index returns.
- Synthetic international indexing.
- Global asset allocation.
- Synthetic indexing as part of a strategy or manager transition.
- Country or capitalization tilts.

2. INDEXING WITH ETFs

As discussed in Chapters 14, 16, and 23, since the first products were listed in the United States in 1992/1993, ETFs have become widely used by institutions and individuals and their coverage has expanded to encompass a broad range of size, style, and sector indexes for the United States and many international indexes. In some cases, investors must trade ETFs rather than futures because of policy restrictions on their use of derivatives. (As stated in previous chapters, although they share some functional characteristics, ETFs are *not* equity derivatives.) In other cases, ETFs provide exposure to a specific index or market segment for which futures do not exist. Many investors find ETFs operationally more convenient than index futures because of their simplicity and similarity to stocks for trading, bookkeeping, monitoring, and performance measurement.

The variety of available ETF products is a major advantage over futures. While only about 10 U.S. equity index futures contracts trade actively, there are now over 120 ETFs listed on U.S. exchanges. Some appeal as trading vehicles, while others fill gaps in longer term portfolio holdings. The most actively traded ETFs include SPY and QQQ as well as a number of HOLding Company Depositary Receipts^{SM} (HOLDRs). Other ETFs—especially those based on the Russell and Wilshire benchmark indexes—have attracted more interest as longer-term portfolio holdings, but are less actively traded.

ETFs have filled a need that is not easily met by index futures: tradable instruments that offer precise exposure to size, style, and sector segments of the market. Whereas both futures and ETFs trade on exchanges, providing efficient matching of buyers and sellers, the "upstairs" ETF markets have provided more flexibility in facilitating ETF trades for customers. This additional source of capital and liquidity provides a significant advantage for ETFs on segments of the market where interest is cyclical.

Buying or shorting an ETF generally provides the investor with exposure to the index that the ETF tracks. As discussed in Chapter 23, some ETFs track modified versions of published indexes because of concentration limits that need to be met for funds organized under the Investment Company Act of 1940, or in order to meet the definition of a diversified fund according to the Internal Revenue Service. For example, the Energy SPDRs and Dow Jones U.S. Energy iShares periodically reset the weight of ExxonMobil so that it does not exceed 25 percent of the funds. This means that the ETFs have performance differences when compared with the standard S&P Energy Index and the Dow Jones U.S. Energy Index, which do not cap the weight of any stocks. The ETFs essentially track modified capitalization-weighted versions of these indexes.

As discussed in previous chapters, ETFs that track some of the broadest indexes, such as the Russell 3000 and the Wilshire 5000, use a sampling approach to construct the underlying stock portfolio. In this case, there is some tracking error relative to the index due to the sampling. Management fees and dividends also influence the performance of ETFs. Some of the fund structures allow for the reinvestment of dividends within the fund; others do not. Some U.S.-listed ETFs on equity indexes pay out dividends quarterly, so both the reinvestment process and the timing of dividend payments may influence the relative performance of ETFs and their underlying indexes. Management fees range from 9 bps to 99 bps on an annualized basis, depending on the fund and are reflected on a pro rata basis in the daily net asset value (NAV).

Another factor to consider in comparing performance is related to the timing of the last ETF trade as compared with the closing price of the stocks that make up the underlying index. Like futures, SPY, QQQ, and many other broad-based ETFs trade for 15 minutes beyond the close of the stock markets, contributing to daily divergence in performance that is often reversed on the following day. Another timing discrepancy is reflected in the tracking errors of less liquid ETFs versus their indexes. In some cases, the last trade for an ETF occurs considerably earlier than the stock market close. As discussed in Chapter 23, ETFs based on international indexes that trade on U.S. exchanges are the most extreme case; because broker/dealers and exchange specialists price these most competitively when they can hedge their exposure in the local markets, the last ETF trade may take place many hours earlier than the U.S. market close.

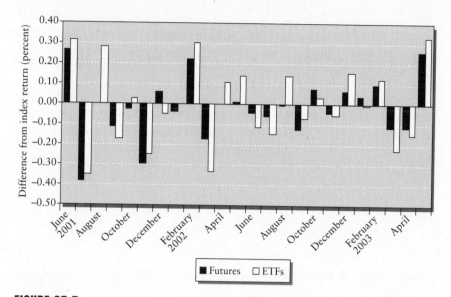

FIGURE 25.7 S&P 500 Futures and "SPY" ETF Tracking Performance versus S&P 500 Index
Source: Goldman Sachs.

Figure 25.7 shows the difference in monthly performance between the S&P 500 index returns and (1) synthetic returns based on S&P 500 futures, and (2) the S&P 500 SPDR (ticker "SPY"), for the two-year period ending May 2003. The returns for the futures, ETFs, and indexes are all based on 4:00 P.M. prices, the "tick" at that time for futures, the average of the bid and ask for ETFs, and the close for the index. In this way, all series are calculated at consistent times and there is no additional "noise" from timing differences between the 4:15 P.M. close for futures and ETFs and the stock market close at 4:00 P.M. For the two years ending May 2003, the annual tracking error based on monthly returns for futures and ETFs as compared with index returns was quite similar: 55 bps for S&P 500 futures and 71 bps for SPY.

Transaction Costs for ETFs

ETF investors typically pay commissions on ETF transactions comparable to those on stocks, and may experience market impact related to the liquidity of the ETFs or the underlying stock portfolio. Upstairs market makers may also quote a bid/ask spread for ETFs, and investors would not then incur a market impact. As with traditional index funds, ETF investors pay a management fee that is reflected daily on a pro rata basis in the NAV.

ETF PRICING ESSENTIALS

As discussed in Chapters 14, 16, and 23, ETFs trade like stocks and, therefore, offer a greater degree of flexibility than traditional mutual funds or other index funds. Investors can trade ETFs intraday and employ the usual order types, such as limit and market on close orders that are available in single-stock trading. In contrast, investors can only purchase traditional mutual funds at the fund's NAV, which is published at the end of each trading day. As discussed in Chapters 16 and 23, unlike traditional funds, investors buy and sell ETFs at the market price, which is determined by supply and demand just as it is for stocks, with an important difference: The amount of outstanding ETF shares can be adjusted each day. The exchange-designated Specialist and certain broker/dealers who are Authorized Participants (APs) may create or redeem ETFs in large lot sizes known as creation units (and described in previous chapters). These transactions are conducted by sending baskets of stocks (to create ETF shares) or ETF shares (to redeem for a stock basket) to the trustee of the ETF. The following figure depicts the trading and hedging function of the ETF market makers (Specialists and APs) and shows how they will use a variety of index products (index futures/options, ETFs, and physical securities) to hedge their positions:

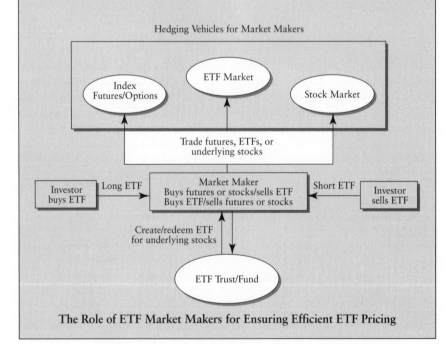

Hedging Vehicles for Market Makers

The Role of ETF Market Makers for Ensuring Efficient ETF Pricing

The opportunity to create and redeem shares enables ETFs to function like open-end funds and keeps market prices close to NAV. The *fungibility* of ETFs with baskets of underlying stocks makes their liquidity equivalent to or better than the liquidity of the stock baskets. Furthermore, because these APs can commit capital to their positions and easily hedge long and short ETF inventory with the most appropriate and efficient vehicle at the time, ETF transaction costs are typically equal to or lower than those for the corresponding stock basket. Therefore, the creation/redemption process typically leads to convergence within a price band around the ETF's net asset value, driven primarily by the cost of transacting in the underlying shares at creation or redemption. As stated in Chapter 23, the cost of transacting in the underlying stock, therefore, represents the upper bound on the cost of a large ETF transaction. For this reason, the dollar volume of the trading activity in the underlying stocks is more significant in assessing liquidity than the dollar volume of the ETF.

ETFs are also actively traded on exchanges and in the OTC (or upstairs) market which is a large factor in the success and liquidity of ETFs and is enhanced by the ability of specialists to hedge risk intraday. As indicated in this figure, this hedging can be done with stocks, futures, options, or other active ETFs and by exchanging long and short inventory through the creation and redemption process with the ETF fund at the end of the day. This ability to easily manage market-making risk increases the liquidity of the ETF shares.

Other Considerations

Unlike most traditional index funds, ETFs can be readily purchased on margin and can be sold short. Like futures, ETFs are typically exempt from short-selling restrictions that disallow short selling on a downtick.

ETFs have some advantages relative to futures including much smaller minimum investment sizes than futures contracts. For example, the S&P 500 SPDR has no round-lot requirements and trades at a price of about $100, or about ¹⁄₁₀ the size of the S&P 500 futures, while the S&P 500 e-mini futures, the smaller of the CME contracts, trades at 50 times the level of the S&P 500, or about $50,000.

ETF Liquidity

ETFs and HOLDRs trading in the United States had more than $100 billion in assets as of December 2002, with an average daily volume of over $8 billion (see the E-ppendix at www.ActiveIndexInvesting.com for updated asset and volume data). The growth has been dramatic, but is built on a steady foundation. Figure 25.8 shows the trend of volume and asset growth since the early 1990s. The editor's predictions in Chapter 31 can help readers extrapolate the probability of the continuation of this trend.

As of end-2002, the largest ETFs in terms of assets are the SPDR (SPY), followed by the QQQ and other broad-based products (Figure 25.9). Nasdaq-100 "cubes" account for the majority of ETF trading volume (48 percent), with the SPY accounting for 25 percent. As of end-2002, international

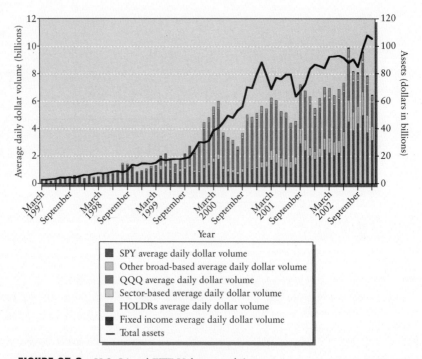

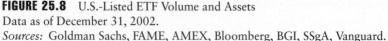

- SPY average daily dollar volume
- Other broad-based average daily dollar volume
- QQQ average daily dollar volume
- Sector-based average daily dollar volume
- HOLDRs average daily dollar volume
- Fixed income average daily dollar volume
- — Total assets

FIGURE 25.8 U.S.-Listed ETF Volume and Assets
Data as of December 31, 2002.
Sources: Goldman Sachs, FAME, AMEX, Bloomberg, BGI, SSgA, Vanguard.

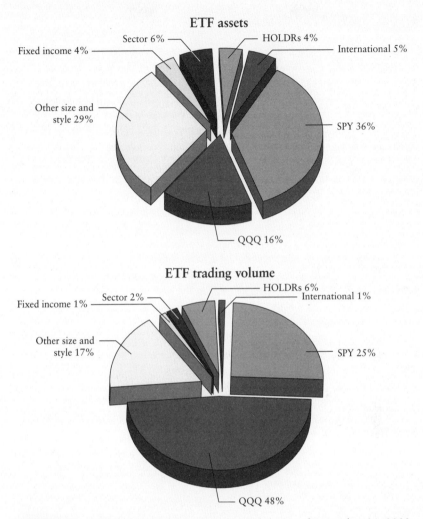

ETF assets

Sector 6%
HOLDRs 4%
Fixed income 4%
International 5%
Other size and style 29%
SPY 36%
QQQ 16%

ETF trading volume

HOLDRs 6%
Fixed income 1%
Sector 2%
International 1%
Other size and style 17%
SPY 25%
QQQ 48%

FIGURE 25.9 Breakdown of ETF Assets and Volume as of December 31, 2002

equity products traded in the United States accounted for 1 percent of volume and 5 percent of assets. Other broad-based ETFs, sector and fixed-income ETFs and HOLDRs made up the balance. This market share is certain to change over time—it is important for users to stay in touch with their brokers and tap into industry resources such as IndexUniverse.com and exchange web sites to follow market trends.

3. INDEX SWAPS

Swaps may be the most flexible means of capturing index returns, but the products are not appropriate for all users. An equity index swap is a contract between two counter parties to exchange an interest payment for the return of an index at some future date. Swaps are typically conducted between financial institutions and an institutional investor, who must be an "eligible contract participant," as defined by the Commodity Futures Modernization Act. The International Swap Dealers Association (ISDA) has attempted to standardize some of the basic terms of swap agreements, but features such as underlying index, term, collateral requirements, and funding rate can be fully customized for each swap. Figure 25.10 shows the mechanics of a simple equity index swap based on the S&P 500 index. Swaps may even be based on customized baskets of stocks, rather than on a published index.

Like futures, swaps generally represent forward transactions and so do not require payment at the outset. There may, however, be collateral requirements, which are typically determined by the seller of the swap who, by convention, is the payer of the index return. Among the factors that go into determining collateral are: the credit-worthiness of the buyer of the swap, the riskiness or volatility of the underlying index, and the term of the swap. The swap could also have predetermined reset dates, which typically would reduce the collateral requirements, since profits and losses would then be exchanged at intermediate points in the life of the swap, reducing the accumulated risk to the seller over the term of the swap.

Swaps are usually quoted as annualized LIBOR (London Interbank Offered Rate) yields with a plus or minus LIBOR spread added (as shown in Figure 25.10 as LIBOR + 10 bps). The index returns are most commonly based on total returns, including index dividends. The basic mechanics of an S&P 500 index swap are shown in Figure 25.10, with a sample interest rate of LIBOR + 10 bps. The swap returns are equivalent to the index returns received net of the interest rate paid to the swap dealer. In order to match the returns of the index, the buyer of a swap would need to invest the desired

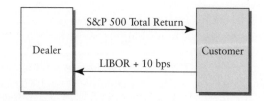

FIGURE 25.10   Sample Mechanics of an S&P 500 Index Swap

notional exposure in a strategy that pays interest. To break even, this interest rate should equal the funding rate, or the interest paid to the swap dealer.

The price of a swap is typically based on the swap dealer's cost to establish the hedge for the swap position plus some profit. A dealer offering a swap on the S&P 500 index might hedge the exposure by buying a basket of index-tracking stocks, an S&P 500 ETF, or index futures. Which hedge is used will depend on the dealer's judgment of the cheapest instrument at the time. Because of the differences in margin that apply to stocks or ETFs and futures, it is often cheapest for the dealer to hedge with futures where available, as futures tie up less of the dealer's capital.

Since swaps are contractual agreements and not traded on an exchange, they must be opened and closed with the same swap dealer. This means that swaps are not liquid in the same sense that exchange-traded instruments are, even when the position underlying the swap is liquid.

4. INDEX OPTIONS

Unlike futures, ETFs, and swaps, index options provide asymmetric exposure to index returns. There are two varieties of index options: a call, which gives the right to buy an index; and a put, which gives the right to sell an index. Like futures, options have an expiration date when the right to buy or sell can be exercised; they also have an exercise price, or index level at which the put or call can be exercised. The value of call or put options fluctuates with the index level prior to exercise and converges to the intrinsic value, or difference between the index and the exercise price, at expiration.

Options can be listed on organized, regulated exchanges—such as S&P 500 and S&P 100 options on the Chicago Board Options Exchange (CBOE)—or over-the-counter (OTC) options, which are structured by broker-dealers in a similar way as OTC index swaps.

For example, if an investor buys a December 2004 call option with a strike price of 1000 on the S&P 500 and the index is at 1050 on the expiration date, the call option will be worth 50 index points and the investor will receive cash in his or her options account equal to the index multiplier ($100 for the S&P 500 index options), multiplied by 50 index points. A put holder with a strike price of 1000 would receive nothing, since a put at expiration is worth the greater of nothing or its intrinsic value which, in this case, would be −50 index points.

Because a call option provides index exposure only above the strike price and a put option only below, the index returns can be separated into upside and downside exposure. This asymmetrical pay-off is the most important feature of options as illustrated in Figure 25.11. However,

OPTION PRICING ESSENTIALS

Prior to expiration, option prices reflect an expectation about future index volatility, because volatility affects the chance that the index will move above or below the exercise price at expiration. The higher the volatility, the greater the value of the option because the higher the probability that the index will move beyond the strike price by expiration. The time to expiration also has a positive impact on the option premium, because the longer the time period, the greater the chance the index can move to a level favorable to the holder. Additional factors affecting the option price are interest rates and the dividends expected through expiration. The various factors are summarized in the following table:

Factors Affecting Option Prices

	Calls	Puts
Current stock price	+	−
Strike price	−	+
Market interest rates	+	−
Dividend yield	−	+
Expected volatility	+	+
Time to maturity	+	+*

*Time value is positive for both Puts and Calls.

Although dividends are not paid directly on options, they are implied in the price of an option in a way similar to futures.

There is extensive literature on option pricing. One of the most authoritative references on the topic which we recommend is *Options, Futures, and Other Derivatives* (5th ed.) by John C. Hull (Upper Saddle River, NJ: Prentice Hall, 2002).

investors sometimes find it useful to combine the purchase of a call option with the sale of a put option to simulate the purchase of a futures contract, often called a "combo." This is essentially a "synthetic future." This is one way for U.S. investors who are authorized to enter into OTC agreements to gain synthetic index exposure to markets whose futures which have not received a CFTC "no-action" letter. By simultaneously buying an OTC call and selling an OTC put with the same strike, investors can get an equivalent

Buy Call Option

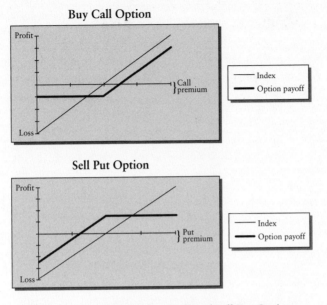

Combo: Buy Call and Sell Put Options

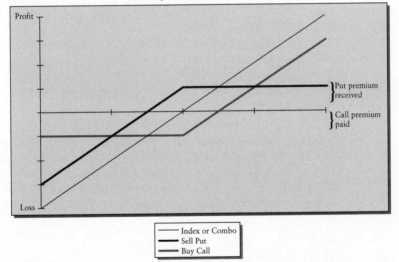

FIGURE 25.11 Asymmetrical and Symmetrical Exposure with Index Options

return to that of the overseas futures contract. Typically, the options are structured to expire simultaneously with the listed futures, so that all calendar-spread risk is borne by the investor. Alternatively, the investor can ask an OTC option dealer to price longer term options, or structure the agreement as a longer term swap, where the dealer takes the calendar roll risk for an agreed-upon premium.

Options offer leverage in that they provide exposure to index returns without making a notional investment in the underlying index. The investment is the option premium, or the price of the option at the time of the transaction. As with other leveraged products, the investor needs to earn interest on the portion of the investment that is not needed to pay for the options to match the returns of an unleveraged index strategy.

Options are usually used to express a directional view on an index, while limiting the loss to the cost of the option, rather than as a way to track an index. However, options, as discussed in Chapter 15, can also be combined with indexing as a way to enhance returns. Strategies can be constructed from a combination of puts and calls to benefit from an increase or decrease in the volatility assumption embedded in an option price prior to expiration. Covered call strategies combine index exposure with a short call position on all or a portion of the underlying notional amount; these types of strategies enhance returns for a range of index levels below the strike price by the premium collected on the short call, as shown in the upper payoff diagram in Figure 25.12. This enhancement comes at the expense of limiting upside to the strike level of the index plus the premium received from selling the call option. Another commonly used option strategy provides index exposure with downside risk hedged using a long index put position, this effectively provides a floor at expiration for the index exposure, since the investor has the right to sell the index to the seller of the put option at that level. This pattern is illustrated in the lower payoff diagram in Figure 25.12. The cost of the put reduces index returns for levels of the index at expiration above the floor index level, but limits the downside to the cost of the put. *(Editor's note: There are some enhanced index funds that use these strategies, either to achieve "index alpha" or for "modified beta"—the latter which is discussed further in Chapter 31.)*

Transaction Costs for Options

Buyers and sellers of exchange-listed options are typically charged a commission and incur a market impact cost, which reflects the liquidity of the option. Unlike futures, as stated previously, options may also be traded OTC, which may offer advantages in customizing terms and strikes, as well as providing additional liquidity from dealers' commitment of capital. Dealers'

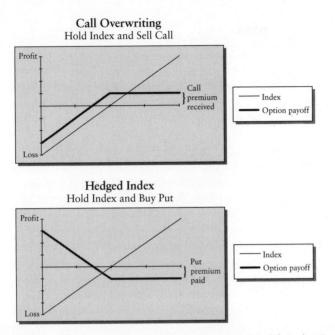

FIGURE 25.12 Common Option Strategies That Can Modify Index Returns

prices for OTC options are typically quoted with a bid-ask spread and investors incur no market impact.

OTC options are traded mainly between financial institutions and institutional investors. Like swaps, they are legal contracts with terms agreed between the parties. Because of their flexibility and anonymity, they are a significant source of liquidity in index options, in addition to exchange-listed option activity.

Option Liquidity

Listed index options trade on major exchanges such as the CBOE, the American Stock Exchange (AMEX), and the Philadelphia Stock Exchange (PHLX) and are used for both investing and hedging underlying index exposure. Other index options covering sectors or style segments of the U.S. equity market are traded on several additional exchanges in the United States, including electronic markets like the International Securities Exchange (ISE). Many of the major international markets also have liquid listed index options. For indexes that have listed futures, options on these futures may also exist and options are now available on an increasing number of ETFs (which is discussed

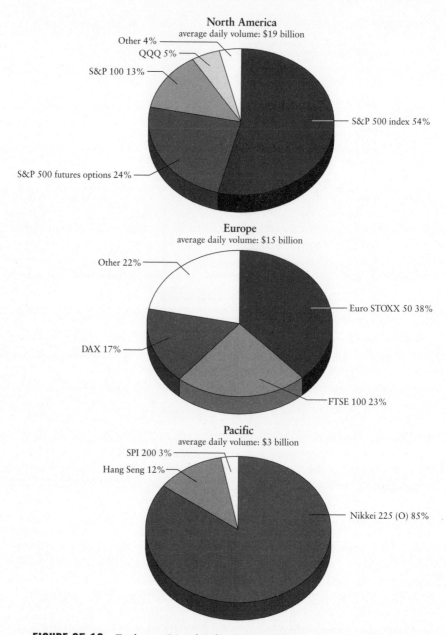

North America
average daily volume: $19 billion

Other 4%
QQQ 5%
S&P 100 13%
S&P 500 index 54%
S&P 500 futures options 24%

Europe
average daily volume: $15 billion

Other 22%
Euro STOXX 50 38%
DAX 17%
FTSE 100 23%

Pacific
average daily volume: $3 billion

SPI 200 3%
Hang Seng 12%
Nikkei 225 (O) 85%

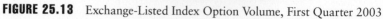

FIGURE 25.13 Exchange-Listed Index Option Volume, First Quarter 2003

later in this chapter and further in Chapter 31. Figure 25.13 shows the most active listed index options and their percentage of daily average volume in major global trading regions for the first quarter of 2003.

HOW DO INVESTORS CHOOSE AMONG THE AVAILABLE INDEX PRODUCTS?

The choice of index products is driven by the specific requirements and limitations of the investor, the strategy, and the investment horizon. Not all the index vehicles discussed in this or the following chapter are available to all investors, so the first hurdle is to determine what policy, legal or regulatory authorization is necessary to use each product, and which is most appropriate. The tax treatment of each of the products, worthy of a chapter of its own, may be critical for taxable investors (and is discussed in Chapter 27). The type of investment strategy may also determine the best choice of vehicle. Options, with their asymmetric index exposure, are the best way to implement a directional view on an index while limiting risk. As noted previously, swaps, with their ability to be customized, can be structured on any index, even those with no listed instruments. Table 25.1 summarizes the basic features and advantages/disadvantages of these four "direct access" products and strategies. The discussions in Chapters 14 and 26 about the benefits and tradeoffs of index funds and securities-holding institutional index portfolios should be considered along with these four possible routes to exposure.

As discussed in Chapter 15, the higher levels of leverage available with futures, swaps, and options make certain types of enhanced index strategies possible. In the late 1980s when S&P 500 futures traded persistently cheap, returns in excess of the S&P 500 index were possible from simply combining futures with basic cash management strategies. As discussed in Chapter 15, these opportunities continued to present themselves in non-U.S. markets—especially emerging markets—through the 1990s, and still occasionally appear. As also discussed in that chapter, futures and swaps are commonly employed where the enhancement or "alpha" is earned from managing the funds not used for margin requirements in one of a number of strategies, including short-term fixed-income strategies, volatility or relative index trading strategies, long/short equity strategies, convertible bond arbitrage, risk arbitrage, and market-neutral hedge funds strategies.

From the perspective of a more sophisticated investor intent on implementing a medium or shorter term view, futures may be preferable to ETFs. As stated previously, futures markets are highly liquid, and commissions are low; therefore, initial per-trade costs are substantially lower with futures

TABLE 25.1 Comparison of Features of Index Products[a]

	Futures	ETFs	Swaps	Options
Flexibility				
Underlying indexes	About 20 in the United States; much fewer in non-U.S. markets	More than 100 in the United States; more than futures in non-U.S. markets	Any index	About 15 for listed; any for OTC
Leverage	Greater than stocks	Equal to stocks	Greater than stocks	Greater than stocks
Anonymity	Limited	Limited	High	Limited for listed; high for OTC
Ease of Use				
Regulatory requirements	CFTC registration or "no action" for non-U.S. products	Typically same as for stocks; some 12d(1) fund limits	Limited to eligible contract participants[b]	Accredited investor for OTC[c]
Daily mark-to-market	Yes	No	No	Limited to selling uncovered options

Transaction Costs				
Entry/exit costs	Lower than stocks	Lower or equal to stocks	Lower or equal to stocks	Higher than stocks
Holding costs	Interest rates embedded in nearby contract price + calendar spread price	Management fee	Funding rate	Option time decay may need to roll into next contract
Trading Efficiency				
Liquidity	Higher than stocks	Higher than or equal to stocks	Lower than stocks	Lower than stocks
Capital commitment	Limited	Yes	Yes	Limited for listed; high for TOC
Shorting	No uptick, no borrow	No uptick, borrow-like stock	Depends on underlyer	n/a
Minimum size	About $25,000 and up	No minimum	Varies	No minimum
Tracking				
Sources of performance difference	Nearby mispricing + calendar spread mispricing	Premium/discount to NA OR market maker spread	None	Based on strike and term of option
Dividends	Forecasts included in price	Paid quarterly	Included in capital return	Forecasts included in price

[a] Direct-access index products—table does not cover index-tracking portfolios that directly hold securities, which are discussed in Chapter 26.
[b] As defined by Section 1a(12) of the Commodity Futures Modernization Act of 2000.
[c] As defined by Section 4(2) of the Securities Act of 1933.

than with ETFs. Index futures have cost and operational advantages over ETFs for overlay and high turnover strategies. The lower commissions and the frequently higher liquidity of futures relative to stocks and ETFs may reduce the cost of initiating a position; however, on an on-going basis, the cost of rolling futures should be compared with the ETF management fee.

Initial margin requirements are typically much lower for futures, providing more leeway for index enhancement strategies. Futures can sometimes be used to gain access to several developing markets where direct stock investment is highly restricted. Shorting is relatively simple with futures: There is no need to borrow as with stocks and no need to wait for an uptick and cash settlement of index futures eliminates the risk of a short squeeze. Although mispricing introduces risk for the investment strategy, to the extent that there is persistent and predictable mispricing due to regulatory differences, tax inefficiencies, or other structural reasons, the basis may be captured and added to the investment return.

On the other hand, as stated previously, futures are only available on a limited number of indexes; to the extent that a substitute index must be used, there is tracking risk as compared with the investor's benchmark. Futures expiration requires ongoing management for rolling positions. Daily mark-to-market means that excess cash may need to be set aside for meeting variation margin and unpredictable mispricing adds risk to the strategy. The performance measurement of the futures positions is somewhat more complicated given the need to track futures prices, calendar spread, and interest income. Finally, for international equity index exposure, U.S. investors are limited to those futures contracts with CFTC "noaction" letters, and currency exposure must be managed separately to match a stock portfolio.

For investors who do not need or want the leverage in futures and swaps, or who can achieve leverage in other ways, ETFs provide the operational ease of trading stocks combined in a single traded instrument. If the investor wants to implement a longer term view, futures contracts must be rolled every three months because of expiration, which may lead to higher trading costs through additional commissions and potential mispricing of the calendar spread. As discussed in Chapters 16 and 23, capital commitment by specialists and APs, and the structural ability to create and redeem ETFs typically keeps the cost of trading ETFs lower or equal to stocks and the liquidity equal to or better than trading the underlying stocks. ETFs can also provide access to restricted markets and share the shorting advantages of futures (although they must be borrowed). Perhaps most importantly, ETFs are available on many more indexes than futures, providing vehicles for sector, size, and style-based strategies that are not available through futures products. *(Editor's Note: This last advantage is growing steadily as ETFs on an ever-expanding range of indexes and asset classes are launched.)*

As discussed earlier in the chapter, ETFs can experience tracking error versus stock portfolios due to the premium or discount relative to NAV or from a market maker spread, although the daily creation and redemption process ensures that arbitrage is frequent and efficient. More persistent tracking errors can arise from sampling methods used to construct the underlying stock portfolio for the ETF and from concentration issues in some products. This was discussed in Chapter 23. The holding costs include a management fee and dividend reinvestment can cause some tracking. For liquid futures and ETFs, we have found that the tracking error relative to their underlying indexes is generally small and comparable between the products.

Recently, new products have been launched that combine features of more than one of the index product types. There are now single stock futures contracts on ETFs trading on the NQLX and OneChicago exchanges, which provide for physical settlement into the exchange-traded funds. As noted earlier, options on ETFs are also growing in popularity, and options on the QQQ and Dow Jones Diamonds (ticker: DIA) are now among the most actively traded "single-stock" options (although investors use them as equivalent to index options).[3] New hybrid vehicles will provide even greater alternatives for investors. Rather than fragmenting liquidity, the introduction of more index products seems to have bolstered the volume in many of them. For example, the growth of the exchange-traded fund market—in S&P 500-based and Russell Indexes-based ETFs in particular—has provided alternative index vehicles, but has also increased the volume of index futures since ETF market makers often use futures to hedge the risk of their positions.

Index swaps can be fully customized with respect to benchmark index and term, and a single contract can bundle many features, including long and short exposures. Swaps can also be used to alter the nature and timing of gains or losses for better tax efficiency. There is greater potential for leverage with index swaps than with any other product and, because swaps are private OTC contracts, investors can preserve anonymity for sensitive transactions.

On the other hand, investors must be eligible contract participants and even if they are, the initial documentation requirements can be complex. Unlike exchange-traded vehicles where the investors counterparty is an exchange or clearinghouse, the seller of a swap is the counterparty. This could expose the investor to higher credit risk than with an exchange-listed product. Because swaps are private contracts, their prices are typically not observable in the market, and investors may experience back office and reporting constraints.

CONCLUSION

Thus, just as with the choice of underlying benchmark index that was discussed in Chapter 6, there is no one "best" or "one size fits all" solution for all situations. In fact, the differences among the products provide valuable choices and additional arbitrage opportunities. All of the index products discussed in this chapter are commonly used by institutional investors, including active managers, hedge funds, global-asset allocation managers, proprietary traders, and financial institutions managing their equity risk. Even further choices are available to asset-owning institutions, as the following chapter will discuss. But the availability of this myriad of choices is part of what makes index-based products so useful for all types of investors, creating a virtually limitless range of applications.

NOTES

1. Some investors use "tailing" to adjust the number of futures contracts for the sensitivity of futures to interest rates, which causes them to move more than the index, all else being equal. Investors who tail would buy slightly fewer contracts than the number given in our example.
2. For more information on the acronyms of various "flagship indexes" used in Figure 25.6, see Chapters 5, 6, and 14, as well as the *Index Research* and *Futures/Options* sections of IndexUniverse.com.
3. As the new area of options and single stock futures on ETFs is quite dynamic, please consult a broker-dealer for updates or the Futures/Options and Links sections of IndexUniverse.com for more information.

How and Why Large Pension Plans Use Index-Based Strategies as Their Core Investments

Nancy Calkins

_____ **Editor's Note** _____

Indexing is for savvy investors. The world's largest and most sophisticated investors are public and private pension funds, university endowments, charitable foundations, and other major asset-owning institutions such as government-linked entities, (for example, the Hong Kong Monetary Authority, the Government of Singapore Investment Corporation, and the Abu Dhabi Investment Authority). In late 2002, U.S. pension plan sponsors controlled approximately $10 trillion in investable assets with the top 25 global pension funds stewarding assets in excess of $50 billion each.[1] As a group, pension plans committed over $1.4 trillion to index-based strategies—approximately $1.1 trillion to indexation and another $300 billion to enhanced-index strategies.[2] Index and index-based strategies represent over 20 percent of the investments made by these large and sophisticated institutional investors. This chapter helps the reader understand why these institutional investors commit so much capital to index-based strategies.

Written from the perspective of a pension plan executive with over 20 years of experience, this chapter provides insight into the principles and

The author and editor would like to acknowledge the substantial assistance provided by Mark Friebel in developing this chapter. Thanks also go to Christina Polischuk for her valuable comments on both the content and style of the chapter.

concepts described in Part One as they are put into action. You will also gain a better appreciation of how the use of seemingly simple index-based strategies provide enormous unseen benefits to institutional investors, from crossing to securities lending revenue. Nancy also explains the pros and cons of the different types of index strategies available to pension plans. This assessment, combined with the analysis of the four ways investors can directly get index exposure in the previous chapter, provides readers with a comprehensive overview of the choices. Finally, consistent with the theme of this part of the book, it will become apparent that having indexing at the core of an investment strategy provides a strong foundation for the entire investment program.

The use of index-based strategies by large institutional investors is anything but monolithic. Two enlightening sidebars are included within this chapter. The first, by the assistant treasurer responsible for Oregon Investment Council's plans, shows how Oregon blends index and active strategies to achieve the right balance of risk and return for their pension plan. The second sidebar is written by Yasuchika Asaoka, executive director of the Japan Pension Fund Association—Japan's largest pension fund. Mr. Asaoka highlights some of the same principles, and you will see the logic behind PFA's decision to index a major portion of its domestic and international investments. The strategies employed by these large institutional investors provide the best proof that indexing is indeed a strategy for sophisticated investors.

WHY DO PENSION PLANS USE INDEX FUNDS?

Index-based strategies are an increasingly valuable investment vehicle for plan sponsors because of two key factors: First, rapidly changing global markets are causing institutions to rethink their investment strategies, and second, there are significant improvements in the management of costs and risks associated with investing by large pension plans. Although index products may sometimes seem simple and straightforward, when combined with other investment vehicles, they can form rather sophisticated and cost-effective frameworks for implementing the asset allocation policies of the large institutional investor. This chapter provides insight into our specific thinking, considerations, and objectives in utilizing index funds.

Operating in the real world, plan sponsors must manage a multitude of issues and opportunities while working with a variety of constraints. Plan sponsors seek to deliver superior investment returns while controlling for risks and costs. We seek administrative efficiencies while balancing and integrating any number of special interests. Consequently, solutions that can satisfy more than one objective are highly desirable. Index funds provide such multifaceted solutions. The advantages of using index-based strategies for large institutional investors are numerous, and include:

- Lower management fees.
- Lower transaction costs.
- Delivery of market returns with a highly transparent process.
- Facilitation of asset exposure.
- Risk control on the total investment portfolio.
- Fewer managers to hire and monitor.
- The opportunity to create strategic partnerships with index fund managers.

While market returns are fickle—up, down, sideways—management fees and transactions costs are consistent, and *always* negative—essentially dead-weight costs. Nevertheless, management fees and transactions costs are expenses that cannot be avoided and directly reduce net returns to a plan. Compared to active management, however, passive management offers a lower cost structure with regard to both of these types of expenses. Management fees on index funds are quite low. Depending on the size of a particular institutional investment mandate or the size of the total relationship with the manager, domestic index management fees can be a single basis point or lower on the total assets under management. This compares to an average of stated fees of 42 basis points (bps) for a typical "traditional active" large-cap U.S. equity mandate. While negotiated fees are closer to 30 bps, that remains significantly higher than fees on index funds. Similarly stated fees are over 50 bps for a typical active international equity mandate, with negotiated fees of about 40 bps. Institutional international equity index strategies for large plans are also usually in the single-digit basis points fee range, with the exception of emerging market indexing, which has a substantially higher cost.[3]

Transaction costs are also lower for index funds, which is attributable to two key factors: lower turnover and crossing. Transaction costs are not just the commission charged on a trade, but also include the less visible bid/ask spread and the even more difficult to ascertain market impact of that trade. The lower turnover of indexed portfolios reduces the amount of necessary trading as compared to active management. For example, the annual turnover in the S&P 500 averages about 4 percent. Compare this to a traditional active U.S. equity portfolio that averages 100 percent turnover annually.

While indexing reduces the need for individual security research, trading is still a very important factor to address for optimal benchmark performance. Since indexes change over time, considerable skill is necessary to manage the index changes and minimize the impact on portfolio performance. Traders should seek to minimize all execution costs, commissions, spreads, and market impact.

One method of reducing execution costs that is available primarily through index managers is *crossing*. Simply defined, securities crossing matches buyers and sellers at a preagreed price such as market close, thus eliminating commissions spreads, and market impact. This greatly reduces the costs of transactions necessary to produce the market return and keeps the fund's return closer to that of the index, which as discussed in Part Four, does not incur or reflect the frictional costs of real-world transactions.

The enormous benefit of crossing is best illustrated with an example. However, a bit of explanation about the structure of a typical commingled index fund is first required.

Index-based portfolios lend themselves to pools of commingled funds in which like-participants invest in the same fund. While mutual funds are the dominant commingled vehicle in the retail investor's world, the collective trust and commingled trust are the prevalent vehicles in the institutional investor's world. Legally, institutional investors are deemed to own a proportional undivided interest in each of the securities held by the fund. Practically speaking, the participants own their undivided interest through units of the fund and these units are usually priced proportionately at a net asset value (NAV). These types of funds and their activities are highly regulated. Crossing is one activity that is permissible under regulatory exemptions that are very specific as to how and when the activity can be conducted.

An ironclad truth of investing is that if we reduce the total cost of investment, we increase the value gained. Crossing is the most powerful technique available for reducing the cost of investment, whereby internal trades are free of transaction costs. Large index managers have vibrant internal marketplaces that provide ongoing opportunities to eliminate or reduce the normal costs associated with securities transactions. The following example illustrates the five steps taken by an investment manager to minimize trading costs when taking on new client assets:

1. The fund will accept securities from a client's previous investment portfolio that overlap the targeted portfolio to the fullest extent possible without creating unacceptable weight biases relative to the index.
2. A private or *internal crossing* then takes place on the security level among all of the manager's clients' index commingled funds and separate account strategies that hold the same securities and are in opposite buy/sell positions.
3. External crossing opportunities are then explored for all remaining securities. Examples of external public security crossing through fourth market networks are POSIT, Instinet, and AZX.
4. After all crossing opportunities have been completed, the residual activity is traded in the open market using strategies designed to minimize transaction costs. These strategies are a function of the sector and liquidity of

the stocks being traded. In these cases, we most often employ *package* or *portfolio* trading techniques, whereby brokers are asked to bid on an entire list of securities based on size and structure. Some managers have found that brokers are willing to bid more aggressively for an entire package than for individual securities. Large index managers can use their significant amount of daily trading activity to aggressively negotiate favorable commissions for clients.

5. Finally, with residual cash raised in the open market trade, *unit exchange* crossing opportunities with clients who are withdrawing cash from the fund are identified. In this case, the incoming client would receive units of the fund in exchange for cash.

All types of crossing ("in-kind," unit exchanges, and internal security) are performed *free* of all commissions, bid-ask spreads, and market impact costs to the client. The only trading costs born by the client involve the few securities that need to be traded in the external marketplace.

The Washington State Investment Board (WSIB) retirement account's holding of a U.S. Equity market index fund has, over time, saved 130 bps in transaction costs due to internal and external unit-level and security-level crossing. As an example of crossing savings in action, for a $100 million buy or sell of the S&P 500 Index Fund, total trading costs are approximately $170,000 or 17 bps (10 bps commission + 7 bps spread). An estimated 50 percent internal cross would eliminate 50 percent of those costs for a savings of $85,000.

For long-term investors, such as pension funds, *closely tracking an index* while minimizing fees and trading costs is a prudent method of managing large sums of money. In discussions about active management, value-added alpha seems to focus on the *positive* addition of return over a benchmark or indexed portfolio. There is another side—the *negative* alpha or "value-not-added" of active management, which can detract from benchmark returns. As discussed in Part One, over the long run, investment managers as a whole will receive average market returns.

Effective management of all fees and costs is critical to the success of any asset owners, especially those who seek to match the market return. Closely tracking an index return, coupled with low costs, often provides an excellent combination when compared to active management. After all, net returns after fees and trading make active management, *on average,* less attractive than indexing. As discussed in Chapter 2, the mathematical logic of this was most elegantly demonstrated by William Sharpe.[4]

Indexing is a low-cost method to gain precise *asset and/or subasset class exposure.* Grey Baer and Gary Gensler provide an excellent example of the U.S. government's Thrift Savings Plans for federal employees' use of index funds in Chapter 29. Using index-based products for smaller programs provides equity and fixed-income exposure in the most cost-effective way. This is the case not only for defined benefit and defined contribution pension funds, but also for other public and private-sector programs such as worker's compensation insurance, college savings, endowment, permanent, and other funds.

Pension funds are concerned about the risk of meeting their pension obligations. Viewing *risk control* at both the total portfolio level and within asset classes is extremely important. Indexing can assist in controlling risk by providing a core of assets that closely track the specific target market. The structure of active equity management programs often includes specialty managers by region, style, sector, and/or capitalization. If one or two of these components is out of favor, risk can increase at the portfolio level. Indexed strategies, along with an optimal combination of active managers, can often reduce the overall risk of a portfolio. Similar approaches can be constructed for fixed-income strategies.

Indexing also tends to be very transparent. Part Four highlighted the various ways an index fund can be managed—for example, fully replicated, optimized, or stratified sampled. Each provides the investor with a very clear and predictable sense of the securities held, risk profile, and so forth. Furthermore, plan sponsors can usually have a *look through* into their holdings on a daily basis if needed.

With large sums of money to invest in a primarily active management equity program, pension funds are often forced to hire numerous managers to reduce the risk of exposure to any one manager, or to reduce the risk of a large concentration in a region, sector, style, or capitalization. Hiring, monitoring, and changing active investment managers is an expensive and time-consuming process. Using a core indexed portfolio reduces the number of managers to hire and monitor. Since index management varies only slightly (with portfolios that use stratified sampling or optimization) from manager to manager, even the exposure risk of one manager is significantly reduced because the index portfolio can be transferred to another index manager with relative efficiency.

The plan sponsor should also not overlook the value of creating a *strategic relationship* with its index manager. Large institutional index managers generally invest in most of the world's investable equity and bond markets. Therefore, they research a wide variety of investment topics, and they tend to be especially attuned to operational risk and overall risk management. Consequently, these index managers are particularly well equipped to support their clients with many of their client's investment issues, especially those related to benchmark issues and the plan's total portfolio.[5] We have often relied on these managers to advise us on the implications of major benchmark changes and/or new index product offerings.

Index managers and pension plans share the experiences of building portfolios or programs, evaluating the pros and cons of investing in various markets, assessing benchmark methodology, analyzing the costs of investing, and managing asset allocation.[6] As with index managers, pension plans that invest money internally experience the same uncertainties of the marketplace, trading and operational complexities, the challenges of tracking error, and the necessity to thoroughly analyze and understand performance attribution. In addition, index managers often act as a liaison to connect their clients who share similar experiences. Index managers and pension plans encounter many common experiences, although sometimes from different perspectives. Thus, sharing information is beneficial for both the manager and the pension plan.

HOW DO PENSION FUNDS USE INDEX FUNDS?

As discussed in Chapters 3, 14, and 18, index funds offer virtually limitless flexibility in portfolio design and construction. Popular uses include program structuring, implementing asset-allocation strategies, and as building blocks to create various strategic and tactical *active index* portfolios.

Program Structuring

Many pension funds use the core/satellite concept to structure their defined benefit portfolios. The core is often a large, low-cost index fund. The satellites are smaller actively managed portfolios designed to add value around the indexed core. The combination of the core and satellite creates the opportunity for increased returns, without significantly increasing risk. Sophisticated financial advisors and individuals have started to emulate this core/satellite approach, which is discussed in detail in Chapters 28 and 30.

Traditionally, pension funds use this concept for the structure within an asset class. For example, a core domestic equity index fund is combined with actively managed combinations of domestic mid-cap, small-cap, value, growth, and/or thematic equity portfolios to potentially add value above the index returns.

A few pension funds have made a strategic decision to index all of their domestic equity assets. From this, it may appear that the fund has foregone opportunities in areas of capitalization or style that would add value to the overall portfolio. However, viewing the total asset allocation picture, not just each asset class, provides insight to where a pension fund prefers to take risk and seek additional return.

We can use the WSIB's approach to illustrate several of these points. WSIB is well known for its 1997 decision to index 100 percent of its U.S.

equity allocation to the Wilshire 5000 Total Market Index for its defined benefit retirement assets. The WSIB target allocation to private markets totals 29 percent (17 percent to private equity and 12 percent to real estate), while the U.S. equity asset-allocation target is 31 percent. The sizeable exposure to private markets is balanced with the large, diversified, broad-market indexed core portfolio. The U.S. equity allocation, combined with the WSIB's target allocation to less liquid private market assets provide a diversified exposure to active management and less efficient markets, such as small/mid-cap stocks. Private market investing is the area in which the WSIB prefers to take risk and believes there is additional return potential.

Within its 15 percent non-U.S. equity allocation, the WSIB uses the more traditional core and satellite structure. In 2003, the WSIB approved a new international program structure that will be implemented over a 9- to 12-month period. Ninety-five percent of the international assets will be allocated to developed markets and 5 percent to actively managed emerging markets. Forty percent of the developed markets assets are indexed, with the remaining 60 percent invested in satellite portfolios using active core, value, and growth investment styles. Currently, the emerging market component includes the use index-based funds in lieu of stock selection, with alternative country weights within the overall strategy. (This approach is a variant of the structured-tiered emerging markets strategy described in Chapter 18.) This noncapitalization weighted, index-based approach is used in tandem with traditional active portfolios, with the combined allocation to managers/strategies providing a well-balanced approach to this dynamic asset class. An extensive discussion of all the variants of alternative-weighting indexing techniques for international equities can be found in Chapter 18.

Another approach is the one taken by Washington's neighbor just to the south, Oregon. The following sidebar describes Oregon's use of index, risk-controlled active and active strategies, and how they are blended to produce a more efficient overall portfolio.

THE STATE OF OREGON'S BLEND OF INDEX, ENHANCED INDEX, AND ACTIVE EQUITY STRATEGIES
Michael Mueller

One irrefutable truth about equity investing is that the aggregate efforts of all active managers is *the market*. Investment management boards, consultants, and managing fiduciaries are forever trying to identify the silver bullet that will enable them to identify *tomorrow's* best managers; they have been quite adept at identifying *yesterday's* winners. In a zero-sum game, being right only slightly better than half the time seems like an easy proposition, until you try to accomplish that feat. While studies can demonstrate that only one of four active managers exceed the median manager in two consecutive years and one out of eight for three such years, within our industry, woefully little is done with this knowledge.*

The Oregon Investment Council (OIC), the board charged with investing the state's $41 billion pension fund, and the state treasury staff believe that successful active managers *can* be found, but we have hedged that decision by setting up an asset-allocation continuum that begins with a passive core, followed by a slice of risk-controlled active, and topped off with a dose of full active strategies. As stated in the OIC's policies: The Council uses passive management to control costs, evaluate active management strategies, capture exposure to the more *efficient markets,* manage the risk of underperformance and facilitate re-balancing to the strategic policy asset mix. Efficient markets have been defined in the traditional sense, as a market in which security prices rapidly reflect all information about securities and, by implication, active managers find it more difficult to pick stocks that consistently beat the performance of an index fund. Practically, we have defined efficient markets as large cap (Russell 1000) on the domestic side and developed markets (EAFE + Canada) on the international side.

The overall objective of the domestic equity strategy is to achieve a portfolio return of 50 bps, or more, above the Russell 3000 Index over a market cycle of three to five years on a net-of-fee basis, with no more than 3 percent tracking error. Within the confines of this risk budget for the domestic equity asset class, the following additional gradation is made: a 43 percent target to passive, large-cap, index funds; a 14 percent target to controlled risk funds (up to 1 percent of expected excess return with 1 to 2.5 percent risk); and a 43 percent target to traditional active managers (2+ percent expected excess return with 3+ percent risk) (see the figure that

---

*John L. Maginn and Donald L. Tuttle, *Managing Investment Portfolios: A Dynamic Process,* 2nd ed. (Charlottesville, VA: Association for Investment Research and Management, 1990), pp. 36–39.

(Continued)

follows. While most pension funds do not explicitly carve out an allocation for controlled-risk strategies (i.e., they are a component of the active core), the discipline we follow clarifies the role of all the managers in the portfolio and acknowledges that risk-controlled active is better defined as active-"light," not as enhanced indexing (or passive "heavy"). On this point—in words and actions—we agree with the definitions for both enhanced indexing and risk-controlled active set forth by Steven A. Schoenfeld and Joy Yang in Chapter 15 of this book.

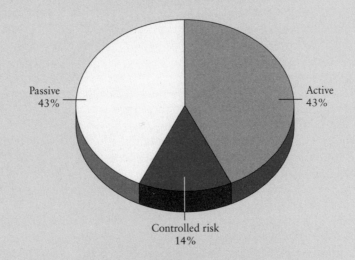

Passive
43%

Active
43%

Controlled risk
14%

Oregon's U.S. Equity Strategy Allocation

In the developed international equity markets, we allocate 20 percent to a passive indexed core, tracking our MSCI World ex-U.S. benchmark, with a 10 percent allocation to an international controlled-risk strategy (see the figure at the top of p. 545 in this sidebar). The majority of the plan is allocated to a variety of active international managers, with the goal of outperforming the policy benchmark for this asset class.

While this strategy does not position the public equity portion of the Oregon pension fund to "shoot the lights out," it does provide a discipline to increase the likelihood that the domestic and international equity portfolios will be able to deliver their portion of the portfolio's total return at a defined and acceptable level of risk.

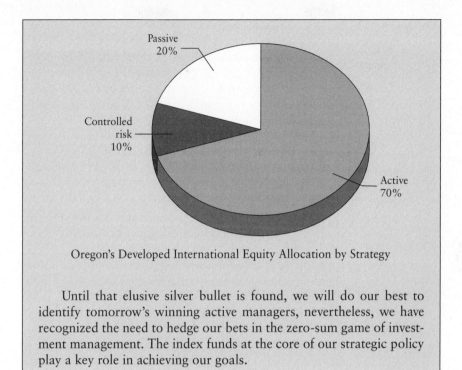

Oregon's Developed International Equity Allocation by Strategy

Until that elusive silver bullet is found, we will do our best to identify tomorrow's winning active managers, nevertheless, we have recognized the need to hedge our bets in the zero-sum game of investment management. The index funds at the core of our strategic policy play a key role in achieving our goals.

Implementing Asset-Allocation Strategies

Index funds can facilitate the implementation of rebalancing, changing asset allocation strategically or tactically, or developing a completion portfolio.

As covered in detail in Chapter 18 and especially in Chapter 30, asset allocation is the biggest factor in determining long-term performance.[7] Therefore, adhering to the stated asset-allocation policy is crucial. Purchasing or selling index funds provides a quick, efficient, and cost-effective method to *rebalance allocations* in the public market asset classes, with minimal disruption to the actively managed portfolios.

In the case of major, long-term *asset-allocation changes* or in the situation of changes in the active manager lineup, index funds are used as a low cost and efficient "parking place" until assets are redistributed to the desired asset class or new manager. On a shorter-term basis, pension funds may tactically shift between asset classes. Using indexed vehicles to implement the shifts avoids interfering with the potential value-added from the active managers. Aje Saigal highlighted GSIC's (Government of Singapore Investment Corp.) use of index-based products for some of these applications in his interview in a sidebar in Chapter 18.

When active management is usually the focal point of a pension fund strategy, index funds can still play an important role in reducing the risk between the chosen mix of managers and the selected benchmark. In this way, the pension plan is free to hire specific managers to take significant active bets, manage concentrated portfolios, or who are niche players. While the active managers invest their portfolios in a relatively unrestricted manner, the index funds can be used to "fill the gaps" or *complete a portfolio* and thus reduce the active risk to the underlying benchmark. This risk budgeting approach, discussed in more detail in Chapter 3, has gained wide acceptance among large pension plans. The sidebar within Chapter 18 by John Krimmel of Illinois SURS provides an excellent example of the use of index funds to plug "risk holes" in an overall investment strategy.

Building Blocks to Create Active Portfolios

As the variety of index funds increases, so do their uses in investors' portfolios. As discussed extensively in Chapter 18, index funds can be used as components to build a variety of active portfolios with passive stock selection.

Within an asset class, different portfolio attributes can be over/underweighted to create style, capitalization, country, and sector tilts. In U.S. equity, index funds may be broken into components of large, mid-, or small capitalization; market sectors; and value or growth styles. For example, a pension fund may take a long-term view that value outperforms and, therefore overweights the value style across all capitalizations. As a tactical strategy, the pension fund could develop a model to shift from value to growth and/or from large-cap to small/mid-cap during the period of their forecasted outperformance. With the growing emphasis on sectors in the developed markets, sectors may be the next basis on which to build index components. In non-U.S. equity, a pension fund can use indexed country funds to take active country bets. As discussed earlier and in Chapters 14 and 18, over/underweighting countries can be especially effective in the emerging markets.

Target allocation portfolios can be created with index funds and targeted to a conservative, moderate, or aggressive risk profile. The portfolios are rebalanced to the target allocations, a strategy that sells the overperforming asset classes and buys the underperforming asset classes. Using a target allocation portfolio as an option in a defined contribution program provides a disciplined investment strategy and relieves the individual participant of the rebalancing task. Chapter 30 provides some examples of this approach, implemented with index funds or ETFs.

Portfolios for lifestyle goals are one of the most valuable uses of index funds to create an active portfolio or series of portfolios. Two examples of these "evolving" portfolios are retirement or college savings plans. A series of portfolios are developed based on the number of years to reach a goal (years to retirement) or a target year for the goal (start college in 2020) or based on age (investing today for birth to three-year-olds, four- to seven-year-olds, etc.). Index components or asset allocation portfolios are used as the building blocks. The weights of component parts of funds are reallocated over time as the portfolio moves closer to the goal. For example, investing for retirement in 20 years or investing for a one-year-old's college would start out with an aggressive portfolio, possibly 100 percent equity. Over time, the portfolio would evolve to a moderate then conservative strategy gradually adding more and more bonds as the terminus date of the long-term goal draws nearer. A wide variety of investment managers provide such products, and others are assembled "a la carte" by public and private-sector sponsors of retirement plans. Chapter 18 provides more details on these investment strategies and the logic behind using *portfolios of indexes* with different asset allocation strategies for maximum investment efficiency.

THE BEST APPROACH TO IMPLEMENT INDEX-BASED STRATEGIES

After a plan sponsor decides how indexing best fits into its program, implementation begins. Chapter 25 discusses some overall considerations for deciding between available index vehicles for direct access to index returns, but the vast majority of public and private pension plans (as well as many foundations and endowments) have legal guidelines that require them to invest in physical securities with voting and lending rights. Thus assuming that the plan chooses "traditional" index strategies—where the plan is the beneficial owner of the underlying securities tracking the index—there are two key decisions: (1) whether to manage the money internally or to use an external index manager, and (2) if an external manager is employed, whether to invest in a commingled fund or a separate account. The answer to each of these questions has a significant impact on how the plan's resources are deployed. We discuss both considerations next.

Internal versus External Management

Pension plans often begin to manage money internally with an indexing strategy. Many plans believe that managing money internally is a way to attract and retain talented staff as well as reduce the cost of managing the plan. Although pension plans invest billions of dollars for beneficiaries, they are frequently run with small staffs and small budgets. When considering whether to manage an index fund internally or employ an external index investment manager, there are numerous staffing and cost issues to consider.

Arguably, to manage each indexing strategy internally, a minimum of four staff people would be necessary. Two *investment professionals* would be required to ensure that modeling and trading could be accomplished at any time and that there would be adequate redundancy. Generally, at least two back-office personnel are needed to assist in processing trades, investment accounting, and coordinating with the custodian.

Experienced back-office personnel may be difficult to hire due to the specialized nature of investment accounting and trade settlement. Depending on the amount of money to be indexed, the technology necessary, the index used and strategy employed (replication, optimization, stratified sampling), the countries indexed, and whether proxy voting is outsourced, staff levels could be much larger.

Additionally, transaction costs would almost certainly increase. The advantage of a robust internal crossing forum with numerous buyers and sellers would no longer be available to the lone plan sponsor, although they could access external crossing platforms. This would invariably increase the underlying costs of managing an in-house fund.

Another unpleasant reality that increases the cost of managing a fund internally is the dreaded *operating error*. The most common operating error for an internally managed fund would be related to trading—whether for cash flows or index changes. For example, errors could include buying or selling the wrong amount of securities and/or creating trades based on incorrect cash balances. Errors could also result if there were a missed index change or corporate action. If a pension plan staff errs and a loss results, the fund would absorb the loss and its asset value would be reduced. On the other hand, if a third party, that is, the external manager, errs resulting in a loss to its client, invariably the client is made "whole" by the manager. If an error results in a gain (oh lucky day!), the external manager would also be obliged to remit any benefit to the fund and ultimately its participants.

The pension plan must evaluate its present technological capabilities and its commitment to investing in future technology and training employees, as well as its ability to maintain the necessary modeling tools and research software.

When evaluating the internal versus external management issue, all costs and benefits must be examined closely, and when *noneconomic* objectives are being pursued, this should be acknowledged. For example, some plan sponsors might want an internally managed capability to motivate and retain staff, or in order to meet a local statute. These policy goals are acceptable, as long as all parties recognize the explicit and implicit costs and benefits of them.

Considerations for Using Institutional Separate Accounts versus Commingled Funds

Index products lend themselves to pools of commingled funds in which like-participants invest in the same fund (e.g., commingled trusts, collective trusts, and in the retail world, mutual funds). The participants do not directly own the underlying securities in the fund, but own units in the fund priced usually at a net asset value. Commingled trust funds are used by boards that invest for numerous stakeholders with similar objectives, and it is advantageous to pool money and resources.

The separate account allows the investor to have maximum control and flexibility to customize the portfolio guidelines, and easier access to security level data; however, there are disadvantages, such as potentially higher management and trading costs. There are numerous considerations when comparing separate accounts and commingled funds, which are discussed next, and summarized in Table 26.1.

Ownership is one major difference between separate accounts and commingled funds. A separate account acquires shares of stocks and securities and bears all the responsibilities of direct ownership. On the other hand, the plan holds units in a commingled fund and, as such, the plan has exposure to, but not direct ownership of, the underlying securities.

Commingled funds are designed to accommodate numerous *participant investors* with similar needs and objectives, while a separate account focuses on the plan sponsor as the sole participant investing internally or with its external index manager. Especially for smaller plan sponsors, commingled funds may afford economies of scale with lower management fees and less direct costs.

While commingled funds have many advantages, the participant must agree to *conform with the structure and process associated with the funds.* Investors must accept all the conditions of the fund as it is established. Participants do not have the ability to establish unique terms and guidelines for

TABLE 26.1 Commingled Funds versus Separate Accounts for Institutional Investors

	Commingled Fund	Separate Account
Ownership	Plan acquires units in fund	Plan directly acquires shares of stock and securities
Participants	Designed for numerous	Plan and manager
Control	Little input or control by plan	Input to portfolio guidelines by plan
	Accept fund agreement	Easier to monitor
	Day-to-day by manager	Day-to-day by manager
Terms/guidelines	Set by fund	Substantially set by plan
Custody	Fund's custodian	Plan's custodian*
Registration	In fund's name	In plan's name
Country	In fund's name	In plan's name
Timeliness of performance and account data	Dependent on fund's manager and custodian	Dependent on plan's custodian
Security level information	Stock exposure based on plan's percent of fund	Easily attainable
		Use in vendor's analytics programs
	Some mutual funds provide security data only twice a year	
	Difficult and time-consuming to integrate with other data and to calculate plan's gain/loss on individual stocks	
	Fund's manager must provide special reports as required	
Proxy voting	Voted by fund*	Voted by plan or designee
Securities lending	Managed by the fund	Managed by the plan or designee
	Securities lending returns may be higher due to lending power of large, stable pool of assets	Split may be more favorable; but returns may not be as high as commingled fund (smaller pool)
	Cash collateral guidelines according to fund	May have more choice related to cash collateral pools/guidelines
Securities litigation	Handled by the fund	Handled by the plan or designee
Directed commissions	Generally not available; trading focuses on minimizing costs	Handled by the plan or designee
Costs	Management cost lower	Must analyze all costs to compare benefits—custody, proxy voting, registration, data needs, securities lending
	Trading cost lower due to greater crossing opportunities	

* Some flexibility for plan-directed proxy voting, depending on asset manager.

the account. Situations do occasionally arise that eliminate the use of commingled funds as an option. For example, if a pension plan is invested in an S&P 500 index fund and is required to sell its tobacco stocks, it can no longer invest in the S&P 500. A "standardized" tobacco-free S&P 500 fund may be available, yet the pension plan must accept the fund's definition of a tobacco company and the stocks that would be eliminated from the S&P 500. Similarly, plan sponsors with broader social goals, such as religious organizations, usually require a separate account structure to achieve their combined policy and investment objectives.

Commingled funds are held by the fund's custodian and listed as a one line-item (the value of the investment in the commingled fund) with the plan's master custodian. Separate accounts are held by the pension plan's custodian and contain the underlying securities held in the portfolio. Fees and services will vary by custodian.

Country registration for international equities is an important consideration, especially in emerging markets. For a separate account, the pension plan is the direct owner of the securities and must register in each foreign country. The process is time-consuming and costly. Furthermore, the ability to invest is often restricted until the administrative process is completed. If investing through a commingled fund, the pension plan is transacting in units of the fund and not directly purchasing or selling securities. Thus, registering in each country individually is no longer required. The manager of the fund handles the registration and all other attendant local requirements. Once again, the pension plan can recognize significant cost and time savings by using the scale advantages of a third-party manager.

The timeliness of performance and accounting data was once a significant factor, but has steadily become less of an issue. Advances in technology have greatly enhanced accessibility to the data; however, the speed, access and accuracy continue to be highly dependent on the managers and custodians involved. There remains a significant difference in the level of detail available between separate accounts and commingled funds. One disadvantage of a commingled fund is its limited access to the detailed underlying *security-level information.* Calculating a pension plan's exposure (market value) to an individual stock at one point in time is relatively easy. Knowing the weight of the individual stock weight in the fund and applying it to the total value of the pension plan's total investment in the fund is the easiest method to calculate the exposure. However, it is more difficult to estimate a pension plan's gains and losses with respect to individual stock's held in a commingled fund.

Although some managers offer other options, most commingled funds vote *proxies* on behalf of their shareholders. Since index investment managers are institutional investors, their objectives are aligned with the pension fund on most economic issues: both look to maximize share value. Different viewpoints most often arise on social and political issues. For example, recent proxy issues have centered around compelling Bermuda-headquartered companies to reincorporate in the United States. Some shareholders feel that the superior shareholder rights in the United States justify the change, while other shareholders find the economics of a Bermuda incorporation to be a significant advantage to running a competitive global business. Both are valid viewpoints that institutional investors may take (some of these corporate governance issues related to indexing are discussed in the sidebar within Chapter 13). Separate accounts are usually the better option if a pension plan wants to vote its own proxies. The next decision is whether to use internal staff resources to vote proxies or hire an external proxy voting firm. Using an external firm still requires staff time to develop the plan's view on standard proxy voting issues, to provide advice on nonstandard proxy issues, and to oversee the process.

As discussed within Part Four, an integral part of investing an index portfolio involves capturing the securities lending "enhancement" available to these large, stable asset pools. Securities lending is the temporary transfer of a security by its owner (in this case, the commingled fund) to another investor or financial intermediary. Securities are borrowed to settle failed trades, engage in dividend arbitrage, or short a stock. Securities are lent to maximize the value of the portfolio. Index funds provide a large pool of relatively stable and lendable securities. Commingled funds will generally have their securities lending program managed by the asset manager.

There are three parties in a securities lending transaction—the beneficial owners (the participants in a commingled fund), the lending agent (the commingled fund represented by the asset manager), and the borrowers (broker/dealers). The borrowers must provide collateral on the borrowed securities (102 percent for United States equities and 105 percent for international stocks) that is invested in a cash investment vehicle. The difference between the net cash earnings and the interest paid to the borrower for their collateral posted (rebate rate) represents the gross return on the securities lending trade. The income is split between the lending agent (usually the asset manager for a commingled fund) and the beneficial owner. The split may be equal (50 percent to owner/50 percent to the lending agent) or any negotiated amount. Splits range from 50 percent/50 percent to 80 percent/20 percent depending on the market, the lending agent and the negotiating leverage that the plan sponsor has with their index manager.[8] The lending agent bears all the operational costs related to the securities lending transactions.

If the pension plan invests in commingled funds, the plan sponsor must evaluate whether the *securities lending* program associated with the index fund is managed and priced according to its investment and possibly statutory requirements. If a separate account is used, the pension plan's custodian or a third-party lender may lend securities. Whether commingled fund or separate account, the plan sponsor must understand the securities-lending split and the investment strategy used for the collateral pool. It is also very important to examine the cost and risk profile of the underlying collateral pool.

Securities litigation is handled within a commingled fund. Therefore, if a pension plan wants to take an active role in a securities litigation process, it is advisable to hold the securities in a separate account. The reasons for this are varied but include quick and clear access to information that a commingled fund may not have been required to collect and retain.

If *directed commissions* or *commission recapture programs* are important elements to the pension plan, a separate account is necessary. Generally, directed commissions and commission recapture programs are not available with commingled indexed funds. This is because these sorts of programs consider other aspects of value when obtaining "best execution," which a fund manager has a fiduciary responsibility to achieve. Index fund managers have an investment imperative to minimize execution costs to better track the index. In any event, the free and low cost trading available through crossing opportunities in commingled funds can significantly reduce execution costs, making the net benefit to the fund at least as advantageous as directed commissions and commission recapture programs.

Fees and costs are always a major factor in any decision. Just as numerous clients can use one commingled fund vehicle, one fund can be used for numerous investment programs, large and small. Having a separate account for smaller programs may be expensive. Using a commingled index fund can reduce costs significantly. In addition, large pension funds can negotiate very low fees on index funds and often develop strategic partnerships with its index managers. When comparing the costs and fees, it is important to be careful to include all the costs/services that may be attributed to a commingled fund or separate account structure.

One pension plan that has both the scale and need to use a separate account is Japan's Pension Fund Association (PFA)—the largest pension fund in Japan. To close this chapter with another robust example, Yasuchika Asaoka describes PFA's rationale for using index-based strategies. PFA was one of Japan's pioneers in adapting a rigorous benchmark framework, and in using index-based strategies at the core of their investment strategy.

THE BACKGROUND AND LOGIC OF THE JAPAN'S PENSION FUND ASSOCIATION'S USE OF INDEX STRATEGIES

Yasuchika Asaoka

As many chapters in this book have detailed, there are various reasons for selecting index-based investment strategies. From a major pension-fund perspective, we have identified five key reasons, as follows:

1. There is little chance to gain added value over the market (or benchmark) with active strategies since the market is highly efficient.
2. Our judgment that excess return over the market is not expected with active strategies even in cases where the market is not highly efficient.
3. In connection with the second factor, the larger the asset size of a pension fund, the higher the optimal ratio of passive strategies relative to active funds.
4. There might be a case where pension funds do not have sufficient knowledge of the market to appropriately judge the skill of active managers in stock selection and asset allocation.
5. There might also be a case where the passive strategy plays an important role in pension funds for implementing efficient asset allocation changes.

Taking all this into consideration, it is no easy task to determine whether the market is extremely efficient, or even just how efficient the market is. The more diversified the investors and their management targets are, the more difficult it is to create the standards to judge the level of efficiency in the market. Even the U.S. market, which is highly efficient with defined benefits pension plans as major investors, could be considered less efficient with the expansion of defined contribution pension plans.

The Japan Pension Fund Association (PFA) currently manages 5.4 trillion yen (over $50 billion as of early 2003). PFA follows a policy for strategic asset allocation as shown in the figure presented next. PFA is currently not adopting any additional tactical asset allocation or market timing strategies and we implement rebalancing strategies, which allow returning to a policy of strategic asset allocation when an asset allocation ratio exceeds its pre-set limit.

The four major assets in the strategic asset allocation policy are Japanese bonds, Japanese equities (both labeled as domestic in

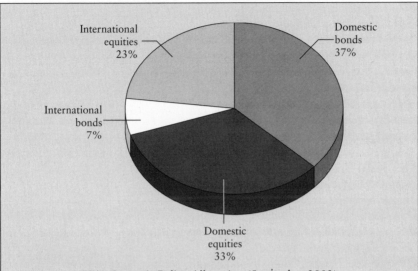

PFA's Strategic Policy Allocation (September 2002)

previous figure and the following table), foreign bonds, and foreign equities. As shown in the following table, a benchmark that represents the complete broad market is used for each asset class.

**PFA Benchmarks Used for Strategic Asset Allocation and
Passive Implementation**

Asset Class	Policy Benchmark
Domestic equities	Tokyo Stock Price Index (TOPIX) including dividends
Domestic bonds	Nomura Bond Performance Index
International equities	MSCI Kokusai (World ex-Japan)
International bonds	Nikko Salomon Smith Barney WGBI (ex-Japan)

Currently, passive investment strategies comprise approximately 35 percent of the total assets of the plan, using the representative benchmark index of each asset, adopted in Japanese equities, foreign bonds, and foreign equities (comprising the core developed market benchmark as well as emerging markets). Indexing is therefore indispensable for the effective management of returns, risk, and cost in PFA's investment strategy.

(Continued)

PFA's adoption of index strategies is not based on the premise that the target markets are too efficient (i.e., that we cannot gain excess returns over the market by active strategies on medium and long-term perspectives). In fact, we *are* confident in gaining excess returns in the medium and long-term by efficiently combining indexing with well-managed active funds, and are steadily making efforts to achieve this objective. However, as noted above, our assets under management are quite large, and it is accepted wisdom that there is a natural ceiling on the amounts mandated to active strategies depending on the characteristics of investment strategies and the market scale of each investment target.

Accordingly, it is crucial for PFA to ensure an efficient manager structure. Successful development of this structure depends on how we can achieve the highest level of "excess return after management fees" within our allowable risk budget. Also, as discussed in other parts of the book, the phenomenon of *closet indexing* must be avoided when we aggregate active strategies in total. In line with these basic principles, the current ratio of passive to active strategies was determined after reviewing a full range of efficient manager structures. In emerging markets equities, however, our lack of sufficient infrastructure to fully evaluate and confirm long-term performance of active strategies has led us to select only an index-based strategy.

Finally, in passive strategies for Japanese equities and foreign developed-market equities, securities lending services provide us with an indispensable level of revenue. As discussed in this chapter, this revenue is a critical factor in considering optimal manager structures. Similarly index-based strategies are an efficient way to adjust overall asset allocation through rebalancing, which like all asset owners, we will implement on a regular basis.

CONCLUSION: WHERE DO PLAN SPONSORS GO NEXT?

This chapter provided details on the ways that pension plans use index funds—whether as a core holding complemented by active satellite portfolios or with actively managed portfolios playing the lead role and index funds filling the gaps and reducing overall portfolio risk. This chapter also depicted some of the ways the basic index funds can be used as building blocks to create *active index* portfolios. Chapters 15, 18, and the sidebars within this chapter and Chapter 18 give some robust examples of sophisticated blending of active and index strategies. Controlling risk, reducing costs, and efficient strategy and program implementation all make index funds a vital component in the management of pension plans and other large asset owners.

The bearish and volatile market environment of the early 2000s resulted in many pension plan assets falling and their liabilities rising, and even with 2003's major global equity rally, the problems persist. Although there are no easy solutions to the challenges of this environment, being cognizant of the pension plan's risk exposure, understanding the asset/liability characteristics, and maintaining a long-term perspective will assist in the development of a structure that fits the plan's needs. Furthermore, in an uncertain return environment, rigorously controlling costs is one of the only "sure things" that a pension fund—or any investor—can do to improve overall performance.

Clearly, index-based strategies, with the flexibility, transparency, cost-control, and risk management they provide will continue to have a critically important role in the structure of each pension plan. And these benefits will ensure a growing role for indexing in individual investing, whether professionally advised or independently directed. It is inconceivable that either the largest or the smallest investors could achieve their long-term objectives without indexing as part of their strategies.

NOTES

1. *Pensions & Investments* and Watson Wyatt, "World's Largest Pension Funds," *Pensions & Investments* (December 23, 2002).
2. See note 1, p. 18.
3. Higher securities lending revenue from international developed market index strategies almost always can offset most or all of the higher management fees for these strategies.
4. See Chapter 2, and/or William Sharpe, "The Arithmetic of Active Management," *Financial Analysts Journal*, vol. 47, no.1 (January/February 1991): 7–9.
5. Information on research resources from the major institutional index fund managers is available from their web sites. Links are provided on IndexUniverse.com.
6. For example, our index managers were a vital resource in helping plan our strategy for the 2001/2002 MSCI benchmark evolution (see Chapters 9 and 21), and regarding economic developments and market mechanisms in emerging stock markets. (See sidebar within Chapter 21.)
7. Gary Brinson, L. Randolph Hood, and Gilbert L. Beebower, "Determinates of Portfolio Performance," *Financial Analysts Journal* (July/August 1986).
8. At least one large public pension fund has negotiated a 90/10 securities lending split with its lending agents.

CHAPTER 27

Tax-Efficient Indexation

Mark A. Zurack

_____ **Editor's Note** _____

In this chapter, a former Goldman Sachs managing director who helped build that firm's formidable index and derivatives research and strategy area, details the trade-offs and choices an investor faces when adding tax considerations into the index-based investment equation. The chapter builds upon the descriptions and tradeoffs between various index products provided in Chapters 25 and 26, as well as some of the tax management techniques described in Chapter 24. Mark Zurack reviews the core benefits of indexing for tax-sensitive investors, and details the advantages and disadvantages of the various products and approaches. He focuses on the situation faced by three types of investors in the U.S. equity market—taxable institutions, namely, corporations; individuals; and non-U.S. residents. The author now lectures on derivative products and investment strategies at Columbia University, but retains a strong passion for tax-efficient investing.

As evidenced by its heightened coverage in the popular press, indexation is becoming an increasingly important strategy for individual investors, and its appeal for institutions remains strong. As discussed in Part Four, the goal of an index fund is to match the performance of an agreed-upon benchmark, which is usually a market index. The attractiveness of index-based strategies lies in their cost structure. The management fees and transaction costs of running an index fund are always cheaper, usually well under half the cost of investing in an active portfolio.

For tax-sensitive investors, index funds and related products may offer additional value. Turnover in index funds is typically lower than in active portfolios, so capital gains tend to be deferred for a long time. In fact, it is possible to use an individually managed index fund (separate account) as part of a strategy to accelerate capital losses in the fund while allowing gains to remain. Those losses can be used to offset other taxable gains the investor may have.

There are five basic ways to establish exposure to a benchmark index, as highlighted next. *(Editor's note: These five approaches differ slightly from the categories laid out in Chapter 25, which included a category for options-based strategies. Instead of including options, Mark makes the distinction here between index mutual funds and separate accounts, which are better suited for the tax-related analysis in this chapter, as few investors would use exclusively options-based strategies for tax-efficient index exposure.)* For purposes of illustration and consistency, we will use the popular S&P 500 Index as the benchmark for strategies described throughout this chapter:

1. *Mutual fund.* Many of the major mutual fund families offer funds that track an index, usually the S&P 500.
2. *Separate account.* In this case, an investment manager would run the index fund as a separate account for a specific investor.
3. *Exchange-traded funds (ETFs).* ETFs trade like stocks, but represent shares of ownership of a 1940 Act vehicle or a "Unit Investment Trust" that holds the index's constituent stocks and closely tracks the performance of the index.
4. *Futures.* In this case, the investor combines a long position in S&P 500 futures with a fixed-income security. Consider the case of a manager who wants to invest $10 million into the market. With the index at 1350, each contract is worth $337,500 (the multiplier 250 × the index level of the cash). Therefore, approximately $10 million of S&P 500 exposure could be achieved by establishing a long position of 30 S&P 500 futures contracts.[1]
5. *Equity index swaps.* Here the investor combines a fixed-income portfolio with an S&P 500 equity index swap. Most equity swaps are structured to provide the investor the total return of the index times the notional amount of the swap at its termination. In return, the investor makes periodic payments (usually quarterly) to the counterparty, the quantities usually linked to the three-month London Interbank Offered (LIBOR) rate.

Analysis of how tax considerations could impact which index strategy a taxable investor chooses is a critical issue for many types of investors to explore. In this chapter, we focus on three types of taxable investors: individuals, corporations, and non-U.S. residents.

Investments like mutual funds and hedge funds are pass-through vehicles for tax purposes. That is, how the income is taxed depends on the profile and residence of the investor in the fund—namely, whether they are an individual, corporation, or nontaxable investor.

HOW ARE INDEX-BASED INVESTORS TAXED?

Index strategies on U.S. stocks generate different types of income, including dividends, interest, and short-term and long-term capital gains. Some investors, such as U.S. pension and endowment funds, do not pay taxes on any source of income (the type of investors that the previous chapter focused on); others such as some non-U.S. investors incur withholding tax on dividends, while U.S. individuals and corporations pay taxes on all sources of income, albeit at different rates. Table 27.1 compares how different sources of income are treated for each type of investor.

As Table 27.1 shows, individuals benefit most from long-term capital gains versus other sources of income; corporations benefit from qualified

TABLE 27.1 Maximum U.S. Federal Tax Rates by Type of Income and Investor

Income Source	Individuals (%)[a]	Corporations (%)[b]	Non-U.S. Residents[c]
Long-term capital gain (LTCG)	15.00[1]	35.00	n/a
Short-term capital gain (STCG)	35.00	35.00	n/a
Dividend income	15.00[2]	35.00[d]	Withholding tax varies by country[e]
Interest income	35.00[3]	35.00	n/a

[a] U.S. persons only.

[b] Includes industrial corporations, banks, and insurance companies, although banks and insurance companies are also subject to special industry-specific rules.

[c] In addition to their local tax treatment.

[d] Subject to complex limitations, U.S. corporations generally may effectively exclude 70 percent to 100 percent of dividends from income by claiming a "dividends-received deduction."

[e] In addition, dividends paid to a non-U.S. recipient in respect of U.S. shares or a U.S. recipient in respect of non-U.S. shares may be subject to withholding at source. Such withholding may be subject to reduction/modification by applicable tax treaties. Rate varies by country, generally ranges between 15 and 30 percent.

[1] For sales or dispositions after May 5, 2003.

[2] Qualified dividend income.

[3] Except for interest on tax-exempt state or municipal bonds, certain ESOP loans expenses and interest on U.S. Savings bonds used to pay qualified educational expenses.

dividends but are indifferent to holding period on capital gains; while foreign investors much prefer interest income over dividends and often are indifferent to the character of capital gains. These differing incentives guide the decision on optimal vehicle and strategy for each type of investor. The specific approaches are reviewed in the remainder of the chapter.

OPTIMAL INDEX STRATEGIES FOR INDIVIDUALS

Individuals would ideally prefer never to recognize capital gains and to minimize dividend and interest income. If capital gains are to be recognized, the individual has a strong preference for long-term capital gains (LTCG) over short-term capital gains (STCG).

Each of the five index strategies described earlier potentially generates LTCG, STCG, dividend, and interest income. The reasons for these four types of potentially taxable income are described in Table 27.2.

Mutual funds, separate accounts, and ETFs have a similar tax profile since they all invest in stocks and only turn over the portfolio when there is a change to the index. However, there are some differences between the three alternatives, as described next.

TABLE 27.2   The Four Types of Income Emanating from Index Strategies*

	LTCG	STCG	Dividends	Interest
Mutual funds	Removal of stocks from the index. Mergers for cash. Large withdrawals	Large withdrawals (highly unlikely)	S&P 500 yield minus expenses	Only on spare cash
Separate Account	Removal of stocks from the index. Mergers for cash	Large withdrawals (highly unlikely)	S&P 500 yield minus expenses	Only on spare cash
ETFs	Removal of stocks from the index. Mergers for cash	Large withdrawals (highly unlikely)	S&P 500 yield minus expenses	Only on spare cash
Futures	60 percent of any gain or loss on futures	40 percent of any gain or loss on futures	None	Fixed income return on portfolio
Swap	Gain/loss on swap contract	Gain/loss on swap contract	None	Fixed income return on portfolio

* In addition, there is turnover for index changes—additions, deletions, changes of shares outstanding, corporate actions. Any index change that changes benchmark weights will cause turnover, and therefore, would generate STCG and/or LTCG.

Mutual Funds versus ETFs

Both mutual funds and ETFs represent a simple, low-cost way to establish index exposure. On a pretax basis, the performance of each product will depend on the management and administration fees each charges. In addition, the investor pays a commission when buying or selling ETFs.

On an after-tax basis, both mutual funds and ETFs incur taxes on the dividends paid, as well as any capital gains resulting from the selling of stocks leaving the index. To offset all or a portion of recognized capital gains, some mutual funds and most ETFs have the ability to employ a degree of loss harvesting to offset gains, by selling stocks with specific *tax lots* with losses when redemptions occur. *Loss harvesting* is a strategy we describe in the next section.

The main difference between a mutual fund and an ETF is the way they handle redemptions. When a mutual fund incurs large redemptions, it may have to liquidate a material portion of its holdings to raise cash. It is very possible that some of the securities sold will generate capital gains. Those gains will create taxable gains for *all* shareholders, not just investors redeeming their shares.

By contrast, most ETF holders never redeem their fund shares, but instead sell them into the open market, leaving remaining shareholders unaffected. Large ETF holders can redeem their shares, but will not receive cash as a result. Instead, as described in Chapters 16 and 23, they will usually be delivered "in-kind"—actual physical delivery of the portfolio of securities underlying the ETF to the ETF's fund manager. The delivery of physical stocks to or from a single shareholder does not create a taxable event for remaining shareholders.

It should also be noted that the ETF manager doesn't always deliver a full portfolio of securities to meet in-kind redemptions. When the ETF manager learns that some stocks are expected to leave the index, he may heavily weigh those securities in any portfolios delivered to meet in-kind distributions. This implies that the ETF manager may generate fewer capital gains from index changes than his or her counterpart at a mutual fund.

Mutual Funds/Exchange-Traded Funds versus Separate Accounts

A separate account is potentially the most flexible alternative to index mutual funds and ETFs, since it provides the investor full control over when gains and losses can be taken. Its benchmark can also be customized. If the investor wants to eliminate or adjust the weights of industries or specific securities, that is easily accomplished. Most important, it provides investors with a vehicle for harvesting losses and potential gifting securities with gains if those strategies are compatible with the investor's overall needs.

Any well-diversified portfolio of equities will generate some unrealized capital losses because, even in a bull market, not every stock in the index increases in value. An individual can recognize or *harvest* those losses to offset any gains generated by the index fund or any other investment they have.

In some cases, the stocks in question may still be viewed as an attractive long-term investment. Ideally, the client would like to sell the stock, realize the loss (to offset realized gains), and immediately buy it back. Unfortunately, the IRS's *Wash-Sale Rule* does not allow this action. Any stock sold at a loss cannot be repurchased for a minimum of 31 days, in order for the loss to be realized immediately. Similarly, the investor *cannot* replace the stock with the purchase of any call option (irrespective of strike) or convertible bond or preferred and recognize the loss. This leaves the investor with three alternatives during the 31-day period:

1. Hold cash.
2. Buy exposure to a different stock or a broad market index.
3. Replace the stock with the sale of a put with a term greater than 31 days. For this purpose, the put cannot be deep-in-the-money.

All three of these alternatives create additional tracking risk versus the index and, potentially, additional transactions costs. However, in many cases the tax benefit of loss harvesting outweighs the risks and costs, because you are trading off certain "tax alpha" for tracking error that can be negative or positive. (The concept of tax alpha is discussed in more detail in Chapters 14 and 24.)

Stocks with large capital gains can also be used as part of a philanthropy-oriented strategy. That is, the investor can gift stocks with large, unrealized capital gains to charity, which not only avoids the recognition of a capital gain, but generates a charitable deduction equal to the fair market value of the stock at the time it was gifted, as long as the stock was held for more than a year. Investors should note that the IRS's *Wash-Sale Rule* only applies when capital losses are recognized, so the stocks gifted could immediately be repurchased.

Futures versus Swaps

Synthetic indexation strategies using futures or equity swaps—described in detail by my former colleagues in Chapter 25—have different tax properties than either mutual funds, ETFs, or separate accounts. First, the fixed-income return on the portfolio generates interest income that is taxed at a relatively high rate. Any gains or losses on futures are recognized either when the futures contract is closed out, expires, or at year-end, whichever occurs sooner. Sixty percent of those gains are taxed as long-term capital gains, 40 percent as short-term capital gains.

This implies that synthetic indexation strategies using futures are unattractive on an after-tax basis for individuals with long-term holding periods. Mutual funds, ETFs, and separate accounts generate less dividend income than the interest income of a synthetic index and only recognize a small portion of the capital gains, which are usually long-term gains. However, for *individuals with holding periods less than a year,* 60 percent of any capital gains on a futures strategy are taxed at the long-term rate. By contrast, 100 percent of all gains on mutual funds, ETFs, and stocks are taxed at the higher short-term rate.

The taxation on equity swaps depends on how long the swap is held, but also on when payments are made. If all payments are made at maturity and the swap is held for more than a year, then the net gain or loss on the swap will be long term. Remember, the fixed-income component of the strategy still generates interest income. If payments are made periodically, those payments could generate a combination of short-term and long-term capital gains, interest income, and interest expense. This implies that individuals with longer term holding periods (over a year) will probably prefer synthetic indexation using swaps rather than futures and the reverse.

To summarize the key points of analysis, Table 27.3 compares the five different indexation strategies from an individual's after-tax perspective, and highlights the major advantages of each approach.

TABLE 27.3   When Different Index-Based Strategies Are Most Tax-Efficient for Individual Investors

Mutual fund	Long-term investor, generally costs lower than ETF, offsets potential tax disadvantage.
ETF	Long-term investor concerned about large potential redemptions.
Separate account	High to ultra-high net worth investor willing to pay potentially larger management fees for building portfolio with existing holdings, tax loss-harvesting, customization of portfolio, and tax-efficient charitable giving.
Futures	Short-term trading strategies.
Equity swaps	Higher pre-tax return, when holding period of investment matches term of swap.

OPTIMAL INDEX STRATEGIES FOR CORPORATIONS

Most U.S. corporations do not directly invest in a diversified portfolio of common equities like an index fund. Their equity investments tend to be in concentrated cross shareholdings resulting from private investments or other corporate transactions. Their pension funds are active equity index fund users, but those portfolios are nontaxable and off the corporation's balance sheet.

Insurance companies are the broad exception to this general rule. Banks, by regulation, do not hold common equities, but insurance companies do.

The major differences in tax treatment between individuals and corporations that affect index strategies are:

- Corporations pay taxes on 30 percent of dividend income coming from U.S. corporations. Subject to complex limitations, U.S. corporations generally may effectively exclude 70 percent to 100 percent of dividends from income by claiming a dividends-received deduction.
- Corporations are indifferent between short-term and long-term capital gains, both are taxed at 35 percent.

As a result of these differences, corporations find all three of the stock strategies—mutual funds, ETFs, and separate accounts—attractive, and the derivatives-based strategies less attractive. That is because the interest income on a synthetic index fund using futures is fully taxable while 70 percent of the dividend income from stock is excluded from tax.

INDEX STRATEGIES FOR NON-U.S. RESIDENTS

Non-U.S. residents face tax considerations that differ from U.S. individuals or corporations, and these may drive their indexing strategy in a different direction. The non-U.S. resident is by no means a homogeneous investor when it comes to tax-efficient investing. In each country, capital gains, interest, and dividends are taxed differently. And like the United States, within a country, individuals and corporations may be taxed differently.

However, there may be some components of the tax law that drive indexing strategies for non-U.S. residents across jurisdictions and investor types. For example, dividends paid to a non-U.S. recipient for U.S. shares may be subject to withholding tax at source. Such withholding may be subject to reduction/modification by applicable tax treaties. The rate varies by country, generally ranging between 15 percent to 30 percent.

This implies that many non-U.S. residents lose between 15 percent and 30 percent of the dividend yield of the index in addition to any local taxes they pay. With the S&P 500 yielding approximately 1.5 percent as of the end of 2003, that translated to a cost of 23 to 45 basis points per year.

In contrast, a synthetic index strategy generates interest income and capital gains, neither of which trigger a withholding tax. For some investors, withholding tax is the only tax they incur, so the synthetic strategy will be the more attractive alternative. However, for the non-U.S. resident who pays ordinary income and/or capital gains tax, the after-tax comparison of alternatives depends heavily on their local tax regime.

CONCLUSION—INDEXING AS THE COMMON DENOMINATOR

The important conclusions for investors are quite simple and powerful. As we have seen in previous chapters, indexing is a proven strategy for the world's largest and most sophisticated tax-exempt investors. But it is an even more compelling approach for taxable investors. Even in "plain vanilla" form, indexing can provide substantial tax-related benefits over traditional active strategies. Using indexing's "full potential," in a customized, active-tax managed format, the strategies can even deliver more—*tax-alpha*. This chapter has shown that there are different optimal solutions for diverse types of taxable investors (and different time horizons). But indexing is the common denominator for all of these users and applications, and remains the most flexible framework and technique to minimize costs and maximize investment efficiency.

NOTE

1. A futures position requires the payment of initial margin, which equals a small fraction of its notional value. In addition, it is marked-to-the-market each day. See Chapters 14 and 25 for more background, or *A Guide to Synthetic and Enhanced Index Strategies, Equity Derivatives Research* (Goldman Sachs & Co., August 4, 1998), for a detailed exploration of the topic.

CHAPTER **28**

Indexing for Advisors

A Sophisticated Strategy for Professional Investment Advisors and Their Clients

Michael J. Chasnoff

———————————— **Editor's Note** ————————————

A heavy emphasis throughout the book has been geared toward institutional investors. This is by design as a major theme of the book is that indexing is a highly sophisticated investment approach, and the best proof of this is the extent to which large pension plans, foundations, and endowments use indexing. With this chapter and the two that follow, the emphasis shifts toward individual investors—whether they are do-it-yourself investors, or have professional advisors assisting their efforts. The author of this chapter offers the perspective of a financial advisor who has introduced the core-satellite concept into his practice, and implements much of it with exchange-traded funds (ETFs). And in the concluding parts of the chapter, Michael Chasnoff traces his experiential "journey" toward this approach. The sidebar by Joyce Franklin builds on some of the issues discussed in the previous chapter, and shows how ETFs can provide tax benefits to the clients of advisors. To further supplement this chapter, the experience and opinions of other advisors who use index-based strategies can be surveyed by viewing the relevant features in the "Advisor Research" section of IndexUniverse.com.

This chapter demonstrates how advisors add value to the investment management process by actively employing index funds and passive investment strategies. By gaining a better understanding of these applications, more advisors will develop and implement intelligent index investment programs. The chapter *does not* contain schemes to attain wealth without risk, nor does it attempt to describe how to select the best-performing index investment. Rather, it provides a logical case for indexing, as well as a sensible framework for establishing a long-term investment program utilizing index funds. Such a program must take into account: the investment objective, the investment time-horizon, and a realistic expectation of the returns available from the securities markets over the long run.

The chapter makes reference to many of the concepts and products described throughout this book. While minimizing references to any specific index products, it will be obvious that much of the philosophy is influenced by the advancement of indexing contributed by the development of index mutual funds and ETFs.

THE PROFESSIONAL BIAS FOR ACTIVE MANAGEMENT

Why have advisors historically preferred active management? The lure of outperforming the market, rightly or wrongly, has been the benchmark for measuring success. Indexing is considered to be a bland, lackluster investment strategy. It flies in the face of The American Way: "I can do better."

Clearly the stated objective of active management is to add value by producing investment returns that are in excess of the funds' designated target benchmark or index by researching and trading individual stocks or bonds. Each manager follows a stated strategy for trying to beat the market.

The only way to beat the market, after adjusting for market risk, is to discover and exploit other investors' mistakes. Very few investors have been able to outsmart and outmaneuver other investors consistently enough to beat the market over the long term. To achieve market-beating returns, the manager must identify a successful process and replicate the activity consistently over time. There are several techniques that active managers use to try to beat the market. One way to improve performance is to be a smart stock picker. Typically, active managers either utilize a "top-down" or "bottom-up" selection approach.

Top-Down and Bottom-Up

Top-down managers start by looking at economic trends to help them predict which industries will prosper in the future. Once they've zeroed in on some industries, they further sift through them to find the most promising companies. In contrast, bottom-up managers look for outstanding companies in any industry, thereby assuming that a great company will do well even if it is in an industry that is not thriving at the moment.

Some managers take a more general view by focusing on the markets as a whole, rather than attempting to pick individual stocks. To be successful, these investors must accurately and consistently predict the future by anticipating economic trends.

Market Timing/Tactical Asset Allocation

While seeking to improve returns, active managers will modify the level of cash holdings within a portfolio. Many active managers keep some cash on hand ready to invest when new opportunities arise, as well as cover periodic or unscheduled distributions. Other managers may increase the amount of cash on hand if they anticipate a market downturn in the near future, hoping to later buy stocks at lower prices. Or, if they expect stocks to do well, they may invest all available money or even leverage their assets to take full advantage of the hoped-for market upturn.

ACTIVE MANAGEMENT FAILS TO MEET EXPECTATIONS

Studies on market timing conclude that an active investment manager would have to be right on his market forecast 75 percent of the time for his portfolio just to break even after measuring the costs of mistakes and transaction costs.[1] With 55 days accounting for 90 percent of the stock markets net gain in the 10 years ending June 2002, the odds are definitely against this strategy.[2]

Equally challenging has been the art of stock picking. One study revealed that a stock picker who uses his or her intuitive skills had a *one in 36 chance* of success in beating the market.[3] Only 3 percent of professional managers beat the market. Chance alone can explain this outcome. Chapters 3 and 4 provide much more insight and detail on the never-ending "index versus active" debate.

Rather than picking stocks or timing the market, advisors who employ asset-allocation strategies believe their "value added" comes from selecting best-of-class managers. Many advisors have narrowed their manager selection to perceived less efficient market sectors like small-cap and international fund categories. Claims that the average small-, mid-cap, and international managers outperform index funds have been greatly exaggerated. According to Morningstar, neither fund group collectively outperformed its benchmark index during the past 10 years, and both groups had higher risk scores.[4] As discussed in Chapters 3 and 4, "survivorship bias" (where the historical data of poor-performing funds is often eliminated) inflates mutual fund performance averages, so the spread is actually larger than it seems. In other words, funds that are closed or merged out of existence due to poor performance *should be* included in studies that compare active manager performance against relevant benchmarks. Not taking these funds into account artificially inflates active manager performance as a group. IndexUniverse.com has regular updates on this issue, including the quarterly survey of index versus active performance calculated by Standard & Poor's.

BUILDING THE CASE FOR INDEXING

Although indexing has demonstrated its worth, the majority of assets managed by advisors continues to be deployed in actively managed portfolios—whether in mutual funds, ETFs or separate accounts. As stated in Chapter 2, the logic of indexing is based on a simple fact: Before expenses are counted, investors as a group earn the market return. If one investor—through luck or skill—gets an above average return, he necessarily achieves it at the expense of another investor who is left with a below average return. In other words, markets are a zero-sum game where every transaction involves both a winner and a loser.

While some actively managed funds have done better than average, most have done worse. Since all investors collectively own the entire stock market, then active investors, as a group, can do no better than market returns. As further stated in Chapter 2, and reinforced in Chapters 3 and 4, since management fees and transaction costs incurred by index-based investors are substantially lower than those incurred by active investors, and both provide equal *gross* returns, then passive investors must earn the higher *net* returns.[5] To overcome the costs of portfolio management and transactions, Charles D. Ellis estimated investment managers would have to beat the market by about 2 percentage points a year, which he regarded as an unlikely prospect.[6]

The Industry's Shift to Indexing

As described Chapter 2, institutional use of indexing began in the early 1970s. The Vanguard Group popularized the strategy starting in 1976 by making the S&P 500 Index Fund available to consumers on a direct retail basis. Academic and popular discussions of the subject, such as Burton Malkiel's *A Random Walk Down Wall Street*, Paul Samuelson's *Challenge to Judgment* and Sharpe's *Arithmetic of Active Management*, have helped expand awareness of passive investment strategies among investors and their advisors.[7]

In addition, indexing enjoyed a relatively favorable performance result during the bull market of the late 1980s and 1990s, whether in large-cap,

TABLE 28.1 Active U.S. Equity Funds versus Relevant
Index Benchmarks

Index/Fund	Total Return— 15-Year Annualized (%)
S&P 500	10.83
Average Large-Cap Equity "Blend" Fund	9.15
S&P MidCap 400	13.66
Average Mid-Cap Equity "Blend" Fund	11.14
S&P SmallCap 600	9.35
Average Small-Cap Equity "Blend" Fund	9.61

Source: Morningstar Principia Pro, data as of 3/31/03.

mid-cap, or small-cap, as is visible in the 15-year performance data portrayed in Table 28.1. *(Editor's note: Comprehensive updates on the performance of active mutual funds versus their appropriate benchmark index is now provided via Standard and Poor's Index Versus Active [commonly known within the industry as SPIVA] database and research which is regularly posted on IndexUniverse.com and www.spglobal.com.)*

TRADITIONAL INDEX APPLICATIONS

Most advisors have become familiar with the benefits of indexing and its basic applications. It is now more common for advisors to include an S&P 500 index fund in a large-cap allocation. However, uses of indexing are rapidly proliferating as providers of ETFs roll out new products and as innovative techniques are developed and implemented by visionary advisors. Some of the more popular applications are described next.

Allocation and Rebalancing

Most advisors are familiar with Modern Portfolio Theory and the oft-cited Brinson, Hood, and Beebower study that examined the relative importance of investment policy. The study compared the performance of actively managed portfolios with that of passively invested funds and found that 93.6 percent of the *variation* in performance between active and passive portfolios was attributable to investment policy decisions.[8] Chapter 30 provides more detail and nuance on the importance of the policy allocation decision. To determine the appropriate investment policy, advisors consider the investor's objectives, time horizon, and risk tolerance. Once the investment policy is set between a balance of stocks, bonds, and cash reserves, the decision as to the asset allocation and underlying investment alternatives is made.

Whether the portfolio is structured partially or exclusively with index-based components, it's vitally important to rebalance the holdings in order to maintain the appropriate risk characteristics. Rebalancing is essential and, as discussed in Chapter 18, helps not only to maintain an appropriate strategic allocation, but also capture "mean reversion," which can enhance long-term performance. Over a period of time, diversified portfolios will have asset classes generating various returns. To reset the portfolio to its original risk characteristics, leading asset classes must be sold back to their original targets and the proceeds are then deployed to the lagging investment categories. Index funds greatly simplify rebalancing activity, since their risks are precisely quantified and their liquidity allows for seamless transactions.

As Figure 28.1 shows, a portfolio evenly divided between stocks and bonds that was rebalanced every six months would have generated an average annualized return of 9.4 percent over four decades—only marginally lower than the 9.6 percent return of the same initial portfolio that was never rebalanced. However, as is also visible in the diagram, rebalancing substantially

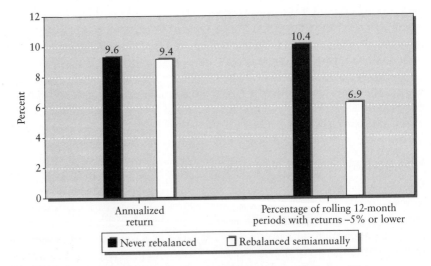

FIGURE 28.1 Systematic Rebalancing: Similar Returns with Lower Risk over Four Decades
Source: The Vanguard Group, *In the Vanguard* (Winter 2002).

lowers risk. Over 12-month rolling periods, the rebalanced portfolio had returns of −5 percent or lower about 7 percent of the time, compared with more than 10 percent of the time for the other portfolio.

EVOLUTIONARY DEVELOPMENTS

Because the first retail index fund was tied to the S&P 500, many investors still equate *only* the S&P 500 with indexing. However, as discussed in the interview in Chapter 2, Vanguard's retired founder John Bogle believes that the ideal indexing strategy is to own the entire market, and he now recommends the Wilshire 5000 index as a better representation of the "total market"*(Editor's note: As of final editing, there were no fewer than five comparable broad-market ETFs, representing the Wilshire, S&P, Dow Jones MSCI, and Russell index series. While they have a variety of differences, they all serve the objectives sketched out by Bogle in Chapter 2.)*

Today, with the emergence of index-linked ETFs, advisors can precisely weight underlying investment alternatives with portfolios that closely mirror the asset category's benchmark. These new vehicles provide advisors with a tremendously flexible and cost-effective investment tool. (See Chapters 16 and 25 for a discussion of ETFs and their advantages.) Advisors can allocate between large-, mid-, and small-cap stock classifications as well as the total market indexes. Just as importantly, advisors can balance or tilt a portfolio in the direction of value or growth investment styles. Portfolios can even be allocated by popular benchmark providers such as Standard & Poor's, Russell, Dow Jones, Wilshire, and others.

Depending on the advisor's investment approach, he or she can diversify or emphasize specific industries or economic sectors. Further, advisors may spread their portfolio exposures across borders into country-specific funds, global sectors, and international benchmarks. The introduction of fixed-income ETFs in 2002 now allows advisors to build balanced portfolios with duration specific fixed-income funds. Many advisors are replacing traditional index funds with ETFs, and they are using them more actively than before.

ETFs: CHANGING THE WAY PROFESSIONAL ADVISORS USE INDEXING

With ETFs, advisors can fluidly build cost-effective portfolios from a broad selection of alternatives to structure an exact allocation that is appropriate

for the client or obtain targeted exposure to a specific sector or market—
and the advisor can change the allocation as goals and objectives evolve.

Trading Hedging and Shorting Flexibility

Unlike mutual funds, ETFs can be traded intraday using market orders, stop
orders, and limit orders. With intraday trading, advisors can make an ETF
investment in the morning and sell it an hour later; traditional mutual fund
transactions, on the other hand, are typically executed after the market is
closed. When allocating or rebalancing, advisors can make real-time investment decisions. Buys and sells can be placed on a simultaneous basis or
scaled in over the trading day.

Investors and advisors can also sell ETFs short or trade them on margin. Some ETFs are the basis for options, offering a wide variety of investing
and hedging strategies. Advisors can add leverage to the portfolio by using
margin. They can hedge the portfolio by selling calls, buying puts, and selling short.

Portfolio Transitioning

ETFs can be useful during the manager selection process, allowing the
client to remain exposed to the market during a manager firing or hiring.
When the time comes, as it unfortunately does, that a particular investment
manager needs to be removed from the client portfolio, one trade into an
ETF allows the portfolio to remain fully invested while due diligence on
other managers is performed. The manager selection process does not
occur overnight, and can often take a month or even more. Remaining fully
invested during the selection process will ensure that the investor will not
miss out on a market rally by sitting on the sidelines.

Another use of ETFs is in the allocation of new client portfolios. When a
new account is opened at any firm, the investment plan may take time to implement. Given initial client timelines and risk tolerance, a new account can
be quickly exposed to the market while manager due diligence and specific
goals are discussed with the new client. In addition, some new accounts may
not meet certain minimum asset sizes that a separately managed account
(SMA) requires. These accounts can be deployed with confidence using a few
ETFs as substitutes for the SMA category (see Chapter 24 for more details
and background on SMAs). Finally, another method might be when an advisor has new cash to deploy to the market. Rather than leaving the money in
cash reserves, he may purchase the S&P 500 index to gain exposure to the
large-cap allocation.

TRANSITIONS AND TAX SWAPS

There are several methods advisors can use to transition client assets. When advisors realize a loss from the sale of securities, they must wait at least 30 days before they repurchase the holding to avoid the wash-sale rule. Should this wash-sale rule be neglected, however, the tax loss benefit would be lost, and consequently the position's tax basis would remain unchanged from the original purchase. To gain market exposure during the 30-day period, advisors can purchase ETFs that correlate closely to the security sold.

A swap or replacement strategy relies on the desire to remain fully invested. This is a vital concept as the mentioned previously, the bulk of a market's return in a given year may often be concentrated in a few trading sessions If the securities are not substantially identical, it is possible to implement the following tactics to garner the benefits of tax loss harvesting and remain invested in the market.

Tax management is an important tool when managing a taxable portfolio such as a personal account or trust. As discussed in Chapters 24 and 27, a dollar saved in taxes is a direct increase in wealth.

One way to increase total return is to manage a portfolio of index funds using a tax-swapping strategy. The idea is to buy a specific dollar amount of an index fund each quarter, thus establishing different tax lots. If the market turns down during the quarter, sell the tax lots that are at a loss and simultaneously buy a similar index fund managed by a different fund company to replace the position. Using a tax swap strategy, you can increase your overall return by saving on taxes while never losing your position in the stock market.

The concept of tax swapping index funds is very similar to a common strategy of bond swapping. In a bond swap, you sell a security that is at a loss in your portfolio while simultaneously replacing it with a bond that has similar yield and maturity. As long as the bond bought is not "substantially identical" to the bond sold, it is not considered a "tax wash" by the IRS. For example, if you sold a 5 percent coupon, A-rated, five-year corporate bond of one utility company at a loss and simultaneously bought a 5 percent coupon, A-rated, five-year bond of another utility company at the same yield, it is perfectly fine. The loss can be used to offset a realized capital gain, or can be used to reduce adjusted gross income by up to $3,000 per year. By lowering taxes, you increase wealth.

It is important to understand that the new security cannot be "substantially identical" to the one sold. If the two are substantially identical, you would need to wait 30 days before buying back the new one, possibly losing your tax deduction. The definition of a "substantially identical" security is a matter of interpretation, however. Tax courts have ruled that if you swap the securities of one company for the securities of an unrelated company, then the securities are not identical and a tax loss is allowed. Therefore, swapping a Vanguard index mutual fund for a Schwab index mutual fund should not create a tax wash.[9]

Strategies for Index Fund Tax Swapping

Most people put money into the markets over time, a little here and a little there. I recommend saving your taxable dollars and making regular quarterly investments on the first day of every quarter. Buying at regular times of the year establishes different "tax lots" for your shares. Since it is unlikely that the market will trade at the same level the first day of each quarter, you will be buying index fund shares at different net asset values and establishing different tax positions. It is important to keep track of the cost basis of each tax lot, so you can later take advantage of tax swaps.

Tax Loss Harvesting Opportunities

The selling of a security, whether a single stock or an index investment, to harvest an unrealized loss is a time-tested strategy. The benefits are two-fold: not only can a harvested unrealized loss be set against realized gains in the same portfolio, the sell proceeds can be reinvested either in a similar position or a newly desired position. Further, tax loss harvesting can improve the overall tax efficiency of a portfolio even if the amount of the unrealized losses harvested exceeds the maximum allowable amount an investor can offset against realized gains.

When realizing capital losses from the sale of an index, advisors can replicate the index by creating a proxy basket of other exchange-traded funds. For example, to create a mirror image of the Russell 3000 Index, advisors can purchase 46 percent Russell 1000 Growth, 46 percent Russell 1000 Value, and 8 percent Russell 2000. This gives the investor the same exposure. Chapters 24 and 27 discuss other ways that taxable investors can realize active tax loss harvesting with index-based strategies.

INCOME DISTRIBUTION AVOIDANCE STRATEGIES

One of the disadvantages of mutual funds is the requirement to distribute its realized gains prior to the end of the year. To avoid receipt of the taxable gain, many advisors either look for other funds that may have already paid-out their capital gains distributions or hold cash until the distribution is made. With ETFs, advisors can gain immediate exposure to the capitalization

MAXIMIZING THE STRUCTURAL BENEFITS AND MINIMIZING THE COSTS OF USING INDEX FUNDS AND ETFs—HELPFUL TIPS FROM A FINANCIAL ADVISOR

Joyce L. Franklin

Minimize ETF Trading Costs

Although exchange-traded funds have razor-thin expense ratios and are generally cheaper than comparable traditional index funds, trading costs can be a trap for the ETF investor. ETFs trade like stocks, and most brokers charge either a per-share trading fee or a minimum trading fee. However, you can purchase many ETFs through discount online brokers for less than $15. A large dollar, one-time ETF trade is preferable to dollar-cost averaging into a small ETF position, due to minimum trading fees. And remember that trading fees will be imposed for both buying and selling an ETF. For the small investor who invests a set amount over fixed time periods (for example $100 each month), a no-load index-based mutual fund may be preferable to an ETF. You can easily do a breakeven analysis by comparing expenses, holding period, and trading fees for each alternative to determine whether an ETF or a no-load index fund is best.

Harvesting Tax Losses Using ETFs

Selling a fund with an unrealized loss allows you to offset capital gains from other investments. Current tax law permits capital losses in excess of capital gains to reduce your income by up to $3,000 per year; any excess loss is carried forward for use in a future year. Remember that if you sell stock with a loss, the *wash sale rules* (discussed in this chapter as well as Chapters 24 and 27) bar deducting a loss on that security when a substantially identical one is purchased within 30 days of the original sale.

Buying one S&P 500 index fund, taking a loss, and immediately buying another S&P 500 index fund will likely be considered a wash sale. However, ETFs can be used to harvest losses while maintaining exposure to a specific asset class. For example, IVV is an S&P 500 Index ETF. Selling IVV and immediately purchasing IWB, the Russell 1000 Index, will allow you to maintain exposure in large-cap U.S. stock while avoiding the wash sale rule. These two funds track similar, but yet not identical, indexes that are highly correlated. Note that at

(Continued)

the time of this writing, there has been no official IRS pronouncement specifically approving or disapproving this strategy. Be sure to consult with a CPA or other tax expert for the most recent news on this issue.

Beware of Distributions

Before purchasing a fund or an ETF, find out when dividends and capital gains will be distributed, as shareholders must pay tax on any distribution. Although many stock index funds and ETFs are now managed to reduce capital gains, there still can be some nasty surprises, especially for specialized sector, style, or country funds. Avoiding distributions will minimize your taxes. The most popular time for a mutual fund to make a distribution is at year-end, although anytime during the year is considered fair game.

Avoid making a purchase just before the fund's record date to avoid current tax. If you buy the fund after the record date, you're safe from that round of taxable distributions. The payable date is the date on which the distribution will actually be paid out to all shareholders of record. The reinvest date is the date that the distribution will be reinvested in more shares of the stock. You may choose not to reinvest dividends, but you're still on the hook to pay tax on the distribution.

To research dividend and capital gain distributions, call the fund company or custodian, or check out the fund's distribution schedule on their web site. Investors who buy an ETF in a retirement account, such as an IRA or 401(k) will not be currently taxed on any distributions.

Consider Index-Based Separate Accounts

A recent innovation, now available to investors with just over $100,000 to invest, is the *index-based separate account*. Essentially, this is a personal index fund where the individual owns the actual securities in the index-based portfolio, and the manager actively harvests the portfolio for tax losses. While this approach may carry higher explicit fees than a traditional index fund or ETF, the tax-loss benefit can often be worth significantly more than the added fee expense. Furthermore, these accounts can be customized to accommodate an investor's existing holdings. Chapter 24 discusses this concept in more detail.

and style of the manager by selecting a specific index that highly correlates to the fund.

As noted in Chapters 16, 23, and 27, *in-kind distributions* are used by ETFs when shares of the fund are created or redeemed by institutional investors. This in-kind mechanism allows the fund to remove lower cost basis shares from the portfolio, therefore lowering the embedded capital gains in the portfolio.

The retail investor in an ETF realizes a benefit from this by potentially having a lower tax bill at year-end from their ETF investment than their traditional mutual fund. The conventional wisdom that says you should not purchase a mutual fund at year-end (when capital gains are distributed) does not necessarily apply to ETFs. When was the last time a product was introduced that benefited retail investors when institutional investors traded?

THE TALE OF A REFORMED ADVISOR

Initially, I must admit, I thought that I could identify best-of-class managers from each asset category. We carefully considered the manager's tenure, relative performance and risk scores, style and cap adherence, and annual expense ratio. When we allocated the portfolio, we gave special attention to the distribution between large- and smaller-cap funds, as well as to the balance between value and growth styles.

But after a number of years of inconsistent results, I realized that I needed to improve on my investment process. I analyzed our recommendations and found we had a significant level of success when we identified smaller-cap managers. In most cases, these managers had solid track records in down markets, exhibited a strong adherence to their market cap, and maintained a disciplined style preference.

This evaluation resulted in replacing our large-cap managers with index funds. Today, this approach is referred to as a *core-and-satellite* strategy. Like other contributors to this book, I believe combining these two seemingly mutually exclusive strategies (passive and active) results in an important middle ground that furthers the diversification process.

The benefits of combining active and passive strategies result in a lower weighted-average portfolio cost. We apply a disciplined approach, rebalancing our holdings on a contingent basis when our minimum or maximum guidelines are violated. Portfolios concentrated with trailing-fund winners and passive funds fail to achieve a core-and-satellite strategy. It is not core-and-satellite unless the portfolio is balanced with the appropriate component funds.

The first step to develop a core-and-satellite portfolio is to determine how "benchmark sensitive" you wish your portfolio to be. Human nature being what it is, most people aren't too concerned when their funds are doing much better than the relevant market index. Benchmark sensitivity becomes a factor when a fund performs worse than the index. With actively managed funds, this is almost certain to happen from time to time.

That is why extremely benchmark-sensitive investors favor index funds, which track their target indexes closely. Investors who aren't benchmark-sensitive at all may favor active funds, whose returns can deviate considerably—in both absolute and relative terms—from year to year. However, many people are in the middle: They are willing to accept returns that vary by a few percentage points from the overall market performance, but they don't want to risk having their portfolios get way out of line. These investors may favor a core-and-satellite approach, which is visually portrayed in Figure 28.2.

Deciding how to split your portfolio between passive and active funds depends, in part, on your confidence in the ability of active managers to earn returns that consistently outpace the market. Of course, as discussed in previous chapters, it's extremely difficult to identify funds that will outperform in the future.

One approach to satellite selection would be to allocate 50 percent of the total portfolio among four active funds that correlate closely to the core fund, have style purity, and are in market-proportional weightings. For example, if the core were a total-market stock index fund, the satellites could be a large-capitalization growth fund (20 percent of the satellite portion), a large-cap value fund (20 percent), a mid-/small-cap growth fund (5 percent), and a mid-/small-cap value fund (5 percent)—each with characteristics similar to

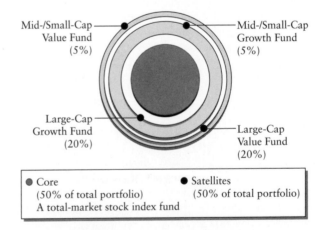

FIGURE 28.2 A Core-Satellite Strategy

its sector of the broad market. Such a portfolio would be broadly diversified and would offer a chance (albeit a small one) of earning a return that was far ahead of—or behind—the overall market's performance. In the worst-case scenario, the portfolio would slightly underperform the broad market. In the best-case scenario, it would slightly outperform the market without having assumed a significant amount of additional risk.

A contrasting approach would be to choose active funds that don't correlate highly with the core holding—or with each other—in hopes of picking up higher returns than index funds would provide. This approach increases the chance of significantly outperforming or underperforming the core fund. No matter how the satellites are selected, two overarching factors apply: costs and diversification.

First, costs are as important in a core-and-satellite portfolio as in any investment context. A high-cost fund simply faces too high a performance hurdle to be able to enhance the overall portfolio's performance over time. Second, advisors should not expect every component of the portfolio to perform well at the same time. After all, it's the differing returns that build strength for the overall investment strategy. As Steven A. Schoenfeld articulates in Chapter 30, having "indexing at the core" is the key to minimizing costs and maximizing diversification. This is why sophisticated financial advisors are increasingly using index-based products to benefit their clients' portfolios.

NOTES

1. *Source:* SEI Investments.
2. Using Russell 3000 daily data, the best performing 55 days from 6/30/92 to 6/30/02 produced 90 percent of the returns during that period.
3. Robert H. Jeffrey and Robert D. Arnott, "Is Your Alpha Big Enough to Cover Its Taxes?" *Journal of Portfolio Management* (Spring 1993).
4. Morningstar data from Principia Pro, as of September 2002.
5. William F. Sharpe, "The Arithmetic of Active Management," *Financial Analysts' Journal,* vol. 47, no. 1 (January/February 1991): 7–9.
6. Charles D. Ellis, *Investment Policy* (Homewood, IL: Irwin Publishing, 1993).
7. See bibliography at end of book and in "E-ppendix" at www.IndexUniverse.com.
8. Gary Brinson, L. Randolph Hood, and Gilbert L. Beebower, "Determinants of Portfolio Performance," *Financial Analysts Journal* (July/August 1986); and Gary Brinson, L. Randolph Hood, and Gilbert L. Beebower, "Explanation of Total Return Variation," *Financial Analysts Journal* (May/June 1991). Subsequent research on this topic is discussed in Chapter 31—"Indexing at the Core."
9. Government policies change regularly. Always consult a tax specialist before implementing any of these tax-related strategies.

CHAPTER 29

Indexing for Individual Investors

Greg Baer and Gary Gensler

_____ **Editor's Note** _____

This chapter is an edited excerpt of an important book written for individual investors, The Great Mutual Fund Trap. *The authors, both former U.S. Treasury Department officials, recount the many pitfalls that sensible people seem to fall into when it comes to making investment decisions. With a handful of insightful statistics and humorous anecdotes, they remind individual investors that past performance really isn't indicative of future performance, and that paying front loads and back loads for mutual funds defies common sense. Readers should keep in mind that Gary and Greg worked on this book during 2001 and 2002, long before the mutual fund scandals of 2003 hit the headlines. They conclude that while index investing may be less fun, it can certainly be more profitable, as U.S. civil servants participating the government's Thrift Savings Plan know very well. And the chapter is filled with colorful analogies, too. Written in a direct and informal style, if there is one chapter in the book that you should consider sharing with your friends and family who want to know why you've become an enthusiastic proponent of indexing, this is it.*

_____

This chapter is predominately excerpted from *The Great Mutual Fund Trap* (New York: Broadway Books, 2002), paperback published in January 2004, with permission from the publisher. Yasue Pai assisted the editor and authors in developing this excerpted chapter, and we acknowledge her valuable contribution.

The world's best putters (the golfers on the PGA Tour) make only about half of all their putts from six feet away. There are good reasons for putting results to be uncertain and hard to understand. And those reasons don't change much over time. Once you understand them, they are easy to accept as part of the game. But putting is, was, and likely always will be difficult to comprehend for those who don't understand the true rules of the game.

—Dave Pelz, *Dave Pelz's Putting Bible*

This chapter is written for the millions of Americans who invest in the stock or bond markets to help achieve their long-term financial goals—perhaps a home, a college education for their children, or a secure retirement. We believe that the vast majority of these investors are investing the wrong way—paying billions of dollars in unnecessary costs and running needless risks in a quest to outperform the market. How are so many intelligent people wasting so much money? By making the perfectly understandable mistake of trusting the experts.

In the great majority of cases, however, expert money management advice simply leads investors to underperform the market and enrich Wall Street.

So, what's an investor to do? You *cannot* improve your returns by spending more time or money trying to pick funds or stocks. You *can*, however, significantly improve your returns by choosing investment vehicles that offer the lowest possible costs and the greatest tax efficiency, and you can reduce your risk by choosing vehicles that diversify your portfolio.

The good news is that financial products have emerged that allow you to achieve these goals through *passive* investing with index funds and exchange-traded funds (ETFs). Index funds now offer the choice of investing in the market as a whole—achieving broader portfolio diversification than the original mutual funds—at very low cost and with minimal taxes. ETFs offer the same diversification and similar cost advantages with even better tax consequences. Investing with these products over a lifetime, you can yield nearly twice as much return as the same amount invested actively. Assume, for example, that you're investing $250 per month ($3,000 per year) and that you can expect to earn 8 percent annually after the cost of passive investing. You end up with a retirement nest egg of about $872,000. Actively pursue the same goal and you'll end up earning at least 2 percent *less* per year on average, or $497,000 in all. Because of costs and compounding, you will have forgone fully *43 percent* of your potential future retirement money, as shown in Figure 29.1.

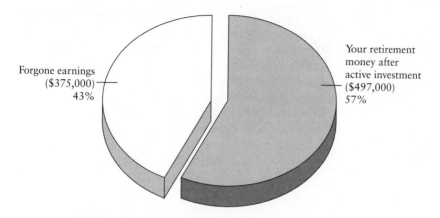

FIGURE 29.1   The Big Bite of Traditional Active Investing

Considering that the stakes are so high, you owe it to yourself to climb out of the mutual fund trap and reinvigorate your common sense. It means comparing your stock fund's performance to a meaningful (and investable) benchmark like the Wilshire 5000 or S&P 500 and doing the same with your bond funds. It means coming to grips with the fact that past performance really isn't predictive of future performance. It means viewing with a critical eye the blizzard of advice from the fund industry and a co-dependent financial media. It also means checking your records to see how much you're paying in fees, loads, and unnecessary taxes. Yes, that's a lot to ask, but protecting your hard-earned savings is worth at least that much.

THE GREAT MUTUAL FUND TRAP

What upsets me is not that you lied to me, but that from now on I can no longer believe you.

—Friedrich Wilhem Nietzsche

Americans currently have over $3 trillion invested in actively managed stock mutual funds.[1] They have another $800 million invested in actively managed bond funds.[2] These mutual funds are held by 50 million American households directly or in brokerage accounts, 401(k)s, IRAs, or variable annuities. Yet by any objective measure, these funds are failing their millions of devoted clients. That's entirely predictable, given that the mutual fund companies run up at least $70 billion per year in costs for investors in their attempts to beat the market. Over a five-year period, only about 20 percent of actively managed stock funds perform well enough to earn back their fees and loads. Furthermore, five years later, the identity of the fortunate 20 percent will have changed. This point is crucial. It turns out that the government-mandated disclaimer that accompanies every fund's reported results—"past performance is no guarantee of future results"—is *absolutely true.*

So, why do so many people keep investing in ways the evidence shows is counterproductive? We believe that there are four simple answers:

1. We are by nature optimistic and confident. We are all too willing to believe that poor past experience will reverse itself or in the future apply only to other people.
2. Our optimism and overconfidence are reinforced by a constant, consistent message from the financial industry and the financial media: Try to beat the market. The message can be direct, even crass, such as when in late 1999 a TV commercial promises that frequent stock trading will earn you a Caribbean island of your own.
3. We tend to focus on *returns* and ignore the *costs* of investing. You probably know about how much you pay each month for electricity, housing, and other services. If you're like most people, though, you've never totaled up your costs of investing—all of them, including management fees, transaction costs, and taxes. Why? Because mutual funds and brokers have constructed a system where the costs are practically invisible.
4. Investors do not understand how markets work, and how very difficult it is to beat them consistently, even by a little bit. When individual investors think about picking stocks, they believe that they can do research on the past performance and current management of companies and pick winning companies a majority of the time. Or they believe they can give their money to an expert money manager who probably can do even better, in exchange for a fee.

THE GRIM REALITY OF POOR PERFORMANCE

> *Does history repeat itself, the first time as tragedy, the second time as farce? No, that's too grand, too considered a process. History just burps, and we taste again that raw-onion sandwich it swallowed centuries ago.*
>
> —Julian Barnes, *A History of the World in 10½ Chapters*

The grim reality of mutual fund performance is shown graphically in Figure 29.2. We see that in the 5- and 10-year periods ending September 2001, the

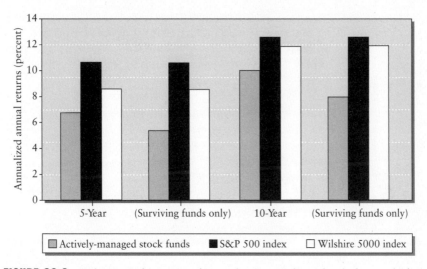

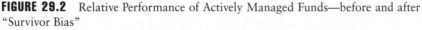

FIGURE 29.2 Relative Performance of Actively Managed Funds—before and after "Survivor Bias"
Source: Morningstar Principia Pro, data through September 30, 2001.

average stock fund trails far behind the market (updates on the ongoing manager/index performance battle are available via S&P's "SPIVA" analysis on IndexUniverse.com and www.spglobal.com). Only a small percentage beat the market over a multiyear period, especially after adjusting for those funds that did not survive during the period (the right-side set of bars in both the 5- and 10-year analysis).

Consider these results from the point of view of an individual investor trying to select an actively managed fund that will beat the market. The average actively managed fund trails the market considerably (see Chapters 3 and 29 for more on this). Even an above-average fund only stays even, beating the market by enough to offset its fees and expenses. Only a few funds beat the market by a significant amount, and then not for long. More specifically:

■ Over the five-year period ending December 31, 2001, only 33 percent of surviving actively managed stock funds beat the market. Only 25 percent beat it by more than 1 percent per year.
■ Over the past 10-year period ending December 31, 2001, only 28 percent of surviving actively managed stock funds beat the S&P 500. Only 11 percent beat it by more than 2 percent per year.[3]
■ Adjust for survivorship bias and those numbers drop even further. It's likely that fewer than 20 percent of all funds actually beat the market

over a five-year period, and fewer than 10 percent over a 10-year period. The "surviving funds only" bars on Figures 29.2 make this dramatically apparent.

Risk and the Life of an Active Portfolio Manager

Not only have actively managed funds underperformed the market, *they have done so while incurring greater risk for their shareholders.* Actively managed funds are more volatile (as measured by standard deviation) than the market, as shown in Table 29.1.

The returns of actively managed funds were 20 to 25 percent more volatile than the broad market. Why are actively managed funds so much riskier? We have three explanations:

1. Actively managed funds are not as diversified. Sector funds obviously are not fully diversified, but even *diversified* actively managed funds have considerably higher volatility than the market—a standard deviation of 24.9 percent for five years and 18.8 percent for 10 years.
2. A lot of money has flowed into—and out of—growth funds, which tend to be more volatile than other funds. Still, even excluding growth funds *entirely,* the remaining funds still have higher risks than the broader market.
3. Another possible explanation has to do with the economics of mutual fund companies and the personal incentives of fund managers. Consider the following:
   - The revenues of mutual funds depend on building up a large amount of assets under management. Mutual funds generally increase assets when their style or sector of the overall market is doing well.
   - A mutual fund in a hot sector or style will see significant inflows only if it is ranked toward the top of its group.

TABLE 29.1 Relative Risks of Actively Managed Funds

	Standard Deviation (%)	
	(5-Year)	(10-Year)
Actively managed funds	25.5	19.4
S&P 500 Index	19.9	15.8
Wilshire 5000 Index	20.4	16.2

Source: Morningstar Principia Pro, data through December 31, 2001.

TABLE 29.2 The Worldview of a Sector-Based Mutual Fund Manager

	Sector/Benchmark	
	Doing Well	**Doing Poorly**
Fund outperforming sector/benchmark	Cash flows into fund; manager gets big bonus, promotion	Cash flow stagnant; manager keeps job
Fund underperforming sector/benchmark	Fund misses opportunity to grow; manager gets fired	Cash flow stagnant; manager keeps job

■ The most likely way for a fund manager to generate a high ranking is to take on additional risk. A manager's greatest fear is to turn in mediocre performance during a bull market in his or her sector. In fact, some fund managers refer to this concept among themselves as the "fear of the upside."

Note the perverse incentives implied by that last point and illustrated by us regarding a sector fund manager in Table 29.2. Lesson: The risk-taking incentives of fund managers are likely to generate greater risk than you would choose for yourself.

FROM BAD TO WORSE: SECTORS, LIES, AND TICKERTAPES

To generate more business, the mutual fund industry has opened up three other tables in the great fund casino. These funds divide the stock universe in three ways: by industry or sectors (e.g., technology, energy), by size (e.g., large-cap, mid-cap), or by style (growth versus value).

It's tempting to pick a few slices of the market. In roulette, some gamblers don't like the risk of picking a single number and instead prefer to bet on red or black. In other words, to gain a bigger reward one has to take on increased risk of losing everything (nothing ventured, nothing gained). The bet with sector funds is that you know more about what sector will outperform than you do about what stock will outperform. Let's take a look at the average performance of the three main categories of sector funds.

Industry Funds

Industry or sector funds offer investors the lure of specialization. These funds are based on the notion that a fund manager focused on just one area of the economy will use the resulting expertise to outperform fund managers invest-ing in all areas of the economy. In reality, though, many of the large fund companies (particularly Fidelity) use such funds as a training ground for new fund managers. Only a couple of years out of business school, they're trying to move up the ladder to larger, diversified funds. Once they gather experi-ence in one sector, they're usually transferred to a new one.

The record seems to show that, expert or not, sector fund managers cannot do any better against the market than any other active managers. Table 29.3 shows the returns of all actively managed funds focusing on a particular sector or industry over the past 5 and 10 years.

As poor as all these figures are, they don't tell the whole story. Industry/sector funds have significantly higher standard deviations than those of the average actively managed diversified fund so their risk-adjusted returns are far worse than absolute returns. Furthermore, if we were able to adjust for survivorship bias—estimated to be as much as 1.4 percent to over 2 percent per year when looking at the performance of all mutual funds and even higher for industry funds—these figures would be *much* worse. A sector-focused index fund or ETF would be a much better bet.

Size Doesn't Matter—And Neither Does Style!

If you don't want to invest in particular industries, companies can also be categorized by size. The fund industry now offers us large-, mid-, and small-cap funds focusing on companies with large market capitalizations, mid-sized capitalizations, and small capitalizations.

TABLE 29.3   Performance of Actively Managed Industry/Sector Funds (Load-Adjusted)

	Average Annual Performance (%)	
	(5-Year)	(10-Year)
Industry funds	7.5	12.0
S&P 500	10.0	12.7
Relative performance	−2.8	−0.7

Source: Morningstar Principia Pro, data through December 31, 2001 (399 funds: industry funds, ex-cluding index funds, ETFs, institutional funds, multi-ple classes of the same fund, and funds holding more than 20 percent of their assets in bonds).

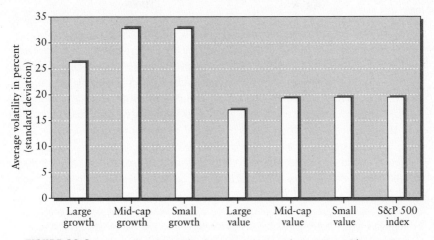

FIGURE 29.3 Annualized Standard Deviation Based on 5-Year Observation
Source: Morningstar Principia Pro as of September 30, 2001.

Another popular way to pick funds is by *style*. The notion is that companies with higher potential growth in revenues and profits (so called "growth" companies) will trade differently from those with lower growth (so called "value" stocks). Wall Street uses many different definitions for growth stocks and value stocks. We find them all a bit arbitrary. As seen in Figures 29.3 and 29.4, which show average annual volatility and average

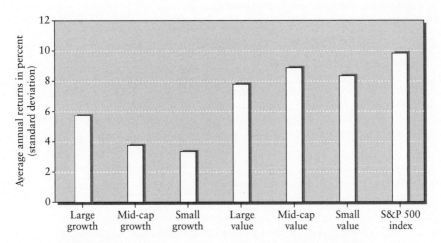

FIGURE 29.4 Annualized Returns Based on 5-Year Observation
Source: Morningstar Principia Pro as of September 30, 2001.

annual returns, respectively, growth funds historically tended to have more volatility and risk than value funds.

Over 5 and 10 years, every major size or style fund underperformed the S&P 500, generally by significant amounts. All but mid-cap value underperformed the Wilshire 5000 as well.[4] Here, it's the anti-Wobegon—all the children really are below average.[5] The reason is not difficult to understand. While in any year, growth may be up and value may be down, over time the performance evens out. The ankle weights of fees and costs, however, are a constant inescapable drag.

Looking at risk, the higher relative standard deviations for the funds mean they are more risky than the market. None was noticeably lower, so in every case, the risk-adjusted returns fall far short.

THE TRIUMPH OF HOPE OVER EXPERIENCE

Faith may be defined briefly as an illogical belief in the occurrence of the improbable.

—H. L. Mencken, *Prejudices*

Faced with the grim statistics about the average actively managed mutual fund, many investors will naturally respond, "I'm not going to pick one of those average or below-average funds; I'm going to pick an above-average fund." In general, individual investors will use two methods: (1) buying funds whose past performance is good and (2) buying funds recommended by experts. If it were only that easy. . . .

Looking at the Big Picture

Perhaps the most important study of the factors affecting mutual fund performance was conducted by a researcher named Mark Carhart, a former professor at the University of California.[6] The study is important for several reasons. First, it examined mutual funds over a very long period, from 1962 to 1993, through both bull markets and bear markets. Second, it looked at a very large number of funds of the type in which we're most interested: 1,892 diversified (non-sector/size/style) equity funds. Finally, unique for a study of this size, the study is free of survivorship bias. Finding all the old, dead funds requires a lot of detective work. Carhart did that work.

What did he find? Basically there isn't much hope for those looking to use past performance to predict future performance. The winning funds of the past are unlikely to be the winning funds of the future. Carhart found that if you take the top 10 percent of funds in a given year, by the next year 80 percent of those funds have dropped out of that top 10 percent ranking. For the top 20 percent of funds, 73 percent drop out the next year. For the top 50 percent of funds, roughly 45 percent fall out the next year. That's not much different from what you'd expect from random chance.

A follow-up study by economist Russ Wermers attempted to gain further insights into the stock picking skills of fund managers. Starting with Carhart's fund database, he then examined the performance of the individual stocks held by the funds in addition to the performance of the funds themselves.[7] Thus, he was better able to focus on how much of a fund's persistence was attributable to stock picking skill, as opposed to other factors. The results of Wermers' study provide no comfort to investors in actively managed mutual funds. He found that the average mutual fund net return trailed the market by 1 percent per year. Risk adjusted returns were 1.6 percent worse.

Wermers' study does include some solace for fund managers. He found evidence of modest stock picking skill that the Carhart study had not. In particular, he found that the underlying stocks held by mutual funds outperformed the broad market (when risk adjusted) by 0.7 percent per year. The problem, however, is that 0.7 percent of stock picking skill is woefully inadequate in the face of mutual fund costs.

What about "Hot" Funds?

"Hot" funds—those that performed well over the past year—are the focus of inordinate media interest, industry advertising, and investor money. The best known of these lists is *Money* magazine's annual ranking of the top 50 funds of the previous year, but even the rather less passionate *Consumer Reports* has gotten into the game of ranking mutual funds. So, a closer look is in order. Hot status says everything about the risk of a fund and its place in a hot sector. It says little about the skill of its manager or its *long-term* prospects.

We looked at *Money*'s lists for the years 2000, 1999, and 1998. Of the 50 top-performing funds in 2000, *not a single one appeared on the list in either 1999 or 1998.* There were seven mutual funds that appeared on the list in both 1998 and 1999, all in the Internet area, which had remained hot for two years. Heaven help you if you thought this was a sustainable trend. They fell an average of 41 percent in 2000 and another 46 percent in 2001.

This result is extremely significant. Investors looking at the top 50 might infer that these were the best managed funds over the past year—that their managers, at least for one year, had the magic touch. In fact, that's not the case. Yearly results reflect what economic sector outperformed the rest of the market that year. Almost any fund devoted to that sector is going to score well, regardless of the stock-picking talents of its fund manager. Conversely, even the most brilliant fund manager cannot hope to crack the top 50 if he or she is in a "cold" sector. In the late 1990s, you never saw an energy, financial services, retailing, or aerospace fund ranked among *Money's* winners. Did the fund managers in those sectors have lobotomies at the beginning of the year? No, they were just following the wrong sector.

What about Proven Funds?

Confronted with the poor record of the mutual fund industry as a group, many folks with whom we've spoken respond, "But I stick with the proven funds." So, does it work?

In his classic book, *A Random Walk Down Wall Street,* Burton Malkiel took the top-20 best-performing equity mutual funds of 1978 to 1987 and tracked them for the next 10 years. His results showed that while those funds had beaten the S&P 500 by 5.8 percentage points a year, during the 10 years they grew to fame, they trailed by 0.8 percentage points. We can look at those funds to see how they have performed for the 10 years through 2001. In other words, if you'd read a profile 10 years ago of the 20 very best mutual funds for most of the 1980s, and decided to buy them, how would you have done?

Here it is in a nutshell: if you'd bought and held a portfolio of the 20 best diversified mutual funds 10 years ago, you would have trailed an S&P 500 Index Fund by 1.2 percentage points per year. The index fund outperformed 12 of the 20 funds for the period.

Is Bigger Better?

Another possible approach to choosing an above-average fund would simply be to buy the largest funds. There is some logic to this approach, as there are economies of scale in the fund industry. So, we identified the 10 largest funds in 1991, and tracked them to see how they did over the following 10 years.[8]

While we've certainly seen worse strategies, this one is not a winner. As a group, the 10 largest funds trailed the S&P 500 by 0.6 percentage points per year over the next 10 years, before considering taxes. None of the funds beat or trailed the index by a whole lot: the best (American Funds' Growth Fund of America) led the index by only 1.3 percentage points per year; the worst (Pioneer Value) trailed by only 3.5 percentage points per year.

These results are not surprising, however, given how large funds are run. *Funds get to be big because they were once successful. They do not get to be successful because they are big. Once a fund gets big, beating the market becomes much harder.* First, the person at the fund who is responsible for the success often retires, moves onto another company, or opens a hedge fund, where the pay is better. Second, successful funds inevitably grow larger, as investors flock to them. The influx of assets forces the fund to choose between closing to new investors (as both Fidelity Magellan and several Janus funds have done) or changing how they invest.[9]

Another factor actually prompts large fund managers to track their benchmark index closely. With all the assets they need, managers at the largest funds are more concerned than those at smaller funds with retaining assets than with taking large risks to generate inflows. Our earlier chart on fund manager incentives doesn't apply here.

The phenomenon is known in the United States as "closet indexing." In the United Kingdom it's more vividly called "index hugging." What it means is getting passive investing at the cost of active investing. *(Editor's note: When investors buy several large, diversified actively managed mutual funds, they also essentially get the same thing—an overall portfolio that has become an expensive index fund.)*

Morningstar's Five-Star Funds

Morningstar ratings are wildly popular with investors and the media. They come from a respected source of mutual fund information and have an outward simplicity. Morningstar rates mutual funds according to its "star" system. The star system is a computer-generated rating based on a fund's risk-adjusted return over the past 10, 5, and 3 years. Five-star funds are the best, and one-star funds are the worst.[10] These ratings have great influence, as highly rated funds routinely use their Morningstar stars prominently in their advertising.

Since Morningstar has all the data, you might have assumed they are more likely than anyone to pick winning mutual funds. The history, however, suggests otherwise:

- Of those funds receiving a four-star or five-star ranking in one year, between 40 to 60 percent of those funds had fallen to a three-star ranking or below by the next year.
- Tracked as a group over a seven-year period, Morningstar's top-ranked no-load equity funds—the cream of the crop—lagged the market by an average of almost 3 percentage points a year.
- The performance of Morningstar's five-star funds is indistinguishable from its four-star funds, and even its three-star funds. That is, any differences are statistically insignificant.

■ Morningstar's stinkers—the one-star and two-star funds—do underperform persistently. Thus, Morningstar's system could serve investors
as a warning sign for funds to avoid. Unfortunately, however, *75 percent
of no-load funds receive a three-star ranking or above.* Furthermore,
many of the one-star stinkers are simply those charging appallingly high
loads, something investors can determine pretty rapidly themselves.[11]

Morningstar itself has recognized this problem. It cautions investors
against using their ratings as buy recommendations. They liken their star
ratings to an achievement test, rather than an aptitude test. They say that
the ratings, which tell you who delivered good performance in the past, are
not prologue to the future. But this still doesn't prevent investors and advisors from basing their fund purchase decisions on the rankings.

THE ANKLE WEIGHTS OF RUNNING AN ACTIVELY MANAGED FUND

*How come it's a penny for your thoughts, but you have to put your
two cents' worth in? Somebody's making a penny.*

—Steven Wright

Mutual fund managers are considered the Olympians of investing, well-
conditioned market analysts with access to all the best research. Yet we've
seen that they seem to lose just about every race. Now we'll see why: They
rack up over $70 billion per year in costs for their investors. Money managers
simply can't consistently keep up with the markets while running with such
ankle weights. In total, expect something in excess of 4 percent of your fund
assets to disappear in costs per year for a load fund. If you are good about
picking only no-load funds you should still expect costs totaling close to
3 percent per year. Compound these costs over your lifetime and you'll see
the serious, serious bite they take out of your savings. . . These are ankle
weights that would have brought Carl Lewis and Bruce Jenner to their knees.

Paying the Piper

Ask most people about their actively managed stock funds and they may
have some vague notion that the fund charges an annual management fee.
That fee is a bigger drag on returns than most investors realize. Yet, it is
only the beginning of the costs that you pay by having a mutual fund manager do your investing for you.

Some of these costs are disclosed to investors:

- Monthly management, administrative, and distribution fees averaging over 1 percent per year.
- Sales loads, which are commissions charged by over half of all actively managed mutual funds when you buy or sell shares. When you do pay, the average load is 4.1 percent.[12] With an average holding period of only three years, the average load fund investor is paying an additional 1.4 percent per year.

A review of the 2,216 actively managed stock funds in the Morningstar database shows an average expense ratio of 1.33 percent. This figure assumes that all holders of multiclass funds choose the A shares, which generally have the lowest expense ratio. Look at all classes and the average rises to 1.61 percent.[13] The Securities and Exchange Commission (SEC) arrives at a similar figure of 0.9 percent to 1.4 percent.[14] The industry does not dispute these numbers. In congressional testimony in 1998, the Investment Company Institute (ICI), the trade group for the mutual fund industry, said that the simple average of fees equals approximately 1.52 percent.[15]

So, if you invest in an *actively managed* equity mutual fund, you will probably pay an average annual management fee somewhere around 1.3 percent to 1.6 percent of the value of your investment. You pay it whether that investment makes money, loses money, or stays the same. In Vegas, whether you win or lose, at least you get free drinks, a great hotel room, and the adrenaline rush that comes with the turn of the wheel. Invest with a money manager, however, and he's guaranteed free drinks, a big house, and the adrenaline rush that comes with investing *your* money.

Paying Some Guy Who Introduces You to the Piper

About half of all mutual funds also charge a sales commission, which you generally will pay any time you purchase a fund through a broker, planner, or other intermediary. These commissions are called *front-end loads* (if paid at purchase) and *back-end* or *deferred loads* (if paid at sale). For stock funds charging loads, the average load (front-end plus back-end) is 4.1 percent.[16] Investors pay about $20 billion in loads per year.[17]

There is absolutely no reason to pay these loads. They are not like brokerage commissions, which are necessary to execute a trade on an exchange. Your mutual fund is charging you to issue you its own shares. Loads don't even help to offset other costs. Expense ratios for such load funds are also high, with an average of 1.75 percent. And as a group load funds actually earn lower average returns than no-load funds, *even without taking the load into account.*[18]

So why are so many investors paying loads? The mutual fund industry increasingly relies on others—brokers, insurance companies, and financial advisors—to sell its products. This trend accelerated when Charles Schwab offered a mutual fund "supermarket." Full-service brokerage firms then began letting their sales forces offer competing funds in addition to their in-house funds. While initially hesitant to promote a competitor's products, the brokers later developed revenue-sharing agreements whereby they would get paid for every new sale they made. Most mutual fund families feel they have to pay, lest they lose access to new assets and market share.

Editor's Note

Many of the most exorbitant of these aforementioned costs—especially sales loads' revenue-sharing agreements and 12(b)1 fees—are finally coming down a bit, based on public and regulatory pressure emanating from the mutual fund scandals of 2003, which are discussed more in the following chapter. But the changes to-date have been relatively minor, and do not significantly reduce the burden of these multiple "ankle weights."

Undisclosed Costs

While investors may not pay particular attention to these costs described above, they are at least disclosed at the outset of the relationship. There are also very important costs that go undisclosed including:

- Trading costs—the approximately 0.5 to 1 percent of assets that an actively managed fund pays out in brokerage costs and bid/ask spreads each year.[19]
- The opportunity cost of holding idle cash, about 0.5 percent of assets each year during the 1990s bull market, though perhaps less now.
- Excess capital gains taxes incurred as the portfolio is turned over each year. While difficult to estimate, they probably cost active fund investors 1 percent to 2 percent of assets per year for taxable accounts.

Many investors might not ever think of these last three as "costs." They're hard to measure. They don't show up on any statement. After all, the fund pays the trading costs. Nobody "pays" an opportunity cost, and it's hard to measure exactly how much a fund costs you in capital gains taxes. Yet all these costs stand between you and the market-beating performance you crave.

PASSIVE INVESTING FOR *(LESS)* FUN AND *(MORE)* PROFIT

Two men are camping, asleep in their tents, when they here a loud crashing sound. One of them peeks outside the tent and says, "Oh, God, it's a bear!" The other begins lacing up the running shoes he's brought along. The first asks him, "What are you doing? You can't outrun the bear. They can run 20 miles an hour and climb trees!" The second man responds, "I don't have to outrun the bear; I just have to outrun you."

Just as you cannot win and should not enter a footrace with a bear, you cannot win and should not enter a performance race with the stock market. Rather, as expounded on in Part One of the book, you should *buy the market as a whole* and stop trying to outrun it through active fund management or stock picking. Just take satisfaction in outrunning all of your peers, who still have the ankle weights of active management slowing them down.

The Right Way to Do Things

What is the right way to achieve your financial goals? Believe it or not, the best example is the defined-contribution plan operated by the U.S. government, known as the Thrift Savings Plan (TSP). Set up in 1986 for civilian employees, it now includes military employees as well. As of late 2001, the plan held over $100 billion in assets, with over half of it invested in the stock market.

Over the 10-year period of 1991 to 2000, the TSP's return on stock investments was a 17.43 percent compound annual rate of return, *including all expenses.*[20] That compares to a 17.46 percent return for the S&P 500 Index and exceeds the returns of the average actively managed stock fund by over *4 percent per year.* The return on bond investments was 7.87 percent versus 7.96 percent for the Lehman Brothers U.S. Aggregate bond index. That too far surpassed the average actively managed bond fund for that period.

So how were the government managers of the Thrift Savings Plan able to achieve such stupendous returns? Tech heavy? Early in biotech? Much simpler: the TSP decided to (1) index and (2) bargain for the lowest possible cost. The government puts the TSP contract out for competitive bid every three years. The TSP's administrative costs plus the index fund management *fees currently total only 0.03 percent to 0.09 percent,* depending on the fund.

Judging from the average expense ratios of 401(k) assets in mutual funds, Corporate America could learn a lot from the TSP. In particular,

Corporate America (1) does not generally index, and (2) does not bargain for the lowest possible cost. When the SEC studied mutual fund fees, it found that 401(k) participants pay significant expense ratios. A sampling of retirement-oriented funds found that their fees averaged 0.96 percent per year. While that number is lower than the fees of the average actively managed stock fund, the SEC found that this was primarily due to their size, as the average retirement-oriented fund in their sample had $20 billion in assets. These fees are actually in line with other large actively managed mutual funds.[21]

The sad fact for most workers is that the government probably does a far better job with its employees' savings than your employer does with yours. Keep in mind, too, that most public and private pension funds in the country now have a significant portion of their assets in index funds as highlighted in Chapters 14 and 26. The failure of many employers to allow employees the same option is therefore inexcusable.

BREAKING UP IS HARD TO DO—MOVING FROM ACTIVE TO PASSIVE INVESTING

> *Freedom's just another word for nothin' left to lose.*
>
> —Kris Kristofferson, "Me and Bobby McGee"

Your conversion from the active to the passive investment bandwagon is easy to manage if you have new money to invest. If you have small amounts, then you should use an index mutual fund. If you have larger amounts and your investment returns are taxable, then you should consider an exchange-traded index fund. But now comes the hard part: what to do with all the money you've *already* invested actively? Here, moving to passive investment may end up costing you a little bit.

That cost comes primarily in the form of taxes. If you're fortunate, then the actively managed equity mutual funds and individual stocks that you hold have appreciated in value since you bought them. Selling them and reinvesting passively means realizing that gain and having to pay taxes earlier than you might otherwise have paid them. You're going to want to do a little thinking before you take that step, or use some of the tax minimizing strategies that were discussed in Chapters 24, 27, and 28. We suspect that in most cases you'll find the end result well worth the cost.

If your stocks or actively managed funds are within a tax-deferred investment account—a 401(k), 403(b), or IRA—or if they have not appreciated in price, then you have no tax worries and should sell them immediately and begin investing passively.

If you have unrealized taxable capital gains in your funds or stocks, then matters get a little more complicated. There are two fairly easy steps you can take. First, you should immediately begin reinvesting any dividends or distributions from your existing investments in an index fund. Simply tell your actively managed fund or dividend reinvestment program (DRIP) that you'd like to begin receiving cash distributions. Then reinvest them. Second, if you have capital losses in other stocks, then you can sell those stocks along with stocks with corresponding gains, thereby negating any tax effects.

If you have unrealized gains that are not offset by losses, however, then you face a choice. You probably should not sell any stock that you have held for less than a year, if it has significant gains. After one year, the lower, long-term capital gains rate applies, and you will save on your taxes by waiting for it to kick in. As for long-term gains, your course of action should depend on the amount of unrealized gain, the volatility and risk of your portfolio, and the current level of your management fees and costs. Basically, the less you have in unrealized gains, the more reason to make a change. The less diversified and more volatile your stocks are, then the more reason there is to sell quickly. The higher your current cost structure, the more reason to sell and switch as well.

Beyond taxes, there may be some brokerage commissions or a back-end load to pay. Commissions shouldn't be enough to deter you from your escape. Back-end loads, however, can be significant. If you're close to the date when the load disappears, you may want to wait for it to pass before you sell. But once that back-end load disappears, we encourage you, move on to the index frontier.

CONCLUSION: AN INVESTMENT RECOVERY PLAN

> *There are just two rules for success:*
> *1. Never tell all you know.*
>
> —Roger H. Lincoln

Bill James, baseball's best-known statistician and historian, released a new edition of his celebrated *Historical Baseball Abstract* in 2001. Like its predecessor, the new *Abstract* included a ranking of the hundred greatest players in baseball history. Many readers were surprised to see that the player judged as the best active major leaguer and the thirty-fifth greatest player of all time—ahead of people like Cal Ripken, Sandy Koufax, and Roger Clemens—was . . . Craig Biggio.

Craig Biggio doesn't hit home runs, and never has. You won't see him interviewed on *Sports Center* or featured on many posters. What Biggio does well is all the little things. He steals bases and almost never gets caught. During the 2001 season, he became only the fifth player in the history of baseball not to ground into a double play. He managed to get hit by thirty-four pitches, the second-highest total in the twentieth century. In baseball, things like that add up.

As you face financial markets, you'd do well to remember Craig Biggio. Markets are the equivalent of a pitcher's ballpark: their fences are deep, the ball is dead, and you won't be able to hit many home runs. What you need to do is what Craig Biggio does: get everything else right. Get your costs down, your diversification up, and your assets allocated intelligently. The following chapter by the book's editor proposes a specific four step plan to make it happen, and we recommend considering some of his ideas and combining them with ours. Most importantly, don't worry about making headlines; *just win.*

If you want to take that course, here are 10 ways we'd start:

1. Ignore all rankings! *Money* magazine's top-ranked funds for last year are funds you should avoid this year. *Stop thinking all it takes to beat the market is a magazine subscription.*
2. *Watch financial news for entertainment value only.* The financial media and Wall Street depend on each other to promote frequent trading and to make the market look complicated and interesting.
3. *Never underestimate the power of an index fund.* Viewed by many investors as boring, index funds are a miracle of innovation and efficiency. You can invest $5,000 in hundreds or even thousands of different stocks that will guarantee you a market return, and the cost is around $10 per year.
4. *Better yet, use exchange-traded index funds.* If you have more than $5,000 to invest, you can take that cost down from $10 to $5 per year, and forget about having unwanted capital gains distributed to you.
5. *If you are paying a percentage of your assets to try to beat the market, stop.* Say good-bye to active fund managers, full-service brokers, and asset-based financial planners.
6. *Take control of your tax situation.* Every year, ask yourself this question, "Have I sheltered every possible dollar of my investments from taxation?"
7. *Sit down and draft an asset allocation plan.* If you need help, then get it (for free online or in a book, or pay by the hour with a financial planner).
8. *Don't try to time the markets.* Wall Street pros do a lousy job predicting when the market will do either. You'll do no better than they do.
9. *If your employer does not include index funds among your 401(k) options, then consider it a pay cut.* Work to reverse that pay cut by buying an additional copy of this book and highlighting key parts of this and

other chapters for the human resources department. (Or save a bit more money—and buy a copy of *our* book, now available in paperback!)

10. *Spend more time with friends and family.* Do you really need to check your stock prices that tenth time today? Do you really care what Wal-Mart's next quarter might look like? Focusing on these things isn't making you any wealthier or any more interesting. Get out a little!

NOTES

1. Investment Company Institute Fact Book (2001). We exclude money market mutual funds because they are effectively deposit accounts. During the 1990s, stock funds attracted 83 percent of the net new cash flow to all mutual funds. As of year-end 2001, equity funds held $3.4 trillion, and hybrid funds holding a combination of equity and bonds held another $350 billion. Bond funds held $825 billion. Money market funds held $1.845 trillion.
2. See note 1.
3. Morningstar Principia Pro (data as of December 31, 2001). Data are for surviving actively managed domestic stock funds, excluding index, exchange-traded, and institutional funds, multiple classes of the same fund, and funds holding more than 20 percent of their assets in bonds.
4. While the mid-cap value funds outperformed the Wilshire 5000, they trailed their own benchmark (the S&P Midcap 400) by 4.3 percentage points over 5 years and 1.9 percentage points over 10 years.
5. Lake Wobegon is a cherished U.S. public radio program developed and hosted by Garrison Keillor about a fictional Minnesota town where "all the women are pretty and all the children are above average."
6. Mark M. Carhart, "On Persistence in Mutual Fund Performance," *Journal of Finance,* vol. 52 (March 1997): 57.
7. Russ Wermers, "Mutual Fund Performance: An Empirical Decomposition into Stock-Picking Talent, Style Transaction Costs, and Expenses," *Journal of Finance,* vol. 55 (August 2000): 16.
8. The funds were Fidelity Magellan, American Funds' Washington Mutual, American Funds Growth Fund of America, Fidelity Equity-Income, Fidelity Puritan, Vanguard Windsor, Lord Abbott Affiliated A, American Funds American Mutual, Templeton World, and Pioneer Value A. Some have changed names since 1991; we give the current name.
9. Why? Funds with growing asset bases must choose between continuing to hold the same number of stocks in increasing amounts or buying a larger number of stocks. Each option has drawbacks for funds attempting to beat the market. To the extent the fund holds a significant percentage of a company's stock, it faces liquidity problems in buying or selling the stock. Selling a large block of stock will push the price down. This will lower returns. On the other hand, to the extent that a fund chooses to hold many stocks in smaller amounts, it is less likely to earn superior returns through a few inspired (or lucky) choices.

10. The top 10 percent of funds get five stars, the next 22.5 percent get four stars, the middle 35 percent get three stars, the next 22.5 percent get two stars, and the bottom 10 percent get one star.

11. Mark Hulbert, "No Stars for Morningstar," *Forbes* (December 29, 1997): 104. Morningstar has recently evolved their methodology to attenuate this problem.

12. Morningstar Principia Pro as of December 31, 2001. Search was for all mutual fund share classes charging a sales load, excluding index funds, exchange-traded funds, and institutional funds—7,389 funds in all. The 4.1 percent came from adding the average front-end and back-end load.

13. Search includes actively managed (nonindex, non-ETF) funds, excluding institutional funds and multiple classes of the same fund. Stock funds are classified domestic stock by Morningstar, and hold less than 20 percent of their assets in bonds. Data are as of December 31, 2001.

14. *SEC Report of the Division of Investment Management on Mutual Fund Fees and Expenses,* January 2001. Fee study released January 2001. The SEC found that the average for all long-term (nonmoney market) funds was 1.36 percent, though this average includes bond funds, which tend to have lower fees. The SEC also measured the average fee weighted by the size of each fund. For this average, they determined that the industry had fees of approximately 0.9 percent. Throughout the chapter, we report data on an unweighted basis, as that is how Morningstar presents it. As the SEC numbers show, the average investor may pay a little less than these averages because our numbers count large and small funds equally. Since large funds tend to have marginally lower expense ratios, asset-weighted numbers tend to be lower. On the other hand, some of the largest funds with below average expense ratios are closed to all or new investment, and thus probably should not be included. So the average fees a new investor would pay probably lie somewhere in the middle.

15. Testimony of Matthew Fink, president of the Investment Company Institute, before the Subcommittee on Finance and Hazardous Materials, House Committee on Commerce, September 29, 1998.

16. Morningstar Principia Pro. Data are for mutual funds charging a front-end or back-end load, excluding index funds, ETFs, and institutional funds.

17. Each year there are nearly $1 trillion each in stock mutual fund sales and in redemptions. With about half of these in load funds and the average 4.1 percent total load, that leads to investors paying about $20 billion in sales loads per year.

18. Mark Hulbert, "Do Funds Charge Investors for Negative Value Added?" *New York Times* (July 8, 2001).

19. Looking solely at diversified funds, Carhart estimates trading costs at 0.95 percent per year. Wermers reports 1.04 percent per year in 1990, dropping to 0.48 percent by 1994. Sector funds have higher turnover than diversified funds, and thus should have higher trading costs.

20. Data available on the Thrift Savings Plan web site at www.tsp.gov/rates history.

21. Equally weighted fees based upon the Securities and Exchange Commission Report on Mutual Fund Fees, January 10, 2001 (cited in note 14).

CHAPTER 30

Indexing at the Core

The Four Key Axioms for Long-Term Investment Success

Steven A. Schoenfeld

_____ Editor's Note _____

Part Five covers a lot of terrain in order to provide a broad range of perspectives on using sophisticated index-based investment strategies. This chapter adds a framework to "pull it all together"—and provides personal views that can be relevant for both institutional and individual investors, though the focus is primarily on the latter group and the professionals who advise them. Thus, I've chosen a universal subtitle, "The Four Key Axioms for Long-Term Investment Success."[1] In these pages, I share opinions that I have shaped during more than two decades in the financial industry, working as a derivatives researcher and trader, index product developer, index fund manager and investment strategist. These ideas build on the key points articulated in Chapter 29 about the true costs of mutual funds and traditional active management. And I believe that the chapter contains useful and practical advice for individuals who want to apply the findings of timeless finance research and the best practices of the world's most sophisticated investors. You be the judge.

The subtitle of this book promises to show readers how to *maximize portfolio performance and minimize risk through global index strategies*. Part Five of the book has shown how highly successful investors use a variety of index-based approaches to do just that. This chapter unifies many of the book's investment concepts and themes into a framework that investors can use to maximize *their* portfolio performance. I also tackle some of the key challenges of establishing and maintaining an effective long-term investment strategy. While the advice is geared toward individuals and financial advisors who want to apply the practices of the institutional investors featured in this book, some of the principles are also relevant for pension funds, endowments, and foundations.

The *four key axioms of investment success* are designed to be simple and straightforward to put in place and maintain. The essential factor for implementation of the axioms is that *index-based approaches should be at the core of a successful investment strategy.* In fact, I believe that placing indexing at the core and adhering to these four simple axioms will assure a more efficient and risk-controlled portfolio than the typical self-directed (or advised) investor following most other approaches.

THE FOUR KEY AXIOMS FOR INVESTMENT SUCCESS

An axiom has an element of self-evident truth, and as it becomes widely understood, it is accepted on its intrinsic merit. Although these four axioms may not at first seem self-evident, after you have read all or most of the book—and this chapter—their truth will hopefully become obvious.

The four axioms focus on the following concepts and are treated in this sequence:

1. Diversified asset allocation.
2. Risk budgeting of managers/strategies.
3. Disciplined rebalancing.
4. Rigorous cost control.

These axioms are intentionally sequenced in steps that even a relatively inexperienced individual investor can follow and maintain over time.

Axiom 1: Establish a Broadly Diversified Asset Allocation Strategy

The first step toward long-term investment success is to develop and maintain a truly diversified asset allocation strategy. This concept has been stressed throughout the book and has been referred to as *strategic asset allocation* as well as *policy allocation* or *policy benchmark.* The concepts are essentially the same—they all refer to the targeted allocation between different asset classes (e.g., equities and bonds) and subasset classes (e.g., large-cap, small-cap, and international equities). I use terms like strategic asset allocation and policy benchmark interchangeably.

I tackle the subject in two steps—a reinforcement of the importance of asset allocation, followed by an exhortation to achieve sufficiently deep and broad diversification.

The Critical Importance of Asset Allocation Numerous times in this book, contributors have referred to the conclusions of the landmark 1986 study by Brinson, Beebower, and Hood to stress the dominance of asset allocation as the primary factor affecting investors' results.[2] I agree with the conclusions of this study and the subsequent follow-up research, but we need to dig deeper to truly understand the magnitude of importance of asset allocation.[3] The reason is that these studies are often misinterpreted into answering the wrong question.

What Brinson and his colleagues were testing was how much a portfolio's *variability* over time was due to asset allocation, and they concluded that it was over 90 percent. An important paper by Roger Ibbotson and Paul Kaplan combined the data in the Brinson studies with other data sets to retest their original question. The authors also added a much more important question: "What percentage of the *return level* [of a pension fund or investor's total portfolio] is explained by policy return [strategic asset allocation]?"[4] This question lies at the heart of the investor's dilemma of where to focus limited time and resources: picking asset classes and allocations or picking managers to deliver outperformance. Their results were stunning, and conclusively confirm the focus of this first axiom—asset allocation matters most.

Ibbotson and Kaplan used the following five asset classes: U.S. Large Cap, U.S. Small Cap, non-U.S. Stocks, U.S. Bonds, and Cash, and assessed both U.S. pension funds and balanced mutual funds. They confirmed the original question of the Brinson et al. studies, that about 90 percent of the variability of the monthly returns can be explained by the variability of the funds' policy benchmarks.

Long-term returns are what matter most to investors saving for retirement or a child's education. Thus, Ibbotson and Kaplan—using a broadened data set—concluded, "On average, policy [asset allocation] accounted for a little more than all of total return."[5] That statement is not a typo—I'll repeat: "... *a little more than all of total return.*" As the authors noted, that means "on average, the pension funds and balanced mutual funds are not adding value above their policy benchmarks because of a combination of timing, security selection, management fees and expenses."[6] Using the four data sets, the average percentage of total return level explained by policy return (asset allocation) was 104 percent![7] This conclusion is consistent with William

Sharpe's "Arithmetic of Active Management" cited previously in the book. The aggregation of all investors *is* the market, and over time and after all costs, it is mathematically impossible for the average active manager to outperform the market—or a properly constructed market benchmark.

The only way to do better than the market is to pick outperforming managers—and previous chapters have shown how difficult this is, even for institutional investors with substantial resources at their disposal. If institutions have accepted that the odds are steep and have chosen to index over 20 percent of their assets—with some indexing more than half of domestic equities—what chance do individuals have? (This is discussed under Axiom 2.)

This detailed discussion on the attribution of the source of returns drives home the point that getting asset allocation right is the primary way to achieve successful long-term performance. Keep this in mind as we move through the other three axioms. But first, let's look at how to create an optimally diversified asset allocation (or policy benchmark). The preceding points should have convinced you that investors need to spend less time picking funds or managers and more time choosing the strategic investment policy with asset class mixes that provide maximum diversification. We now focus on the specific asset classes, subasset classes, and prospective portfolio weights.

Diversification—Make It Broad and Deep   Having balance in one's portfolio is essential. This means having several asset classes that are weakly correlated with each other—one will zig while the other zags. The more noncorrelated asset classes and subasset classes that are included, the more diversified an overall investment strategy will be.

The five asset classes used by Ibbotson and Kaplan are a good start. But two decades of investment experience and the research of others make me certain that investors can do better by going deeper and broader. By adding a few subasset classes and several alternative assets classes, investors gain a more efficient portfolio. They diversify away more risk (as measured by annualized standard deviation) and increase the expected return, thereby producing higher Sharpe ratios.[8]

Burton Malkiel, author of *A Random Walk down Wall Street* and a major proponent of indexing, recently explored the asset classes that are likely to provide the maximum diversification benefit, with a focus on nontraditional asset classes. His research of the period from 1991 to 2001 (which includes both soaring bull markets and brutal bear markets) showed that alternatives like REITs, bonds, and Treasury Inflation-Protected Securities (TIPS) historically have relatively low correlations and high returns when equities are weak.[9]

In addition to those diversifying asset classes, maintaining significant exposure to international equities, including emerging markets, is another important diversifier. Although some—including Malkiel—have questioned the value of significant international exposure, history has proven that including non-U.S. stocks has long-term benefits. Despite the volatility of emerging markets, 2003 was the third year in a row that they have outperformed both U.S. and developed-international equities in a challenging global market environment.

It is essential to remain committed to the asset allocation, even when prevailing sentiment makes it difficult. This would mean sticking with emerging markets when the subasset class is being pummeled, as it was in the 1997-to-1998 period.

Table 30.1 illustrates the concept of a broad and deep strategic asset allocation with three sample allocations—a *conservative*, a *moderate*, and an *aggressive portfolio*. These portfolios are geared to specific investor objectives, which tend to be related to an investor's age, income, number of dependents, and tax situation, among other factors. They are designed to convey the framework for establishing a policy benchmark and should not be construed as specific investment advice. More sample portfolios from professional investment advisors are provided in various sections of IndexUniverse.com and in the book's E-ppendix, at www.ActiveIndexInvesting.com. Other useful portfolio suggestions for different types of investors are provided in books such as Malkiel's aforementioned *A Random Walk Down Wall Street* and David Blitzer's *Outpacing the Pros*.[10]

In the general framework portrayed in the table, the three sample allocations are:

1. *Conservative portfolio.* For investors relatively close to retirement or use of funds.
2. *Moderate portfolio.* For "average" investors, with a longer-term time horizon of at least 10 years. A middle-of-the-generation baby boomer would best fit this definition.
3. *Aggressive portfolio.* For relatively young investors, with a long-term time horizon, or for investors who, in return for potentially higher returns, can handle the added risk.

Unlike the allocations I mentioned earlier in the chapter, I use Short-Term Fixed Income in lieu of cash, partly because of the extremely low-yield environment for cash-like investments at the time of writing.

Further information on the asset classes and viable benchmark indexes for each asset class and subasset class is available in this chapter's E-ppendix entry on www.ActiveIndexInvesting.com, and readers are invited to submit feedback on this framework on the site's discussion board.

TABLE 30.1 Potential Asset Allocations for U.S.-Based Investors

| Asset Class | | Portfolio | | | Potential ETFs (by Ticker) or |
Asset	Sub-Asset	Conservative	Moderate	Aggressive	Index Funds for Allocation[a]
U.S. equities	Large-Cap	15	30	35	SPY, IVV, VV, IWB, SSgA Funds S&P 500 (SVSPX), Vanguard 500 Fund (VFINX)[b]
	Mid/small[c]	10	15	20	**Mid:** IWR, IJH, VO, MDY, Vanguard Mid Cap Index (VIMSX) **Small:** IWM, IJR, VB, Vanguard Small-Cap Index (VAESX)
International equities	Developed	5	8	15	EFA, Vanguard Developed Market Index Fund (VDMIX), SSGA MSCI EAFE Index Fund (SSMSX)
	Emerging		2	5	EEM, Vanguard EM Index (VEIEX)
Fixed income	Short-term	15	5		SHY, Vanguard ST Bond Index (VBISX)
	Long-Term[d]	15	10	5	TLT, Vanguard LT Bond Index (VBLTX)
	Corporate or high yield	10	5	5	LQD, Vanguard IT Corp Fund (VFICX)
	TIPS	15	10		TIP, Vanguard Inflation Protected Securities (VIPSX)
Alternatives	REITs	10	10	5	Vanguard REIT Index Fund (VGSIX) RWR, ICF, IYR

Commodities	5	5	GLD, IAU,[e] PIMCO Commodity Real Return (PCRAX), Oppenheimer Real Asset (QRAAX)
Hedge funds	5		RYDEX SPhinX Fund (Reuters, SPHG)

[a]These are not specific investment recommendations, but are given as notional examples of how an investor can "fill in the boxes" of their strategic asset allocation. These examples are not comprehensive, as in many of the categories there are numerous other index funds and ETFs that could substitute for the ones listed. For example, ETFs based on the NYSE or Morningstar Indexes could be used in some of the U.S. Equity categories.

[b]There are scores of S&P 500 Index Funds from numerous firms. Poential investors should be aware that all index funds are not alike, as should be clear from reading previous chapters of this book.

[c]Investors could choose to combine the large-cap and mid/small-cap categories and simply hold a total stock market index fund such as the TIAA-CREF Equity Index (TCEIX), the Vanguard Total Stock Market Index Fund (VTSMX), or one of many total market ETFs tracking popular total market indexes such as ISI, IYY, VTI, or IWW.

[d]As with equities, investors could choose to combine some or all of the fixed-income categories and instead use a total bond market index strategy, tracking an index such as the Lehman Brothers' Aggregate. Index funds such as the SSGA Bond Market Fund (SSBMX) and ETFs such as AGG could then be held in lieu of the mix of short-term, long-term, and corporate bonds in the table.

[e]GLD and IAU are listed Gold-based investment products still in registration with the SEC as of the time of this writing. For updates on these and other investable commodity products, see the Gold/Commodities section of IndexUniverse.com.

Source: Global Index Strategies LLC.

Any policy allocation should not be considered permanently fixed. As investors near retirement, the policy benchmark should shift toward an increasingly conservative mix. Similarly, as new sub-asset classes (or investable products on the sub-asset class) develop, they need to be considered for inclusion in the overall strategy. For example, as high yield bond index funds and international bond index funds continue to develop, they would be a prime candidate for inclusion in the preceding allocation matrices.

Axiom 2: Use Risk Budgeting to Build an Appropriate Manager/Fund Structure

No matter which asset/policy mix investors choose, they must then "fill in the boxes" with the appropriate fund or investment vehicle, as illustrated in the far-right column in Table 30.1.[11] As discussed in Chapter 3, risk budgeting is a process by which investors (and/or their advisor/consultant) establish customized goals and quantify the amount of active manager risk they find acceptable. Once an investor has a strategic policy, the default allocation is used in the policy benchmark. Thus, in the preceding matrix, the Russell 1000 could be used for the large-cap allocation and the Russell 2000 for the small-cap allocation. Similarly, MSCI EAFE could be used for developed international and MSCI EMF for emerging markets. Many sophisticated investors and advisors will maintain a "composite policy benchmark" that combines these various asset class benchmarks in the desired strategic weight and adjusts for their relative performance.

The investor must now choose managers/funds for each of these asset and sub-asset classes. The tendency has historically been to spend significant effort to choose active managers for each of the boxes, on the assumption (hope?) that they will add incremental alpha to the portfolio. As noted, it is difficult to choose outperforming active managers, especially ex-ante (before the fact). And we know from the "arithmetic of active management" that the aggregate of active managers will underperform after all costs. Thus, not only is the straightforward default option—using index products such as mutual funds or ETFs based on the same benchmarks within the policy allocation—easier and cheaper to implement, it will yield better long-term performance. So, for the "Moderate" example in Table 30.1, the investor could implement the 55 percent equity allocation by investing 30 percent of the portfolio in a Russell 1000 index product, 15 percent in a Russell 2000 fund, 8 percent in an MSCI EAFE index product, and 2 percent in an emerging market index fund. As the far-right column of Table 30.1 illustrates, there are ETFs or index funds for each of the remaining subasset classes in the Moderate portfolio.

This default allocation can actually be the core of a portfolio, in any of the major asset classes. Investors should only replace the indexed core if they have a very high confidence that the alternative actively managed fund for the relevant asset class will deliver the targeted alpha. These noncore allocations become the satellite strategies that complement the performance of the core.[12] And we've seen through the compelling data and examples cited in Chapters 3, 4, 28, and 29 how difficult this can be. There is no need to totally give up trying—we human beings tend to be optimistic about our own abilities—but remember, the better investment of your time is to focus on the allocation decisions.

Indexing at the core is a powerful concept that dramatically simplifies the investment process. This is how many large institutions and a growing number of advisors structure their portfolios. It empowers investors because the core of index-based strategies essentially "buys" some risk budget and enables investors to include active managers with high potential for alpha. But when in doubt on how to fill in the allocation box, keep it simple—index—and you will outperform in the long run.

Axiom 3: Be Disciplined about Rebalancing to Strategic Policy Allocation

Now you have both a policy benchmark and an implemented investment strategy. But markets are dynamic, and the most carefully constructed portfolio will deviate from the policy weights relatively quickly. This need not be a problem. In fact, if investors are disciplined about rebalancing to the originally established strategic policy weights, it actually presents an opportunity. The opportunity is derived from markets' tendencies to mean-revert, as discussed in Chapter 18. Thus, investors should plan on selling the outperforming subasset classes and adding the proceeds to the underperforming subasset classes. Although this can result in "leaving some money on the table" during sustained bull markets like that experienced in the United States in the late 1990s, the long-term benefit of rebalancing is substantial. In hindsight, who would have minded leaving a little on the table in U.S. small-cap stocks in 1999 and early 2000? Disciplined rebalancing prevents performance-chasing in the choice of funds, and dampens the volatility of an overall portfolio.

As discussed in Chapters 1 and 18, institutions can choose from a myriad of rebalancing approaches, including sophisticated trigger-based models that rebalance as a function of the percentage move away from the initial asset allocation. But these complexities are generally unnecessary for individuals and advisors—as Table 28.1 in Chapter 28 demonstrated, the primary long-term benefits of regular rebalancing can be captured through a straightforward temporal-based rebalance.

For self-directed investors, annual or semiannual rebalancing is usually sufficient. I recommend choosing a date that is easy to remember and that comes just before or after a major financial event, such as tax deadlines or bonus payment cycle (two very different types of events!). On such dates, investors are already paying attention to their finances. Also, it is more important to rebalance the major asset class weights (equities/fixed income/alternatives) than the weightings in the sub-asset classes (U.S. large/mid/small-cap).

It is very difficult to tilt against conventional wisdom and sell a winning asset class—or buy into a subasset class that has been bleeding red ink. Yet both investment theory and history have demonstrated that a contrarian approach can pay off handsomely—the time to buy is when a stock, country/market, or entire asset class is in disfavor. I am not recommending recklessness—the beauty of a rebalancing discipline is that you will catch extremes, but you will still retain the "guardrails" of the overall strategy.

A good example of the power of this discipline comes from investors' experience with emerging markets in 1997 and 1998—the nadir of the Asian financial crisis and the general emerging market meltdown that followed, exacerbated by Russia's debt default. Individuals and institutions were dumping emerging market stocks and bonds. Yet those who were bold enough to simply rebalance their strategic asset allocation for emerging markets back to neutral made substantial profits.[13]

Having index-based strategies at the core of your allocation makes this rebalancing relatively simple. Whether through mutual funds or ETFs, a quick update of a spreadsheet (or readily available allocation tools available on the Web) will tell you the rough amount you need to sell and buy.[14] While you are implementing the subasset class rebalances, you should assess the performance of the active managers within the strategy and attribute their source of returns. You can then determine whether to "top up" their allocation or fund the reallocation from that element of your investment.

If you do not have the discipline to rebalance your portfolio regularly, then consider using a professional financial advisor. Having someone help develop and implement your investment strategy can be worth the one or two percent per annum cost, especially if the advisor uses low cost index-based strategies. While that added cost comes right out of returns, having your portfolio unbalanced—as many investors learned in the early 2000s—could create a loss of 15 percent or more, which swamps the cost of advisory fees.

Information on resources to help identify good advisors who use low-cost index-based strategies is available on the advisor section of IndexUniverse .com and is also discussed later in this chapter.

Axiom 4: Rigorously Apply Explicit and Implicit Cost Control

Implementing the first three axioms should have taken out most of the risk of dramatically underperforming the markets. The next thing you want to do is ensure that you are keeping overall costs to a minimum.

Cost control is essential to long-term investment success. It is the only "free lunch" in investing—anything you save translates directly into higher returns. Yet as the previous chapter illustrated, this is the area that investors have generally paid the least attention to—focusing on returns is a lot sexier—and regular double-digit returns compensated for a lot of excessive costs in the bullish 1990s.

There are three elements of costs:

1. Fees.
2. Transaction costs (turnover/commission/rebalancing).
3. Taxes.

The lower a management fee (and overall expense ratio), the more money an investor can pocket. Any active strategy chosen to fill the boxes not only must generate sufficient alpha for the added active risk, but must do so after fees. This is a high hurdle, and it reinforces the case for *indexing at the core.*

Transaction costs have two elements: the costs of turnover and commission within the portfolio as an ongoing expense of management, and the costs of initial investment and rebalancing. As Chapter 29 highlighted, active funds face significantly higher hurdles (or as Gensler and Baer called them, "*ankle weights* to outperformance").

When investors aggregate the expense ratio and turnover costs, they get a clear sense of the impact of these ankle weights. John Bogle conducted a study that encompassed the 10-year period ending June 2001.[15] Like the previously discussed Ibbotson-Kaplan study, it covered a time period that included a wide range of market environments. Bogle looked at the net performance difference between high-cost and low-cost funds in each of the nine Morningstar style boxes.[16] He found that for all funds, the expense ratio differential was 1.2 percent, but the *performance* differential was approximately double that, at 2.2 percent. Lower cost funds had a clear performance advantage that increased further when adjusted for portfolio risk. This pushed the performance differential to 3.0 percent annually for the decade under observation. Each $1 of extra cost resulted in a loss of $2.50 in risk-adjusted return. Bogle's simple but powerful conclusion regarding these results; ". . . it is not possible to understate the significance of these differences. Costs matter."[17]

For individual investors, the added entry/exit cost for an active fund versus index fund is negligible, but the ETF structure makes systematic rebalancing easier because almost all index mutual funds (properly) have transaction fees to discourage market timing. (And since late 2003 we have also seen a variety of traditional active funds scramble to implement similar features to discourage market timers.)

For individuals, taxes are another key element that tilts the scales toward index-based strategies. Most large institutions are tax-exempt investors and don't pay higher taxes for high-turnover strategies. As described in Chapters 1 and 3, these investors commit close to 25 percent of their assets to index-based strategies. These institutional investors were estimated to save between $14 and $18 billion per year by using index strategies during the 1990s.[18] Yet individuals, who have much more to gain because a large percentage of individual investment is taxable, hold significantly less assets in index strategies. Indexing offers a big advantage in tax efficiency, and index-based separate accounts—as discussed in Chapters 24 and 27—have the potential to do even better through active tax-loss harvesting.

With regulators' newfound focus on the costs of mutual funds, we are now in an environment of rigorous transparency for all investment vehicles—so use it to your advantage. As costs are the only element of the investment equation that investors can absolutely control, it is self-evident that individuals and their advisors should follow this axiom and put indexing at the core of their portfolios to improve performance.

THE MOST IMPORTANT ELEMENT OF INVESTMENT SUCCESS—*INDEXING AT THE CORE*

Intertwined with the four axioms is the last major element of investment success. How can you remember it? Luckily it rhymes: *Indexing at the core— 50 percent or more.*

Obviously all investors shouldn't use the same percentage, but you can think of the appropriate amount to index within the following ranges:

- If you have a lot of confidence in your own or your advisor's ability to pick winning active managers or desire a lot of alternative/nontraditional asset classes such as private equity and other partnerships, you should still aim to have at least 40 percent indexed. If you index some or all of the main asset classes, it will free up time (and risk budget) for you to perform the needed research and due diligence on the active managers and/or nontraditional investments.
- If, like many of the contributors in this book, you agree that an index-based approach will provide efficient market exposure and, in effect, purchase the risk budget to enable some satellite active managers, you should index 70 percent or more of the overall portfolio. For the more esoteric asset classes such as emerging markets and commodities (which tend to be more risky in the first place), indexed exposure should be close to 100 percent. The reason for the high percentage

is that you are looking for diversification benefit from the asset class exposure itself, much more than the potential added alpha within the asset class from an active manager.

■ There is absolutely nothing wrong with going 100 percent indexed. Remember the first axiom and the research that supports it—most if not all of your long-term investment returns will come from asset class returns, and index products efficiently deliver those returns. For many investors and advisors, taking this approach is quite liberating and allows them to focus their time and energy into the areas that have the greatest effect on their investment results.

A related element of investment success is to *truly know yourself* as an investor. Money is an emotional subject, and the goals we all have for our investment activity are close to our hearts—financial security, retirement, children's education, and intergenerational transfer. Therefore, you must carefully define your objectives, know why you are investing, and understand the purpose of each major investment account.

Assess your personal strengths and weaknesses as an investor. Desiring to have fun in the market is okay; just be clear about it, and keep this activity separate from the rest of your long-term investment assets. Set aside perhaps 5 percent of your portfolio (but a maximum of 10 percent) for your "adventurous investing," whether it be stock picking, buying hot funds, or even futures trading (which is where I generally deploy my speculative investment efforts). Have fun and feel free to go for home runs; just enter into the endeavor fully cognizant that the arithmetic of active management will still apply to this activity—and remember that long-term gains will come from hitting lots of singles with your core portfolio.

Even with a "play" portfolio, index products such as ETFs, index futures, and options on ETFs may very well be the most efficient way to take size, sector, and country bets.[19] Many speculative investors use these vehicles, and both relatively conservative or very bold *active index* strategies such as those discussed in Chapter 18 can be constructed with these products.

NEXT STEPS—HOW TO ACCESS AND CHOOSE THE BEST INDEX-BASED PRODUCTS

I hope that this chapter, along with Chapters 28 and 29, has given you the philosophical framework and confidence to aim for long-term investment success by *indexing at the core*. You may now be wondering about the appropriate next steps to take.

It is not too hard to get efficient index-based exposure within a solid asset allocation plan, so there is no excuse not to take those steps. There are two basic approaches—and both are valid and reasonable paths.

Do It Yourself

The first approach is to take full control of your investments and build your own long-term investment strategy. Through a new or existing brokerage account, you can build a portfolio of ETFs and/or index funds that are aligned with your policy benchmarks.

In some ways, this "do it yourself" approach was not completely possible until 2002, with the introduction of fixed-income ETFs. While fixed-income index funds were long available, investors can now truly build an all-ETF portfolio spanning multiple asset classes. And as my predictions in the next chapter will detail, the remaining asset and sub-asset classes are likely to be filled in with appropriate ETFs by the end of 2005.

One of the most efficient ways to build an ETF portfolio is through services such as FolioFN.com, Sharebuilder.com, and BUYandHOLD.com. They provide a sharply discounted online brokerage service that enables dollar-cost average purchases as well as regularly timed investment programs (payroll deduction).[20] FolioFN goes a bit further and provides prepackaged ETF portfolios. All the major discount brokerage firms can also provide competitive commissions to build an index-based portfolio, primarily through ETFs, but also through proprietary or name-brand index mutual funds.[21]

Alternatively, you could build a similar portfolio using index mutual funds. Vanguard, Fidelity, Schwab, State Street Global Advisors (SSgA), TIAA-CREF and others all offer a range of no-load index mutual funds that enable investors to build a well-diversified, low-cost index portfolio.

For the do-it-yourself investor, resources, research and allocation tools are accessible via IndexUniverse.com or one of the many links to index data, index providers, and ETF/index fund and derivative product sites that are featured there.

Using Advisors

The second path to creating your investment strategy is to retain a financial consultant—either an independent registered investment advisor or a consultant affiliated with a brokerage/investment firm. Using an advisor is more expensive, one way or another, because it involves one or more of the following: an asset-based fee, higher commissions, or a flat-rate consultation fee. But for investors who don't have the time or discipline to establish the appropriate allocations, "fill in" the boxes with a mix of index and active funds, and engage in a disciplined rebalancing program, the added cost of an advisor is well worth it.

A broker or fee-based advisor can establish a portfolio of index mutual funds (generally from DFA, Vanguard, or Schwab) or mutual funds and ETFs, usually combined with a selection of actively managed funds and alternative asset class investments.[22] Similarly, some advisors/financial consultants specialize in exclusively index-based strategies, either using index funds or ETFs. One potential advantage that can partly offset the higher fees of using an advisor is the availability of "wrap accounts" which can often integrate diverse holdings (funds, stocks, ETFs, etc.) into a single account structure.

Finally, for high-net-worth investors, elite advisors offer index-based separate accounts, the attributes and benefits of which were discussed in Chapter 24. Essentially, this involves the creation of a "personal index fund," with the end-investor owning the actual constituent securities. These strategies are particularly powerful and appropriate for investors with large existing holdings of stock, or those with a need for customized benchmarks within asset classes.[23]

Over the next few years, more and more advisors will be able to offer universal account structures that seamlessly hold stocks, ETFs, mutual funds, separate accounts (both active and indexed), bonds, and specialized investments such as hedge funds. This capability—which likely will grow substantially in the coming years—is briefly discussed in Chapter 31.

Resources regarding advisor services oriented toward index products are available at www.IndexUniverse.com. The web site features research and columns by advisors, as well as information and links to advisor web sites and various ETF-based, mutual fund-based and separate account investment services.

CONCLUSION—ADHERE TO THE AXIOMS TO SUCCEED

This chapter has distilled the results of 35 years of investment research and more than 21 years of market experience into a straightforward plan of action that individuals and advisors can implement. It is subjective by design and personal by intention. But money and investing—even the relatively scientific practice of indexing—*are* deeply personal subjects. The stakes are high, especially after the early 2000s' brutal bear market mauled so many investor portfolios. Therefore, the only course of action is to aim for long-term success by tilting the odds in your favor. And that means following the path highlighted throughout Part Five. So to reiterate, here is the path that sophisticated investors have chosen:

Adhere to the Four Key Axioms

1. Build a diversified asset allocation.
2. Use a risk budget framework to choose managers/approaches for each asset class.
3. Practice disciplined rebalancing.
4. Rigorously control costs and taxes.

This four-step approach—with *indexing at the core*—can help you implement an investment plan that will work for the long term. Discipline is essential. Be sure to set up a reallocation strategy and timetable, ideally at a time you will remember. That might be at year-end to take advantage of the tax-loss harvesting opportunities, or in the spring right after you have paid your taxes.

No matter how risky your *satellites* may be (either high-risk managers in established asset classes or simply riskier asset classes such as hedge funds or commodities), the indexed core will provide the essential ballast of index returns and lower costs for the portfolio. The core index allocation will help stabilize the portfolio and will "buy" the risk budget for the more risky satellites. This approach addresses the missteps that so many investors made in the late 1990s/early 2000s by having too much exposure to technology stocks and other hot sub-asset classes.

Aim to succeed in the only way that counts, by meeting your personal financial goals with indexing at the core of your strategy. This is the beginning of your journey to a more efficient, lower cost, *lower stress,* and ultimately, higher performance investment portfolio.

NOTES

1. The etymology of the noun *axiom* is from the Latin, *axioma,* and the Greek *axióma,* literally meaning worth or something worthy. The definitions of axiom in *Merriam-Webster's Collegiate Dictionary* are (1) "a maxim widely accepted on its intrinsic merit," (2) "a statement accepted as true as the basis for argument or inference," and (3) "an established rule or principle or a self-evident truth."
2. Gary P. Brinson, L. Randolph Hood, and Gilbert L. Beebower, "Determinants of Portfolio Performance," *Financial Analysts Journal,* vol. 42, no. 4 (July/August 1986): 39–48.
3. Five years later, a follow-up study tested the same hypothesis. Gary P. Brinson, Brian D. Singer, and Gilbert L. Beebower, "Determinants of Portfolio Performance II: An Update," *Financial Analysts Journal,* vol. 47, no. 3 (May/June, 1991): 40–48.
4. Roger G. Ibbotson and Paul D. Kaplan, "Does Asset Allocation Policy Explain 40, 90, or 100 Percent of Performance?" *Financial Analysts Journal,* vol. 56, no.

1 (January/February 2000): 26–32. Ibbotson and Kaplan also looked at a third question—How much of the variation between (among) funds is explained by asset allocation policy? These results were interesting, and the reader is encouraged to read the complete *FAJ* article. Another study, cited in Chapter 18, also covers this topic admirably—Dale Stevens, Ronald J. Surz, and Mark E. Wilmer, "The Importance of Investment Policy," *Journal of Investing,* vol. 8, no. 4 (Winter 1999): 80–85.

5. See note 4, p. 32.
6. See note 4, p. 32.
7. See note 4.
8. See Chapters 2 and 3 for more on the efficient frontier and Sharpe ratio.
9. Burton G. Malkiel, "How Much Diversification Is Enough?" in *Equity Portfolio Construction* (Charlottesville, VA: Association of Investment Management and Research, 2002), pp. 18–28. Available from www.aimrpubs.org.
10. Burton G. Malkiel, *A Random Walk down Wall Street,* 8th ed. (New York: W.W. Norton, 2003), p. 364; and David M. Blitzer, *Outpacing the Pros* (New York: McGraw-Hill, 2001), pp. 187–198.
11. As stated in the footnotes in Table 30.1, the funds and ETFs in the far right column are examples to illustrate the point of "filling in the asset class boxes," and are not a comprehensive list of all the potential vehicles to achieve the returns of that allocation. Furthermore, the funds and ETFs listed are the author's own personal opinion of which funds and their benchmarks are the "best fit" for a particular objective and are not specific investment recommendations. Finally, as readers will have learned throughout the book, indexing is a very dynamic field, and some of these funds/ETFs may not be available in the future and other suitable funds/ETFs might have been introduced since the book's publication. Consult a financial advisor or visit www.IndexUniverse.com for updates on new index product developments.
12. A number of "Core-Satellite" hypothetical tools are available from web sites, including www.IndexUniverse.com. One of the best is available from www.ishares.com.
13. For an example of the case for maintaining the strategic allocation to emerging markets during the Asian/emerging market financial crisis, see Steven A. Schoenfeld, Robert Ginis, Ross Hikida, and Binu George, "The Continuing Value of Emerging Market Equities," BGI White Paper (December 1998), available from the authors via the book's E-ppendix, www.ActiveIndexInvesting.com. The paper stresses the need for a longer-term perspective on both the asset class and on rebalancing toward policy benchmarks.
14. ETF allocation tools are available from IndexUniverse.com, www.ishares.com, and www.etfconnect.com.
15. John C. Bogle, "An Index Fundamentalist Goes Back to the Drawing Board," *Journal of Portfolio Management,* vol. 28, no. 3 (Spring 2002).
16. The Morningstar style boxes involve a rigorous methodology that assigns mutual funds (and now separate accounts) to one of nine categories, such as Large-Cap Value or Mid-Cap Growth. More information is available at www.morningstar.com. Morningstar now produces comprehensive indexes that are aligned with these style boxes.

17. See note 15.
18. "25 Years of Indexing—An Analysis of the Cost and Benefits," London, PricewaterhouseCoopers (July 1998). (Report prepared for Barclays Global Investors.)
19. For insight into shorter term trading with index products, see Steven A. Schoenfeld, "The Active Index Strategist" *Journal of Indexes* (first quarter, 2004), pp. 22–27, and some of the index and market strategies columns on IndexUniverse.com.
20. Baer and Gensler's *The Great Mutual Fund Trap* calls these services "discount portfolio companies," and discusses them at length (pp. 205–208), specifically BUYandHOLD (www.buyandhold.com), Sharebuilder.com (www.sharebuilder .com), FolioFN (www.foliofn.com), and E-Trade Baskets. The latter has since been closed, but FolioFN in particular continues to develop and expand its offering of baskets (or folios) of ETFs. The concept of an index-based separate account, discussed in Chapters 24 and 27, is closely related to the original "folio" concept, but has evolved beyond narrow baskets of individual securities.
21. As ETF assets have grown, especially since the start of 2003, more and more discount and online brokerage platforms are offering specialized information and services for ETF trading, research, and portfolio construction. For example, see Ameritrade's *ETF Center* at www.ameritrade.com.
22. Some index funds are only available through advisors, notably Dimensional Fund Advisors (DFA) funds.
23. The pioneers of these strategies were Parametric Portfolio Associates and First Quadrant, but numerous other players have developed the capability, including Dimensional Fund Advisors, State Street Global Advisors, Northern Trust Global Investments, Advisor Partners, Active Index Advisors, and the Aperio Group.

CHAPTER 31

The Future of Indexing

The Revolution Has Just Begun!

Steven A. Schoenfeld

_____**Editor's Note**_____

One of the primary aims of this book has been to convey the dynamism and creativity of the index industry. I hope that readers have gained an appreciation of the many layers of "activeness" of index-based investing, as well as the multifaceted impact that indexing has had on financial markets. Considering how far indexing has come in just over three decades, the only way to conclude a book of this scope and depth is to project the future of the products and usage of index-based investing. That is my goal in this chapter. I have segmented this short discussion (on a very large topic) into five broad areas: index funds (both institutional and retail), enhanced indexing, index derivatives, exchange-traded funds (ETFs) and similar exchange traded products (ETPs), and alternative indexes and index products. In reality, as seen throughout the book, these areas are highly interrelated, and therefore there are many cross-references to the different products—and to many points made earlier in the book.

This chapter places heavy emphasis on ETF/ETP development, as these investment vehicles will play a leading role in the next phase of indexing's expansion. This is primarily because they are uniquely able to accommodate all types of investors (with all ranges of time horizons) without disadvantaging other investors in the products.[1] ETFs will dramatically extend the benefits of indexing to a much broader universe of users.

As Nobel Prize winning Physicist Niels Bohr famously said, "prediction is very difficult, especially about the future."[2] Yet despite the risks, I can't resist the challenge, and I'll live with the consequences. I conclude the chapter

*with some predictions about asset growth and market share for index funds
and ETFs. These predictions might seem bold now, but I believe strongly in
the continued growth potential of index products and thus hope they prove
accurate. Notwithstanding the revolutionary achievements that indexing
has already brought to investment activity, in many ways, the revolution has
really just begun!*

This chapter provides an opinionated, long-term perspective on the past
three decades' development of the index-based product set and makes
some predictions about the future of indexing and exchange-traded products such as ETFs in the global capital markets. It concludes with a vision of
how continuing financial innovation can help solve end users' long-term,
functional finance needs.

With this product proliferation, growth, and flexibility has come another phenomenon—the *democratization* of financial capabilities. Indexing,
ETFs, and the derivatives based on them now enable the creation of sophisticated strategies for smaller investors. These opportunities previously were
only available to large institutions and ultra high-net-worth investors using
specialized financial advisors. The strategies include index-based portfolios
customized for investors' unique risk and return preferences as well as taxation and socially-based investing concerns. Table 31.1—an expanded version of Table P1.1 in the introduction to Part One—provides an overview of
the development of indexing and ETF vehicles, some examples of the increasing democratization of sophisticated strategies, as well as some predictions for the period beyond 2005.

As we go deeper into the fourth decade of indexing, this major trend of
democratization will increasingly mean more choices of index products and
strategies for financial advisors and individual investors. Highly specialized
index funds, ETFs, and derivatives on ETFs will provide substantial benefits,
but will carry the risk of potential complexity and inappropriate use. This
latter "problem of success" will lead to further opportunities for the investment industry to provide real-world solutions to their clients.

Let's start with some specific benefits. As discussed in Chapter 30, increasingly, even relatively small individual investors will be able to build
index-based strategies that are customized to their specific risk and return
objectives. This could be achieved through a portfolio of ETFs and/or index
funds or through index-based separate accounts (or a combination of
the two). The latter format will be particularly appropriate for taxable portfolios. Customized risk management will also be available, particularly
through options and futures on ETFs. *Modified beta* strategies—previously
only available to institutions—will be accessible to individual investors with

TABLE 31.1 The Expansion and Democratization of Index and ETF Vehicles and Strategies

1970s	The first institutional (1971/1973) and retail index funds (1976)
	First International Index Fund (1979)
	First Enhanced Index Fund (1979)
1980s	Listed stock index futures and options (1982-U.S., 1984-U.K., 1986-Japan)
	Expansion of index funds—global, deeper within asset classes
	First Fixed Income Index Funds
	First screened portfolios (South Africa-free)
1990s	Massive growth of index fund assets spurred by bull market
	First Emerging Market Index Funds (1991, 1993, 1994)
	Launch of ETFs in Canada and United States (TIPS, Super-Shares, SPDR)
	Expansion of screened/ custom portfolios for institutions
2000–2002	Global ETF explosion (equity and fixed income)
	Index-based "stock baskets" for retail investors
	Bear market demonstrates utility of index products
2003–2005	Options and single stock futures on ETFs bring liquid derivatives to more specialized/ focused indexes
	Index-based separate accounts and universal accounts (combining separate accounts, ETFs, and mutual funds)
	Launch of quasi-active ETFs (active benchmarks)
	Launch of commodity and currency ETFs
	Proliferation of ETFs in (domestic) emerging markets
	Smaller institutions and individuals able to replicate the most sophisticated cash and derivative strategies
2006 and beyond	Truly active ETFs (initially likely risk-controlled active)
	Mass customization (blending ETFs and ETF derivatives)
	Liability-based products (futures/options)
	Pure and "targeted" solutions for households and firms

the patience to understand the pros and cons of these approaches. This will open the possibility for individual investors to achieve a degree of alpha/beta separation—using index-based strategies for asset class exposure (beta)—while using hedge funds or other pure alpha strategies to achieve above-strategy benchmark performance. Although institutional investors are well along in their ability to separate market exposure and alpha, individuals will have substantially fewer choices for pure alpha strategies, and they will likely have significantly higher fees.

This future vision of democratization has some negative implications. First and foremost, there is a good chance of product overload. Investors need solutions, not infinite choices.[3] This will require financial service companies to structure semicustom solutions, such as the lifestyle funds discussed in Chapter 18, or will require financial advisors to become closer to their clients' needs and have the right tool kit of index products and sophisticated analytics to create *mass-customized* solutions. Another possible direction—products that solve investors' *functional* needs, such as college costs or long-term medical care—is discussed in the closing pages of this chapter. There is also the risk of misuse of the plethora of products, particularly index derivatives.

The financial industry, unfortunately, has a long history of luring investors into inappropriate strategies, such as the surge into technology funds at the top of the 1990's bubble. Indexing shouldn't mean a similar rushing into hot sectors and countries with index products like ETFs or index options. With the plethora of choices, a few broad-based, total-asset-class index funds will still remain the most appropriate choice for many investors. The industry needs to develop educational programs and packaged products that assist investors with these choices. It is my firm conviction that the proper path for the use of index products is a holistic long-term approach, such as those based on the *Four Key Axioms for Success* described in Chapter 30.

The following overview of medium-term prospects for four broad categories of index products suggests where the industry is heading. While the chapter looks at all four categories, it dwells substantially longer on ETFs because the utility and practicality of ETFs will continue to drive spectacular growth in their use. The longer-term outlook presented toward the end of the chapter reflects a belief that we will see a growing convergence of products and strategies.

INDEX FUNDS AND INDEX PORTFOLIOS[4]

This is a broad category, and thus, we will take a high-level look at some mega-trends. Chapters 14, 25, and 26 provide additional insight into product and application trends. For institutions, the desire for low-cost, transparent, and accurate market exposure to complement absolute return strategies will drive significant growth in indexing. In the retail arena, the continual adoption of best practices from the institutional world will drive steady asset growth in both index mutual funds and index portfolios, the latter being an untapped area of substantial growth potential.

Index-based portfolios will remain essential components of investment strategies in the institutional arena (pension plans, foundations, and endowments). In fact, the accelerating trend within the institutional asset management business toward separating beta (or market returns) and alpha (value-added) will likely expose the inefficiency of using numerous traditional active managers to gain a desired market exposure, when the managers are hugging the benchmarks.

The days of closet indexers are numbered, and the institutional world is shifting toward heavy use of index and enhanced index funds to capture market beta in almost every asset class. Alpha will be sought increasingly through market-neutral and other absolute return strategies. As a recent essay on this trend predicted: "Passive management will grow dramatically and become the dominant form by which investors capture market risk premiums. Market returns currently provided by active managers will transition to passive specialists."[5]

Institutions will continue to take advantage of more and more variants of customization, driven both by index vendor capabilities and ideas, and their own unique requirements. As discussed way back in Chapter 1, the interaction of different players in the index industry is driving innovation. This is exactly one of those situations. Index providers are developing their own dividend-tilted benchmarks, addressing a perceived need following a reduction in the taxation of dividends. Similarly, as seen in Chapter 13, index vendors have rapidly developed standardized socially responsible indexes when market demand arises.

The larger degree of customization demand comes from asset owners' unique concerns and preferences. These include corporate governance screening, environmental screening, and even political and economic risk, such as screening for companies with exposure to state sponsors of terrorism.[6]

In the retail investor market, the industry can anticipate continued growth driven by advisors and direct investment from individuals. Many chapters in this book, especially Chapter 14, have traced the growth of conventional indexing, and this story isn't over. Superior relative long-term performance and lower costs will continue to drive growth of standard index mutual funds. The intense scrutiny by regulators and investors in late 2003 and early 2004 on the cost (and ethical) structure of traditional mutual funds can only accelerate the trend. In assessing the impact of the specific charges related to market timing in mutual funds, it is important to remember that index funds were pioneers in the concepts of fair value pricing, low fees, and tools to discourage rapid trading—all of which are now being adapted by traditional mutual funds.[7]

We can anticipate continued growth of broad-market index strategies—this is the right solution for many investors. Vanguard and Dimensional Fund Advisors (DFA) will maintain their large share of this market, but Fidelity, TIAA-CREF, Schwab, State Street Global Advisors (SSgA), and others have strong capabilities and good distribution channels. There are signs that Socially Responsible Investing (SRI) and other social policy-based indexing strategies will continue to gain traction, including the fascinating area of corporate governance-screened indexes mentioned in Chapter 13. There is likely to be substantial deepening of index-based investing for both fixed income and international equities (both developed and emerging markets). For the latter asset class, the conventional wisdom that indexing makes sense only for domestic large-cap will slowly adapt to the reality that the arithmetic of active management works for all asset classes. Index-based approaches for alternative asset classes such as commodities and hedge funds will gain acceptance primarily because of their transparency and lower cost.

Properly used, the innovative rapid allocation and leveraged index funds from firms such as Rydex and ProFunds will gain assets and usage from both advisors and individual active traders. The above-mentioned scrutiny of mutual fund practices can only help these fund complexes, which were built from the ground up to accommodate market timing activity.

Index-based separate accounts are another area that should see substantial growth. These products have unique advantages for taxable, high-net-worth investors, as described in Chapters 24 and 27. Sold by advisors and financial consultants, and managed by behind-the-scenes, technologically enabled index managers such as those cited in Chapter 30, index-based separate accounts combine the best features of index mutual funds and the customized separate account structure. As mentioned in Chapter 24, indexing accounts for less than 1 percent of the half-trillion-dollar separate account business (compared with around 25 percent of institutional assets and about half that in the mutual fund/ETF market).

Retail investors will also have greater access to index-based "total portfolio" solutions: Financial service firms and advisors will assemble multi-asset class strategies, which are now fully implementable via portfolios of ETFs, or index-based separate accounts holding a combination of ETFs and index constituent stocks. Ultimately, advisors and other financial specialists will be able to assemble alternative-weight index strategies and products using the optimal mix of index funds, ETFs, and separate accounts. This trend toward universal accounts is mentioned in Chapter 24 and discussed later in this chapter, and as long as the fees are reasonable, investors stand to benefit from these new approaches.

ENHANCED INDEXING

As discussed in Chapters 14 and 15, enhanced indexing—in all its variants—is one of the most robust and dynamic areas of indexing and is likely to grow in several dimensions. Asset growth can be expected mostly in institutional-oriented strategies. Much of the growth of enhanced indexing has been in domestic large-cap strategies. As the strategy defined in Chapter 15 develops more momentum, firms with the appropriate resources and commitment inevitably will extend the approach deeper into the cap and style ranges of U.S. equities.

Institutional enhanced index offerings will also go broader into international equities, both developed and emerging markets. Despite the industry's skeptical smirks in the early 2000s, developed market benchmarks, such as MSCI EAFE (Europe, Australasia, & Far East) and ACWI ex-U.S. *have* become harder to beat. Some of the star active international strategies/firms of the 1990s are now on plan sponsors "watch lists."[8] Thus, enhanced index and risk-controlled active approaches to developed international equities will continue to gain assets. The steady relative outperformance of emerging markets this decade—and the continued high active risk incurred by traditional managers in this asset class—will eventually lead more investors to gravitate toward enhanced index and risk-controlled active approaches. International equity enhanced indexing strategies will naturally require substantial commitment of resources by asset management firms, but will offer higher margins than domestic enhanced indexing.

Higher costs limit the potential for retail enhanced index products to some extent. The small margin of index alpha created is generally too slim to compensate for the higher cost structure of retail funds. As indicated in Chapter 15, the category is "all over the map," and the lack of consensus on defining the approach in the institutional world doesn't help matters. The sidebar in the chapter also demonstrated that retail enhanced index funds have yet to demonstrate consistent outperformance of their benchmarks. There are some successful offerings, such as PIMCO's StocksPlus fund, and despite the aforementioned hurdles, retail-oriented enhanced index funds will develop. They are still better than traditional active, and the scandals associated with traditional index mutual funds might encourage some retail firms to commit more capital to develop enhanced index products. Furthermore, we can expect more risk budgeting by retail investors. Optimizer-based manager allocations by professional advisors will, therefore, yield a shift to more enhanced index strategies.

Two high-potential areas for retail-oriented funds to use enhanced index strategies are in the lifestyle fund arena (discussed in Chapter 18) and in products targeting the 401(k) market, as this structure neutralizes the tax implications of greater turnover in enhanced indexing.

Finally, the customized strategies that aim to outperform their benchmark index through tax-loss harvesting make compelling investment and economic sense for individual investors. Well-known and boutique investment advisors manage these index-based separate accounts, which increasingly will be available on the major broker/dealer wrap account platforms. For taxable (nonretirement) accounts, this *tax alpha* is an enhancement that investors pocket each and every year—it cannot be lost back to the market in next year's performance.

As discussed in Chapters 24 and 27, index-based portfolios are the ideal platform for active tax-loss harvesting because the investment objective is stock-agnostic. This means that the goal of portfolio managers is to track the pretax index, say the S&P 500. They do not have specific alpha targets for stocks nor do they fall in love with a holding. They are neutral and, therefore better able, for example, to sell one health care stock and replace it with another, capturing a tax loss that goes directly into the client's pocket. As mentioned previously, these enhanced index strategies can be implemented with individual securities, with portfolios of ETFs or a blend of the two approaches.

THE FUTURE OF INDEX DERIVATIVES

Index derivatives—futures, options, ETF options, and swaps—compose a dynamic and very global field of innovation for the financial industry. Numerous changes are underway—new products, regulatory evolution, and brutal competition between domestic and global exchanges.

As discussed in Chapters 14 and 25, index derivatives experienced steady growth during the bearish market environment of the early 2000s. During this period, derivatives demonstrated once again their utility for efficiently adjusting market exposure. The addition of ETFs and ETF derivatives to the mix has extended these tools into narrower slices of domestic and international markets (see Chapter 25 for a description of these trends as well as several useful diagrams).

While index futures and options' strong liquidity trends will continue, the more intriguing potential for the future is in options and single stock futures on ETFs. These derivatives are in the early stages of development, but have significant potential because of the strong liquidity in underlying ETFs. As mentioned in Chapter 25, the number of stock index futures has been relatively small because of the need to concentrate liquidity for futures. But for ETF derivatives, the "solid leg" of liquidity is derived from the underlying ETF, which we have seen (in Chapters 23 and 25) is dependent on the liquidity of the constituent stocks in the portfolio composition file (PCF). This means that derivative structures can be created on a virtually limitless range of underlying indexes/ETFs.

For example, although the industry has long dreamed of having index futures on the MSCI EAFE index, hedging across 21 equity markets, especially from the U.S. time zone, would make this a very difficult future contract for market makers. Thus, despite a license being available, no exchange had launched such a product. In contrast, in 2002, the Chicago Board Options Exchange (CBOE) launched "Options on EFA" based on the iShares MSCI EAFE fund. Traders, market makers, and hedgers know that these options settle into the physical ETF, and thus, pricing has been consistent.

The range of options on ETFs will grow, with the CBOE, International Securities Exchange (ISE), and American Stock Exchange (Amex) all competing for market share. Similarly, OneChicago and NQLX have joined the fray, and while they have not gained substantial absolute volumes, their growth in their first year tracks earlier growth of nascent (and now quite successful) derivative markets.[9]

These developments can be extended in the coming years through linkages between new stock index futures and actively managed ETFs and their derivatives. As ETFs and options/futures on ETFs continue to mature, they will become another anchor of liquidity for dealers/market makers to hedge a stock index future position. As described in Chapter 21, there is demand for index futures on the major global equity benchmarks such as MSCI Japan or MSCI U.K., as these will create lower tracking error for portfolio managers than local indexes such as Topix or FTSE 100. With active ETFs on these MSCI benchmarks, and the likelihood of options and/or single stock futures on the ETFs, exchanges such as the Chicago Mercantile Exchange (CME) or New York Board of Trade (NYBoT) could launch index futures on these benchmarks with greater confidence that market makers would maintain a liquid market. Alternatively, investors may prefer the simplicity of single stock futures on the ETF. These would physically settle into the ETF, which could then be converted into the basket of securities, as described in detail in Chapter 16.

Finally, another area of potentially dramatic expansion of the derivative product set is index futures and options on entirely new asset classes and exposures. This includes both economic and market indicators. While this may sound far-fetched, it is actually happening. The CME is listing futures on the widely followed Consumer Price Index (CPI), which is a benchmark for myriad inflation-adjusted prices in the economy. Similarly, stock market volatility is being securitized with the introduction of options—and more recently, futures—on the CBOE's Volatility Index (VIX).

These economic indicator derivatives can become building blocks for many next-generation financial products that address the underlying functional needs of investors. This possibility is discussed later in the chapter.

THE FUTURE OF EXCHANGE-TRADED FUNDS

As previous chapters have highlighted, exchange-traded funds have been a part of the financial landscape for over a decade and have become invaluable tools for market participants. Their growth has been nothing short of spectacular, and as this book went to press, asset growth was accelerating, in part because of the mutual fund trading and pricing investigations uncovered in 2003.

As a result of their efficient structure and low cost, ETFs are a major part of the future of indexing. More and more index-based activity will converge on ETFs because they are cost-effective and efficient for *both* institutions and individuals. In dramatic contrast to mutual funds and other investment alternatives, the participation of large and small investors with different objectives and time horizons actually benefits the tax management of the products. As we assess this global expansion of ETF products, assets under management, volume, and users, it inevitably leads to the question, "What next?" Is this growth sustainable? Are all the "good indexes" taken? Will quasi-active and actively managed ETFs gain traction?

To say that the industry has come a long way would be an enormous understatement. In early 1993, just three ETFs were listed worldwide: Canada's Toronto Index Participation Securities and two competing products in the United States (LOR's SuperTrust Index SuperUnit, and the AMEX/SSgA SPDR). Combined, they had less than $800 million in assets. In early 2004, there were 297 ETFs (with 358 exchange listings on 28 exchanges). There were 35 firms managing ETFs with approximately $220 billion in assets and about $10 billion in average daily value of volume. Of these 297 ETFs, there were 38 ETFs worldwide with over $1 billion in assets (and 40 if one includes HLDRS).[10] This is dramatic expansion of a financial product and a huge endorsement for index-based investing.

Beyond the sheer growth of assets and activity, the expansion beyond flagship indexes and asset classes has been equally impressive. Although not yet uniform in major markets, there are now ETFs for virtually all capitalization ranges of equity, most international regions (at least from a U.S.

perspective), most types of fixed-income instruments (with the missing ones currently under development), and the beginnings of commodity and currency Exchange-Traded Products (many of these products will not have a "fund" structure, and therefore, I refer to them as "ETPs"). U.S. investors have the widest selection—they can access the full range of capitalization, sectors, and style for the domestic equity market, as well as all non-U.S. regional and individual country equity markets. It should be noted, however, that a variety of non-U.S. investors trade in the U.S.-listed ETFs, both to get finely segmented U.S. equity exposure, but also to access non-U.S. equities and U.S. fixed income. Furthermore, the range of fixed-income ETFs is continually expanding, and the first four quasi-active equity ETFs have been launched.[11] As of this writing, there are no U.S-listed commodity or currency ETPs, but they have been launched outside the United States, and their arrival is imminent, likely starting with a gold bullion ETF.[12]

Another sign of maturation in the ETF marketplace is that major ETF sponsors are willing to close funds, even as they are launching new ones. This process has been underway in the United States since 2002, and the consolidation began in Europe in 2003, starting with UNICO i-tracker's closing of five MSCI European sector ETFs. This has been followed with BGI's iShares and Merrill Lynch's LDRS both announcing the closing of 9 FTSE European sector and 13 FTSE global sector ETFs respectively.[13] Merrill Lynch's subsequent sale of its flagship EuroSTOXX LDRS funds to Barclays/iShares was another strategic milestone for the industry. And in early 2004, the first ETF closings/delistings took place in Japan and Korea. Further consolidation is inevitable, particularly in Europe (where 15 ETF managers remain). Another likely scenario is the shutting down or selling to larger players of entire ETF complexes, such as the closing of the four ETF Advisors' "FITRs" fixed-income ETFs in the United States in 2003.

ETF manufacturers will increasingly prefer to launch funds that have a higher degree of success, and the asset level hurdle for defining success will continue to rise. That will not prevent some firms from ignoring short-term economics to get a toehold in the ETF market. For example, it would not be surprising if other retail mutual fund giants follow in Fidelity's footsteps and launch ETFs to gain an understanding of the product's operational complexities and market mechanisms. Similarly, we can expect "strategic" partnerships between index providers, fund sponsors, and exchanges to develop and list new ETFs based on new index series (such as BGI's iShares partnerships with the NYSE and Morningstar Indexes).[14]

Despite the amazing progress of index-based funds, derivatives, and ETF vehicles since the early 1970s, the developments I have projected for the rest of the decade (even if only some of my expectations are realized) will amply justify the belief expressed in this chapter's title—namely that "the indexing revolution has just begun." The next part of this chapter details likely developments in the coming years. Much focus remains on ETFs as the primary vehicle for accessing index-based strategies and all of their potential. Exchange-traded funds bring it all together—by providing liquid slices of almost every imaginable market category. And once they are listed, the creation of derivatives on them is relatively simple. Thus, we can expect further convergence of product usage and an acceleration of institutional techniques in the broader financial marketplace.

INDEXING IN 2005 AND BEYOND

As we move deeper into the fourth decade of indexing and the second decade of ETFs, three broad trends are driving continued growth and use of index-based products. *First,* intense product development will continue, with innovation, competition (and consolidation), and expansion of asset class coverage. *Second,* ETFs will become standard tools for almost all financial market participants. *Third,* the financial industry will seamlessly use index products, especially ETFs, as a component of other financial products, whether within (active or enhanced index) funds, within separate accounts, or in blends of ETFs and derivatives.

Worldwide Index Product Development

This past decade has seen tremendous strides in index-based and ETF product development, but we are just at the cusp of even greater innovation. Fixed-income ETFs have been listed in the United States only since mid-2002, and yet their growth has been dramatic—in asset gathering and trading activity—with more fixed-income products steadily on the way.[15] The same can be expected for fixed income in Europe.

In the major developed markets, product innovation will occur in four broad areas:

1. Filling out of the asset classes.
2. Continued twists on index-based ETFs with quasi-active products.
3. The move toward pure active ETFs.
4. The continued listing of derivatives on ETFs.

In the "filling out of the asset classes" category, it is still hard to get exposure to some asset class niches, key countries, and regions with ETFs. However, it is becoming clear that ETF manufacturers will no longer let their products cross-subsidize each other just to achieve a complete product set/index family. The recent closure of three families of sector funds in Europe demonstrates this. Many in the industry insist, "All the good indexes are taken." Whereas this is true to a point, markets evolve, newly popular asset classes emerge, and indexes—and the ETFs that track them—will continue to be launched.

Commodities will likely provide a promising area for development of new asset classes. As mentioned, the Gold ETPs listed in Sydney and London (and soon in the United States) could prove popular with both retail and institutional investors, especially as they make holding the yellow metal more efficient. As the rapid growth of the iShares MSCI emerging market ETFs in 2001–2003 has demonstrated, when products ease market participation, investors will move substantial assets, even if the expense ratio is relatively high.[16] Although Gold ETPs will have a direct link to the physical metal, the key to development of other commodity-based ETPs/ETFs, such as for crude oil or nonferrous metals, will be the development and regulatory approval of a futures/derivatives-based product structure. Such a breakthrough would facilitate the launch of ETFs that track well-known commodity indexes such as the Goldman Sachs Commodity Index (GSCI), Standard & Poors (S&P), and DJ-AIG (for more on commodity indexes, see the sidebar in Chapter 10).

Derivatives use within an ETF structure will also be a vital element of the leveraged and inverse ETFs that are pending with the Securities and Exchange Commission (SEC). ProFunds Advisors has filed for eight such funds; four are leveraged, providing a magnified long market exposure, and four provide a leveraged inverse exposure, rising in value when benchmarks such as the Nasdaq-100 and S&P 500 fall. These funds would rely heavily on derivatives to get the magnified long or leveraged short exposure and would follow in the footsteps of the two synthetic ETFs listed in Canada by BGI's iUnits. Once these funds clear the SEC, other firms are very likely to use the same exemptions to launch a myriad of ETFs with derivative-linked exposures. However, an open question for these products—which will only be answered after launch—is whether the market will use these specialized ETFs in the same way that investors use mutual funds to facilitate market timing.[17]

If derivative-based ETPs/ETFs are accepted in a major way, it would open the way for other potentially valuable new products based on market risks (such as volatility for particular asset classes) and variables such as weather, hydrocarbon emissions, housing prices, and economic statistics. These are currently traded primarily in the over-the-counter market. If futures markets develop for some of these risks, products that address individuals and firms' liability streams could be created. This could eventually lead to liability-based products that solve the total needs of end users. Also falling into the more esoteric category is the concept of an ETF (or open-end mutual fund) structure for either a hedge fund "fund of funds" or a hedge fund index fund.[18]

The first pure active ETFs will likely have some index-based element, either a core index component from which the creation/redemption mechanism takes place or a sector rotation or multiasset class rotation approach that actively manages index-based subcomponents. The success enjoyed by the first four quasi-active ETFs mentioned earlier indicates that such products would find market acceptance. But first, the "tough nut" of developing a pure active ETF needs to be cracked—and move through the SEC. Essentially, the challenge is to maintain a robust creation/redemption mechanism that keeps the market price aligned with the ETF's net asset value (NAV), while preserving a reasonable level of opacity to shield/hide the managers' alpha-seeking positions. If, but more likely *when,* this nut is cracked, we could see a *massive* shift of active funds to the ETF structure. This would be due to its greater efficiency and ability to accommodate all types of investors—including short-term investors—without hurting the interests of long-term holders.

In smaller developed markets, and in emerging markets, product development will follow many of the patterns we have seen in major developed markets, but with a faster take-off trajectory. As this chapter is being edited, six emerging markets had ETFs, and they are in development in at least four others, including China, which only launched its first index fund in 2003.[19] In markets such as Korea and Israel, we are already seeing robust competition among ETF providers and different indexes. For example, seven new tradable index products were launched in Israel between the first draft and final edits of this chapter. Developments in emerging markets should not be ignored, as innovative structures often develop in unexpected places. Occasionally, early innovation takes place in emerging markets—Brazil's inflation (cost-of-living deflator) futures and South Africa's currency ETF are good examples.

As product development steadily continues around the world, investors' tool kit of ETFs and derivatives on ETFs will essentially be complete. Thus, the key to further growth will be the deepening and broadening of usage by an expanding group of intermediaries and end users.

EXPANSION OF INDEX PRODUCT USE

As index funds and ETFs become more embedded into the financial tool kit of investors, their use has expanded dramatically. Major broker/dealers in the United States, Europe, and Asia have established dedicated sales/research teams to service the growing institutional users of ETFs, and they have been increasingly integrated with other index-based research and trading operations (as the perspective provided by the authors of Chapters 16 and 25 amply demonstrates). These sell-side groups serve pension funds, mutual funds, institutional asset managers, and hedge funds. Many internally managed pension funds that would never hire external index managers gladly use ETFs for exposure to both U.S. and domestic markets. Even major pension funds that extensively rely on external managers use ETFs for cash equitization, asset allocation, and rebalancing. In the retail/intermediary space, standard institutional-like strategy/manager allocation approaches have become much more accepted by financial advisors. Finally, hedge funds of all types have increased their use of ETFs and derivatives on ETFs substantially. Table 31.2 lists seven common applications of ETFs driving this expansion. The first six were discussed in detail in previous chapters of the book, and the last one is discussed within this chapter (chapter numbers are provided for reference).

Furthermore, significant developments during 2003 have spurred usage—most notably the easing of restrictions on mutual funds in the United States and Europe to include ETFs in their funds. While the number of institutions using ETFs in the United States and Europe in mid-2003 was already impressive at over 1,300, it can safely be predicted that this number will be closer to 5,000 by the end of the decade. There is no reason the majority of mutual funds should not use ETFs for their cash equitization and asset allocation needs.

Another major development, which was reaching a peak as this manuscript went into production, is the controversy and legal action about mutual fund sales practices and accommodation of market timing trades by mutual fund companies. Significant outflows were experienced by many of the impacted mutual fund families (from both their mutual fund and institutional clients), and index mutual funds and ETFs are positioned to gain significant assets from investors seeking transparency, low cost, and lower risk.

TABLE 31.2   Applications of Index-Based ETF Strategies

Core-satellite (28, 30)

Completion strategy (16, 25)

"Ballast" for a separate account strategy (24)

Cash equitization (16, 25)

Alternative weighting schemes [sector rotation, alternative country weightings] (18, 30)

Trading/shorting (16, 25, 30)

Partially protected/modified beta strategies (31)

Note: Numbers in parentheses refer to book chapters where the strategies are discussed.

Finally, speaking of bold predictions, I will be surprised if total worldwide ETF assets are less than $1 trillion by the end of the decade, and I believe they are more likely to be closer to $2 trillion. Other industry consultants and exchanges have somewhat lower estimates, ranging from $500 billion to $1 trillion. My projection is still less than a third of the current size of the U.S. mutual fund industry, although the controversy over mutual fund sales and trading practices could shrink mutual fund assets and further accelerate the growth of ETFs.[20] As another prediction, I believe that retail-oriented index mutual funds, which currently account for around 11 percent of U.S. mutual fund assets, will achieve a penetration rate that is closer to the ratio of 20 percent or more, which is common among institutional investors. The scandals that surfaced late in 2003 involving traditional mutual fund sales and trading practices will likely be a major impetus for investors to move assets to index mutual funds, which had already experienced substantial net inflows throughout the bear market of the early 2000s. Therefore, depending on overall equity and bond market levels, total index mutual fund assets in the United States could surpass $2 trillion by the end of the decade. When combined with my ETF projections, the aggregate of publicly available index-based funds should exceed $3 trillion by 2010.

Hybrid Products

One of the factors that will drive asset growth is the acceleration of *hybrid products:* financial products that seamlessly blend ETFs and other securities and/or products. More and more financial advisors will be providing their clients with total financial accounts that blend separately managed accounts, mutual funds, and ETFs. Citigroup's Smith Barney Consulting Group unit is in the forefront of this development, with the 2003 rollout of their "Integrated Investment Services" platform for in-house brokers.

Another way that ETFs are being integrated into other structures is through privately managed accounts, whether via trust banks or the more common separately managed account products offered by financial advisors. Several firms have introduced index-based separate accounts that track benchmark indexes such as the S&P 500 and the Russell 3000. One such strategy can track a large-cap U.S. or international equity benchmark with just 50 to 60 securities while holding a percentage of the relevant ETF in lieu of cash and to minimize tracking error.[21] We can expect to see more extensive use of ETFs within separate accounts in the coming years, either in this hybrid blend or through a variety of prepackaged portfolios of ETFs assembled by advisors and optimized for client preferences.

Just as the original financial product to include an ETF structure—LOR's SuperTrust—included a risk control vehicle (the different SuperShares, which provided different claims to performance of the Index SuperUnit), investors can now use combinations of ETFs and options/futures on ETFs to construct a virtually infinite variety of return/risk patterns.[22] These structures can be assembled into what I call *modified beta portfolios.*

Particularly in the early to mid 2000s, as equity and fixed-income market direction has been volatile and uncertain, there is strong appeal for combining index products (index portfolios, ETFs, and their related derivatives) to customize exposure and provide protection from extreme market moves. The range of strategies is essentially limitless, but can be grouped into five broad categories, as highlighted in Table 31.3. I have grouped these according to outcome/objective, not by instruments, and it should be noted that these strategies are appropriate for a variety of market environments.

Option overwriting is well understood in the industry (and discussed in more detail in Chapter 25), but in the past, index option overwriting was limited to the most familiar flagship indexes. With the advent of options on ETFs, the range of underlying indexes available for this strategy has expanded dramatically, and by mid-decade, almost all the key ETFs likely will have related options trading.[23] In addition to the more familiar "buy-write" strategies, Put Overwrite strategies are also practical because ETFs can be shorted on a downtick. These strategies are for relatively bearish investors who do not believe a market/sector/style will completely crash.[24]

The infinite flexibility provided by ETFs and their derivatives is undoubtedly a major positive development for the capital markets and financial services industry. But in some ways, this myriad of options (*pun intended*) is way too much choice for the average end user. Most investors don't want infinite flexibility—they want solutions tailored to their own needs. While *mass customization* is an overused phrase, our industry is inevitably heading in that direction, and index products—index funds, customized index portfolios, index futures and options, and ETFs and ETF derivatives—will provide some of the capabilities for developing these "bespoke" solutions.

TABLE 31.3   Flexible Index-Based Strategies for Variable Markets

Index option overwriting for income

Buy-write strategies (downside protection in exchange for capped upside)

Principal-protected and modified-beta strategies (single stock futures and options on ETFs make this possible for more strategies and subasset classes)

Customized index-based strategies (alternative benchmarks, weightings, and trigger/temporal rebalancing)

Quasi-active indexes/strategies: value-screened and dividend-tilt strategies

INDEXING IN 2010

By the start of the next decade, the complete "tool kit" of ETFs and index derivatives will be established, and the technology will have been refined to scaleably deliver customized index portfolios. Thus, while users might be overwhelmed by the variety of products, creative firms will develop efficient packaged portfolios. But financial market innovation will *not* be static in 2010; the growth and proliferation of tradable index products will still be just one component of an even broader tool kit of financial products that can enable our industry to reach its real potential.

The most intense financial innovation will be needed to solve the *real* needs of households, pension funds, and foundations/endowments, corporations, and governments. As expounded by leading financial academics like Merton Miller, Robert Shiller, and others, the most pressing need for financial products is for the *ones our industry has not yet developed.*[25] What end users of financial products really want is not more and more choice of products, but precise solutions that solve their *functional* needs. People have major lifetime income streams and needs—salary, inheritances, college tuition, health care, retirement. There is no reason our industry cannot develop indexes and products based on these indexes to solve long-term financial needs.

Similarly, there is no reason financial engineering cannot produce efficient products linked to macroeconomic variables and microeconomic factors such as household expenses (baskets of goods) and risks (insurance-like products). The resulting products may look like variants of structured notes or a modified ETF vehicle (it would not be surprising if they had some similarities to the predecessors of ETFs—the Americus Trust and LOR's Super-Trust). Whatever structure, these *functional* products have enormous potential for management of lifetime personal risks and expenditures and more predictable financial planning for millions of people.

When such products are developed, index funds, index-based portfolios, ETFs, and their related index derivatives are likely to serve as core holdings in *lifetime portfolios,* as hedges for liabilities, and as building blocks for structures we cannot fully imagine yet. Systems and financial technology will inevitably play a key role. It is highly likely that highly customized portfolios of securities, funds, and ETFs—and perhaps even derivatives—will be constructed by model-driven proposal/portfolio builder systems using optimizers and other models. An advisor or individual should be able to plug in risk parameters, customization factors, and the need—and the custom portfolio will be built. Numerous firms are working on pieces of these future *solution set* functionalities—it is no longer a question of *whether* they will be introduced, but rather *when* they will be available.

PLAYING A PART IN THE REVOLUTION

The penetration of indexation within institutional portfolios is likely to be relatively static for U.S. domestic assets (as the growth curve shifts to enhanced indexing). However, international indexing will experience strong secular growth, both standard and enhanced, particularly as the "arithmetic of active management" asserts itself on traditional active approaches with the application of more appropriate and better-constructed benchmarks.[26] Outside the United States, there is much room for further penetration of indexing in Japan, Asia, parts of Europe, and in almost all the advanced emerging markets.[27]

I can't resist repeating my prediction, but now with a more global perspective. As stated earlier in the chapter, a conservative estimate of the overall ETF asset base in 2010 would assume at least 20 percent of the current U.S. mutual fund market, and a substantial slice of both retail and institutional assets in Europe and Asia. Thus, I will be shocked if global ETF assets are less than $1 trillion in 2010, and it is much more likely that they'll be closer to $2 trillion. When combined with index mutual funds in the United States, U.S. tax-exempt institutional index strategies, and international institutional index strategies (users such as Japan's PFA and Singapore's GSIC), my estimate for 2010's total worldwide indexed assets is over $7 trillion. By my "guesstimate" (this is a multifaceted estimate, which means it is only slightly better than a guess), index-based assets would represent at least 15 percent of total world equity market capitalization in 2010.[28]

Innovation in all dimensions of investment theory, technology, and business practice will lead to continued growth in indexing. I envision two parallel revolutions: The aforementioned institutional paradigm shift toward separation of beta and alpha will drive steady demand for low-cost, efficient market exposure. There is no better provider of this than index-based strategies, and they will be available for every asset class—and many quasi-asset classes such as hedge fund strategies.

An even larger retail/individual investor revolution is brewing. Although it started well behind the institutional curve, this marketplace is steadily catching up, certainly in the United States and Canada. As highlighted by the arguments presented in Chapters 28 and 30, the financial advisor community is slowly but surely adapting a core-satellite approach. This is a huge step forward from the industry's traditional portfolio of expensive, underperforming active managers that was skewered in Chapter 29, and recent disclosures about mutual fund practices will surely accelerate this progress.

Individual professionals working in the marketplace can and will still make a difference. Almost every financial market player will be able to participate in this investment product and strategy revolution. The industry will provide the tools—robust indexes based on every imaginable asset class and economic factor evolving with market developments, liquid products based on those indexes, and their derivatives. Academia and specialized research firms will provide many of the key theories and formulas for new structures and will supplement the other players in the marketplace.

Financial professionals can work to provide for the *functional* needs of their clients—whether it is income and retirement security, health care, or appropriate hedges for long-term liabilities. And as Chapter 30 demonstrated, all investors can benefit by following the Four Key Axioms of long-term investment success if they place indexing at the core of their portfolios. With both professionals and individuals taking more responsibility for investment performance, the future of indexing—index funds, enhanced indexing, ETFs, index derivatives, and alternative asset indexing—is indeed bright. The revolution that started a third of a decade ago has truly just begun!

NOTES

1. Some parts of this chapter were previously published as "The Future of ETFs—The Revolution Has Just Begun," in Institutional Investor's *ETFs II—New Approaches and Global Outreach*, ed. Brian Bruce (September 2003), pp. 110–115. A short excerpt from this chapter was translated and published in Hebrew in *HaBorsa*, the magazine of the Tel Aviv Stock Exchange (March 2004).
2. Renown Danish scientist and humanitarian, Nobel Prize winning Physicist Niels Bohr (1885–1962). A very similar quote is often attributed to world-class philosopher and Yankees catcher Yogi Berra, who was purported to have said: "It's tough to make predictions, especially about the future." In fact, his famous quote in this genre was "the future ain't what it used to be."
3. Just in the time between submitting the final draft of this chapter and reviewing the page proofs, three completely new families of U.S. indexes were introduced as ETFs (MSCI U.S. Indexes, NYSE Indexes, and Morningstar Indexes) in the U.S. marketplace (which already had four index series trading at the end of 2003).
4. I have chosen to add the term *index portfolios* to distinguish between index funds and ETFs. Index portfolios can be institutional separate accounts, or increasingly, index-based separate accounts for individuals. The latter have the potential to bring indexing to a major cross-section of investors who heretofore have not had access to customized index strategies.
5. Eric Brandhorst, "The Future of Asset Management: Separation of Market Returns and Value-Added," SSgA *Point of View* (September 2003). Available from www.ssga.com.
6. FTSE and Institutional Shareholder Services (ISS) announced, as the book was going to print, their intention to launch a series of Corporate Governance-screened indexes, based on ISS's Corporate Governance Quotient factors

previously mentioned in the sidebar within Chapter 13. A commercially available service, the Global Securtiy Risk Monitor, developed by the Investor Responsibility Research Center and Center for Securities Advisory Group, provides a screening tool to determine which global companies have business interests in U.S. government-designated state sponsors of terrorism and/or proliferators of weapons of mass destruction. See www.irrc.com for more information.

7. See John Spence, "Fair Value Pricing in International Index Funds" (IndexUniverse.com, October 2003), available in archives on www.IndexUniverse.com.

8. See Steven A. Schoenfeld, "Watch Out, Active Managers, for the New EAFE," *Pensions & Investments* (November 12, 2001). In the two full years after the publication of this article, EAFE has steadily risen in InterSec's three-year rolling performance ranking for the EAFE Plus Universe, and entered 2004 close to the median.

9. For more information on single stock futures and options on ETFs, see the Futures/Options section on IndexUniverse.com or the exchanges' web sites: www.nqlx.com and www.onechicago.com. For updates on foreign stock index futures permitted for U.S. persons' use, see www.cftc.gov.

10. Morgan Stanley, *Exchange Traded Funds Review: A Global Summary* (London, March 4, 2004), pp. 1–6, 14–21; and Harvard Business School; Leland O'Brien Rubenstein Associates, Inc.: SuperTrust (HBS Case Study 9-294-050), 1994. Updates on the number of ETFs, their listings, and assets under management are available from the ETF section on IndexUniverse.com.

11. By *quasi-active ETFs,* I mean index-based ETFs where the index is not a flagship benchmark (like the DJIA), or a standard capitalization-weighted or capped index. However, it has actively managed elements in its index methodology, such as the RYDEX's S&P Equal-Weighted Index, the iShares Dow Jones Select Dividend Index or PowerShares' Intellidex products.

12. Two sponsors have already applied to the SEC to launch gold bullion exchange traded products—The World Gold Council and Barclays Global Investors. Full coverage and updates are available in the Gold/Commodities section of IndexUniverse.com.

13. See full story in Industry News section of IndexUniverse.com (September 2003).

14. By "strategic" I mean partnerships that go beyond a single ETF listing and will usually involve a commitment to launch a full range/series of index products. For example, with the Morningstar Indexes based on their nine-box "Style Box" (discussed in Chapter 6 and the E-ppendix), it would not make sense to just offer two or three Morningstar Index-based ETFs—the value and flexibility for users comes from having the mix and match capability from all nine ETFs. For more background and updates, see the Breaking News and Industry News sections of IndexUniverse.com.

15. An entire book chapter could be written on the change in fixed-income market dynamics that ETF and ETF derivative trading has begun to unleash. Unfortunately, it will take another book, and probably another author!

16. The most dramatic example of this is with the iShares MSCI Emerging Market Fund—EEM—which tracks the primary benchmark for the entire asset class. It

was launched in early April 2003, and by end-February 2004 had grown to more than $1.6 billion is assets (significantly aided by a major emerging market rally in 2003 and early 2004).

17. There are currently over $12 billion in the combined ProFunds, RYDEX, and Potomac fund families, which all facilitate market timing and feature numerous leveraged and inverse products on a range of size, sector, and style benchmarks.

18. This concept is not as far-fetched as it may sound. As mentioned in the sidebar in Chapter 13, RYDEX Capital Partners launched a 1940 Investment Company Act closed-end fund tracking the S&P Hedge Fund Index—The Rydex SPhinX Fund—in 2003, and it had gathered over $200 million in assets by early 2004.

19. Korea, Taiwan, India, Israel, Mexico, and South Africa. For examples, see stories on indexing in Brazil, ETF development in Israel, and on China's first index fund on IndexUniverse.com.

20. For updates on the mutual fund "market timing" and sales practice issues, as well as updates on U.S. and global ETF assets, see IndexUniverse.com. Some of the industry consultants who have projected somewhat lower ETF asset levels include Financial Research Corporation and PricewaterhouseCoopers.

21. The first such firm was Active Index Advisors, which launched its products in late 2002 and early 2003.

22. For a complete description of the SuperTrust structure and the subcomponents that can be combined to implement various risk-controlled investment strategies, see Exhibit 4 of the Harvard Business School Case Study, referred to in note 10.

23. An up-to-date list of ETFs with listed options can be procured from most brokers, or on exchange and or ETF issuer sites (though they don't list other firms/exchanges' ETF options). These sites can be accessed via the Links section on IndexUniverse.com.

24. A good explanation of the Put Overwrite strategy with ETFs is provided by Murali Ramaswami and Alex Bundy, "ETFs—An Alternative to Futures and a Companion to Options," *A Guide to Exchange Traded Funds,* ed. Brian Bruce (Institutional Investor Journals, 2001), p. 159.

25. See Robert J. Shiller, *The New Financial Order* (Princeton, NJ: Princeton University Press, 2003).

26. See note 8.

27. "Advanced Emerging Market"—like *Active* Index Investing—is decidedly *not* an oxymoron. Not only is it a formal country classification in the FTSE Global Equity Indexes (recently endorsed by a major global country classification survey conducted by FTSE), but equally important, it recognizes the steady progress of developing countries that pursue the appropriate economic liberalization and democratization policies. Previous members of this category, such as Portugal and Greece, have since graduated to developed market status, and many of the current members—South Korea, Taiwan, South Africa, Israel, Mexico, and Brazil—are likely to follow the same path. The above-mentioned country classification effort by FTSE will formally add operational elements (settlement and trading procedures, regulatory structure,

derivative markets) to the criteria for determining a markets status as developed, emerging, or "advanced emerging."

28. First of all, I recognize that indexing will continue to grow in fixed-income and other asset classes as well, but solid numbers are pretty hard to procure, except for equities. I estimated world market capitalization in 2010 by taking the end-2002 figure of just under $24 trillion (according to *S&P's 2003 Global Stock Markets Factbook*), adding 2003's market move, and smoothing an extrapolation from the average of market-cap levels from the previous 5 years. This gets to a range of $35 to $40 trillion in 2010, so my "guesstimate" of 15 percent is very much on the conservative side.

Guide to the E-ppendix

www.ActiveIndexInvesting.com, Partnered with IndexUniverse.com

Steven A. Schoenfeld

When I wrote my first book, *The Pacific Rim Futures and Options Markets*, its appendix was extensive, taking up almost 25 percent of the book, and killing a few extra trees in the process. As I mentioned in the Preface, even more problematic was the fact that the combination of a dynamic derivatives industry and rapidly changing underlying markets doomed much of the information in the appendix to obsolescence by the time the book arrived in stores. That was back in 1992, before the Internet was popularized, and there wasn't much of an alternative. But luckily, today there is, and from the start of this project in 2001, I was determined to develop a web-based complement to the book, especially given the ever-changing nature of the subject matter.

Even today, so many investment books have considerable appendices and data tables that quickly become obsolete in the rapidly changing world of global finance. In the hope of enhancing the ongoing relevance of the book—and saving a lot of trees—I've coined the *E-ppendix* (Electronic Appendix) concept: *an online accompaniment to the book that supplements the printed material and will be updated with developing news, data, tools, and research*. Its URL is www.ActiveIndexInvesting.com, and it is partnered with the broader focused and more regularly updated IndexUniverse.com web site, which aims to be the definitive online resource for index-related topics.

The E-ppendix is also the place where my colleagues at IndexUniverse .com and I will post more detailed information on contributors to the book, updated research from those contributors, an unabridged glossary, and an unabridged bibliography (both of which can be expanded with readers' feedback and contributions). The E-ppendix also features various "Web-Only" sidebars (linked directly to specific chapters and content in

649

the book), data, tools (with links to the IndexUniverse.com data screener), and much more.

Other valuable features of the E-ppendix are the Discussion Boards and the Feedback Tools. These enable readers of the book to interact online with contributors and the editor, as well as with each other. My hope is that over time, many elements of the E-ppendix will reflect the interests and contributions of the book's readers, eventually becoming an integral part of the book experience.

The development of this E-ppendix took substantial effort and generated considerable momentum in related ventures. As noted in the preface, what started as a site designed to support the book has now evolved considerably, and I've partnered with the *Journal of Indexes* and *The Exchange Traded Fund Report (ETFR)* to continue building IndexUniverse.com into the premiere web site for a complete range of global index-related issues. My colleagues and I are gratified that we've received enthusiastic support for the site from across the index industry—from index providers, exchanges, and index fund/ETF managers. Many of the E-ppendix features discussed next will be supplemented by the news, tools, and research that is available on IndexUniverse.com.

Below you will find an outline of the information on the E-ppendix. It is essentially the provisional site map, as the book goes to print, and will give you a sense of the data, research and fun stuff available to supplement the book. The E-ppendix will surely evolve, and the beauty of the web is that a site can grow to suit the needs of its users. So, the following outline is just a rough guide, but you, the reader/visitor can help shape the development of the site.

BOOK OVERVIEW AND CHAPTER BACKGROUNDS

This part of the E-ppendix includes an interactive table of contents, a variety of chapter/sidebar outlines, excerpts from the book, and editorial reviews of the book.

MORE ON THE CONTRIBUTORS AND THE EDITOR

Change is the only constant in the financial industry: People switch jobs, change functions, start new businesses. Some of the book's contributors even changed jobs or functions multiple times during the writing of the book (including the editor!). Thus there are no detailed biographies of contributors in the book—but we provide that and more in the E-ppendix. Bios, photos, and even some fun information on both contributors and the editor are included.

■ Complete biographies and updates on the book's 60 chapter and side-bar contributors.
■ Links to selected contributors' previous writing/research and affiliated institutions.
■ Complete biography of the editor.
■ Previous writing/research of the editor.
■ Reader feedback capabilities to editor and contributors.

SUPPLEMENTAL MATERIAL AND SIDEBARS

Parts One through Five of the book cover an enormous amount of material, yet the scope and scale of the project inevitably yielded a lot more material that could have been included, even in a 700-page book. Thus, this section of the E-ppendix includes:

■ Web-only sidebars.
■ Additional and/or updated tables and figures for selected chapters.
■ Updated data and research specifically linked to chapters.
■ Expanded, unabridged glossary and unabridged bibliography.

This part of the E-ppendix is designed to parallel the structure of the book, with five parts and individual chapters within each part.

Part One—The Indexing Revolution: Theory and Practice (Chapters 2 to 4)

Web-Only Features   Additional interviews, memories, and anecdotes from historic moments in indexing and index-products.

Web-Only Features   Expanded/unabridged versions of selected chapters and sidebars.

Part Two—Benchmarks: The Foundation for Indexing (Chapters 5 to 13)

Web-Only Sidebar   The Balancing Act of Constructing Benchmark Indexes (Chapter 6).

Web-Only Sidebars   Background on the Major Index Families, in the words of the Index Providers (Morningstar, Dow Jones, S&P, MSCI, etc.) (Chapter 7).

Web-Only Sidebar   Is the S&P SuperComposite Super? (Chapter 8).

Web-Only Sidebar Global Equity Benchmarks (Chapter 9).

Web-Only Features Expanded/unabridged versions of selected chapters and sidebars.

Part Three—The Ever-Expanding Variety and Flexibility of Index Product (Chapters 14 to 18)

Web-Only Sidebar European Corporate Bond ETFs.

Web-Only Sidebar Hedge Fund Indexing—A Square Peg in a Round Hole?

Web-Only Sidebar The *Active Index* Strategist—How Investors and Traders Can Use ETFs to Implement Technical Market Signals (Chapter 18).

Web-Only Features Expanded/unabridged versions of selected chapters and sidebars.

Part Four—Managing Index Funds: It's Anything but Passive! (Chapters 19 to 24)

Web-Only Sidebar Managing the Russell Reconstitution (Chapter 20).

Web-Only Sidebar Managing Political and Financial Risk in International Index Funds from B-Z—Brazil, Malaysia, Russia, Zimbabwe 1997–2000 (Chapter 21).

Web-Only Features Expanded/unabridged versions of selected book chapters and sidebars.

Part Five—Pulling It All Together: How to Use Index Products to Build an Efficient, Risk-Controlled Investment Strategy (Chapters 25 to 31)

Web-Only Features Special feature articles from plan sponsors and financial advisors regarding their use of index-based strategies and index products.

Web-Only Features Expanded/unabridged versions of selected chapters and sidebars.

UNABRIDGED GLOSSARY AND BIBLIOGRAPHY

- Enhanced list of useful indexing and quantitative investment terms.
- Expanded and updated bibliography.
- Feedback feature for submission of additional terms and references.
- Links to other useful industry and academic glossaries.

WEB-ONLY SIDEBARS

As mentioned, the following sidebars are already integrated into various book chapters. They will be joined by other features and updates from contributors and will correspond with the content and topics of specific parts of the book and/or specific chapters:

- The Balancing Act of Constructing Benchmark Indexes, by Khalid Ghayur.
- Introduction to the Morningstar Indexes, by Sanjay Arya.
- A History of the Dow Jones Indexes, by John Prestbo.
- The Nasdaq Indexes, by John Jacobs.
- S&P's Growing Index Family, by David Blitzer.
- The Russell Indexes, by Lori Richards.
- FTSE's Unique Approach to Benchmark Maintenance, by Mark Makepeace.
- Is the S&P SuperComposite Super? by Arlene Rockefeller.
- Global Equity Benchmarks, by Hugh Wilson.
- The *Active Index* Strategist—How Investors and Traders Can Use ETFs to Implement Technical Market Signals, by Steven Schoenfeld.
- Hedge Fund Indexing—A Square Peg in a Round Hole? by Adele Kohler.
- Managing the Russell Reconstitution, by Amy Schioldager and Jane Leung.
- Managing Political and Financial Risk in International Index Funds from B–Z—Brazil, Malaysia, Russia, Zimbabwe 1997—2000, by Steven A. Schoenfeld and Robert Ginis.

INDEX DATA AND RESEARCH (POWERED BY INDEXUNIVERSE.COM)

- Updated returns and methodology updates from the major equity and bond index providers.
- Information on alternative asset class indexes (commodities, currencies, hedge funds, real estate).
- Specialized LINKS section, connecting readers to the latest information from index providers, including index research.
- Market commentary and analysis from major index providers.
- Data tools and screeners for various indexes.

INDEX PRODUCTS AND MARKETS (POWERED BY INDEXUNIVERSE.COM)

- Regularly updated information on index funds, ETFs, index derivatives.
- Specialized subsections for:
  —Index mutual funds.
  —ETFs.
  —Index futures and options.
  —Advisors specializing in index-based portfolios.
  —International/global index products.
  —Gold and commodities.

INVESTMENT BOOKSTORE

Contributors and the editor have selected a variety of other important books on indexing, quantitative investing, and overall investment practices. Visitors can browse these titles, and purchase them directly from the site. Additional copies of this book can also be ordered at a substantial discount.

DISCUSSION BOARDS

A full range of topics related to the book can be explored in an interactive way. Readers can discuss topics with contributors, the editor, and each other. This feature is integrated with the specialized discussion boards of IndexUniverse.com.

The E-ppendix also has several **Special Sections** designed to provide targeted information for different readers of the book. Their content is briefly described below.

FOR NOVICES

■ An educational center teaches the basics of index investing.
■ A "greatest hits" of basic background material on indexing provided by some of the world's leading index fund managers and index providers.
■ Links to the best web sites for beginning index investors.
■ Discussion boards on basic indexing topics.

FOR ACADEMIA

■ Much of the research on indexing has come from academic circles—this section of the site is geared for both students and academic researchers, both within and beyond the ivory towers.
■ A special section of this sub-site is co-sponsored by the Duke University Global Capital Markets Center (GCMC) and will include current academic research from Fuqua School of Business. Other academic institutions are expected to join as contributors and/or co-sponsors.
■ Discussion boards for academic topics.

FOR PROFESSIONALS

■ Professionally-oriented investment ideas, asset allocation, index product, and benchmark research, from the top buy-side and sell-side analysts and firms. Some areas of this sub-site will be password-protected and require registration and qualification to enable distribution of *professional-only* research.
■ A special section geared toward pension funds, foundations, and endowments, highlighting institutional use of index and enhanced index strategies.
■ A section focused on the interests and index product opportunities for financial advisors.
■ Premium news, data and tools for qualified and registered site visitors.
■ Discussion boards for professional investors.

FOR FUN

Some people have claimed indexing is boring, but it doesn't have to be. This section of the E-ppendix explores the lighter side of indexing and includes the following features:

- Index Trivia.
- "Really Alternative" asset class indexes.
- Interactive Features:
  —Reader Surveys (in partnership with IndexUniverse.com).
  —Market Direction contests.
  —Test Your Index Knowledge.
  —Indexing "Top Ten" Lists (e.g., "The Ten Stupidest Index Products Ever Launched").
  —Index Haikus.

Abridged Glossary of Indexation and Quantitative Investment Terminology

This glossary addresses a number of specific concepts and terms used in the book that are unique to indexing and quantitative investing. A particular emphasis is placed on terminology regarding ETFs and fixed-income investing, as the chapters on these topics use terms and concepts that might be new to many readers. A more extensive glossary is included in the book's E-ppendix at www.ActiveIndexInvesting.com (also accessible via IndexUniverse.com). This online Glossary of Indexation and Quantitative Investment Terminology will be expanded based on readers' inquiries and input, regularly updated by the team at IndexUniverse.com. Your feedback and contributions are welcome.

12-b1 fees   A percentage of assets paid by mutual fund shareholders to cover marketing expenses for the fund.

active manager   A portfolio manager who attempts to improve the portfolio's risk-adjusted return relative to a benchmark through stock picking, market timing, or other strategies.

alpha   Commonly known as the "extra return" a fund manager can provide relative to the market's risk. Alpha measures the difference between actual returns and expected performance resulting from exposure to specific risk factors. Can be expressed as a positive or negative number.

American depository receipts (ADRs)   Certificates traded on U.S. exchanges that represent shares in a foreign company.

arbitrage   Simultaneous purchase and sale of similar instruments in different markets or categories to take advantage of price discrepancies.

asset allocation   The diversification of investments among various asset classes—such as large-cap U.S. stocks, international equities, intermediate bonds, real estate, precious metals, and so on.

asset class   A type or category of investment (e.g., a stock, bond, or REIT) that has its own particular risk/return profile.

Authorized Participant (AP)   An external broker authorized to place creation/redemption orders for ETFs. APs generally help make markets in ETFs as well.

basis point   ¹⁄₁₀₀ of a percentage point, or 0.01 percent. For example, 20 basis points equals 0.20 percent.

benchmark   An index that serves as a standard against which the performance of a fund or portfolio is measured. For example, a large-cap stock fund may be compared with the S&P 500 Index or Russell 1000 Index to assess how it performs over time. In the same way, a bond fund may be compared to a fixed-income index, such as the Lehman U.S. Aggregate Index, or € Corporates Index.

beta   Measures the sensitivity of a fund's performance to general market movement. A higher beta denotes more risk. For example, a fund with a beta of 1.40 would be expected to rise or fall 14 percent when the market (usually represented by an index) moves 10 percent in either direction.

bid/ask spread   The difference between the bid price and the ask price (or offer price) in a security transaction, whether equities, bonds, or commodities. Also referred to as transaction costs or explicit costs. For example, in the fixed-income market, if a bond is bid at $101.50 and offered at $101.75, the spread is $0.25, in price terms. Bid/ask spreads in bond markets are more frequently quoted in yield terms and equates to the difference between the bid yield and ask yield. For example, if bid yield = 4.20 percent and ask yield = 4.15 percent, then the bid/ask spread is 5 basis points, in yield terms. The spread narrows or widens according to supply and demand and is a good indicator of liquidity. In bond and OTC derivative markets, where institutional investors do not normally pay an explicit commission, the bid/ask spread is cost incurred when buying or selling shares of securities or funds for a portfolio.

call   An options contract that gives the option buyer the right to buy the underlying instrument at a specified price for a certain, fixed period of time. (See also *put*.)

Capital Asset Pricing Model (CAPM)   A model used to value stocks by examining the relationship between risk and expected return. Assumes that investors expect to be compensated for taking more risk through higher returns.

capital gains   Taxable profits on the sale of investments that have increased in value.

cash settlement   A transaction settled in cash payment (rather than the physical delivery of a commodity, currency, or security) depending on profit or loss.

closed-end fund   A fund with a fixed number of shares outstanding, and that does not redeem shares the way a typical mutual fund does. Unlike

ETFs, CEFs often trade at substantial premiums or discounts to net asset value (NAV).

closet index fund   An actively managed fund that "hugs" its benchmark index, so that investors are essentially getting an index fund (at active fees). Called "index hugging" in the U.K.

covered call   The selling of a call option while simultaneously holding an equivalent position in the underlying security or futures.

credit   Nongovernment bonds. The bond market is generally divided into government bonds and credit. Credit being called so, after the credit risk aspect of bonds issued by nongovernment entities. The credit section can be further subdivided into more and more specific subgroups, such as agencies, supranationals, corporates, and securitized.

credit rating   Ratings agencies attribute credit ratings to bonds as an indicator of their general creditworthiness or quality.

depository trust company (DTC)   A corporation that facilitates transfers of U.S. securities and holds securities for member institutions.

diversify   To reduce risk in an portfolio by spreading investments among different bond or stock issuers or issues that are not perfectly correlated so that losses in any one bond/stock/security do not affect the whole portfolio and may be partially offset by gains in other securities holdings.

dividend yield   Annualized rate of dividends paid on a share of stock, divided by its current share price.

dollar-cost averaging   Strategy of investing fixed amounts to a fund on a regular basis (usually monthly) regardless of the market's direction. Many investors and advisors use the strategy to enforce discipline and factor out emotions in investment decisions—forcing investors to buy when shares are low and sell when they are high.

emerging markets   The financial markets of developing countries, usually categorized by World Bank definitions. Also refers to the countries/economies as a whole.

enhanced index fund   A fund that closely tracks an index, but attempts to outperform the benchmark using risk-controlled trading or overweight/underweight strategies (see Chapter 15).

exchange   A regulated marketplace for the trading of stocks, options, futures, commodities, and other financial instruments.

exchange-traded fund (ETF)   A basket of securities generally designed to track an index that trades like a stock and is listed on an exchange (see Chapter 16).

expected return   The result of mathematical analysis involving statistical distributions of stock prices and their impact on the value of an investment.

expense ratio   The percentage of assets paid by fund shareholders to cover the expenses of managing the fund.

float   The number of shares outstanding of a stock available for purchase by the public on open markets. Also called free-float.

future   A standardized agreement, traded on a futures exchange, to buy or sell an instrument at a specified price at a date in the future. The contract specifies the instrument, quality, quantity, delivery date, and settlement mechanism (see Chapters 14 and 25).

growth fund   A mutual fund that invests in stocks whose primary objective is capital (price) appreciation. Growth funds typically experience greater share-price volatility than more conservative funds. (See also *value fund*.)

hedge   The purchase or sale of a futures contract or other derivative as a temporary substitute for a cash market transaction to be made at a later date. The hedge position is designed to protect the investor from temporary price movements in an instrument that the investor already owns or plans to own.

hedge fund   A fund generally available only to institutions and high net worth investors that uses aggressive investment strategies, including selling short, leverage, program trading, swaps, arbitrage, and derivatives. Hedge funds are exempt from many of the rules and regulations governing other mutual funds and other regulated investment pools.

index   See *benchmark* (see also Chapters 5 and 6).

index arbitrage   Investment strategy designed to take advantage of pricing inefficiencies between the price of stocks in an index and the price of index futures contracts.

index fund   Fund with an investment policy of closely tracking the performance of a market benchmark, such as the Wilshire 5000 or Lehman U.S. Aggregate Bond index.

index option   An option whose underlying pricing is based on an index.

index tracking   Correlation between fund's return versus the return of index.

indexation   A so-called passive investment strategy designed to match the returns of a benchmark index. Can be implemented for equity, fixed income, real estate, commodity, and other asset classes.

indicative optimal portfolio value (IOPV)   The value of the securities in an exchange-traded fund plus estimated cash. An ETF's IOPV is reported by Bloomberg and other quotation services every 15 seconds and should closely track NAV.

institutional investor   An entity—such as a foundation, endowment, or retirement plan—that invests a portfolio on behalf of a group of individuals—employees, for example—to achieve specific objectives. Can also refer to the managers of large portfolios, including mutual funds. Trade sizes tend to be much larger than retail trades and are often dealt over-the-counter, particularly in the fixed-income market maker. Pricing is usually more competitive for these larger institutional investors versus retail clients.

investment objective   A stated financial strategy or goal followed by a institutional portfolio manager, a mutual fund, or a financial advisor.

leverage   The use of borrowed money in an effort to enhance future returns (adds more risk).

limit order   An order that can be filled only at a specified price or better.

liquidity   The degree to which a financial instrument is easily and quickly traded. Highly liquid stocks can experience high trading volume without a dramatic change in price.

listed option   An option contract traded on a regulated, recognized exchange.

load   A sales charge added to the purchase and/or sale price of some mutual funds and annuities. Deferred loads are back-end sales charges imposed when investors redeem shares.

long   Owning an asset in the hope that its price will rise, or as a hedge for a corresponding short position. (See also *short.*)

market capitalization   (Often abbreviated as "market cap.") The value of a publicly traded firm; found by multiplying the number of its outstanding shares by the current market price per share. An entire market (e.g., Canadian equities) or market segment (e.g., U.S. small-cap value) can also be measured by market cap, as can entire asset classes (e.g., Emerging Market equities). In these latter three cases, indexes play an integral role in measuring market cap.

market maker   An exchange member whose function is to aid in the making of a market by making bids and offers for his or her account in the absence of or in addition to public buy or sell orders.

market on close order   A buy or sell order to be executed as close as possible to the end of the trading day.

matrix pricing   A security whose price is not explicitly calculated, but is determined by a relationship to other, more liquid securities.

maturity   The date when a debt is due to be paid.

median   A common way of measuring active manager performance (as a whole) relative to benchmark indexes. Not to be confused with average (or mean), the median is found by arranging all the numbers in a set and choosing the middle number. If the set has an even amount of numbers, then the median is the average of the two middle numbers.

net asset value (NAV)   The value of one share in a mutual fund company computed daily. In general, it is calculated by summing the values of all the fund's investments, subtracting its expenses and liabilities, and dividing by the number of shares outstanding.

nonsystematic risk   Stock-specific risk, which is in addition to risk or volatility of the overall market. (See also *systematic risk.*)

option   A contract giving the holder the right but not the obligation to purchase or sell a security on or before a predetermined future date for a fixed price. Options on securities indexes are generally similar, but settled in cash.

over-the-counter (OTC)   Private transactions directly between two parties, not intermediated by an exchange, with details of the transaction not being public either.

p/b ratio   Price-to-book ratio. The p/b ratio of a company is calculated by dividing the market price of its stock by the company's per-share book value.

p/e ratio   Price-to-earning ratio. The price of a stock divided by its reported earnings. It is an indicator of how much investors are willing to pay for an opportunity to share in firm's future earning potential.

passive management   Investment strategy designed to closely track an index.

portfolio composition file (PCF)   This data file is published daily and made available to the National Securities Clearing Corporation (NSCC) participants. A PCF contains the security holdings for one "creation basket" along with necessary cash component information to create one unit of an ETF.

portfolio trade   Sale or purchase of a basket of stocks in a single trade.

put   An options contract that gives the holder the right to sell the underlying instrument at a specified price for a certain, fixed period of time. (See also *call*.)

real estate investment trust (REIT)   A corporation or trust for the securitization of real estate property and loans. REITs are traded on an exchange, so are usually more liquid than individual properties (see Chapter 17).

rebalancing   The process of adjusting portfolio assets back to their original target levels, in response to market movements. Rebalancing can refer to an index portfolio manager's reaction to index changes/corporate actions, or to a plan sponsor or financial advisor's adjustment of overall asset levels within a portfolio. There are a myriad of approaches to both index rebalancing and to overall portfolio rebalancing (see Chapters 19, 20, 21, 23, 29, and 30).

regression analysis   A complex statistical technique used to find relationships between variables for the purpose of predicting future values.

retail investor   A noninstitutional investor. Retail investors encompass individual investors as well as brokers or intermediaries who trade on behalf of individual investors. Trade sizes tend to be much smaller than institutional trades.

risk   The volatility of returns for a security or asset class, usually expressed as annualized standard deviation.

R-squared   A statistic that indicates how much of a fund's fluctuations were attributable to movements in the fund's benchmark index. R-squared ranges between 0 percent and 100 percent. 100 would indicate that 100 percent of the movements in a fund were completely explained by movements in the benchmark index.

Sharpe ratio   A meaure of risk developed by Nobel Laureate William Sharpe. Calculated by dividing the returns in excess of the 90-day T-bill rate by the standard deviation of those returns for a given time period.

short   An investment position that will profit from a decline in price. This position can be speculative, or be part of a hedged strategy, linked to a corresponding long position. (See also *long.*)

specialist   A stock exchange member who makes a market in an exchange-traded security such as stocks or ETFs.

spread   The difference between the best bid and best offer for a given security or financial instrument at a given point in time. Also called the bid-offer spread or bid-ask spread.

standard deviation   A common measure of portfolio volatility or risk. The distribution of returns around the mean.

strategic asset allocation   Long-term commitment to broad asset categories such as stocks, bonds, and commodities. Also known as policy allocation or policy benchmark.

style drift   When a fund moves away from its stated investment objective over time. For example, when a growth fund gradually shifts to a value orientation.

swap   An agreement to exchange of streams of periodic payments over time with a counterparty, according to specified terms (see Chapter 25).

systematic risk   The risk associated with general market movements, rather than the risk associated with an individual security movement. (See also *nonsystematic risk.*) For equity markets, systematic risk can usually be hedged with stock-index futures or options.

systemic risk   The risk associated with the general health or structure of the financial system or its component markets. It occurs as a result of the system's ability to handle large degrees of political market, credit, or settlement risk. A good example of systemic risk was the "contagion effect" of the Asian financial crisis of 1997/1998, which subsequently spread to both the global bond market and other regional stock markets.

tactical asset allocation   To sell asset classes that have strengthened and buy asset classes that have weakened in anticipation of the market returning to equilibrium. Generally shorter term in orientation than strategic asset allocation.

tracking error   The difference between the performance of a portfolio of securities versus an index (see Chapter 14 for a more detailed definition).

transaction costs   Costs incurred when buying or selling an asset, such as broker commissions and the bid/ask spread.

turnover   (Value of security purchases + Value of security sales)/Value of portfolio, for a specified time period. Sometimes expressed in dollar (or Euro) value of turnover.

value fund   Specializes in the purchase of inexpensive stocks—companies with low valuations. Various measures are used to determine "value" characteristics in major value benchmarks (see Chapters 6, 7, and 8).

variance   The second moment around the mean; the expected value of the square of the deviations of a random variable from its mean value.

volatility   The rate at which an asset moves up or down. (See also *standard deviation.*)

volume   The number of shares traded in a given market.

wash sale rule   A wash sale is invoked when a security that was sold for a capital loss is bought back within 30 days of the sale. When a wash sale occurs, the fund or an individual is disallowed from realizing that loss and must defer it until the security is sold out completely for more than 30 days. This rule is designed to prevent investors from amassing capital losses without truly selling out of a security position.

yield   Used in reference to bonds, yield is the coupon payment divided by the bond's face value if held to maturity. Bond yields and bond prices are inversely related. With equities, usually refers to dividend yield (dividend/stock price).

Abridged Bibliography and Research Resources

An unabridged Bibliography and further Research Resources are available on the book's E-ppendix at www.ActiveIndexInvesting.com supported by IndexUniverse.com. This section will be periodically updated, and readers are invited to submit suggested additions to this online supplement to the book via the Feedback feature on the E-ppendix.

Ackermann, Carl, Richard McEnally, and David Ravenscraft. "The Performance of Hedge Funds: Risk, Return, and Incentives." *Journal of Finance* (June 1999).

Amnec, N., and L. Martellini. "The Brave New World of Hedge Fund Indexes." USC Working Paper, 2002.

Anson, Mark. "Symmetrical Performance Measures and Asymmetrical Trading Strategies: A Cautionary Example," *Journal of Alternative Investments* (2002).

Baer, Greg, and Gary Gensler. *The Great Mutual Fund Trap.* New York: Broadway Books, 2002.

Beebower, Gilbert L., Gary P. Brinson, and L. Randolph Hood. "Determinants of Portfolio Performance." *Financial Analysts Journal* (1986).

Bernstein, Peter L. *Against the Gods: The Remarkable Story of Risk.* New York: John Wiley & Sons, 1996.

Bernstein, Peter L. *Capital Ideas: The Improbable Origins of Modern Wall Street.* New York: Free Press, 1992.

Bernstein, William. *The Intelligent Asset Allocator.* New York: McGraw-Hill, 2000.

Biggs, Barton. "Ben Graham Would Be Proud." *Morgan Stanley Investment Perspectives* (April 19, 1993).

Blitzer, David M. *Outpacing the Pros.* New York: McGraw-Hill, 2001.

Bodie, Zvi, Alex Kane, and Alan J. Marcus. *Investments,* 3rd ed. Chicago: Richard D. Irwin, 1996.

Bogle, John C. *Bogle on Mutual Funds.* New York: Dell, 1994.

Bogle, John C. *Common Sense on Mutual Funds.* New York: John Wiley & Sons, 1999.

Brandhorst, Eric. "Problems with Manager Universe Data." *State Street Global Advisors* (November 22, 2002) [available on www.ssga.com].

Brandhorst, Eric. "The Future of Asset Management: Separation of Market Returns and Value-Added." *State Street Global Advisors' Point of View* (September 2003).

Brown, J., W. Goetzmann, and R. Ibbotson. "Offshore Hedge Funds, Survival and Performance, 1989–1995." *Journal of Business* (1999).

Brown, Stephen, William Goetzmann, and Roger Ibbotson. "Offshore Hedge Funds: Survival and Performance, 1989–95." *Journal of Business*, vol. 72 (1999).

Carhart, Mark M. "On Persistence in Mutual Fund Performance." Working Paper, School of Business Administration, University of Southern California (Draft dated September 1, 1996).

Chow, G., and M. Kritzman. "Value at Risk for Portfolios with Short Positions." *Journal of Portfolio Management* (2002).

Courtney, David. *From Forum to Futures, 2000 Years of Britain's Commodity Markets*. London: Metal Bulletin Books, 1991.

Culp, Christopher. *The Risk Management Process*. New York: John Wiley & Sons, 2001.

Droms, William G., and David A. Walker. "Mutual Fund Investment Performance." *Quarterly Review of Economics and Finance*, vol. 36, no. 3 (Fall 1996).

Edwards, Franklin, and Jimmy Liew. "Hedge Funds versus Managed Futures as Asset Classes." *Journal of Derivatives* (Summer 1999).

Edwards, R. "Hedge Fund and Commodity Fund Investments in Bull and Bear Markets." *Journal of Portfolio Investments* (2001).

Ellis, Charles D. "The Loser's Game." *Financial Analyst Journal* (July/August 1975).

Ellis, Charles D., and John J. Brennan. *Winning the Loser's Game*, 4th ed. New York: McGraw-Hill, 2002.

Elton, Edwin J., Martin J. Gruber, and Christopher R. Blake. "The Persistence of Risk-Adjusted Mutual Fund Performance." *Journal of Business* (1996).

Fabozzi, Frank J., and Robert Molay. *Perspectives on Equity Indexing*. New Hope, PA: Frank J. Fabozzi Associates, 2000.

Fama, Eugene F. "Efficient Capital Markets: A Review of Theory and Empirical Work." *Journal of Finance* (1970).

Fama, Eugene F. "Random Walks in Stock Prices." *Financial Analysts Journal* (September/October 1965).

Ferri, Richard. *All about Index Funds*. New York: McGraw-Hill, 2002.

Francis, Jack C., William W. Toy, and J. Gregg Whittaker. *The Handbook of Equity Derivatives*. New York: John Wiley & Sons, 1999.

Fung, W., and D. Hsieh. "Asset Based Hedge Fund Styles and Portfolio Diversification." Working Paper, Fuqua School of Business, Duke University (2001).

Fung, William, and David Hsieh. "Performance Characteristics of Hedge Funds and Commodity Funds: Natural versus Spurious Biases." *Journal of Financial and Quantitative Analysis,* vol. 35 (2000).

Gastineau, Gary L. *The Exchange-Traded Funds Manual.* New York: John Wiley & Sons (2002).

Goetzmann, William N., and Roger G. Ibbotson. "Do Winners Repeat?" *Journal of Portfolio Management* (Winter 1994).

Goldman Sachs & Co., and Financial Risk Management Ltd. "The Hedge Fund 'Industry' and Absolute Return Funds." *Journal of Alternative Investments.* (Spring 1999).

Goodspeed, Bennett W. *The Tao Jones Averages—A Guide to Whole-Brained Investing.* New York: E.F. Dutton, 1983.

Green, Gary. *Beating the Index with Index Funds.* RGB Media (2001).

Grinblatt, Mark, and Sheridan Titman. "A Study of Monthly Mutual Fund Returns and Performance Evaluation Techniques." *Journal of Financial and Quantitative Analysis,* vol. 29, no. 3 (September 1994).

Grinold, Richard C., and Ronald N. Kahn. *Active Portfolio Management: A Quantitative Approach for Producing Superior Returns and Selecting Superior Returns and Controlling Risk.* New York: McGraw-Hill, 1999.

Haugen, Robert A. *The New Finance: A Case against Efficient Markets.* Englewood Cliffs, NJ: Prentice-Hall, 1995.

Henker, Thomas. "Naïve Diversification for Hedge Funds." *Journal of Alternative Assets* (Winter 1998).

Ibbotson, Roger G., and Paul D. Kaplan. "Does Asset Allocation Policy Explain 40, 90, or 100 Percent of Performance?" *Financial Analysts Journal,* Association for Investment Management and Research (January/February 2000).

Ineichen, A. "In Search of Alpha—Investing in Hedge Funds." Research Paper, UBS Warburg (2000).

Ineichen, A. "The Search for Alpha Continues." Research Paper, UBS Warburg (2001).

Janke, William W. "The Development of Structured Portfolio Management: A Contextual View." In *Quantitative International Investing,* edited by Brian Bruce, 153–181. Chicago: Probus Publishing Company, 1990.

Jeffrey, Robert H., and Robert D. Arnott. "Is Your Alpha Big Enough to Cover Its Taxes?" *Journal of Portfolio Management* (Spring 1993).

Kahn, Ronald N., and Andrew Rudd. "Does Historical Performance Predict Future Performance?" *BARRA Newsletter* (Spring 1995).

Lamm, R. McFall, Jr. "Portfolios of Alternative Assets: Why Not 100% Hedge Funds?" *Journal of Investing* (Winter 1999): 87–97.

Lederman, Jess, and Keith K. H. Park, eds. *The Global Equity Markets.* Chicago, IL/Cambridge, UK: Probus Publishing Company, 1991.

L'habitant, Francois-Serge, and Michelle Learned. "Hedge Fund Diversification: How Much is Enough?" *Journal of Alternative Investments* (Winter 2002).

Liang, Bing. "Hedge Funds: The Living and the Dead." *Journal of Financial and Quantitative Analysis* (2001).

Lo, Andrew. "Risk Management for Hedge Funds: Introduction and Overview." *Financial Analysts Journal* (November/December 2001).

Magin, John, and Donald Tuttle, eds. *Managing Investment Portfolios—A Dynamic Process,* 2nd ed. Charlottesville VA: Association of Investment Management and Research, 1990.

Malkiel, Burton G. "Returns from Investing in Equity Mutual Funds; 1971 to 1991." *Journal of Finance,* vol. L, no. 2 (June 1995).

Malkiel, Burton G. *A Random Walk Down Wall Street,* 8th ed. New York: W.W. Norton, 2003.

Malkiel, Burton G., and Alexander Radisich. "The Growth of Index Funds and the Pricing of Equity Securities." *Journal of Portfolio Management* (Winter 2001).

Markowitz, Harry M. "Portfolio Selection." *Journal of Finance* (March 1952).

Murphy, John J. *Intermarket Technical Analysis—Trading Strategies for the Global Stock, Bond, Commodity and Currency Markets.* New York: Wiley Finance/ John Wiley & Sons, 1991.

Park, James, Stephen Brown, and William Goetzmann. "Performance Benchmarks and Survivorship Bias for Hedge Fund and Commodity Trading Advisors." *Hedge Fund News* (August 1999).

Park, James, and Jeremy Staum. "Fund of Funds Diversification: How Much Is Enough?" *Journal of Alternative Assets* (Winter 1998).

Park, Keith K. H., and Steven A. Schoenfeld. *The Pacific Rim Futures and Options Markets: A Comprehensive, Country-By-Country Reference to the World's Fastest-Growing Financial Markets.* Chicago, IL/Cambridge, UK: Probus Professional Publishers, 1992.

Park, Keith K. H., and Antoine W. van Agtmael, eds. *The World's Emerging Stock Markets.* Chicago, IL/Cambridge, UK: Probus Publishing Company, 1993.

PricewaterhouseCoopers. "25 Years of Indexing: An Analysis of the Costs and Benefits" (commissioned by Barclays Global Investors), July 1998.

Purcell, David, and Paul Crowley. "The Reality of Hedge Funds." *Journal of Investing* (Fall 1999): 26–44.

Ross, Barry. "Hedge Funds: A Walk through the Graveyard." Working Paper, Applied Finance Center, MacQuarie University (March 2003).

Samuelson, Paul A. "Challenge to Judgment." *Journal of Portfolio Management* (Fall 1974).

Samuelson, Paul A. "The Judgment of Economic Science on Rational Portfolio Management: Indexing, Timing, and Long-Horizon Effects." *Journal of Portfolio Management* (Fall 1989).

Sauter, Gus. "Index Rex." *Journal of Indexes,* 3rd quarter, 2003.

Schneeweis, T., H. Kazemi, and G. Martin. "Understanding Hedge Fund Performance." Research Paper, Lehman Brothers (2001).

Schoenfeld, Steven A. "Perfection Impossible—Why Simply 'Good' Indexes Can Result in a More Perfect Solution." *Journal of Indexes,* 2nd quarter, 2002.

Schoenfeld, Steven A. "Index-Based Investment in Emerging Stock Markets." *Emerging Markets Quarterly,* (Institutional Investor Journals) (Spring 1998).

Schoenfeld, Steven A., and Edward Strawderman. "Emerging Futures and Options Markets—An Overview of Issues and Prospects in Developing Countries." Research Study Series—International Finance Corporation (World Bank Group), Washington, DC (March 1994).

Schoenfeld, Steven A., Peter Handley, and Binu George. "International Equity Benchmarks for U.S. Investors." *Investment Insights, Barclays Global Investors* (December 2000).

Schoenfeld, Steven A., and Robert Ginis. "International Equity Benchmarks for North American Investors" (updated edition including sector and style indexes). *Investment Insights, Barclays Global Investors* (November 2002).

Sharpe, William F. "Capital Asset Prices: A Theory of Market Equilibrium under Conditions of Risk." *Journal of Finance* (September 1964).

Sharpe, William F. "The Arithmetic of Active Management." *Financial Analyst Journal* (January/February 1991).

Shiller, Robert J. *The New Financial Order.* Princeton, NJ: Princeton University Press, 2003.

Siegel, Daniel, and Diane Siegel. *The Futures Markets.* Chicago: Probus Publishing Company, 1990.

Siegel, Jeremy B. *Stocks for the Long Run.* New York: McGraw-Hill Professional Publishing, 1998.

Standard & Poor's. Standard & Poor's *Global Stock Markets Factbook.* New York: 2003 (and previous editions, published by IFC since 1988 and S&P since 2001).

Standard & Poor's. "Standard & Poor's Hedge Fund Index—Structure, Methodology, Definitions and Practices." Research Paper, Standard & Poor's (2002).

Stevens, Dale H., Ronald J. Surz, and Mark E. Wimer. "The Importance of Investment Policy." *Journal of Investing,* vol. 8, no. 4 (Winter 1999): 80–85.

Stoll, H. R., and R. E. Whaley. "Futures and Options on Stock Indices: Economic Purpose, Arbitrage, and Market Structure." *The Review of Futures Markets,* vol. 7, no. 2 (1988).

Swedroe, Larry. *What Wall Street Doesn't Want You to Know.* New York: St. Martin's Press, 2000.

Tamarkin, Bob. *The Merc: The Emergence of a Global Financial Powerhouse.* New York: HarperCollins, 1993.

Volkman, David A., and Mark E. Wohar. "Determinants of Persistence in Relative Performance of Mutual Funds." *Journal of Financial Research,* vol. 18, no. 4 (Winter 1995).

Weisman, Andrew. "Dangerous Attractions: Informationless Investing and Hedge Fund Performance Measurement Bias." *Journal of Portfolio Management* (2002).

Wiandt, Jim, and Will McClatchy. *Exchange Traded Funds: An Insider's Guide to Buying the Market.* New York: John Wiley & Sons, 2001.

Young, Patrick, and Thomas Theys. *Capital Market Revolution—The Future of Markets in an Online World.* London: Financial Times-Prentice-Hall, 1999.

Zask, Ezra. *Global Investment Risk Management.* New York: McGraw-Hill, 1999.

Index